'King Darius' Palace at Susa is perhaps the least well known yet the most important of the Achaemenid Persian palaces, less perhaps for its remains on the ground than for its architecture and treasures which are to be seen in Teheran and notably in the Louvre. This magisterial volume, the translation of the French edition of 2010, brings together at last a comprehensive account of the architectural remains and the finds, from various scholarly hands. It is a major resource and, with its lavish illustration, a joy to handle and read.'
Sir John Boardman, FBA
Emeritus Lincoln Professor of Classical Art and Archaeology, University of Oxford

'This magnificent volume stretches far beyond the confines of Achaemenid Susa. It puts Susa in the context of the Achaemenid world in general, and in doing so it touches on practically all aspects of Ancient Persia in the 5th and 4th centuries BC. Jean Perrot and his colleagues are to be warmly congratulated for presenting their findings to the public in such an accessible and informative way.'
from the introduction by **John Curtis**, OBE, FBA
Keeper of Special Middle East Projects, The British Museum

'This sumptuous volume provides a richly illustrated, authoritative survey of the key structures and many individual objects found at Susa that can be said to have contributed so much to the advancement of Achaemenid studies, beginning in the second half of the nineteenth century. Above all, students of the evolution of early Achaemenid art and architecture will find this multi-authored volume to be essential reading.'
David Stronach, OBE
Professor Emeritus of Near Eastern Archaeology, University of California, Berkeley

'This lavishly illustrated volume on Darius I's palace at Susa is not only of utmost importance for the specialist in Near Eastern Archaeology. With its chapters on the history of Elam in Achaemenid times, and on the royal builder himself, it is also an indispensable tool for historians of Pre-Islamic Persia. Its comprehensive account of the French excavations provides key insights into European encounters with Iran as well into the history of scholarship.'
Josef Wiesehöfer
Professor of Ancient History, Kiel University

The Palace of Darius at Susa

The Great Royal Residence of Achaemenid Persia

Edited by Jean Perrot

with an Introduction by John Curtis

Translated by Gérard Collon
Translation editing by Dominique Collon

I.B. TAURIS
LONDON · NEW YORK

www.ibtauris.com

Published in association with
the Iran Heritage Foundation

IRAN
HERITAGE

Published in 2013 by I.B.Tauris & Co Ltd
6 Salem Road, London W2 4BU • 175 Fifth Avenue, New York NY 10010
www.ibtauris.com

Distributed in the United States and Canada exclusively by
Palgrave Macmillan, 175 Fifth Avenue, New York NY 10010

First published in French in 2010
Copyright © 2010 Les Presses de l'Université Paris-Sorbonne (PUPS)
English translation © 2013 I.B.Tauris & Co Ltd
Translated from the French by Gérard Collon • Translation edited by Dominique Collon
Introduction © John Curtis 2013

ISBN: 978-1-84885-621-9

A full CIP record for this book is available from the British Library
A full CIP record is available from the Library of Congress
Library of Congress Catalog Card Number: available

Designed by E&P Design • Printed and bound in Italy by Printer Trento

The publishers gratefully acknowledge the support of the Iran Heritage Foundation
towards the publication of this book

FSC
www.fsc.org

MIX
Paper from
responsible sources
FSC® C015829

Sponsors

The publishers gratefully acknowledge the generous support given by the following sponsors of this publication:

- Mohammed Afkhami
- Ata and Lida Ahsani
- Manucher and Mahvash Azmudeh
- The family of the late Mr Cooverji Hormusji Bhabha of Bombay, India
- Ali Reza Erfan
- Aligholi and Emanuela Hedayat
- Iran Heritage Foundation
- Zinat Irvani
- Jawad and Mahnaz Kamel
- Omid and Kimya Kamshad
- Akbar A. Lari
- Mehdi and Soheyla Metghalchi
- Ardeshir Naghshineh
- Ali and May Rashidian
- Ali and Anousheh Razi
- Dr Abtin Sassanfar
- Dr Ali and Monir Sattaripour
- The Soudavar Memorial Foundation

Contents

The Authors

Pierre AMIET | *Honorary Inspector General of the Museums of France* • ch. 11

Béatrice ANDRÉ-SALVINI | *General Curator, Director of the Department of Oriental Antiquities, Musée du Louvre*

Rémy BOUCHARLAT | *Director of the Maison de l'Orient et de la Méditerranée, Lyon* • ch. 11 & ch. 13

Pierre BRIANT | *Collège de France* • ch. 1

Annie CAUBET | *Honorary General Curator of the Musées Nationaux* • ch. 10

Nicole CHEVALIER | *Musée du Louvre, Department of Oriental Antiquities* • ch. 3

Noëmi DAUCÉ | *Institut National du Patrimoine, Paris 1* • ch. 10

Constance FRANK | *Oriental Archaeology Department, University of Lyon 2* • ch. 11

Hermann GASCHE | *Archaeologist, University of Ghent* • ch. 13

Albert HESSE | *Senior Researcher, Université Pierre et Marie Curie, Paris 6* • ch. 5

Daniel LADIRAY | *Researcher, National Centre for Scientific Research [CNRS]* • ch. 6

Jean PERROT † | *Director of the Archaeological Mission to Susa* • ch. 4, ch. 7 & ch. 14

Jean SOLER | *Historian of Religions* • ch. 4

François VALLAT | *Assyriologist, National Centre for Scientific Research [CNRS]* ch. 2, ch. 9 & appendix

Jean YOYOTTE † | *Honorary Professor at the Collège de France* • ch. 8

Acknowledgements

Jean Perrot

Before thanking those, from near and from far, who have contributed to the preparation of this publication, I would like to recall the memories my colleagues and I have of our past at Susa, thirty or forty years ago with Iranian workmen and archaeologists by our side. The workmen were without equal. Every year they would come down in teams with their village headman from their snow-covered mountains to make themselves available to the mission and its master mason, Abbas Ettemadi: a man who could impart his passion for the rediscovery of Darius' Palace and the glorious past of their country. This was an adventure lived through the vision of the young archaeologists and technicians whom Firouz Bagherzadeh, director of the Centre for Archaeological Research at the Iranian Museums, would send to us (with the constant support of the highest government authorities).

The concept of a book accessible to the wider public through its illustrations was encouraged by Louis Faton who, for a long time, had shown his interest in Iran's past, with the intention of extending the knowledge of archaeological discoveries as widely as possible.

This work was able to profit from the enthusiasm of all those archaeologists, historians, epigraphists, technicians and artists asked to contribute to its publication; in particular Rémy Boucharlat and the Franco-Iranian archaeological mission at Pasargadae and Persepolis. It benefited from the advice and attention of Geneviève Dollfus, notably in the presentation of the bibliography, a thankless task which is much appreciated. Thanks are due especially to Loïc Thirion-Lopez and Peter Rupp (Héritage Virtuel) for the care and attention brought to digital imagery, as well as to the photographic service of the National Museum in Tehran for its images.

The difficulties of publication were overcome thanks to support from institutions and individuals whom I thank without being able to name them all;

and to encouragement from a network of people whose goodwill I have often exhausted. My heartfelt thanks go to Danielle Saffar for her precious counsel, and to Sophie Linon-Chipon who, under the direction of François Moureau, took dynamic charge of the final phase of publication at the Presses de l'Université Paris-Sorbonne.

Finally, the realisation of this book owes much to my wife, Manijeh, whose contribution is marked by her aesthetic sense.

Foreword

Jean Perrot

The events of human life, either public or private, are so intimately linked to architecture that the majority of observers can reconstruct nations and individuals in all their habits from the remains of their public monuments or by the examination of their domestic relics. Archaeology is, to social nature, as comparative anatomy is to taxonomy. A mosaic reveals an entire society, as much as an ichthyosaur skeleton implies a whole creation [...] From this, no doubt, stems the prodigious interest which an architectural description inspires, when the author's fantasy does not obscure the facts. Cannot everyone with a bit of deduction use it to call up the past? And, for man, the past resembles the future singularly. Is not telling him what was, almost telling him what will be?
HONORÉ DE BALZAC, THE QUEST OF THE ABSOLUTE

This book brings together and presents the current state of knowledge on Susa in the period of the great Achaemenid Persian kings through the building works of Darius and his successors. The contribution of archaeology is still necessary here. Other than the inscriptions of Darius and the administrative and economic tablets of Persepolis, we suffer from a severe lack of literary resources, even indirect ones. Under Darius I, Herodotus was not yet born. The period from 522 BC to 486 BC is of exceptional interest, as it saw the finishing touches to the formative years of what one might call the Achaemenid period. The new archaeological data allows us to better understand Darius' personality, all too often imbued in a generic way with traits common to all the Great Kings. The data allow us also to define and expand the vision we have of Susa, and its place and role in the organisation and functioning of the Persian Empire.

The discovery of Susa goes back to the middle of the nineteenth century. Indeed, the memory of a palace of the Achaemenid kings had remained strong in the mind of humanity through biblical tales (Esther, Ezra and Nehemiah,

Daniel), the theatre (Aeschylus' *The Persians*, Racine's *Esther*) and Greco-Roman literature. In the Middle Ages, great travellers such as Rabbi Benjamin of Tudela made their way to Susa and admired its ruins. The British archaeologist William K. Loftus was the first to dig at Susa in 1852; then, from 1884 to 1886, Marcel and Jane Dieulafoy uncovered a gigantic capital and elements of a frieze in glazed brick which were, in 1888, the glory of the oriental galleries in the Louvre. From 1897 the excavations of the palace recommenced in a haphazard way, becoming bogged down in an architectural complex which the imagination of successive excavators had trouble in mastering.

It would take luck and the circumstances occasioned by the preparations for the commemoration of the 2,500th anniversary of the monarchy in Iran in 1969, to relaunch interest in the great Achaemenid sites (Pasargadae, Persepolis, Susa). From 1969 to 1979, excavation and research brought Susa to life in all its greatness, with its defensive system and dependencies, a residential palace which had no equal in its time in oriental architecture (Ecbatana's has still not been discovered and the terrace at Persepolis has no residential palace).

Susa, today called Shush-i Daniel, in Khuzestan, was founded 6,000 years ago at a spot where the Iranian plateau widens onto the Mesopotamian plain, north of the Persian Gulf. It had for a long time been the capital of a powerful Elamite kingdom that had united Susiana and the high country of Anshan, which would later become Fars. Destroyed by the Assyrians in 646 BC, the city had little by little disappeared from the political horizon. By the sixth century, it was no more than a staging post from Persia (Fars, Pasargadae, and the region of Persepolis) on the way to Babylonia. Its position, however, remained important strategically, and Darius could not ignore this when planning the great routes of the empire.

It is thanks to the support and encouragement of the Iranian authorities that restoration work was soon followed by systematic excavations that were able to be conducted at Susa from 1969 to 1979 on the Apadana tell. Preliminary reports were published regularly in the Cahiers de la Délégation archéologique française en Iran (DAFI), and also in Persian, in the series of the Iranian Centre for Archaeological Research (ICAR) actively directed by Firouz Bagherzadeh. Students, members of ICAR and of Tehran Museum participated in each season of excavations. Articles also appeared in numerous French and foreign journals as and when discoveries were made.

The events of 1979 led to research being interrupted and the teams breaking up. This affected continuity in the production of excavation reports. Meanwhile, from 1981 to 1984, a Franco-American programme led to a preliminary evaluation of the results, which were presented in 1985 during a Rencontre Assyriologique Internationale organised in France under the auspices of the Centre National de Recherche Scientifique (CNRS) and the National Science Foundation (NSF). An account was published in *Paléorient* (vol. 11/2, 1985) and Assyriologists and Elamite scholars (centred around M.-J. Steve) managed to bring together a general survey in the columns of the *Supplément au Dictionnaire de la Bible*; while 1996 saw the masterly work by Pierre Briant (*From Cyrus to Alexander: A History of the Persian Empire*).

Nonetheless, there was a feeling among the researchers and technicians of the Susa Archaeological Mission of incompletion, and of a debt owed to a country which had welcomed them and entrusted them with the exploration of its prodigious past.

It was at this point, in 2007, that the idea was born of a work, which, while answering to the needs of the diverse disciplines which archaeological research has spawned, would also be highly illustrated to render it accessible to a wider interested public. The present volume therefore represents the results of recent excavations by placing them in the context of earlier work and the interpretations to which it gave rise.

These results have enabled, in a certain measure, a survey of the techniques and methods of Middle Eastern architecture at the cusp of the sixth to fifth centuries BC. In iconographic studies they have advanced our understanding of the way traditional forms of religious symbolism were substituted for a new imagery translating royal ideology. Archaeology here compensates for deficiencies in literary sources and, through Darius' statue, clarifies the singular relationship between Persia and Egypt.

i

Column capitals of the north portico of the Hypostyle Hall
sculptor Pascal Coupot; reconstruction by Héritage Virtuel

Introduction

John Curtis, OBE, FBA

Keeper of Special Middle East Projects, The British Museum

Whether we regard it in a geographical, historical, or scriptural point of view, there are few places throughout the East more replete with interest than … Susa.

Well before the first excavations at the site, the name of Shushan or Susa was very familiar to readers of the Bible. This was principally because the events described in the Book of Esther took place in Susa. According to the story, after Queen Vashti displeases King Xerxes she is deposed and a young Jewish girl, Esther, is selected in her place. In this privileged position, Esther manages to prevent a threatened massacre of the Jews in Persia orchestrated by Haman, a bitter rival of Esther's guardian, Mordecai. The annual festival of Purim commemorates this deliverance. Also, it was at Susa that Daniel had his dream about the ram and the goat – 'In my vision I saw myself in the citadel of Susa in the province of Elam; in the vision I was beside the Ulai Canal' (Daniel 8:2), and Nehemiah was at Susa when he received the news that the walls and gates of Jerusalem had fallen into disrepair (Nehemiah 1:1).

It was also known from the testimony of Classical authors such as Herodotus, Xenophon, Strabo, Diodorus Siculus, Quintus Curtius and Arrian that Susa was an important capital city of the Achaemenid Persians.

Because of the notoriety of the place, there was keen interest in the early nineteenth century in locating it. There were at least three candidates to be the ancient city of Susa: modern Shushtar, on the left bank of the River Karun, where there are impressive ancient waterworks; modern Shush, on the River Shaur; and modern Susan, on the upper reaches of the River Karun, just over 50 km to the east of Masjid-i Suleiman and more than 150 km from Shush. Amongst the early travellers to the site was John MacDonald Kinneir, later to become British envoy to the Persian court 1826–30, who visited Shush in March 1810 and concluded that it was probably ancient Susa. He wrote in his *Geographical Memoir of the Persian Empire* published in 1813:

> *About seven or eight miles to the west of* Dezphoul *(Dezful) commence the ruins of* Shus *… like the ruins of* Ctesiphon, Babylon *and* Kufa *(they) consist of hillocks of earth and rubbish, covered with broken pieces of brick and coloured tile … These mounds bear some resemblance to the pyramids of* Babylon; *with this difference, that instead of being entirely made of brick, they are formed of clay and pieces of tile … Large blocks of marble, covered with hieroglyphics, are not unfrequently here discovered by the Arabs, when digging in search of hidden treasure; and at the foot of the most elevated of the pyramids stands the* Tomb of Daniel, *a small, and apparently a modern building, erected on the spot where the relics of that prophet is believed to rest.*

Despite its potential importance, the site did not make a good impression on MacDonald Kinneir: 'The site of the city of *Shus* is now a gloomy wilderness, infested by lions, hyaenas, and other beasts of prey. The dread of these furious animals compelled Mr Monteith and myself to take shelter for the night within the walls that encompass *Daniel's Tomb*.'

When Austen Henry Layard visited Shush in 1841 he had no doubt that it was the ancient city of Susa. In his *Early Adventures* he wrote: 'The vast mound which marks the site of the ancient city of Susa, the capital of Susiana and Elymais, was visible in the distance, and as we drew near it appeared to me to be little inferior in size to the Mujelibi, the principal ruin of Babylon. We rode first to the tomb – the principal object of my visit'. A little later he adds 'There cannot be any doubt … that the great mound and the remains which surround it … occupy the site of the ancient capital of Susiana; and, consequently, it may be presumed, of Shushan the palace, of the Book of Daniel'. He also visited Susan in the Bakhtiari Mountains, which Colonel H.C. Rawlinson believed to be the site of Shushan the Palace, where Daniel had had his vision, but Layard dismissed this identification, and it is Layard's description of Susan (not Shush) that is quoted below in this book.

Nevertheless, the identification of Shush with ancient Susa was not resolved beyond all reasonable doubt until the commencement of excavations there.

The site of Susa is about 100 km north of Ahvaz, in Khuzistan in south-western Iran. It consists of three gigantic mounds, occupying an area of about one square kilometer, known as the Apadana mound, the Acropolis mound, and the Ville Royale (royal town) mound. The Acropolis rises 36m above the level of the plain. To the east of this cluster of mounds is the so-called 'Tell of the Artisans'. To the west of this complex of mounds, at a distance of about 200m, is the small River Shaur. The space in between was originally filled by the village of Shush, which has now expanded to the north and south and across the river to become a large town of more than 50,000 inhabitants. The tomb of the prophet Daniel is in the centre of the old village, close to the river. Like many similar shrines in the Middle East there is no evidence of a foundation earlier that the medieval period. To the west of the River Shaur is an Achaemenid palace, and further west again, at a distance of several kilometers across a flood-plain, is the River Karkheh.

In May 1850, William Kennett Loftus, a geologist with the Turco-Persian Frontier Commission, accompanied by the artist Henry A. Churchill, made a plan of the ruins. They returned in January 1851 with Lieutenant-Colonel W.F. Williams, the British Commissioner on the Frontier Commission, and in a brief excavation hit upon the Apadana or audience hall of the great palace built by Darius and restored by Artaxerxes II.

In a two-month season from February–April 1852, this time on behalf of the British Museum, Loftus not only reconstructed the plan of the Apadana but dug trenches in all the three main mounds of the site. Amongst other things he found in the south-west corner of the Ville Royale mound about 200 terracotta figurines of a semi-naked woman from the Middle Elamite period and in the north part of the Acropolis mound a large collection of fragments of alabaster vase inscribed with the name of Xerxes in Old Persian, Elamite, Babylonian and Egyptian. Despite these interesting results, at the conclusion of the excavation Rawlinson, then the British Consul in Baghdad, reported that Loftus had 'turned the mound of Susa topsy-turvey without finding much', and the British Museum decided not to continue with the excavations.

More than 30 years were to elapse before excavations were resumed at Susa, now by the French archaeologists Marcel and Jane Dieulafoy, who in 1885 and 1886 found many of the wonderful glazed brick friezes from Darius's Palace showing lions and Persian archers that are now in the Louvre. The academic reports on the work were by Marcel Dieulafoy, but his wife was obviously a spirited and feisty woman who did much to contribute to the success of the enterprise. As well as a detailed daily record of the excavations at Susa, she published a fascinating and informative account of their journeys in the Middle East in 1880–1 under the title *La Perse, La Chaldée and La Susiane*. In 1897 responsibility for the excavations at Susa was given to Jacques de Morgan, and he remained in charge until 1912. During this time, talented people involved in the excavations included Roland de Mecquenem and the architect Maurice Pillet, who has left for posterity some charming watercolour reconstructions. Originally the French archaeologists were operating under the authority of a firman signed by Nasir ed-Din Shah in 1884, but in 1900 after five years of negotiation a convention was signed by Muzaffar ed-Din Shah granting France exclusive excavation rights in the whole of Iran and authorizing the excavators to take all the finds from Susa to France. The only stipulation was that there would have to be financial compensation for gold and silver objects. This convention remained in force until 1927 when the country opened up to other excavators and a division of finds at the end of every season was introduced. It was also during the time of de Morgan that a massive castle ('le château') was built on the northern spur of the Acropolis mound. This building was partly for the use of the dig-team and their equipment, but it also had a defensive purpose as Susa was still subject to attacks from marauding tribes at that time. The result is a building that still dominates the site of Susa and is by far the grandest archaeological expedition house in the Middle East.

After an interruption because of the First World War, de Mecquenem supervised intermittent excavations until the Second World War and then from 1946–67 Roman Ghirshman was in charge of the project. He had already made his name through the excavation of Iranian sites such as Tepe Sialk, just outside Kashan, and Tepe Giyan, near Nahavand in Luristan. Then in 1969 a new programme involving Iranian as well as French archaeogists was initiated under the direction of Jean Perrot. This continued until the Iranian Revolution of 1979. It is to Jean Perrot, of course, that we are indebted for the present book, which serves as a magnificent legacy to his work at Susa. Professor Perrot deserves great credit for initiating and editing this publication, which is a full record of the Achaemenid period at Susa that lasted from 550 BC until 331 BC. The book was first published in French in 2010, and this English translation has been undertaken by Gerard Collon with the assistance of Dominique Collon. Although this book is primarily concerned with Achaemenid Susa, the excavations at the site have also revealed much about pre- and post-Achaemenid levels, and we will briefly discuss these next.

Susa has been inhabited since the Neolithic period, perhaps as far back as 7000 BC. In the millennia that followed, successive civilisations at Susa produced splendid pottery decorated with a range of geometric and figural designs. From

about 3000 BC onwards Susa was one of the main centres of the Elamite civilization that was based in the highland and lowland areas of south-western Iran.
History begins at Susa in the so-called Proto-Elamite period (*c.*3100–2700 BC)
when the burgeoning economic situation necessitated the recording of transactions in the form of clay tablets inscribed with a pictographic writing system that
is still not completely understood. In the Old Elamite period (*c.*2700–1500 BC),
Elam was politically and culturally dominated by powerful dynasties in
Mesopotamia to the west, but in the Middle Elamite period (*c.*1500–1100 BC)
local traditions predominate. From this period there are many cuneiform tablets
written in the Elamite language, and works in bronze such as the statue of
Queen Napirisha weighing 1750 kg, now in the Louvre, testify to the wealth
of Susa. Such was the strength of Elam at this time that in 1168 BC the king
Shutruk-Nahhunte was able to invade southern Mesopotamia and bring back
to Susa many important Babylonian pieces including the Code of Hammurabi
which is also now in the Louvre. Dating from the Neo-Elamite period (*c.*1100–
550 BC) are interesting rock reliefs at places such as Shikaft-i Salman and Kul-i
Farah on the edge of the Izeh Plain, but Susa itself was destroyed by the Assyrian
king Ashurbanipal in 647 BC. For the next 100 years, until the beginning of
the Achaemenid period, little is known about Susa, but Elamite civilization
apparently continued to flourish..

In 550 BC an event occurred that was to have a profound effect on the history
of the Middle East. In that year, Cyrus the Great deposed the Median king
Astyages and proclaimed himself king over the now united Medes and Persians.
So began the Achaemenid dynasty so called after Achaemenes, named by Darius
as the eponymous founder of the dynasty. In a historic battle in 547 or 546 BC
Cyrus defeated Croesus of Lydia which brought much of central and western
Turkey under his control. Then in 539 BC he captured Babylon and the former
Babylonian empire stretching as far as the Mediterranean coast fell into his
hands. He was now master of most of the Ancient Near East. Cyrus built for
himself a new city, at Pasargadae in Fars, and he was eventually buried there in
a splendid stone-built tomb that survives to this day. His son Cambyses added
Egypt to the rapidly expanding Persian Empire, but following his premature
death there was a short period of civil war from which Darius (522–486 BC),
arguably the greatest of the Persian kings, emerged victorious. Under Darius
the Persian Empire reached its greatest extent, stretching from North Africa to
the Indus Valley and from Central Asia to the Persian Gulf. Towards the end
of Darius' reign there was even an invasion of Greece, initiating the so-called
Graeco-Persian wars that were carried on by his successor Xerxes. In line with
his territorial ambitions, Darius was also an energetic builder. He launched at
least two grandiose building programmes, notably at Persepolis and Susa. Of
the two schemes, Persepolis, which was continued by Xerxes, was the more
ambitious, but probably the two centres were intended for different purposes
which are not entirely clear to us. In any case, they served different constituencies:
Persepolis was on the Iranian plateau in the heart of the modern province of
Fars, whereas Susa was in the lowlands, facing Mesopotamia. The building works
of Darius at Susa were extensive, as we shall see from this volume, and Xerxes
made some effort to complete them, but Darius' enthusiasm for the site does not
seem to have been shared by all his successors. It is recorded that his palace was
burned down in the reign of Artaxerxes I (465–424 BC) and the only king after
Darius and Xerxes who we know for certain to have sponsored building work
at Susa was Artaxerxes II (404–359 BC). Nevertheless, it is likely that Susa
remained an important centre down to the end of the Achaemenid period.
Indeed, it is sometimes suggested that Susa was the main treasury of the Persian
Empire.

Darius' palace at Susa consisted in part of a columned hall with column capitals in the form of bulls, and this type of columned hall or as it is often but erroneously called Apadana, has come to typify Persian architecture of this period. Whether the columned hall was an Iranian invention is not entirely clear, but certainly the Achaemenid columned hall had its direct antecedents in North-West Iran in the late second or early first millennium BC. In the Achaemenid period it appeared as a monumental public building in an area which had previously been dominated by the large mud brick palaces of Assyria and Babylonia. But this was not the only innovation at this period. Persian art was eclectic, that is to say forms and motifs were deliberately drawn from contemporary or near contemporary cultures such as Babylonia, Assyria, Egypt and Elam, and combined with native Persian features to produce a new and highly distinctive art style. There were also other innovations, for example the worship of Ahuramazda, the introduction of Old Persian cuneiform, a vast improvement in land, sea and canal communications, and the wider use of coinage. It can fairly be claimed, therefore, that the Achaemenid period was a time of change, and the evidence for many of the new practices can be found at Susa.

The Achaemenid period was brought to an end by Alexander's invasion of the Ancient Near East. Following a string of victories over the armies of the Persian king Darius III, Alexander reached the gates of Susa in late 331 BC. He entered the city without a struggle, and proceeded to loot the royal treasury. This event is graphically described by a number of classical authors including Arrian in his *Anabasis of Alexander*, who wrote

> *Alexander reached Susa in twenty days from Babylon; he entered the city and took over the treasure, up to fifty thousand talents of silver, and all the rest of the royal belongings. A good deal was captured there in addition, all that Xerxes brought back from Greece, notably bronze statues of Harmodius and Aristogeiton, which Alexander sent back to the Athenians.*

In the ensuing Hellenistic (Seleucid) period, Susa remained an important city known as Seleucia on the Eulaeus. A Greek inscription on one of the reused Achaemenid column bases is a memorial to Arreneides, the governor of Susa. As the Palace of Darius had not been destroyed by Alexander it presumably continued to be occupied during the Hellenistic period and probably later, but archaeological evidence for this is scant. During the Parthian and Sasanian periods, when Iranian dynasties reasserted themselves, Susa was an important centre, and throughout this time coins were minted here. This continued even after Susa was captured by the invading Arabs in AD 638, and the wealth of the city at this time is shown by the discovery of Ummayad coins, glass vessels and pottery. Almost certainly the grand Achaemenid buildings would have collapsed by this time and they would have been covered up by successive Islamic occupation levels. There were also flourishing Christian and Jewish communities. From the fifteenth century onwards however the city was in decline, and eventually the dwindling population moved from the high archaeological mounds to the area around Daniel's Tomb on the banks of the river Shaur.

In this sumptuous volume, the excavations of the Achaemenid buildings and levels at Susa are described mainly by Jean Perrot himself, Daniel Ladiray and Rémy Boucharlat. Dominating the site, on the Apadana Mound, was the Palace of Darius, consisting of a columned hall, built in the Iranian style, to one side of a vast mud brick building owing more to the Mesopotamian tradition. In this way there was a neat fusion of highland and lowland, new and old. In an inscription in Old Persian, Darius provides an account of how the palace was built. He describes in detail how the foundations were dug, and relates how materials and workmen were brought from different parts of the empire. Amongst the materials were cedar wood from the Lebanon, ivory from Ethiopia, lapis lazuli and carnelian from Sogdiana, and gold from Sardis and Bactria, while the specialist workmen included Ionians, Sardians, Medes, Egyptians and Babylonians. The columned hall was first stumbled upon by Williams and Loftus, and Loftus was able to reconstruct a ground plan with commendable accuracy. In the central hall, measuring about 58m square, there had been 36 columns in six rows of six, on square bases, with porticoes on three sides. Each portico had two rows of six columns on circular bases, giving a grand total of 72 columns in all. The bases would have supported fluted stone columns surmounted by bull-shaped capitals. Perrot estimates that the columns would have stood to a height of 20m. Four of the column bases in the central hall had inscriptions recording that the palace was originally built by Darius, had burnt down in the time of Artaxerxes I, and was rebuilt by Artaxerxes II. While this hypostyle hall is likely to have been used for formal receptions and affairs of state, the adjoining palace was apparently residential and administrative. It is an enormous building, measuring 246 x 155 m and constructed from mud brick. Essentially, the rooms are arranged around three large courtyards, very much in the Assyrian and Babylonian style.

On the south side of the west court there are two large rooms that have long been interpreted as the royal apartments. These two rooms both have pilasters near the four corners, a distinctive plan that leads to such rooms being known as 'salles à quatre saillants'. It is usually suggested that the purpose of these pilasters is to enable large rooms to be covered over with mud brick vaults. In fig 217 on p. 211, Hermann Gasche shows in an interesting sketch how this worked – the pilasters would have supported transverse vaults at either end of the room and a barrel vault for most of the length of the room between the two pairs of pilasters. This distinctive plan of a hall with four pilasters can be traced back beyond the middle of the second millennium BC at Susa, and although examples are lacking from the intervening period, this may be due to the inadequacy of the archaeological evidence. Interestingly, a similar plan with two long rooms opening into a smaller room, and with the same doorways, is found at Babylon, in buildings that are usually attributed to the Babylonian king Nebuchadnezzar (604–562 BC). It is often supposed that Babylon provides the inspiration for the occurrence of the 'salles à quatre saillants' plan at Susa, but Gasche rejects this possibility. For him, the tradition is Elamite, and Darius' builders are drawing on a longstanding local practice. How, then, to explain the similarities with the palaces at Babylon? Gasche concludes that the west part of the Southern Palace at Babylon was constructed or at least remodeled in the Achaemenid period, possibly even by Darius himself, as was the Northern Palace and the Summer Palace at Babylon. There would, then, be more evidence for Achaemenid building activity at Babylon than the very small columned building known as the 'Perserbau' tacked on to the west side of Nebuchadnezzar's Southern Palace. This is an attractive theory, but it remains hypothetical; it is unfortunate that it cannot be supported by inscriptional evidence or the presence of more material of Persian date in the palaces at Babylon.

The French excavators conclude that the rooms in the Residency would have had vaulted mud brick roofs generally around 12–13 m above floor level but possibly as high as 20 m, that is the same as the hypostyle hall, in the case of the royal apartments and the great halls to the south of the East Court.

Although built in mud brick the Residence was not devoid of decoration. There were red plaster floors in the private area of the Residence, and there was glazed brick decoration principally in the courtyards. This must originally have been very extensive: we learn from Annie Caubet's chapter that there are now no less than 13,000 bricks in museum collections, divided between France (Louvre) and Iran (Shush-i Daniel Museum in Susa and the National Museum in Tehran). Many of these bricks belong to the friezes of archers, sometimes thought to be the 'Immortals' who formed the king's personal bodyguard, and friezes of lions. In addition there are panels showing pairs of winged human-headed lions seated beneath a winged disc, composite monsters such as winged bulls and griffins, and bricks which are thought to have belonged to scenes showing figures climbing a staircase bearing food and drink and animals. The figures are dressed alternately in Persian and Median costume and are usually – as here – identified as servants, but Shahrokh Razmjou has convincingly argued that they are more probably priests carrying offerings and animals to be sacrificed at a religious ceremony. In the scenes on these glazed bricks there is an interesting contrast between Mesopotamian motifs represented by the fabulous monsters and Persian motifs represented by the archers. Caubet describes in detail the different techniques that are used to make these bricks which will be of great interest to those interested in ancient technology. Another matter of much potential interest has received little attention. These are the ancient fitters' marks that are to be found on top of the bricks painted in one of the colored glazes. There are also incised marks. The purpose of these marks was presumably to indicate to the ancient bricklayers the number of the course and the exact position in that course of the individual bricks. Loftus produced a chart of these marks, but it seems little record was kept of the marks found by Dieulafoy and Mecquenem before the bricks were cemented into reconstructions. As these marks are of absorbing interest, and could even be based on some kind of writing system, they would certainly repay further investigation.

Before leaving Darius' Palace we should note that during the years of the Franco-Iranian programme between 1969 and 1979 the extensive investigation of Darius' Palace provided much information, as described by Daniel Ladiray, about the building foundations, drainage arrangements, construction techniques, floor treatments, and much else of considerable interest. Also, it is gratifying that electrical resistivity surveys undertaken by Albert Hesse produced successful results in the areas of the Hypostyle Hall and the Residency, largely because the Achaemenid builders laid down beds of gravel for their foundations. Nevertheless, it remains the case that the plans as presented here are mainly the results obtained through excavation.

A short distance to the east of Darius's palace, on the very edge of the Apadana Mound, is a monumental gateway that gives access to the palace. This Gate of Darius is a rectangular building with two long rooms on either side and in the middle a square hall with four column bases. There was an inscription here by Xerxes reporting that he had completed the building begun by his father Darius. In 1972, a stone statue of Darius was found against one of the doorjambs in this gateway. The head of the statue is missing, but it is still a magnificent work of art and now occupies pride of place in the National Museum in Tehran. Darius is shown wearing a Persian robe, and with a dorsal pillar (an Egyptian device) at his back. The stone to make the statue came from Waddi Hammamat in Egypt, and the style and workmanship are clearly Egyptian. The king stands on a rectangular base which has on its two long sides 24 'fortress cartouches' with names in Egyptian hieroglyphs of the peoples belonging to the Persian empire, and above each cartouche is a kneeling figure with arms upraised dressed in the traditional costume of his country. Here we find representations of Bactrians, Babylonians, Egyptians and many others. On the short sides of the base are Egyptian fertility figures. There are inscriptions on the folds of the dress in Elamite, Old Persian, Babylonian and Egyptian which record that 'the Persian man has conquered Egypt'. Jean Yoyotte (now sadly deceased), who has written a detailed description of the statue in this volume, originally suggested that it must have been set up at Heliopolis on the site of modern Cairo, but here he concludes that a more likely location was Pithom (Tell el-Maskhuta) to the east of the Nile Delta. The Egyptian text on the statue mentions the god Atum and there were temples to Atum in both places. Pithom seems more likely because it is on the line of Darius' canal that connected the Nile with the Red Sea (otherwise known as the Canal of the Pharaohs or Necho's Canal), and it is thought that the statue was originally made to commemorate the inauguration of this canal. Exactly why the statue was brought to Susa, when it was brought and by which route are still unanswered questions but the consensus seems to be that it was brought to Susa at the end of Darius' reign or at the beginning of Xerxes' reign, probably by sea all around the Arabian Peninsula and into the Persian Gulf.

Access to the Gate of Darius was apparently through a building known as the Propylaeum, so-called because it appears to have been a porch or gatehouse leading to the royal enclosure. It was situated on the north-west corner of the Ville Royale mound, and must have been linked to the Gate of Darius by a bridge or causeway. The Propylaeum is a small building with a passage through the centre and two-column porticoes at either end. These column bases are inscribed with the name of Xerxes. On the east side of the Ville Royale mound, at a distance of about 400 m from the Propylaeum, is yet another gate, known as the Gate of the Artisans. Beyond this gate to the east, at a much lower level, is an area supposed to have been inhabited by 'artisans' and others, hence the name of the gate.

In the south part of the Ville Royale mound, known as the Donjon, many Achaemenid remains have been discovered by successive excavators, such as column bases and fragments of fluted column, together with miscellaneous small objects of probable Achaemenid date. It was here that Achaemenid ivories were discovered, thrown into a well. They are described, with other artefacts, by Piere Amiet. The presence of these Achaemenid remains has led many archaeologists to suggest that there was an important Achaemenid building, probably a palace, in this location, but Boucharlat demonstrates that the architectural fragments were probably brought from Darius' Palace and the Shaur Palace. Nevertheless, the existence of Achaemenid-type foundations on the Ville Royale apparently shows there was probably an Achaemenid building here, even if the architectural fragments that have been discovered do not come from it.

The Acropolis mound was surrounded by a substantial Achaemenid wall that was traced by Jacques de Morgan. The height of the Acropolis mound, and the fact that it was strongly defended, has led to speculation that the Treasury referred to by the Greek authors and the garrison might have been housed here. This is an attractive hypothesis but it has not yet been supported by archaeological investigation. It may be significant, however, that a magnificent bronze lion weight and a large bronze weight in the form of a knucklebone were found on the southern flank of the Acropolis, testifying to the presence of wealthy artifacts in this area. Also on the Acropolis Mound, Jacques de Morgan found a rich tomb in 1901. The body had been buried in a bronze coffin, accompanied by an assortment of gold jewellery. A torque, a pair of lion-headed bracelets, a pair of earrings and a pair of roundels all had the inlaid polychrome decoration that is a hallmark of the Achaemenid period. In this tradition, pieces of jewellery are inlaid with semi-precious stones such as turquoise, lapis lazuli and carnelian, and with glass and paste, all of different colours. These inlays were fitted into cavities (cloisons) on the surface of the gold jewellery.

On the west bank of the River Shaur that flows through the site, and nearly 500 m to the west of the Hypostyle Hall of Darius, is another cluster of Achaemenid period buildings only a few metres above the level of the plain that has come to be known as the Shaur Palace. This complex, measuring about 220

x 150 m, was excavated by Audran Labrousse and Rémy Boucharlat in the 1970s
and significant additions to the plan were made through electrical resistivity
surveys conducted by Albert Hesse. The best-preserved building in this complex
(Building I) has a hypostyle hall, about one third the size of that of Darius'
Palace, with eight rows of eight columns on round stone bases surrounded on
four sides by porticoes with double rows of columns on square stone bases. A
surprising discovery was made in some of the bricks of the west wall of the
hypostyle hall in the form of mercury which is thought to have been placed there
as a foundation deposit. In the north-west part of the hypostyle hall fragments
of painted plaster were found showing the heads of life-size figures in profile.
One shows a Mede, and another has been identified as an Arachosian. The
dominant colours are blue and red. These paintings are very significant because
they are the best evidence for wall painting in Achaemenid palaces that has been
recovered to date. Building II in the complex was not well preserved, but also had
columns, while Building III was represented only by traces of its foundations. Of
the pieces of sculpture found in this area the most remarkable is a stone panel
with relief decoration showing a half life-size figure mounting a staircase. This
sculpture provides an interesting parallel with Persepolis but as it was found in
a secondary context we do not know where it would have been placed originally
and how it would have fitted into a decorative scheme. The same problem applies
to a stone staircase found some 800 m to the north of the Shaur complex that is
thought probably to come from here. About 300 fragments of glazed brick were
also found in the complex, and although none was found in context they provide
a strong indication that there were originally glazed brick panels here as in the
Palace of Darius.

How should we interpret the Shaur Palace? On the Shaur mound 14 fragments
of inscribed column base were found coming from at least eight square bases.
They all bore parts of a trilingual inscription of Artaxerxes II. Unfortunately all
of these pieces were in secondary contexts, but it seems clear that some if not all
the buildings in this complex were constructed or restored by Artaxerxes II. There
is some controversy about the inscription. Older scholars such as Roland G. Kent
believed that Artaxerxes says he built the palace as a 'pleasant retreat' or paradise.
This is denied by François Vallat, who here provides a more prosaic translation.
Whatever the truth of this matter, we may well imagine that this palace was
situated in an idyllic spot on the banks of the River Shaur and would have been a
perfect retreat for Artaxerxes, well away from the large complex of Darius' Palace
which he had himself restored and was probably where official and administrative
business was conducted. The Shaur Palace may well have been a paradise, even if
the inscription does not say so.

We should also consider a now vanished columned building 4 km north-
east of Susa that Marcel Dieulafoy excavated in 1886. He called this building
the Ayadana (Old Persian 'sanctuary') and interpreted it as an Achaemenid fire
temple for practising the Zoroastrian religion. As Rémy Boucharlat has shown,
however, it is more likely to be a non-religious building dating from the Seleucid
or Parthian periods.

This book is much more than a survey of the archaeology, art and architecture
of Susa in the Achaemenid period. Thus, there is a chapter by Pierre Briant,
the master historian of the Achaemenid period, titled 'Susa and Elam in the
Achaemenid Empire', and chapters by François Vallat, 'Darius the Great King'
and 'The Main Achaemenid Inscriptions at Susa'. In fact, 36 different royal
inscriptions have been found at the site, represented by numerous fragments.
They are mostly from the reign of Darius I (Darius the Great) (522–486 BC), but
also date from the reigns of Xerxes (486–465 BC), Darius II (424–404 BC), and
Artaxerxes II (404–359 BC). The majority of these inscriptions were trilingual,

written in Old Persian, Elamite and Babylonian. In addition, in an appendix Vallat presents a new translation of the Elamite version of the Bisitun inscription. Some of the theories presented as a result of these studies relate to subjects that are of fundamental importance for Achaemenid studies, so they should be briefly highlighted here.

The first concerns the ancestry of Darius I and his claim to the throne. It will be remembered that Cyrus the Great was succeeded by Cambyses. After the latter's premature death in 522 BC a civil war broke out from which Darius emerged victorious.

Vallat accepts Darius' claim that he belonged to a noble family that could trace its ancestry back to Achaemenes, the eponymous founder of the Achaemenid dynasty. Thus in the great inscription at Bisitun, Darius says 'my father was Hystaspes; Hystaspes' father was Arsames; Arsames' father was Ariaramnes; Ariaramnes' father was Teispes; Teispes' father was Achaemenes.' Now, it is known from the Cyrus Cylinder that Cyrus was a descendant of Teispes, so if Darius's stated genealogy was correct he would not only have had a strong claim to the throne but his branch of the family may even have had a better claim than Cyrus and his descendants. This is shown in the genealogical table reproduced on page xxxii. However, many scholars still follow the view that Darius was an imposter and that his genealogy was fabricated. Much has been written about this intriguing question, but the matter still remains open. For an authoritative discussion of the question, the reader is referred to Pierre Briant's magisterial *History of the Persian Empire.*

The second controversial question also centres on Darius I and his Bisitun inscription. It is nowadays commonly believed that the Old Persian script was introduced in the time of Darius, partly because Darius says in the Elamite version of the Bisitun inscription 'I [Darius] made another inscription, in Aryan (i.e. Old Persian), which before did not exist'. Now, however, Vallat renders this sentence 'I translated this inscription differently in Aryan, it did not previously exist here' (i.e. there was no Old Persian inscription *in this place* before). Partly based on this, Vallat suggests that Old Persian existed already in the time of Ariaramnes, the great-grandfather of Darius. For Vallat the Old Persian inscriptions at Pasargadae were carved in the time of Cyrus and not in the time of Darius, as generally thought, and he accepts the authenticity of two gold tablets from Hamadan with Old Persian inscriptions of Ariaramnes and Arsames, the grandfather of Darius. These tablets are often regarded as forgeries, made later in the Achaemenid period by Darius (to support his legitimacy) or by Artaxerxes II, or even as forgeries made in modern times. Again, there is much that remains unresolved, but for the time being the gold tablets must be treated with caution. The gold tablets also impact on the question of religion. Because they purport to show that both Ariaramnes and Arsames paid homage to Ahuramazda, Vallat concludes that the 'senior branch' of the Achaemenid family (i.e., Darius' family) were followers of Ahuramazda. Cyrus the Great and his family, by contrast, he thinks, were followers of Mithra, and the Median *magi* (priests) only came to prominence with Cyrus' accession. Whatever the truth of this, it is certainly the case that the accession of Darius does seem to mark some kind of watershed in religious matters, and it is not impossible that events such as the filling-in of the temple at Nush-i Jan should even have happened at the beginning of Darius' reign.

This magnificent volume, then, stretches far beyond the confines of Achaemenid Susa. It puts Susa in the context of the Achaemenid world in general, and in doing so it touches on practically all aspects of Ancient Persia in the fifth and fourth centuries BC. Jean Perrot and his colleagues are to be warmly congratulated for presenting their findings to the public in such an accessible and informative way. It will be clear to the reader of this book that although Susa is one of the most important sites in Iran, its exploration was undertaken largely by foreign archaeologists, first British and then French. Since the Iranian Revolution in 1979, however, the work has been taken up by Iranian archaeologists. I am indebted to Dr Shahrokh Razmjou for supplying me with information. He tells me that Mr Mir Abedin Kaboli worked at Susa in 1982–1983 and from 1995 until 2005 (see also p. 113 and n. 18 on p. 123). Work was concentrated on the west side of the Apadana Mound, and some important additions were made to the plan of the Apadana itself. Certain evidence for a tower was found at the north-west corner of the building, rather larger than the reconstruction suggested by Jean Perrot, and there were remains of another tower in the south-west corner. There were staircases in the vicinity of both towers. The wall between the two towers, which was found to be not completely straight, acted partly as a retaining wall, behind which were deposits of the earlier Elamite levels of the mound containing Elamite artefacts such as glazed bricks. Mr Kaboli also restored some parts of the Apadana that had not been restored by the French Mission. Restoration work at Susa was also undertaken by Mr Ehsan Yaghmaee and Mr Mehdi Rahbar. The latter restored some parts of the Apadana Palace and the Shaur Palace that were damaged during the Iraq–Iran war, and he was also responsible for restoration work on the 'château'. To celebrate all this work, an archaeological conference was held at Susa in 1994.

While this volume in English was in course of preparation, the sad news was received that Jean Perrot had passed away on 24 December 2012, aged 92 years. What had started as a tribute has now become a memorial volume. Jean Perrot was born at Landresse in France on 10 June 1920, and he studied at the Sorbonne and the École du Louvre, in the latter case with René Dussaud and André Parrot. His introduction to Near Eastern archaeology came in 1945 when he went to Palestine, shortly to become Israel, and for the next 23 years he worked in the Levant, Turkey, Cyprus and Afghanistan. During this time he excavated at many important sites, mostly dating from the Neolithic and Chalcolithic periods, and his interest in prehistory is reflected in the fact that he co-founded the important journal *Paléorient* in 1973. In 1968 he was appointed Director of the Délégation Archéologique Française en Iran, in succession to Roman Ghirshman, and from 1969 until 1979 he led the joint Franco-Iranian Archaeological Mission to Susa. After the Iranian revolution he returned to Israel and was the first director of the Centre de Recherche Française de Jérusalem 1979–1989. During his long and distinguished career, many honours came to him. He had joined the CNRS as a research assistant in 1946 and eventually became the Director of Research in 1972. As early as 1965 he was made a corresponding member of the French Académie des Inscriptions et Belles-Lettres. In a lifetime replete with achievements there were many highlights, but undoubtedly the crowning glory of his career was the excavation at Susa. It is particularly appropriate that an issue of *Dossiers d'Archéologie* (hors-série no. 23), written by Jean Perrot himself and devoted to Darius the Great, was published shortly after his death. This contains a selection of illustrations from the present book, and provided an opportunity for several colleagues, including Nicolas Grimal of the Collège de France, to write glowing tributes about the life and work of Jean Perrot. Undoubtedly there will be many more.

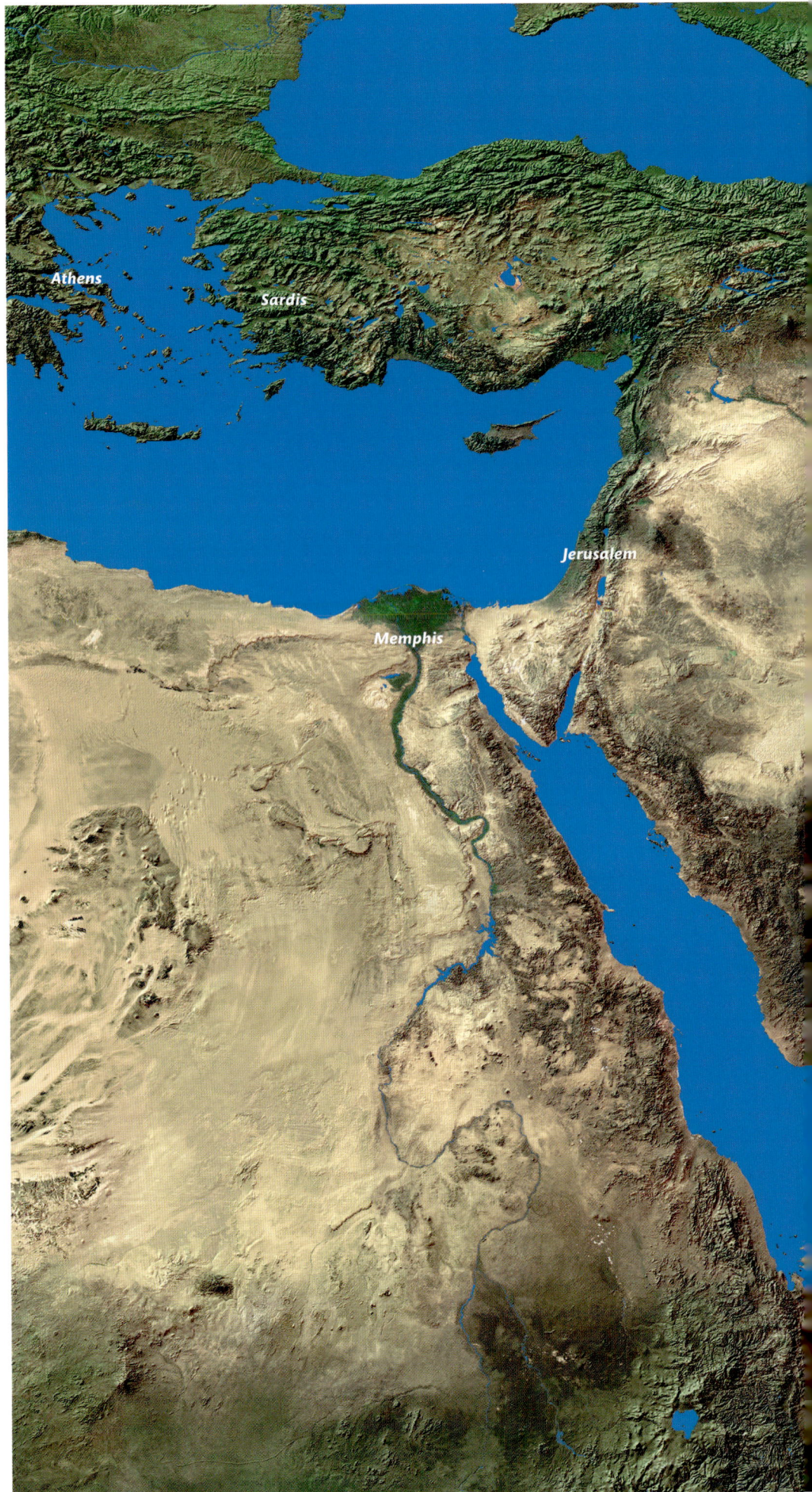

Athens

Sardis

Jerusalem

Memphis

Balkh

Ecbatana

Babylon

Susa

Persepolis

Persian Gulf

iii
Shush-i Daniel (Susa)

What the ancients called 'The River of Susa' is probably not the Shaur, but the Karkheh – the Ulai river of the Book of Daniel (8:2: 'In my vision I saw myself in the citadel of Susa in the province of Elam. In my vision I was beside the Ulai Canal.' NIV). The Greeks called the river the Eulæus, since it sounded similar to the name of a river in Macedonia. The River Shaur is actually a left-bank tributary of the Karkheh and part of its flood plain.

The course of the Karkheh has varied, due primarily to tectonic instability in the region. The Arabian plate dives under the Iranian plate in an easterly direction, the convergence producing anticlinal ridges on the Susiana plain, oriented North-North-East, South-South-East, parallel to the folds in the Zagros mountains. The altitude of the plain is 25 m north of Ahvaz and 100 m in the region of Dizful.

The Susiana plain is fertile. The rains in the spring are abundant, with annual rainfall averaging between 250 and 400 mm, and with a very dense hydrographic network draining the waters of the Iranian plateau. Those of the Karkheh go on to lose themselves in the marshes of southern Iraq, which constitute a barrier between Susiana and southern Mesopotamia. Those of the Dez and the Karun reach the Persian Gulf to the south, the Dez offering a navigable route to within a few of miles of Susa.

River Karkheh

River Shaur

*Shaur
Palace*

*Apadana
tell*

Acropolis

*Ville
Royale
tell*

*Tell
of the
Artisans*

Elam

François Vallat

Cuneiform inscriptions clearly show that the word Elam, in the narrowest sense, originally represented what is now the province of Fars (including Pasargadae and Persepolis). In a wider sense it covered the entirety of the Iranian plateau. The political definition did not correspond to the geographical situation. Thus Susa had long been part of Elam. It is therefore only important to define Elam according to period.

With the discovery of the 'proto-Elamite' tablets we obtained a vague idea of what Elam was in 3000 BC. These documents were found in a geographical area that stretches over most of present-day Iran. The distribution does not necessarily imply political ties; it does, however, suggest commercial links.

The first real image of an Elamite 'Empire' appears towards the end of the third millennium BC, during the Akkadian period, with tales of Sargon the Great's campaigns. At that time Elam comprised western Iran, from the Caspian Sea in the north to the south of the Persian Gulf, incorporating the deserts of the Dasht-i Kavir and the Dasht-i Lut. It was composed of different geopolitical entities: Awan in Luristan, Elam (in its narrowest sense) in the province of Fars, and Shimashki in Kerman. Susiana was then an integral part of a Mesopotamian empire.

In the second millennium BC, and until almost the eighth century BC, we know only that Elam comprised Susiana and Fars Province. No written record provides us with the eastern and northern limits of an Elamite empire then at its peak.

We then have to wait until the end of the first quarter of the first millennium BC for further elements that might contain geographical data. At this time the determining factor was the slow progression of the Median and Persian tribes onto the Iranian plateau. It was then that Susiana assumed the name Elam. At this ultimate stage references appear in the annals of the kings of Assyria, in books of the Bible and the inscriptions of the Achaemenid kings, particularly those of Darius. In his vast empire, Elam is but a province – a satrapy.

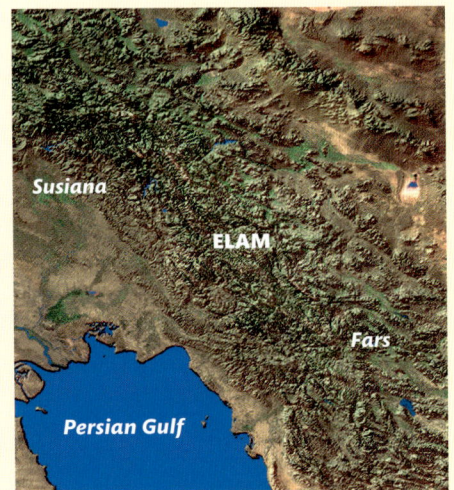

iv
Location of Elam

Key events in the Achaemenid Period

562 Death of Nebuchadnezzar II, King of Babylon

556 The Persian Cyrus II seizes control of Media

555 Nabonidus King of Babylon

546 Conquest of Lydia and Sardis in Asia Minor

539 Cyrus II occupies Babylon. End of Nabonidus' Reign

529 Death of Cyrus II, the Great

529 Cambyses II King of Persia

525 Cambyses II, first Pharaoh of the XXVIIth Egyptian dynasty

522 Death of Cambyses, seizure of power by Darius

519 Beginning of building works at Persepolis and Susa

518 Libyan and Scythian campaigns

500 Opening of the canal between the Red Sea and the Nile

493 Ionian revolt

490 Defeat of Persians at Marathon

486 Death of Darius. Egyptian revolt. Reign of Xerxes (486–465 BC)

480 Defeat of Persians at Salamis and in the Aegean

479 Xerxes crushes the Babylonian revolt

465 Assassination of Xerxes. Reign of Artaxerxes I (465–425 BC)

460 Revolt in Egypt

424 Reign of Darius II (424–405 BC)

405 Reign of Artaxerxes II (405–359 BC)

401 Battle of Cunaxa and death of Cyrus the Younger

399 Egypt escapes from Persian domination

359 Reign of Artaxerxes III (359–338 BC)

343 Reconquest of Egypt

336 Reign of Darius III (336–331 BC)

334 Alexander in Asia Minor

333 Defeat of Darius III at Issus

331 Defeat at Gaugamela

330 Alexander at Persepolis

323 Death of Alexander

Genealogical Table of the Achaemenid Dynasty

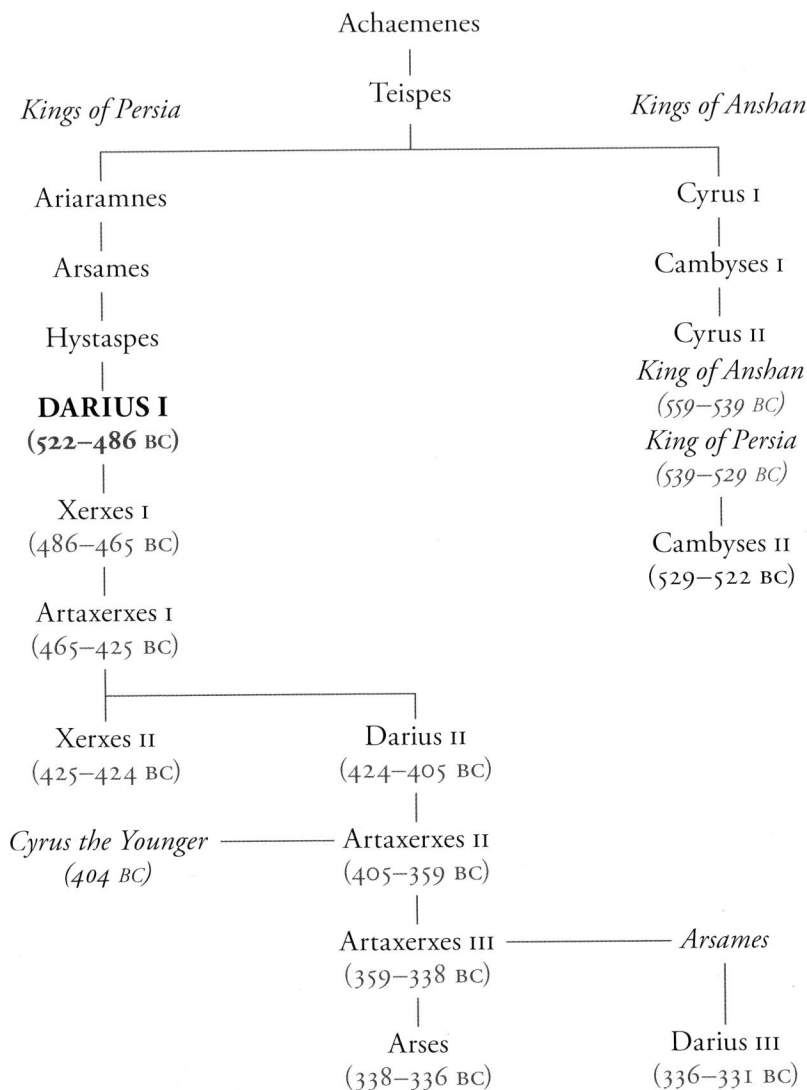

Achaemenes

|

Teispes

Kings of Persia   *Kings of Anshan*

Ariaramnes   Cyrus I

| |

Arsames   Cambyses I

| |

Hystaspes   Cyrus II
                                    King of Anshan
| *(559–539 BC)*
DARIUS I   *King of Persia*
(522–486 BC)   *(539–529 BC)*
| |
Xerxes I   Cambyses II
(486–465 BC)   (529–522 BC)
|
Artaxerxes I
(465–425 BC)

Xerxes II   Darius II
(425–424 BC)   (424–405 BC)
                              |
Cyrus the Younger ———— Artaxerxes II
(404 BC)   (405–359 BC)
                              |
                         Artaxerxes III ———————— *Arsames*
                         (359–338 BC) |
                              | |
                            Arses   Darius III
                         (338–336 BC)   (336–331 BC)

The Palace of Darius at Susa

1

Jules-Georges Bondoux, *Les fouilles de Suse*
1905, oil on canvas, h 4.63 m

1

Susa and Elam in the Achaemenid Empire

Pierre Briant

SOURCES AND PROBLEMS

For many years historians dreamt of seeing a series of 20 or so works, neatly arranged in alphabetical order on their library shelves, each volume dedicated to one of the great regions or satrapies of the Achaemenid Empire. This wish, already expressed over a century ago by Michael Rostovtzeff whilst reflecting on the Achaemenid foundations of the Hellenistic world, has never been realised despite remarkable progress since then. The number of written, archaeological, iconographic and numismatic records has expanded considerably, while websites and online databases are now available,[2] and in different regional and thematic subdivisions, Achaemenid history is covered by a large number of specialists. Regions such as western Asia Minor, Trans-Euphrates and especially Babylonia are better documented and known. There remain, however, considerable documentary lacunas which, in my view at least, explain the reticence in presenting regional syntheses.

This statement is equally relevant to three of the countries where the kings set up their palaces and residences, specifically Persia proper (Persepolis, Pasargadae), Elam (Susa) and Media (Ecbatana). What we know today of Achaemenid Media fills only a few paragraphs. Putting aside the discovery (out of their original context) of a few inscribed bases, the recent excavations at Ecbatana have not led to the discovery of the town nor the palaces frequented by Cyrus and his successors.[3] The palaces of Pasargadae, Persepolis and of Susa are, on the contrary well known, both through archaeology and epigraphy (this book attests to this), but the towns and/or agglomerations themselves are so poorly attested that they have long been referred to as 'empty capitals'. The recent prospecting at Pasargadae suggests another strategy and other avenues of research,[4] but much work remains before we can really understand what the town of Susa was actually like, and its place in the region of which it was the centre and in the wider empire in which it represented one of the power bases of the Great King.[5]

At Susa, we do not have at our disposal the immense wealth of documentation represented at Persepolis by the thousands of associated tablets and seals. These offer, and will offer us in the future, an analytical picture of the stages of construction of the Terrace buildings, the organisation of work on the site, in the workshops and in the Fars countryside,[6] the administrative geography of the region, religious life and cults,[7] the role of the king, the royal family and nobles, as well as of the political, economic and ideological organisation of Persia.[8]

Although there can be no doubt that Susa contained one or several archives, there are only scarce residual testimonies.[9] In addition, Elam was outside Persepolis' administrative sphere.[10] Only some of the tablets from Persepolis can give us information, indirectly: for example, travel ration texts (Series Q) often cite Susa (or Elam) as a point of departure and arrival, or a staging post for the caravans travelling the roads of the empire, and particularly between Susa and Persepolis.

In an indirect and elusive manner, Babylonian records, or those written in Babylonian, offer a few suggestions on the question of the 'town' of Susa and its population. Private contracts have been found, dated to one of the Artaxerxes 'King of Countries' and written in Susa. Associated tablets and seals indicate that there was at least a sedentary population, of very diverse ethnic composition (Babylonian, Egyptian, Persian, etc.). One of the parties to a contract was in the retinue of an officer who had a well-attested Iranian title (*ustarbar*). One of the texts testifies to the relations between Susa and Ecbatana.[11] The presence of a market is implied by the fact that a certain number of debts contracted in Susa had to be reimbursed in Babylonia 'at Susa rates'. It was understood that the money collected in Susa was to be reimbursed at the rate prevailing in Susa.[12] Other Babylonian tablets attest to the existence of a 'Royal Canal of Susa', which connected Babylonia and Elam.[13]

The documentary harvest from Greco-Roman narratives is limited and often problematic. The main reason is that in no episode of Greco-Persian military confrontation was Susa a theatre. It is the same with Persepolis: no Greek writer cites or even describes it before Alexander's first stay between January and May 330 BC. Furthermore, unlike Persepolis, Susa was never subjected to pillage or destruction by Alexander's troops. The only exception happened during the king's absence in India. On his return, measures were taken against local officials who had abused the country and the population. Amongst those sentenced to death was Herakon, who was 'convicted by some people of Susa of having destroyed the town temple'.[14] Of this temple, we sadly know nothing.

In 331 BC, Alexander had been peacefully welcomed by the Satrap, but he only passed through quickly in his haste to reach the high country and Persepolis. No writer therefore thought it necessary to give the least detail of this town, its topography, its extent, the palaces or even its terrace, brought to light by archaeologists. There is an isolated reference in Diodorus to the 'famous palaces of Susa' (*ta preiboeta en Sousois basileia*), where Alexander seizes the treasures of Darius III.[15] The Greek historian Arrian's reference to a citadel (*akra tôn Sousôn*),[16] is confirmed by Diodorus and Polybius.[17] It is no doubt what Strabo, who also evokes a citadel (*akra*), termed the acropolis (*akropolis*). According to this same author, the perimeter of 200 stadia was not fortified (*ateikhistos*); he adds, however, that there was a 'wall, which, like the temples and like the royal palaces (*ta basileia*), was made of brick and bitumen more or less the same as those of the Babylonians'.[18] Apparently, Strabo juxtaposed references from various heterogenous sources (Aeschylus, Simonides and Polykleitos are cited at brief intervals, but many other authors were used).[19] In addition, whilst developing his argument, he established a contrast between Susa, and residences which, in Persia, were sited in 'naturally stronger positions'.[20] This could simply indicate that this

2
Principal routes of the Achaemenid Empire
after BRIANT, 1996: 378

was not the case with Susa. However, the existence of a citadel obviously cannot be doubted.[21] It is therefore difficult to harmonise this information with the result of the excavations.[22] One can even ask, in the case of Susa, whether it is worth the effort. As we can see, in fact, the accounts of Classical writers had a primary role in the image formed and transmitted by travellers in 'pre-archaeological'[23] centuries, but the prodigious progress in field research since the last decades of the 19th century has removed much of the interest in the incomplete, confused and uncertain evocations of Alexander's chroniclers, now lost and often used second or third hand by writers of the Roman period. If on one hand, relevant archaeological work can be useful to commentators on Strabo, on the other hand, literary references contribute nothing, or almost nothing, to the archaeology of today.

Such a remark does not mean that classical sources should not be used, since they are sometimes extremely informative, and their interpretation on other points can lead to reflexion and discussion, even when they do not always impart precise information.[24] Let us say simply that in this domain, like many others, progress comes rather from the comparison of Susian epigraphic and archaeological sources with all the written sources: the Susian, Persepolitan and Babylonian sources, just as much as the Greco-Roman literary testimonies when they exist and are judged pertinent.

FROM THE CAPITAL OF THE KINGDOM OF ELAM TO THE ROYAL ACHAEMENID RESIDENCE

We are incredibly badly informed about the conditions in which the ancient neo-Elamite kingdom came to be integrated into the new Achaemenid Empire, and how its capital became a royal Achaemenid residence. The contacts between the high country of Anshan and the Elamite low country were ancient, and the intercultural exchanges were extremely decisive in the evolution of the culture,

3
**Seal of 'Kurash of Anshan'
on tablet PF 694 from Persepolis**
© OI Chicago;
drawing by L. Sterner after M. Garrison
Ars Orientalis, 21 (1992), p. 4

4
**Susa, on the border of the Mesopotamian
plain and the Iranian plateau**
© WorldSat International Inc.1008
(www.worldsat.ca all rights reserved)

ethnicity and ideology of Achaemenid Persia. This is illustrated by the tablets from the Acropolis at Susa, the tomb of Arjan, Neo-Elamite inscriptions, Neo-Elamite and Achaemenid glyptic and, of course, the thousands of Elamite tablets from Achaemenid Persepolis.[25] One of the most remarkable testimonies is the seal of 'Kurash of Anshan, son of Teispes' which was reused at Persepolis on tablets of Series J (PFS 93*).[26] Beyond the current discussions, there is a broad consensus in favour of the theory of a specific and powerful Elamite contribution – via the region of Anshan – before the affirmation (under Darius) of a 'Persian' identity.

Great uncertainty remains as to the date and the context of the capture of Susa by the Achaemenid Persians. A passage by Herodotus (I.188–189), is sometimes thought to suggest an annexation by Cyrus before the capture of Babylon, but this is really not pertinent.[27] It is true that a Hellenistic text, the *Dynastic Prophecy*, designates Cyrus as 'King of Elam', but it could simply be a literary archaism. In all the other known Babylonian occurrences, his title is 'King of Persia'.[28] For his part, Darius claims that on his accession Elam was part of the Empire (DB § 6). However, such a declaration does not exclude the possibility that under Cyrus and Cambyses, a small Elamite kingdom survived as a close dependency of the Achaemenid kings. In any case, prior to Darius' building works, there is no evidence of Achaemenid culture at Susa.

Susa and Elam only appear in the narrative records during the great revolts at the time of Darius' seizure of power.[29] The Elamites rebelled three times. They were

5

Bisitun relief
Darius facing the 'liar kings'
photograph by Y. Majidzadeh

amongst the first, with the Babylonians, to manifest their desire to free themselves from Persian domination. The first revolt was in 522 BC under the leadership of Asina who, although having a Persian name, is called an Elamite in the Babylonian version of Darius' Bisitun inscription. He took the title of King of Elam and the population rallied to him (DB § 16). In December 522, Darius was content with sending an Elamite 'messenger' against him, according to the Babylonian and Elamite versions. 'This Asina was taken and sent to me. Then I killed him' (DB § 17). With many others (including Persia itself), Elam was once again in revolt when Darius was at Babylon and was attempting to coordinate the counter-offensive of his lieutenants on different fronts (DB § 20–21). The chief rebel once again has a Persian name, Martiya. He is also termed 'Persian' by Darius (DB § 52), and it is in Persia from which he originates, that he starts the revolt; more precisely in the village of Kuknakan, well known in the tablets of Persepolis as being a royal staging post,[30] where Princess Irtasduna had her domains.[31] Then, in Elam proper, he proclaimed himself king under the name of Imanish. According to the account of Darius, the Elamites became fearful due to the proximity of the king (then in Babylonia), and they themselves killed the rebel king (DB § 22–23). The two rebels figure in first (DB*c*) and fourth (DB*f*) positions on the Bisitun Relief in the procession of 'Liar Kings', both guilty of having proclaimed themselves 'King in Elam'.

Things did not end here, however, because after the crushing of the great revolts and the erection of the Bisitun monument, Elam was in revolt for a third time.

On this occasion, Darius' narrative is much more detailed, and it seems that he is describing the gravity of the situation. The chief rebel is called Atamaita. Darius sent an army, under the command of the Persian Gaubaruva (Gobryas), who won a victory over the Elamite army: 'Then Gaubaruva beat and crushed the Elamites and he captured their chief, and sent him to me. Then I killed him. Afterwards the people were mine.' (DB § 71). As in the case of the Sakas, referred to immediately afterwards (DB § 74–75), Darius added a religious justification for his victories in DB § 72: 'These Elamites were perfidious and they did not venerate Ahuramazda. I venerated Ahuramazda. By the grace of Ahuramazda, I treated them according to my pleasure.'

It is not a case here of the great king 'persecuting' the Elamite religious rites and cults, especially when one considers the importance of Humban and the Elamite cults, and the royal patronage from which they benefited in the Persepolis Tablets.[32] It was simply a case of restating, in another fashion, that he owed his power and his supremacy to the protection of the one who was proclaimed the Great God of Persia and of the royal and imperial power. Be that as it may, this latest regaining of control marked the end of an independent Elamite royalty (if it had survived thus far),[33] and the definitive integration of Elam into the empire, even if the Persepolis Tablets reveal the persistent usage of both place names: Anshan and Elam (*Hatamtam*).[34] Henceforth, Elam was a subject state and satrapy of which Susa was the capital, and the term Anshan designates not the ancient kingdom but the region of the same name.[35]

It was then that Darius decided to make Susa a royal Achaemenid residence. This caused an immediate change in the urban structure. Neither the date of the beginning of the works nor the speed of construction are known with any precision.[36] Despite their considerable interest, the numerous primary sources do not allow us to reach any great certainty in this domain. It is certainly not a few lines from Herodotus which will allow us to date the start of construction.[37] A passage from the biography of the Egyptian Udjahorresnet indicates that he was sent to Egypt by Darius 'whilst his majesty was in Elam', so possibly in 519 BC, if one accepts that his return was linked to a royal decision concerning the bringing together of the Egyptian judiciary.[38] However, the text does not imply that a palace already existed at this date in the town. It seems more likely that the first proof of existence of the royal palace (*ulhi sunkina*) can be detected in a Persepolis Tablet dated 500/499 BC.[39]

Tablets from different Babylonian cities, mentioning the sending of men, soldiers and taxes to Susa (Shushan), tell of an interesting evolution in the toponymic terminology.[40] From 504 BC at Borsippa and certainly in the last years of the reign of Darius, then from around 496 BC at Sippar, the dispatches are no longer 'to Elam' but 'to Susa'. This dual naming exists also in the Persepolis Tablets of Darius' reign, where one finds, in amongst the large number of occurrences of 'Susa', a few tablets referring to 'Elam'.[41] The specific importance of these records from Borsippa and Sippar is that they give us a Babylonian perspective. It appears then, that seen from Babylonia around 500 BC, the building works were sufficiently advanced for Susa to be considered a political and financial centre of the empire.

We can only conjecture as to the reasons for Darius' complete remodelling of Susa more or less at the same time as he launched the works at Persepolis. The question had already perplexed Strabo who, bearing in mind the importance of Susa in the empire, thought that one could almost say that 'the region of Susiana is a part of Persia' (XV.3.2). He went on to explain that after their victories, the Persians considered that their country was situated at the extremity of their empire (*ep' eskhatiai*) and that Susa was more central and closer to Babylonia and

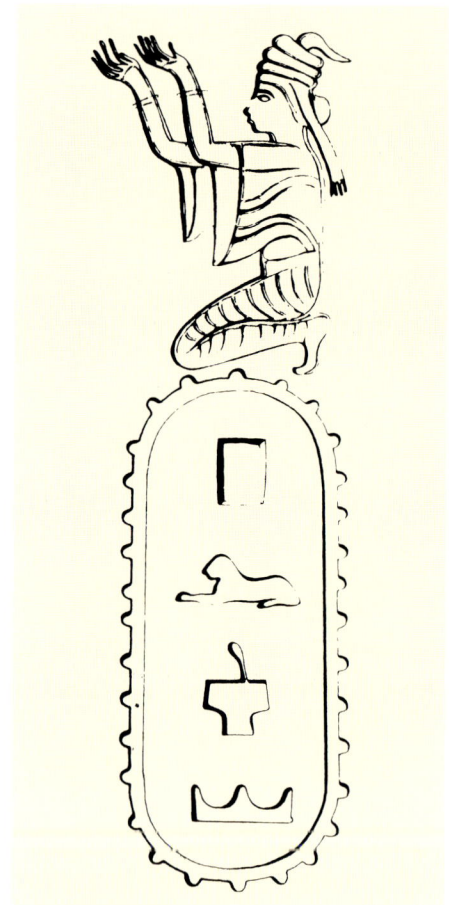

6
The Persian (top) **and the Elamite** (below) **on the base of the Darius Statue**
Cahiers DAFI, 4, 1974

7
The Elamite delegation at Persepolis
photograph by Pierre Briant

the other population centres, which was why they established the royal seat of their dominion at Susa. In addition, the Persians were impressed by the beauty and the prestige of the city, the more so because Susa had never taken any action of importance, but had always been subject to other powers: 'except perhaps in times long gone, in the time of heroes!' Strabo's reasoning reveals a Greek vision of the imperial universe, where the centre is determined by its distance from the Mediterranean, and the countries of the Iranian plateau are reputed to be at the end of the world, according to the uncertain limits known to the Greeks as *eskhatiai*. Nonetheless, Strabo does not fail to note that the Persians did not accord less importance to their palaces at Persepolis and Pasargadae, 'there where the treasures were, the stores and the tombs of the Persians; these were sites which were at once hereditary and more naturally fortified' (xv.3.3).

In one of his inscriptions (DSe § 5), Darius affirms that he had wanted to restore some buildings and the walls, which were in a very bad state. Understandably, however, it was fitting, first and foremost, to create an entirely new royal town: 'towards the bottom, the earth has been dug until I reached the bedrock' (DSf § 7), and several royal declarations underline that all the countries and peoples of the empire participated in the work through their products or their specific skills: from Lydia, Bactria, Sogdiana, Chorasmia, the Lebanon, and Egypt. Only Elam and the Elamites are not particularly lauded for their participation: although 'the columns and stone […] were brought from a village by the name of Abiradu in Elam', it was Babylonian and Carian specialists who carved the stone (DSf § 11; DSz § 11). It is very possible that the role given to Elam (simply a provider of primary materials without prestige)[42] and the Elamites (without specific skills) gives an illustration of the royal will to erase the memory of the ancient grandeur of the country, whilst Darius restored and remodelled a famous centre of the world of antiquity to serve his own glorious ends.[43]

Elam, nevertheless, a country (*dahyu*) amongst other conquered countries (*bandaka*), retained an important position in the empire. This is attested first by the status of Elamite writing: not only was Elamite the first version carved on the cliff at Bisitun, but practically all later royal inscriptions were trilingual (Old Persian, Elamite, Babylonian), and it is in Elamite cuneiform that the majority of the tablets of the Persepolis archive were inscribed. In addition, in the lists of countries and on the reliefs (Persepolis, Naqsh-i Rustam, Egyptian monuments), Elam is part of the first order, cited generally just after Persia and Media, or sometimes before Media when Persia and the Persians are absent.[44] It is interesting to note that the same order (Persian-Median-Kissian/Elamite) is adopted in the catalogue of Xerxes' army presented by Herodotus (VII.61–62).

Herodotus explains that 'the Kissians were equipped like the Persians, except that they wore mitres (*mithrephoroi*) instead of bonnets (*piloi*).' It is true that on many monuments the clothing of the Elamites does not differ from that of the Persians.[45] This is the case, for example, on the statue of Darius at Susa. Both wear a long robe with multiple pleats, and a tunic with very large sleeves. The principal difference is in the headdress, since the Elamite has neither bonnet nor turban. On other monuments (Bisitun, the Tripylon and the royal tombs), the Persians and Elamites are almost identical. It is therefore often difficult to distinguish one from the other, so much so that the designation of 'Susian Guards', habitually given to all Susian archers, no doubt deserves to be revised.[46]

The Elamites are also represented on the so-called Tributary Reliefs on the Apadana at Persepolis, where 23 nations of the empire are represented bringing tribute to the Great King. In second position, behind the Medes, is the Elamite delegation, introduced by a 'Median' usher, who holds in his right hand the left hand of the first Elamite delegate that he is to introduce. The delegation is composed of six members divided into two groups, separated by a lioness held on a leash by the first delegate of the second group (delegate 4). Bearded, hair bunched into a bun, and covered by a round cap, they wear a long pleated robe and high laced boots. Like the other delegations, the Elamites bring objects and animals that represent their country. This is the case with the short sword (delegate 3) and, even more so, with the bow decorated with duck heads, such was the reputation of Elamite archers in the Near East (delegate 2). Then comes the lioness, who, with a backward glance seems angry, either with the delegate who holds her by the leash and threatens her with a stick, or with delegates 5 and 6 who both hold a lion cub in their arms, the right hand holding the front right paw of the animal, the left hand its belly.

The similarity of the robes of the Persians and Elamites, and the importance given to the bow carried by both, seems to imply a political nicety, which would make Elam a separate country – perhaps simply because of Elam's ancient links with Anshan – but henceforth signifying its submission to the Persians. The lioness also points towards Elam; a later writer recounted that, in the sanctuary of Anahita in Elymais, 'there are tame lions which joyously welcome and fawn upon those on their way to the shrine'.[47] Did these animals represent future occupants of a royal 'paradise' or garden, especially the lion cubs, future playmates of the princes?[48] Or is not the message much more elaborate, with the scene of the lioness and the cubs to be understood as a metaphor for the inclusion of ancient Elam into the new empire of Darius?[49]

THE GREAT KING AT SUSA AND ELSEWHERE

As a body, Classical sources attribute to Susa an exceptional place in the imperial political organisation. Diodorus realised this perfectly when he qualified the palaces of Susa as 'very famous'. Strabo estimated that the Persians had taken great care with their decoration.[50] Was it not at Susa that, according to Greek writers, the famous Golden Vine of the Great King was to be found – the vine that, in 316 BC, Antigone discovered whilst making an inventory of the treasures in the Citadel?[51] All the tales give an account of the incredible quantity of riches in the treasuries and stores when Alexander captured Susa. According to Strabo (citing Polyclitus) each king had a residence built in the citadel (oikesis), as well as treasuries (thesauroi) and storehouses (parathesis) in which to deposit his royal tribute. These buildings were considered by each king as a record of his good administration (hypomnèmata tès oikonomias).[52] The rest of the passage (tributary reforms by Darius) may suggest in the reader's mind that Susa was the only imperial centre where provincial tribute was brought and stored, whether it was gold and silver or different precious stones, gems or crowns.

According to Aeschylus, it was at Susa that Queen Atossa learnt of the disaster that had befallen Xerxes' army at Salamis. According to Herodotus, it was at Susa that royal audiences were granted; it was there that refugees and ambassadors came to find the king; it was there that the seven hatched their coup; that the 'the intrigues of the harem' unfolded; it was at Susa that 'the Great King had his residence (diaitan poiéetai) and his treasure trove' (v 41). At least this is the testimony borrowed by Herodotus from the tyrant Aristagoras, come to Sparta to convince King Cleomenes to launch a campaign against the Persians. As soon as he found out that it required 'three months' march' to reach the Great King, the Spartan dismissed Aristagoras without further ado. It is in this context that Herodotus dedicates a long passage to the description of 'the route that goes from the sea to the king', that is to say the Royal Road that leads from Sardis to Susa (v 52–54). Linked to so many others, this passage from Herodotus has done much to embed the idea that Susa in fact held, par excellence, the role and place of 'capital of the empire'.

It is perfectly possible that many Greek ambassadors met the Great King in his palace at Susa. However, this proves nothing, because it was up to the king to decide the date and place, and to assemble the foreign ambassadors at Susa or elsewhere, and the ambassadors also depended on the goodwill of the satraps charged with delivering to them the necessary authorisation.[53] This choice was not linked to any permanent supremacy of Susa in the empire. It would then be poor methodology to postulate that all delegations from a foreign country or province of the empire would go automatically to Susa 'capital of the empire'.[54]

In reality, the term 'capital' is completely inappropriate to a state where the ruler and his court moved around frequently from palace to palace. Indeed, for the Greeks, one of the most recognized Persian customs was the nomadic nature of the court, which toured throughout the year from palace to palace, specifically Persepolis, Susa, Babylon and Ecbatana. The Greek writers make the court migrate in accordance with the seasons, the Great King escaping the extremes of heat and cold in line with the recurring Greek theme which denounces the luxury and cowardice of Persian kings.[55] The custom is well illustrated by the rules that held sway at the royal table; a variant was anticipated, depending on whether the king was at Susa or Babylon. Instead of having to supply 500 marriš of wine, the quantities had to be delivered half in palm wine, half in grape wine.[56] For the Classical writers, the large number of anecdotes relating to the variations in court etiquette illustrate the custom perfectly.[57] The question is more to determine if the Great King had, for example, fixed periods of residence, and how long these were. From one writer to the next, the seasons vary. The king and court were at Susa either in spring or winter. An examination of the Persepolis Tablets should have answered the question.[58] The results of the investigation were rather disappointing due to the uncertainties and gaps in the available samples. In the texts of travel rations, only a form such as 'They went to the king at Susa' (PF 1486, 1787; PF-NN 382, 1564, 2511) was used. It also revealed that, of 23 distant journeys organised from Susa,[59] 14 (thus 70 per cent) received authority from the king (*halmi sunkina*); (22 per cent for the journeys from Susa to Persia). We are tempted to infer that the king was then at Susa, but this conclusion is not a certainty, as the inscription could be an authorisation for the return journey.[60] On this basis we only have 11 almost certain confirmations of Darius' presence at Susa between 501 and 494/3 BC. It seems that in general the king resided at Susa during the winter, and it seems that from 500–498 BC Susa was probably his residence of choice.

The touring of the kings and their presence at Susa is also illuminated by certain Babylonian tablets. Two tablets in particular, which refer to the official entry of Artaxerxes II into Susa in 398 BC (UET 4. 48–49), should be highlighted.[61]

Levy of taxes in Babylonia on the occasion of the entry of Artaxerxes II into Susa (398 BC)

Kidin-Nabû, son of Sumaia, will start his journey to carry the bāra-contribution due for the entry of the king into Susa in Year 6 of Artaxerxes [II] and perform the service of contributions agent for the offerings, and he will transport this on Kusurēa's account, son of Sin-ahhê-bullit. Kidin-Nabû, son of Sumaia, has received from the hands of Kusurēa, son of Sin-ahlê-bullit, the payment of his salary and his complete equipment corresponding to that of contributions agent for the offerings. Zakitu, his mother, daughter of Anu-uballit, guarantees that Kidin-Nabû, son of Sumaia, will begin the journey and transport the bâra-contribution due for the entry of the King into Susa in Year 6 of the King Artaxerxes on Kusurēa's account, son of Sin-ahhê-bullit. If Kidin-Nabû, son of Sumaia, does not journey and transport the bâra-contribution due for the entry of the king into Susa in the Year 6 of the King Artaxerxes on Kusurēa's account, son of Sin-ahhê-bullit, Kidin-Nabû, son of Sumaia and Zakitu, his mother, will have to pay ⅓ of a mina [around 166 g] of refined silver to Kusurēa, son of Sin-ahhê-bullit. They are joint guarantors for this payment. Kusurēa will be paid in the place of his choosing [witnesses]. Drawn up at Ur on the 4- [...] of Year 6 of Artaxerxes [II] King of countries.

JOANNÈS, 2000: 153

Here, as is often the case, the information is only indirect, and it only figures in private correspondence because an agreement was reached between two people. One of these, Kidin-Nabû, took on the task of transporting, on Kusurēa's account, 'a contribution (*bâra*) for the king's entry' to Susa. This contribution was raised from offerings to the sanctuary at Ur in southern Babylonia.[62]

It is the same for the tablets with evidence of business carried out by the representatives of Babylonian enterprises at various royal palaces. It is, in fact, extremely probable that journeys then undertaken to Susa, or also to Persia and Ecbatana, took place at the time the king and court sojourned there, between the reigns of Darius I and Darius II.[63] This is perhaps the reason that the head of the Murašu family of Nippur, in February 423 BC, rented a house in Babylon for several months until the 'king's exit' *(adi muhli ase šarri)* (BE X, 1).[64] In any event, it appears that, generally speaking, Babylonians journeyed to Susa by choice at the end of the year and returned in the spring.[65]

As a result there were not one but several centres of power: power was where the Great King happened to be, whether in one of his palaces at Persepolis, Susa, Babylon or Ecbatana, or in some other palace,[66] his tent, for example, a true mobile palace,[67] the sumptuous decoration of which struck the minds and

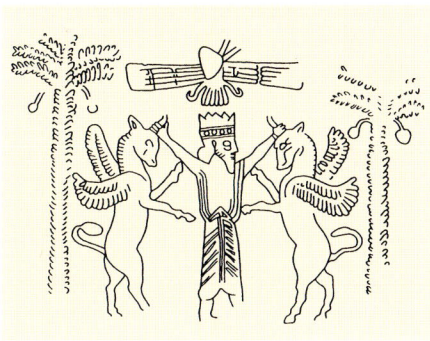

8
Seal (PFS 7*) impressed on an Elamite tablet from Susa (Sb 13078)
A royal hero wearing Persian court dress and a crenellated crown, holds in each of his outstretched hands a composite animal whom he masters. The trilingual cuneiform caption reads: 'I, Darius, King' (Great King in the Babylonian version)
Musée du Louvre © RMN/Franck Raux; drawing by M. Garrison, *JNES* 55/1, 1996, p. 27

imagination of the Greek chroniclers. Wherever he was, the king carried on official correspondence.[68] The Achaemenid state was an itinerant state and had, therefore, no fixed or precise capital. All things considered, the Greek writers never used the term 'capital': the term *to basileion/ ta basileia* referred to Palace X, that is to say, more generally to the royal residence.[69] If we accept this, then Susa was not the imperial capital; it was but one of the royal residences.

These movements from one residence to another were not specific to the king. Not only did he travel with the entire court, but we know that the wives of the royal family also stayed at Susa, and not necessarily at the same time as the king. In 500 BC, Princess Idrabama has no less than 236 *marriš* of wine delivered to Susa (PF 737). The tablet in question is classified in Series J, which deals with the product 'consumed in front of X', more often the king, that is to say the king's table, or the table of a very important individual at court.[70] The tablets of this series prove the existence of a specialist service charged with overseeing all the preparations related to catering for the king, his court and all those who were involved in the move from one residence to another.

The best example is a tablet discovered at Susa, now in the Louvre (sb 13078), which was first published by V. Scheil in 1911 (MDP XI, no. 308).[71] As Hallock has already noted, the text of the tablet is very similar to the Series J tablets at Persepolis. It reports that: '64 *marriš* of top quality purified butter[72] provided by Maštetinna, were consumed in front of the king, in Susa and five villages, in the 22nd year'. The king in question was Darius, and the year was 500/499 BC. The text implies that the king and court were on tour, as the butter was delivered in different stages, here called *humanuš*, traditionally 'translated' as 'village'.[73] What is notable is that the seal used on the Susian tablet is the one which was recorded with the abbreviation PFS 7* at Persepolis. Along with seal PFS 66*, PFS 7* was exclusively used by a very high official of the crown (anonymous), to seal the tablets of Series J. Another official, PFS 93*, was charged with the management of the animals whose meat was reserved for the royal table.[74] The clearest implication is that there existed a royal administration at Susa, as in all the satrapic capitals, and an archive for which this seal provides an eloquent if somewhat erratic testimony.

FROM BACTRIA TO SARDIS VIA SUSA
Furthermore, it is clear that not only Herodotus but also the other Greek writers give an account of the imperial universe which was bounded in the east by Babylon and Susa, thus ignoring a good half of the empire of the Great Kings, including Persia proper, the whole Iranian plateau and Central Asia.[75] By contrast, in a work now lost, Ctesias gave an account of the stages on the roads from Ephesus to Bactria and India. In combination with the Persepolis archives, this permits us to place Susa at the heart of a network of royal roads. The inscriptions of Series Q record the travel rations which were given to travellers who had an official permit (*halmi*), and who were therefore authorised to stop at stations along the route. The name of these stops is sometimes indicated (this was where travellers received their rations from the administrative stores). This authorisation was generally given by the person in charge of the region at the point of departure, most frequently the satrap; it might be, however, the king himself or a high administrative official (e.g. Parnakka).[76] By bringing together the available data, we find that the results are very clear.[77] Numerous official movements to and from Susa, are registered to and from the northern (Kerman), and eastern satrapies (Aria, Bactria, India, Gandara, Drangiana, Arachosia, etc.) As can be expected, Susa, like the other large centres of the empire, was the hub of a network of royal routes,[78] no more and no less than Persepolis, Ecbatana or Babylon.

We should not be surprised that the table mentions only the countries east of Elam, as though it were a mirror image of the Greek view of the imperial universe. This is not the case. On one hand, we must remember that the Persepolis archives are not the imperial archives, but those that reflect different productive and administrative activities in Fars. So when the satrap of Susa gave an authorisation for a journey from Elam to Ecbatana, to Sardis, to Damascus, or to Memphis, the duplicate permit (*halmi*) was registered at Susa. By contrast, journeys from Susa to the east were also registered at Persepolis simply because the rations were allocated by the stations in Fars.

In addition, there is no doubt that Susa, or a nearby staging post, saw the groups authorised to go to Sardis (PF 1321). One can presume the same of travellers authorised by the satrap of Sardis, Artaphernes, to go to Persepolis (PF 1404; 1455; NN 1096), who stopped for rations at Hidali, on the borders of Elam and Persia;[79] or even groups going to Babylon from Persia (PF 1512), to Syria (PF 1574), or even to Egypt (PF 1544). Generally these journeys via Susa are undetectable in the Persepolis records, unless the Susian satrap provided a permit to a group which, coming from Babylon, seems to have stopped off in Susa (PF 1357), or to an official who then joins a group coming from the east (PF-NN 901). There is no doubt that there were stores managed by the administration,[80] where travellers could resupply. A single journey from Susa to Babylon with mention of rations is perhaps attested thanks to a Babylonian tablet.[81] Another Babylonian record from the reign of Artaxerxes II refers to a journey (perhaps royal) between Babylon and Susa.[82]

To these medium and long-distance connections, it is worth adding the far more frequent journeys between Susa and Persepolis (or other locations in Persia), on a total of 238 ration tablets. As with many of the batch from the Fortification Archive, the greater part date from Years 21–23 of Darius (501/499 BC); 29 date from the Years 26–28 onwards (496/494 ff.). Only one tablet dates from a later reign, from Year 3 of Artaxerxes I (461 BC): it concerns the movement of an artisan between Susa and Persepolis described in a tablet from the Treasury Archive (PT 78). Of 238 tablets, 99 described a journey between Persia and Susa, 139 a journey in the opposite direction. High ranking courtiers (including the king and his family), or administrative officials (*kurtaš*), or even men accompanied by animals (PF 1418, 1442, 1571; PF-NN 1076, 1402, 1656, 1706, 1803 etc.), made the journey. It could be very small groups, sometimes one person (10 occurrences) or, on the contrary, very large groups, up to 1980 men from Susa to Persepolis in 499 BC (PF-NN 934) or, indeed 1014 *kurtaš* on the same journey in 499/8 BC (PF-NN 1126), or 416 stonemasons sent from Susa in 499 BC (PF-NN 2426). The picture is essentially the same for journeys over a longer distance.

TAXES AND ADMINISTRATIVE TRANSFERS

Persepolis records have the added advantage of providing us with information, however indirect or modest, on the administration of Elam. Elam was included by Herodotus amongst the groups paying tribute,[83] and was certainly the satrapy of which Susa was the capital. From the Series Q tablets one can infer that in the years 504–494 BC the satrap was Bakabana [Bagapāna]; one of the subordinate officers was Marunda;[84] among the lower ranks, certain officers have Elamite names.[85]

Some tablets raise very interesting questions, the answers to which are not always easy to find. For example, in 500 BC, a treasurer (*ganzabara*) by the name of Mannuya, accompanied by one companion and two 'pages' (*puhu*), was sent from Susa to Matezziš (very close to Persepolis). He was charged with taking money there from Susa. For this reason they received 16 consecutive days' worth of rations

TABLE 1
**The relationships of Susa with the different regions of the Empire other than Persia (500–492 BC)
from the fortification tablets of Persepolis** (Series Q)

i. FROM THE PROVINCES TO SUSA

Tablet	Seal(s)	From	To	Halt	Halmi	Number and quantity	Year/month (Darius)
PF 1287		Bactra	Susa		Irdabanuš	50 men	22/12
PF 1289		Kerman	Susa		Karkiš	10 men, 5 puhu[1]	28/8
PF 1318	49, 84	India	Susa		King	20 men, 1 elite guide	23/2
PF 1351		Arachosia	Susa		Bakabaduš	4h men, 5 puhu	28/5
PF 1358		Gandara	Susa		Bakabaduš	7h men, 2 puhu	
PF 1377	18, 223	Kerman	Susa		Karkiš	Hindukka and 100 puhu from Bakeya	23/1(?)
PF 1399	84, 223	Kerman	Susa	Hidali	Karkiš	Hindukka and 100 puhu	23/1
PF 1436		Kerman	Susa		Karkiš	Ukakka and 9 men, šalup, his companions	
PF 1439		Arachosia	Susa		Ziššawiš	Kunda, 1 šalup,[2] 26 puhu	22
PF 1529	136, 219	India[3]	Susa		Irdubama	Mipušda and 2 men Indians	23
PF 1552		India	Susa		Parnakka	Batakanduš, 3 men Indians, 23 puhu	23
PF 1555		Bactra	Susa		Irdabanuš	Munna and 24 men	22/2
PF 1953 (34)	1586	Arachosia	Susa			[2910] (?)	
PF 2050	1612, 1613		Susa	Makkaš	King	6 men, 41 puhu	27/8
PF 2051		[India]	Susa		Irdubama	1 elite guide, 11 šalup, 23 puhu	23
PF 2056		Aria	Susa		King	1 elite guide, 588 men, 18 horses, 100 mules	28/11
PF-NN 317		India	Susa		Irdubama	4 men, 20 puhu, 4 dogs	22/10(?)
PF-NN 431		Gandara	Susa		Irdatakama	170 men, 120 puhu, 12 camels, 31 mules	20/10
PF-NN 809	95, 223	Kerman	Susa		Karkiš	1 Chief of Treasure, 100 puhu	22/12
PF-NN 881	1047, x	Arachosia	Susa	Several villages		23 kurtaš, 2 puhu, 1 elite guide	
PF-NN 901	95, 192	Sardis	Parnakka	[via Susa]	Bakabana	94 men	23/10
PF-NN 946	24, x	Kerman	Susa		King	4 men, 36 puhu	4
PF-NN 1044	84, 284 (?)	Kerman	Susa	Hidali	Karkiš	1060 men šaluip-porters (taššup)	23/1
PF-NN 1081 (74)	[x?]	Makkan	King at Susa			12 men (?)	
PF-NN 1081 (81–82)	[x?]	Kerman	Susa			75 men (or more)	
PF-NN 1264	x	[India]	King at Susa		Irdubama	1	23
PF-NN 1571	84, x, (y)	India	Susa	Hidali	Irdubama	1 men, 2 elite guides, 20 puhu	23/1
PF-NN 1580	84, x	Kerman	Susa	Hidali	Karkiš	19 men	23/1(?)
PF-NN 1585	18, x	Kerman	Susa		Karkiš	13 men, 4 puhu	23/10
PF-NN 1621	1276, x	Kerman	Susa		Karkiš	1 men, 4 puhu	22/1(?)
PF-NN 1713	10, x	Aria	Susa		King	1 + 9 men	23/7(?)
PF-NN 1898	1393, x	Arachosia	Susa		Bakabaduš	20 men	
PF-NN 1939 (=PFa14)	x, y	Kerman	Susa	Mistukraš		71 (?) puhu from Irtašduna and from Irdabama	
PF-NN 2040 (4–6)	x	Sagartia	Elam		King	taššup hallinup	22
PF-NN 2062	x, y	Arachosia	Susa		Parnakka	10 kurtaš	
PF-NN 2139	223, x	Kerman	Susa	Mistukraš	Karkiš	100 puhu	
PF-NN 2323		India	Susa	Uzikurraš		1 elite guide, 5 men, 67 puhu	23
PF-NN 2584	8, x	India	Susa		Parnakka	4 men, 37 puhu	

1. In principle 'young' in the sense of dependency (HALLOCK, 1969: 746; BRIANT, 1996: 444–445, 950 and HENKELMAN, 2003: 129–131.
2. In principle 'free', 'noble'; translated as 'gentleman' by Hallock.
3. The point of departure, Hinduš, is proposed because of the name of the officer who grants the halmi, Irdubama, must be the satrap of the region; also in PF 2051, PF-NN 1264.

Continued overleaf

ii. FROM SUSA TO THE PROVINCES

Tablet	Seal(s)	From	To	Halt	Halmi	Number and quantity	Year/month (Darius)
PF 1332	1275, 1276	Susa	Kerman	Bessit-me		1 man, 2 puhu	
PF 1348		Susa	Kerman		King	1 + 20 men, 12 puhu	23/10
PF 1361	10, 1290	[Susa][4]	Arie		Bakabana	1 man	22/12
PF 1383	18, 1306	Susa	India		King	1 + 2 men, 9 puhu	23/12
PF 1385	24, 1308	Susa	Arachosia		King	1	1
PF 1398	84, 289	Susa	Kerman	Hidali	King	52 šalup, 51 puhu	23/1
PF 1440	213, 1332	Susa	Kandahar		King	1 man, 1 woman, 5 puhu	22
PF 1484		[Susa]	Arachosia		Bakabana	2 šalup, 1 puhu	7
PF 1540	10, 1433	Susa	Aria		Bakabana	1 man + group of stonemasons	22/11
PF 1550	213, 940	Susa	Gandara		King	1 woman, 1 elite guide	22/2
PF 1556	49	Susa	India			1	23/3
PF 2057	1622, 1623	Susa	India	From Dašer at Hidali	King	1 guide, 3 men Indians	
PFa 17 (=NN2095)	21, x	Susa	Makkaš		Parnakka	62 šaluip and 100 puhu Arabs	22/2
PF-NN 615	289, 940	Susa	Kerman		King	50h. šaluip	22/2
PF-NN 765		Susa	Kerman		King	1 + 9 man., 3 libap[5]	23/11
PF-NN 944	48, x	Susa	Gandara		King	1 man, 15 puhu	23/12
PF-NN 1458	110 (?), x	Susa	India		King	1 woman, 2 šalup, 5 lbap Indians, 1 elite guide	23/1
PF-NN 2096	33, x	Susa	Drangiana		King	1 šaluir, 1 libair	23/11
PF-NN 2383	18, x	Susa	Gandara		King	1 + 59 men	2
PF-NN 2503	10, x	[Susa]	Arachosia		Bakabana	1 puhu, stonemason	22/11

4. For the same reasons as in the previous note, Bakabana was most probably the satrap of Elam.
5. The term includes a sense of dependency: see HALLOCK, 1969: 720 ; also MISSIOU, 1993: 385–387.

9
Three ration tablets for journeys to Susa
© 'Persepolis Fortification Archive Project'
photographs by OI Chicago

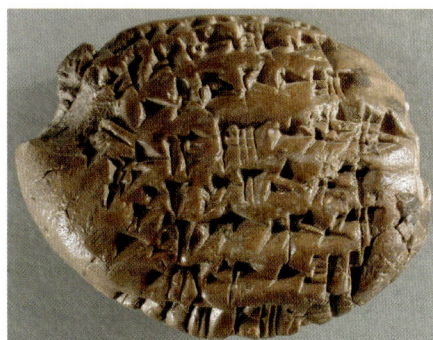

PF 1287: in 500 BC, 50 workers received rations for a journey from Bactria to Susa authorised by Irdabanuš (Artabanos), no doubt the satrap of Bactria

PF 1293: distribution of flour rations for two men and two young people (*puhu*) going to Susa with a sealed authorisation (*halmi*) from Parnakka

PF 1295: Mitrabada, accompanied by 262 men, received flour rations on a journey to Susa, most certainly from Persepolis, where Ziššawiš held office

(PF 1342). The next year (499 BC?) Bakabana granted an authorisation (*halmi*) to a certain Batteša accompanied by one man and eight *puhu*. They were charged with transporting 'the Babylonian treasure (*kapnuški Bapilira*)' to Persepolis (PF 1357).[86] Both the texts mention the transfers of treasure to Persepolis, but why was the satrap of Susa given the task of delivering the 'Babylonian treasure' to Persia? When the Egyptian satrap sent a treasure to Babylon (**ganza = kapnuški*), the task was entrusted to his own subordinates. The same applied when two princesses (Artystone/Irtašduna, and Irdabama) transferred a treasure from Kerman to Susa (PFa 147).[87] The answer to the question might be suggested by Babylonian records in which one sees that the taxes raised in Babylonia had to be transferred to Susa for the official entry of Artaxerxes II.[88] One is tempted to deduce from this that these satrapic frontiers were porous – when it concerned offering service to the king, it was the court administration which took charge – which would explain why the operations undertaken at Susa and in Elam could leave archival traces in the Persepolis Tablets.[89]

In 500 BC the proceeds of a tax in Persia known as *baziš*,[90] payable in principle in small livestock, were sent to Susa from a town or village of Fars called Maturban (PF 57). The text can be associated with PF 1495: in December 500 BC, on authorisation (*halmi*) sent by Bakaduš, Miššabada was ordered, with the help of 31 men, to convey the *baziš* of Udana collected from Barrikana in Persia, to Susa. The two officers in question are confirmed elsewhere as being administrators of small livestock in Persia (PF 62, 66). This time, however, the hides collected from slaughtered livestock were not conveyed to Persian treasuries; the flock was herded to Susa. Such a procedure seems to imply that there were functioning relationships between the administrators of Persepolis and those of Susa. This is also suggested by records detailing the delivery of rations of different types of poultry at Susa,[91] or further still by the mention of quantities of flour delivered to Susa and allocated on site for local use (PF 89–92). The tablets also mention the transfer of animals (camels, horses, mules) either between Susa and Persepolis, or in the opposite direction.[92] The case of a train of 33 camels that came and went between the two centres, from one month to the other, is interesting because one of the documents (PF 1787) shows that the transfer was due to the presence of the king at Susa. Sent to Susa in the first month of 500 BC, they were returned the following month to Matezziš by the satrap of Bakabana (PF 1786; PFa 26).

It is tempting to think of an identical circumstance, when examining the contents of tablet PF 1442: some shepherds (*batera* / pl. *batep*) are ordered to herd 'the king's sheep' from Persia to Susa, that is to say, animals probably belonging to the king's household (*ulhi sunkina*).[93] It is possible that these thousands of animals were destined to feed the court during its residence in Susa.[94] There is no doubt that the entrance of the king into the town, and the ensuing residence of thousands of court followers and the army, was extremely costly to the region and its inhabitants.[95] The two Babylonian tablets already mentioned confirm this: on the entry of Artaxerxes II into Susa in 398 BC, Kusurēa, a celebrity from the town of Ur, was compelled to pay a specific contribution to the royal administration. He had to deliver it to Susa (*ana Zabēli ša nēreb šarri ana Šušan*). To this end he paid a certain Kidin-Nabû to deliver the tax (*bara*), *due for the entry of the king into Susa in Year 6 of the reign of King Artaxerxes.* In case of default, Kidin-Nabû and his mother had to pay Kusurēa compensation amounting to 1/3 of a mina of pure silver.[96] One can see, therefore, that Susa and Elam were not the only ones to cover the costs of the royal presence; the neighbouring provinces of Persia and Babylonia were also asked to contribute.

We find further interesting confirmation in the payment of another tax, *the ulkpiyataš,* a term of Iranian origin (**upa-yata*) which specifies, though imprecisely, a specific contribution which must be paid to the king in commodities (cereals, wine, etc.), possibly for the royal table. In the Persepolis Tablets the tax is sometimes called 'royal'. It was generally transported from one place to another (Liduma, Tandari, etc); some of the villages mentioned are in Elam. On one occasion at least, the levy (more than 200 *marriš* of wine) was sent to Persia via Elam (PF-NN 28),[97] according to wording which implies that 'Elam' signifed only 'Susa'. We can observe the same movement of the same levy, this time from Babylon to Susa.[98] In Babylonia the documents were tax receipts. They contained not only the *upijatu* but also the taxes and labour which enabled the levy to be transported to Susa as, for instance, from Borsippa, according to a formula such as *urāšu ša zebēlu ša upiyātu Elam [ša Šušan]*, meaning 'the service of *urāšu* (*corvée*) for transporting the *upiyātu* from Elam [from Susa]'. We have eight records from Borsippa mentioning the formula, from years 15 and 33 of Darius' reign. They even reveal, indirectly, the raising of a commodities tax in Babylonia, which had the same name as the one raised in Persia (and elsewhere no doubt); of another tax, in the form of an obligation to supply transport for merchandise to Susa. Transport was by water. Money had to be raised for the hire of boats, and the buying of provisions for those who, by way of forced labour (*urāšu*) hauled the boats. Numerous taxes, which added considerably to the costs, also had to be paid, for the use of canals, bridges, harbours, and the embarkation of merchandise.[99] In 507 BC works are attested on the 'Royal Canal of Elam' (*nār-šarri ša Elam*). The travellers had to change boats at Bāb-Nār-Kabari, then follow this river/canal to the 'quay at Susa' (*karum ša Šušan*). A record from the period of Xerxes (Year 1) indicates that there was a customs house there, headed by a director of payments, *rab miksi* (VS 4, 194). The port of Susa was also involved in traffic from the Persian Gulf. During the period of Alexander (but this was certainly true of earlier periods) one could sail down the Ulai/Eulaios towards the sea, and up river to the bridge-of-boats, over which the road from Susa to Persepolis ran. There was also a canal between the Ulai and Tigris rivers.[100] Contrary to traditional interpretation, nothing indicates that Susa was ever under threat of attack by fleets from the Persian Gulf.[101]

WORKMEN AT SUSA

In his inscriptions, Darius aims to affirm or to make it understood that all the peoples and countries of the empire collaborated in a communal work effort, as if the labourers had come there to work of their own volition and initiative.[102] The texts of the Treasury Tablets and the Fortification Tablets show that the workers at the building sites of Persepolis came from numerous parts of the empire, but all indicate that they had been sent by order of the imperial authorities and that in the main they had no liberty: these texts were known as *kurtaš*.[103] We do not have comparable records at Susa, not even isolated examples. By contrast, the Persepolitan and Babylonian records provide indirect but first-hand accounts, in that they mention the sending of workers to Susa during the reign of Darius. We have every reason to think that these workers were destined to work on the building sites.

There are a dozen examples of the dispatch of *kurtaš* from Persepolis to Susa during Years 22–23, in groups that vary from 10 to 500 (Table 2), to which can be added the arrival at Susa of *kurtaš* from Kerman and Arachosia. They can be simply called by their generic term *kurtaš*, sometimes with their gender (M/F) indicated, or their ethnicity (Lycians, Skudrians, Cappadocians), or their specialisation (leatherworkers). Some groups do not have subgroups designated as *kurtaš*, but they do, however, have categories (*puhu*, for example) which are also indentured to the imperial administration, but without their specialisation being

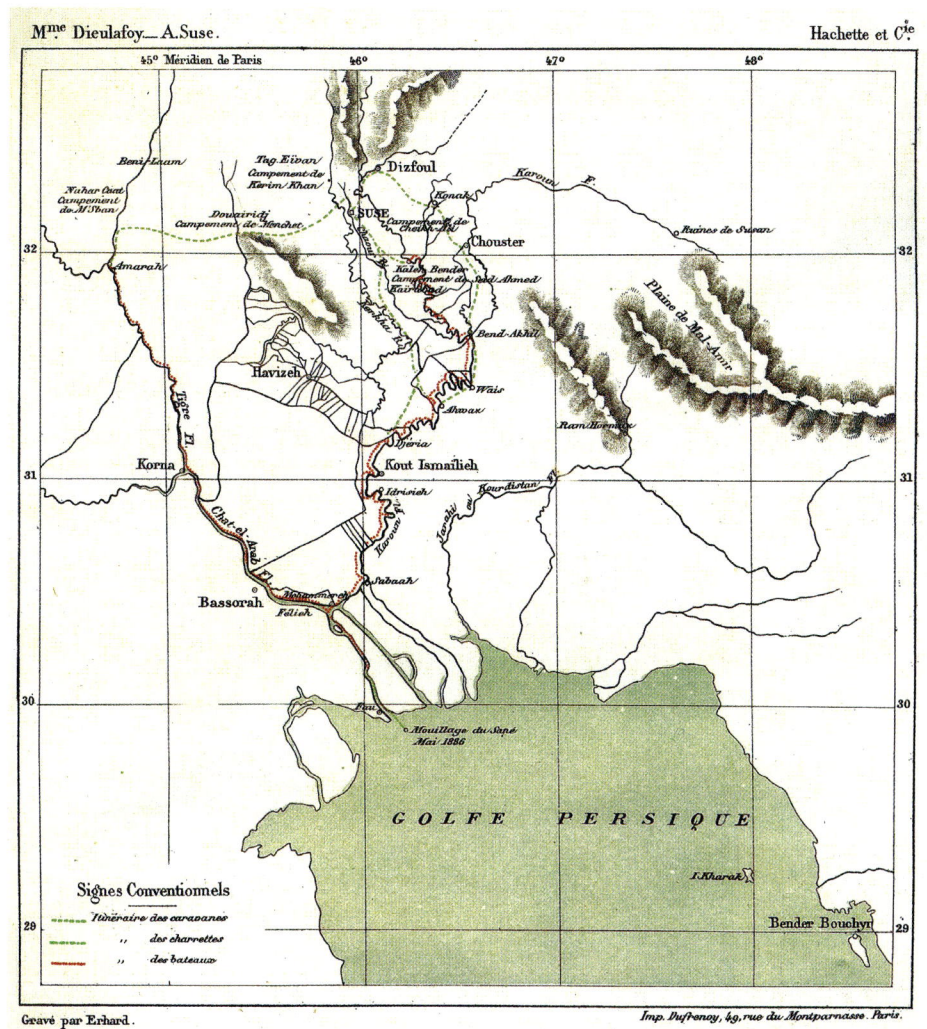

10

Map showing the route used by Marcel
Dieulafoy's mission to transport antiquities
by boat from Susa to Paris and the Louvre
J. DIEULAFOY, 1888

necessarily indicated. There are some exceptions such as the *puhu*, a stonemason,
sent to Susa from Arachosia in 500/499 BC (PF-NN 2503). These groups can be
very large, for example from Persepolis to Susa: 262 male carriers (PF 1295); 1500
men (PF 1542): 129 men and *puhu* in 500 BC (PF-NN 980); 260 men, *šalup and
puhu* in 501/500 BC (PF-NN 1564: 'to the King at Susa'); 131 men *šalup* (PF-NN
1906). Sometimes their specialisation is explicit, such as five woodworkers sent
to Susa (PF 1487). Large numbers are also sent from the provinces to Susa: for
example, perhaps 2910 (men? *kurtaš?*) from Arachosia (PF 1953[34, 35]);[104] 588 men,
18 horses, 100 mules, from Aria in 494/493 BC (PF 2056); 170 men and 120 *puhu*
from Gandara in 502/501 BC (PF-NN 431); 1060 *šalup* (carriers) from Carmania in
499/498 BC (PF-NN 1044) etc.

Table 2 brings together only the examples of transfers to Susa. Other, more
numerous, tablets detail *kurtaš* and workers sent from Susa. Table 3 is a sample
of the movement of *kurtaš* between Susa and Persia. We can see that the size of
the groups is no smaller; for example, the 416 stonemasons sent from Susa with
the king's authority in 499 BC (PF-NN 2426). In certain cases, it can be a return
journey to Persepolis for certain groups who had previously been sent to Susa
(cf. PF-NN 839 where the official who delivered the *halmi* had his post in Persia).
To these examples one must add all those groups of workers, sometimes very large,
who were not categorised as *kurtaš*: 560 *šalup* and *puhu* (*taššup*)[105] to Tamukkan in
year 22 (PF-NN 271); 1980 men to Persepolis in year 23 (PF-NN 934) etc. Sometimes
a text concerns sending a single skilled artisan: one stonemason to Atek in Persia
(PF 1246); one goldsmith to Persepolis in year 28 (PF-NN 1361); a decorator of
the first order to Persepolis in 461 (PT 78); a stonemason and one companion to

TABLE 2
Movements of *kurtaš* to Susa/Elam

i. FROM PERSEPOLIS TO SUSA

Tablet	Seal(s)	From	To	Description	Number	Halmi	Year/month (Darius)
PF 1396			Susa	Kurtaš of Mauparna		Parnakka	
PF 1428				Maurada companions, men, kurtaš	4, 38, 20	Bakabana	23/10
PF 1497		Persepolis	Elam	Kurtaš-zappan [copper workers][1]	50	22	
PF 1565	17, 1447		Elam	Lycian kurtaš	100	Ziššawiš	
PF 1575	18, 1459		Elam	Skudran kurtaš	26	Parnakka	21/4
PF 1577	17, 1460		Elam	Cappadocian kurtaš	108	Parnakka	
NN 123		Persepolis	Elam	Lycian kurtaš	500	Ziššawiš	22
NN 550		Persepolis	Elam	Kurtaš-zappan [copper workers]	255	Irupiya	22
NN 803	1047, x		Susa	Men (kurtaš?)	720	Bakabaduš	
NN 1311	x, y	Persepolis	Susa	Kurtaš			22/9
NN 1807	x, y		Susa	Kurtaš	10	Parnakka	4
NN 1856		Persepolis	Susa	Kurtaš-zappan [copper workers]	70	Parnakka	22

ii. FROM OTHER REGIONS TO SUSA

Tablet	Seal(s)	From	To	Description	Number	Halmi	Year/month (Darius)
NN 881	1047, x	Arachosia	Susa	Kurtaš, puhu, elite guide	23, 2, 1		
NN 2062	x, y	Arachosia	Susa	Kurtaš		Parnakka	

1. About this translation see HENKELMAN, 2005: 24

TABLE 3
Dispatch of *kurtaš* from Susa to Persia

Tablet	Seal(s)	From	To	Description	Number	Halmi	Year/month (Darius)
PF 1475	110, 192	[Susa]	Persepolis	Kurtaš	155	Bakabana	23/9
PF 1489	109, 1386			M. (purkurzapï), elite guides Kurtaš, puhu	22, 2, 16, 2	Bakabana	23/6
PF 1547	1439	Susa	Matezziš	Egyptian kurtaš	30	Bakabana	22
PF 1557	17, 1442	[Susa]	Tamukkan	Egyptian kurtaš	547	Bakabana	21
NN 327		Susa	Persepolis	Artisan kurtaš	23	Bakabana	21
NN 362		Susa	Persepolis	Kurtaš	78(?)	Bakabana	22
NN 364		[Susa]	Persepolis	Babylonian(?) kurtaš	22	Bakabana	22
NN 435		[Susa]	Persepolis	Artisan kurtaš ?)	[5]	Bakabana	
NN 487		Susa	Persepolis	Kurtaš [...]	140	Bakabana	23/12
NN 786		[Susa]	Persepolis	Babylonian kurtaš		Bakabana	
NN 839		Susa	Matezziš	Kurtaš		Ziššawiš	22/12
NN 1126	107, x	Aksuštiš		Skudran kurtaš	1014	Bakabana	21
NN 1216	x, y	[Susa]	Persepolis	Kurtaš zamip[1]	3(?)	Bakabana	28/1
NN 1798			Susa	Persepolis	Kurtaš (m.)	40+41	Bakabana	28/4
NN 1969	x, y (N 54)	Susa	Persepolis	Kurtaš		Parnakka	21/12
NN 2132	(?)	Susa	Persepolis	Babylonian kurtaš	124	Bakabana	22
NN 2426	x, y	Susa(?)	Persia(?)	Men libap (stonemasons)	321, 95	King	23/1

1. Forced labour? 'Exerters', HALLOCK, 1969

Arachosia in Year 22 (PF-NN 2503); in reverse order (from Persepolis to Susa) one goldsmith in Year 22 (PF 1519).

As 72 per cent of the tablets of Series Q are concentrated in Years 22 and 23 of Darius I,[106] the available sample does not allow us to paint an exhaustive picture of the movement of workers from Persia to Susa, which would otherwise illustrate with great precision the phases of works undertaken in the ancient capital of Elam. Certain specialisations leave no doubt as to the reasons for the transfer (for example the 416 stonemasons sent to Susa in 499: PF-NN 2426). Amongst all the groups, however, a large number could comprise unskilled labour or indeed labourers working in other sectors (agriculture and animal husbandry for example). We have here, rather, an illustration of the management of labour available at an imperial level comparable to what we know was in operation inside Persia itself.[107]

Groups of workers were moved from one place to another according to the necessities of the time (which almost always elude us), and, depending on politics, involving the transfers/deportations known equally from Classical and earlier Neo-Assyrian and Neo-Babylonian sources.[108] We have some information on the settlement in Elam of Greek and Asiatic communities: the Eritreans at Arderika 'in Kissia', about 40 km from Susa on the banks of the Tigris, where naphtha was produced on royal lands; the Milesians were settled on the shores of the Persian Gulf near the town of Ampe, close to the mouth of the Tigris.[109] At the time of Alexander, we also know of villages of Carians in nearby Babylonia, which Diodorus places on the opposite bank of the Tigris when coming from Susa; of settlements of Boeotians placed by Diodorus several days march past Sittacene. At Gaugamela, a group of 'deported Carians' were integrated with a contingent of Babylonians alongside the inhabitants of Sittacene.[110] There is no doubt, therefore, that Elam, like Babylonia and other regions, had accepted foreign communities, amongst which were to be found Greeks, Ionians and other inhabitants of Asia Minor, all equally well represented amongst the *kurtaš* of the Persepolis Tablets. Our knowledge of the presence of these communities in Babylon and Elam substantiates Darius' claims in his inscriptions that it was the Carians and the Ionians who were charged with transporting wood from the Lebanon between Babylon and the building sites of Susa (DSf 9 and DSz 8).[111] In any case it is clear that Susa was perfectly integrated within this political system. There is therefore no doubt that other than the resident communities, one part of this multi-ethnic and multilingual Susian population of labourers came from Persia and other provinces, not necessarily close by, in the form of groups defined by their ethnicity, their professional qualifications, and/or a statutory definition (*kurtaš*, men, women, *puhu*, etc.). These very mobile groups were split up and sent off by the administration to different parts of the empire, sometimes several hundred miles away.

Once more the Babylonian records can be used profitably: the groups mentioned were subject to various taxes and levies which sometimes had to be carried to Susa, either by a royal treasurer,[112] or by the subjects themselves, as we have seen previously. Temples and individuals were also subject to the corvée or the service of *urāšu*. The participation of teams composed of the dependents of large sanctuaries in the building projects of the Great Kings is attested in Babylonia under Cyrus and Cambyses: for example at Abanu, near the Persian Gulf, as well as at Lahiru, situated on the overland route between Babylonia and Susa.[113] The similarity between a Babylonian tablet (YOS 7, 187) and the tablets from Persepolis has even allowed us to demonstrate recently that, in the reign of Cambyses, Babylonian labour was used in Persia, at the site of Matanan.[114] It is this type of labour that the royal and satrapal administration requisitioned when, under Darius, they dug the 'Elam Canal' which linked Babylonia and Susa via

Bab Nār-Kabari (cf. vs 6.302). In this manner, one can see that the Great Kings attempted to link Babylonia, Elam and Persia more efficiently by improving both land routes and waterways.[115]

We know that the pool of labour from the sanctuaries was also used by the administration to complete works and building projects in Elam and Susa.[116] The first mention dates from Year 5 of Darius, and the records carry on through to the beginning of the reign of Xerxes, but journeys and exchanges between Babylonia and Susa are also mentioned under Darius II and Artaxerxes II. A contract signed in 516/515 BC makes reference to silver for the king's corvée (*kaspu ana dulli ša šarri*), owed by the chariot house of the principal administrator (*qipu*) of the sanctuary of Esagil (vs 6.155). In another case, a Babylonian pays to enrol a substitute who will perform his service in Susa (KU 14); a text from the Ebbabar of Sippar gives record of 'rations and provisions (*rikis qabli*)[117] for the labourers who are working at Susa, and for those who transport provisions and rations';[118] a record from the same source is an order for the delivery of rations of wool to workers of the Ebabbar who are doing their service in Susa;[119] another letter mentions workers who are returning from Susa (CT 22 59); a contract mentions that, amongst all the taxes imposed on a Babylonian, there is one called *allaku ša Elam*, that is to say the obligation to fulfil a period of labour in Elam (BM 27789).[120] As disparate as they may appear, these records lead us to presume that a large number of the labourers brought to Susa from Babylon had been recruited to complete work on the terrace of Darius' Palace: 'the men who made the bricks were Babylonians' (DSf § 13; DSz § 7, 12).

FROM DARIUS TO ALEXANDER

During the reign of Darius there is a relative abundance of archaeological and epigraphic data which is properly Susian and is supported by Babylonian and Persepolitan sources. However, Susa moves into the shadows during the reigns of his successors.[121] Certain tablets of the Murašu Archive give an account of the day-to-day activities of Babylonian businesses in the capital of Elam under Darius II. Some contracts signed at Susa illustrate the presence of a Babylonian community there during the reign of one of the Artaxerxes. The first of these kings is hardly mentioned other than in relation to the fire at Darius' Apadana, which he neglected to restore during his reign; it is not impossible, however, that he built a palace at the location of the Donjon (D2sb), where carved Achaemenid ivories have been found.[122] It was Artaxerxes II who gained glory by rebuilding Darius' Apadana (A2sa). Known from a Babylonian text, the entry of this same king into Babylon in 398 BC shows, unsurprisingly, that the kings continued their occasional visits. This is confirmed in a roundabout way by a Babylonian chronicle which mentions that, after the crushing of the Sidonian revolt by Artaxerxes III, the prisoners were sent to Babylon and Susa.[123] Two astronomical records allude to Susa: one, dated to 347 BC, gives an account of an individual's departure from Babylon for Susa (it might even be the king himself);[124] the other, dated 367 BC, alludes to Susa and its governor(?), but in an unknown and obscure context.[125]

Artaxerxes II, not content with rebuilding the Apadana of Darius, had a new palace constructed below the terrace (A2sd), known as the Shaur.[126] Perhaps it was here that in 387/386 BC he convened the ambassadors of the Greek cities during a congress at Susa, which ended with a royal edict reintegrating the cities of Asia Minor into the Achaemenid fold ('Peace of Antalcidas'). A well-known passage from Berossus, quoted by Clement of Alexandria, attributes a notable religious initiative to Artaxerxes II: it is said that he was the first to erect statues in honour of Aphrodite Anaitis (Anahita). To do this he chose the largest centres of the

11
Susa: loading cases for transport to the Louvre
J. DIEULAFOY, 1888

empire: the provinces of Bactria, Damascus and Sardis, and the royal residences at Babylon, Ecbatana, Susa and Persepolis. It is tempting to mention the inscriptions from Susa where, for the first time, Artaxerxes II invoked Mithra and Anahita alongside Ahuramazda (A2sa; A2sd).[127]

The arrival of Alexander at Susa in the autumn of 331 BC went off smoothly. As had been the case with Babylon, Susa had been carefully prepared. Immediately after his defeat of Darius III at the battle of Arbela (1 October 331 BC) the Macedonian king had sent a messenger (Philoxenus) to Susa to open negotiations with the Satrap of Elam, Abulites. Philoxenus told Alexander what the inhabitants of Susa had explained about their town, that the treasure was intact and entirely at Alexander's disposal.[128] Quintus Curtius Rufus adds that on his arrival Alexander was greeted outside the town by the son of the Satrap; Abulites himself came to salute him on the banks of the Choaspes 'with gifts of all royal opulence. There were amongst these presents, dromedaries of an incredible speed, as well as 12 elephants that Darius had had brought from India…'.[129] Alexander laid hands on the treasure and took the usual administrative measures: Macedonians were put into military and financial posts and he left the satrapy of Susiana to Abulites, to which, a while later, he added the territory of the Ouxians of the plain.[130] The Great King did not fail to make gestures of friendship towards the Greeks: he sent back to Athens objects which had been carried off by Xerxes. The inscribed bronze knucklebone of Didyma, however, stayed in the stores.[131] Finally, on his departure, he allowed Darius' mother, son and daughters to remain at Susa, where one may suppose that the royal princesses had their residence.

On his return from India, Alexander stayed at Susa, where he arrested and executed Abulites and his son Oxathres who, like many others, had made the most of the king's absence to abuse their positions, as was the case with Herakon who had been accused by the inhabitants of Susa of having destroyed the temple/sanctuary of the town (Arrian VI.27.5). We also know of the celebrated weddings of Susa.[132] We do not know anything, however, of the precise use which he made of the palace, nor where his troops were encamped. It is probable that from this date, and under his successors, the palaces were not properly maintained and therefore, in a relatively short time, these buildings disappeared.[133] Only the citadel (*akra*) was maintained; it is mentioned several times during the battles of the Diadochi, and then again in 221 BC when the rebel Molon failed to capture it, such was the strength of its fortifications.[134]

12
The tells of Susa
Ghirshman archive

1. I should like to thank Caroline Waerzeggers (Amsterdam), Mark Garrison (Austin, Texas) and Wouter Henkelman (Collège de France, Paris) for their remarks and suggestions. It goes without saying that any remaining errors are my own.
2. See especially: www.museum-achemenet.college-de-france.fr.
3. BOUCHARLAT, 2005b: 253–254.
4. BOUCHARLAT, 2001, 2003b.
5. See the excellent remarks by POTTS, 1999a.
6. BRIANT, 1996: 434–528 and 962–972.
7. Regarding this, from now on see the remarkable monograph by HENKELMAN, 2008.
8. See BRIANT, HENKELMAN and STOLPER, 2008.
9. See also my remarks in BRIANT, 1982: 207–209; BRIANT, 1996: 1151, *s.v.* 'archives satrapiques'; see above, pp. 11–19.
10. Regarding this point, which is still disputed, see the analysis by HENKELMAN, 2008: 65–69, and § 5 below.
11. JOANNÈS, 1990.
12. See the texts assembled by WAERZEGGERS, 2010, Table 1; it concerns transactions carried out by Babylonian businesses in the imperial residences at Susa, Ecbatana and Matezziš. STOLPER, 1990; JOANNÈS, 2005.
13. See below, pp. 13–14.
14. Arrian VI.27.5: *to en Sousois hiéron*. Normally, this Greek term refers more to a 'sanctuary' than to a 'temple', but Arrian uses this term, as here, for a temple (cf. Arrian III.16.4: at Babylon, Alexander 'ordered the rebuilding (*anakodomein*) of the temples (*to hiéra*) that Xerxes has destroyed').
15. Diodorus XVII, 65.5.
16. Arrian, *Anab.* III.16.9; cf. Quintus Curtius Rufus, *Hist. Alex.* V, 2.16 (*arx*).
17. See Diodorus XIX, 17.3 (*akra*) and 18.1 (*akra*); Polybius V, 48.14 (*akra*).
18. *Geog.* XV.3.2.
19. The first two describe the mythological history of Susa, founded by Memnon, son of Kissia, from which Susa received the name 'city of Memnon' (Herodotus VII. 151), or that of Memnonion, attributed to the Acropolis (Strabo XV.3.2). Polukleitos was used by Strabo predominantly for what he had to say about the use of bricks and bitumen [in STEVE, GASCHE and VALLAT, 2002, col. 489, read 'Polyclète' rather than 'Philoclète'].
20. XV.3.3: *en topois erymnotérois*.
21. Also in Esther IX: 6.11 and 12, where the term *birah/birtha* is used, as in many other Aramaean texts of the period, whatever the importance of the town or settlement: LEMAIRE and LOZACHMEUR, 1987, and BRIANT, 1996: 1161, *s.v.* 'byrt'.
22. BOUCHARLAT, 2006: 448–450.
23. To quote Chardin: 'There is nothing that is easier for us to know in the descriptions of Arrian, Quintus Curtius Rufus and Diodorus Siculus, than the situation of Persepolis; and it is a very great pleasure to travel through this country with the ancient authors to hand'; or again, a century later, Choiseul-Gouffier, on the eve of his journey to Greece: 'I had the pleasant foretaste of travelling through this beautiful region with copies of Homer and Herodotus to hand'.
24. See especially the importance of Classical sources in the reconstruction of the hydrographic networks of Susiana: MORGAN, 1900: 10–16; LE RIDER, 1965: 161–267; see also BRIANT, 2006 and 2008.

25. I had already considered all these points in my 1984 study and they have recently been very much revived and discussed. See now, however, the fundamental study by HENKELMAN, 2008 (with bibliography), and many important articles assembled by ALVAREZ-MON and GARRISON, 2011.
26. GARRISON, 1991: 3–7, and now GARRISON, 2011.
27. BRIANT, 1994: 55, n. 20.
28. See the list of texts in WATERS, 2004: 94–95, who, however, draws the conclusion that Cyrus adopted this title after having vanquished and subjugated the Elamites; see more recently the detailed discussion in POTTS, 2005, who insists on the Elamite identity of both Anshan and Cyrus.
29. BRIANT, 1996: 127–140 and 927–929.
30. PF 718; PF-NN 2089 (Series J).
31. PF 1836, 1837.
32. HENKELMAN, 2008: 305–384.
33. Following Waters' suggestion in this direction (WATERS, 2000: 85) and the very interesting study by Tavernier (TAVERNIER, 2004), Henkelman has found the latter's hypothesis very appealing (HENKELMAN, 2008: 362–363), namely that the rebel Athamaita and the Neo-Elamite king known in inscriptions by the name Atta-hamiti-Inšušinak were one and the same person (see also POTTS, 2005: note 98). According to this hypothesis, until his revolt he would have been the last Elamite king of Susa. VALLAT (2006) forcefully rejects this hypothesis.
34. PF 1780; horses moved between Anshan and Elam.
35. HENKELMAN, 2008: n. 817.
36. See the presentation and bibliography in BRIANT, 1996: 177–179 and 934 and, more recently, STEVE, VALLAT and GASCHE, 2002–03: col. 486–495.
37. Despite some attempt to do so by STEVE, 1974: 27–28, followed by VALLAT, 1986: 281; also by BRIANT, 1993, followed by POTTS, 1999a: 323.
38. POSENER, 1936: 22 and 175–176, and BRIANT, 1993.
39. PF-NN 1573; concerning Susa if we agree to associate this text with PF-NN 2383: TUPLIN, 1998: 93, no. 69; but W. Henkelman (personal communication) informs me that more likely concerns Persepolis. Note that tablet sb 13078 (published below) attests that at this date Darius was indeed at Susa.
40. I am borrowing this interpretation in its entirety from Waerzeggers' remarkable article (2010) where she demonstrates that 'Susa' in the Babylonian-Achaemenid texts is indeed the capital of Elam, and not a city with the same name that might have existed in Babylonia. In my opinion, her study settles once and for all a discussion that has continued for a long time among Assyriologists (see previously ABRAHAM, 1997: 81–82).
41. PF 1497, 1565, 1575, 1577, 1780, 1858; PF-NN 208, 1443, 20404–6 etc; HENKELMAN, 2008: 343–347. The two terms are not necessarily used as synonyms, in that the region of Elam cannot be reduced to the city of Susa (HALLOCK, 1969: 695, *s.v.* 'hatuma').
42. In contrast to cedarwood (Lebanon), *yaka*-wood (Gandara and Kerman), gold (Lydia and Bactria), lapis lazuli and carnelian (Sogdiana), turquoise (Chorasmia), silver and ebony (Egypt) and ivory (Ethiopia, India, Arachosia), or decorative elements (Ionia): *DSf; DSz*.
43. It may have been then that the Elamite hydronym Ulā was changed into an Iranian

hydronym, Huwaspa (Choaspes): POTTS, 1999b: 35; 1999b: 35; compare with Strabo XV.3.6. (metonomasia of the Agradatas river into Cyrus by the king of that name).
44. See the synthesis by BRIANT, 1996: 184–194 and 934–935.
45. This was already noted many years ago. For an update see HINZ, 1969: 70 ff.
46. Here I am closely following ROAF 1974: 94–98 and 104–105.
47. Elien, *Animals* XII.23, with HENKELMAN, 2008: 436–438.
48. See the remarks by HENKELMAN, 2008: 439 no. 1016.
49. ROOT, 2003, now expanded in Root (in press). The author bases her interpretation on two observations on Elamite specificity: 1. It is the only relief at Persepolis that includes a display of femininity, namely the lioness' teats; 2. This is the only delegation where the movement of the lioness looking back at its cubs, introduces some form of narrative.
50. Strabo XV.3.3: 'They adorned the palace of Susa with decoration more than any other'.
51. BRIANT, 1996: 249 and 941.
52. XV.3.21.
53. BRIANT, 1991: 70–72.
54. This simple observation weakens the proposal by GIOVINAZZO 2000–2001.
55. BRIANT, 1988; 1996: 196–207.
56. See Polyaenus' famous text, *Stratagems* IV.3.32, on which I have commented at length (BRIANT, 1996: 297 ff.) and which S. Amigues has reexamined in a very remarkable study on palm wine (AMIGUES, 2003: 54–55).
57. BRIANT, 1994 (water from the Choaspes which accompanied the king on his journeys), and BRIANT, 2003: 357 ff.
58. David Lewis had focused his research on this question and, before his death in 1994, he had constructed a database of all the Series Q tablets that R. Hallock had published or transliterated. C. Tuplin continued this research to its conclusion, and published the results in great detail (TUPLIN, 1998: 90–102). I have summarised them here.
59. See below, § 4, Table 1.
60. See, for instance, BRIANT, 1991: 70, no. 13. This is one of the arguments that invalidates many of the conclusions of GIOVINAZZO, 1994b; TUPLIN, 1998: 83, no. 50; 1995, nos 84–85 and 99, no. 102.
61. See framed in JOANNÈS, 2000: 153.
62. On the place of these documents in the 'archive of the Barber of Ur', see JOANNÈS, 2005: 127–128; see also the Gallâbu (barber's) Archive from Ur described in Jursa 2005, in 7.12.1.2 on pp. 133–134. To be published by F. Joannès (no. 1026), and JOANNÈS, 2005: 183–186.
63. See especially STOLPER, 1990 and 1992.
64. It is difficult to know what exactly this expression means, and whether it does refer to the king's departure (see the discussion in CARDASCIA, 1951: 142), especially as the text belongs to a very difficult period of transition, namely the accession of Ochus-Darius II, between the death of Artaxerxes and the elimination of Sogdianos (STOLPER, 1985: 122). Nevertheless, the hypothesis remains a possibility.
65. ABRAHAM, 1997: 60–64 and WAERZEGGERS, 2010, II.2.

66. Strabo (xv.3.3) does not forget to mention that, apart from Susa, Persepolis and Pasargadae, the Great King also had palaces at Gabae and Tawuka.
67. BRIANT, 1988: 267–269 ('mobile palace'); compare with the description of an Ottoman camp by the Englishman, Paul Rycaut: 'The pavilions of the Grand Vizier and of others of high status would be better termed palaces than tents; they are of prodigious size … [They are] portable palaces' (*The Present State of the Ottoman Empire, 1670*)
68. See Elien, *Varia Hist.* xiv.12 and BRIANT, 1992a.
69. In Diodorus Siculus xix, 21, 2, the translation of *to basileion* (Persepolis) as 'capitale royale' is a nonsense (Collection des Universités de France, p. 35).
70. HALLOCK, 1969: 24–25, and HENKELMAN's update (in press) (§ 3 for Irdabama, with the remark in note 90); also HENKELMAN, 2008: 110, no. 243.
71. See a transliteration and translation by HALLOCK, 1969: 25 (who admittedly expresses many doubts), and a presentation by M. Stolper (STOLPER, 1994). The latter describes as 'sensational' the discovery by M. Garrison of the seal impressed on the tablet. What follows is taken essentially from his remarkable publication (GARRISON, 1996: 17–20; for its almost certain Susian origin, as well as that of the uninscribed tablet: 32).
72. The translation of the name of the product is due to W. Henkelman (HENKELMAN, 2010), with notes 199–202.
73. See the remarks by HALLOCK, 1969: 698. See also PF 1573, 2057, where the author uses the term 'stopping places'; HALLOCK, 1969: 439 ('3 villages, i.e stopping places'); in PF 1460, the rations are distributed in a 'village' (*humanuš*), and also in PF 736 (Series J); in favour of Princess Irdabama, away in Elam in 501–500 BC); the recent publication of an administrative tablet in Old Persian (Fort. 1208–101) demonstrates that Old Persian equivalent of the Elamite *humanuš* is *vardana*, also known in DB (STOLPER and TAVERNIER, 2007).
74. HENKELMAN, 2010, 2011, note 75.
75. BRIANT, 1984a: 64–66.
76. BRIANT, 1991, and 1996: 369–389; TUPLIN, 1998: 80–81.
77. In order not to confuse the situation, I have not included the category that is by far the largest, that of the journeys Susa-Persepolis-Susa.
78. See also the earlier remarks by GARRISON, 1996: 33–34.
79. The same applies to Datis who, in January or February 497 BC, armed with the king's *halmi*, travels express (*pirradaziš*) between Sardis and Persepolis, and receives rations at Hidali (PF-NN 1809; LEWIS, 1980).
80. PF 57, 88–92, 136, 318, 737, etc.
81. Amherst 258; DANDAMAYEV, 1972: 262–263, note 8 (with en error in the numbering); BRIANT, 1996, p. 526.
82. *Astronomical Diaries* no. 346; WAERZEGGERS, 2010, Table 2, bottom line.
83. 'From Susa and the rest of the country of the Kissians, came 300 talents; it was the eighth department' (III.97).
84. KOCH, 1993: 8–12.
85. Šatin-Kitin (PF 88, 92), Tep-Kitin (PF 91) and many others.
86. Concerning these texts, see also the remarks by TUPLIN, 2008.
87. See parallels and remarks in BRIANT, 1996: 477 and 970.

88. UET 4, 48 and 49.
89. Perhaps this explains why Mirinzana affirms that he must not go (into the country of Elam' (*Hatamtám hatuma*), but the accounts will be prepared there by someone else (PF 1858, with comments by HENKELMAN, 2008: 346).
90. The Elamite equivalent of the Old Persian *bāji* ('tribute'); on the nature and collection of *baziš* in Persia, see BRIANT 1996: 452–454 and 966–967 and, recently, TUPLIN, 2008.
91. PF 1752–1753, with remarks by HENKELMAN, 2008: 110–111.
92. See especially the category 'travel rations for animals' (S3): PF 1780–1784, 1786–1787; PF-NN 1148, 1443 etc.
93. BRIANT, 1996: 478–486 and 970–952.
94. On the basis of the daily flour ration distributed to the group by the administration, it has been possible to evaluate the number of shepherds at about 700, and the number of sheep at 100,000 (BRIANT, 1982: 331–356 (p. 144), with references); but W. Henkelman (personal communication) pointed out to me that the rations were allocated for several days, and the calculations must be revised; according to him, the number of animals should not have exceeded 5,000 to 10,000 head.
95. BRIANT, 1996: 413–414.
96. JOANNÈS, 1988; 2000: 153 (translation); 2006: 127–128; WAERZEGGERS (2010).
97. See the remarks by HENKELMAN, 2008: 346–347.
98. On this matter, see especially STOLPER, 1977: 254–259; JOANNÈS, 1989: 151–159, and 2005; the texts have been assembled and discussed by WAERZEGGERS (2010); see also ABRAHAM, 2004: 17 ff.
99. See especially the text edited and translated by ABRAHAM, 2004: 251–255, no. 27 (around 500/498 BC).
100. See, for example, Arrian, *Indica* 42, and *Anabasis* vii.7.1–2; on Achaemenid interest in the Gulf, see recently the preliminary remarks by JOANNÈS, 2005: 187–189.
101. See most recently BRIANT, 2008.
102. BRIANT, 1996: 189–190.
103. Concerning the workmen on the Persepolis building sites, and by extension on the *kurtaš*, see BRIANT, 1996: 442–452 and 965–966.
104. See the *ad loc* notes by HALLOCK, 1969: 557, notes j–k.
105. Like the Babylonian *sabe* (see below, note 117), the Elamite *taššup* used here (also PF-NN 1044) can refer to a troupe of soldiers as well as to a troupe of civilians/workers (BRIANT, 1996: 115, 444, 925).
106. HALLOCK, 1969: 41.
107. BRIANT, 1996: 443, 449–451, 966.
108. BRIANT, 1996: 1169, *s.v.* 'Déportation', and KULESZA, 1994.
109. Herodotus vi .20 (Milesians); vi. 119 (Erythraeans, about whom there is a rich ancient tradition); see also HOGEMAN, 1991.
110. Diodorus xvii.110.3–5 (villages); Arrian iii.8.5 (contingents of 'deported Carians'). Sittacene was part of Babylonia, separated from Elam by the course of the Tigris): LE RIDER, 1965: 268–269 (Hellenistic period) and KESSLER, 2002; the latter recalls the well-attested Carian communities in Babylonia, concerning which see the exemplary study by WAERZEGGERS, 2006.
111. The term Ionian must not be translated as 'Greek'.

112. PF 1357: After having probably stopped off at Susa (authorised by Bakabana), a small group of 8 *puhu* accompanying Battesˇa and his Companion receive rations from Susa to Persepolis where they have to convoy the 'Babylonian Treasure' (*kapnukiš Bapilira*).
113. JOANNÈS, 2005: 185–190.
114. HENKELMAN and KLEBER, 2007; see also TOLINI, 2008.
115. On this matter see the interesting comments by F. Joannès (JOANNÈS, 2005: 189, 195–196).
116. BONGENAAR, 1997: 37–38 and notes; MacGINNIS, 2002; JOANNÈS, 2005: 193–194; WAERZEGGERS 2010; (the texts cited here are taken from his article, and from that of MacGINNIS, 2002; see previously DANDAMAYEV, 1972).
117. The terminology is used frequently to refer to the equipment and rations of soldiers, possibly summoned to Susa. In some cases, the term used for designating the men, *sabe*, is ambiguous, as is the term in Elamite (see above, note 105); it is all the more ambiguous in that troupes of soldiers could be used for non-military work (for instance, the digging and dredging of canals).
118. MacGINNIS, 2002: 177–179, no. 1: rations and provisions include: barley, dates, cress, wool, 53 pairs of second-category sandals.
119. MacGINNIS, 2002: 177–179: no. 2.
120. Text edited and translated by WAERZEGGERS, 2006: no. 13 (pp. 18–19) with brief comments p. 5.
121. Concerning this period of construction, see the update in STEVE, VALLAT and GASCHE, 2002–03; col. 293–4.
122. See the discussion and bibliography in POTTS 1999a: 335–337 together with R. BOUCHARLAT's update.
123. See the translation in GLASSNER, 1993: 205; also FINKEL, VAN DER SPEK: www.livius. org/cg-cm/chronicles /abc9/artaxerxes.html. Very naturally the Babylonian writer refers mainly to the entry of women into the 'royal palace' of Babylon.
124. ADRTB no. 346: WAERZEGGERS (2010).
125. ADRTB, no. 366.
126. R. Boucharlat, ch. xii.
127. BRIANT, 1996: 695–696 and 1024–1025.
128. Arrian, *Anab.* iii.16.6; for the name of the satrap, see BRIANT, 1996: 744–745.
129. Quintus Curtius Rufus, *Hist. Alex.* v.2 8–10.
130. BRIANT, 1982: 161–173.
131. ANDRE-SALVINI and DESCAMPS-LEQUIME, 2005.
132. On Alexander and Susa at Susa, see Arrian, *Anabasis* vii.4–6.
133. I return to R. Boucharlat's expression in his 1990 article.
134. Polybius v.48.14: 'This city he also took at the first assault, but the assaults he made on the citadel were unsuccessful, as the general Diogenes had thrown himself into it before his arrival. 15: Abandoning this attempt, he left a force to besiege it…'

The Cyrus Cylinder

Jean Perrot

Found in 1879 amongst the ruins of Babylon, the 'Cyrus Cylinder' contains a vital inscription. Drafted shortly after the capture of Babylon by Cyrus II in 539 BC, the account comes from the religious quarter of the town, probably from the priests attached to the cult of Marduk, 'The Great Lord'. The priests of Marduk accused Nabonidus, their king, of having forsaken the temples and despoiling them. They wished for the intervention of Cyrus, King of Persia; they saluted his arrival in the town and inspired the inscription of the cylinder according to a template set down by Ashurbanipal when he restored the walls and gates of the city.

The second section is a proclamation by Cyrus: 'I am Cyrus, king of the universe, the great king, the powerful king, king of Babylon, king of Sumer and Akkad, king of the four quarters of the world, [...] all kings who sit on thrones, from every quarter, from the Upper Sea to the Lower Sea, those who inhabit [remote districts] (and) the kings of the land of Amurru who live in tents, all of them, brought their weighty tribute into Shuanna, and kissed my feet. From [Shuanna] I sent back to their places to the city of Ashur and Susa, Akkad, the land of Eshnunna, the city of Zamban, the city of Meturnu, Der, as far as the border of the land of Guti – the sanctuaries across the river Tigris – whose shrines had earlier become dilapidated, the gods who lived therein, and made permanent sanctuaries for them.' (Translation by Irving Finkel, Assistant Keeper, Department of the Middle East, British Museum, London).

We find an echo of this account in the Bible (2 Chronicles, 36:22–23 and Ezra 1:1–2):

1. Now in the first year of Cyrus king of Persia, that the word of the Lord spoken by the mouth of Jeremiah might be accomplished, the Lord stirred up the spirit of Cyrus king of Persia, that he made a proclamation throughout all

13

The Cyrus Cylinder
A terracotta barrel cylinder, 23 cm long
British Museum no. ME 90420

his kingdom, and put it also in writing, saying,
2. Thus saith Cyrus king of Persia, All the kingdoms of the earth hath the Lord God of heaven given me; and he hath charged me to build him an house in Jerusalem, which is in Judah.

The biblical text recreated, in its own way, the decree by Cyrus expressing the king's desire to return the gods looted in war to their original places of worship; also to return the deported populations to their countries of origin. Yahveh had 'woken Cyrus' spirit' in the same way that Marduk 'took the hand of Cyrus' and called him to the kingship of the whole... 'Thus saith the Lord to his anointed, to Cyrus, whose right hand I have holden, to subdue nations before him' (Isaiah, 45:1).

The Cyrus Cylinder does not teach us anything about the religious beliefs of the Persians in the time of Cyrus and Cambyses. Cyrus venerates Marduk, which does not mean that he made him his personal God; his approach was political. It must be noted that the text does not mention Ahuramazda.

Bibliography:
SMITH, 1963; ELLERS, 1974;
KURHT, 1983; FINKEL, 2013

14
Darius on the Bisitun rock
photograph by Y. Majidzadeh

2

Darius the Great King

François Vallat

Darius the Great reigned over the Persian Empire from 522 to 486 BC.[1] He was one of the great figures of Near Eastern antiquity, but his image over the last few decades has been tarnished largely by the erroneous analysis of various inscriptions. It is therefore necessary to try to re-establish a certain degree of truth, knowing well that in history the truth of today may not be the truth of tomorrow. Therefore, rather than present the campaigns of the King of Kings, write at length about his six official wives and his numerous progeny, or expose the ostentation of the court – which can be found in all good history books – it would seem useful to highlight certain records which have never been properly translated and allow us to paint a very different portrait of the monarch than that currently presented to us. However, before taking on the analysis of these inscriptions, we should attempt to sketch the image that Darius would have wished to leave us.

A PORTRAIT OF THE KING BY HIMSELF

In various inscriptions, in particular those carved on the cliffs of Naqsh-i Rustam, Darius enumerated his qualities. It was in one of these rock carvings (DNb) that Darius painted a picture of his gifts. The passage begins (§ 1) by paying homage to the divinity:

> *Ahuramazda is the great god*
> *who has created the beauty that we see,*
> *who has created happiness for man,*
> *who has bestowed intelligence and courage on King Darius*

If we browse through all the inscriptions left to us by Darius, it is intriguing to note what seems to be the sovereign's abhorrence of the opposite of truth – the lie. The

15

**Illustration of the layout of inscriptions
(Babylonian, Elamite, Old Persian)
on the Bisitun relief**

Inscriptions from the first phase of the work
Inscriptions from the second phase of the work

El. = Elamite · O.P. = Old Persian · Bab. = Babylonian

16
Bisitun relief
photograph by Y. Majidzadeh

king seems to have been obsessed by the lie, considering it the source of all injustice, all turpitude and misfortune. This hatred of the lie (*drauga* in Old Persian), inherited from ancient Indo-Iranian civilisation, consequently makes truth a paragon of virtue. The king believed that all the revolts that he had to put down following his accession to the throne were the fault of the liar kings. He clearly asserted that, in DB § 54: 'those that lying had raised up'. Not only did he fight lying, source of injustice, but he asked his successors to imitate him in DB § 56/57:

And you who later will read this inscription, believe what I have done,
What is written in this inscription!
Do not think it is a lie!
I swear by Ahuramazda that it is the truth and no lie
that I have accomplished [all] this in a [single] year.

He added in DB § 58

other things [...] are not written in this inscription,
The reason is: he who later will read this inscription
Might think that it is too much, that which has been accomplished by me.
He would not believe it and would think it was a lie.[2]

Besides, Darius wished to be just and equitable towards all the subjects of the empire. After having enumerated the 23 peoples which made up the empire (DB § 6), he declared (DB § 8):

Within these countries, the man who is loyal I reward well;
He who is hostile, I punish greatly.

In his administration of justice, he claimed that he was not choleric and that he was capable of self-control; he also added (DNb § 5) that he acted with level-headedness and equity:

What a man says against a man,
that does not convince me,
until I hear the statements of both.

Darius had benefited from a physical education, as he was happy to report at Naqsh-i Rustam (DNb § 8 and 9):

I am skilled both with hands and with feet.
As a horseman, I am a good horseman.
As a bowman, I am a good bowman, both on foot and on horseback.
As a spearman, I am a good spearman, both on foot and on horseback.

If his physical education seems excellent, we know nothing of his intellectual capacity. Was he literate? We might doubt it when we read in a Bisitun inscription (DB L): 'this very inscription which I sent to all the lands after it was written and read before me.'

However, this sentence does not necessarily imply that he was illiterate. It may be that it was an Elamite or, more broadly, a Near Eastern custom. At that time one did not address the king directly. One wrote to his scribe who read him the document. The letter started with: 'To my Lord so-and-so, so speaks such and such…' or 'To the King, so speaks such and such'.[3]

Besides which, as the reliefs at Bisitun can testify, Darius seems to have had a high opinion of himself. He had himself depicted physically as far larger than others. But we should also note that the two attending officers were also larger than the liar kings, yet without being taller than the King of Kings. We find the same proportions on the door jambs of his palace at Persepolis. Similarly, the statue found at Susa which had been carved in stone from Wadi Hammamat is clearly larger than life.[4] It is in the same spirit that he had throne bearers carved on his tomb at Naqsh-i Rustam (DNa § 4), as he explained himself:

If you think: 'How numerous are these people that Darius[5] subdued?'
Look at the depictions of those who bear the throne.
In this manner you will know them.
Then shall you know, then shall it become known to you: the spear of the Persian
Man has gone forth far; then shall it become known to you: the Persian Man has
delivered battle far indeed from Persia.

It seems somewhat pretentious when he asserts that no other king had accomplished as much as he had in a single year. One must, however, see in this assertion an unspoken attack on Cyrus, whom he never mentions in his inscriptions.

Darius also states that he rewards the one who does good and punishes his enemies. His punishments were sometimes more than harsh. The Babylonian and Aramaic versions of the inscription at Bisitun detail the number of his victims, killed or taken prisoner after each battle,[6] but this claim does not feature in the Elamite or Old Persian versions of the text. These totals run from a few hundred to several thousand individuals. Even if some of these numbers may be exaggerated,

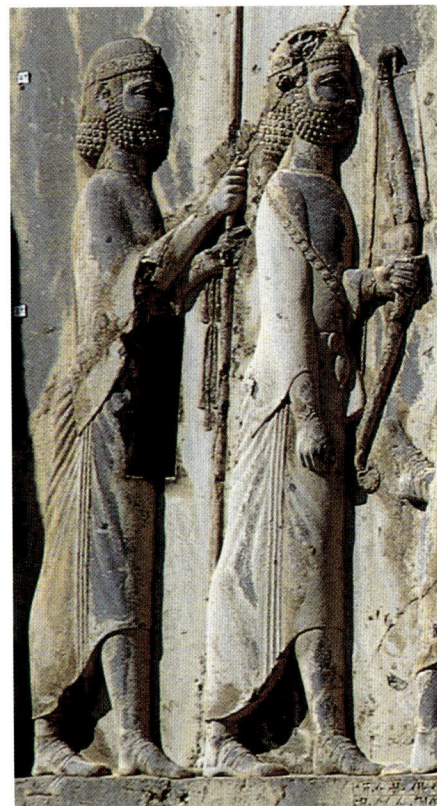

17
Bisitun relief
Two dignitaries standing behind the king carrying symbols of royal power, the bow and spear
photograph by Y. Majidzadeh

18
Bisitun relief
The 'liar kings' with ropes
around their necks
photograph by Y. Majidzadeh

other elements illustrate the cruelty of the period. In DB § 32 the text is clear when he refers to one of the leaders of the revolts: 'I cut off his nose and ears and tongue, and tore out one eye; he was kept bound to my door, everyone saw him. Then, at Ecbatana, he was impaled.'

Sometimes he became menacing. Thus in DB § 61: 'And if […] you hide this proclamation and you do not tell it to the people, may Ahuramazda kill you, and may you not protect your family!'[7]

On the other hand, he could reward, as in DB § 60: 'if you do not hide this tale from the people but if you tell it to them, may Ahuramazda favour you as well as your family and may you live long!'

He could be generous to those who had served him well, as he stated in DB § 63: 'The man who installed himself in my palace, I protected ardently.'

He went even further: the last two paragraphs of the first large inscription at Bisitun (DB § 68 and DB § 69) were dedicated to the reward of the six Persian nobles who had supported him during the elimination of Gaumata the Magus. After having named them and their ancestry (DB § 68), he declared (DB § 69): 'You, who later will become King, protect the families of these men.'

In his Letter to Gadatas, Darius lectured the satrap who had dared raise a levy on the sacred gardeners of Apollo and had made them cultivate secular land. Darius asserted his piety on every possible occasion. It is always by the grace or with the help of Ahuramazda that he won his battles, conquered the lands, or built palaces; that he has punished the wicked and rewarded the good. In the Bisitun inscription the name of Ahuramazda is mentioned 72 times. We should not be surprised, therefore, when he mentions in DSK: 'Ahuramazda is mine, I am Ahuramazda's'.

THE TARNISHED IMAGE OF DARIUS

If we go back to the image of the king suggested by contemporary historians, it is important to analyse the inscriptions by putting the sources into a hierarchy. We will find that the Elamite version of the royal inscriptions, the first to have been written, allows us to re-establish a badly misinterpreted historical truth. Most of the translators of these texts thought that the principal version of these trilingual inscriptions was the Old Persian because Persian was the monarch's mother tongue. This approach has led some research to a dead end. We have too often forgotten that at the time of Darius, Old Persian was a recent written language. Elamite had a 2000-year-old history with a scribal school far older than Achaemenid civilisation. It is enough for us to look at the Persepolis archives to be convinced – the thousands of excavated tablets in this capital are all inscribed in Elamite. The only exceptions are two Akkadian tablets, a small Greek text incised on clay, and one single tablet in Old Persian. But the most pertinent evidence, as we will see, is furnished by Darius himself who wrote his first royal inscription in Elamite – an inscription which is the source of many a misunderstanding. It is the one carved above the King on the rock at Bisitun, the one now identified by the letters 'L: El'.

On this subject, the reasoning of G.G. Cameron, the decipherer of the Persepolis Tablets, is very significant. In his 1959 publication of what is known as the Daiva Inscription (which we will examine later), he claimed that the original text for the trilingual inscriptions was Old Persian, even though he appeared to be somewhat confused (*sic!*). About 15 years later, he claimed the contrary, asserting that the first text to be composed was the Elamite version. It is therefore the Elamite version that we will favour. It is not a question, however, of denying the elements contained in Mesopotamian tablets or eliminating information from Classical sources. The important thing is to order the sources.

The majority of modern historians think that Darius was a usurper, and consequently that all the writings that he left us – carved on rock or marble, on gold or silver tablets, or simply on clay – at Bisitun, Susa, Persepolis or elsewhere, contain only untruths designed to demonstrate or prove a fallacious legitimacy. All would then be lies. He would not then be the ninth king of a family that had reigned in two lines, as he claimed. He would not be the legitimate heir to Cyrus the Great, founder of the Persian Empire, as he attested. His own lineage could not go back to Achaemenes because the latter was only the mythical founder of the dynasty.[8] And for some, he would be the sole sovereign of the Achaemenid dynasty not to have a single drop of Achaemenid blood in his veins![9]

THE ANCESTORS OF DARIUS

To try to understand the complexity of the situation, we must go back to the beginning. In the second half of the nineteenth century, when a first decipherment of the cuneiform inscriptions was attempted, experts from various disciplines proposed an outline of the Achaemenid dynasty that favoured the information given by Darius in the trilingual inscription (Old Persian, Elamite and Babylonian) carved on the rock face at Bisitun. It is therefore important to recall these words. Darius presented himself in the first four paragraphs of this important inscription:

> [§ 1] *I am Darius the Great King, King of Kings, King in Persia, King of the peoples, the son of Hystaspes, grandson of Arsames, the Achaemenid.*
> [§ 2] *Darius the King says: My father was Hystaspes; Hystaspes' father was Arsames; Arsames' father was Ariaramnes; Ariaramnes' father was Teispes; Teispes' father was Achaemenes.*
> [§ 3] *Darius the King says: For this reason we are called Achaemenids. (So) from long ago we have been noble. From long ago our family has been royal.*
> [§ 4] *Darius the King says: There were eight of our family who were kings before me; I am the ninth; nine in two lines have we been kings.*

The second paragraph is particularly interesting for the genealogy of Darius as it lists all his ancestors: Hystaspes, Arsames, Ariaramnes, Teispes and Achaemenes. In the fourth paragraph, the king explained that his family could count eight kings before him, and that these reigned in two lines, but he did not mention them all by name. Knowing that his father Hystaspes did not reign, we have, with Arsames, Ariaramnes, Teispes and Achaemenes, four Achaemenid sovereigns. From there it was not hard to find the other four monarchs because we know that Darius inherited the empire created by Cyrus.

Cyrus himself, in his famous Cylinder, gave us his own genealogy. He called himself, in effect: 'the son of Cambyses, the great king, king of the city of Anshan,

```
                    Achaemenes
                        |
                     Teispes
              _____|_____
             |                     |
        Ariaramnes              Cyrus I
             |                     |
         Arsames              Cambyses I
             |                     |
        Hystaspes              Cyrus II
             |                     |
         Darius I             Cambyses II
```

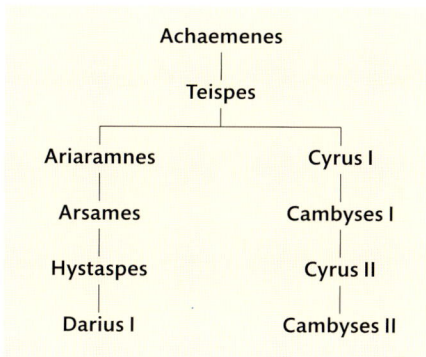

grandson of Cyrus, the Great King, ki[ng of the ci]ty of Anshan, descendant of Teispes, the Great King, king of the city of Anshan.'

By going back to Teispes, Cyrus linked himself with the Achaemenid family and at the same time he gave us the four kings not mentioned by Darius: the two named Cyrus and the two named Cambyses. Even before the Cyrus Cylinder was known (1879), in 1851 Jules Oppert had proposed the outline illustrated here, by suggesting that Teispes had split his kingdom between his two sons Ariaramnes and Cyrus I.

This outline, with some modifications, was generally accepted. However, the discovery of the Cyrus Cylinder at Babylon in 1879 should have changed this. Indeed, in the Cylinder, Cyrus indicated that he and his ancestors were but the 'Kings of the city of Anshan'. This should have led to questions about who the king of this region was. The prestige of Cyrus, however, was such that historians seem to have been much influenced by the story of Cyrus' life as transmitted to us by the Classical writers, the foremost being Herodotus. Indeed, the 'Father of History' narrates the adventures which surround the birth and youth of the future Great King, and his actions until his death.

This view was universally held until 1932, when a new text, written in Akkadian, was published.[10] The text states that the Great King of Assyria, Ashurbanipal, had, after his campaign in Elam, received the submission of 'Cyrus, King of Parsumas' who had sent him tribute brought to Nineveh by his son Arukku. It was then supposed that 'Cyrus King of Parsumas' and 'Cyrus King of Anshan' were one and the same. Cyrus I thus became the contemporary of Ashurbanipal who reigned from 668 to 627 BC. This record, however, dates from around 646 BC and as it was known previously that Cyrus II had taken Babylon in 539 BC, it appeared that more than a century separated the two kings of Anshan named Cyrus, as it did grandfather and grandson. The new text seemed to contradict all the elements given by Darius in his different inscriptions. Thereafter all the statements made by Darius became suspect and much historical and archaeological received wisdom was considered questionable.

In this view Darius became a usurper whose main concern was to forge a link with Cyrus' family, his illustrious predecessor. He cheated by linking Ariaramnes to Teispes, son of Achaemenes, because Teispes, father of Cyrus I, was another person altogether and had nothing to do with Teispes father of Ariaramnes, Darius' ancestor. Indeed, doubt was cast on the existence of Achaemenes, father of Teispes, because Cyrus did not mention him in his Cylinder. But as Cyrus called himself 'Achaemenid' on the inscriptions at Pasargadae, the natural deduction was that these lines, carved in many places in the palace of Cyrus' capital, had really been added by Darius. It is here that another problem in our understanding of the period arises: the date of the creation of the Old Persian script. Obviously if Old Persian had been created by Darius, Cyrus would not have been able to carve the inscriptions of Pasargadae.

The reality, as we shall soon see, is very different: it was not Darius who was a usurper, but Cyrus who instigated a coup against his Lord, Arsames, the grandfather of Darius.

THE CREATION OF THE OLD PERSIAN SCRIPT

Even today, most specialists think that it was Darius who was the inventor of Old Persian writing. This interpretation, however, is based on the erroneous translation of the 70th paragraph of the Bisitun inscription. The text is, indeed, problematic.

To start with, the Elamite version, which was the first to be incised, has only 69 paragraphs. This is the same as the Babylonian translation which succeeded it.

The number of paragraphs in Old Persian, which was carved later, is 76. It is the 70th paragraph which is the subject of controversy. If the Babylonian version, which does not include this paragraph, is discounted in this argument, a small Elamite inscription carved above the representation of Darius at Bisitun (the inscription called 'DB L') contains almost the same text as that of paragraph 70.

Additionally, it is important to highlight that this paragraph in Old Persian is situated at the bottom of the panel which has suffered more from the ravages of time and weather than the parts higher up, so that only a partially reconstituted segment is available to specialists. Finally, a significant element of the Elamite text does not figure in the Old Persian version. Usually, following W. Hinz,[11] the paragraph is translated as follows:

1 *Darius, the king, says:*
2 *By the grace of Ahuramazda,*
3 *I made another inscription, in Aryan,*
4 *which before did not exist.*
5 *On clay as well as on leather,*
6 *I made both [my] name and genealogy [to be inscribed].*
7 *and this was written and read before me.*
8 *To all the provinces I then sent this very inscription.*
9 *People learnt it.*

However, this translation contains errors which change the sense of the message that Darius wanted to transmit. It is important therefore to pick these out without going into philological detail, which is too important to be dealt with here and will be developed elsewhere.[12] Thus line 3 should read: 'I translated this inscription differently in Aryan,' .

What had not been understood until recently is that the verb *hutta* 'to do', constructed with the directional *ikki* 'beyond, towards' means 'translate'. We have identical verb constructs in several languages. Thus, for example, **trans**late is **über**setzen in German, **tra**duire in French, from the Latin **traducere, and meta**graphy in Greek, **pere**vodith in Russian.

All these verbs are constructed with a directional. The existence of composite verbs is well documented in Elamite. Line 3 does not deal with the creation of a new form of writing, but with the translation of an inscription.

The problem that now needs to be resolved is to know what text has been translated 'differently' into Aryan. The sentence (line 4): 'which before did not exist here' raises an interesting point. Indeed, initially only the Elamite inscriptions were carved on the relief. The Elamite inscription DBa ('A: El' on the preceding drawing), the one situated immediately above the king, whom it identifies, is without doubt the first to have been inscribed. This inscription is apparently identical to the first four paragraphs of the large inscription (DB) translated in the Appendix.[13] 'Apparently' only! Because no one had noticed the profound differences between the first Elamite text and its translation into Old Persian as we can see: DBa in Elamite says:

I am Darius, the king, the son of Hystaspes, the Achaemenid.
I am King of Kings (because) I am descended from a Persian king.

Whilst DBa in Old Persian proclaims:

I am Darius, the Great King, King of Kings,
The King in Persia, the king of all peoples,
The son of Hystaspes, the grandson of Arsames the Achaemenid.

Elamite DBa contains the first of Darius' titles, but as this one had become obsolete by the time he translated it into Old Persian in the last phase of the Bisitun project, he modified it. In other words, the king said that he had translated Elamite DBa into Old Persian DBa 'differently', that is to say, replacing his first title with the new one certified here. Finally, it is interesting to note that this line 4, 'Which before did not exist here', does not appear in the Old Persian, which is to be expected, because the adverb 'here' indicates the top left-hand corner of the panel whilst paragraph 70 of the Old Persian text is engraved at the bottom right-hand corner.

The remainder of the analysis of these lines will confirm this new interpretation. The second problem is on line 6, which is generally translated 'I made name and genealogy' (which means nothing) or, more seriously: 'I made [my] name and genealogy [to be inscribed].' But even if this last translation is accepted and it makes sense, it does not do justice either to the genius of the Elamite language or to Darius' character. Indeed, the King is never economic with possessives, especially those in the first person. Everything belongs to him. The apparent absence of a possessive pronoun in this context is all the more awkward if one of the words is badly translated. Literally, the sentence is made up of four words which it is important to quote and to analyse, although three of these pose no problem: *hiš kutta eippi hutta*. The noun *hiš* 'the name', the conjunction 'and' as well as the verb *hutta* 'I made' are elements of the Elamite language that are perfectly well known and therefore do not present any difficulty. It remains for us to consider *eippi*. This noun has been confused with other Elamite words phonetically similar but with different meanings. It was Hinz who proposed the meaning 'origin, genealogy' for *eippi*, and therefore translated *hiš kutta eippi* as 'name and genealogy'. In reality, the expression *hiš-eippi*, in ancient times as in the inscriptions of Shilhak Inshushinak (c.1150–1120 BC), meant 'identity'. It was the identity, the lineage of his ancestors, who built or restored the temples of Susa, that the king was looking for, not their titles: all were kings because the construction of a palace or a temple was a royal privilege. Furthermore, when Shilhak Inshushinak referred to these individuals he always labelled them 'the kings my predecessors'. Here the two terms are separated by the conjunction 'and', whence the literal translation 'name and genealogy' which does not, at first glance, make any obvious sense. But in Elamite, the possessive suffix of the third person -*i* is not apparent when attached to a word ending in-*i* like *eippi*. We can therefore remodel the sentence: 'I have established (made) a name and its lineage' or better still 'I have (re-)established a name and its lineage'.

This way Darius establishes a major distinction in the analysis of these documents. He distinguishes the two branches using different terms. The members of his direct ancestry constitute his lineage (*eippi*) whilst the rest of the Achaemenid succession belongs to Darius' family in a broader sense. This family is indicated in the Elamite inscriptions by the Sumerogram NUMUN. The Cyrus and Cambyses kings belong to his NUMUN, as confirmed by certain passages in the great inscription at Bisitun (DB). Thus when Darius makes allusion to Cambyses he says (DB § 10): 'One named Cambyses, son of Cyrus, of our family'.

And when he mentions the revolt of Gaumata the Magus, he specifies (DB § 12): 'This kingdom that Gaumata the Magus had taken from Cambyses, this kingdom had belonged to our family from long ago (NUMUN)'.

Darius therefore considers all those named Cyrus and Cambyses to be amongst the members of his family NUMUN and ipso facto they are part of the eight kings, his predecessors, whom he alludes to.[14] The 'name and his lineage' that Darius has re-established upon taking power, is therefore the one belonging to the ancestor of the direct line of the Achaemenids, Achaemenes (the name) and his succession to the throne of Persia (his lineage).

The remainder and the end of the inscription do not present any major difficulty. Only the verb *sapi* has been interpreted in various ways. But it is clear that Darius has sent these words into all the countries to illustrate his legitimacy by bringing to light the ancestors of the Achaemenid family, without, it must be noted, ever mentioning Cyrus, the creator of the empire that he has inherited. We can also highlight the material aspects of this inscription. Contrary to the majority of this sovereign's inscriptions, Darius is king by his ascendancy and not 'by the grace of Ahuramazda' as he so often proclaims elsewhere. In the great inscription of Bisitun, it is only in the fifth paragraph (a paragraph which does not figure in the short text sent to all the lands!), that the king says:

> By the grace of Ahuramazda, I am King.
> Ahuramazda bestowed the kingdom upon me.

This Elamite inscription DB L (partly repeated in paragraph 70 of the Old Persian text) can therefore be translated:

> Darius the king says:
> By the grace of Ahuramazda,
> I translated this inscription differently in Aryan.
> It did not previously exist here.
> Thus, on tablets as well as on parchment,
> The people learnt that
> I [re]-established a name and its lineage,
> [Thanks] to this very inscription which I
> Sent to all the lands [after]
> It was written and read before me.

This new translation changes many current theories. The foremost is the evidence put forward for the coup by Cyrus, and confirmed by several external sources which we will examine. Other falsehoods can be definitively done away with. First, it is perfectly clear that Old Persian was not created at the time of Darius because the sentence generally translated as 'I have made another inscription in Aryan' must henceforth read 'I translated this inscription differently in Aryan'. This Old Persian script existed at the latest under Ariaramnes, Darius' great-grandfather.

Next, it implies that the inscriptions of Cyrus at Pasargadae, and of Arsames and Ariaramnes discovered at Hamadan, must not be considered as fakes, and that they can be integrated into the historical canon.

Finally, we can no longer maintain that Darius sent a copy of the great inscription of Bisitun to all the regions of his vast empire; he only sent his first royal inscription (DB L = DB § 70) translated into Old Persian, the one which justifies his legitimacy.

We could also add that it shows that the more senior branch of the Achaemenids is that of Darius and not that of the Cyrus and Cambyses kings as was asserted until now.

CYRUS' COUP D'ÉTAT

The transfer of supreme power from the senior branch to the junior branch was made under Cyrus II. There are several arguments to support this. First, he calls himself 'King of the city of Anshan' on the Pasargadae inscriptions: 'I am Cyrus, the King, the Achaemenid (CMA)' or 'Cyrus is the Great King, the Achaemenid (CMC)'.

We can also note that the third line of the Cyrus Cylinder reads: 'in place of the great, a low person was put in charge of his country'.[15]

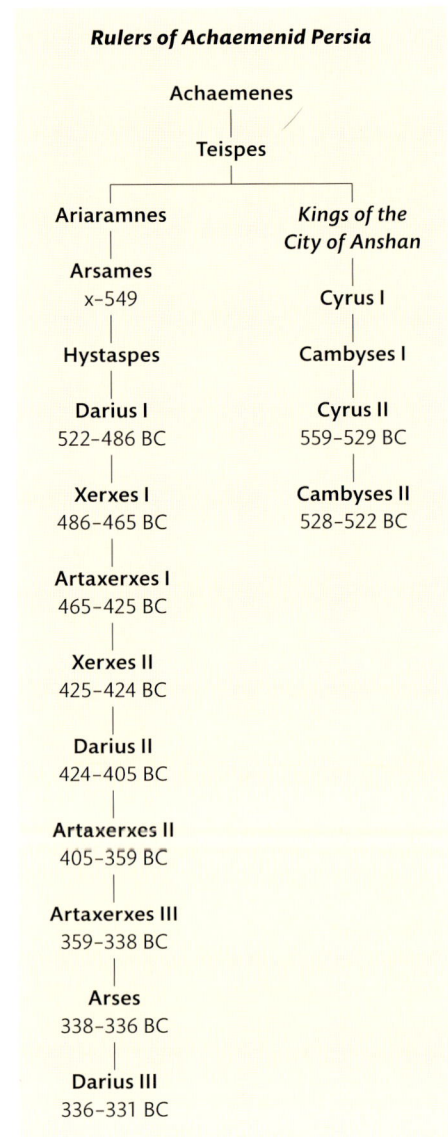

Rulers of Achaemenid Persia

Achaemenes

Teispes

Ariaramnes

Arsames
x–549

Hystaspes

Darius I
522–486 BC

Xerxes I
486–465 BC

Artaxerxes I
465–425 BC

Xerxes II
425–424 BC

Darius II
424–405 BC

Artaxerxes II
405–359 BC

Artaxerxes III
359–338 BC

Arses
338–336 BC

Darius III
336–331 BC

Kings of the City of Anshan

Cyrus I

Cambyses I

Cyrus II
559–529 BC

Cambyses II
528–522 BC

19
Bisitun relief
The Elamite version DB L (cream dot)
photograph by Y. Majidzadeh

In all probability this sentence alludes to the seizure of power in Persia by Cyrus, the low '"King of Anshan" who appropriated the Crown and became the "Great King" of Persia.'

Another record, the Nabonidus Chronicle,[16] even provides an approximate date for the usurpation. When Astyages marched against Cyrus, Cyrus is called 'King of Anshan', but when Cyrus crosses the Tigris on his way to Lydia, he is 'King of Persia'. The coup therefore took place between these two events.

According to the legend passed on by the Greek historians, in particular by Herodotus, Cyrus was the offspring of the marriage of Cambyses I and Mandane, the daughter of Astyages, the celebrated Median king to whom the Persians were linked. Profiting from a revolt in Media, Cyrus overthrew his father-in-law Astyages and seized his capital, Ecbatana, around 550 to 549 BC. He then attacked the Lydian king Croesus, who supported Astyages, and defeated him in 547 BC. Confident of his new power, of his newly gained riches and notoriety, the petty king of Anshan became King of the Medes and seized power over Persia by dethroning his sovereign, Arsames. From there he was in a position to subjugate Babylon, which fell without a fight in 539 BC. This whole saga lasted only about ten years. Thus Cyrus put an end to the senior branch of the Achaemenids. With his characteristic political astuteness, Cyrus allowed Arsames and his family to live. Arsames and his son, Hystaspes, were still alive when Darius, at the beginning of his reign, had the foundation plaques of Susa inscribed (DSf and DSz): 'And by the grace of Ahuramazda, my father Hystaspes and Arsames my grandfather were still alive when Ahuramazda made me king on earth.'

From this we can understand why he bore a grudge against Cyrus for having dethroned his grandfather and prevented his father from reigning. Since Cyrus' successor, his son Cambyses II, had died without a successor, Darius believed that the crown and the empire were his by right. After having crushed several revolts, of which the details are presented in three languages on the cliff of Bisitun, he established himself at Susa, and then a few years later he began the construction *ex nihilo* of Persepolis. Darius nurtured a real anger towards his illustrious predecessor and it is because of this *damnatio memoriae* that he inflicted on Cyrus, that certain passages of his inscriptions seem so enigmatic. Why, when he said that eight members of his family were kings before him, did he not name them all? Although he listed his direct lineage, he did not mention indirect ancestors. He seems to have wanted to expunge Cyrus from the collective memory. Besides, the name of Cyrus does not appear in any of his inscriptions. Darius mentioned Cyrus only in the expression 'I am so-and-so, son of Cyrus', a sentence which he attributed to the Liar Kings whose rebellions he crushed.[17]

Never does Darius mention Cyrus when describing the different provinces of his immense empire, built up essentially by his predecessor. He does not say that it is Cyrus who conquered the Median Empire which extended as far as Afghanistan, and who, to the west, conquered Lydia and Ionia. Furthermore, Darius mocked Cyrus, the creator of the empire, by asserting that none of the ancient kings had ever realised as much as he himself had in the course of a year (DB § 59). After the restoration of Susa, Darius conceived of a capital in his own country, Persia. With the old tradition of the 'Kings of Anshan and Persia', he could have settled in Anshan and restored the ruins of Tell-i Malyan or chosen to refurbish and embellish the grandiose site of Pasargadae. There was no question of restoring Anshan, the fiefdom of the junior branch of Achaemenids and even less of living in Cyrus' former quarters in Pasargadae. As he said himself, in an inscription at Persepolis (DPf), he preferred to build a new capital:

> *In this place where this fortress is built,*
> *beforehand no fortress had been built.*

Thus he created a total break with Cyrus, his eminent predecessor.

DARIUS AND THE ECONOMY

Amongst the many economic reforms initiated by Darius, some are well known. It was he (not Cyrus) who introduced the use of metal coinage into the day-to-day economy, as many tablets from Persepolis testify. The labourers were sometimes paid in money, sometimes in commodities. In addition, economic exchanges were helped by the road network, where at each halt travellers were greeted in caravanserais where they found all they needed for themselves, their retinues and their animals. For some functionaries the lodgings were free. It was enough for them to show their orders, drawn up for them by a meticulous administration. In reality such an order was a 'circular letter of credit' which worked like our present-day credit cards. This network also faciliated the movements of tax collectors, military units and caravans taking tribute to Persepolis for the New Year (21 March in our calendar). To improve communications further, Darius ordered the digging of the 'Suez canal', as declared on the Chalouf Stele:

> *King Darius says: I am a Persian; setting out from Persia, I conquered Egypt.*
> *I ordered the digging of this canal from the river that is called Nile and flows*
> *in Egypt, to the sea that begins in Persia. Therefore, when this canal had been*
> *dug as I had ordered, ships went from Egypt through this canal to Persia, as I*
> *had intended.*

20
Pasargadae, 'The winged genie'
The inscription reads:
'I, Cyrus, the King, an Achaemenid...'
drawing by C. Texier

He could not have known that the statue that he had had made in Egypt 'to show that the Persian man held Egypt' would, some decades later, use this route to reach Susa. It was Xerxes who brought his father's statue back, once he had completed the monumental Apadana.[18] What is less well known and more surprising is the overseeing of the production and distribution of goods. As an example we can choose a financial tablet from Persepolis. In this letter, Parnakka, the senior economic administrator (the Pharnaces of Greek sources), orders the shepherd to provide a monthly sheep to a goldsmith (whose name has been lost through damage) working in Persepolis:[19]

To Harrena, the shepherd:
So speaks Parnakka:
'The goldsmith at Persepolis named X
should receive as salary 6 sheep
for the second month, the third month,
the fourth month, the fifth month, the sixth month, the seventh month.
For six months of the 18th year, for each month he shall receive a sheep.'
Kamezza has registered the order after receiving double from Maraza.

The most interesting are the last two lines of this letter which were written in the margin. Indeed this document, which is a clay tablet (*tuppi*) written in Elamite, is in reality a copy of the original (*halmi*) which was sent to the recipient. The original was written in Aramaic on parchment. A second copy in Aramaic (*dumme*) was also stored, on parchment, in the administrative archives, according to an ingenious system known elsewhere in the Near East. Clay tablets had string extending out from both flat sides of the flattened oval, a unique type of tablet in the history of cuneiform tablets. The string was used to suspend the tablet from a stick. To consult the archives, one needed to look at the seal which was impressed on the flat side of the tablet and which was visible without touching the record. In addition, the copy of the Aramaic text was also attached to the stick. In the case of litigation, all ambiguities could be resolved by consulting the tablet.[20]

So, on these records the information was complete. The name of the sender and of the recipient were in the first lines of the document. All intermediaries were listed in the codicil, which, when it was complete, indicated the name of the

21
Persepolis tablet
In Freiburg, Switzerland, lines 11–16

person who gave the order, the one who transmitted it, the one who wrote it in Aramaic on the *halmi* and, finally, the one who registered it on the clay tablet which has come down to us.

This bureaucratic system, in three languages, allowed the administration to oversee all the expenses and income of all kinds which were due to the royal household. Whilst thousands of tablets were dug up at Persepolis, the site at Susa has provided us only with two, and the second is fragmentary.[21]

DARIUS AND RELIGION

It is always to these texts (whether at Bisitun, Persepolis or Naqsh-i Rustam) that we must return when we speak of Achaemenid religion. In truth, it is a strange phenomenon to see the obstinacy with which certain historians neglect these inscriptions, to give preference to the sayings of Herodotus or to project the ideas of the Avesta.[22]
ÉDOUARD DHORME

It is hard to understand the religious situation in the country when Darius ascended to the Persian throne because of the paucity of the primary sources, However, the surviving records and iconographic representations offer a few outlines. The two inscriptions that date from before Cyrus, those of Ariaramnes and Arsames,[23] are clear. The only divinity mentioned is Ahuramazda, the Great King who had given them kingdom and kingship. Indeed, after the King's titles, one can read on the golden plaque of Hamadan (AmH):

Ariaramnes the King says: This country, Persia, which I hold, which is possessed of good horses, of good men, the Great God Ahuramazda bestowed it upon me. By the favour of Ahuramazda I am king in this country.

For his part, Arsames, also on a golden plaque at Hamadan (AsH) added:

Arsames the King says: Ahuramazda, great god, the greatest of gods, made me king. He bestowed on me the Persian people, with good armies, with good horses. By the favour of Ahuramazda I hold this land. May Ahuramazda protect me, and my royal house, and may he protect this land which I hold.

And the two inscriptions end by soliciting the protection of Ahuramazda. The Achaemenids of the senior branch were therefore followers of Ahuramazda.

Meanwhile the situation was not as simple for the junior branch, that of the kings Cyrus and Cambyses. It appears that Cyrus II received a Median education and the analysis of certain fleeting elements of Darius' inscriptions leads us to the following hypothesis. When he placed himself on the Persian throne, Cyrus also imposed worship of the god of his childhood, Mithra. He put the Magi – the Median religious cast – in charge of religious affairs. The imposition of the worship of Mithra in the place of Ahuramazda must have distressed some people, amongst whom was a certain Zarathustra, the Zoroaster of Classical sources. The sudden change of the official master of the pantheon of the Gods allows us to understand the first stanza of Yasna 46, sometimes called 'Ushtavad Gatha'.[24]

To what land shall I escape? Whither shall I go? I have been separated from my relatives and from my tribe. Neither the village, nor the wicked leaders of the land are favourable towards me. O Lord, how can I assure myself of your favour?

Zarathustra appears here like an outcast – it is likely that many of his followers rallied to the new power. After having been thrown out of his clan and his tribe he found himself in a land where the villagers and their chiefs were hostile to him. This sounds logical when we know that Zarathustra was a Persian who had to leave his family because he remained faithful to Ahuramazda. But in fleeing to the east, he arrived in the regions held by the Medes and where Mithra was lord.[25] It was to avoid harassment by the Magi that he had to seek exile in the eastern provinces of the empire where it is thought he came from.[26] There was another aspect that resulted from Cyrus' coup: Darius's hatred for the usurper. It would be unsurprising if Darius' father also harboured such feelings; it is even possible that the prince who brought aid to the rebels, Vishtaspa/Hystaspes, was in fact Darius' father. Indeed, in Yasna 46, stanza 14 we read:[27]

> *O Zarathushtra, what righteous man is your friend for the great covenant? Who wishes to be heard? It is the prince Vishtaspa at the moment of the decisive test.[28] Those whom you will unite in one House with you, good Lord, these I salute with words of Good Thoughts.*

Hystaspes may have rebelled because of his father's downfall and then forged links with Zarathustra, either from religious conviction or for political motives. It must be noted that during the first Parthian revolt in March 521 BC Vishtaspa/Hystaspes was in the region in a private capacity. One must wonder whether Darius' father and the prophet did not meet on that occasion. It seems that Hystaspes stayed a while in the region because several months later, in July 521 BC, Darius sent a Persian army to support Hystaspes' efforts during the second Parthian revolt, at Ray, south of present-day Tehran.

So, with Darius, it was a return to the *status quo ante* characterised by the omnipresence and omnipotence of Ahuramazda whilst Mithra, the great God of the Indo-Iranians, the principal deity of the Medes and the personal god of Cyrus, disappeared completely from Darius' inscriptions. The absence of Mithra in the Achaemenid inscriptions is as complete as in the Gathas. This observation led J. Duchesne-Guillemin to view this phenomenon as a 'white revolution':

'Darius' inscriptions represent the penetration of Ahuramazda into the religion of the bagas [gods], or, if one wishes, the promotion of Ahuramazda to the first

religious tolerance to all the people of the empire by respecting their habits and customs, would not have done the same for the followers of Mithra. Finally, there could have been a strategic reason: there were far more Medes than there were Persians, as demonstrated by the name 'Median Wars' used to denote the wars against the Greeks, launched by Darius and carried on by Xerxes. Whatever the reasons, Darius was unable to eliminate the Magi and impose the worship of Ahuramazda over the whole of his territory, as is proved by the difficulties encountered by Xerxes on his succession. But we can say that the Achaemenid Persians were Mazdaean before becoming Zoroastrian.

DARIUS AND HIS HERITAGE: XERXES AND THE DAIVAS

The famous 'Daiva Inscription' (xph), sometimes called 'the Harem Inscription' from the name of the palace where it was found at Persepolis in 1936, has already caused many to put pen to paper – almost on a par with Paragraph 70 – and its contents have never been entirely clarified. This deficiency is due to two particular reasons. First, the inscription is carved on four stone blocks with two Old Persian versions (of which one is complete), one Babylonian version and one incomplete Elamite version. Hence the first studies were based on the Old Persian version which does not correspond directly with the Elamite text. It was not until a new and complete Elamite version was discovered at Persepolis copied by G. G. Cameron in 1957 and published in 1959,[34] that progress could be made.

The second reason is that the original version of the royal inscriptions was written in Elamite, under both Darius and Xerxes. The other versions are more or less faithful to the original, and more or less fantastic than the original. It seems sometimes that the scribes responsible for the Old Persian or the Babylonian texts did not always fully understand the words they were asked to translate. Whatever the reasons, until now, the translation of the disputed passage (xph § 4) of the Old Persian is generally accepted as:

King Xerxes says: when I became king,
there was among the peoples who are listed above
one that was in rebellion.

Naturally, studies have been dedicated to this enigma: which of the 30 countries listed in the previous paragraph had fomented a rebellion? Amongst other hypotheses, Egypt, Babylonia and even Athens have been proposed. The Elamite version, once again, is very clear because it can be translated (xph § 24–26):

Xerxes the King says: 'When I became king,
there was, in the country cited
before the others, confusion.'

The country first in the list is Persia as lines 11–13 mention:

King Xerxes says: By the grace of Ahuramazda
these are the countries of which I was king apart from Persia.
I had lordship over them. They brought me tribute.

There then follows the list of 30 countries. This interpretation is confirmed by lines 29–31 of the same inscription: 'And among these countries there was a place where previously daivas were worshipped. Afterwards, by the grace of Ahuramazda, I destroyed that sanctuary of daivas.'

To my knowledge, the *daivas*, who are Indo-Iranian deities, were not worshipped in Babylon, Egypt or Greece; but they were in Persia. Xerxes makes allusion to a war of succession which followed his accession to the throne. There is nothing strange about this when we know that Xerxes was designated Darius' heir, even though he was not the eldest son. Darius had two or three children from his first wife, the daughter of Gobryas. Xerxes was the eldest child of the second wife, Atossa, the daughter of Cyrus. Some Greek sources tell us that Artobarzanes, the eldest son, relinquished his rights to the throne. It is possible that the followers of Mithra had attempted to steer politics towards religion by re-establishing the worship of the *daivas* and thus opposing the omnipresence of Ahuramazda imposed by Darius. The reappearance of the Magi, so hated by Darius and by Zarathustra, illustrates a challenge to the Great King who, during the course of his 35-year reign, had not been able to eliminate from the political scene the Magi who, in his eyes, represented Cyrus. The victory of the Magi was even more complete when Artaxerxes II reintroduced Mithra into the official religion of the Achaemenids. In his inscription at Susa (A2sa), which narrates the restoration of the Apadana which had burned down under Artaxerxes I, the King wrote:

> *May Ahuramazda, Anahita and Mithra protect me from all harm*
> *and that which I may have caused!*

Certainly Ahuramazada remains the principal deity in the pantheon of the gods at this period, notwithstanding the return of Mithra, accompanied by Anahita, to the religious scene. This sentence was also taken up by the same king in Inscription A2sd, whilst his successor Artaxerxes III, in his Persepolis Inscription (A3Pa) was content with calling upon only two gods:

> *May Ahuramazda and the god Mithra protect me, as well as the people*
> *and that which I have done!*

1. As he said himself at Hamadan (DH § 2) and
at Persepolis (DPh), his empire stretched 'from
the Scythians to Ethiopia, from India to Sardis'.
Epigraphists have conventionally designated the
inscriptions by two or three letters, of which the first
represents the name of the king, sometimes followed
by a number. Thus A2 is used for Artaxerxes II. The
second capital letter stands for the place of discovery:
s for Susa, P for Persepolis, B for Bisitun. Lower-case
letters designate the different inscriptions of the same
king within the same site. Numbers may be used to
indicate the paragraph or verse in the original text.
2. It may be that Darius is referring here to the
restoration work undertaken at Susa from the
beginning of his reign.
3. The first is an Akkadian text; the second is an
Elamite translation.
4. As attested by petrographic analysis (TRICHET
and VALLAT, 1990; J. Yoyotte, this volume, ch. VIII.
5. One should note that most of these countries had
been conquered by Cyrus, and Darius deliberately
ignores this.
6. For the Akkadian version, see MALBRAN, 1994;
for the Aramaic version see GREENFIELD and
PORTEN, 1982.
7. This last threat is perhaps derived from Elamite. In
numerous curses in classical Neo-Elamite times there
are, indeed, formulae such as: 'that no descendants
may be borne' or 'let him not have any descendants'.
8. This theory was most recently proposed by
P. de Miroschedji (MIROSCHEDJI, 1985: 282–283).
9. This theory is endorsed by M.W. Waters
(WATERS, 1996: 18).
10. WEIDNER, 1931–1932.
11. HINZ, 1968: 95–98.
12. VALLAT, 2011.
13. F. Vallat, this volume, Appendix.
14. It is indeed surprising to read in E. Pirart
(PIRART, 1996) the following remark: 'Darius I
affirms that he is the 9th Achaemenid. However,
there have not been eight Achaemenids before him,
whichever way of counting one adopts'!
15. CB § 2. See, for example, LECOQ, 1997: 181.
16. GRAYSON, 1975.
17. I am most grateful to Jean Yoyotte for bringing
to my attention an Egyptian text. It is a fragmentary
inscription (POSENER, 1936: 60) that refers to
a 'residence that Cyrus has built [...] and Posener
(POSENER, 1936: 60) adds: 'The absence of any
royal title preceding Cyrus is strange'.
18. On Darius' activities in Egypt, see J. Yoyotte,
this volume, ch. VIII.
19. VALLAT, 1994.
20. Concerning this particular system, see VALLAT,
1997a.
21. The complete tablet has been published by
V. Scheil (SCHEIL, 1911: 101, no. 308), but for the
translation see R.T. Hallock (HALLOCK, 1969: 25).
22. DHORME, 1913: 15.
23. These two inscriptions have been considered to
be forgeries by those who thought that Darius had
created the Old Persian script. Now that this theory
must definitely be abandoned, there is absolutely no
reason for not completely rehabilitating these two
texts and making use of them in the same way as
the other inscriptions.
24. Translated by DUCHESNE-GUILLEMIN,
1975: 190.
25. Indeed, he had no other option, because Cyrus
lived more in the western part of the empire,

spending his time between Ecbatana, Pasargadae
and Babylon when he was not in the battlefield.
26. GNOLL, 1980.
27. Translated by DUCHESNE-GUILLEMIN,
1975: 194.
28. Avesta.org, English translation:
http://avesta.org/yasna/yasna.htm#y43.
29. DUCHESNE-GUILLEMIN, 1953: 15.
30. This peculiarity did not escape P. Lecoq
(LECOQ, 1997: 160).
31. LECOQ, 1997: 277.
32. This was recently suggested by S. Razmjou
(RAZMJOU, 2001: 10).
33. KELLENS, 1997: 288.
34. CAMERON, 1959.

Convention of the Persian Antiquities Concession

Jean Perrot

In archaeology, the official relationship between France and Iran goes back to 1884 with the firman of Nasir ed-Din Shah authorising Marcel Dieulafoy to excavate the 'tumuli' in Susiana where the British archaeologist W.K. Loftus had discovered the site of Susa in 1852. The operation led to the despatch of fragments of a large capital with bulls' heads, and of parts of a glazed brick panel to the Louvre. These restored pieces were the highlights of the 1888 exhibition. The Shah, irritated, accused Dieulafoy of 'having robbed him'. The negotiations for a convention permitting further excavations were lengthy. They resulted in 1895 in a convention that met with a mixed response from Jacques de Morgan who, whilst finding the convention 'highly advantageous', regretted that it did not give him 'all the guarantees or facilities that an archaeologist could wish for'. The brutal death of Nasir ed-Din Shah in 1896 delayed the ratification. When he arrived in Tehran in 1897, de Morgan attempted to modify the convention with the new sovereign, Muzaffar ed-Din Shah, all the while hoping for a firman enforcing the clauses of the first convention. A new treaty was signed in Paris in 1900 which incorporated de Morgan's suggestions (as he boasts in his Memoirs), highlighting specifically that: 'the government of his Imperial Majesty the Shah of Persia grants France exclusive and perpetual rights to excavate over the whole of the Persian Empire'. With regards to Susa and Susiana, the excavators had the right, barring a few financial arrangements, to take to France the entirety of their discoveries. Such were the times.

The effects of the convention lasted until 1927, when Iran opened up to foreign excavations, with the finds shared between Iran and the excavators. The situation became increasingly intolerable, with archaeological research becoming more and more objective and conscious of the need for widespread investment, not to mention a growing and justified Iranian national sensitivity. In 1968 French researchers agreed to the entirety of the requests of their Iranian colleagues and

24
Facsimile of the beginning (above) **and end** (above, right) **of the
Convention relating to the Concession of Persian Antiquities,
signed in Paris in 1900**
Archives of the Foreign Affairs Ministry

25
Photograph from Maurice Pillet's album, 'At Susa in 1913'
© Musée du Louvre/Christian Larrieu

26
Nasir ed-Din Shah
painting on leather by Bahram Kizmanshani
Department of Islamic Arts, Musée du Louvre,
MAO 776. © RMN/Hervé Lewandowski

France decided to renounce its share of finds. In 1969 steps were taken to execute these measures in close cooperation with the Iranian Ministry of Culture, the Antiquities Service, the Centre for Archaeological Research, and the National Museum of Iran. Furthermore, the French proposal to protect the vestiges of Darius' Palace at Susa was well received; it was actively supported by the Iranian government from 1969 until 1979, at the same time as measures were taken to protect the site and its antiquities.

27
Jules-Georges Bondoux, *Les Fouilles de Suse*
1905, oil on canvas, h 4.63 m
© Musée du Louvre, paintings department: inv. 20803

3

The Discoverers of the Palace of Susa

Nicole Chevalier

The relics of the Achaemenid palaces were not torn from a splendid monument, but resurrected from the avaricious entrails of the earth and acquired at risk to our own lives.

JANE DIEULAFOY

THE TRAVELLERS

The origins of archaeological exploration in the Middle East during the first half of the nineteenth century lay in the political interests of the European powers, a deep understanding of the Bible and a general intellectual curiosity for exotic locations and periods. It was for political reasons that, at the beginning of the nineteenth century, British travellers were the first to reach Susa: namely Colonel John Macdonald Kinneir (1808–1810) accompanied by Major Montieth, Robert Gordon, a member of the Ouseley mission (1811), and Sir Robert Ker Porter (1817–1820). Situated at the edges of the Ottoman and Persian Empires, Susiana was home to rebel tribes and was a difficult region to access. In 1836, following a force of 2,000 soldiers sent by the Shah to pacify the region, Major Rawlinson managed to reach the area.[1]

In the middle of the nineteenth century, the few French travellers who reached Persia were not so fortunate. It was in vain that first, Charles Texier (1838), and then the architect Pascal Coste, together with the artist Eugène Flandin (1839–1840) attempted to reach Susa. On their arrival in Shiraz, Coste and Flandin were still hopeful, but since they had run out of resources, they had to be content with the scant information imparted by the Baron de Bode, Councillor at the Russian Embassy. From the drawings and information imparted to them, they decided that the monuments must be of little interest.[2] This opinion on the mediocrity of the Susian remains was confirmed by Austen Henry Layard. It was without enthusiasm that that the future excavator of Nineveh and Nimrud explored the ruins. He wrote his account in a letter to the Orientalist Eugène Boré, who communicated it to the Société Asiatique on 1 June 1841: 'I visited Susa, which Major Rawlinson believes to be the Shushan of the Holy Scriptures, as well as Daniel's tomb; but the ruins are of no importance, and there is only one inscription in cuneiform, which I was unable to copy as it was with difficulty that I escaped, [having been] robbed and fleeced by the Dinarounis tribe who live in this savage and desert land. Other than the similarity between the name and the tomb of the prophet, there is nothing to indicate that a great city lies here.'[3]

WILLIAM KENNETT LOFTUS (1850–1852)

Layard's opinion did not affect the belief that the hills that hid the ancient city also held the vestiges of important Achaemenid building works. Since Susa had lost its position as capital after the Macedonian conquest, the first excavators hoped to gain easy access to the Achaemenid remains by attacking the tell from above. The British explorer William Kennett Loftus (1820–1858), was the first to undertake the exploration.[4]

When Loftus began his research into the location of the capital of the Persian kings, he was already an experienced explorer. He had been travelling in the East since 1849 and knew it well. As a geologist, he had been engaged as an expert on the Turco-Persian Boundary Commission led by Lieutenant Colonel W. F. Williams.

Loftus' account, *Travels and Researches in Chaldaea and Susiana; with an Account of Excavations at Warka, the 'Erech' of Nimrod, Shûsh, 'Shushan the Palace' of Esther, in 1849–52*, which appeared in 1857, shows that he had already excavated several sites in southern Mesopotamia. Thus it was that at the beginning of 1850 he was con-ducting a survey at Warka-Uruk, in the company of the artist Henry A. Churchill. Colonel Williams followed the activities of his subordinate with interest and suggested he explore the site of Susa. At the end of May 1850, in Churchill's company, Loftus began an initial survey of the site; next to the 'Citadel' (the Acropolis) and 'great platform' (the Ville Royale) he identified the tell of 'Shushan the Palace', later known as the 'Apadana'.[5]

After a break during the summer, and having obtained a *firman* granted by Nasir ed-Din Shah, work resumed in January 1851, this time in the presence of Colonel Williams. Orders were given to the local authorities to favour the work of the archaeologists and ensure their protection. However, the local population was reluctant to take part in the excavation, and appalling climatic conditions were detrimental to its smooth operation. The trenches opened up on the Acropolis by the Commission's servants delivered on the one hand traces that Loftus identified as belonging to the Sassanian period, while others – essentially glazed bricks – belonged to the Elamite period.[6] Due to a lack of funds, however, Colonel Williams was very quickly forced to curtail his scientific ambitions and had to content himself with a surface exploration of the Apadana; this proved to be very fruitful. Blocks of limestone and column drums having attracted his attention, at a little more than a metre below the surface, he cleared three bell-shaped column bases resting on slabs. Close to traces found on the surface, he opened up four trenches, but without further results. Called back to their work, the Commission members abandoned their research, just as it was beginning to bear fruit.

A year later, in mid-February 1852, Loftus recommenced his work at Susa under the aegis of the Trustees of the British Museum, who had just designated Henry Creswick Rawlinson, consul in Baghdad, as 'supervisor' of all British excavations in Mesopotamia. Rawlinson, who had authority over the the excavations at Susa, obtained a new firman, and a grant of £500 from the Ministry of Finance. For

28
W.K. Loftus (1820–1858)
The first excavator of Susa
British Museum

29
Capital in the shape of a double bull protome belonging to column number two of the Apadana
drawing by H. A. Churchill, *Susa drawings*, pl. 8
© British Museum, London

30
Plan of the principal tells of Susa
LOFTUS, 1857: 340

two months, on his own, with occasional help from Churchill, Loftus explored
the tells of Susa, particularly the Apadana. There was no shortage of labour and
the numbers rose from 70 to 350 workers, recruited primarily from the Lurs of
the neighbouring villages and the inhabitants of Dizful. During a visit to Susa,
Lieutenant Jackson of the Indian Navy painted two interesting watercolours of
the excavations. Loftus was particularly keen to identify the building to which
the column bases, uncovered the previous year, belonged. In addition to the three
columns found by Colonel Williams in the eastern colonnade, he discovered eight
columns in the porticoes and twenty in the Hypostyle Hall. These elements were
sufficient to permit him to reconstruct the general layout of the Apadana.[7] The
plan he drafted showed a central hall with thirty-six columns in six rows of six,
resting on square plinths, surrounded on three sides by porticoes made up of two
rows of six columns on bell-shaped bases. Following his excavations, Loftus formed
the impression that the Hypostyle Hall at Susa, like that of Xerxes at Persepolis
(the similarity struck him) had never been enclosed by walls; he searched for a
wall, but in vain, digging several trenches between the central hall and the lateral
porticoes.[8] Loftus was also interested in the building's elevation. From fragments
of fluted columns and column capitals in the form of double bull protomes scattered over the whole site, he concluded that all the columns, both in the colonnades
and the central area, had had bull capitals.[9]

Another trench, to the south-west of the Apadana, revealed a brick pavement at
a depth of 3.35 m, lying on top of which were fragments of glazed brick decorated
with different motifs, rosettes and winged discs. With great intuition, Loftus deduced that these bricks must have ornamented the palace itself. In addition he

Plan of the Great Hall of Columns at Susa.

■	Column bases or basement slabs actually discovered.	⊠	Column bases with trilingual inscriptions.
▦	Positions of columns not sought for.	☐	Position of a column, no portion of which was found.

31
Plan of the Apadana
LOFTUS, 1857: 366

justifiably interpreted a whole series of signs as being masons' marks serving as a guide to the assembly of the large decorative panels, and he compiled a chart of them.[10]

One of Loftus' major discoveries is both epigraphic and historical. To the north of the middle passage of the central hall, he uncovered four column bases carrying trilingual inscriptions – Old Persian, Elamite and Babylonian – revealing that this building, called an Apadana, was built by Darius I (521–486 BC), was burnt down under Artaxerxes I (465–425 BC), and was rebuilt by Artaxerxes II (405–359 BC).[11] Different soundings in various places across the site allowed him also to bring to light other pieces of evidence from the Achaemenid period: amongst these were architectural elements found at the southern point of the Ville Royale tell.[12] On the Acropolis he collected a large number of fragments of alabaster vases of which some examples are inscribed with the name of Xerxes (486–465 BC).

In April 1852, Loftus interrupted his excavations and moved the focus of his research to Mesopotamia. Apparently Rawlinson was disappointed with the results obtained at Susa; the famous Orientalist had hoped to see Loftus excavate the whole site. The results, however, were not negligible: it was proved Susa was biblical Shushan; a map of the ruins was produced; on the Apadana mound, bases were revealed on which one could read the names of Artaxerxes and Darius; and the Apadana was identified. Loftus immediately connected this building with Xerxes' great hypostyle hall at Persepolis.[13] Rawlinson's judgement was unfortunately supported by a lacklustre publication which did not do justice to the pioneering work which Loftus had accomplished at Susa; the report contributed to his research being underestimated for many years.[14] Even so, in 1890, the Hellenic scholar Georges Perrot,[15] well-informed and full of admiration for the work of Loftus at Susa, described him as 'one of the most intelligent and astute travellers there has ever been'.[16] He was astonished at how little was made of certain aspects of his discoveries: 'Loftus had already brought back to Europe fragments of the glazed decoration of the Palace of Susa, which he deposited at the British Museum. It is astonishing that they have not been more noticed. Amongst the motifs which are on the glazed earthenware he draws our attention to the winged disc, which I cannot find on the bricks which belong to the Louvre'.[17]

MARCEL AND JANE DIEULAFOY (1884-1886)

The memory of Susa haunted my husband's nights. He rebuilt these Achaemenid palaces in his memory, where Greece, Egypt and western Asia had brought their tribute and their treasure; before him was assembled the vast army of Xerxes, leaving Susa for the shores of Ionia; he heard the lamentations of Atossa when she learnt of the disaster at Salamis and the paeans of victory sung by the Greeks over the smoking ruins of Persepolis.[18]

JANE DIEULAFOY

When Marcel and Jane Dieulafoy arrived at Susa on 26 February 1885 it was not the first time that they had set foot in the ancient city. Three years before, at the end of a long journey through Persia and Mesopotamia, they had managed to do what no other French travellers had done before, finally cross into Susiana.

32
**Marcel Dieulafoy (1844-1920) and
Jane Dieulafoy, née Magre (1851-1916)**
The first French excavators of Susa
© Musée du Louvre, photographic archives
of the Oriental Antiquities Department

First contact with Susa (1882)

Having left in February 1881, Jane and Marcel Dieulafoy reached Susa on 14 January 1882 after having studied Pasargadae and Persepolis on the way. Finally they explored the site that Loftus had had to abandon 30 years before: 'There, our guide, moving aside abundant brambles, showed us the pedestals of several columns in staggered rows. Four of these were decorated with trilingual inscriptions in cuneiform characters. [These pedestals had allowed Loftus to reconstruct] a Hypostyle Hall surrounded on three sides by porticoes and having close similarities to the Apadana of Xerxes at Persepolis. The general disposition, the column bases more or less intact, the paw of a colossal animal folded under its stomach, are the indisputable signs of the Achaemenid origins of the Susian monument. Even without these signs, the reading of the trilingual inscriptions, of which we were able to learn the meaning, would tell us that this palace, built at the time of Artaxerxes Mnemon, replaced the throne room of Darius, burnt down

33
Jane Dieulafoy
'With the Khassérés between the Kerkha
and the Shaur, 4 April 1886'
photograph by Marcel Dieulafoy

34
Engravings from Jane Dieulafoy's Journal
J. DIEULAFOY, 1888

during the reign of one of his successors. It would therefore have been in the shade of these colonnades that the radiant beauty of Esther dazzled the King of Kings and that the sovereign lowered his golden sceptre to her.'[19]

According to Jane, Marcel Dieulafoy was able to draw a certain number of conclusions from this first and brief contact with the vestiges of the palace: 'According to my husband, the exterior façade of the palace was not facing north towards the Bakhtiari mountains, as the English archaeologists seem to have thought; the view of the mountains was reserved for the King, but the main entrance, the monumental doors stood to the south of the Apadana. The position of the trilingual inscriptions carved on the East, South and West faces of the bases is the proof of this. If the throne had been facing north, visitors would have found themselves facing the smooth side and would only have been able to read one line with any ease. Let us turn the royal seat 180°: the happy mortals admitted to the presence of the sovereign arrived by a route that skirted the fortress; as soon as they crossed the threshold of the Palace, they would see the monarch at the end of the hall in all his glory, and, if they were permitted to approach the throne, they would easily be able to decipher the three cuneiform texts.'[20]

After this 13-month trip around Persia and Susiana, carefully described by Jane in *La Perse, la Chaldée et la Susiane*, Dieulafoy reported the results of his mission to the Académie des Inscriptions et Belles-Lettres in 1882. He explained his theories on Persian architecture and its links with the architecture of the Middle Ages, a theory which he developed in *L'Art antique de la Perse*, a considerable work that caused a sensation.[21] As highlighted by René Dussaud, curator of the Department of Oriental Antiquities in the Louvre, in his history of the *Académie des Inscriptions et Belles-Lettres*, an institution of which he was the life chair, 'his geometric mind would henceforth attempt to derive everything from Persia'.[22] His theories did not go unchallenged: 'ingenious ideas', commented Georges Perrot, 'of which more than one is worthy of discussion'.[23] Susa, for which Dieulafoy provides a plan of the Apadana, is only an example. Curiously, this plan is not only different from Loftus' but it also differs from the one described by Jane in her account of their journey.[24] This was Marcel Dieulafoy's first contact with ancient Susa; despite the fleeting visit, he was certain that the site deserved further investigation.

The first campaign (1885)

On his return to Paris, Dieulafoy did everything to bring his project to life, finding the necessary funds and obtaining the indispensable authorisation from the Persian government. Louis de Ronchaud, director of the Musées Nationaux,

ACROPOLE DE SUSE

Plan figuratif du terrain
levé par Mᴿ BABIN ingénieur des Ponts et Chaussées
attaché à la mission
sous la direction de
Mᴿ DIEULAFOY
Ingénieur en chef des Ponts et Chaussées

35
Susa Acropolis
Relief map modelled by M. Babin,
civil engineer
M. DIEULAFOY, 1893: plan I

36
The west colonnade of the Apadana
J. DIEULAFOY, 1888: 306

37
**An outline map of the Susa tells
with trenches indicated**
M. DIEULAFOY, 1893: 424

supported Marcel Dieulafoy and provided him with a grant of 31,200 francs, from a special fund set aside for the acquisition of works of art destined for the national museums. This was topped up with the sum of 15,000 francs granted by the Minister of Education.[25] Other than Jane, who was naturally part of the mission, Marcel Dieulafoy appointed two collaborators: Charles Babin, a civil engineer, and Frédéric Houssay, a naturalist. In her *Journal*, Jane told the tale of this perilous adventure. It was she who reported on the unfolding research, and a large number of these passages were reused in a more academic form by Dieulafoy.

Obtaining the authorisation necessary at the Persian end was not easy. Having been refused once by Nasir ed-Din Shah, René de Balloy, French Minister in Tehran, managed to convince the reticent shah who had at first refused because 'Muslim rites prohibit the excavation or opening of graves'. Agreement was finally given 'on condition that the mission will not touch, under any circumstance, the sacred tomb of Daniel […] Unless the tomb in question is in need of repairs, when the French government will undertake these at its own expense.'

Pressed for time, the mission boarded the *Tonkin*, a military transport which took them to Aden; the firman granted by the sovereign was picked up at Bushir, and the excavators arrived at Susa on 26 January 1885. They pitched their tents at the south-western corner of the Apadana, a long way from Daniel's tomb so as not to upset Muslim sensibility. 'Having reached this land of Susa, camped on the ruins of the palaces of the Great Kings, is that not already a victory!'[26]

At the end of the first season, the results were encouraging, even though the difficulties had increased – excessive heat followed by heavy rains which flooded the trenches and cut the mission off from the rest of the country, difficulty recruiting workers, and the fanaticism of the devotees of Daniel.

For Dieulafoy, the city of Susa once extended on both banks of a large river, now called the Kerkha, with the important part developing on the left bank. A relief map showing the main contours of the terrain, made by Charles Babin, led him to identify – like Loftus before him – three large mounds covering an area of about 100 hectares: in the north-west, 'Tumulus no. 1' or Apadana; in the south, the 'Citadel' (later called the Acropolis) whose summit still rose 36 m above the valley floor; in the south-west 'Tumulus no. 2' or 'Elamite tumulus' (the future Ville Royale) where he thought could be found the main palace and its

38
Dieulafoy trenches
J. DIEULAFOY, 1888

outbuildings.[27] As can be seen on the plan published by Jane, later taken up by Dieulafoy,[28] on which the excavations are marked, not only 'Tumulus no. 1' was explored. Dieulafoy opened up various trenches at several points on the 'Citadel' and on 'Tumulus no. 2'. It is, however, where Loftus had worked with success that he concentrated his efforts; from the word go the finds were remarkable.

Dieulafoy's excavations were based on two unquestioned assumptions; following his first journey to Persia, on the strength of what he saw at Pasargadae and at Persepolis and based on the position of the trilingual inscriptions engraved on the column bases uncovered by Loftus, he argued that the grand entrance of the throne room must look towards the 'Citadel'. Situated towards the south, it would be preceded by a pylon 'analogous with the *Viçadayou* [northern] portico of Persepolis'. Elsewhere, from the inscriptions discovered by Loftus he realised that the remains brought to light were those of a fourth century building, under which there must be the remains of buildings by Darius.

Thus, when on 27 February 1885 Dieulafoy began his excavation he decided to look: 'a long way from the English excavations for the doors and stairways, certain to find them if some vestiges of the palace had survived the centuries and the revolutions.' These considerations led him to cut a thin exploratory trench, positioned in relation to the Apadana, where the Persepolitan portico would be. This first excavation was 4 m wide by 60 m long (trench C).[29] Having to abandon this trench for a while due to the heavy rains and in order to gather more information on 'the position of the doors – if they are not ruined – on their shape and decoration', he opened another trench (B) in the same sector, perpendicular to the southern façade of the Apadana starting from the last row of columns in the Central Hall. At a depth of 2.3 m, he discovered 'large bricks placed on a thick bed of stones, a sort of foundation layer which seemed to extend uniformly under the Palace and its outbuildings'.[30] In fact, the result was not the one he had banked on; nothing revealed the presence of a door.

On 21 March 1885, in trench C, where Dieulafoy had been looking for the pylons, decorated glazed bricks appeared in large quantities: 'here are white palm fronds tied by a yellow ribbon, blue and green dentils, then embossed enamelling, enhanced with colours enlivened by a matt turquoise background. [...] The whole makes up a complete frieze, 72 cm high, but whose length we can only imagine, as the fault-line which extends parallel or perpendicular to the façade of the Palace cuts sideways into the trench. Have we found the long-sought doors?' When collapsing, the frieze would have forced down the paving slabs found to the south of the Apadana by more than 50 cm. An examination of the rubble allowed Dieulafoy to discover 'a very precious fragment. [...] In profile, on the same matt turquoise background, a white snout, yellow nostrils, the ferocious whiskers of a fantastic beast. A round eye, clearly outlined, surmounts the jaw muscles, beautifully observed, represented in white enamel. The colours are vivid and bold.'[31]

Thanks to a reinforcement of 50 or so men, on 4 April 1885 Jane Dieulafoy took on the rubble covering the frieze which 'extends parallel to the façade of the palace, 60 m in front of the southern portico'. To uncover it, a new trench was required, cutting across the first; Jane extended it for 36 m.[32] The decorated bricks lay face-down on the paving slabs underneath a hard layer of earth – 3 to 3.5 m thick – from a collapsed wall. The clearing of the decorated bricks, broken into many fragments, was a delicate task. Each fragment was excavated with the tip of a knife, drawn on squared paper then placed in a basket with a reference number. This way, a lion 1.75 m high and 3.5 m long was reconstructed along with the friezes that framed it. Fragments of two other animals showed that it was part of a procession estimated by Dieulafoy as nine strong.[33] 'Based on the enamelling and

39
Fragments of frieze
M. DIEULAFOY, 1893: pl. XIII, 5

40
**Lion and Griffin reconstructed
by M. Dieulafoy**
M. DIEULAFOY, 1893: pl. III and XI

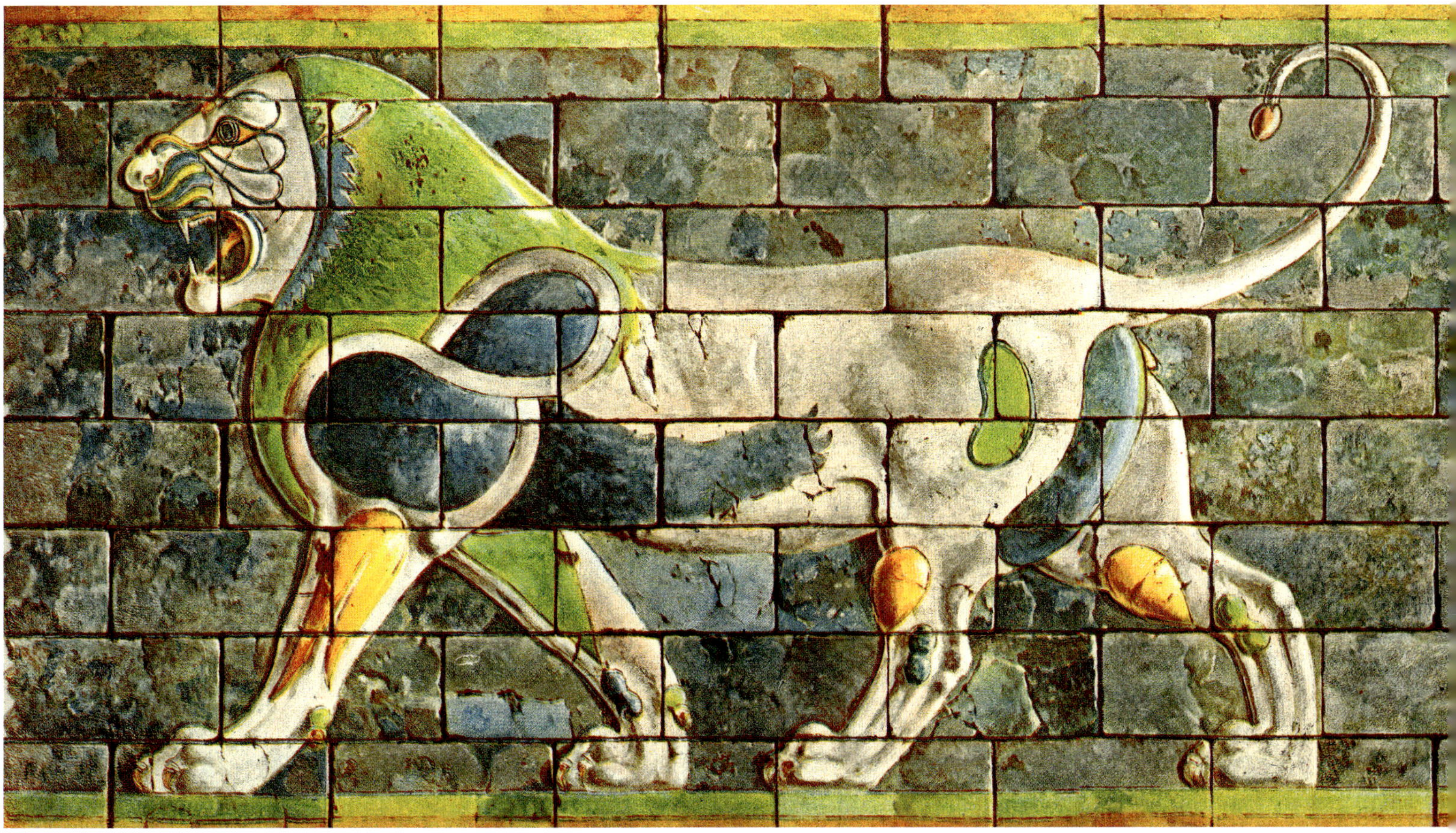

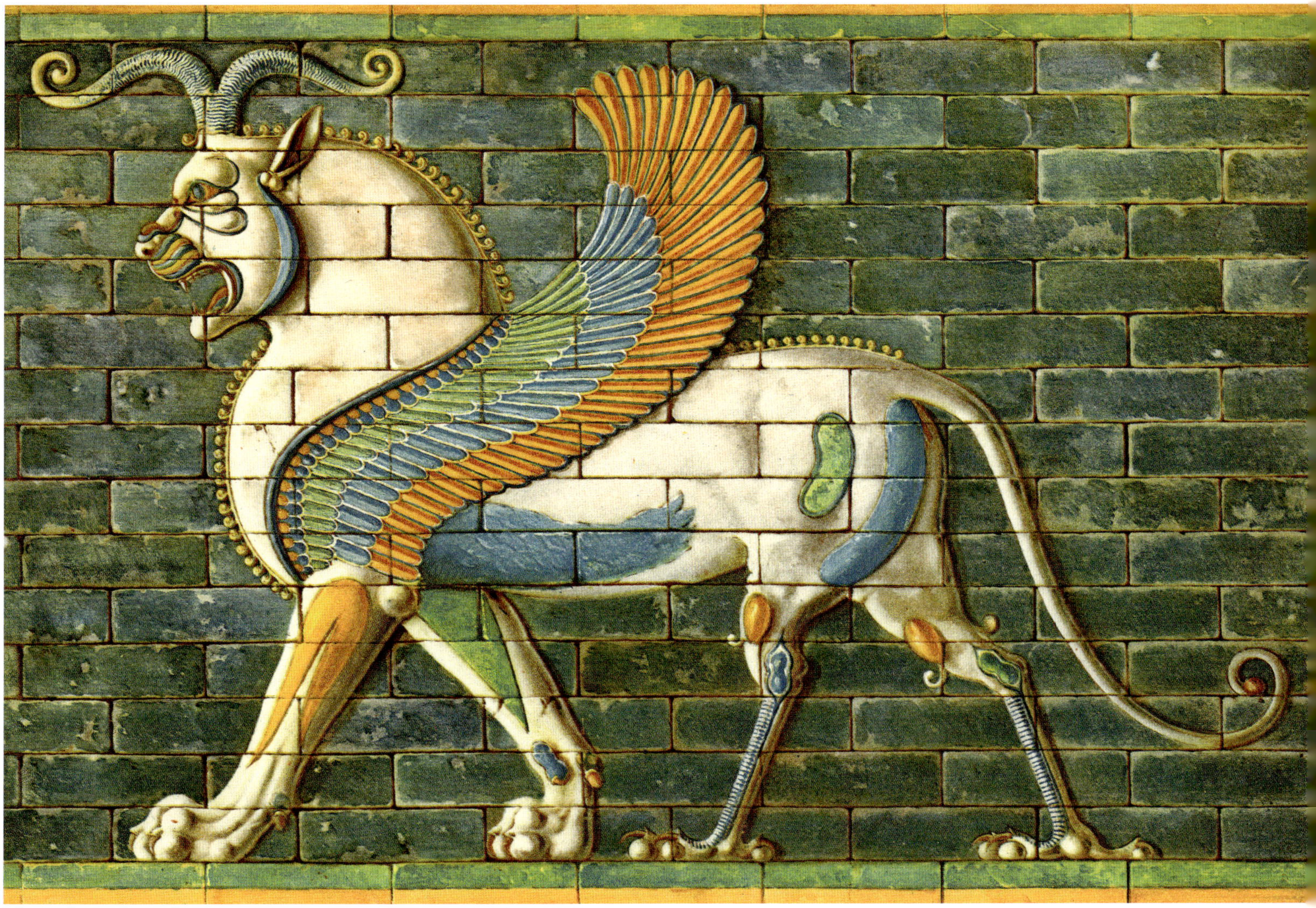

41

Susa Acropolis

Restoration of the outline of the curtain wall and fortifications by Marcel Dieulafoy

M. DIEULAFOY, 1893: plan II

the coloration of the upper and lateral faces, [Jane Dieulafoy judged that] the merlons stood out against the sky. The frieze crowned an isolated wall, a high wall, because the paving slabs at palace floor level were broken and deeply indented by the fall of the bricks. The earth, so hard and compact above the rubble, came from the mud brick wall which supported the frieze. The baked bricks laid in a double row with the enamelled blocks had been taken from older palaces. Based on these facts and the nature of the merlons which he had found, Dieulafoy concluded that he had discovered the outside door of the throne room…'[34]

Finally, one evening, a fortuitous event occurred. Whilst closing down the site, Jane slipped on a hard surface which, on investigation, turned out to be glazed bricks 'of a new colour and design'. They were laid in courses along a parapet repaired by the Sassanians. Dieulafoy was convinced that he was uncovering a ramp whose shapes and ornamentations 'reminded him of the handrests at the palaces of Persepolis'. Scattered around were parts of figures – shoes, a hand with a bracelet and holding a staff, drapery – as well as white cuneiform inscriptions on a green background.[35]

When Marcel Dieulafoy ended his first excavation on 13 May 1885, the results from the Apadana seemed to confirm his hypothesis; to the south of the Apadana, would be the pylons which he thought he had brought to light, to the west one of the parts, decorated by a frieze of lions; further to the south, on the slope of

42
Glazed bricks with inscriptions of 'archers'
M. DIEULAFOY, 1893: pl. XII

43
**Reconstructed elevation
of a rectilinear Susian façade**
M. DIEULAFOY, 1893: 205, fig. 102

the tell would have been the monumental staircase. Marcel and Jane Dieulafoy returned to France with 55 cases (the lion frieze and the staircase banister), cases which were held up for a while, much to the explorers' despair, by Turkish customs at the port of Basrah.

The second campaign (1885 to 1886)

Work began anew on 15 December 1885. They had to be quick. Nasir ed-Din Shah had heard too much about the wonders brought to light and the misgivings of a population whose worries he was unable to appease. It was with reluctance that he had consented to a second and final excavation; in addition the mission would have to have broken camp by the time of the annual pilgrimage to Daniel's mausoleum. In this hurried state of affairs and through a lack of funds, Marcel Dieulafoy decided to concentrate his efforts on the 'Achaemenid tumulus' (the Apadana), calculating that the embankment was less than 2 m thick. With some bitterness Jane Dieulafoy explained: 'As it was managed until now, the direction given to the excavations was perfect. It would not cross my husband's mind to look for small monuments, as does an antiquities dealer. Only the great lines of architecture, constructive art, the supreme manifestation of a people's economic and intellectual development, seemed to him worthy of his efforts. The reconstruction of the palace, the house, the study of the fortification are far more important than badly dated records of doubtful origin. Besides, Marcel thought that the building having been discovered, the objects for display cases would also roll in. Had not the discovery of the pylons been the prelude to the unearthing of the lions?'

With barely four months, it was not a question of a broad-reaching study; the works on the 'Citadel' and 'tumulus no. 2' were abandoned; as to the fortification, the idea of uncovering it completely was rejected. The new programme was based around four points: (1) reconstruct the outer wall and the defensive works; (2) continue clearing the Apadana; (3) look for the site of the great staircase of which the ramp had been partially discovered in a repaired Sassanian wall; (4) follow up the work in the zone with the lion frieze and find the foundations of the pylons.[36]

On 20 December 1885, the dig restarted in the lion trench where bricks reappeared in a position which made their extraction difficult. Whilst pieces of the frieze discovered during the preceding excavation had fallen onto the paving slabs in a certain order, here it was *an indescribable mess*. The reason given was that 'the extremity of the pylon had twisted before falling in a disorderly heap'. The template established by the lion that had already been uncovered allowed each piece to be fitted into place although the situation was complicated by variations in colour between different animals, as well as animals walking in the opposite direction to the first.[37]

According to Dieulafoy, the rectangular courtyard to the south of the Apadana, between the throne room and the pylons, must have been bounded to the east and to the west by two buildings. The western one would have given on to terraces and gardens, the other would have given access to 'tumulus no. 2' – the Ville Royale – where the sovereign's palace must have been.

On 21 December, they began to dig the hypothetical eastern wing in an extension of trenches c where there was raised ground. On 31 December, having dug up a funerary urn, Dieulafoy believed he was close to the level of the Apadana. Then they discovered fragments of glazed brick of an exceptional quality. Soon 'huge walls covered in magnificent enamelled bricks' appeared. The first elements of the frieze of the archers were discovered. Others were 'heaped up in irregular piles on a tiled floor 4 m below the floor of Artaxerxes' Apadana.'[38]

44
The 'immortals'
On the left 'the Susa contingent',
on the right 'the Persian contingent'
M. DIEULAFOY, 1893: pls VI and VII

Susa in Paris
1888

Nicole Chevalier

On 6 June 1888, the President of the Republic inaugurated two rooms in the Louvre dedicated to the discoveries made at Susa; exhibited amongst others were the capital composed of the front end of two bulls, the lion frieze, the parade of the 'archers' and various antiquities: cylinder seals, glazed vases, weapons, lamps, marble cups, bronze and agate statues, and so on. A third room, opened in 1891, presented a clever reconstruction of the great Hypostyle Hall, the Apadana. Displayed in this way the discoveries created a resounding impression, the hundreds of glazed bricks were a surprise and a revelation for the public and artists alike, if not for archaeologists. This ancient decoration in glazed bricks enthused fans of polychrome architecture. Émile Müller, industrialist, engineer and architect, in collaboration with the sculptor Charles-Louis Lesueur, immediately began reproducing the lion frieze and then the archers in his porcelain factory 'in an indestructible material', stoneware, so as to exhibit them at the universal exhibition of 1889.

At the same time, Marcel Dieulafoy worked on a large volume, *L'Acropole de Suse*, which appeared in 1893. In it he looked at the questions which he had asked himself during the mission: ethnographic (on the peoples of the country), military (on fortifications in the ancient Orient) artistic (on the polychrome decoration used by the Assyrians and Babylonians), and on their architecture, the study and restoration of the palace at Susa. He paid a lot of attention to the reconstruction of the frieze of the archers, which he reconstructed initially in the Louvre; unfortunately, very quickly the glaze started to crumble in the Parisian climate. The bricks had to be restored using blubber from whales ('blanc de baleine') and baking them at 100°C. The lion frieze was a precious guide for placing the figures between decorative bands. As with the lions, the archers march towards each other,

45
Reconstruction of the Apadana
M. DIEULAFOY, 1893: pl. XV

46
Large staircase banister
M. DIEULAFOY, 1893: pl. VIII

47
M. Pillet, *Sphinx in enamelled bricks from the palace*
1911–12, watercolour on paper, 68 x 57 cm
Etienne Pillet Collection. © Musée du Louvre/Christian Larrieu

48
'The new Dieulafoy rooms at the Louvre'
Monde Illustré, 30 June 1888, p. 4

separated by a trilingual cuneiform inscription. This is attested on several bricks where the cuneiform characters are adjacent to the archers' hands. Although fragmentary, the names of Darius and Otanes can be identified. The restoration of the bodies of the figures was achieved by taking account of the continuity of the drawing and the modelling. As to their height, by using the row of green, blue and white triangles of the vertical frame and after having worked out the implications of adding or subtracting several bricks from certain details of the figures, a height of 21 horizontal rows could be attributed to each 'archer'.

As to their original siting, Marcel Dieulafoy considered a number of ideas. He believed that the stepped merlons on a white background, which border the top of the frieze of the archers, proved that the frieze crowned the outside of the wall of the porticoes which was covered in a fawn-coloured stucco of which samples had been discovered mingled with pieces of the archers. Working from the fact that the archers wore clothes which corresponded with descriptions given by Classical historians, that they wore bracelets, earrings, and coronets, and, most importantly, that they held the spear upright, with a distinctive silver ball attached to the bottom end of the shaft, Dieulafoy identified in the frieze a contingent of the 10,000 immortals of the royal guard described by Herodotus (vii, 41). Such was the magnificent vision reconstructed by Marcel Dieulafoy for the Louvre and in his *Acropole de Suse*. However, without underestimating the richness of the finds, the initial hypotheses were far from being verified. The study of the architecture of the palace of Darius still remained to be undertaken, but ten years later, when Jacques de Morgan resumed the excavations at Susa, exploration of the Achaemenid period was no longer the order of the day.

In accordance with the decision of the Persian government, on 29 March 1886 work came to a halt; the discoveries were packed up and with a heavy heart taken to the Shatt al-Arab. On 26 May the expedition, together with its finds (327 cases containing fragments of double-headed bull capitals, the archers and the lions discovered during the last excavation) were loaded onto the cruiser *Le Sané*, sent to meet them by the French Navy. There remained the task of making these artefacts known to scholars and the general public.

JACQUES DE MORGAN (1897–1912)

While the magnificent discoveries made by Jane and Marcel Dieulafoy were welcomed in France, the future of excavations at Susa was uncertain. The shah, hostile to continued work, which was breeding disquiet among the population, was particularly antagonised by the attitude of two explorers who had not conformed to the terms of the firman. In September 1891 when, at the end of a vast exploration of Persia, Jacques de Morgan (1857–1924), entered Susiana, the French legation in Tehran had been fighting to keep the site in French hands for five years. It was only in 1895 that the misgivings of Nasir ed-Din Shah were finally overcome. In exchange for 50,000 francs, he conceded all excavation rights in the country to France. In 1900, his successor Muzaffar ed-Din Shah signed a retrospective treaty granting France all the finds made in Susiana; financial compensation was only requested for the gold and silver objects. It was against this background that, in 1897, the Minister of Education created the Délégation scientifique française en Perse (DSFP; French scientific delegation in Persia) which Jacques de Morgan would run for the next 15 years (1897–1912).

A prehistorian by vocation, Jacques de Morgan, a former mining engineer, did not think it useful to pursue his predecessor's work,[39] with the exception of a few trenches in the Apadana sector during the first excavation.[40] It was only in 1908 that he would resume the investigations on the Apadana tell, mainly to the south of the hall of columns.

GUSTAVE JÉQUIER'S TRENCHES

Following the excavations undertaken by Dieulafoy certain points were open to discussion. (1) There were doubts about the existence of walls dividing and enclosing the central hall of the Apadana;[41] (2) although the northern portico was not contested, a change in ground level to the north of the hall of columns could call

49
Jacques de Morgan (1857–1924)
General Director of Excavations in Persia
© Musée du Louvre, photographic archives
of the Oriental Antiquities Department

50
Jacques de Morgan, *The Susa Château*
oil on canvas, 33 x 53.5 cm
Andrée Jaunay collection

51
Works carried out in 1898 by Gustave Jéquier
The trenches are shown on the plan
previously drawn by Babin
JEQUIER, 1900: fig. 80

into question its existence; (3) the presence of glazed brick decoration; (4) traces of Darius' first building under the hall of columns attributed to Artaxerxes II.

Jéquier challenged Dieulafoy's theory about the existence of walls in the Hypostyle Hall; he advanced the hypothesis of a single row of columns in the northern portico. As to possible decoration for the throne room, the fragments of polychrome brick (all with geometric decoration), were too small in number to warrant the idea of monumental decoration. On the slope of the tell, in the axis of the Hypostyle Hall, he found no evidence allowing him to confirm the existence of the monumental staircase reconstructed by Dieulafoy. However, Jéquier's work enabled him to conclude that the column foundations were pits filled with gravel.

For a decade, investigations on the Apadana were not the order of the day. In 1908, however, Jacques de Morgan's attention was drawn to the southern flank of the Apadana by a sort of plaster faced with red ochre; he decided to resume excavations and charged Roland de Mecquenem with the task; Mecquenem was a colleague and mining engineer like himself and had been part of the delegation since 1903.[42]

ROLAND DE MECQUENEM AND THE DISCOVERY OF DARIUS' PALACE

Under a mass of thick clay (averaging 2.5 m), remnants of the walls of the palace and other buildings, Mecquenem, assisted by Paul Toscanne and Maurice Pézard, both attached to the Délégation, uncovered large areas of red ochre-faced plaster which corresponded to the flooring of halls and corridors, while the courtyards were covered in brick tiles. These different floors were interrupted by what remained of mud brick walls with foundations of one ot two rows of baked bricks: 'these remains resting on a vast layer of gravel and sand'.[43] During the first excavation of 1909, Mecquenem proceeded to clear the West Court (c1) and a section of the adjacent rooms. He noticed that the hard red ochre floors corresponded to huge rooms. Large grey flagstones[44] and numerous fragments of a stele (in grey limestone) were brought to light.[45] In 1910 and 1911 work concentrated on the 'Central Court' (c2) and especially the great hall to the West (A).[46] By the end of the season, thanks to the use of a Decauville railway (tilting skips on tracks), the clearing of the palace was well advanced and Mecquenem believed he had almost finished. At the end of the 1911–1912 excavation the passageways to the north of the courtyards and the eastern zone were cleared but other remains indicated an extension towards the east. Trenches were opened up in the eastern section (c2) to search for glazed bricks. It was then that they discovered 'under a large stone threshold slab of the Apadana' a large tablet inscribed in old Persian with what would come to be called the 'Foundation Charter of the Palace of Darius'.[47] By 30 March 1912, the final day of the last season of the French delegation, the courtyard had been identified as well as parts of the surrounding rooms. In three years an area of roughly 200 m by 100 m had been cleared.[48]

THE PLAN OF DARIUS' PALACE BY MAURICE PILLET

The 1912–1913 season was a time for important discoveries amongst which were three statue fragments – part of the bottom of a face, the hem of a robe and a foot,[49] some fragments of inscription and column bases, two stepped merlons, and so on. More importantly the architectural details of the palace were largely clarified thanks to the presence of Maurice Pillet, a qualified architect.

Mecquenem initially believed that the palace walls had been completely destroyed in antiquity. But when Maurice Pillet joined the expedition, before the beginning of the works he voiced some doubt about their non-existence: 'for several seasons, the mission was committed to the clearing of this building, without, however, worrying about its mud brick walls which had all been removed bit by bit. They must have been several metres high, but the excavators did not distinguish them from the surrounding earth and they destroyed them, stopping only at the tiled floor of the building'.

Mecquenem recognized that his interpretation was difficult to sustain, and that the wall foundations often had important gaps.[50] Pillet wrote bluntly: 'Mecquenem's findings were inexact and incomprehensible.'

52
Roland de Mecquenem (1877–1957)
Member of the French Delegation in Persia from 1903 until 1912, then director of the Susian mission from 1912 to 1946. From 1908, he assumed the direction of the site at Susa in Jacques de Morgan's absence and began the work of clearing the palace of Darius
© Musée du Louvre, photographic archives of the Oriental Antiquities Department

53
Clearing court C1
Maurice Pézard and the winged Griffin bricks
MECQUENEM, 1947: pt. III-1

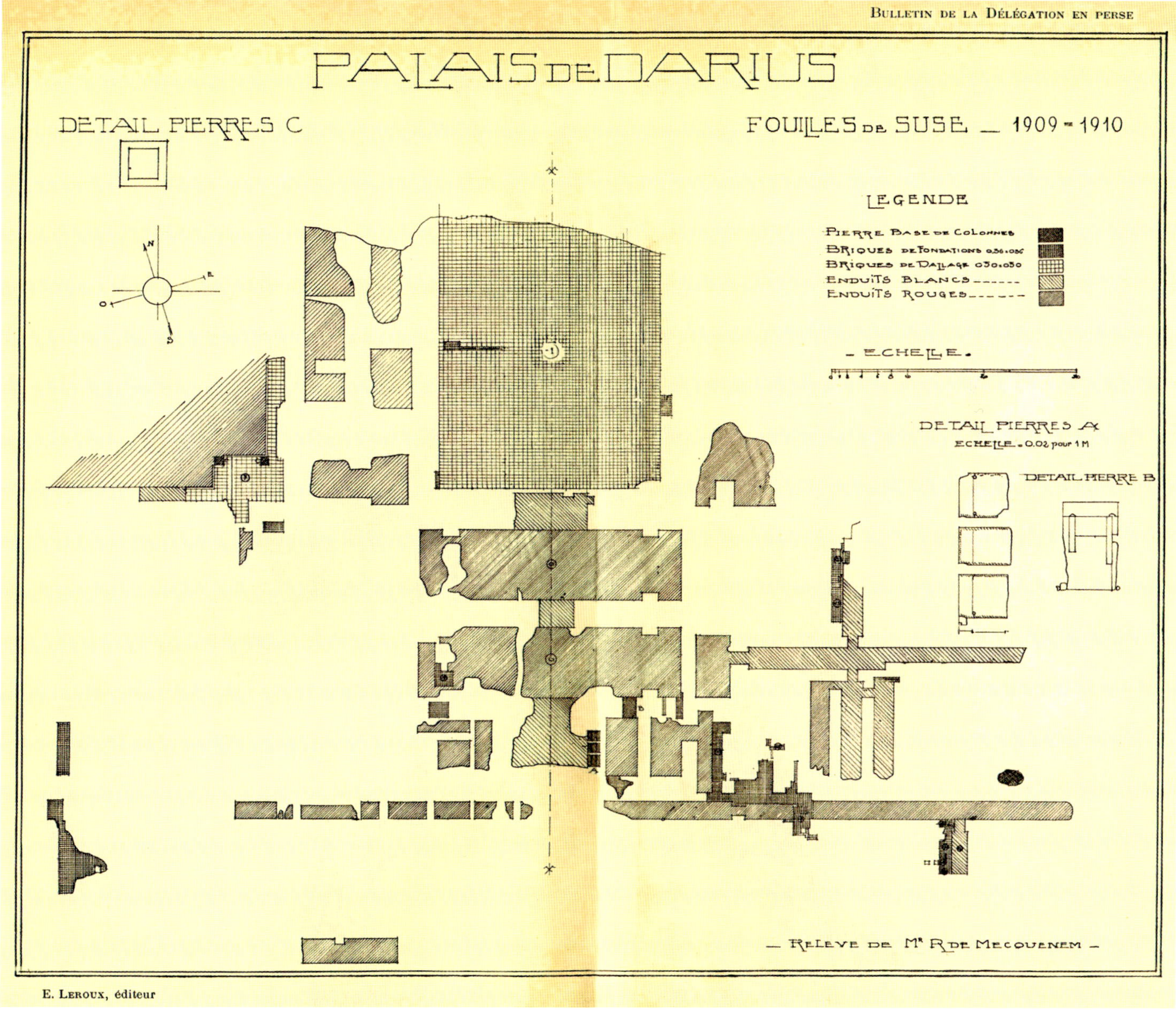

PALAIS DE DARIUS

DETAIL PIERRES C

FOUILLES DE SUSE — 1909–1910

LEGENDE

PIERRE BASE DE COLONNES
BRIQUES DE FONDATIONS 0.36.0.36
BRIQUES DE DALLAGE 0.30.0.30
ENDUITS BLANCS _____
ENDUITS ROUGES _____

— ECHELLE —

DETAIL PIERRES A
ECHELLE = 0.02 pour 1 M

DETAIL PIERRE B

— RELEVE DE Mr R DE MECQUENEM —

E. LEROUX, éditeur

54

**First plan of the palace drawn
by Roland de Mecquenem**
This appeared in 1910 in the
Bulletin de la Délégation en Perse,
fascicule I

55

**Floor of the private part of the residence
coated in red ochre**

Maurice Pillet

Nicole Chevalier

Maurice Pillet (1881–1964) studied architecture at the École des beaux-arts de Paris, from which he gained his degree in 1911. From then on he practised his profession at numerous sites in the Orient. After initial work experience at the Institut français d'archéologie orientale in Cairo, in December 1912 he left for Persia with Roland de Mecquenem who had recently been named head of the Susiana mission. During the winter of 1912–1913, Pillet completed the clearing of the Achaemenid palace and plotted the results. He also put together an important photographic record which allowed him, on his return to France, to attempt a reconstruction of the palace. He presented the initial findings to the Académie des inscriptions et belles-lettres during the winter of 1913. The following year, the Salon des artistes français gave him the opportunity to show the results of his research to the public in the form of a remarkable series of architectural watercolours, recognised officially by the presentation of a gold medal. However, because of a disagreement with Mecquenem, Pillet did not return to Susa, and could unfortunately not complete his work. Finally, the declaration of war the next year contributed to the shadow cast over the major contribution made by Maurice Pillet to the study of Darius' Palace.

56
Maurice Pillet (1881–1964)
Architect to the French mission at Susa, 1912–1913

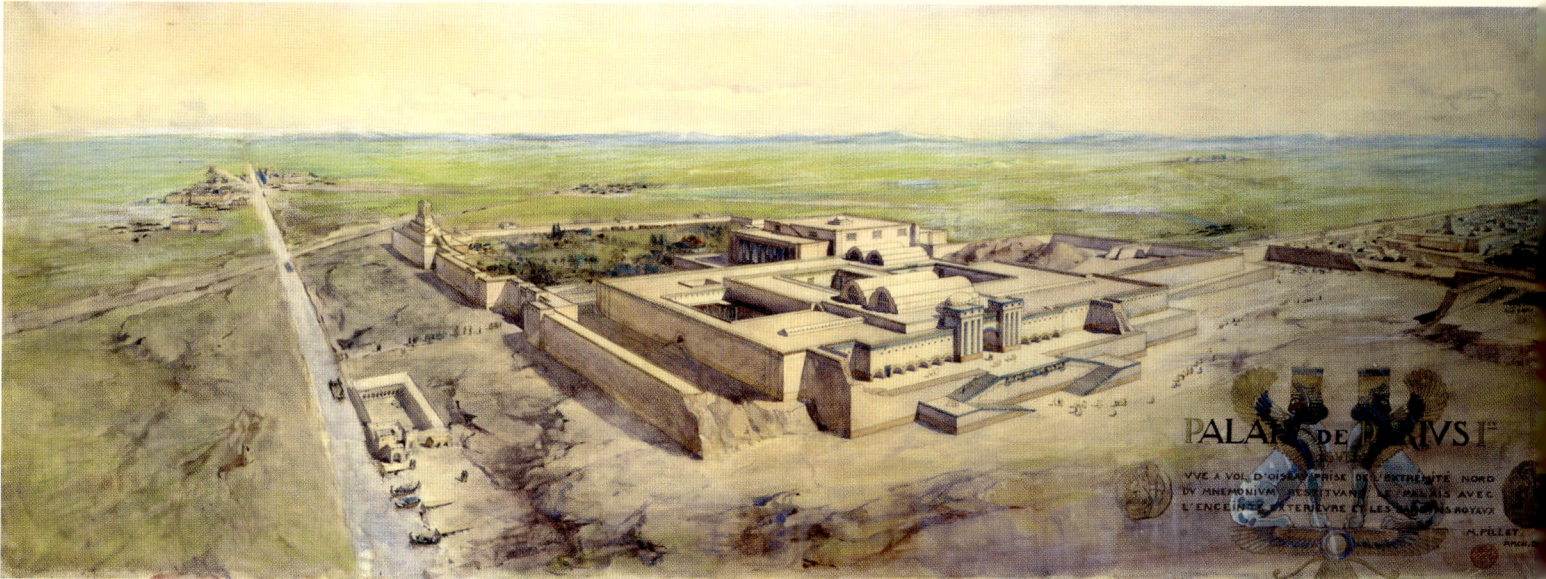

57
Maurice Pillet, *General view of the palace of Darius I* (top),
Grand south entrance (centre) and
Cut-away view along the north–south axis of the palace (bottom)
watercolours on paper
Étienne Pillet collection. © Musée du Louvre/Christian Larrieu

I realised that I had to draw up the plans brick by brick, on a fairly large scale, and so I adopted that of half a centimetre to one metre, as the palace on its own did not measure less than about 200 x 300 m.'[51] It became Pillet's task to supervise the clearing and to revise earlier plans, to continue the drafting and to excavate part of the eastern sector.[52] In Mecquenem's view, Pillet 'did some wonderful work which he exhibited at the 1914 salon and he presented a paper to the Academy at this time'.[53]

Whilst walking the site after heavy rains, Pillet was able to identify traces of the building's walls, which appeared as darker lines in the ground because the clay retained moisture. He drafted the plan of the royal residence, recording every brick. Then, once the plaster floor of the halls and the tiling had been recorded, he busied himself by looking for the doors that the previous excavations had not found: 'without doors we only had foundation plans without internal connections; I therefore focused on this investigation and after having carefully recorded all the breaks in the plaster, I was struck by the following fact: in the northern passageway, circular cracks were appearing in pairs opposite the Central Court; these holes were filled with earth and gravel, and they blended with the surrounding earth. After it had rained, however, they remained darker. Two workmen made quick work of emptying the holes. At first I found burnt wood mixed with bronze nails, then several sandstone bricks of a known type, with a notch with an arrow-head indentation, the symbol of the god Marduk; finally, stone resounded under the pick and a slab of grey marble appeared whose upper surface was perfectly horizontal. It had a square hollow cut in its centre: it was the socket for door pivots. The second hollow provided the same debris, the same notch, the same stone.'[54] Thanks to the stones having served as door sockets for bronze pivots, Pillet identified 35 doors, of which 26 were double doors to which numerous paved passages ran. The plans that he drew up show that the

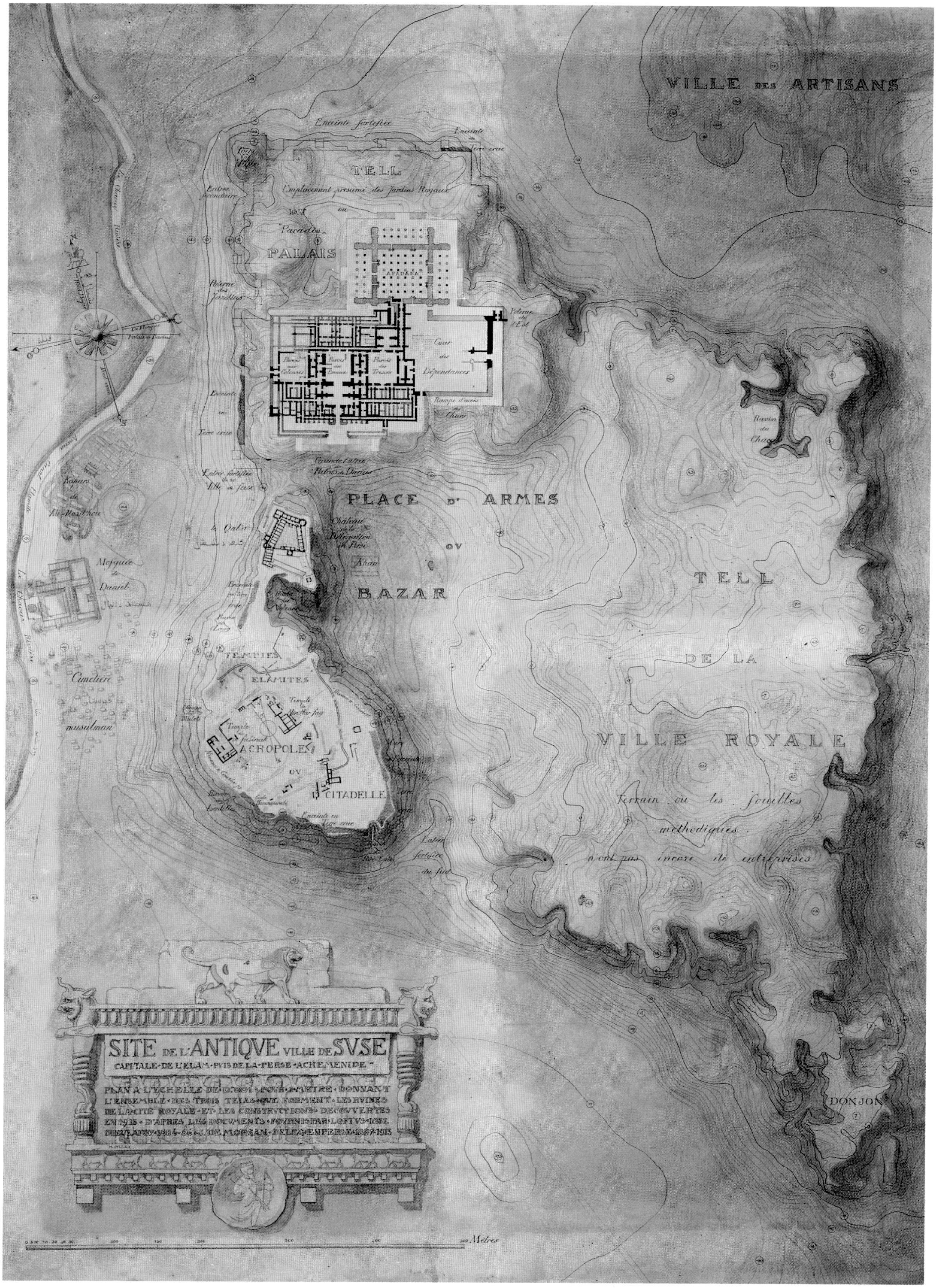

VILLE DES ARTISANS
TELL
Emplacement présumé des Jardins Royaux ou Paradis
PALAIS
APADANA
Cour des Dépendances
Grande Entrée du Palais de Darius
PLACE D'ARMES
OV
BAZAR
TELL
DE LA
VILLE ROYALE
Terrain où les fouilles méthodiques n'ont pas encore été entreprises
Ravin du Chaour
TEMPLES ELAMITES
ACROPOLE
OV
CITADELLE
Mosquée de Daniel
Cimetière musulman
DONJON
SITE DE L'ANTIQVE VILLE DE SVSE
CAPITALE DE L'ELAM PVIS DE LA PERSE ACHEMENIDE
PLAN A L'ECHELLE DE 0.001 POVR 1 METRE DONNANT L'ENSEMBLE DES TROIS TELLS QVI FORMENT LES RVINES DE LA CITE ROYALE ET LES CONSTRVCTIONS DECOVVERTES EN 1915 D'APRES LES DOCVMENTS FOVRNIS PAR LOFTVS 1852 DIEVLAFOY 1884-86 J. DE MORGAN DELEG EN PERSE 1897-1913
M. PILLET
Mètres

60
Palace of Darius I at Susa
draft plan of the excavations: scale 1:1000
photograph by Maurice Pillet of the plan
he drew in 1914
former Maurice Pillet collection.
© Musée du Louvre/Christian Larrieu

large Hypostyle Hall, the Apadana – unlike those at Pasargadae and Persepolis – was not an isolated building, open to the south as Dieulafoy had stated, but that on that side it abutted the royal residence. Thanks to the precision of his plans, Pillet was able to produce a general description which underlined its regular layout.[55]

Although this restoration of the palace was based on clearing a large area (110 rooms), there were still gaps, especially to the south and east of the building, and, inevitably, there were errors of interpretation. The main error concerned the southern sector of the residence where Pillet, following Dieulafoy's theory, placed the principal entrance to the palace (shifted slightly to the west) which would have been reached by a large double ramped staircase. Even so, on this precise point, Pillet recognised that 'the access ramps or staircases as well as the pylons or posts of the entrance have been washed away by the rains which flow in deep crevasses over the edge of the tell'.[56]

Despite this, the reconstruction proposed by Pillet was remarkable considering the state of the excavations and the little time at his disposal. The water-colour plan – and more so the on-site drawings which remained in his portfolio

61
Palace of Darius I at Susa scale 1:2000
from the photographic album
'Palace of Darius I at Susa, 1913'
former Maurice Pillet collection.
© Musée du Louvre/Christian Larrieu

awaiting publication – are a testimony to the importance of his contribution in our understanding of Darius' Palace.

AFTER THE FIRST WORLD WAR

For over six years French excavators could not return to Persia. It was only in the spring of 1920 that Mecquenem made his way to Susa for a brief inspection; in the meantime the site had been occupied by English troops who had ensured its protection.

In 1921, the clearing of the Apadana mound was actively pursued since the Acropolis remained inaccessible until barracks housing a company of sepoys had been removed. Until 1926 work was conducted with two principal aims: the complete clearing of the Achaemenid palace and, under the courtyards, reconnaissance of the Elamite levels.

An external event was the reason for resuming work in 1935–1936. Excavations at Persepolis having brought to light two precious foundation deposits of Darius in two corners of the north side of the Apadana, Iranian officials thought that

63
**The east entrance in 1967 after
a search for foundation deposits**

similar deposits might exist at Susa.[57] Mecquenem therefore went ahead with investigations under stones which flanked the eastern doorway of the palace and Apadana, and under several column bases, but in vain. He did notice, however, that a number of sculpted fragments from capitals were buried underneath the foundation level.

MECQUENEM'S CONTRIBUTION

Mecquenem wrote in 1922: 'Apart from an unexcavated reference mound left above the outer wall (of the Residence) in the north-east, the clearing is complete.'[58] He presented the palace of Susa as being made up of two parts: one part, buildings surrounding three courtyards (Western Court, Central Court, Eastern Court) linked by east–west and north–south passageways, and built on an artificial terrace of around 4 hectares; elsewhere, to the north, as an annex of around 1 hectare, there was a Hypostyle Hall with two porticoes. A north–south passageway permitted communication between these two complexes, level with the third court and the eastern portico of the Hall of Columns. According to

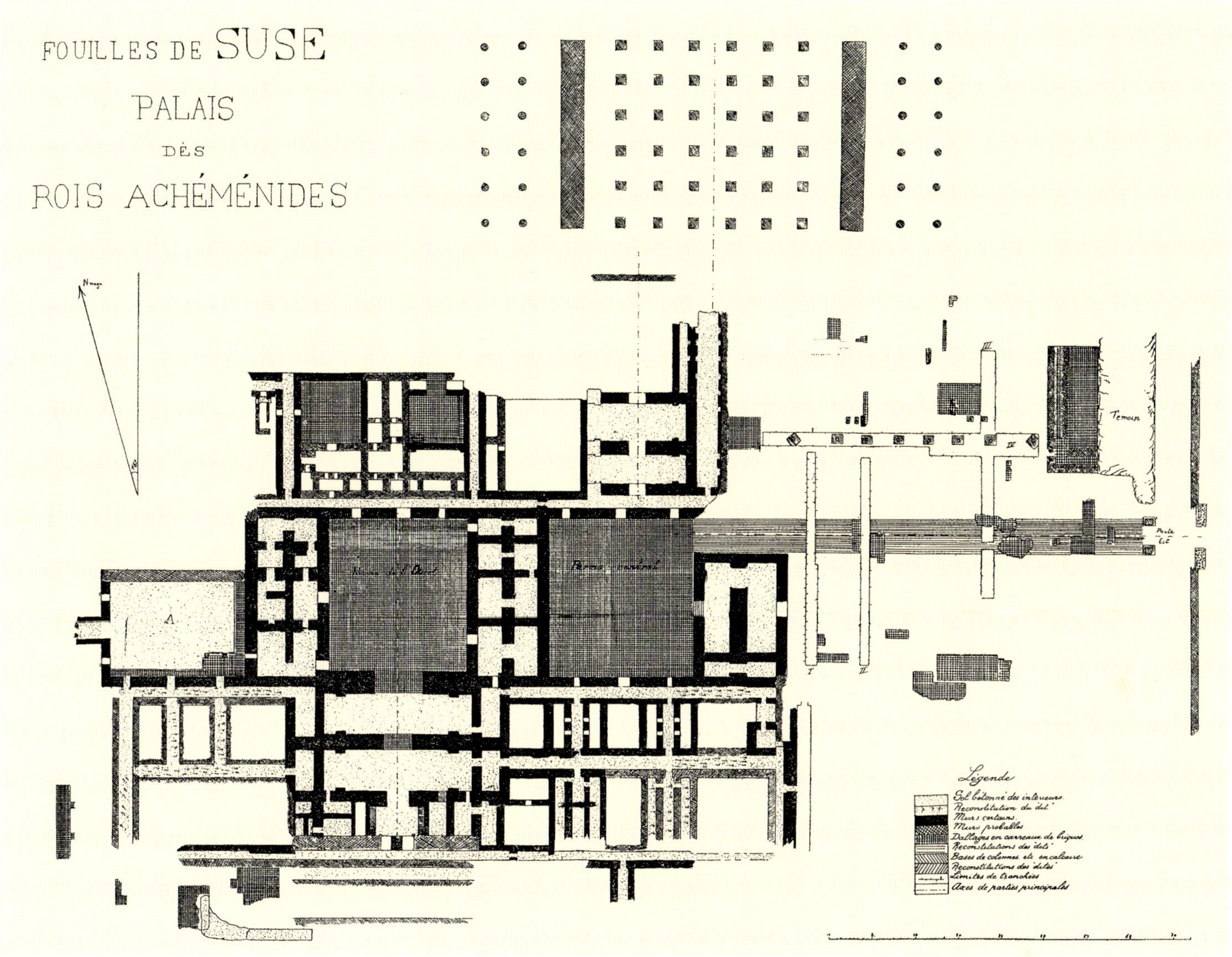

FOUILLES DE SUSE

PALAIS

DÈS

ROIS ACHÉMÉNIDES

64

Plan of the palace of the Achaemenid kings
MECQUENEM, 1922: pl. II

Mecquenem, three monumental doorways (two to the west and one to the east) gave access to the palace; it was impossible, however, to say anything about the southern side.[59] Mecquenem also identified several mounds in the northern part of the Apadana, the tallest of which, in the north-western corner, was identified as a bastion of the curtain wall; gardens were supposed to extend between this wall and the Hypostyle Hall. The ground level was 17 m above the water table.[60]

As regards the interior layout of the palace, Mecquenem insisted that the wide passageways – he identified five – went from the east, that is to say from the Ville Royale, to the west and that a large tiled avenue bordered by badly preserved outbuildings was accessible to chariots and led to the Central Court. The Royal Apartments, more enclosed, surrounded the West Court. Although nothing of the southern wall had been identified, the eastern side of the Palace was bordered by a long, straight mud-brick wall with baked-brick cladding, the foundations of which he said he had found.

As for the Hypostyle Hall, with the exception of an un-excavated reference section between the fifth and sixth rows of columns to the east, it was completely cleared. The clearing of the north of the central hall had not uncovered the traces of the northern portico that Loftus and Dieulafoy had reconstructed. Likewise, the walls between the great Hall of Columns and the porticoes were not found. Nonetheless, Mecquenem estimates that Pillet and Dieulafoy before him were right to reconstruct these walls, which he judged necessary to access the terrace in order to enjoy it and maintain it.[61] He put the staircases in the thickness of

PALAIS DES ROIS ACHÉMÉNIDES]

PLAN I. — ÉTAT DES FOUILLES

Légende des lettres

A	Grande salle de l'Ouest
B, G	Ensemble de Salles de réception
C_1, C_2, C_3	Cours dallées.
D, E	Pavillons.
F, H	Salles hypostyles.
L	Porte orientale.
M	Salle dallée.
N	Ligne de fondations (cote — 1 m.,80)
P_1, P_2, P_3	Appartements.
R_1 à R_5	Circulations bétonnées.
S	Corridor bétonné.
T	Témoin non fouillé.
m1	Massif en briques cuites.
m2	Massif en briques crues.
p1 à p'30	Portes à support de gonds.
aq	Aqueduc.

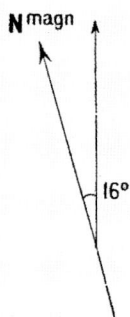

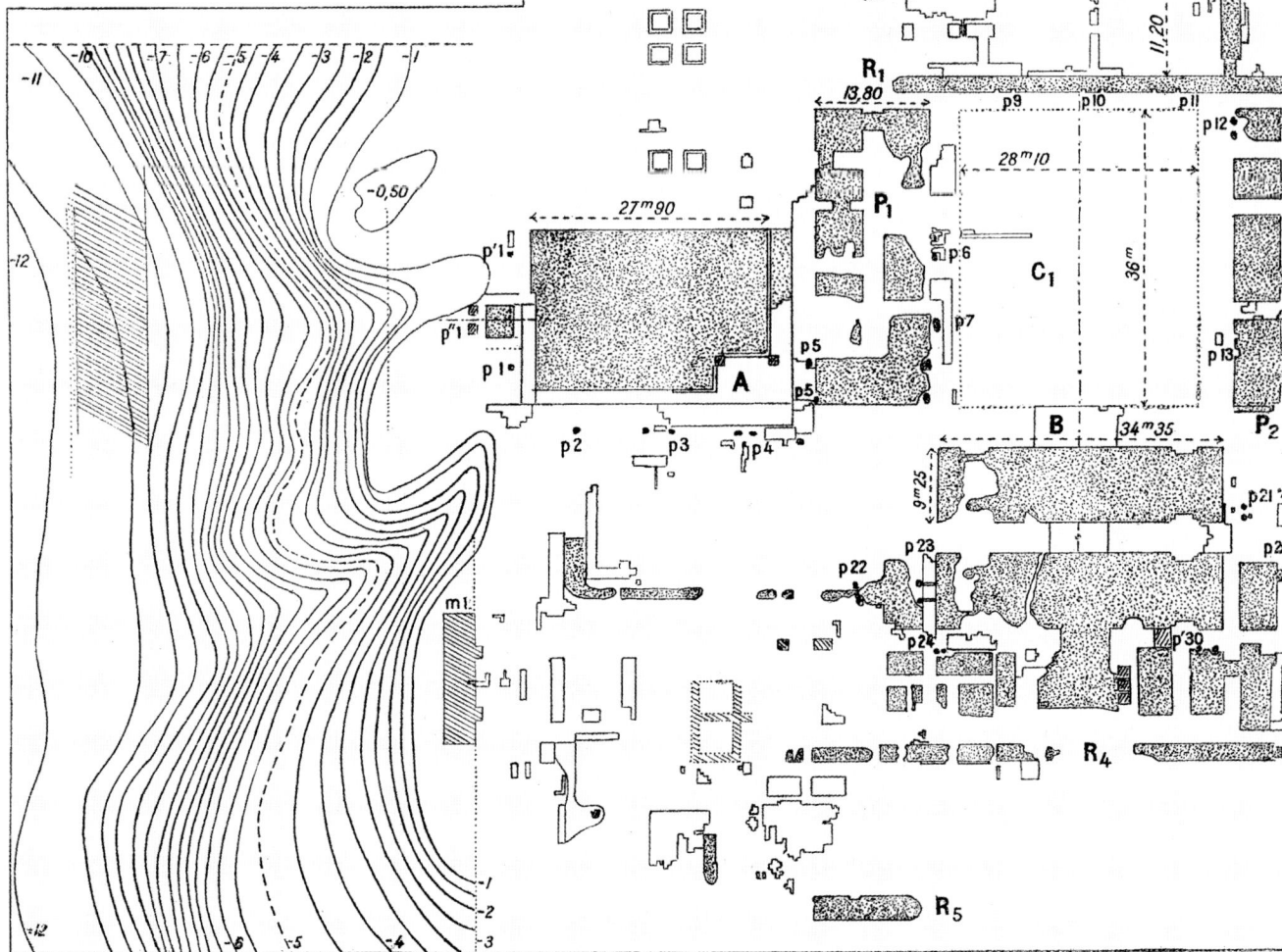

65

Palace of the Achaemenid kings

Plan 1, as excavated

MECQUENEM 1947: 8–9

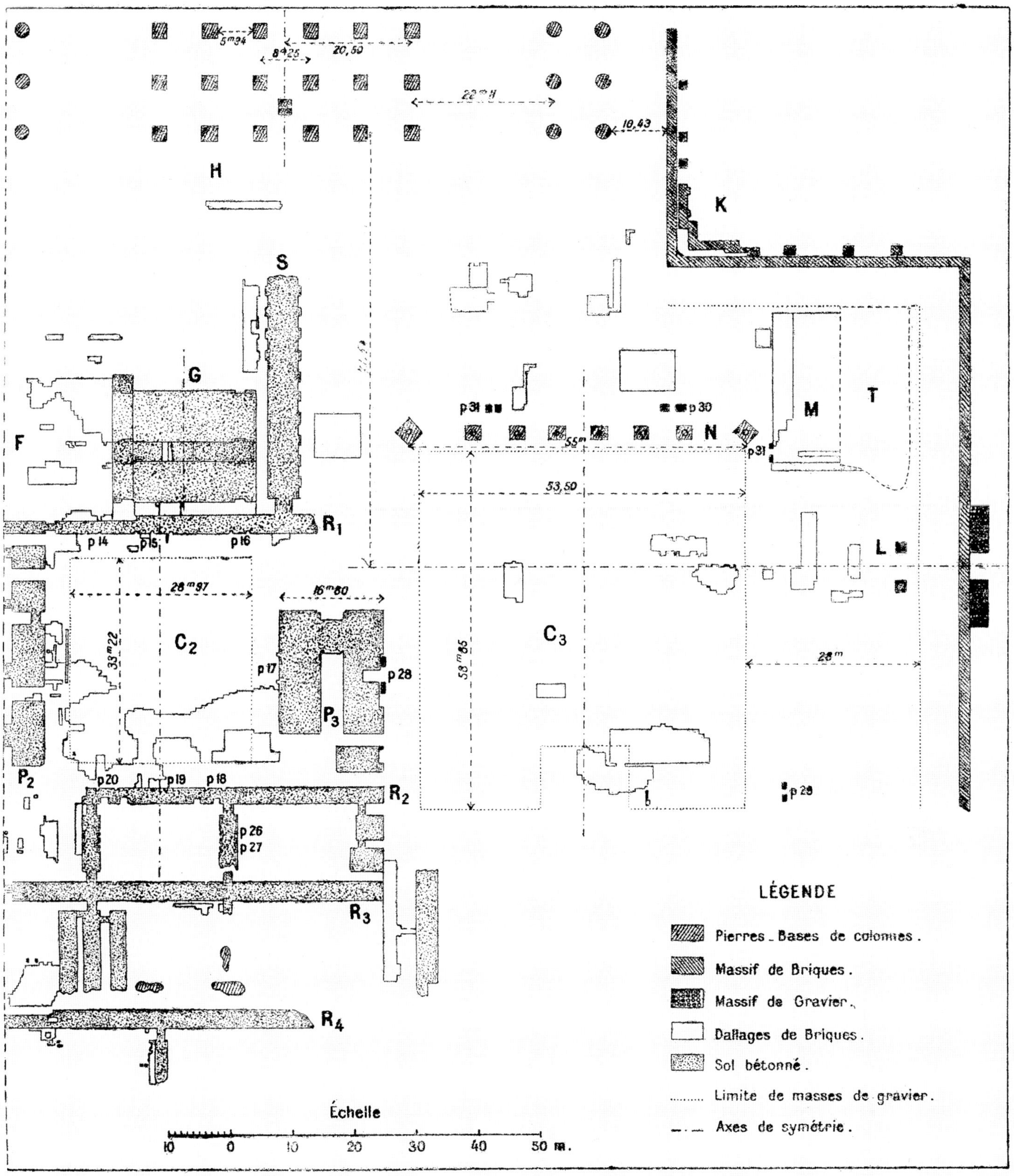

H
K
S
G
F
M
T
N
p31
p30
R1
p14
p15
p16
L
C2
C3
P3
P2
p17
p28
p20
p19
p18
R2
p26
p27
R3
R4
I
28m97
16m60
33m22
58m85
53,50
55m
28m
5m94
8m25
20,50
22m11
10,43
LÉGENDE
Pierres _ Bases de colonnes .
Massif de Briques .
Massif de Gravier .
Dallages de Briques .
Sol bétonné .
Limite de masses de gravier .
Axes de symétrie .
Échelle
10 0 10 20 30 40 50 m.

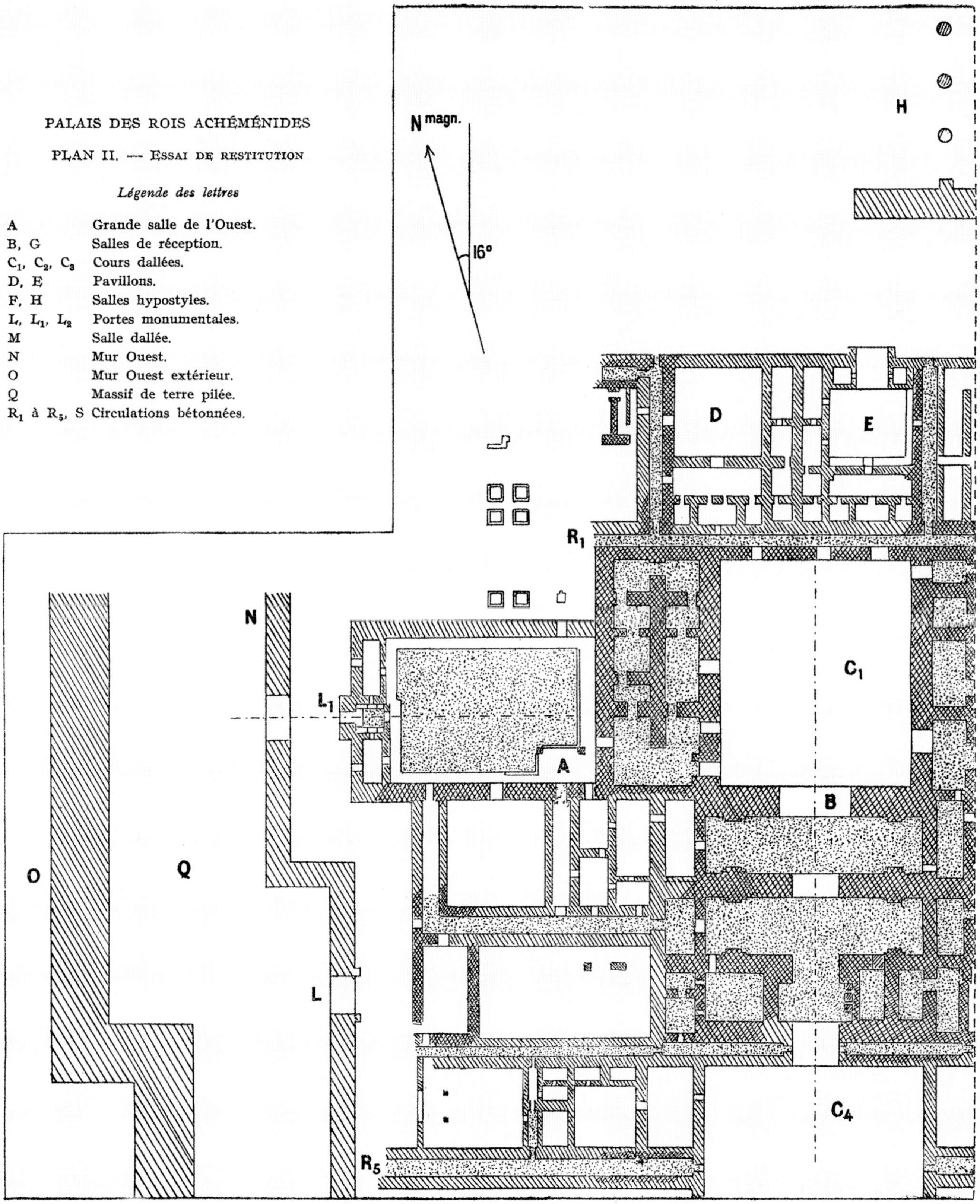

PALAIS DES ROIS ACHÉMÉNIDES

PLAN II. — ESSAI DE RESTITUTION

Légende des lettres

A   Grande salle de l'Ouest.
B, G   Salles de réception.
C_1, C_2, C_3 Cours dallées.
D, E   Pavillons.
F, H   Salles hypostyles.
L, L_1, L_2 Portes monumentales.
M   Salle dallée.
N   Mur Ouest.
O   Mur Ouest extérieur.
Q   Massif de terre pilée.
R_1 à R_5, S   Circulations bétonnées.

N magn.

16°

H

D   E

R_1

N

C_1

L_1

A

B

O   Q

L

C_4

R_5

66
Palace of the Achaemenid kings
Plan 2, attempt at reconstruction
Mecquenem 1947: 24–25

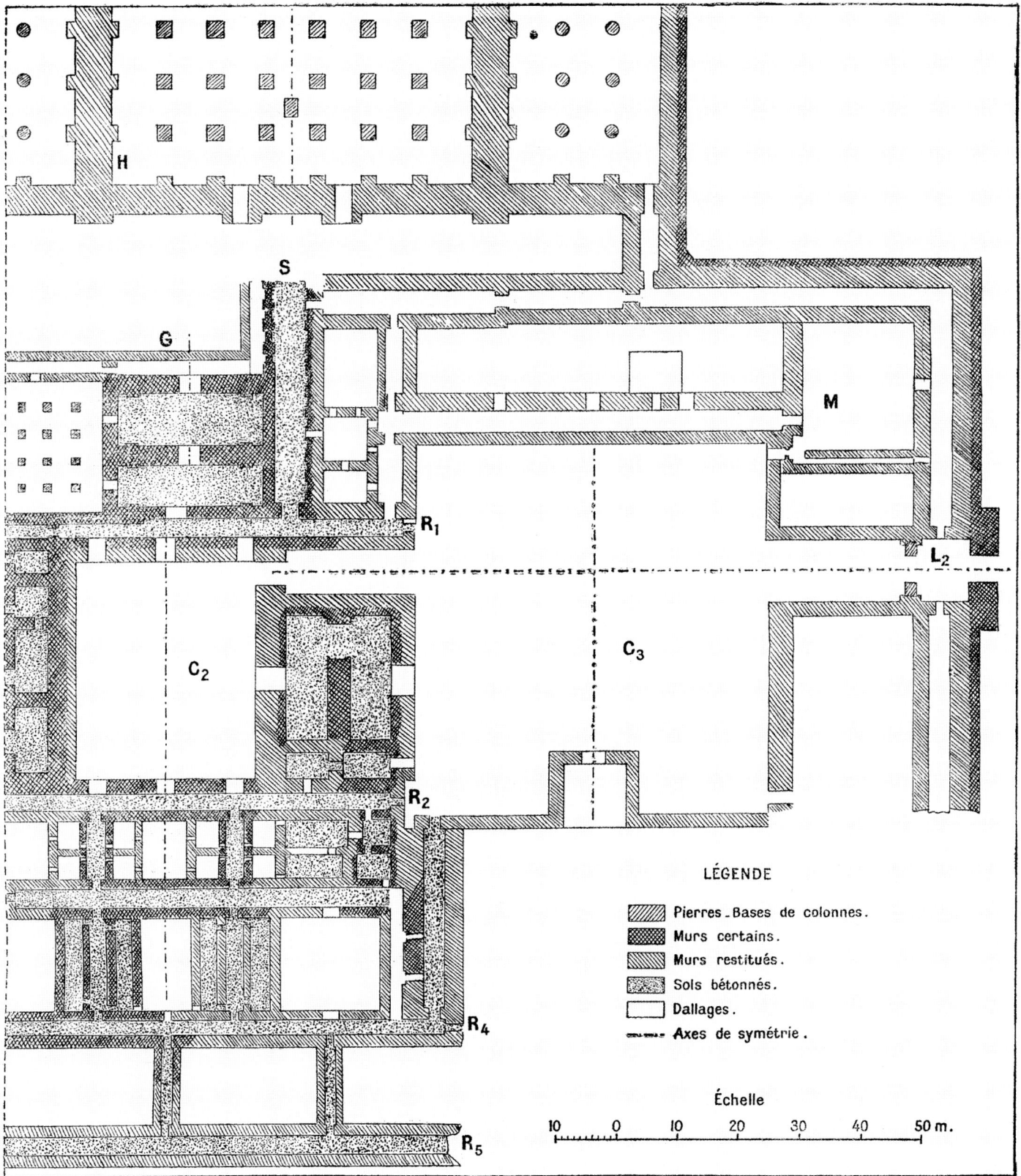

LÉGENDE

Pierres _ Bases de colonnes.
Murs certains.
Murs restitués.
Sols bétonnés.
Dallages.
Axes de symétrie.

Échelle

10   0   10   20   30   40   50 m.

- quai du Chaour · *Chaour. Riv.* · *Tépé Souleiman* · *Imam Zadé* · *Parvis aux colonnes* · *Apadana Parvis central* · *Parvis des trésors* · *Kapar de Hussein Khan*

Murs d'enceinte en briques crues · *déblais*

Vue générale du Tell du Palais Février 1913.

Nota l'horizon est borné par les montagnes du Pouch.e.Kouh

67
General view of the palace tell, February 1913
from the photographic album
'Palace of Darius I at Susa, 1913'
former Maurice Pillet collection.
© Musée du Louvre/Christian Larrieu

the walls which he estimated at 5.5 m. As regards the capitals, he remarked that very few of them had survived; other than those already found by Dieulafoy and Jéquier, he indicated having found a fifth one (a little less well preserved than the one in the Louvre) to the east of the eastern portico next to the highest piece of a fallen column. Noting that the passageways linked the palace and the Apadana, he judged that the palace, which he compared, like Pillet, to the one at Khorsabad (later he would also compare it to the one at Babylon), could have been occupied by all the Achaemenid kings from Darius down to Alexander's conquest and because of this would have been repaired and restored regularly.

At the end of the investigations carried out in the courtyards since 1921, Mecquenem noted that there had existed, under the Apadana tell, a natural hill chosen previously by the ancient inhabitants of Susa as a place for settlement and burial, the evidence going back from the end of the Elamite period to the beginnings of civilisation at Susa.[62] Darius would have had the hill razed to a level chosen for the base of his palace and surrounded the area he wanted to use as a foundation with mud-brick walls. The area would have been infilled with gravel, and on the resulting terrace the plans for the building would have been marked out. The excavated earth could then have been used to make the mud mortar for the walls and so become part of the construction, or was removed to create a wall for the gardens to the north. As for ornamentation, Mecquenem noted that the palace walls were in mud brick rendered on the inside and that the principal decoration came no doubt from glazed brick facing made up of panels with multiple decorations. However he insisted on the fact that during his excavations, no panel had been found *in situ*. It was on the basis of a percentage of bricks relating to a common subject found in the same place that he based his ideas on the location of the panels. He therefore advanced the hypothesis that the winged griffons decorated the West Court; the bricks of the winged human-headed lions found in the north-eastern corner of the Central Court could have decorated the walls of the passageway between the Central and East Courts. The lion frieze, found by Dieulafoy and of which Mecquenem found remnants, would no doubt have been on the north wall of the East Court.[63] As for the winged bulls in glazed brick of which rare examples were found in the East Court (c3), Mecquenem did not suggest a location. This leaves the archers of which Dieulafoy had been the first to discover elements near the eastern gate; Mecquenem thought that they could have graced the surface of the exterior or interior walls, or those of the outer courtyard or, finally, of the 'guard room'. Such was the level of knowledge of the Palace of Darius in 1922.[64]

It was not until 1947, when Mecquenem came to hand over the direction of the excavations to Roman Ghirshman, that his *Contribution à l'étude du palais de Suse*' was published as volume xxx of the *Mémoires*.[65] Mecquenem justified this long delay by the fact that he had published the plan of the Achaemenid palace for the first time in 1922, and that he published it again in 1938.[66] However, the restoration of the decorative panels, completed thanks to the care and attention of the Louvre, gave [him] the opportunity to add a complementary and corrective study.'[67] At the end of this work, Mecquenem concluded with a form of scientific testament: 'The Achaemenid palace of Susa is no longer that of Darius I, neither is it that which the Book of Esther presented as the setting for the intrigues of Mordechai, it is the palace that Alexander the Great captured; it is presented as a royal dwelling, perfectly ordered, with a logical floor plan which was remodelled by the Persian kings according to the needs of the day.

Research is still needed before we can make certain claims; yet it is possible to determine the outline of the platform; the gravel terrace can be explored with the expectation of interesting results, especially to the north and east of the palace; exploration to the east of the eastern gates could recover material which would complement our reliefs in stone and brick.'[68]

THE ROMAN GHIRSHMAN PERIOD (1946-1967)

The interruption to excavations due to the war corresponded with a change of director. At the end of 1945, Roman Ghirshman, who had never worked at Susa but had excavated several sites in Iran, was named director of the French mission in Iran by the Foreign Ministry's excavation commission.[69] On 4 December 1946 he began work.[70] There were few traces of the palace left by then; he wrote that 'it is no more than a chaos of holes and trenches', remnants of his predecessor's work. 'The Achaemenid palace could offer nothing more than limited additional information on its substructures, but the Apadana remained to be studied.'[71] His work on the Apadana mound aimed at finding answers to certain questions that were still pending. The exact plan of the Apadana remained to be drawn: the question of the northern colonnade had not been resolved. The Jéquier and Mecquenem plans 'were not only contrary to the findings at Persepolis but simply anti-architectural, lacking as it was the northern colonnade'.[72]

From 1947, the Hypostyle Hall (site 2) was cleared of its rubble and the excavations began in a sector untouched by previous excavations.[73] 'The hall contained six rows of six columns. To the east, to the west and the north, rose 3 rows of 12 columns each, leading on to depressions which were probably courtyards or gardens from which one climbed via three staircases, today lost. The walls, 5.25 m thick, which separated the hall from the three porticoes, were in mud brick placed on a double row of baked bricks with a continuous foundation of gravel 5 m thick. They were plastered on the inside with a thick coating of mud and straw, painted in green, white, blue, and red.'[74]

Between 1947 and 1950 (first to third excavations), a series of soundings were made at various points on the Apadana mound. During the second excavation, there were nine soundings: to the north-east and to the west of the Hypostyle Hall (sites 5–9); on the western slope of the tell, to find the Achaemenid ramparts (site 10) and to the east of the palace court (trench 15). The majority of the soundings confirmed the existence of Islamic remnants above those of the Achaemenid period. The large wall of baked bricks bonded using bitumen, already noted by

68
Roman and Tania Ghirshman
Ghirshman (1895-1979) was director
of excavations at Susa, 1946-1967
Ghirshman archives

69
Plan of the palace after the excavations, 1964–1965
GHIRSHMAN, 1968: fig. 4

Mecquenem, was cleared along the entire length of the north-western wall of the palace (site 17). Finally investigations took place on the western ramparts of the tell, near the western door to the palace (site 20).[75]

Between 1956 and 1960 Ghirshman undertook a series of excavations below the three porticoes, using aerial photographs produced by the Anglo Iranian Oil Company together with topographic data from the architect A. Julien.[76]

A test trench, to the north of the hall, brought to light what appeared to be 'a large Islamic ditch' which would have destroyed remains from the fourth to second millennia BC. Rubble from earlier excavations of the palace and of the columned hall, that had been piled up to the north of the Apadana, was removed in 1957, leading to the discovery of fragments of columns and capitals below, which confirmed the existence of the northern portico.[77] No staircase having been found, he concluded that the grand entrance to the Hypostyle Hall could only have existed on the side, facing the Palace. As to the large surfaces further down the slope from the hall, he finally identified them as gigantic terraces later than the Achaemenid period. The porticoes could not have been 'suspended' several metres high without being weakened, the same went for the walls of the Hypostyle Hall, and the later building works led to the collapse of the columns. These later building activities must have taken place after Alexander the Great and before the final centuries of the Parthian dynasty.

From 1963 to 1967 Ghirshman focused his attention on the area between the western peristyle of the Hypostyle Hall and the curtain wall, of which it touched the inner face (sites 27, 30, 32, 34).[78] In 1964, he excavated the outer face of the curtain wall, looking for a large gate which, according to him, could have led straight to the Apadana; none was found in this area. The external Achaemenid wall was, however, identified and studied, thus allowing important post-Achaemenid changes to the external defence works of Susa to be recognised.[79]

On 10 April 1967 Roman Ghirshman ended his 21st and final excavation at Susa, and handed over the baton to Jean Perrot, 70 years after the arrival of Jacques de Morgan.

70
Susa in 1947
At the top left is part of the Apadana tell
with the Residence; top right is the 'Château'.
The location of the Artaxerxes II Palace is
in the bend of the Shaur
Ghirshman archives

71
**Aerial view of the Acropolis
taken from the south**
In the foreground is the Acropolis;
in the top right the 'Château' of the mission;
on the left the Tomb of Daniel
photography by Hunting Aerosurvey Ltd.
Ghirshman archives

1. RAWLINSON, 1839.

2. Pascal Coste's albums include copies of some drawings by Baron de Bode, notably of the Mosque of Daniel that the latter had reproduced in his account of his travels; BODE, 1845: 334–335. Coste also recopied an Achaemenid column base and an animal relief which was then in the mosque. The relief had already been published by KER PORTER, 1821–2, vol. 2: 417.

3. BORÉ, 1842: 334–335.

4. A complete report has been published by CURTIS, 1993: 1–55 and 1997: 36–45. For a comprehensive survey of the excavations at Susa from the time of Loftus to the end of the French excavations led by Jean Perrot, see CHEVALIER, 1997.

5. LOFTUS, 1857: plan facing p. 340. It also shows a series of mounds with uncertain contours that correspond to the tell later known as the 'tell of the Artisans'. The position of the trenches is indicated, but only those identified by a letter of the alphabet produced results.

6. CURTIS, 1997b: 37.

7. LOFTUS, 1857: 366 and CURTIS, 1993: 7, fig. 2.

8. LOFTUS, 1857: 374–375.

9. Churchill drew some of the column bases and capitals. When he was preparing his volume on Persia, Georges Perrot consulted these drawings in the British Museum in the portfolios of what was then the Department of Oriental Antiquities – *Second supplementary volume of drawings from objects found at Susa*, drawn by A. Churchill, W.K. Loftus and Lieutenant Jackson. At the time he felt that despite the merits of certain of them, the drawings had lost their interest since the journey of M. Dieulafoy. PERROT and CHIPIEZ, 1890: p. 442. cf. the publication of them by CURTIS, 1993: 1–55.

10. LOFTUS, 1857: 398; CURTIS, 1993: pl. 20a–d, and 1997b: 40.

11. *Lithographic Facsimilies of Inscriptions in the Cuneiform Character from the Ruins of Susa*, London, 1859: pl. 1–5.

12. On the site of what subsequently came to be known as the 'Donjon'. BOUCHARLAT, ch. xii; CURTIS, 1993, 1997b: 41.

13. LOFTUS, 1897: fig. 25–31.

14. The publication of archival records has finally given him credit for his work. CURTIS, 1993: 1–55.

15. Georges Perrot and the architect Charles Chipiez undertook a huge publication in several volumes on *L'Histoire de l'art dans l'Antiquité*. Volume v, published in 1890, deals with Persia. This is probably the fragment published by CURTIS, 1993: 33, no. 105, pl. 20b belonging to a piece with similar decoration discovered by Mecquenem in 1911. See HARPER *et al.*, 1992: no. 157.

16. PERROT and CHIPIEZ, 1890: 759 n. 1.

17. PERROT and CHIPIEZ, 1890: 373, and LOFTUS, 1857: 396–398.

18. DIEULAFOY, J. 1887: 2.

19. DIEULAFOY, J. 1887: 363–364.

20. DIEULAFOY, J. 1887: 364.

21. *CRAIBL*, 1885: 240; 1886: 369.

22. DUSSAUD, 1914, I: 439.

23. *CRAIBL*, 1884: 569

24. DIEULAFOY, M. 1884, II: 22, fig. 17.

25. CHEVALIER, 2002: 118–122.

26. DIEULAFOY, J. 1888: 88.

27. DIEULAFOY, M. 1913: 2–3 et 1885 II: 57.

28. DIEULAFOY, J. 1888: 87 et DIEULAFOY, M. 1893: 424, 46–55.

29. DIEULAFOY, J. 1888: 91. TALLON, 1997a: 46–55, has presented a very clear summary of Marcel Dieulafoy's excavations.

30. DIEULAFOY, J. 1888: 109 and 112.

31. DIEULAFOY, J. 1888: 131–133.

32. DIEULAFOY, J. 1888: 158–160 and 177.

33. DIEULAFOY, M. 1885a: 62–63.

34. DIEULAFOY, J. 1888: 159–160.

35. DIEULAFOY, J. 1888: 167.

36. DIEULAFOY, M. 1886a, II: 200 and DIEULAFOY, J. 1888b: 264.

37. DIEULAFOY, J. 1888: 273.

38. Dieulafoy believed the whole to be the baked-brick foundations of an entrance that Artaxerxes II had built on the ruins of earlier walls belonging to the time of Darius. DIEULAFOY, M. 1886a: 201 and 1893: 280. Mecquenem contested the 4 m attributed by Dieulafoy because, he wrote, 'the trenches were never extended beneath the gravel'. According to him, one should read: '4 m below the surface of the tell'. MECQUENEM, 1947: 32.

39. 'It has been said and printed a hundred times that the Délégation en Perse had taken over at Susa the work of the Dieulafoy excavations. It is an error which I would not discuss here were it not for its, by now, obsessive frequency. The Dieulafoy excavations were focused on the Achaemenid period, and it was on the ruins of this period that they concentrated their efforts; the Elamite ruins were not touched. The palaces of Xerxes, Artaxerxes and others had nothing to do with my choice of site at Susa; it was the history of Elam that I was seeking' (MORGAN, 1905a: 10).

40. JÉQUIER, 1900b: 69–80 and fig. 80. Trenches: 4, 5, 6, 9, 10, 11, 12.

41. Such walls do not appear on the reconstructions proposed in PERROT and CHIPIEZ, 1890: 474–477.

42. At the end of 1908 Mecquenem replaced Morgan on the excavation site of Susa until the latter's resignation as head of the Délégation en Perse on 12 October 1912. During the last two seasons that preceded the First World War, it was as Director of the Mission de Susiane that Mecquenem, in association with Vincent Scheil, led the excavations in the palace area. The progress of the work can be reconstructed thanks to the regular, though often laconic reports sent to the Ministère de l'Instruction Publique which was now responsible for missions abroad.

43. Mecquenem (MECQUENEM and PÉZARD, 1911), has provided a plan of the Palace of Darius for the 1909–1910 season.

44. These are probably the paving slabs of the alcove in the king's chamber (see fig. 137 on page 149 in the present volume).

45. Roland de Mecquenem's reports are in the Archives Nationales (an) f17 17246, 17247, 17255, 17257–58. Many are accompanied by photographs and plans. The Département des Antiquités Orientales in the Louvre has a copy, but without the illustrations. An overview of Mecquenem's excavations based on these archives was produced by L. Martinez in 1996. an f17 17255. Compte-rendu de la campagne de fouilles à Suse, 1922: 1 and MECQUENEM, 1910: 46.

46. an f17 17255, Compte-rendu … 1922:1 and MECQUENEM, 1910: 46–47. This 'Room A' was identified by Pillet as a courtyard, his 'Parvis aux colonnes'.

47. Mecquenem's 1912 Report. For the 'Charter' see F. Vallat, ch. ix; MECQUENEM, 1947: 91

and SCHEIL, 1929: 18 ff., pl. 8, 9; KENT, 1953: 142–144; STEVE, 1974: 145–147.

48. PÉZARD and POTTIER, 1926: 29; MECQUENEM, 1910: 45–47; MECQUENEM and PÉZARD, 1911: 55 and 1922: 109–117.

49. The Report for 1913 does not include the fragment of robe referred to in the 1922 Report. These fragments, which certainly do not belong to the same statue, were first published by SCHEIL, 1929: 57, pl. 13, then by MECQUENEM, 1938: 324 and 1947: 47, pl.5. It is regrettable that, even in his final publication, Mecquenem failed to give the exact locations for even his most important discoveries.

50. M.PILLET Archives.

51. MECQUENEM and PÉZARD, 1911: 51–58.

52. Figs 56–61 in this chapter.

53. MECQUENEM, 1922 Report: 2. Mecquenem refers to the watercolour restorations of the palace that were shown at the 'Salon des artistes français' where Pillet was awarded the gold medal. A brochure was prepared for visitors on this occasion; PILLET, 1913: 641–653. TALLON, 1997b: 132–139.

54. PILLET, 1913: 644.

55. M. PILLET Archives. A remnant of the palace walls survives north of the great hall to the south of the West Court.

56. PILLET, 1913: 647.

57. For his part, Mecquenem was in favour of the resumption of the excavations; there had been few finds previously: only two deposits of no real importance: an inscribed tablet of unbaked clay, and a mass of glazed amulets; MECQUENEM, 1934 Report: 4.

58. MECQUENEM, 1922 Report: 2.

59. Mecquenem noted that south of the most southern room of the West Court there still remained traces of circulation. He therefore thought that the gravel terrace continued south-wards for at least 17 m, and to this had to be added the 9 m thickness of the retaining wall in order to obtain the southern limits of the palace. MECQUENEM, 1947: 26–27.

60. Thus about 18 m above the level of the waters of the Shaur at the Tomb of Daniel.

61. D. LADIRAY, ch. vi.

62. MECQUENEM, 1947: 11–13 and fig. 12. Another aspect of Mecquenem's work consisted of excavations he initiated under the palace. He explains his decision as follows: 'When we looked at the general plan of the palace, we got the impression that the whole eastern wing, where we had failed to find a plastered court [parvis bétonné] had been altered, or even added to the original plan. Furthermore, we could not but wonder whether the Achaemenids might not have built their palace over the ruins of Elamite royal dwellings so far unknown. Thus a sounding below the terrace became part of our programme' (MECQUENEM, 1922 Report). Since the beginning of the excavations, Mecquenem had been interested in the nature of the terrace. In his 1912–1913 Report, he had suggested that it consisted entirely of gravel that was held in place by retaining walls of unbaked brick with a cladding of baked brick. It had been possible to carry out soundings in the central part thanks to the presence of numerous Parthian wells, indicating an average thickness of 12 m. Further north further elevations of the same type had been noted. This had led him to write: 'If we remember that nowadays we have to go to the bed of the Kerkha River, some three kilometers away in order to obtain similar gravel, we cannot but wonder at such an expenditure of effort. Perhaps, among the clay mounds of Susa, there were once deposits of alluvial gravel, such as exist around Dizful' (1913 Report: 4).

63. On his plan, Pillet places them to the west.

64. MECQUENEM, 1947: 47–64.

65. In a personal letter addressed to Mecquenem in 1912, Jacques de Morgan gave instructions as to the conduct of the excavations at the Palace of Darius, and concluded: 'I should very much like you to provide us with a Memoir that will remain the most important testimony concerning the Achaemenid monuments. It could be made into a special volume in which you would review all the Achaemenid discoveries at Susa. It would be a wonderful work. I would have undertaken it myself had we had begun work on the Palace of Darius sooner. It is you who discovered it, and it is you who should have all the credit. Next year I shall go to Susa, and you will be able to make a good start on your volume during your 18 months' leave in France. Therefore, this winter, make all notes that you might need, and open up trenches wherever you think they may be useful for your work' (Mecquenem Archives). The head of the Délégation en Perse, who is in the habit of driving the publications agenda at break-neck speed, has no doubt that a forthcoming volume of the *Mémoires* on the Palace of Darius will soon be added to the twelve already published.

66. MECQUENEM, 1947: 4; MECQUENEM, 1922: 109–117; MECQUENEM, 1938: 322.

67. MECQUENEM, 1947: 4.

68. MECQUENEM, 1947: 117.

69. Ghirshman had excavated at Tepe Giyan (1931–1933), Tepe Sialk (1933–1937) and Bishapur (1935–1937, 1940–1941). In 1942, the tragic death of Joseph Hacklin had resulted in his becoming his successor as head of the Délégation archéologique française en Afghanistan (1941–1943). Regarding the context of Ghirshman's arrival at Susa, see T. GHIRSHMAN 1970. For a clear overview of Ghirshman's activities at Susa, see GASCHE, 1997: 168–179.

70. GHIRSHMAN, 1947: 444. A summary of Ghirshman's activities at Susa between 1946 and 1967, together with a plan locating the various different excavation sites, the numbering of which will be used here, is given in STEVE, GASCHE and DE MEYER, 1980: 107–109.

71. GHIRSHMAN, 1954: 1.

72. GHIRSHMAN, 1947: 445.

73. GHIRSHMAN, 1947: 445–446.

74. GHIRSHMAN, 1947: 446.

75. STEVE, GASCHE and DE MEYER, 1980: 107–109.

76. GHIRSHMAN, 1954: plan 1. He first suggested that the Hypostyle Hall might have stood on a terrace surrounded by courts, with stairways as at Persepolis. He also wished to establish whether the palace had been built on a natural outcrop, or on a prehistoric mound, or on ancient Elamite princely dwellings that had not, so far, been identified (Areas 24 and 25). GHIRSHMAN, 1968b: 13–14.

77. GHIRSHMAN, 1957: 240–241.

78. GHIRSHMAN, 1968b: 15.

79. GHIRSHMAN, 1968b: 16–17 and fig. 38–39.

72

The 'Château' photographed in 1969

The 'Château' of Jacques de Morgan

'The need for a house became apparent and, on 1 January 1898, the foundations were laid on the northern point of the Acropolis mound. The mud-brick building was nearly finished by 1 May. There were two levels of construction, 2 m apart. The more elevated to the north had a wall that followed the contour of the tell, forming a trapeze; to the west a corridor lit by narrow, barred windows gave onto seven vaulted rooms of 2.5 x 4.3 m; to the east lay the drawing-room-cum-library of 7 x 3 m, a dining room of 3 x 3 m, an office, a kitchen of the same dimensions and a woodshed. To the south, a small room was dedicated to natural history and a small darkroom allowed photographic processing by infra-red light ('à la lanterne rouge'). These rooms gave onto a trapezoid courtyard, under which two basements served as store-rooms for the

73
The 'Château' in 1978

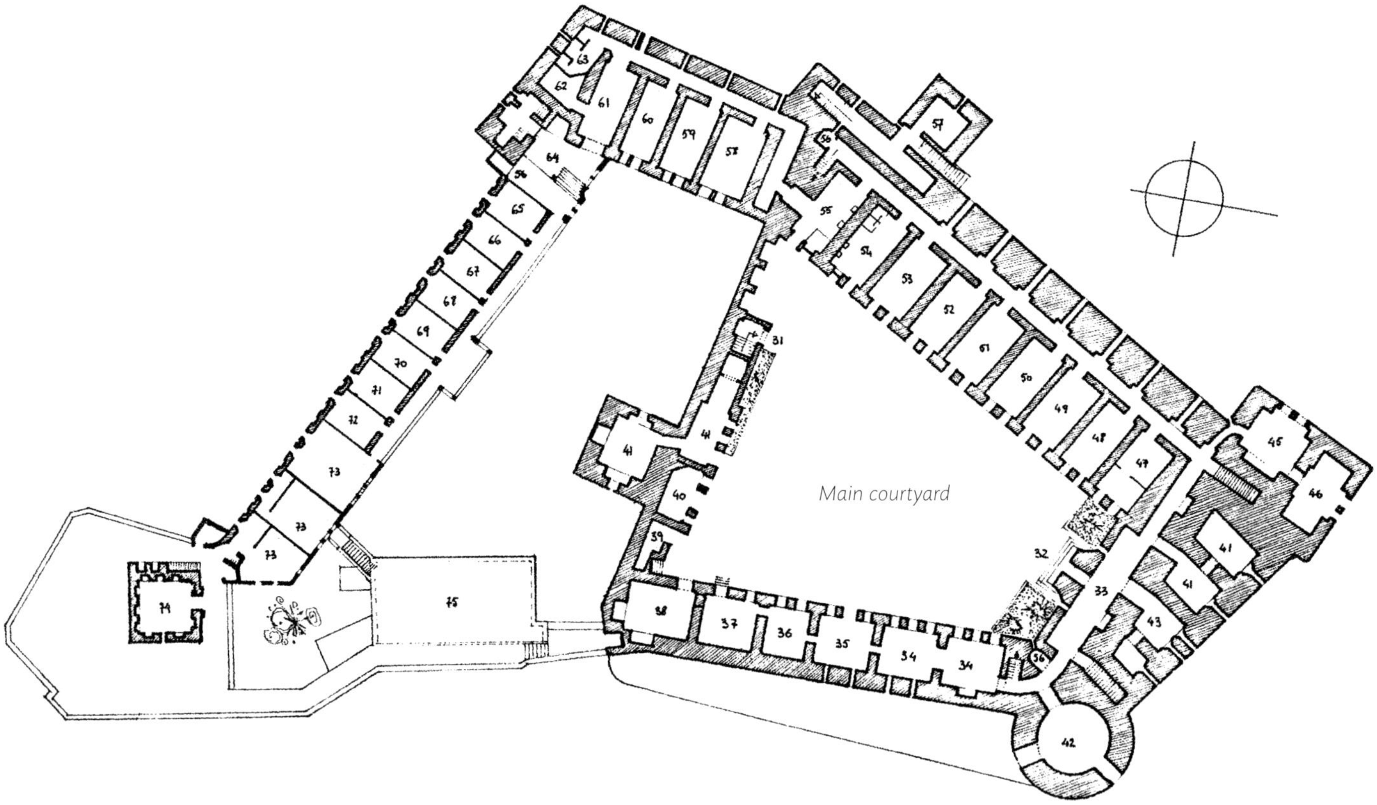

Main courtyard

74
Plan of the 'Château'

Ground floor		*Upper storey*	
1	main entrance	31	entrance
2	small door	32	porch
4	stone museum	33	vestibule
5	conservation laboratory	34	sitting-room
6	photographic laboratory	35	dining room
7	collections	36	office
8	access to the upper courtyard	37	kitchen
10	photographic studio	38	office
11	work room	40	laundry
12	work room	41	library and reading room
13	work room	42	conference room
14	work room	43	epigraphy
15	work room	44	map room
16	garage	45	office
17	Decauville railway shed	47	room
18	stables	48	room
19	work room	49	room
20	work room	50	room
21	work room	51	room
22	staff room	52	room
23	staff room	53	room
24	staff room	54	showers
25.	collections	58–72	rooms
27	carpentry workshop	73	porter's lodge
28	workshop	74	room
29	garage-workshop	75	studio
30	gas oven for baking tablets	76	conference room

antiquities. The lower level comprised a courtyard with living quarters to the west and a workshop; to the south were the stables and a tool shed; to the east were the guards' quarters; to the south-east a bastion was reserved for the garrison. A postern gate gave on to the Acropolis; a double door opened out to the east at the end of an access ramp.

Around 1903, the mud-brick walls started to crack; as baked bricks were being excavated in large numbers, it was decided to build a supporting wall and the northern flanks of the tell were cut back accordingly; despite the gradual shrinkage and the additions made to the wall, there was enough space to allow for a large cellar, two bedrooms, a store room and a photographic workshop; to the west a terrace for our hundred wagons and to the east, a terrace to enjoy the breeze. Crenellations and towers give the place a feudal air. It was completely finished in 1911, but the maintenance of the terraces and the gutters requires the constant attention of a stonemason.'

MECQUENEM, 1912

75

The oldest houses of Shush-i Daniel and the
floodplain of the Karkheh (on the horizon)

4 The Franco-Iranian Programme

Jean Perrot

In 1968, the objective of the programme of the archaeological mission to Susa was not to look at the Achaemenid period; rather, it was to research the recent prehistory of the Near and Middle East.[1] In Susiana, my colleagues and I shared the same interests in the Classical period which, 70 years earlier, had attracted Jacques de Morgan to Susa in search of Oriental sources for Egyptian civilisation.[2] We were also conscious of the responsibilities of the mission towards a country that had entrusted to France the exploration of its past and the conservation of a prestigious heritage for a long period. In the winter of 1968–1969 we began a clean-up of the site, specifically the remains of the Palace of Darius, remains that were disappearing under the grass and brambles covering the Apadana mound. In 1971, on the eve of the celebrations to mark the 2500th anniversary of the monarchy in Iran, the names of Cyrus, Darius and their successors, and of Persepolis, Pasargadae, Ecbatana and Susa were on everybody's lips. In anticipation of the event, visitors arrived every morning at the foot of the 'Château' (the excavation house) which tourists often took to be Darius' Palace. Under the pressure of circumstances, I called the National Centre for the Protection of Iranian Antiquities and the Iranian Centre for Archaeological Research in Tehran,[3] proposing to rebuild a few walls of the palace as had been done at Persepolis. The answer was positive and the support ongoing; archaeologists and Iranian technicians actively participated in the work.[4] The first results were very encouraging, and were to lead to the reopening of excavations that continued until 1979.[5]

FIRST CHECKS

During the winter of 1968–1969 heavy rains caused serious floods in Khuzistan; the rivers of Susa, the Kerkha and the Shaur, broke their banks and flooded the

76
Satellite photographs showing Shush-i Daniel and the tells of Susa

77

The approach road to the Apadana tell (on the right) and the 'Château'

78

Visiting day at Susa

79

The 'Château' and the garden of the archaeological museum on the main road in 1978

80
The village square of Shush-i Daniel
during the winter floods of 1968–69

81
The excavated East Court and the support bases for the 'masts'
along the northern side, below the floor level of the palace

82

Bases and column drums of the western portico of the Hypostyle Hall recognised by Loftus in 1852

village (Shush-i Daniel), the waters destroying a number of houses by eroding the bases of their mud-brick walls. On the flanks of the tells, where men and animals had taken shelter, the run-off had deepened the ravines, most notably on the Apadana mound, exposing, at 2.5 m under the floor of the palace, a large baked-brick wall bonded with bitumen. The old question of a palatial residence, older than the Achaemenid one, was back on the agenda.

The ruins at Susa are not spectacular, unlike those of Persepolis in the mountains of Fars where the stone used in construction gives an impression of the buildings that had once stood there. At the eastern limits of the vast alluvial plain through which flow the Tigris and Euphrates, Susiana is a land of earth and water where the mud-brick structures disappear as soon as people cease to care for them. Susa and its region may have the advantage over Mesopotamia by being close to the Zagros mountain chain and to the Iranian plateau and its resources, but stone is rare; as soon as the palace was abandoned its columns were looted. On the Apadana tell, in 1968, only a few pieces remained, hidden amongst the scrub or under soil that had been furrowed for more than a century by the trenches of archaeologists. Of the Residence of the Great King only a few courses of baked brick and the remains of plaster floors were visible. Its courtyards were full of craters marking ancient digging for Elamite tombs and resembled a moonscape

83
The Apadana tell in the area of the Residence
with some remains of plaster floors
(1968)

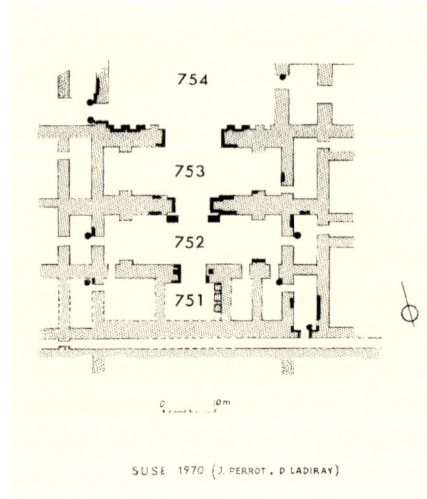

84
To the south of the West Court (C1),
the sector interpreted as comprising the
entrance of the palace was found to be the
King's Apartment (750) with vestibule (753),
antechamber (752) and royal chamber (751)

85
Pieces of column filling an old trench
in the Hypostyle Hall sector

**Tells and principal buildings
of the Achaemenid period**

which made it difficult to read the site as a whole. The existing archaeological documentation was considerable, as the review presented by Nicole Chevalier in the previous chapter has demonstrated; but on location we only had Mecquenem's report on the excavations published in 1947. This lack of information had some positive aspects in that it allowed me to tackle the problems with serenity, away from the hypotheses and projections on the subject by previous generations.

For the informed visitor, what one then called 'the palace' appeared to be organised around three courts: to the south were remains of the large Hypostyle Hall which an inscription of Artaxerxes II had designated by the word 'Apadana'. The first archaeologists had placed the main entrance to this palace on the south side; this view, solidly anchored in subsequent archaeological literature, had been acted upon by Dieulafoy in 1886, when he opened trenches to the south of the Hypostyle Hall, and dug through the Sassanian and Parthian layers in his search for an architectural complex which he imagined to be of Egyptian influence with courts and pylons. Access appeared to be from the south, with on this side, on the flanks of the mound, a grand double staircase of the same type as the one to be seen at Persepolis. Later on, the discoveries by Mecquenem and Pillet of a small door to the west (l1) overlooking the river, and of a more important door to the east (l2), did not change the opinion that the main entrance was in the south.[6]

87
Foundation tablet with the name of Darius inscribed in Elamite (DSz), under the foundations of a wall of the Royal Apartment, west side of the entrance to the King's Chamber (751)

THE EXCAVATIONS FROM 1969 TO 1972

Right from the start of the works,[7] which were followed very closely by Daniel Ladiray, and which naturally began with the 'entrance', we were greatly surprised at the laxity of certain ancient surveys. We observed that the doors between the two great halls (752 and 753b of the plan by Mecquenem) which we expected to open towards the north if the entrance was in room 751, opened in fact towards the south, onto room 752. At Susa, as at Persepolis, the doors pivot inwards; they are pushed to enter a room. Room 751, to the south of the two great halls, could not therefore be an entrance; it was also clear that its southern wall had been eroded (this affected the entire southern wall of the palace). The relative sophistication of the part of the building surrounding the West Court (c1) soon confirmed that this court was part of an architectural whole that could be nothing other than the King's Apartments. From its layout and ornamentation, this sector appeared to be the central element of the palace. This suggestion gained support with the discovery, under the walls of the passage giving access to room 751, of two grey slabs of grey marble inscribed in cuneiform script, in both Elamite and Akkadian, with a text relating to the foundation of the palace (DSz and DSaa). It became apparent then that the 'clearing' of the floors and the walls that Mecquenem had undertaken had not always allowed for the plotting of the exact location of passageways and doorways; the heavy stones that supported the door sockets had often sunk into the earth under their own weight. In their absence, the reading of the plan, the sense of flow, the function of various parts and the interpretation of the whole were completely wrong.

At the time that we were making these observations as well as others relating to how the terrace supporting the palace had been constructed, soundings made under the supervision of Denis Canal had identified the walls and doors of the great Hypostyle Hall (Apadana). Their position had, until then, not been located,

88
Remains of the Hypostyle Hall in 1970

89
**The Hypostyle Hall of the Shaur Palace,
on the right bank of the river,
in course of excavation**

90
Excavation trenches opened in 1969 to 1979
APADANA EAST and APADANA VILLE ROYALE
by Monique Kervan for the Islamic levels
and Rémy Boucharlat for the Parthian levels;
VILLE ROYALE APADANA by Mir Abdin Kaboli

and the first excavators had even had doubts about the existence of walls between the central hall and the porticoes. Elsewhere on the right bank of the Shaur, several hundred metres to the west of the Apadana mound, a great hall of one hundred columns, together with outbuildings, had been fortuitously discovered. According to the fragmentary inscriptions, the complex was possibly the work of Artaxerxes II, the restorer of Darius' large Hypostyle Hall. This new palace, which Audran Labrousse and later Rémy Boucharlat excavated, had been built a century after that of Darius. This discovery opened up a new perspective on the evolution of Achaemenid architecture at Susa and at the same time it shed new light on the problem of dating another 'palace' called the 'Donjon'.[8]

EXTENDING THE SEARCH

Between 1972 and 1979, work extended over the Apadana mound and beyond, towards the east, on the Ville Royale tell. The excavations were preceded by an electronic survey directed by Albert Hesse,[9] with the assistance of Serge Renimel and the cooperation of Mohieddin Sadjadi. At the same time, a methodical audit of the remains and foundations of the palace enabled Daniel Ladiray to clarify and complete the plan, most notably in the area to the east and the sector of door L2.

To the east of the palace, on the eastern edge of the Apadana mound, there was an area that had only been disturbed by the narrow trenches opened by both Loftus and Dieulafoy through the Islamic, Sassanian and Parthian layers. The

91

Clearing the baked brick foundations
of a wall of the Residence

92

Ghirshman's 'stratigraphic trench' (A) at
the south-east corner of the Propylaeum,
exposing the foundations of the building

Parthian layers, represented most notably in this sector by thick foundation walls, had quickly discouraged the excavators. A site opened in 1948 by Ghirshman had been abandoned at the level of the Islamic layers. To the north Mecquenem had left a deep excavation between the palace and the retaining wall of the terrace. This retaining wall, whose outer face formed a glacis, dominated the depression between the two tells of the Apadana and Ville Royale. It was tempting to see in this depression (where the curtain wall surrounding the mounds joined the retaining wall) a possible way in, running north–south towards the centre of the square. One could imagine ramps hugging the retaining wall on the right, and climbing to the Apadana, and to the left giving access to the Ville Royale. This hypothesis made sense because of the presence of a large Achaemenid construction on the Ville Royale which had been spotted several years earlier when the big 'stratigraphic trench', opened up by Ghirshman in the north-west of the tell, had reached the foundations of this monument, prompting a collapse of its foundation gravel into the big trench. Assuming the Achaemenid architects had a sense of symmetry, one might suppose that there was an unknown edifice on the Apadana mound mirroring that on the Ville Royale tell. It was decided to reopen the small trench started by Ghirshman on the Apadana (site Apadana-East), at the same time as clearing, on the Ville Royale mound (the Vilapa site), the building glimpsed on the edge of the Ghirshman trench, under the supervision of Mir Abdin Kaboli.[10]

On each tell the Achaemenid levels were uncovered at a depth of several metres, below the remains of an apparently uninterrupted occupation until the Mongol invasion. For the excavation and the study of these layers I called upon the Centre d'études islamiques de l'université Paris-Sorbonne who sent Monique Kervran to Susa. The Parthian and Seleucid periods were under the control of Rémy Boucharlat and Mehdi Rahbar.

THE DISCOVERY OF THE DARIUS STATUE AND GATE

The Apadana-East site was opened on 21 December 1972, it was cleaned and a grid was marked out. We were stunned the next day by the discovery, at the level of the Islamic walls already exposed by Ghirshman, of a grey stone which soon revealed itself to be the broken top of a colossal statue of Darius; its excavation

93
Discovery of the Darius statue in 1972
The top of the statue, broken, was level with the base of an Islamic period wall

94
Excavation of the Statue of Darius
and first decipherment of its cuneiform
inscriptions by François Vallat (DSab)

under the direction of Monique Kervran, assisted by Denis Canal, quickly showed
that this statue was still upright set against an unknown building. This building
was later revealed to be a monumental gateway (40 x 28 m) with a central room,
with four columns bearing a trilingual inscription by Xerxes, repeated on their
bases, attributing it to his father Darius. As to the statue of Darius, it was covered
in cuneiform inscriptions and hieroglyphics. Following an initial examination
by François Vallat, and by Jean Yoyotte who had been called to Susa, it was immediately evident that it was of exceptional importance for the study of relations
between Persia and Egypt during the Achaemenid Empire.

The access to the terrace of the Apadana mound had therefore been found, but
it remained unclear what shape it was, since the gate was some 15 m above the
level of the plain. A third site, Apadana Ville-Royale (Apavir), was then opened
up to the east of the Darius Gate,[11] across the depression separating the Apadana
tell from the Ville Royale mound in order to check the ramp access theory.

The eastern wall of the gate rested on a spur jutting out about 5.5 m from the
terrace retaining wall; the wall had been destroyed at the top but it was found
again several metres lower. This extension of infill could have served as a buttress
for ramps gently climbing up the retaining wall.[12] Despite being cleared right

down to the water table, this wall showed no sign of ramps. By contrast, in the axis of the gateway, there appeared a vast, solid mass of mud brick, the apparent remains of a wide road linking the platform of the Apadana to the Ville Royale tell. This structure, about 40 m long, on the Ville Royale side lent against a cutting in the Elamite layers.

THE PROPYLAEUM AND THE ARTISANS' GATE

Meanwhile, on the Ville Royale mound, the excavation of the Achaemenid building, led by Mir Abdin Kaboli, was progressing through a tangle of walls and foundations dating from the Parthian era. In 1976 it reached the Achaemenid level where the important remains of a building of 24 m², flanked by two columned porticoes, were brought to light. On the column bases was a trilingual inscription by Xerxes attributing the construction to his father Darius. It was a passageway on a north–south axis at right angles to that of the road and the monumental gateway.

Our rekindled interest in the Ville Royale led to a more intensive investigation of the outline of a gravel surface already noted by our predecessors; this surface marked the internal face of the solid embankment wall outlining the contour of the tell. This investigation led to the discovery, on the eastern edge of the tell, of a small angled gateway situated on the high curtain wall and accessible via a ramp: the Artisans' Gate.[13]

THE CAUSEWAY, THE DARIUS GATE AND THE ESPLANADE

From the Ville Royale one passed to the terrace of the Apadana on the same level (18 m), via a solid causeway built of mud brick and earth in line with the Darius Gate. This causeway, whose outer aspect would have been that of the glacis, itself formed part of the area's curtain wall.

The Darius Gate is so named because of a trilingual inscription by Xerxes on the column bases of the gate's central room.[14] It gives onto the Esplanade, a vast tiled area, apparently open on all sides.

The centre of the Apadana terrace is occupied by the large audience hall which the trilingual inscription of Artaxerxes II (A2 sa) calls the Apadana. The absence of any traces of construction or even foundations in the surrounding areas to the north, to the east and to the west, suggests that this hall could originally have been surrounded by courtyards or gardens on three sides. The Residence extends towards the south – a complex of courtyards and buildings – described until now, along with the Hypostyle Hall, as forming 'the palace'. This complex, the work of Darius I, went through a few minor alterations and, to the west, an important restoration attributed to Artaxerxes II.[15]

THE WALL AND ITS GATES

The three mounds cover a total area of around 70 hectares. They are linked at the base by a thick mud-brick wall and thus form a defensive system. The sides of the Ville Royale were cut almost vertically, and the cut was then covered by a thick wall of compacted earth, encased in a mud-brick embankment, creating a glacis 15 m high. This wall, described differently by the first excavators, was explored most notably by Ghirshman in 1963–1964 on the northern edge of the Ville Royale where it is 27 m thick and sits 'on the remains of the Elamite ramparts'.[16] The whole of the Apadana terrace had the same appearance, but here it was very much a supporting wall to hold the earth taken from the top of the tell and scattered around the central core.

95
Access to the Apadana terrace was controlled
on the Ville Royale tell by the Propylaeum,
at the head of a causeway leading to the
Darius Gate and the Esplanade

96
The edges of the 'Ville Royale' tell were
smoothed before being protected by a
thick mud-brick glacis separated from the
archaeological layers by a gravel 'sleeve'
60 cm thick

97

The walls and pavement of the Propylaeum
These appeared under the foundation walls of the Parthian period,
preserved in the east to a height of more than a metre

98
**Clearing the north-west bastion
of the Apadana terrace**

We cleared this curtain wall in the north-west corner of the terrace where it formed a bastion projecting a few metres. To the south, on the western side, it appeared to present a few projections and salients. The central part of its outline had been traced by Ghirshman over a length of 50 m,[17] and more recently, beginning in 1994, by Mir Abdin Kaboli of the Office for the Protection of Cultural Heritage.[18] This wall is slightly inclined and rises 18 m from the water table to the terrace.

Within this enclosure, and more precisely inside the mud-brick wall that links the three mounds and which has not completely disappeared, one is tempted to place gateways where logic would suggest that they would have been, that is to say to the west, in the wall (still partly visible) close to the museum, between the Acropolis and the Apadana; also to the south between the Ville Royale and the Acropolis. However, no traces of such gates have been found. The only gateway identified with any certainty was the pedestrian gate perched on the glacis at the

99
The retaining wall of the Apadana was
preserved to a height of more than
15 m above the water table

THE FRANCO-IRANIAN PROGRAMME **115**

16 m level, where it was accessible via a ramp of rammed earth and mud brick. This gateway we named the Artisans' Gate, not so much because it gives onto the tell of the Artisans to the east (which did not exist before the Achaemenid period), but because it was the link to the only area out of reach of the floods. It therefore gave access to the local population who had been forced to leave the tells, and to the encampments of the foreign workers brought to Susa by Darius. One access point was essential in this sector of the enclosure. As to the vast depression that separated the tell Ville Royale from what would become the tell of the Artisans, it is unlikely that it corresponds, as has been written, to a ditch filled with the waters of the Shaur and dug by Darius. Aerial photographs make clear that it is a dried up tributary of the river. That is not to say that Darius would have been unable to open up a ditch, but the necessity here is not obvious.

OTHER ELEMENTS

It is not inconceivable that in addition to the elements that we have just examined, the initial project also comprised secondary structures. One can imagine the presence of a small military structure at the southern extremity of the Ville Royale tell, acting as a lookout over an area that was out of range of those on the Acropolis. Elsewhere, the excavation of the Palace of Artaxerxes II on the opposite bank of the Shaur suggested to Rémy Boucharlat a building on the site that could pre-date the works by Artaxerxes II: a sort of pleasure pavilion in the middle of gardens.[19] Several small column bases carrying the names of the first kings of the dynasty could have belonged to smaller structures that have disappeared.[20] No other Royal Achaemenid residence, however, appears to be awaiting discovery on the tells of Susa.

100

The tells of Achaemenid Susa
The three tells were linked by massive mud-brick walls of which imposing traces remain. The Apadana terrace was protected by its retaining walls; the Ville Royale tell by the glacis with salients which surrounded it on exposed edges

101

Remains of the mud-brick wall linking the tells
of Ville Royale and the Acropolis to the south

THE REALITY OF THE 'PALACE OF DARIUS'

As the clearing of the Achaemenid buildings progressed on the Apadana and the ground plan of the Residence was revealed, there opened up an increasing gulf between the archaeological realities and the recent interpretations of the Palace of Darius. In 1947, for Roland de Mecquenem, 'the Achaemenid Palace of Susa was not that of Darius I'; nor was it 'that which the book of Esther presented as witnessing the intrigues of Mordechai; it was the palace which Alexander the Great had seized [...] renovated by the Persian kings according to the needs of the day'. In addition, for Mecquenem, 'the most important building works at Susa had been accomplished by the Babylonians'. This was an assertion rejected by his successor, Roman Ghirshman, for whom 'the palace was built, not by the Babylonians as was generally thought, but according to Elamite architectural principles' (which in reality is not contradictory, the method of building in both regions, in the same environment, being practically the same). Ghirshman thought that the palace had been 'entirely exposed after a half-century of work'. He accepted the broad concept of the restoration proposed by his predecessor and only undertook the search for 'the grand external entrance which must have opened onto the princely residential quarters and their gardens' on the western flank of the Apadana; a fruitless search and hypothesis which collapsed with the discovery of the Darius Gate to the east of the Residence.

In 1980, following the interruption to the excavations, views and ideas about the Royal Residence of Susa differed profoundly from the vision that was current a decade earlier, when it rested largely on the collections brought back to the Louvre in 1886 by Marcel Dieulafoy: the friezes and glazed bricks, and the bull's head capital. This material, as well as fantastical reconstructions and literary references taken from distant sources, fed these daydreams. In Darius' time, Susa was at its lowest ebb. Cyrus II, in his conquest of Babylonia, had perhaps passed by, but had not stopped. It is not even certain whether the Susa complex had a king or royal palace worthy of that name. Judging by the rare remains of this period, termed neo-Elamite III (585–539 BC), the region was not densely populated. The country had recovered after the destructive swathe cut by the Assyrians in 646, as testified by a total of 300 administrative tablets found on the Acropolis. There was evidence

102
Residence
The modification of the plan of rooms in G was evident by a repair to the plaster floors

103
Eastern edge of the Ville Royale tell on the now
silted-up branch of the river, towards the north

104
Dieulafoy's 'parade ground' between
the three tells of ancient Susa

of agricultural and artisanal activity in the area but the Elamite kingdom, of which Susa was the capital, was disintegrating. The records that we have from this period are from elsewhere: the 'Nineveh Letters', the Arjan tomb, the Samati treasure, the bronze plaque at Persepolis, the rock inscriptions at Malamir, etc. For François Vallat, 'the royalty of Susa still had economic relationships with various geo-political entities distant from Susian power', but even the term 'king' tends to disappear from the rare brick inscriptions found on the site.

To remodel the site, Darius' architects could not help but evacuate the population, several thousand people at the most, who were evicted and founded a new district in the north-east which would become known as the tell of the Artisans. The problem we are faced with today is not the palace as such, but the position and role of Susa in Darius' Empire. Before trying to solve it, however, it is important to define our vocabulary and the function of each separate element that makes up the whole.

A NECESSARY ADJUSTMENT TO THE TERMINOLOGY OF SUSA

We found ourselves in the presence of a vast architectural complex to which the traditional Susian terminology could no longer be applied. The image of a sumptuous 'Palace of the Achaemenid Kings' at the heart of an all-encompassing Persian Empire tends to fade behind that of a fort with a royal residence and a large audience chamber, indispensable elements in the exercise of power. A detailed description of the whole demands more rigour in the choice of the terms used. Epigraphists agree that a certain laxity reigned in the Royal Achaemenid chancellery where it seems they haphazardly used words such as *hadish* or *taçara* to designate the same building.[21] To translate these terms with the word 'palace' does not reduce this ambiguity; a palace can be residential, a place of justice, or designated for some other function. The size of the building also needs to be taken into consideration: there are large and small palaces; the Residence at Susa covers almost 4 hectares; the area covered by what is called 'the Palace of Darius' at Persepolis is no greater than that of the 'Darius Gate' (the latter was called like that of Xerxes at Persepolis).

There are, understandably, some reservations about the use of the term 'Propylaeum' at Susa. This is not incongruous, however, given Susian terminology which uses the word 'Acropolis' without qualms. Propylaeum (propulaion) means 'that which is in front of the door'; the word is normally used to designate the vestibule of a temple, the portico that forms the entrance; it also has a place in the military architect's vocabulary. The word 'Propylaeum' admittedly evokes the sanctuaries of Athens,[22] but in this context it is not wrong; its function stems from its position with regard to the palatial complex. This building marks the symbolic line in the sand separating from the outside a domain whose privileged nature could make it sacred like everything associated with royalty.[23]

A bird's eye view of the Achaemenid complex shows a very different geographic reality to that described in the Classical literature. Other than the works dating to the reign of Darius, and perhaps also from the beginning of the reign of Xerxes, no residential palace was built at Susa. Apart from the royal buildings, the scarcity of the remains of human occupation is particularly striking; the few potsherds found here and there do not allow us to define a characteristic pottery for the period. The deeper levels of the tell of the Artisans have not been sufficiently explored, but the promontory of the tell, which is the only one in the area safe from flooding, does not date from the Parthian period. According to the surveys, Susa's surrounding plains do not seem to have had a significant population at the time. Susa was no doubt the administrative and economic centre of the satrapy

105
**North-western bastion
of the Apadana terrace**
Cleared of its facing the stepped
mud-brick courses are evident

of Susiana, but its extent and population can at no time compare with those of centres like Babylon, Pasargadae or Persepolis; and one can better understand the biblical chroniclers who made constant reference to 'Shushan ha-birah', 'Susa the citadel', the fortress. Darius does not seem to have spent time at Susa before the 22nd year of his reign. Artaxerxes II was probably the only king to take an interest in the region and to live there to the point of giving it, in the fourth century BC, the importance accorded it by Greek historians.

106

Participants in the Franco-Iranian programme at Susa, 1974

1 Jane Wheeler Pires Ferreira, paleoethnozoologist
2 Edgardo Pires Ferreira
3 Albert Hesse, civil engineer
4 Geneviève Dollfus, archaeologist
5 Pierre de Miroschedji, archaeologist
6 Massoud Azernoush, archaeologist
7 Serge Renimel, geophysicist
8 Mohieddin Sadjadi, trainee geophysicist
9 François Vallat, epigraphist
10 Jean Perrot, director of the archaeological mission
11 Alain Rempfer, photographer
12 Monique Kervran, archaeologist
13 Yolande Vernes-Crowe, ceramicist

14 Mohammad Akbary, general secretary
15 Martine Maillard-Azernoush, trainee archaeologist
16 Jean Martin, stonemason
17 Jane
18 Joël Mallet, archaeologist
19 Jacques Decroix, draftsman
20 Daniel Ladiray, lead archaeologist
21 Zahra Djaffar-Mohammadi, trainee archaeologist
22 Sema Baykan, archaeologist
23 Bathya de Miroschedji, research assistant
24 Claire Hardy, archaeologist
25 Mme Rempfer
26 Mme Decroix

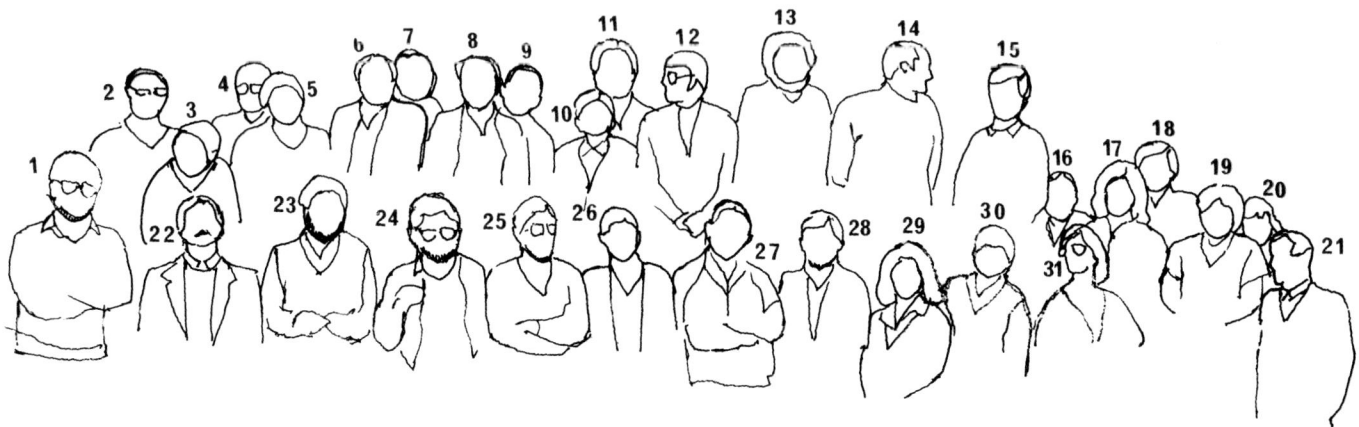

107

**Participants of the Franco-Iranian programme,
Bellevaux Rencontre Internationale, 1985**

1	Gregory Johnson	12	Ezat Negahban	22	Hans Nissen
2	Frank Hole	13	Louis D. Levine	23	Matthew Stolper
3	Carol Kramer	14	Henry T. Wright	24	François Vallat
4	Alain Le Brun	15	Rémy Boucharlat	25	Daniel Ladiray
5	Geneviève Dollfus	16	Marie-Joseph Stève	26	Naomi Miller
6	David Stronach	17	Monique Kervran	27	Jean Perrot
7	Donald Whitcomb	18	Robert Wenke	28	Richard Redding
8	Firouz Bagherzadeh	19	Elizabeth Carter	29	Haydeh Eghbal
9	Pierre de Miroschedji	20	Guitty Azarpay	30	Bernadette Dremière
10	Helen Kantor	21	Pierre Amiet	31	Claire Hardy
11	Hermann Gasche	22	Hans Nissen		

1. The programme of the Mission archéologique de Suse was part of the 'Unités de recherche coopérative' no. 19 and no. 50 of the Centre national de la recherche scientifique (CNRS) concerning the prehistory of south-west Asia.

2. J. de Morgan had discovered Egyptian prehistory during the years he had spent in the Egyptian antiquities service (1892–1895), and was convinced of the importance of Middle Eastern influence on early Egyptian civilisation (MORGAN, 1900).

3. The first under the high authority of former minister Dr Mehran, and the second actively directed by Dr Firouz Bagherzadeh.

4. See the list of participants, p. 121.

5. Regular reports on the excavations were published from 1972 onwards in the *Cahiers da la DAFI*; there were also many poular articles between 1970 and 1985 (see the general bibliography under the names of the contributors to the present volume).

6. Pillet still adopted this view in his reconstructions (N. Chevalier, this volume, ch. III).

7. They consisted in raising the height of the walls by more than 1 m using mud brick.

8. R. Boucharlat, this volume, ch. XII.

9. A. Hesse, this volume, ch. V.

10. Ghirshman took this to be an 'Achaemenid villa', the excavation of which was not on the programme.

11. Thanks to help from the Fondation Patek, and especially to greater assistance from the Iranian government, research into the Islamic levels was carried out by Monique Kervran and Claire Hardy.

12. PERROT, 1974: 43.

13. D. LADIRAY, this volume, ch. VI.

14. This inscription adopts the Median word, also used at Persepolis for the Gate of Xerxes.

15. J. Perrot, this volume, ch. VI, pp. 205–206.

16. GHIRSHMAN, 1968b: 15–17.

17. GHIRSHMAN, 1968b: 15–17, fig. 39. While searching in this sector for direct access to the Apadana from the west, Ghirshman stumbled upon 'gigantic alterations of Susa's outer defences at a period after the Achaemenids'.

18. At 22 m south of the north-west bastion, at the foot of a retaining wall, M. Kaboli (KABOLI, 2000: 161–162) cleared 'a doorway of semi-circular plan' built of bricks measuring 11 x 9 cm. This feature was interpreted as the beginning of a passage and, supposedly, a stairway, leading to the terrace from a door that had not yet been cleared. Almost 1000 large and small fragments of glazed brick are said to have decorated this 'doorway'. They bore floral, geometric and human motifs; these last were arranged in two groups, one with figures of normal height, and the other with figures that were a third of the size. They could be compared with the figures that decorated the ramps leading to the Apadana at Persepolis. M. Kaboli also reported finding '80 fragments of stone balls 10 to 25 cm in diameter, carved from pieces of columns and column bases', as well as 'almost 500 fragments of arrow-heads and darts of Greek, rather than Iranian, manufacture'. This search for access to the Apadana terrace from the west seems to have been motivated by the inconvenience caused to visitors using the Darius Gate on the east to reach the Esplanade, and therefore approaching the Darius Statue with their backs to it. One could counter this argument by pointing out that Darius was dead and his statue was no longer a manifestation of his power; it was placed there by Xerxes in a demonstration of filial piety. As to the discovery of some structures, built of baked brick bonded with bitumen, at the foot of the western rampart and level with the Shaur river: while awaiting a more complete clearance one could suggest a probable relationship with the drains from the terrace.

19. R. Boucharlat, this volume, ch. XII.

20. See 'The small column bases' , pp. 434–435.

21. Darius' inscription qualifies it as *hadish*, and that of Xerxes, on the same building, as *taçara*.

22. In any case it seems preferable to the word 'pavilion'. R. Boucharlat suggests the word 'kiosque', from the Turkish ('pavillion de jardin').

23. In the Orient more than elsewhere perhaps, the properties of land are affirmed by the elevation of a gateway more than by that of an enclosure; the latter can even be absent.

108
**Albert Hesse taking measurements
on the Apadana terrace**

5 The Geophysical Survey of the Achaemenid Foundations

Albert Hesse

THE HISTORICAL CONTEXT OF A NASCENT DISCIPLINE: ARCHAEOMETRY

The surveying of archaeological sites using geophysics is part of a series of disciplines that has come to be called archaeometry. I first visited Susa in March 1968, but the term had been proposed a few years earlier (1958) by Martin Aitken on the suggestion of his colleague Christopher Hawkes.[1] Our British colleagues wanted to gather all the aspects of physics and chemistry capable of playing a part in the archaeological process under one nomenclature. However, the French translation of the term soon extended to the entirety of scientific methods that could contribute to the progress of archaeological understanding. Today we know the importance and the rapid expansion of this discipline which, at the time, was revolutionising the field with promising experiments and short-lived illusions. Some were highly technical; others consisted simply of examination by a fresh pair of eyes that had been trained in calculations, logic and scientific methods, but produced conclusions that could be of fundamental importance. Together they contributed to a real change in tools and archaeological reasoning which, despite reservations, could only evolve.

Initially I was employed by Centre national de la recherche scientifique (CNRS) to develop geophysical techniques, so I was naturally interested in other contributions I could bring to archaeology. Following several seasons in the Sudan with Jean Vercoutter,[2] a move to Susa was a logical step in the broadening of my archaeometric experiences. Certain far-sighted archaeologists were beginning to appreciate the innovations and it was with high expectations that I arrived at the mythical site of Susa to explore its potential. Surveying being my official speciality, this was the principal reason for my visit at the invitation of Jean Perrot.[3]

During my first season in 1968 I was only able to assess the potential of the site. Using a magnetometer, a day of arbitrary tests in the area around Roman

Ghirshman's excavations, at Site A on the mound of the Ville Royale, threw up a series of anomalies which were difficult to interpret in an uncertain context – perhaps Islamic remains.[4] At the end of this visit, it was decided to devote the next season's main survey efforts to the Achaemenid platforms, using electrical resistivity techniques which already seemed original and promising. In the meantime the temptation remained strong to busy myself with various other subjects relating to the field of Achaemenid archaeology, such as the marks and stamps on the baked bricks,[5] and their measurements, as well as those on the stone column bases.[6] My metrological curiosity was also aroused by much older stone hoes found at Jaffarabad, Bandebal and Jowi.[7]

I quickly realised that the three large stratigraphic excavations conducted at Susa and Jaffarabad offered an unparalleled opportunity to collect samples of pottery from areas covering a long period in time from the fifth to the third millennium BC and which, in the absence of very precise dating, at least presented the advantage of being situated very exactly in their relative chronology thanks to the stratigraphy. This opened up the (very broad) field of archaeomagnetism.[8] This we know is based on the variations in the orientation of terrestrial magnetic fields at a given place over time.[9] Finally, at the request of Firouz Bagherzadeh, director of the Iranian Centre for Archaeological Research, an Iranian technician Moheiddin Sadjadi came to Susa to train. He then joined me in taking a series of test and demonstration measurements at the sites of Bishapur and Firuzabad from 7 to 16 February 1974.[10] Difficulties arose first from interruptions to the survey timetable because of my limited availability. To this were added difficulties inherent in the terrain, particularly at Darius' Palace: where soundings were taking place, there were temporary piles of rubble; some walls had already been restored, and there was a brick-making workshop to facilitate this restoration; well-preserved floor tiles made a good barrier against the electrodes and so on. These were some of the obstacles that had to be overcome, or examined at a later date, in order to achieve as complete a coverage as possible, although still incomplete, of the explorable area. Finally, the events of 1978 did not allow us to finish the plans. We thought it would be interesting, however, to present them as they stand, but with a few improvements made possible through advances in information graphics.

SURVEY CONDITIONS

The first campaign gave us the opportunity to make several observations regarding the sites of Susiana in relation to geophysical survey.[11] They present some particular constraints, being like many sites in Mesopotamia and other places of occupation in the shape of artificial hills, otherwise known as 'tells' or 'tepes' depending on whether one uses Arabic or Persian.

The first of these observations results from stratification over a long period due to the piling up of occupation layers. Thus only the latest remains are accessible and can be examined in sufficient detail to satisfy the needs of significant archaeological interpretation, and to all practical purposes they hide the deeper remains. The second constraint comes from the fact that the main building material was mud brick. When the walls are destroyed, the upper layers of brick are washed away, pile up at the base of the walls and gradually cover them until an even layer is formed. As the sediment is of the same nature as the bricks, it shows practically no physical contrast with the wall: the difficulties of excavation in this context are well known, as are the risks of cutting through these mud-brick constructions without realising it. The absence of an appreciable difference in electrical resistivity or magnetic susceptibility must be added to the observations

109
Formation of a 'tell' through the destruction of the mud-brick walls
drawing by A.Hesse

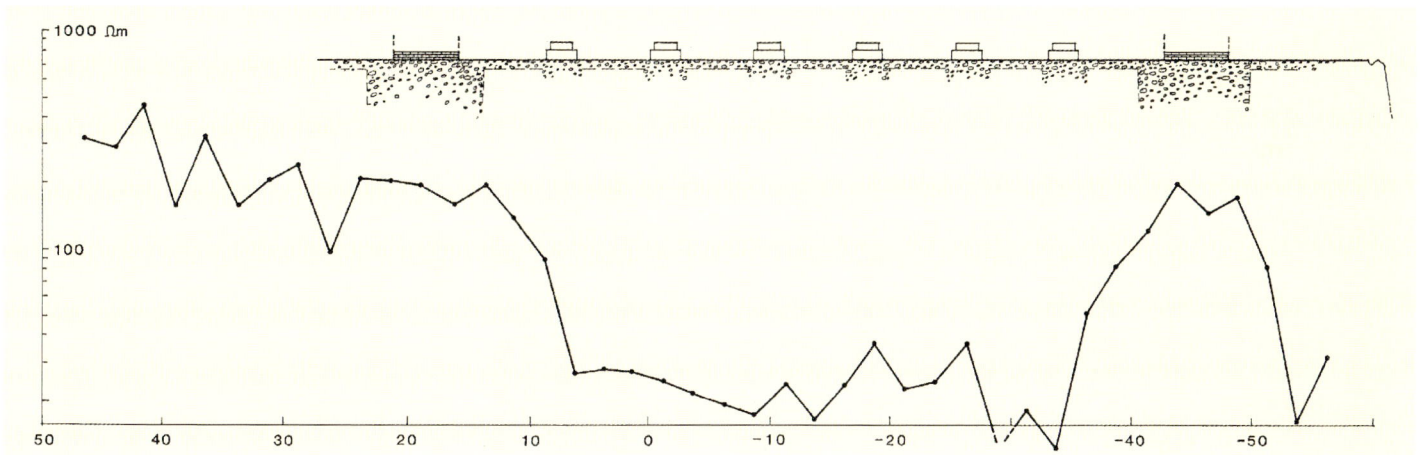

110
Resistivity profile of the Hypostyle Hall
drawing by A.Hesse

111
Foundations in the Palace of Darius

above, and they considerably limit the application of such methods in the geo-physical recording of sites in Susiana.[12]

Luckily at Susa itself, there were a few peculiarities which permitted, in the following cases, a satisfactory detection of certain remains in a somewhat un-orthodox manner.

The first and most original of these situations resulted from the fact that the Achaemenid architects felt the need to use stone for their foundations in order to ensure the seating of the imposing and palatial buildings of the site. Due to a lack of rock on site, imported stone was reserved for the columns or capitals. So they used a clever alternative: they filled pre-sunk pits with large volumes of gravel and pebbles, thus adding an interesting drainage function to the mechanical support under the walls of mud brick.[13] These foundations of shingle, whose plan matches that of the structures above, constitute an excellent marker for the measurement of resistivity: the stone itself and the large proportion of intervening voids are so many obstacles to the passage of electric current that they provoke characteristic spikes. The excavations have shown that the topology of these foundations was quite varied. For the purposes of this chapter we can content ourselves with two principal types. The first is the *galette* (pancake-shaped) foundation, as at the Shaur Palace,[14] where it was flat, of a uniform thickness of around 2 m and where it described the general plan of the palace by carefully skirting the courtyard spaces which, fairly logically, did not have them. The other form looked more like a proper foundation and was sunk deeply for the bases of the main construction walls; we found several examples at the Palace of Darius where the building works were of another magnitude and in a different situation with regard to the water table. In this sector the excavations also identified a third type of foundation called 'en chemise',[15] but we will not discuss this here because the large size of the quadripole used to measure the resistivity did not allow them to be mapped clearly.

The second of these situations is more conventional: it concerns only the re-mains of baked-brick structures. Other than in the Islamic constructions already mentioned in the introduction, this material is not present in the Palace of Darius except as floor tiles or in double courses as wall footings,[16] but a specific search for them was not considered necessary because of their small estimated contribution to the establishment of a geophysical anomaly: the small number of courses and the often incomplete nature of the tiles turned them literally into sieves with regard to the electrical current emitted into the earth for the resistivity measurements. None of the plans drawn, moreover, ever gave a definite indication of their detection, in comparison with the effect of the gravel pits. Indeed, these extremely flat structures, which were shallow in proportion to their width, are barely detectable using magnetometry since, despite the well-known magnetic response to baked clay, this method is better suited to vertical structures with greater depth than width.

TECHNICAL ASPECTS OF MEASUREMENT

These explorations did not happen until later, immediately after those of the Shaur Palace,[17] where there were fewer problems and information-rich data. After this the work was more piecemeal for the reasons stated above.[18]

All the measurements obviously suffered due to a lack of continuity. They also lacked a grid reference system; ignorant as we were at the start of the eventual success of the enterprise, we did not foresee the work extending over such a wide area. Each one of the plans was drafted immediately at Susa, from the record of the measurements and manual transfer of the iso-resistivity curves (i.e. resistivity contour curves) onto graph paper; the topographical reference of each established

112
Serge Renimel at Susa
Copying the measurements onto graph paper
by tracing the isovalue curves

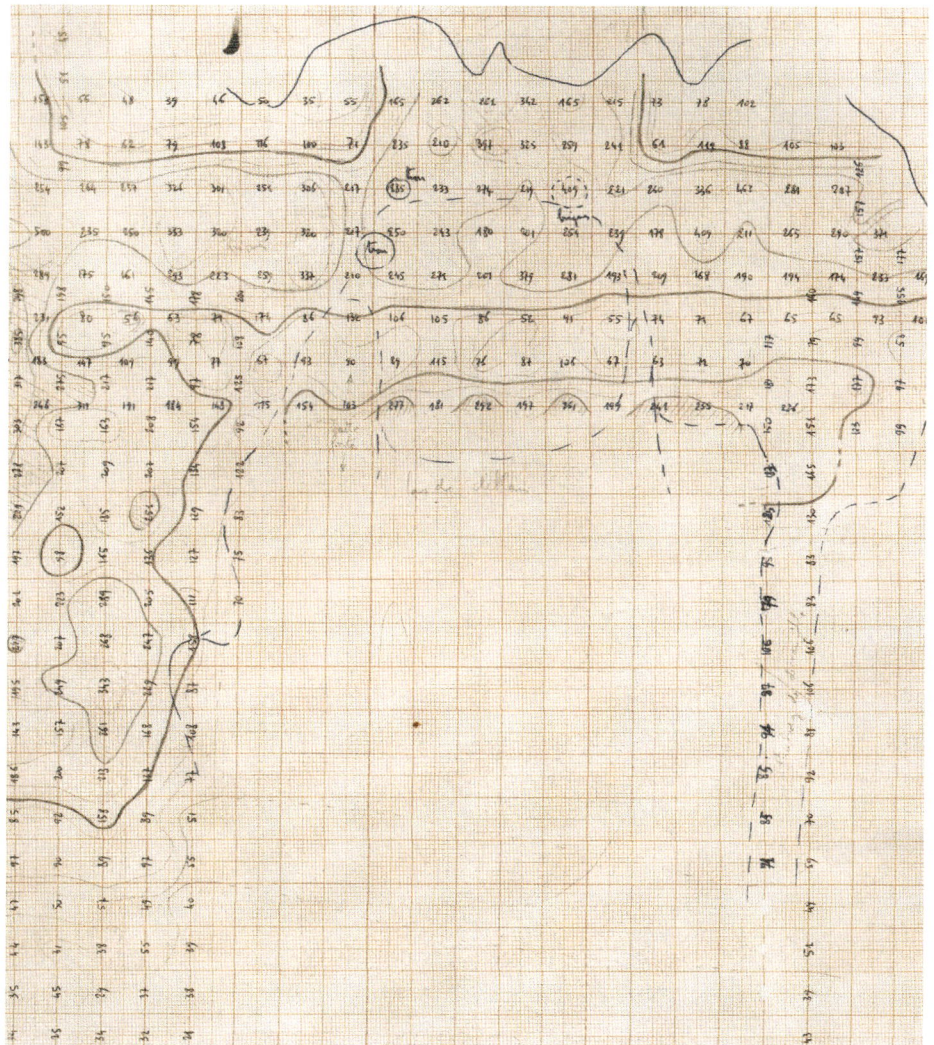

113
Example of an original map
of the terrain south of court C3

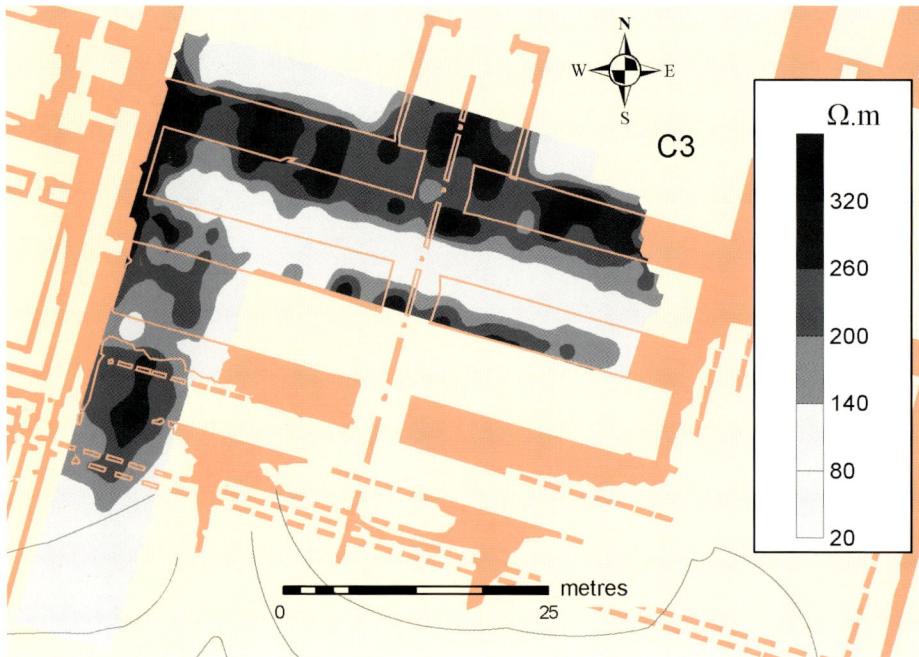

114
**Redrawing of the original map
of the area south of court C3**
drawing by A.Hesse

115
**Composite plan of the resistivity maps
of the Palace of Darius**
produced by Cécelia Bobée

network was made either by linking it to the excavation grid or to the well-preserved or recently restored remains, relying on the still unfinished plans of the Palace of Darius by Daniel Ladiray. This allowed us to draft a first incomplete and therefore provisional plan of the survey. Thirty years later, it has not been easy to bring this work to a close because it has been necessary to insert the last series of measurements which remained, after 1977, in a pretty obsolete manuscript form, waiting for the final publication which only now sees the light of day. It was not thought realistic, or wise, however, to revisit the interpretation of all the data, written by hand on this often incoherent topographical network, both in position and often in spatial density. An exception has been made, however, for one detail, which has been given, for example, a more modern graphic treatment. It must be noted that the illustration of the results benefits hugely from the progress in information technology, because it has been possible to present the old resistivity plans in a remarkably readable way by superimposing the architectural plans.[19]

The first issue normally to be tackled by a surveyor using the resistivity method is the distance between the electrodes, since this will regulate not only the depth of the investigation but also the final resolution of the plan: a short distance means a small quadripole, which will only penetrate to a shallow depth but will allow, with a great number of measurements and so a fair amount of time, a good spatial definition of the anomalies; a large quadripole will give the opposite results. From experience, the quadripole of 3 x 1 m (Wenner array, a = 1 m), used at the time on a large number of European sites to establish what lay beneath a layer of arable earth 20 to 40 cm deep, was not adaptable to the exploration of the gravel pits that formed the foundations. It would at best have identified only the surface differences in the Palace of Darius, caused by the excavations and spoil heaps from previous campaigns. The process of 'electrical sounding' whereby one takes a series of measurements at one point, with an increasing distance between the electrodes, generally gives a fairly precise idea of the width of the quadripole best suited to the task. The choice is even more pertinent when one can make two soundings, one on an already identified part of the structure to be explored, the other outside it. This was possible at the Shaur Palace,[20] where the existence of the *galette* foundations provided the necessary 'tabularity' (i.e. a series of horizontal strata with different resistivities) needed by the theory, whilst at the Palace of Darius it was not. A few electrical soundings were nevertheless made here without any assurance that they were sited in a satisfactory position in relation to the structures, nor that they would come up with the appropriate shapes. For want of a better choice, the same distance of 2.5 m, which had just given us excellent results at the Shaur Palace, was used.

Several partial plans drafted over the course of the excavation campaigns have finally been put together in two places (to the south of the Residence and at the Hypostyle Hall); all the others are in distinct sectors. These results will therefore be analysed sector by sector, progressing from east to west and south to north, without consideration for their date of execution mentioned above.

THE PROPYLAEUM SECTOR

This exploration was undertaken without prior knowledge of the remains that were found under the artificial level, already mentioned above, at the western extremity of Ghirshman's 'site A' of the Ville Royale.[21] The area considered here, although small (one quarter of a hectare), was better suited to tests as it had been cleared to a level compatible with that of the Achaemenid level on the Apadana tell. Furthermore, a collapse of pebbles visible in the section above the Ghirshman excavation was an attractive clue.

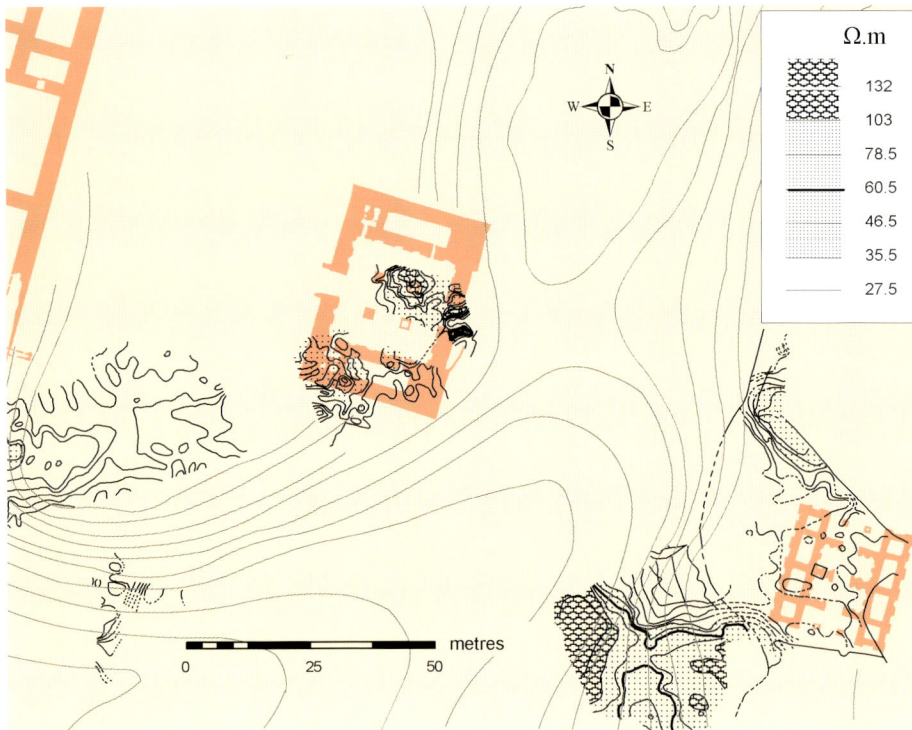

116
**Resistivity map of the
Propylaeum and Darius Gate**
produced by Cécilia Bobée

A first series of measurements in 1972 had shown, in the northern part of the sector, a clear anomaly, which seemed to extend under the unexcavated levels of the tell. The continuation of the exploration to the south produced a second anomaly of the same type, widespread but with no clear geometric shape. The relatively weak resistivities of the anomalies (60–130 Ω.m) did not suggest a mass of gravel constituting a foundation of which we had been able to evaluate the specific resistivity at near 500 Ω.m in a well-drained location such as on the Apadana tell (those on the Shaur are more or less saturated with water from the water table and do not go, for their part, above 200 Ω.m).[22]

THE DARIUS GATE SECTOR

Following the discovery of the monumental statue of Darius in 1972, Serge Renimel was hired to examine the context of the excavation. He put together two small, unconnected, plans which had been drafted using the same level as those chosen for the Propylaeum (covered with black dots above 35 Ω.m). These conveyed a low level of resistivity, much lower than what we would find further on in the Residence and the Hypostyle Hall. At the extremity of the small plan drafted slightly to the west, it was satisfying to see the resistivity rise to the level of 150 Ω.m on the approach to the south-western limit of the Residence. It is worth noting that the higher values corresponded to the top of an anomaly which, parallel to the contour lines that described the slope of the neighbouring gully, ended in an elongated promontory in a north-easterly direction, that is to say, towards the Darius Gate. This was not compatible with the very rectilinear plan of the palace complex and can be explained as reflecting the structural complexity of the terrace embankment or the scree slopes of gravel caused by erosion.

THE SOUTHERN SECTOR OF THE RESIDENCE

Things were very different as soon as, a little to the west, we examined the collection of plans which, at the end of the day, covered the whole of the south

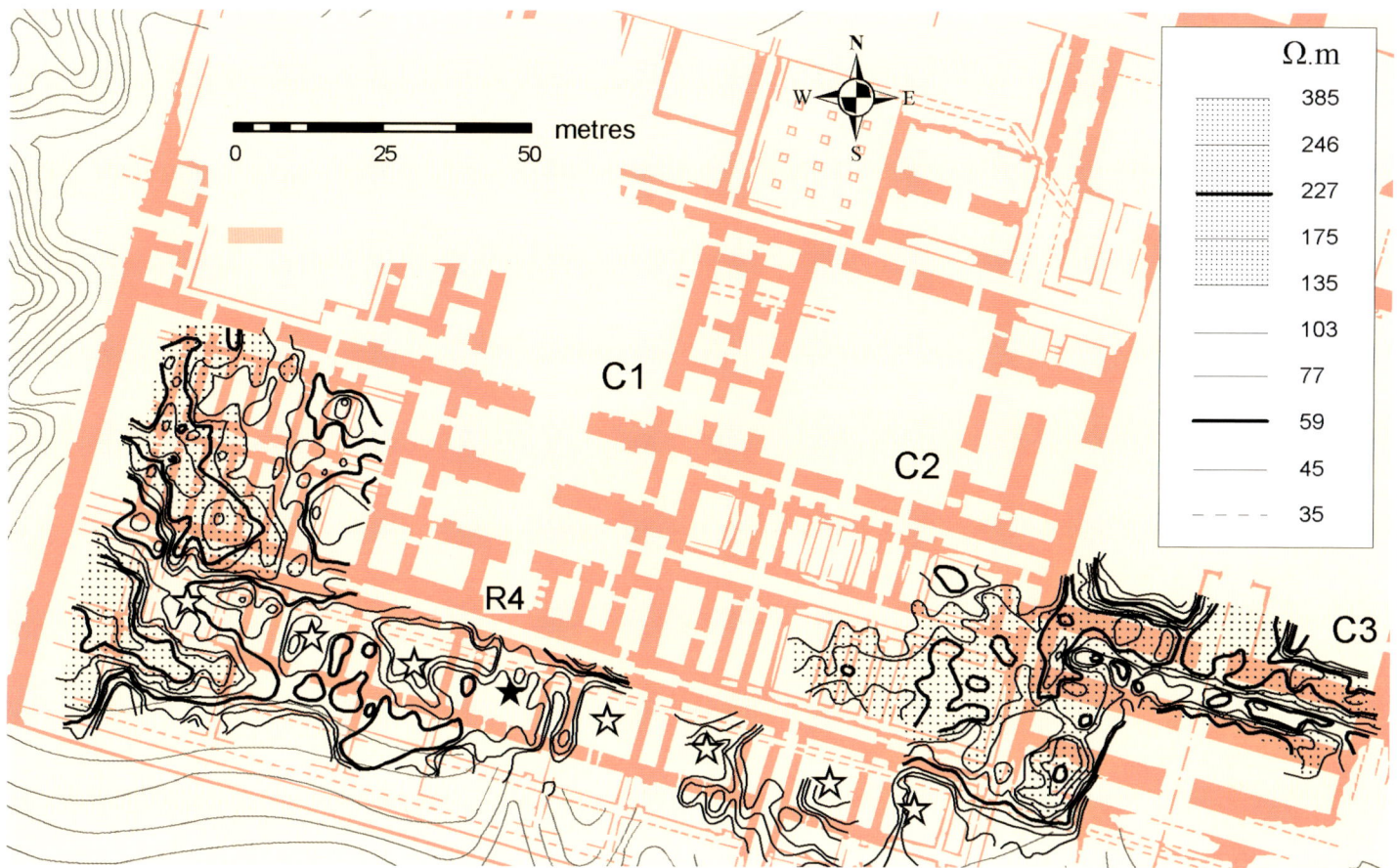

117

Resistivity map of the southern sector of the Royal Residence
produced by by Cécelia Bobée

of the Residence.[23] The first plan drawn up concerned the south of Court c3. Realised as early as 1971, it was welcomed because it was the legibility of this plan that led to the continued exploration of the palace.[24] The commentary here is almost superfluous: one could distinguish a very good anomaly running east–west, very regular in its width (8 to 10 m, a resistivity of 212 Ω.m) and in amplitude (above 300 and as high as 600 Ω.m). It corresponded to the position of the wall that enclosed Court c3 to the south and, although incomplete, clearly showed the upward curve towards the centre of the court in the axis of the doorway. Obviously, the wall, which has disappeared, was not responsible for the anomaly and it was its foundations that were revealed.[25] On the left of the plan, to the west, we can see a sharp right angle of high resistivity heading south. Here we are not distinguishing the outline of the walls but the signal given off by a zone of high resistivity which corresponded with all the foundations and the row of stores of the Royal Residence.

Immediately to the south of the long anomaly described above, we find the northern fringe of another anomaly which is exactly parallel to it and running east–west; it was not possible to continue the measurements and obtain its width, but it obviously corresponds to the second of the three walls that are to the south of Court c3. It does appear, however, to be interrupted at its extremities in a not altogether symmetrical manner and is not linked to a sharp angle of resistivity such as that we have just described.[26]

Further towards the west, the survey was extended to the entire width of the Residence, right to the edge of the terrace on the Shaur. The final plan is the result of piecing together several small surveys undertaken in 1973 and 1974. Control measurements were taken on profiles common to the different plans, showing very weak variations in register from one season to the next, in the same place. This result was to be expected, as the quadripole (a = 2.5 m) investigations were mostly deeper than the levels influenced by surface humidity. In any event, these

THE SECTOR TO THE EAST OF THE HYPOSTYLE HALL

Although the recorded results turned out, in the end, to be a complete sideline in relation to the initial objective, the low resistivity plan of this sector, below the portico and the Hypostyle Hall, fits in perfectly with the operations conducted at the palace. At the time, one could observe, on the surface and on the edge of the terrace, several Achaemenid architectural blocks, whole and broken.[31] A geophysical survey had been requested and measurements were recorded by Serge Renimel before my arrival in January 1974. The plan showed a high reading over an area 5–10 m in diameter, which was more than three times higher than in the surrounding area. It was too great to be an answer to the question asked, unless one imagines an improbable pile of architectural debris. The curiosity generated by this anomaly did not lessen, and the strange results obtained were worth the wait: when the archaeologists excavated they discovered a pottery kiln dating to the fourth millennium BC.

Pierre de Miroschedji was given the responsibility of excavating this kiln.[32] If we look at the kiln's dimensions (1.4 m at its widest), we can see that it was not the only thing responsible for the extent of this anomaly. With regard to its size, it is very likely that the mass of baked clay of the firing chamber itself as well as its contents are a sufficient explanation. The contents were made up of debris from the floor of the firing chamber as well as from the roof of the kiln, together with a vast amount of pottery, mostly coarse bowls. These materials clearly contributed to the high resistivity of the place, the contribution of the ashes and the other fine materials used in the infill being less certain. The extent of the anomaly can no doubt be explained by the role of the ditches (A and B, but excluding the small later ditch C) which, though not distinguishable on the resistivity plan, were also abundantly filled with ceramic material. This discovery was extremely unusual, possibly even unique, leading to its rapid publication.[33] It is important, however, not to generalise by making geophysical surveying a rule in searching for this kind of structure. Magnetometry remains, in principle, the method best adapted to the specific search for structures relating to combustion such as kilns and furnaces.[34]

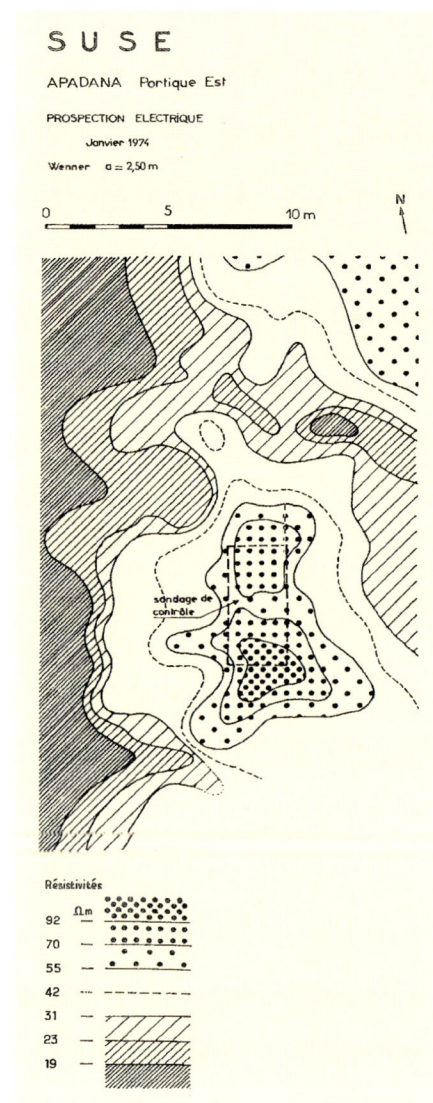

119
Resistivity map of the fourth millennium kiln to the east of the Hypostyle Hall
produced by Cécelia Bobée

1. HESSE, 1990.

2. HESSE, 1975a.

3. Although other subjects drew my attention, from then on Jean Perrot and some other archaeologists to whom I am very grateful, generously allowed me free rein. Thus it was, that between the years 1968 and 1977 (excluding 1969 and 1976), I was able to go ten times to Iran, and for eight of those years I was able to work at Susa, during the winter seasons of the Délégation archéologique française en Iran (DAFI), on sites which can be considered to have been, according to Jean Perrot, true 'field laboratories' (HESSE, 1975b and 1989).

4. See note 7.

5. N. Daucé, this volume, ch. x.

6. HESSE, 1972.

7. Geophysics remained, however, my principal occupation, and with the help of some colleagues, I was able to conduct work not only on Achaemenid foundations but on other topics such as Islamic buildings made of baked brick. As the latter are more recent, they are naturally more favourably located in the upper stratigraphic levels that were the first to be identified in the excavations. Thus, in 1974, Serge Renimel was able to draw up a magnetic plan in connection with Monique Kervran's excavation of a vast area on the periphery of the mosque cleared by R. Ghirshman on the mound known as the Tell of the Artisans. The resulting plan, which has only been very partially published (HESSE, 1979a), reveals walls set at right-angles according to an urban grid whose details are difficult to grasp. This is either because fallen bricks have affected the measurements, and blurred the outlines of the buildings, or because, due to the low magnetic latitude, the anomalies in the magnetic field had two lobes of almost equivalent amplitude, one maximum and one minimum, that were relatively difficult to represent in a way that could be read by an excavator without the use of a system known as 'polar reduction'. The latter was already well known at the time, but was difficult to apply to a large number of measurements without the computer facilities that are now at our disposal.

8. THELLIER, 1966.

9. A programme of sample collection for archaeomagnetism, followed by measurement at the Saint-Maure-des-Fossés laboratory took place regularly from that time, under the auspices of Alain Lecaille, until the last season in 1977, and has resulted in the publication of some informative notes (HESSE and LECAILLE, 1974; HESSE, 1975c; HESSE, 1987 and HESSE, 1989) and an article (DOLLFUS and HESSE, 1977). We had even ambitiously begun to broaden the scope of this programme by gathering samples from other prehistoric sites around Susa (Choga Mish and Haft Tepe), other parts of Iran and even outside Iran: Tepe Malyan and Mureybet in 1974, then Ganj-e Dareh, Godin Tepe, Seh-Gabi and Sagzabad in 1975 with the help of Geneviève Dollfus. Unfortunately, various unavoidable problems not only interrupted the project, but especially compromised the use of the information that had been acquired, and ruined the hopes vested in the project.

10. HESSE, 1975c.

11. For all that relates to the principle and the technical aspect of the geophysical prospection methods, see HESSE, 1978, HESSE, 2000, and SCOLLAR et al., 1990.

12. This was true at the time of our tests when we only had proton magnetometers at our disposal, with a relatively low sensitivity (1nT) which was subject to perturbations in diurnal variations of the terrestrial magnetic field, due to the lack of a differentially mounted double probe. Since then, cesium magnetometers and magnetometers of the *fluxgate* type with two superimposed probes have become available and allow far more precise measurements to be taken, so that under favourable conditions remains with very weak magnetic contrast can be detected.

13. R. Boucharlat, ch. XII.

14. R. Boucharlat, ch. XII.

15. D. Ladiray, ch. VI.

16. The only major exception is the thick wall of baked bricks along the west side of the Apadana terrace.

17. R. Boucharlat, this volume, ch. XII.

18. They can, however, be summarised as follows: Hypostyle Hall and south of Court c3 of the Residence (second half of March 1971); Residence, up to the south-east corner and on a platform that was cleared to the west of Ghirshman excavations on the 'Ville Royale' tell (end of February to mid-March 1972); Additions to the west of the Residence, and close to 'chantier A' (for a few days in February–March 1973, together with Serge Renimel); Additional measurements at the periphery of the preceding plans and resistivity soundings (over a dozen days between the end of January and the beginning of March 1974, together with Mohieddin Sadjadi); Additional measurement at the Palace of Darius (some days in February and March 1975). The material used for these measurements was extremely simple, for good reason: the more complex equipment with automatic recording that we now use did not then exist; transport was limited, because of weight, to a small resistivity meter (either a Tellohm or a Norma), a small hand-commutator to accelerate communication with the various extensions and the necessary lengths of cable. The electrodes were iron rods used for concrete and were made on site by the local blacksmith from Shush-i Daniel.

19. I particularly wish to thank here all those who have helped me in the preparation of this publication, especially C. Bobbée and J. Tabbagh without whom I would not have been able to superimpose the resistivity plans onto the plans of the Palace; P. Briant, who provided me with the digitised records of these plans; R. Boucharlat and J. Perrot for re-reading this text and for their editorial advice concerning its contents and illustrations.

20. R.Boucharlat, ch. XII.

21. Some long sections, illustrating work through the upper parts of this tell, will be drawn up later, but they do not show any anomalies that might indicate foundations. The chances of finding any were probably, in any case, minimal because any later remains of possibly Achaemenid date are buried beneath later Parthian, Sassanian and/or Islamic levels.

22. However, we know that the size of an anomaly is not a sufficient indication of its extent, since a layer of silt above it will act as a conductor and can reduce its impact considerably. The criterion of form is a greater constraint and it must be admitted that, objectively, we could not find much in these anomalies to recognise the remains of foundations on an orthogonal plan. The discovery in the excavation of the remains of various periods and the remains of a Propylaeum founded on a system of foundations apparently far more complex than those which were observed elsewhere (Dieulafoy, ch. VI and D. Ladiray, ch. VI), explain, no doubt, the lack of legibility on the resistivity plan.

23. This sector had functioned as a workshop full of bricks for the restoration of the walls. Once these bricks had been removed, it was possible to complete the exploration.

24. Its legibility was a good reason for publishing it as an example, in a widely distributed volume (SCOLLAR et al. 1990), without waiting for the present publication with its broader remit. As it remains a reference publication, it was tempting to enter these data into a computer and show not only the quality of the depictions but also the even greater readability of the images that can be produced nowadays.

25. As with every geophysical anomaly, we are not dealing with an architectural sketch, such as can be extrapolated from what appears in archaeological soundings. Nevertheless, in this case we can appreciate the interest of a resistivity plan which visualises the physical reality of what is present below the ground before any archaeological sounding has taken place. We must, however, avoid using a series of dots to extend what is always the somewhat hypothetical nature of the results.

26. Two soundings at this point reveal the presence of pebbles, but do not exactly coincide with the weaker resistivity values. We therefore remain uncertain as to whether we are dealing with a partial erosion of the foundations or with an intentional interruption of the mass of pebbles.

27. In accordance with common usage, the measurement grid is generally given the same value as **a**, that is 2.5 m on the walls, whose height had not yet been restored at this stage. The grid was reduced to profiles of 10 m so as to navigate between the surviving column bases at the centre of the Hypostyle Hall. As a result, there was no way that the small foundations of these column bases could appear, either in the Hall, or in the western, northern or eastern peristyles.

28. Jéquier's Trench 9 (see the plan in MECQUENEM, 1947 and N. Chevalier, ch. III, fig. 51).

29. It is also difficult to take into account the possible restorations claimed by Artaxerxes II in a text discussed by J. Perrot, among others, because it is so imprecise (J. Perrot, ch. VII).

30. The other anomalies seem interesting, but their layout leaves much to be desired; they do not describe the forms of construction that might have completed the Hypostyle Hall, nor do they coincide convincingly with the fragments of plan recovered with difficulty during excavations in this sector. The only firm conclusion is that this area is very disturbed.

31. Early photographs show a greater number, notably two capitals.

32. MIROSCHEDJI, 1976.

33. HESSE, 1980.

34. SCOLLAR et al., 1990.

In the hollow left on the perimeter of the Apadana by the defenders of Susa in the third century BC (where the columns of the porticoes, whose fragments are being collected, fell) the geophysical prospecting located a potters' kiln of the fourth millennium BC excavated by P. Miroschedji

6 The Archaeological Results

Daniel Ladiray

This palace which is at Susa, I built it. The materials for it were brought from afar. And the earth was dug deep until it reached hard earth. When it had been completely dug, then its foundations were made of gravel.
DSf § 7, 20–22, VALLAT

I N 1969, the first objective of the Franco-Iranian programme was to protect the meagre remains, whilst still allowing them to be visible, of what was then called the 'Palace of Darius'. Only a shadow of it remained: a few column bases from the Hypostyle Hall, a few plaster floors, a picture distorted by the deep excavations of Roland de Mecquenem right across the courtyard. Our first concern was to find the palace walls using the published plans, so as to raise these walls one metre high in mud brick, whilst always being conscious of protecting them against rain. These operations, under the direction of the mission's chief mason Abbas Ettemad, needed to be accompanied by a graphic diary of photographs and records, but without the necessity of establishing a grid over that already formed by the rooms of the palace. Even so, the discoveries were so important that it became indispensable to have recourse to a more complete system of recording, let alone for the new excavations that were being conducted at the gate on the Ville Royale mound. The excavation of the Palace of Artaxerxes II, on the opposite bank of the Shaur, was independently directed by Rémy Boucharlat.

The purpose here is not to give a detailed account of the operations conducted on the Apadana tell, for which separate reports have been published, notably in the *Cahiers de la Délégation archéologique française en Iran*; furthermore, graphic and photographic documentation is accessible at the University of Paris X–Nanterre as well as in Iran. This chapter presents the results of an analysis by category of the archaeological results concerning the infrastructure and the surface remains of the Residence, the audience hall and the other building works of Darius at Susa.

THE FOUNDATIONS

The old Elamite tell which accommodated the Residence and the Hypostyle Hall was levelled; the earth taken from the summit was redistributed around the edges where it was contained by strong, beaten earth and mud-brick walls. A platform was established 18 m above the waters of the River Shaur, a place to build on, with courtyards and gardens, an area of more than 100,000 m². The problem of foundations varied according to whether they were above the infill, at the periphery, or on top of the Elamite tell, whose millennia of levels (Susa was founded around 4000 BC) formed a solid core at the heart and centre of the platform. These levels rest on a natural rise in the terrain which reaches some 10 m above the level of the river in the central sector; their depth was around 7 m. In this sector, for each wall and for each column, a deep trench was cut, often down to virgin soil, then filled with gravel as was indicated in the foundation charter; on this solid gravel base a double course of bricks for the walls or the supporting stone for the column bases was laid. It consisted of seating the structure solidly on the soil bed, the rock in the earth, the hard earth, as was written in the foundation charter.

The filling of the trenches was done in an orderly fashion; the amount of gravel was reduced to the minimum required; it was controlled, where necessary, by small mud-brick walls in each trench which were raised in time with the gravel, the space between the wall and the angled sides of the trench being infilled. At ground level, the foundations only exceeded the seating of the wall by a few dozen centimetres. The area was levelled on the surface by laying gravel to an average depth of 60 cm. In the area of the Hypostyle Hall, where the subsoil was particularly compact (with earth, walls and floor tiles), the foundation trenches for the columns were vertical, without corrective walls.[1] They were individual and measured 4.8 x 4.8 m. For each column a large stone slab rested on the gravel.

121
Schematic cross-section through the
Apadana terrace

122
The mud-brick walls of the Residence rested on a foundation of baked bricks placed above a trench lined with mud-brick walls and filled with gravel

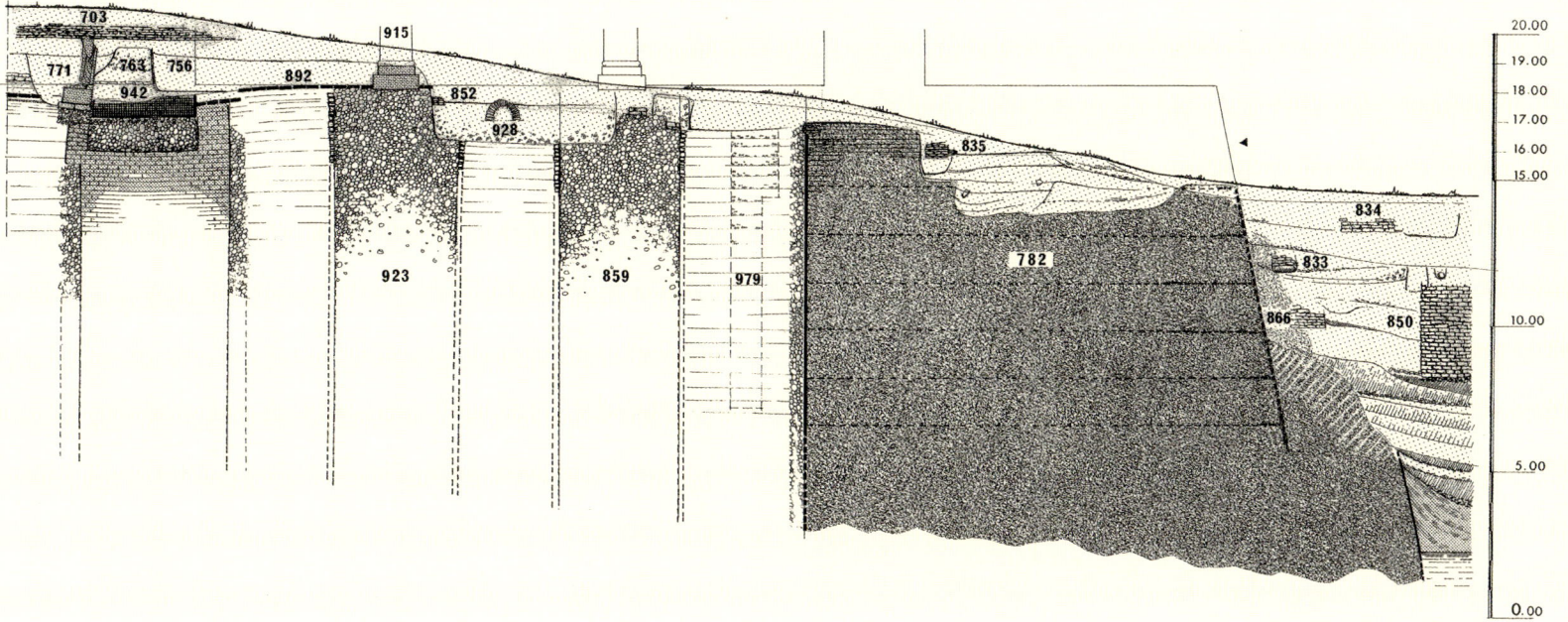

123
Cross-section through the foundations of the Darius Gate
and the retaining wall of the Apadana terrace.

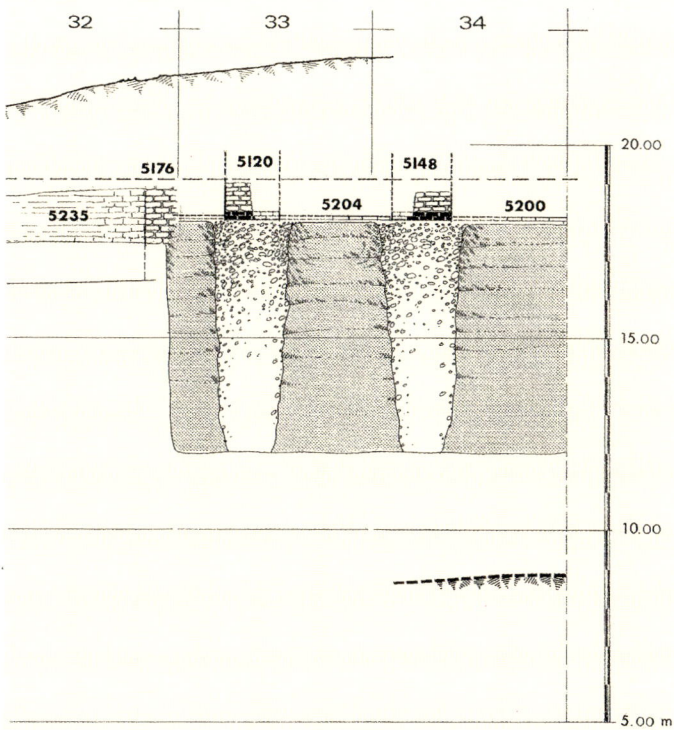

124
Cross-section through the Propylaeum
foundations

125
Section through the Apadana terrace embankment in the area
of the Darius Gate
The earth, which was probably taken from the levelling of the highest part
of the tell, was laid in roughly 60 cm layers (marked with white arrows)

Passage **1460**

Mur **847**

Mur **846**

Sondage **1443**

126
Cross-sections through the large cistern south of the Residence
The baked bricks, bonded with bitumen, were looted from below floor level leading to the collapse on the surface of the walls and the floor tiles

The different types of foundation

The foundations differed according to the nature of the subsoil and according to the weight they had to carry. At the Darius Gate, it was the retaining wall of the Apadana platform, with a width of 22 m at its base, that served as a foundation for the east wall of the gate. The other walls of this monument, raised above the level of the backfill, rested on unusual foundations – for each wall a strong mud-brick wall, 5 m thick, and each flanked by its own gravel sleeves, retained by small mud-brick walls, down to natural soil at a depth of 7 m. This large basement wall had a 'channel' about 1 m deep dug into its top; this channel was filled with gravel and it was on this heightened gravel that the walls of the gate were raised, without an intermediate course of baked bricks, but separated from the foundation by a layer of bitumen. The bases of the four columns of the Central Hall were each raised on a pebble foundation of 4 x 4 m, also bordered with mud bricks made from virgin soil. The totality of these structures lies buried in the regular layers of infill.

Another technique was used at the Propylaeum on the Ville Royale mound.[2] For the foundations of this building, which measured 24 x 24 m, a ditch was dug first measuring 25 x 25 m and 6 m deep; the outline of the structure had been traced in some form on the bottom of the ditch and raised with particular care to the surface (nearly 18 m) by using compacted *pisé* earth for the rooms and gravel for the walls; there are no intermediary walls here. As at the Residence, the walls rest on a double course of baked bricks. The extreme care accorded to the Propylaeum foundations, as indeed to the whole building and its decoration, could indicate a later date. Xerxes dedicated the building, but he attributed its construction to his father.[3]

Underground drainage

The drainage of rainwater must have been a problem in a region where the spring thunderstorms, often violent, could precipitate thousands of cubic metres of water in a matter of minutes onto the Apadana. We often wondered about this, but the question was answered towards the end of our excavations when, in one of the apartments reserved for the royal family, a small drain was noticed. It was made of baked bricks bonded with bitumen, and it led towards what until then we had thought was, and described as, a long 'fault line' running east–west, parallel to passageway R4. This 'fault line', and others marked by the collapse of the ground or the brick courses, we first interpreted as a sign of the fragility of the mud-brick infrastructures.[4] I hope that Darius' engineers may forgive us for having doubted their ingenuity; we swallowed our pride when the perfection of this drainage system was finally brought to light. Cleared first at one point, the 'fault line' soon

127
Small channel made from baked bricks (1426) flowing into the large cistern south of the Residence in the 'princely apartments' sector

128
Collapsed walls and floor tiles in the trench
filled by the tank south of the Residence

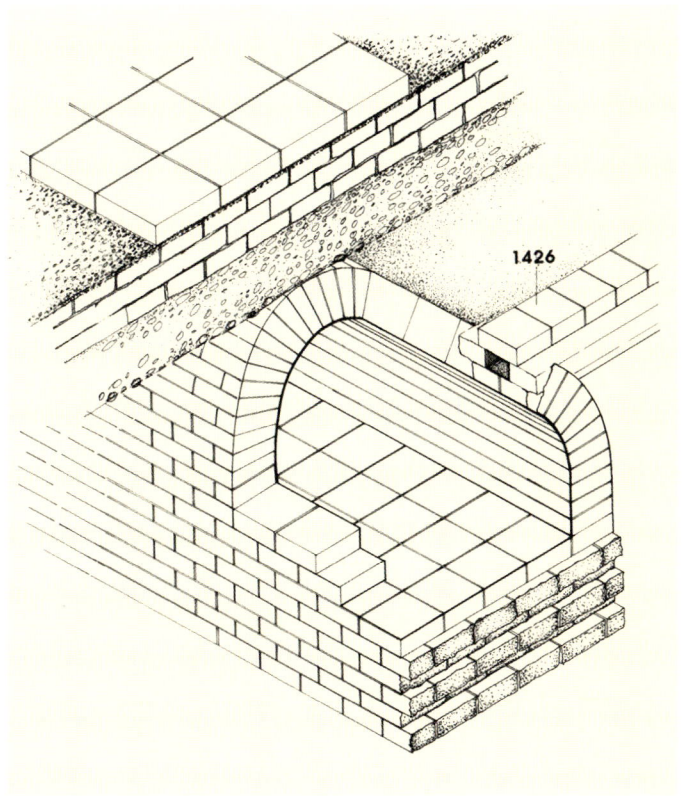

129
Reconstruction of a large drain
drawings D. Ladiray

130
**Plan of the drains of the Residence
with their intakes in the courtyards**
The stone supports for the door sockets are
in red. It should be noted that each sector
of the Residence could isolate itself behind
closed doors

appeared under the floors of the Residence, in the form of a powerful sewer system of baked brick bound with bitumen, vaulted, resting on a thick sub-floor. We noticed then that the line of the drains followed the axis of the passageways and the doors or a parallel one. This would provide us with an indication when we were doubtful of the existence of a passageway. For instance, in the north-west corner of the East Court (C3), in an area where it had already appeared logical to place a door leading directly to the Apadana, in this very corner was the water supply for the courtyard.[5] It was the same for each court and on the Esplanade. There are two main-drains on the Esplanade, close to the walls of the Residence. The first (main-drain I) also served the apartments of the southern sector.[6] Main-drain II also led from the Esplanade; its intake was to the north of the entrance. It had to cross the East Court (C3) before dividing, one branch towards the north-west, to service the apartments of the northern sector of the Residence, and the other branch towards the west, under building complex P2, between the Central Court (C2) and the West Court (C1), from which it collected water before heading towards Court A.[7]

Stone door sills and other elements of the infrastructure

To the north of the 'East Court' (C3) Mecquenem had uncovered, at about 2 m under the floor of the court, some 'foundation stones' which he thought belonged to an older 'palace'. It was, according to the description he gives of the first stone found,[8] 'a stone foundation, formed by two sections of cylinder, the flat sides, face up, were joined together with lead along the edges and formed a square with sides of around 2 m in length, with a central circular socket of about 1 m in diameter and 10 cm deep. In an east–west trench, seven similar foundations were

131
Stone supports
Discovered by Mecquenem, these bases were interpreted by him as evidence of an older palace which he attributed to Darius, while that which he was clearing above he thought the work of Artaxerxes II. They were, in truth, stones destined to hold the bases of eight large 'masts' below ground level, flanking the north face of the East Court (C3). These bases were formed by two adjoining sections of cylinder. The diameter of the sockets was close to 1 m.

132
Stone supports for the hinge sockets in a doorway on the northern side of the East Court (C3)

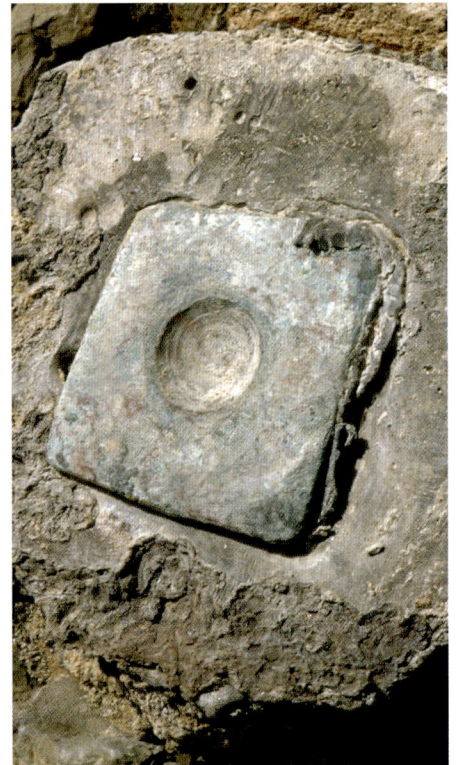

133
Bronze door sockets fixed with lead on stones for the doorway to the King's Apartments, giving onto the passageway R4
The blocks designed to support the door sockets often have a flat surface in the middle of which a square cutaway housed a bronze socket attached with lead. Half cylinders were joined to act as foundations for the columns of the hypostyle hall or to firmly hold the bases of the large masts flanking the northern façade of the East Court (C3).

Stone support for the hinge socket of a door to the antechamber of the Royal Apartments
The flattened surface shows traces of chiselling

uncovered; there was therefore a line of foundations; the two extremities were at 45° to the others and the distance of their axes to the neighbouring foundation was 10.5 m, whilst the following axes were 6.95 m apart'. These stones with the round sockets had seemed to him, by being underground, to be older than the columns of the Hypostyle Hall which he attributed to Artaxerxes II in accordance with their inscription.[9] In fact in c3 they could not be column bases (these do not need to be held in a round socket); more realistically they are the seating for the bases of large masts (a diameter of 1 m at the base suggests a shaft of 15–20 m in height) placed here, following the example of those to be found, in the Mesopotamian and Egyptian tradition, in front of temples. These stones were initially associated with the foundations of the north wall of the court.

A fixing for a hinge socket cut into a stone block, perhaps originally destined to be a column drum

The supporting stones for the door sockets

The identification of the doors (as opposed to simple passageways) was indispensable to the understanding of internal movement and even the function of various parts of the buildings. The bronze-covered wooden doors had disappeared a long time ago,[10] but the sockets remained in place as huge stone blocks sometimes weighing several tons. Often these supporting blocks had sunk under their own weight, thus being missed in the rapid earth clearance which seemed to be the hallmark of the earliest archaeologists. Each of these blocks encased a small bronze cup (the socket), sealed with lead, in which the door's hinge-post turned.[11] The support stones had often been deprived of their precious metal. It would seem that originally the stones, which are more or less cylindrical, had been destined to become column drums (some have a diameter of 1.4 m and a length of nearly 2 m); they could have been abandoned as they were during the course of their manufacture, because they were deemed unsuitable or due to breakage. They were placed on their sides, and into their flattened top the square cavity holding the bronze socket was carved. The dimensions and appearance of these support stones were not linked to the importance of the door that they fitted; thus in the Hypostyle Hall, the supports were just great blocks of stone. This contrasts with their quality at the entrance to the Residence, at the doorway from the 'East Court' (c3) to the Central Court (c2), and in the doorway leading from the latter to the Honour Court (c1); also in the King's Apartments, at the doorway between the vestibule and the antechamber; in short, along the obligatory path from the entrance gate of the Residence to the 'King's chamber'.

Other foundation stones

Here we will discuss several other stones buried at ground level. They are to be found respectively at the centre of the Hypostyle Hall, at the entrance to the Residence and in the King's Apartments.

In the central alley of the Hypostyle Hall, between the bases of the two southern rows of columns, there was a big square stone slab made up of two half-cylinders which, together, had the same dimensions as a column base (2.4 x 2.4 m). This stone slab has been the subject of curiosity for a long time; it seems to have been dug up several times by archaeologists, and it had been left surrounded by debris; it marks the ideal spot for a throne.

On the Esplanade, the entrance to the Residence was flanked by two, large, more or less square, stones (2.24 x 2.25 m and 2.24 x 2.18 m) with a rectangular cutaway 2 cm deep at their centre (1.63 x 1.21 m and 1.6 x 1.25 m). These stones could have served as supports, not for doorposts as Mecquenem proposed, but more likely for human or animal figures on either side of the entrance.[12] The top surfaces of the two stone slabs, as well as their sides, were carefully polished.

In the King's chamber itself, the floor of an open alcove in the eastern wall (over 4 m long and 1.7 m deep) was formed of three slabs of grey limestone, separated from each other by the red cement of the room's floor.[13] Their surface was polished, and a slightly projecting band formed a plinth; anchor points showed, according to Mecquenem, that on the wide part 'a throne, and altar or a statue' had been fixed. It was more than likely the place for a ceremonial bed.[14] A seat could have occupied the centre of the room, in the axis of the doorways. Another slab, 1.72 m wide and 2.5 m long, constituted the threshold of another room (842) next to the King's chamber; in grey limestone with a polished surface, it is made up of pieces held together by two clamps.

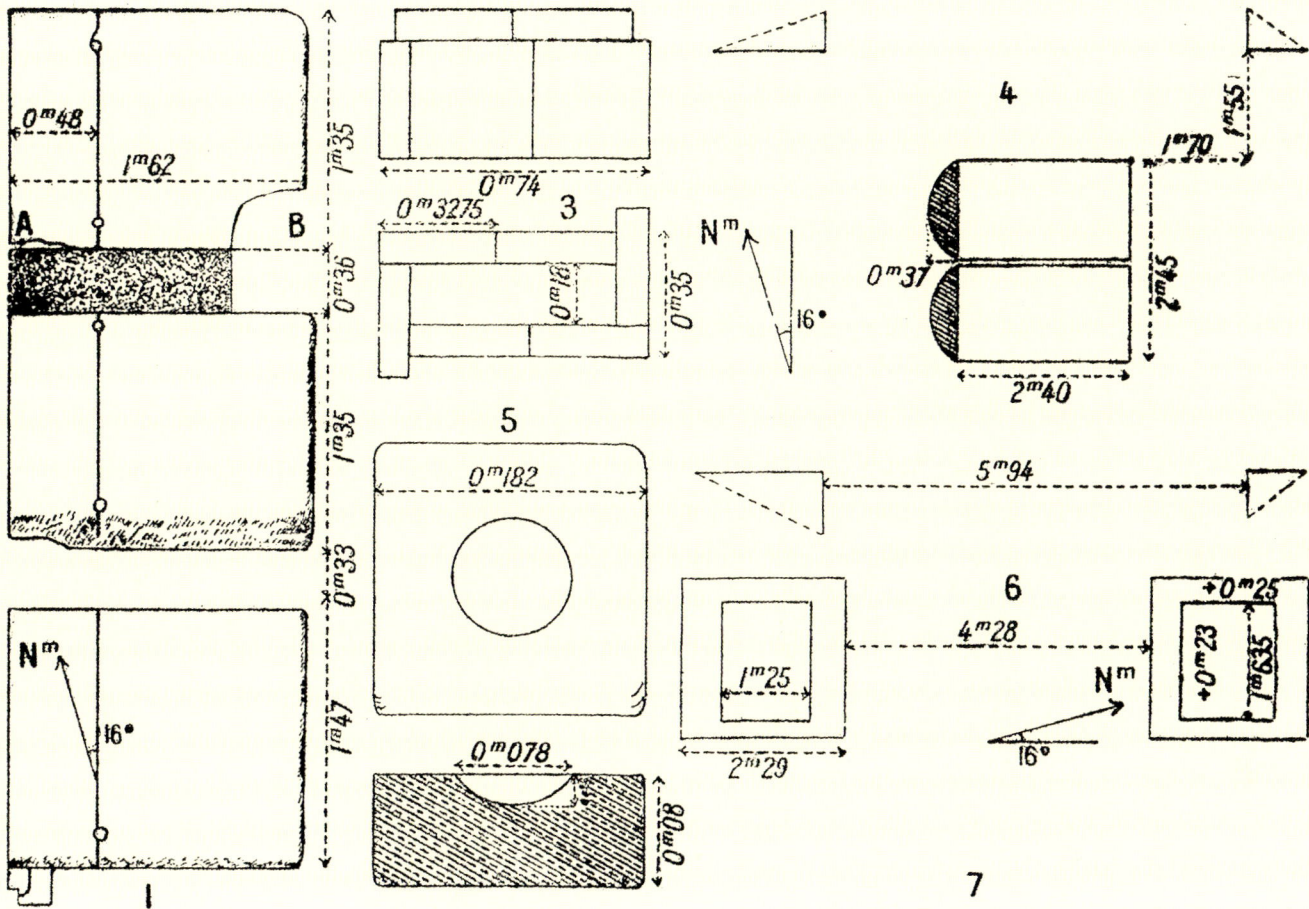

136
Paving slabs from the alcove of the King's Chamber
Sketched and published in 1947 by Roland de Mecquenem
MECQUENEM, 1947: fig 17.7

137
Grand east entrance with the two marble socles
(above) **and paving slabs from the alcove of the**
King's Chamber (right)
from the photographic album
'Palace of Darius I at Susa, 1913'
Former Maurice Pillet collection.
© Musée du Louvre/Christian Larrieu

THE CONSTRUCTION

After the earth had been dug deep, and the gravel foundations were laid, then bricks were moulded by the Babylonians.
DSf 8, VALLAT

At the same time as the earth was being dug out and the trenches filled with gravel from the nearby rivers, thousands of bricks were moulded. It is hard to estimate the quantity and scale of the effort, but a simple calculation shows that, just for the Residence, several hundreds of thousands of baked bricks and several million mud bricks were necessary. Hundreds of workers must have been engaged over several years in the realisation of this great work, whilst others gathered together the materials necessary for construction: stone, wood, lime, metal. It is clear that the population of Susa was not up to the task of providing the materials and artisans necessary. For this work, Darius had recourse to Babylonian masons, their techniques and their models, whilst the working of the stone was entrusted to artisans from Ionia and Sardis; the overall planning was entrusted to architects whose concepts, compared with the ancient palaces of Babylon, carried the mark of a new rigour.

The walls

The walls, made of mud brick, were laid on a double course of baked bricks; these were square, measuring an average 33 cm on each side, and 8 cm thick. They were made with an appropriate mud mixed with chopped straw and were constructed on the ground, or sometimes on mats, in wooden moulds according to the techniques practised in the East over millennia.[15] Thinner tiles (7 cm) and larger ones measuring 50 cm each side were also made.[16] The dimensions of the bricks and tiles, large and small (cubit and foot?), seem to have constituted the units of measurement of the architects, in preference to abstract numbers.

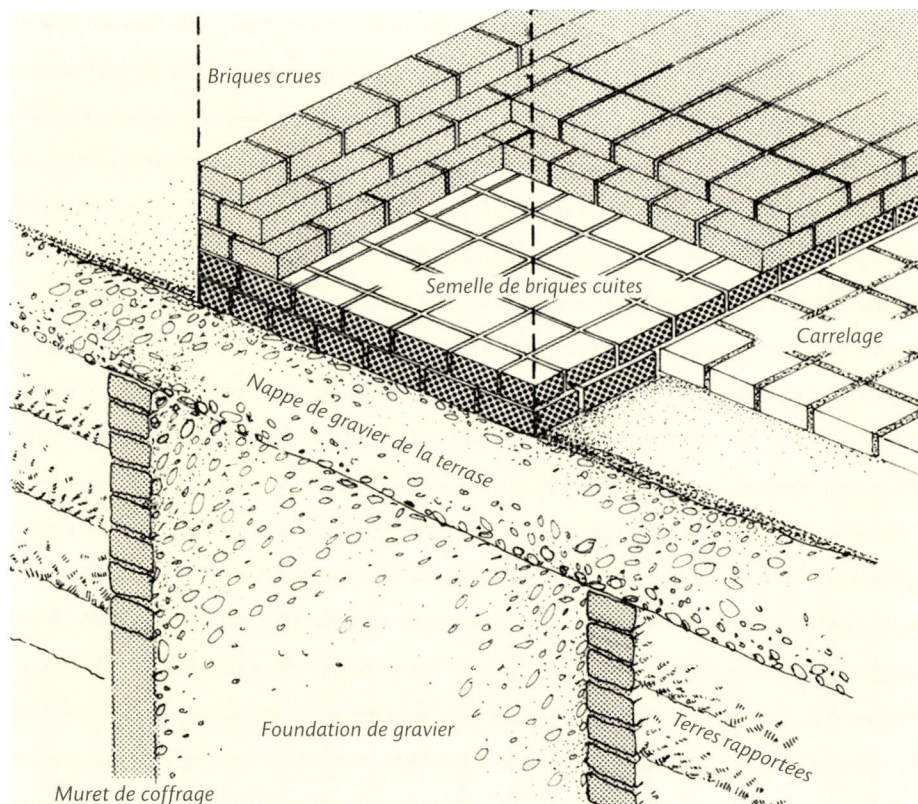

Plan of the brickwork of the walls of the Residence

139

Each wall of the Residence was built on a double course of baked bricks, as here at the entrance of the vestibule in the King's Apartment

The wall was around 3.5 m wide (10 bricks) and over 15 m high

Everything seems to have happened as though the instructions given to the masons concerning the width of the walls, hence the size of the rooms or the courtyards, had been given according to numbers of bricks: here, a wall of four, five or ten bricks; even 15 bricks (5.2 m) for the walls of the Hypostyle Hall. The string-line was stretched over a layer of fine sand,[17] and the mason would align some half-bricks, thus tracing the face of the wall and marking eventual doorways, niches or pilasters. The first course was established behind this row and then covered by the second with a sideways shift of a half-brick to bond the joins; the second course was finished off with a row of half-bricks on the opposite face; the wall was then raised with mud bricks. These walls have disintegrated but have not completely disappeared. Remains, already noted by Mecquenem,[18] were still visible in the King's Apartments, in the left jamb of the doorway separating the vestibule from the antechamber; we also found some in the north-east corner of the Residence (following Mecquenem's testimony) and, outside this edifice, at the Darius Gate, at its south-western corner where the mud-brick walls sit directly on the gravel foundations. At the Propylaeum, the middle wall's eastern section was preserved to a height of over a metre. The faces of the wall were covered in a coating of green mud; this coating had been observed at the Darius Gate and had also been found at the Shaur Palace, notably on a wall of the Central Hall where it shows signs of painting.[19]

Recesses, pilasters and frames

The door frames were all based on a similar principle; they were also marked in the wall courses. Though relatively rare, they were found at the Residence: in the middle passage between the West Court (c1) and the Central Court (c2; this doorway marked the entrance to the private part of the Residence); in the Honour Court (c1), at the great access portal to the vestibule of the Royal Apartments,

140
Entrance to the King's Apartment
The south wall of the King's Chamber that had eroded away is reconstructed

141
Brick production
The partial reconstruction (over 1 m) of the walls of the Residence required the production
of tens of thousands of bricks. The technique has not changed in millennia

142
**The foundation of baked bricks indicate
the recesses in the face of the wall**

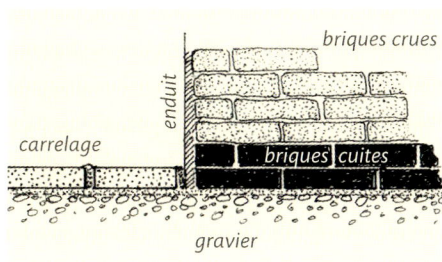

143
Brickwork cross-section

and at the door from the vestibule to the antechamber. Several of the doors giving onto this court (door 795 towards Court A to the west of CI, and the three doors opening to the north and also that of the guardroom 880) display the same recess of one brick around the door frame.

The recesses, simple or stepped, were the principal component of the architectural decor. At the Residence, this was manifested in recesses, simple and narrow (three bricks wide and one and a half bricks deep), which framed the entrance to the Royal Apartments. At the Darius Gate, the walls of the Central Hall were each pierced by four recesses, each with two steps. At the Propylaeum, the exterior and interior walls have stepped recesses at regular intervals.

The western exterior wall of the Residence was embellished with pilasters (five bricks wide and half a brick deep); they stood in pairs at 3.5 m from each other, each pair 9 m from the next.[20] These pilasters are seen, for example, in the southwestern corner of the Residence. The eastern wall of the Residence did not have any pilasters, and the southern wall has completely disappeared.

144
Foundation boxes next to the doors giving onto the West Court, or Honour Court, and the King's Apartment

Foundation boxes

A relationship seems to exist between the framed doors of the Honour Court (c1) and the presence, at their doorposts, under the floor tiles, of small square boxes framed by four bricks set on edge. Mecquenem points out another box at the centre of this courtyard, and an additional one, rectangular and made with six bricks, in the middle of the Central Court (c2). These boxes could have contained foundation deposits, but all were found empty.

Plaster floors and tiled floors

The cement floors are only found at the Residence where they are characteristic of the private areas, rooms and hallways. The plaster is made of a lime mortar and broken brick fragments; its depth varies from 12 to 20 cm and its surface is covered in a carefully polished, wine-red coating. This technique is not unknown in Babylon,[21] but it seems that it is more widely used in Susa.

The courtyards are tiled; the tiles are generally the same size as the bricks, 33 cm on average, but we also find larger tiles, from 49 to 52 cm²; this is notably the case in the Honour Court (c1). The floor of the Esplanade was also tiled between the Residence and the Darius Gate; the gate's passage, relaid several times, had a final flooring of large tiles. At the Propylaeum, the tiling borders the structure so as to protect its foundations and extends further out at the entrance and exit. The tiles of the audience chamber have completely disappeared. Mecquenem thought that the few tiles of aragonite could have belonged to it as well as 'fragments of broken tiles in a veined glaze';[22] we did not find traces of them.

The column bases

In its initial state, the Residence had no columns; at the most we can envisage a few posts to support an awning at the entrance to the great halls to the south of the East Court (c3) where the existence of a gravel foundation permits us to deduce a superstructure. The only column bases found *in situ* within the confines of the Residence were, in the corner of Court A (to the west of c1), those of an awning which are evidence of either a restoration or an addition attributable to Artaxerxes II.[23] In the gravel of 'Court' F (to the north-west of c2), 'places encrusted with limestone' appeared to indicate to Mecquenem the position of *small column bases*; on the ground of this same 'court' he claims to have picked up 'debris of bases' and 'fragments of fluted shaft' which could have belonged to a 'small hypostyle hall' or to a 'portico'. The present state of this sector does not allow for any comment to be made; it would not, however, be very likely that such an installation, were it verifiable, could be attributed to the Babylonian architects at the time of Darius.

145
The Residence:
part of the red covered plaster floor

146
Column bases supporting the
loggia canopy of the small West Court
(addition by Artaxerxes II)
from the photographic album
'Palace of Darius I at Susa, 1913'
Former Maurice Pillet collection.
© Musée du Louvre/Christian Larrieu

THE BUILDING

The Artisans' Gate

On the eastern face of the Ville Royale tell (730°N 950°E on Jullien's 1948 plan), the Artisans' Gate rises on top of the glacis (at the 16 m datum level), 1 m in front of the gravel layer. It is a building of solid construction with a rectangular plan, measuring 35 m long by 18.8 m wide, and made up of two long rooms flanked at their extremities by smaller rooms. The base of the walls is made of square baked bricks (with sides between 32.5 and 33 cm, and 7 to 9 cm thick). The type of the gateway is known as 'pincered',[24] improved here by the addition, at the extremity of the long rooms, of internal passageways which would considerably increase the mobility of the defenders. It was not possible to measure the width of the central corridor with any precision (between 4.5 and 5 m). It seems that a barrier only existed on the entrance side, where we found traces of the socket supports. Access to the gateway was via a mud-brick ramp, still visible today at the highest point of the depression that separates the Ville Royale tell from the tell of the Artisans. This depression was described as a 'ditch' dug by Darius' engineers, which seems highly improbable.[25] The door was necessary in this sector to facilitate access to the 'palace' for the population of the suburb.

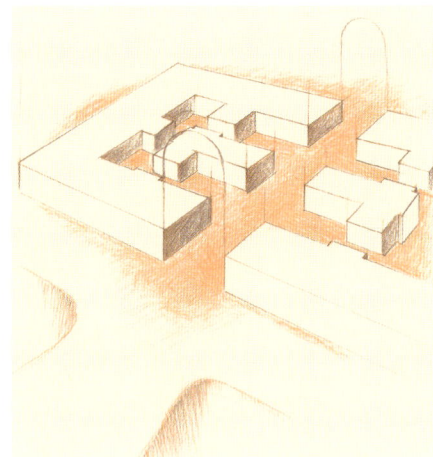

148
Axonometric view of the Artisans' Gate

147
Plan of the Artisan's Gate
drawing by Daniel Ladiray

149

The eastern slopes of the Ville Royale
The white dot indicates the access ramp to the Artisans' Gate.
In the foreground, the silted branch of the Shaur

150

Mud-brick ramp giving access to the Artisans' Gate

151
The Artisans' Gate on the eastern edge of the Ville Royale

The Propylaeum

This building[26] is square with sides of 24 m, and it is made up of two long rooms with offset walls, flanked by porticoes. Overall the work is particularly fine; the techniques used for the foundations as well as the architectural ornamentation (stepped recesses, both interior and exterior) appear more sophisticated than those apparent in the Residence. These improvements may come from a later date during the course of Darius' reign. The structure may have benefited from experience and an evolution in aesthetic taste. The floors of the rooms and the porticoes are tiled, as is the outside border of the structure so as to protect its particularly fragile foundations. The tiling extends out from both the entrance and the exit to the north. The columns, 70 cm in diameter, were probably wooden; they rested on square, grey stone bases with sides of 90 cm. They carry an inscription of Xerxes (xs a).[27]

To the north-east of the Propylaeum, in the higher levels (VII–X) of Ghirshman's 'stratigraphic trench', Hermann Gasche suggested interpreting a solid mass of *pisé* earth, filling a trench dug several metres into the pre-Elamite levels, as the foundations of an east–west way which could have communicated with the palace complex.[28] In fact, the orientation and the exact position of this mass is still imprecise. We do not have elsewhere at Susa any examples of Achaemenid causeways. As for the access route to the Propylaeum, it most likely came from the Parade Ground which, even today, is the most 'natural' route up to the Ville Royale.

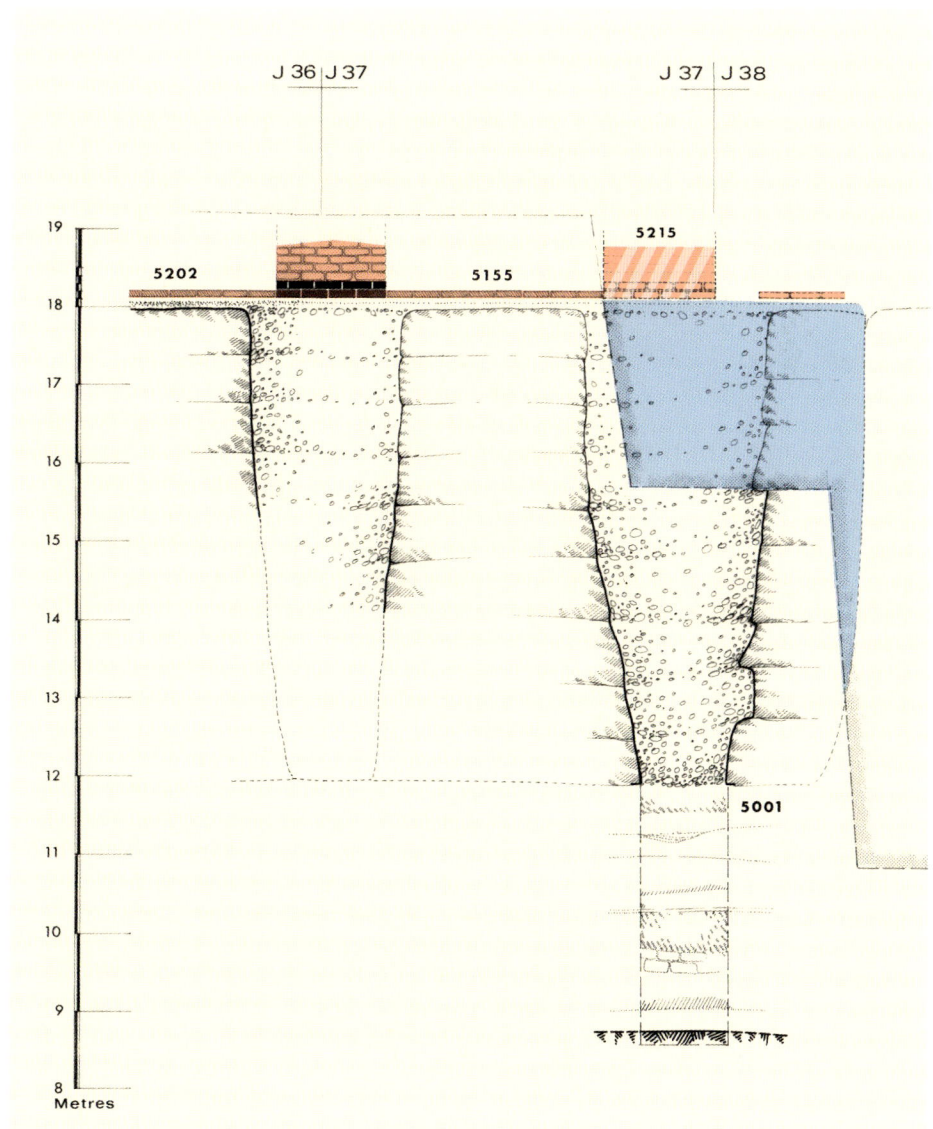

152

East-west section through
the Propylaeum foundations

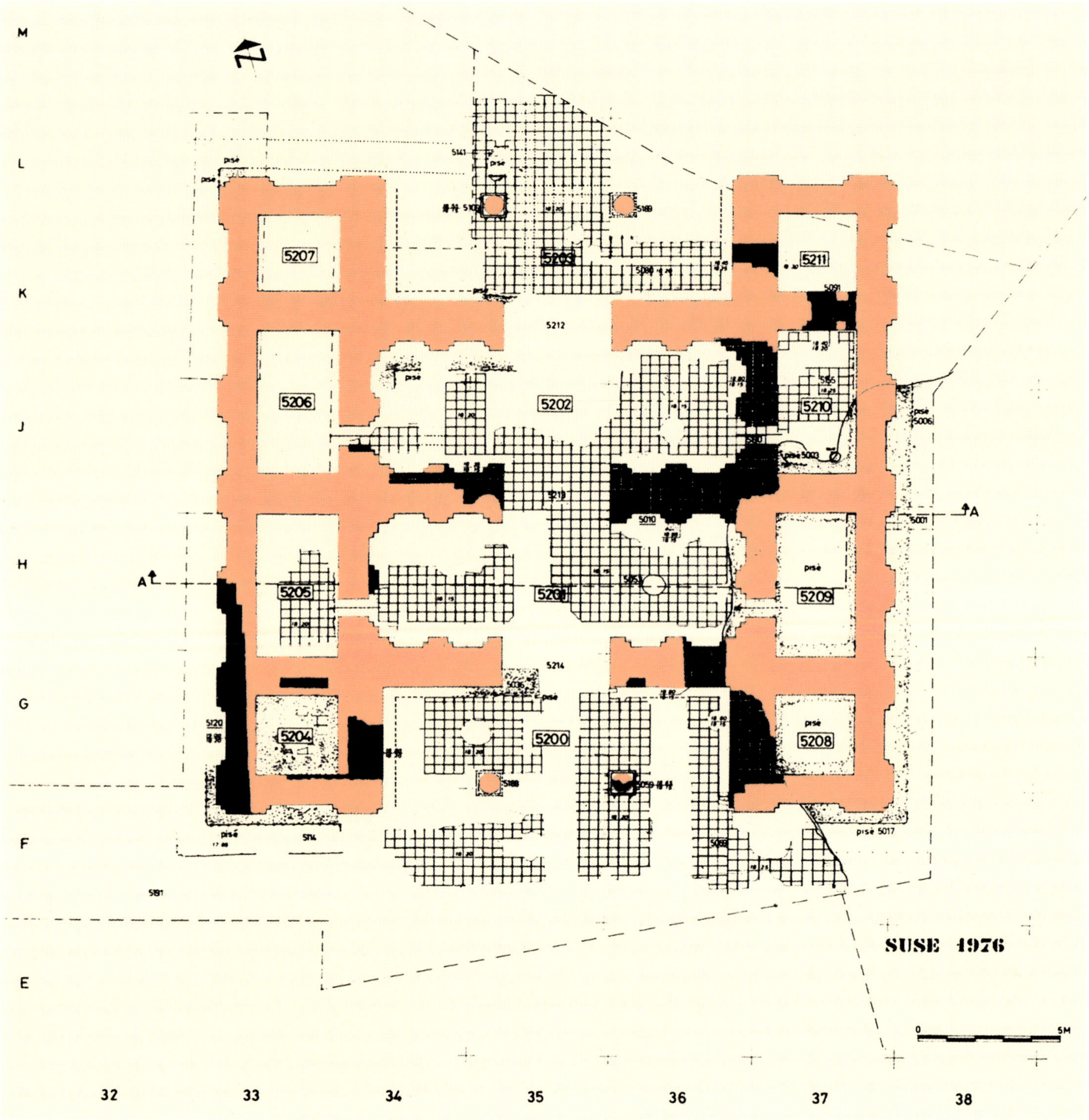

SUSE 1976

153
Plan of the Propylaeum
drawing by Daniel Ladiray

154
Axonometric view of the Propylaeum

155
Base of a column of the southern portico

156

Central sector 'East' of the Propylaeum
Some of the wall facing was preserved

157

Passage from the central hall to a side room

158

Wall with stepped recess in the central hall

159

Interior wall of the Propylaeum
Preserved to a height of nearly 1 m

The Causeway

From the Ville Royale platform there was a route to that of the Apadana, at the same level (about 15 m above the plain and 18 m above the waters of the Shaur), via a sturdy mud-brick road. In the axis of the Darius Gate, it in fact constituted part of the curtain wall due to its position; it was an earthen embankment whose external aspect must have been the same as that of the glacis. Its spread of around 17 m (it is currently below the water table) suggests a causeway with a width at the summit of 10 m. On a compact foundation at datum level 10, rise two large longitudinal walls, in mud brick, linked by two supporting walls forming three large caissons filled with earth and debris, one following on from the other over 30 m. On the Ville Royale side the work rests on a cut in the Elamite layers (from datum levels 13 to 10); on the Apadana side, it leans on the retaining wall starting at level 10. Repairs seem to have been made to the top part of the structure during the Parthian era.[29]

160
Western caisson of the thoroughfare emptied of rubble

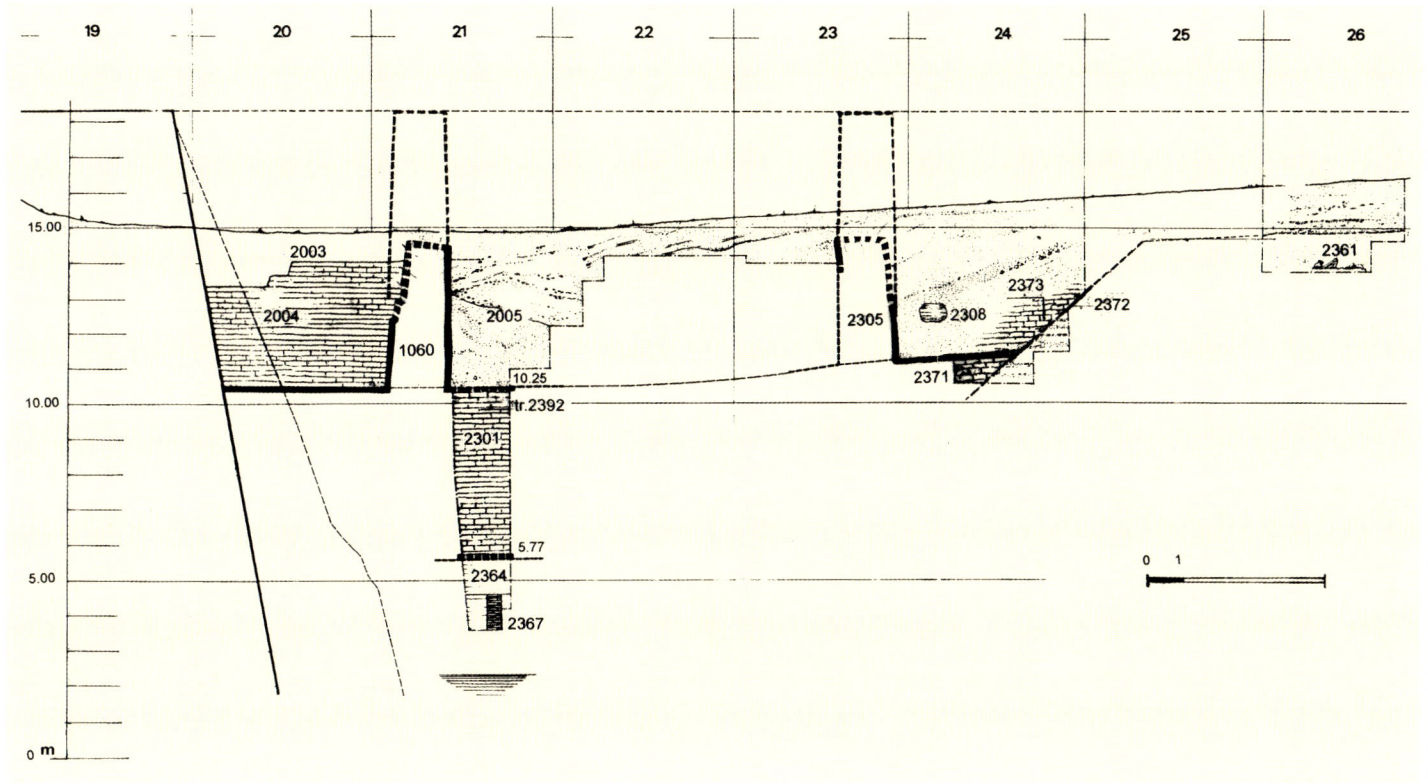

161
Longitudinal cross-section of the causeway
linking the Ville Royale and the Apadana terrace

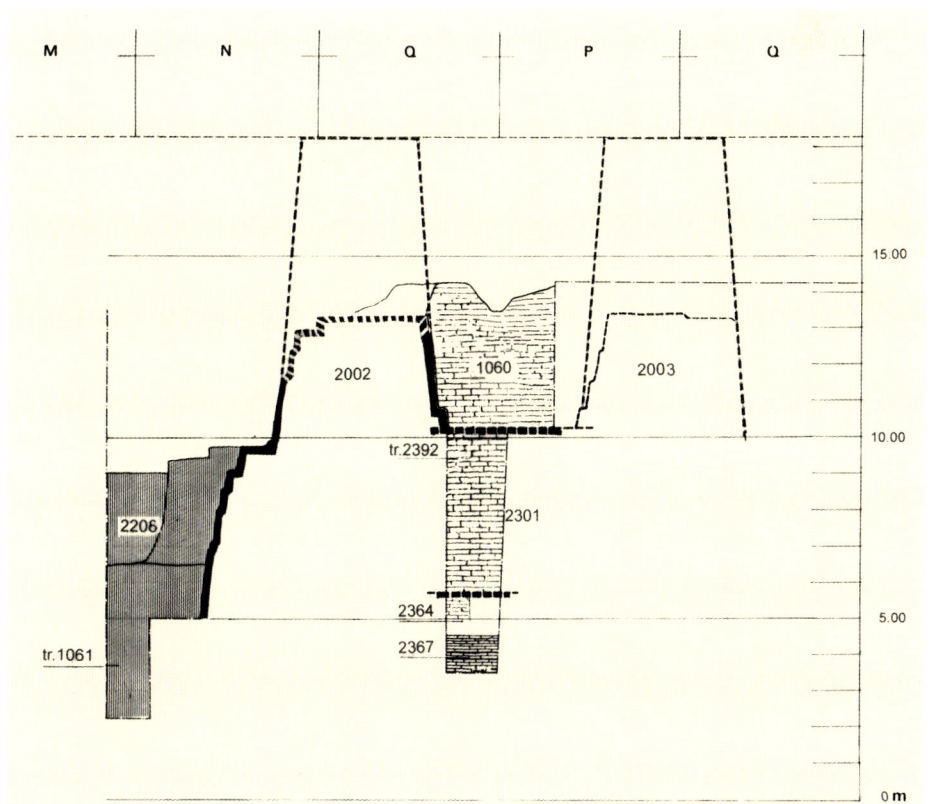

162
Transverse cross-section of the causeway

163
Longitudinal cross-section of the causeway
from the Propylaeum to the Darius Gate

164
The face of the retaining wall of the Apadana terrace
where the causeway abutted, cleared down to the water table

165
The face of the retaining wall of the Apadana terrace
where the causeway abutted, cleared down to the water table

The Darius Gate

The Darius Gate is an independent building measuring 40 x 28 m; its height must have been at least 15 m. It rises on the eastern edge of the Apadana terrace, on a projection of the retaining wall; the façade of the structure rests directly on this wall. The foundations of the gate are, as we have seen above,[30] remarkably complex. The construction of the building is intimately linked to that of the terrace; and the walls of the gate are inseparable from the terrace's retaining wall. The axis of the eastern passage is in line with the extension of the access route and, like it, is orientated east–west. The entrance (5 m wide) must have been flanked by two large sculptures, judging by the size of their foundations;[31] it must have had a door of which the displaced sockets remain. This part of the building had suffered particularly from erosion which had removed almost 3 m from the top of the terrace edge.

The structural plan consists of the central square room (21.1 m sides) with four columns carrying a trilingual inscription by Xerxes (xs a) attributing the building of the gate to Darius his father.[32] The exit onto the Esplanade, the same width as the entrance, is a simple passage; the continuity of the floor tiles indicates that it did not have a door. The central room (450 m²) was flanked on each side by long rooms (14 x 3.5 m) communicating with it via narrow passageways; the north-west and south-west corners of the building had stairwells that circled around a central pillar, and the first steps are preserved. The floor of the lateral rooms, like that of the Central Hall, is covered in 33 cm² tiles grouted with plaster; in the passageway towards the Esplanade the tiling has been renovated with large tiles of 51 cm; these bear the traces of cart or chariot wheels.

The exterior walls were smooth, unlike those of the Propylaeum which had off-set recesses; they were made of mud brick and were 3.3 m thick; their internal

166

Eroded summit of the retaining wall of the Apadana terrace at the height of the Darius Gate

The gravel sleeve separates the terrace from the mass of the causeway. Also visible are the foundations for the sculptures which flanked the entrance of the Darius Gate.

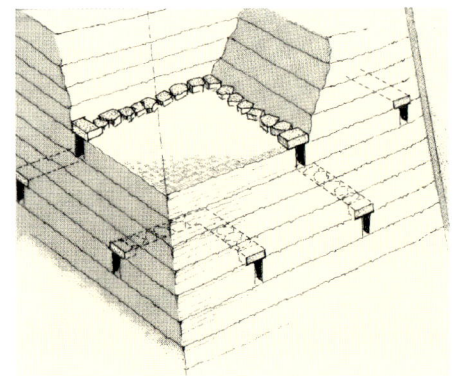

167

Sketch showing the drainage system of the retaining wall of the Apadana terrace in the Darius Gate area

168
Plan of the Darius Gate

169
Axonometric view of the Darius Gate

170
The Darius Gate
Foundations and gravel damp course

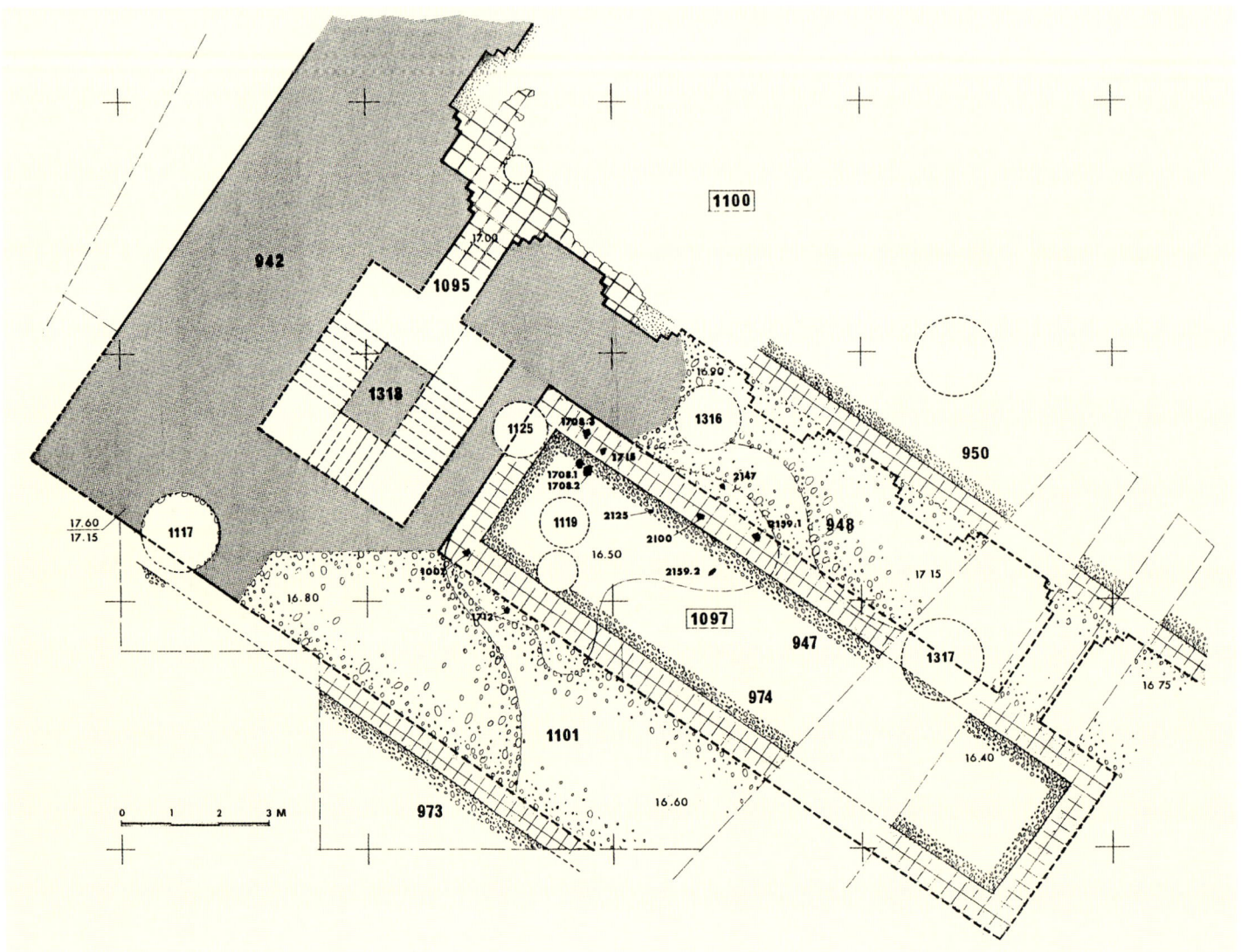

171

Plan of the Darius Gate
Restored by Daniel Ladiray

172

The Darius Gate
Column of the central hall broken
by a foundation wall of a building
of the Parthian or Sassanian period

173

The Darius Gate
Inscribed plinth of a column base
of the central hall

1/4

Plan of the passageway through the Darius Gate
towards the Esplanade

175

East-west cross-section of the passageway
whose floor was repaired on several occasions

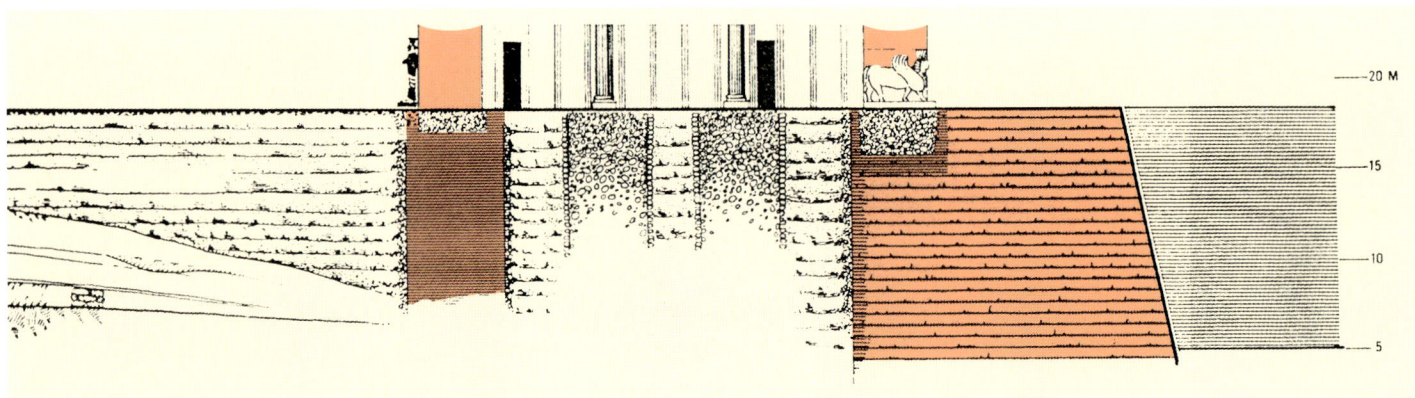

176

Schematic east-west cross-section of the Darius Gate

177

**The passageway through the
Darius Gate towards the Esplanade**
Wheel tracks are visible on the pavement

surface was covered by a thin layer of green clay acting as a bond for a layer of plaster. A few fragments of mud plaster bear the traces of red and blue paint. The walls of the large room had regularly spaced, double-stepped recesses cut into them; these recesses excluded the presence of a bench.

The columns rested on square bases with sides of 1.52 m; two of them, on the western side, were still in place. We cannot confirm that the shafts were made of stone; several fragments that were found had fluting which made them indistinguishable from those of the large Hypostyle Hall; they could be from there, and so could a small fragment of a column with volutes. In the best-preserved south-western part of the building, the excavation produced several fragments of glazed brick and stone tablets with cuneiform signs. As for the exit towards the Residence, it was flanked on the outside by two colossal statues of Darius.[33] That on the southern side was of Egyptian origin and was still *in situ*;[34] of the other, most probably a replica of the first in local stone, we have only a few fragments.[35]

178
The Darius statue *in situ* against the wall of the gate
The foot of the wall was protected by a row of large baked brick tiles

179
The Darius statue on its stone and gravel foundations
One stone had been moved

How the Statue of Darius broke

Jean Perrot

The statue was found *in situ*, standing on its base and leaning back slightly. Its position seems to have been the result of a movement of the earth subsequent to the settling of the soil under the gate. Excavation in this area showed that the gate had been removed at the end of the Achaemenid period,[1] and the foundations, which are known to have been vulnerable,[2] had rapidly been affected by water seepage from drains and sewage coming from successive levels of Seleucid, Parthian and Sassanian housing.[3] As a result the floor levels had collapsed to 1.25 m in the south-west corner of what had been the Central Hall, a few metres behind the statue; the latter's base had progressively sunk to datum level 17.44 (as against an original datum level of 18.25 in the axis of the passage). This change in levels had brought about a shift of soil towards the east and eventually resulted in the statue's breaking under the weight of the soil that had completely covered it by Sassanian times. These breaks are the result, not of blows, but of pressure exercised from the front towards the back, following the lines of fracture in the stone:[4] blows would have left more evident traces.

Furthermore, there is no reason to suppose that those who made the original discovery had lifted the statue in order to be able to tilt it backwards.[5] This was not necessary, as its weight rested on the back of the base, so that the front stone could be moved without any difficulty. Shahrokh Razmjou has given too much weight to the suggestion that the statue had been subjected to attacks by Alexander's soldiers. The damage to the statue is likely to have been accidental. Indeed it is surprising that the statue was not knocked over when the gate was razed in Seleucid times. Not only was the statue treated with respect over the centuries, but so was the space it occupied: the surrounding houses were built at a respectful distance.

The gate area seems to have remained unoccupied from the end of the Sassanian period until the ninth century AD. During this time, erosion was active

180

The foundation stone of the statue against the wall of the gate
In the angled indent formed by the passageway towards the Esplanade there was an iron spike (red marker), possibly used as a reference marker by the builders

181
Position of the statue on its discovery
The front foundation stone had been pulled
forward; it had a cup-shaped depression which
could have held a small foundation deposit.
To the left, associated with a Parthian period
floor, was a child's burial in a jar

182
State of the upper fracture of the statue

here, along the edges of the tell, and must have laid bare the upper part of the statue; it was at that time that the head may have become detached and rolled into the gap separating the Apadana from the Ville Royale tell.[6] The edge of the upper break may even have been exposed for a time as it has suffered some wear and some secondary chipping. It is possible that the stone attracted attention at the time when wall 703 was built in the ninth century AD, and curiosity may have led to the partial clearance of the statue. The excavators would then have partially backfilled the ditch (711) which they had just cleared (the fill of the ditch contained some Islamic sherds), and an occupation level hid the spot.

The history of the Statue of Darius after the Achaemenid period belongs to specialists in Seleucid, Parthian and Sassanian history. It is worth recalling, however, that in Parthian times, when the level of the earth was rising around the statue, several cylindrical jars containing child burials were interred around the statue, suggesting that it may, for a time, have been an object of veneration.

1. The only remains of wall 942, against which the statue had been placed, were its lower courses of unbaked brick.
2. D. Ladiray, this volume, ch. VI.
3. BOUCHARLAT, 1974 : 111.
4. J. Yoyotte, this volume, ch. VIII.
5. RAZMJOU, 2002.
6. We searched for it there with the only certainty that, in view of the metamorphic nature of the stone, it could not have ended up in the lime kilns of the Shaur 'sugar refineries' where were burnt most of the column bases of the audience chamber of Artaxerxes II (R. Boucharlat, this volume, ch. XIII).

183
**Cross-section through the ditch in which
the Darius statue was uncovered for the
first time in the eighth or ninth century AD**
drawing by Daniel Ladiray

Beyond the gate lay a vast Esplanade, devoid of buildings, extending over 60 m to the entrance of the Residence which is staggered 45 m further towards the north. This space, paved with 33 cm tiles, seems to have been open to the elements, and had a view restricted only to the north by the Zagros mountains. It had been ravaged by earlier trenches and more particularly by an excavation by Mecquenem.[36] The platform of the Esplanade was made up of layers of earth brought in from elsewhere, whose thickness extended in places to between 7 and 8 m.

The digging of the pit (1.5 x 1.1 m) destined for the foundations of the Egyptian statue, seems to have damaged the side of the 'upper foundation' of foundation wall 942 and a repair was necessary. The statue was found smothered in the infill of a ditch (771) which had been dug to examine it. The edges of this ditch had appeared under a layer of ashy earth containing Islamic potsherds. On this thick layer, facing east–west, less than 1 m to the north of the statue, ran wall 703, built of baked bricks and attributed to the ninth century AD by Monique Kervran.

The support of the statue is made up of two slabs 20 cm thick, the largest measuring 87 x 75 cm; this slab has two lateral ledges 11 cm thick and 4 cm high running north–south; the width between these ledges corresponds to the width of the base of the statue. The stone at the front had been pulled forward; it measures 70 x 47 cm and has a slight cavity on its upper face, cut with a pick when the stone was carved and probably destined for a small deposit. The sides of the two stones needed to be aligned and were carefully carved. When complete, the support must have measured 1.23 m, so a few centimetres more than the base of the statue (1.04 m). The latter, having been put in position, had been sealed in lead, poured from the northern end between the base of the statue and the stones of the support; several kilos of metal were recovered.

184
General view of the central hall and remains of the wall footings in the north-western corner of the Hypostyle Hall

The Hypostyle Hall (Apadana)

The structure had a square ground plan, with sides of 109 m. It comprised a central hall with six rows of six columns flanked, to the west, to the north and to the east, by porticoes with two rows of six columns; to the south, between the corner towers, was a hall or corridor about 5 m wide.[37] Several questions regarding this structure still remain without any clear answers: we do not have traces of the corner towers in the north other than the crumbling mass of their foundation gravel; only the north-east corner of the north-east tower has been identified. The floor plan of the southern towers remains uncertain. For a long time the walls of the hall evaded the excavators, who sometimes even doubted their existence. R. Ghirshman was the first to identify them at the same time as he confirmed the existence of the northern portico. In the north-western angle of the central hall we uncovered the baked brick coursework of the main wall (326) which was at 5.2 m (15 bricks) wide. Its outline was followed along the north side (325) where, halfway along, D. Canal brought to light the doorpost sockets of what was then the only doorway, before discovering those of the east (342) and west (340), buried under their own weight 30 to 40 cm deep.[38] The support blocks for all the building's door sockets were relatively small and badly squared off.

Each of the three porticoes communicated with the main hall via a single doorway. On the south side communication was made via two identical doorways (343 and 344) giving the peculiar sensation of being within the thickness of the wall. These doors opened towards the Residence. The passageway widened from 4.6 to 5.2 m to accommodate the door battens, unlike the other doors which opened onto the central hall.[39] Coming from the south, what M. Pillet called the 'royal passage' (s) opened out into this long hallway.

tr.751

tr.750

336

7   8   11   337

tr.752

325   341   400

753   755

14   37   38   39   40   41   42   25   tr.853

326   324

16   43   44   45   46   47   48   27   tr.799   tr.830

18   756   50   51   52   53   54   758   29   30   tr.841

340   H   342

757   55   56   57   58   59   60   759   31   32

61   62   63   64   65   66   33   34

401   402

331   791

68   69   70   71   72   35

767   768   769   770

403   344   323   343   404

774   775   776   780   829   786

339   773   777   338

771   772   349

785

782   801   347

353   350   352

802   S

363   805

358   800

G   804   806   942

359   362   807

351   808

365   357   364   811   348   809

810

360   361   812   C3   Nord

R1   872   814

849   879   10 m

817   818   819

185

Plan of the Apadana with access and dependencies
(control trenches in grey)

The Apadana foundations

Jean Perrot and Denis Canal

Among the questions concerning the Apadana was one related to the ground on which the building had been built. During the 1972–1973 season, two stratigraphic trenches were opened under Denis Canal's supervision,[1] with the aim of checking whether the Hypostyle Hall had its own terrace,[2] as had frequently been suggested, possibly with an older underlying Neo-Elamite palace. Two trenches 2.5 m wide were opened, with the first (750) being perpendicular to the north side of the building, between the second and third rows of north–south columns; the second (830), on the east side of the hall, was aligned with the third row of east-west columns. Both trenches reached virgin soil at the 13 m datum level (the floor of the Central Hall and porticoes was at the 18.25 m level, which was the main level of the palace floors).

TRENCH 750

This trench reached the foundations of columns 2 and 8 of the north portico, and these foundations reached virgin soil (826), which they penetrated at the 12.75 m datum level. A small wall of ten courses of unbaked bricks (22 x 16 x 7.8) rested on virgin soil (at 827), forming the corner of a room or courtyard. Two floors of hard-packed earth were related to this small wall which dated to the 4th millennium BC. Above, there were layers of ashy soil (822–823) containing fragments of coarse bowls and other pieces of pottery characteristic of levels 21 to 16 of Acropolis site 1 (Susa II, second half of the 4th millennium).[3] The following levels continue without interruption into the Middle Elamite period (second half of the 2nd millennium BC) and the corner of a large building and a courtyard (803–805) with a floor paved with baked bricks measuring 33/34 cm square and 7/8 cm thick; the corner tile is covered with bitumen. A hearth (in 824) had been cut into by the foundation of column 8. The pottery here was similar to that of levels A XIV–A XV of Ghirshman's stratigraphic trench (the so-called Sukkalmah period). Above there were several occupation levels which contained archaeological material comparable to that of levels A XIII and A XII of the same Ghirshman trench. Further up, the levels had been touched by the erosion that had also affected the Achaemenid levels. They included inhumation burials (801) containing material that can be dated to the late second millennium BC.

Beyond the portico, to the north, the Achaemenid and underlying levels were marked by the deep cut of a post-Achaemenid ditch right down to virgin soil (as far as the 6 m datum level). The digging of this ditch, which extended around the building, must have weakened its foundations and we can see, as deduced by Ghirshman, the reason for the collapse of the columns of the porticoes; numerous remains were found at the bottom of the depression, several metres below the level of the Hall. Ghirshman suggested that the digging of this ditch was the work of the defenders of Susa, either in 317 BC, when the city resisted the attack of Antigonus Monophthalmus, satrap of Phrygia, who sought to rebuild, for his own ends, the empire of Alexander the Great, or in 223 BC, at the time of the revolt of the satraps against the young king Antiochus III. Molon, satrap of Media, laid siege to Susa; according to Polybius (*Histories*, 48, 13–14), he seized the lower town but failed to capture the 'citadel'; the latter may have comprised, together with the Acropolis, the imposing mass of the Residence and the Apadana.

TRENCH 830

On the eastern side of the Hypostyle Hall, trench 830 also reached virgin soil at datum level 13, the maximum height of the natural mound in the Apadana sector which was first settled towards the middle of the fourth millennium BC.[4]

The objective of this trench was to verify the existence, on this side, of a 'retaining wall' for the 'terrace' of the Hypostyle Hall described by Mecquenem.[5] 'This mud-brick wall, 3.5 m in height, followed by a baked brick wall, 1.37 m wide, rested on imported soil or on ancient terrain.' This wall would have been 'built exclusively through excavation'; there would have been no external difference in level with the supporting wall. The eastern edge of this wall passed at 10.43 m from the north–south line of the column bases of the eastern portico.

SUSE. APADANA. 1973.

Tranchées 830, 841, 853. Plan.

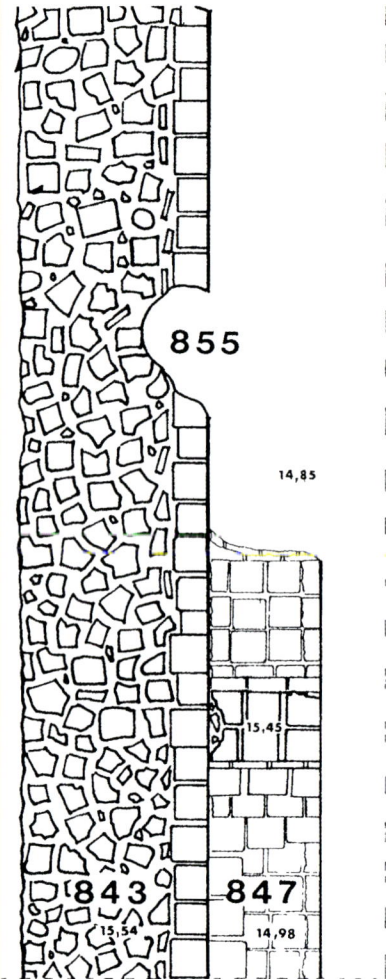

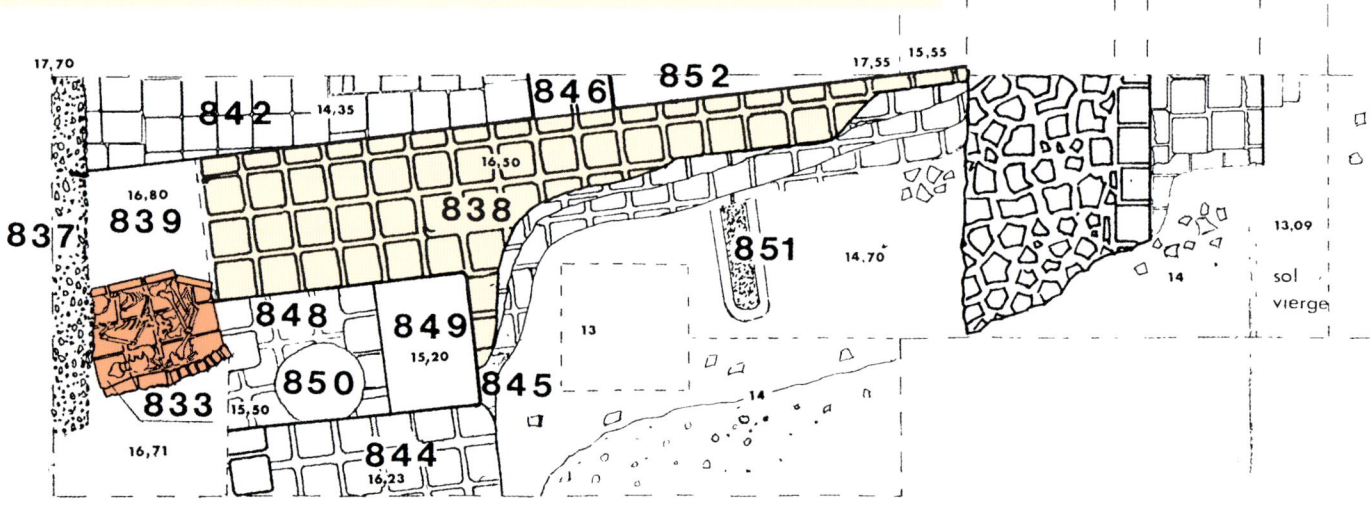

186
Plan of the structures of the second millennium BC unearthed in trench 830

187
**Trench 750 across the northern portico
of the Apadana**

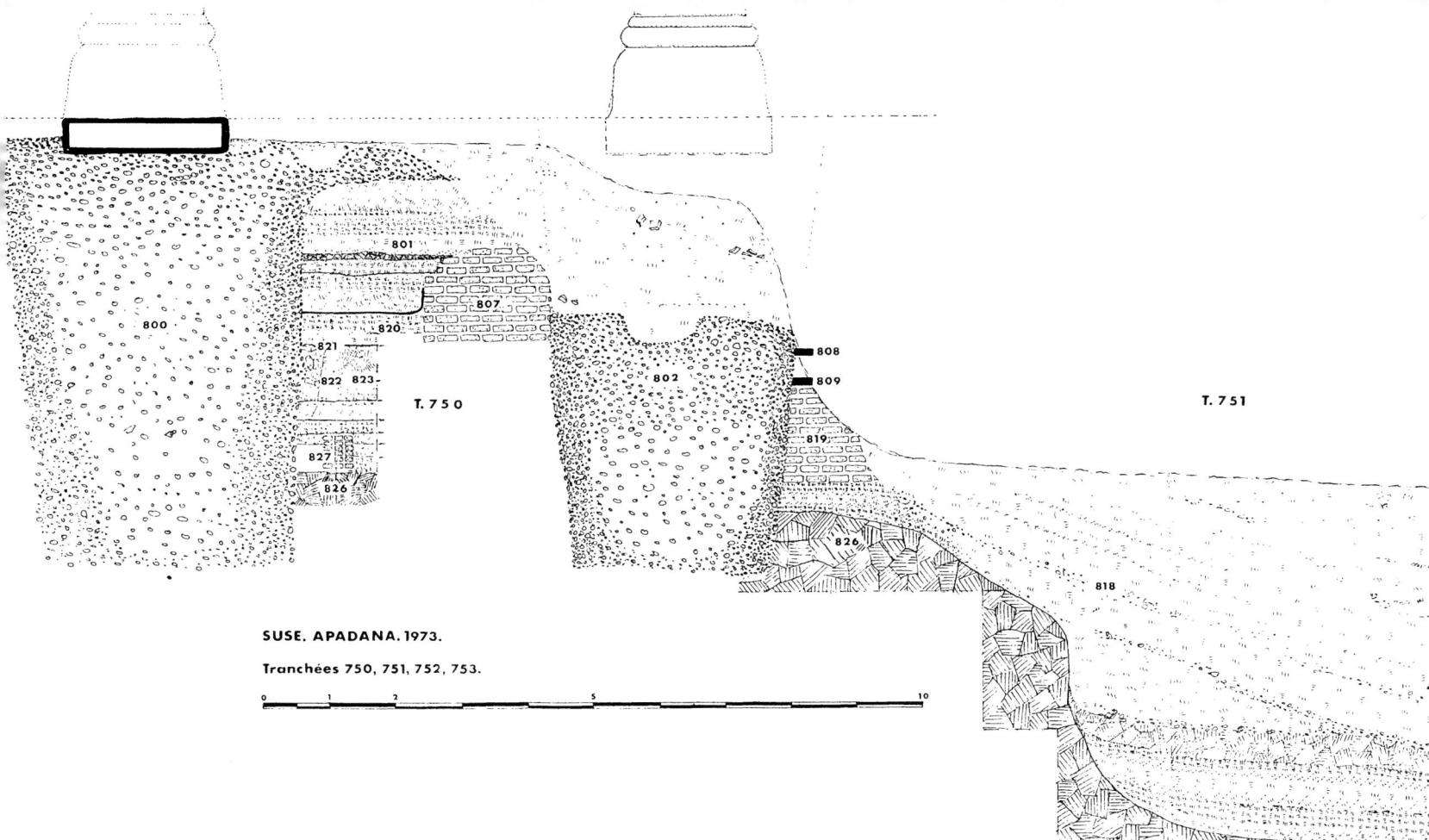

SUSE. APADANA. 1973.

Tranchées 750, 751, 752, 753.

188
Section through trench 750
Dig report, Denis Canal

Trench 830 showed that above the fourth millennium BC levels, one passes without transition (the same as in trench 750) to levels of the second half of the second millennium BC with two or three occupation layers, the last (at level 14.7) with a hearth (851) made of half mud bricks placed end-on and bonded with clay. The structures of this level were cut in the south by the excavations of Mecquenem. Above (at datum level 16.5), there are walls of a large building (838–844 and 845–846) delimiting three spaces (842, 849 and 852). Location 842 seems to be a courtyard tiled with variously sized baked bricks. Along wall 838 there are two hearths. Rooms 849 and 152 show a succession of beaten earth floors with, *in situ*, material comparable with that of levels A XIII and A XII of Ghirshman's site on the Ville Royale tell. This building was cut across (in 837) by the foundation of column 30 of the eastern portico. Further to the east, the trench encountered walls (843 and 847) which correspond to the description given by Mecquenem, but they are post-Achaemenid.

Thus the archaeological data furnished by stratigraphic trenches 750 and 830 clearly show that there was no retaining wall around the Hypostyle Hall. The floor of the hall was on the same level as the surrounding area. There was no trace of a stairway or access ramp. The structure rested on the Middle Elamite layers of the end of the second millennium BC, a period during which the tell became a cemetery. These layers were exposed by the leveling off of the top of the mound when the

189
Trench 830 across the eastern portico of the Hypostyle Hall

site was being prepared by Darius' architects. There is no reason, therefore to search for a Neo-Elamite palace under the Hypostyle Hall. Such a palace, if it had existed, would have been swept away with the upper part of the tell by the palace builders. In any case, it would have been of modest proportions and would not have been sufficient for Darius' needs.

TOMB 833

Above wall 833, at level 16.8, there is a tomb of a type well known at Susa.[6] It rests on tiling consisting of three rows of four baked bricks with sides of 32/33 cm and a thickness of 0.75 cm. It lies in an east–west orientation and is open to the east. Its sides are made of trapezoidal baked bricks of which there are only a few fragments on the southern side. Three skeletons with ornaments were found, and burial goods, including a fragment of a figurine of the 'naked goddess' type. This tomb is of the same period as the burials of level 3 of trench 750 (end of the second millennium BC). It was dug into and partially destroyed by the foundations of column 30 of the eastern portico.

190
Tomb 833
(second half of the second millennium BC)

1. Trainee archaeologist. The pottery from the Elamite levels was examined on site by Elizabeth Carter.
2. Mecquenem (MECQUENEM, 1947: 34).
3. LEBRUN, 1971.
4. A. HESSE, ch. V: 155; MIROSCHEDJI, 1976.
5. MECQUENEM, 1947: 32.
6. GHIRSHMAN 1965: fig. 15, 17 (tomb no. 4; loc. 52 level A XIII).

The 'royal passage' (s) was a gallery about 40 m long whose walls were decorated with recesses or pilasters. This gallery ensured communication between the East Court (c3) and the Hypostyle Hall. One gained access to it via a double door (in 807–808) which also gave access to passageway R1. The 'royal passage' was flanked east and west by a narrow corridor (358–356), 2 m wide, which led to a ceremonial chamber G (358). On either side of these corridors, covering several hundred square metres, the ground had been dug over. The geophysical surveys were a great help in showing the organic link between the construction of the Hypostyle Hall and the Residence. To the east were remnants of tiling (in 347). To the west, there were traces of the pillage of baked bricks from the large northern main-drain (800) as well as old excavation trenches.

The columns of the Apadana

At present, 45 supporting stones are still in place: 32 in the Central Hall, 7 in the eastern portico and 3 in each of the northern and eastern porticoes. These stones, which measure approximately 2.4 x 2.4 m, rested on individual foundations measuring 4.8 x 4.8 m. They were carved with picks, and bore masons' marks on all faces. Two of these (numbers 25 and 27) were round. Between the four middle bases of the two southern rows, there was a large square slab, made up of two half-cylinders (331) that had no foundation. It could mark the location of the throne.

The columns of the central hall rested on square bases (plinth, die, torus). The bases of the portico columns were bell-shaped. With a height of 1.75 m, they were a little larger than the column bases of the central hall. The ornamentation of the bases in the porticoes differed but the style was the same. Those of the western portico had double ribbing which then fanned out into palm fronds; these were surrounded by globes from which sprouted inverted palm fronds; underneath were leaves with prominent veins. Those of the northern portico had a simpler decoration with ribs below an oval motif. Those of the eastern portico had more ribs under a row of palm fronds.

The column shafts consisted of four or five segments with 48 grooves, 15 mm deep. The smallest diameter of the column shaft was 1.6 m, its height was close to 13.5 m, there was no entasis and the shafts were straight. The capital, itself over 8 m high, was composed of three elements: the fronts of two reclining bulls facing outwards (2.32 m high) rest on a 'pillar decorated with volutes' (height 3.2 m), square and fluted, with above and below, on each face, a double spiral the centre of which is decorated with a rosette. The third element is bell-shaped and also measures 3.2 m in height.

191
Column base of the north portico
after restoration

192
Pieces of column of the west portico
Already identified by Loftus

193
**Rosette decorating a volute
on the upright part of the column**

194
Bulls head from a capital
Susa Museum

195
Column base of the central hall

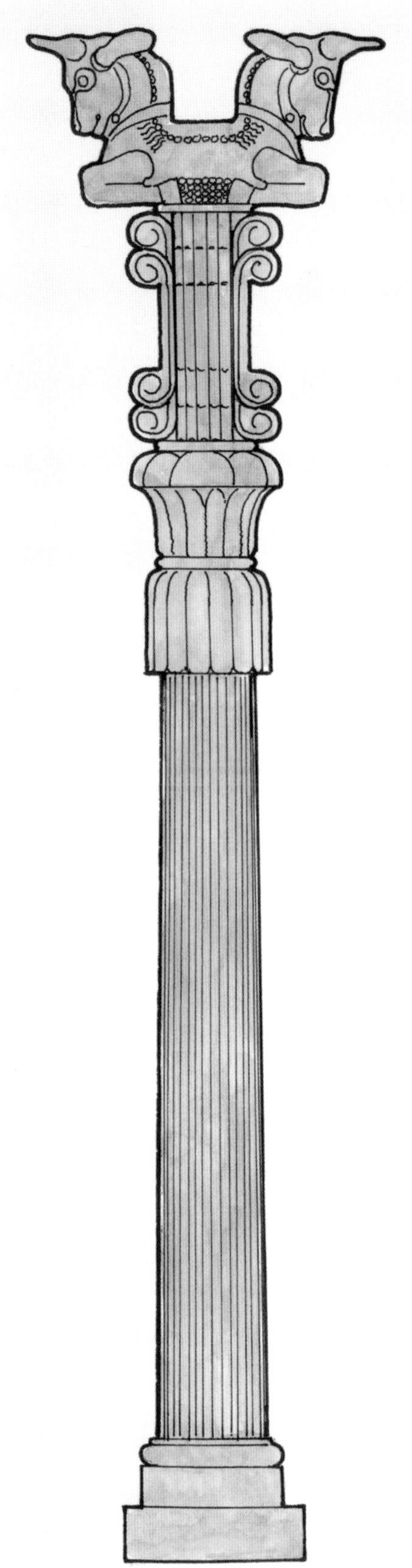

196
Column of the Susa Apadana
drawing by MECQUENEM, 1947

Stoneworking

Jean Perrot

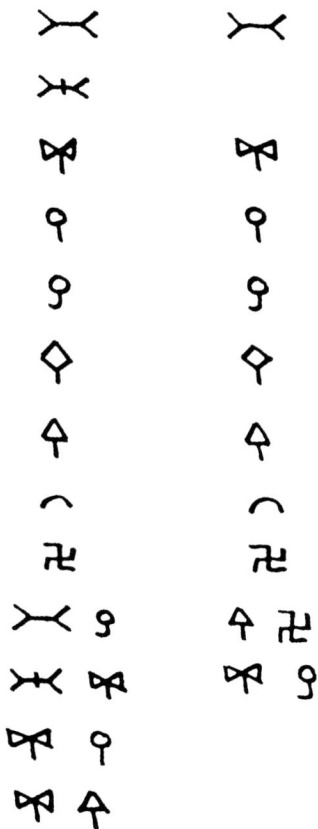

Comparison of stonemasons marks from Susa (left) **and Persepolis** (right)
NYLANDER, 1975: pl. XXXIV

The stone columns which were made here were brought from a village named Hapiratush, in Elam.
DSf § 12

On the borders of the Mesopotamian plain, Susiana is, like Babylonia, a land of earth and water. The only stone to be found is imported. At Susa, the quarries from which the stone was taken have not been found; they are at least 50 km to the east. The rock used is light grey in colour, and fragile – it cracks and splits – but it can be polished to a certain degree. It was extracted as large cylinders, which was practical for the carving of the various elements of the columns; these were rolled (the traces are still there), but were also no doubt transported on the rivers Kerkha and Dez to Susa. Judging by the frequency of flakes on the ground at Susa, the carving was done on site with pick and chisel. Cracks in the stone were fixed with metal staples that were of two different types: one with a large head and dovetail, the others with a slim head. The first and older one was of Greek origin, and was generally used at a Pasargadae; the other replaced it progressively; we find both types next to each other at Susa on the same column base, the second possibly serving to reinforce the first during the restoration by Artaxerxes. The staples and the defects of the stone disappear under a layer of yellowish paint, of which traces still remain.

The stone-cutters who carved this stone were Ionians and from Sardis.
DSf § 12

They used their usual tools, the pick and the chisel and, for the first time, it seems, toothed chisels to trim the blocks. This instrument, which first appeared in Greece towards the middle of the sixth century BC, does not seem to have

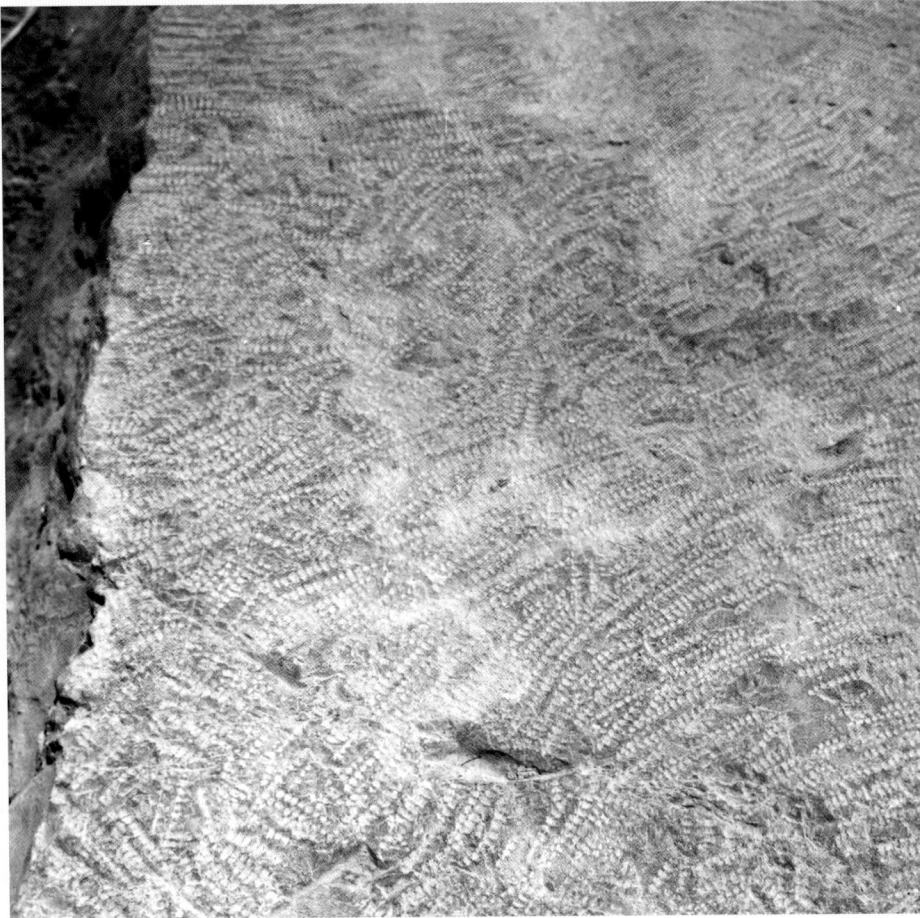

198
Claw-toothed chisel marks on a hinge socket stone in the King's Apartment

been used at Pasargadae under Cyrus. It was, without doubt, used at Susa right from the beginning, if one looks at the support stones for the door sockets in the doorways of the antechamber to the Royal Apartment, probably carved around 515 BC. We also find traces on the bases of the masts of the East Court, and naturally at the Apadana, where the works must have extended over two decades (they were scarcely finished in 500/499 BC, date of the first confirmed sojourn by the King according to the Persepolis Tablets; it mentions the departure for Susa of 400 stonemasons at this date).[1]

In the Hypostyle Hall, each of the 45 stone supports still *in situ* (of the original 72) carries masons' marks on all four sides, carved with a pick. Nine individual signs,[1] or paired signs, can be interpreted as the 'signature' of individuals or workshops. These signs, some of which are known in Ionia, can also be found at Persepolis where several hundred have been counted, which could mean that the stone carvers having worked at Susa, also worked at Persepolis.

A CHANGE OF PROGRAMME

Some of the support stones of the Central Hall of the Apadana at Susa are round, but most of them are square. Their upper surface has been smoothed to receive the column base. Some of the preliminary work, however, is circular as though the stone supports had been destined to receive a round base, like those of the porticoes. Therefore it seems that there was a change of programme during the works; as though at a certain moment the overseers had decided to place columns in the Central Hall on square bases rather than the round bases originally envisaged. This event could also have taken place around 515/514 BC, at the time when it has been suggested that Darius may have been at Susa and decisions were made regarding the appropriate iconography. In any case, this change in the programme could not

199

Selection of column plinths from the Hypostyle Hall, showing the treatment of their surfaces and the marks on their sides

be attributed to Artaxerxes, whose intervention at the Apadana hardly touched anything other than the roofing structure. The building of the Hypostyle Hall at Susa could have taken two decades: the first two of Darius' reign – namely, the last two of the sixth century BC. The Apadana of Susa represented an experience from which the Persepolis Apadana would have gained, commissioned no doubt at the same time, but whose realisation was delayed by the preliminary works to the platform, laboriously carved from the rock.

1. C. Nylander recorded these signs and listed them (see figs 197 and 199) during a visit to Susa in 1973. We are most grateful to him for his help on that occasion and for his remarks concerning the preparation of the columns' stone foundations (NYLANDER, 1975: pl. XXXIV; see also C. NYLANDER, 1966, 1975, 1991).

The Residence

The checks that we were able to make in the sector with the red-coated plaster floors (which correspond to the private quarters of the Residence) led to significant changes in the old plans, most notably in the area of the Royal Apartments and the immediate surroundings. The present state of the area in the north-western sector, to the north of corridor R1, did not, however, permit anything other than a superficial re-examination of the area and the remains designated D, E, F and G on the Mecquenem and Pillet plans.[40] There were some important modifications to the original plans here. In the south-western quarter of the Residence, especially to the south of corridor R4, where the ancient remains were no more than a few patches of floor tiles or plaster floor,[41] our research allowed us to produce a reasonable restoration of the plans of the 'stores' and, to the south of corridor R4, an alignment of apartments, to whose layout we will return.

To the west, Mecquenem had seen in Court A, a 'very large hall' (28 x 20 m). Impressed no doubt by the fact that, under the grey plaster that covered its surface, there appeared fragments of a red surface similar to that which he normally found in the rooms and corridors of the Residence, the link seemed obvious. Pillet described this space as a courtyard (the 'columned parvis') on the basis of the two square bases supporting, in the south-west corner, a canopy which Mecquenem called a 'vestibule' or 'porch', measuring 6 x 4 m and tiled with 33 cm tiles. This tiling carried on to the south and east sides of the court, over an area of 1.85 m to the south and 2.37 m to the east.

Of the 'East Court' (C3) and the buildings that surrounded it, there were only fragmentary remains visible. This area had suffered from excavation works carried out in the past by Mecquenem in the Elamite layers just below and from the

Sections of the plan of the Residence

1 The East Court (C3) and the north-eastern quarter
2 The sector to the south of the East Court
3 The north-western quarter of the Residence and the small West Court (A)
4 The Central Court (C2) and its surroundings
5 The Royal Apartment and its surroundings

16.25 1146

1155

1068

1145

18.30 1148

17.45

1141 948

949

1152 1144

TÉPÉ ÉLAM.
13.00

1004

18.25 1135

1137 1070 1138

17.45

1077 1142 1153 1005

1143

1149 1136
puits 1150
SOL VIERGE
10.25

1133

1126
18.00

1129 SOL VIERGE
11.25

1113 1114

18.25 1119 1134 1154

1123 1122 1139

17.65 1128 1115 17.65

12.75

18.25 1127 1131

1124 17.15

17.55 1121 16.75

1132

SOL BÉTON 18.00

0	10	20 M

1130

1125

12.25 15.00

201

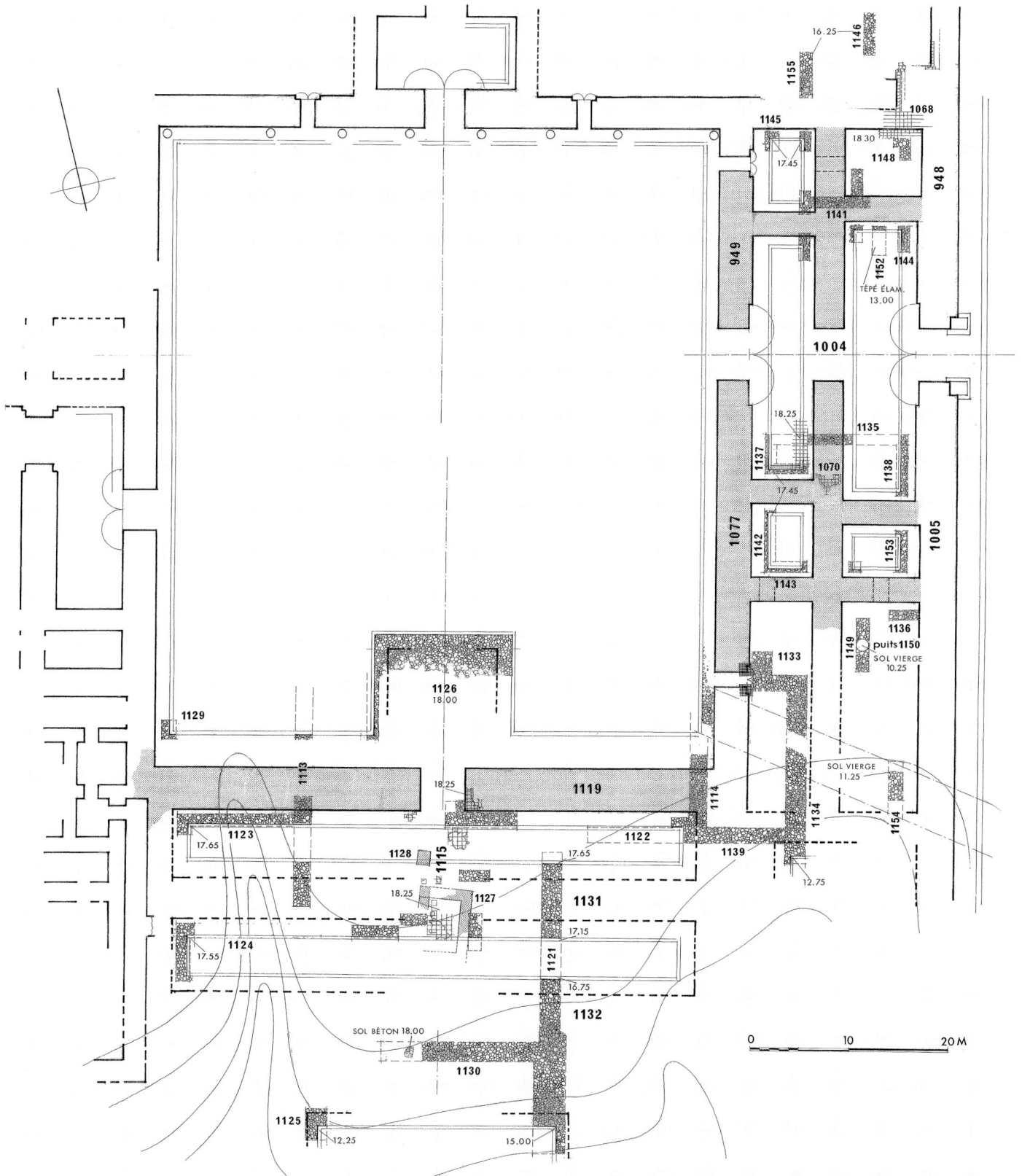

The Residence
The East Court, its southern sector,
and the north-eastern quarter
plan by Daniel Ladiray

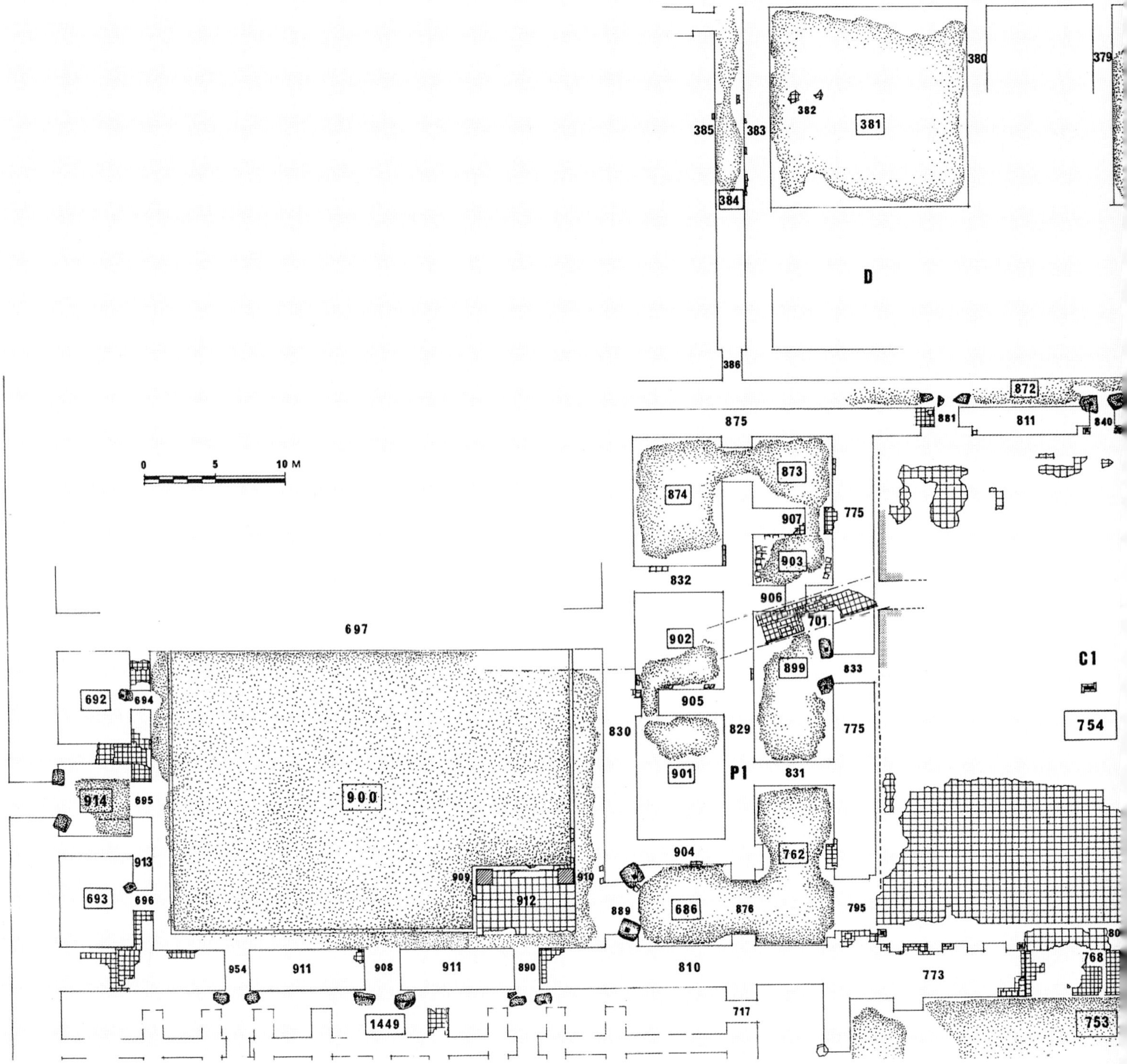

380

379

385   383   382   381

384

D

386

872

881   811   840

875

873

874   907   775

903

832

906

701

902   899   833

C1

905   833

830   829   775   754

901

P1   831

904   762

686   876   795   80

909   910

912   889   768

954   911   908   911   890   810   773   753

717

1449

0   5   10 M

697

692   694

914   695

913

693   696

900

202

The Residence
The north-western area with the small West Court (A) (left)
and the Central Court (C2) and its surroundings (right)
plan by Daniel Ladiray

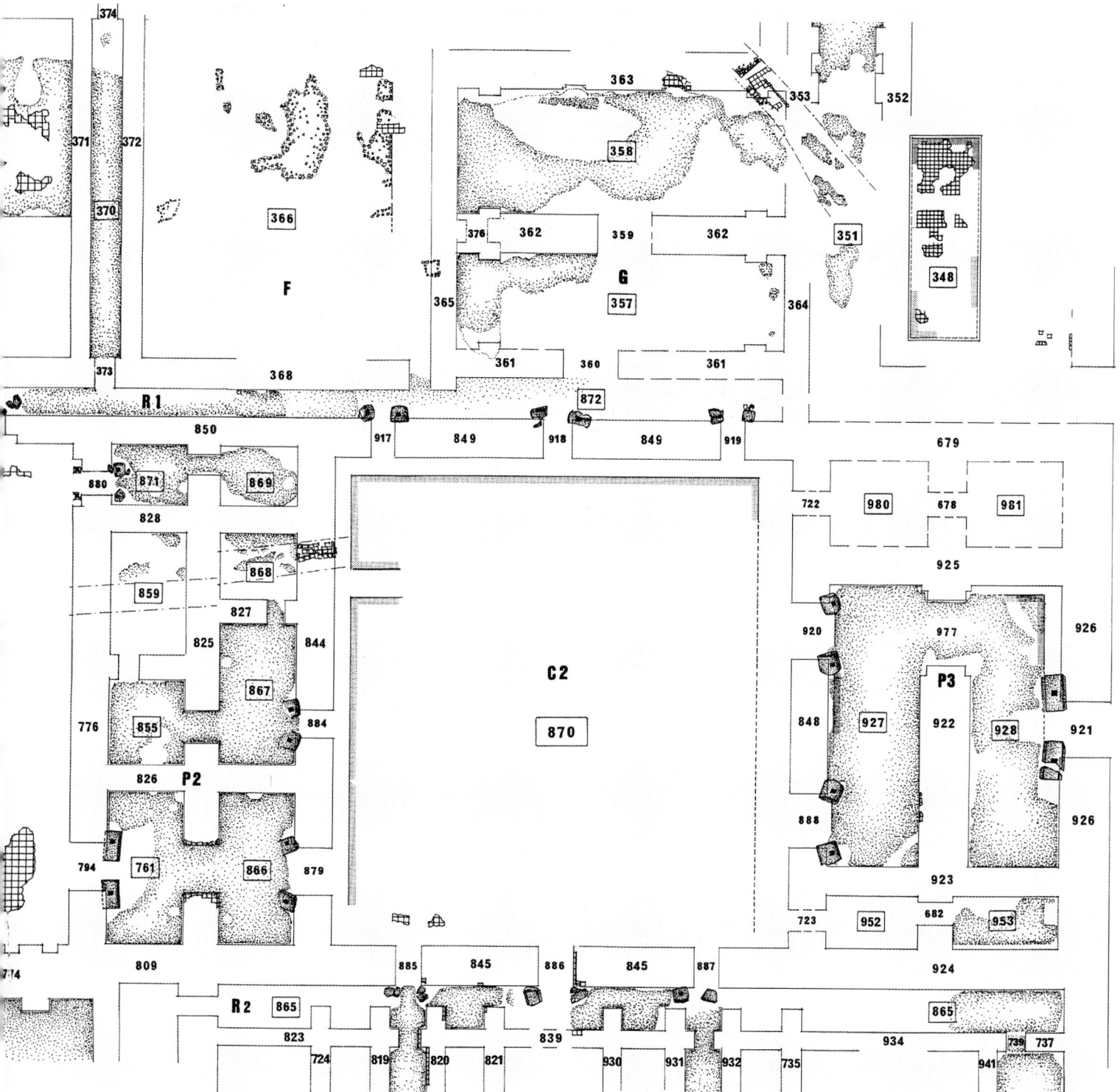

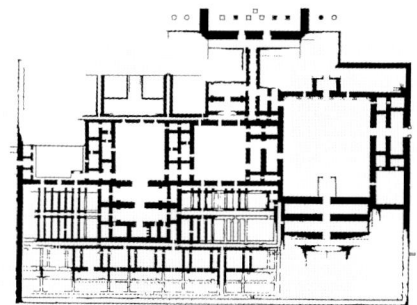

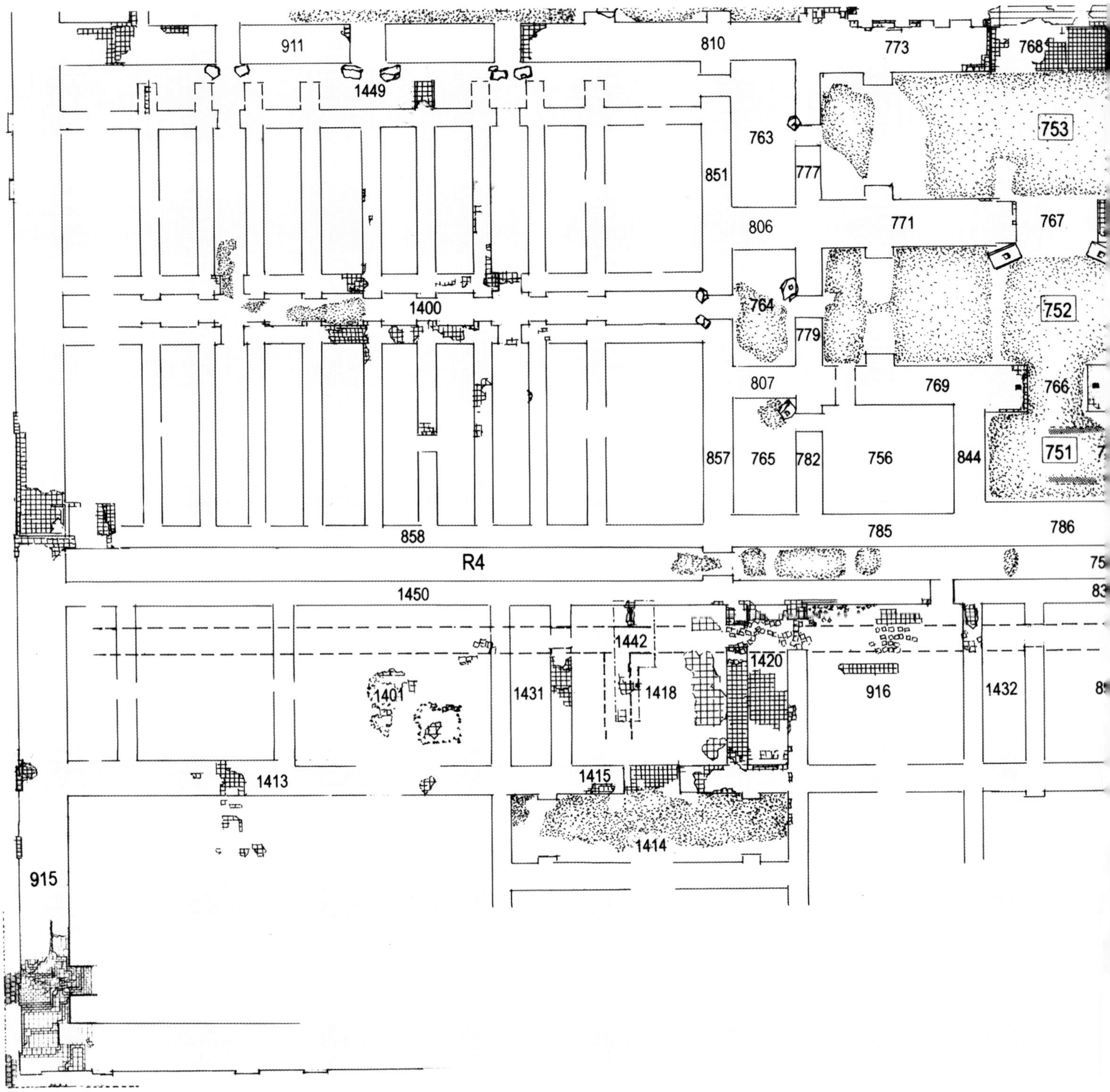

911 810 773 768

1449 753

763

851 777

806 771 767

764 752

779

807 769 766

857 765 782 756 844 751

785 786

858 75

R4

1450 83

1442

1420

1401 1431 1418 916 1432 8

1413 1415

1414

915

203

The Residence
The Royal Apartment (751–753) and its dependencies.
To the south, accessible by corridor R4, the 'women's quarters'.
To the east, the 'great chancellery'. To the west the 'small chancellery'.
plan by Daniel Ladiray

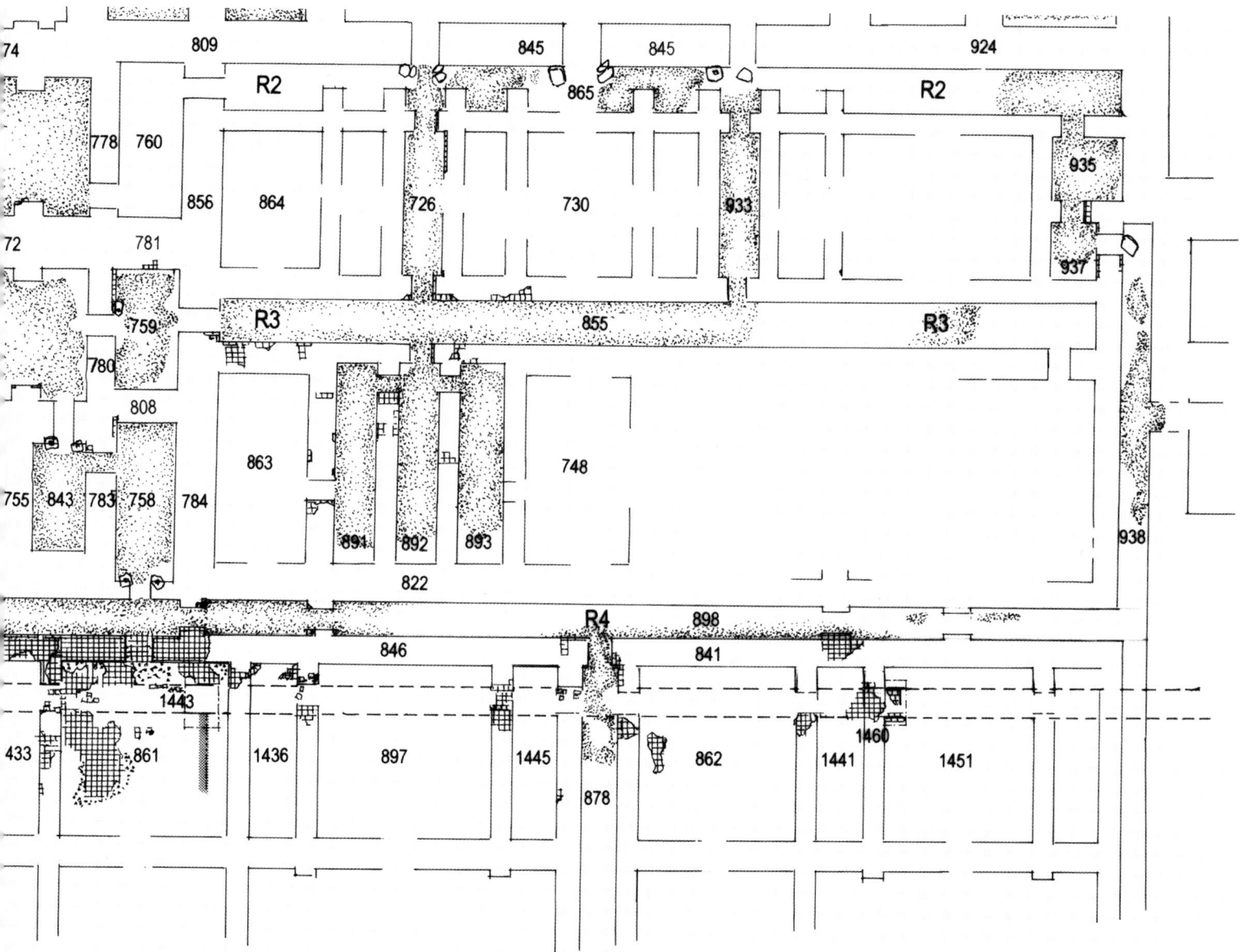

0   5   10   20 M

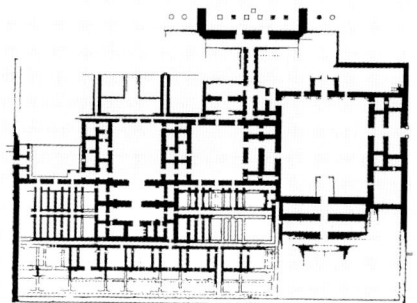

204

The Apadana tell

1 The Hypostyle Hall
2 The Residence
3 The Darius Gate
4 The Propyaeum
5 The Ghirshman trench

205
The 'royal passage' from the East Court to the Apadana
In the foreground: collapse of the plaster floor into the north drain

opening of a large and deep trench in the south-west corner of the court, for the evacuation of the spoil coming from the excavation of its substratum.

The geophysical survey led by A. Hesse and the excavation of the remains of the foundations of the buildings surrounding this court allowed the verification of its dimensions: 64.5 m from north to south and 56 m from east to west.[42] In the north-east corner of the courtyard, the excavation of Reference mound т, left unexcavated by Mecquenem,[43] confirmed that there had been important repair works in this area after the Achaemenid period.

The 'pincer doorways' (portes à tenaille)

There are four 'pincer doorways' in the Residence. They were of similar layout, becoming smaller in size from the first entrance; they could be closed with double doors. The chambers of the first door (948–949) covered 200 and 150 m² respectively; two doors and a central passage were 5.5 m wide; the entrance was probably flanked by ornamental sculptures of which, as we have seen, the supporting stones remain. One could walk from the East Court (c3) to the Central Court (c2) – that is to say from the semi-public sector to the private area, characterised by the red plaster floors – via a second door (927–928) of which the middle passage (977) was staggered so as to hide the view of the interior from the exterior. This passage, whose width was 4.5 m, had a double frame. The first chamber of the second door was 100 m², the second was 135 m²; the exit onto the Central Court had two distinct doorways (888–920), of equal importance. The size of the doorways diminished still further in the passage from the Central Court (c2) to the Honour Court (c1), in the south-west corner of c2. The two chambers of this third door (761–866) measured no more than 60 m² each. The width of the doors was 3.5 m. Between the Honour Court and the small West Court (a) there was a fourth door whose chambers measured 60 and 30 m², and the doorway was 3.5 m wide.

206
The Residence
Doors, corridors, guarded passageways
and guard rooms

The passageways

Independently of the main east–west axis, punctuated by the 'pincer' doorways from the entrance to the Residence to the Royal Apartments, passageways allowed for movement within the confines of the private areas. The two corridors R1 and R4 of the Mecquenem plan serviced the apartments to the north and south of the block that constituted the Royal Apartments and their ancillary rooms. The width of these corridors was around 2 m, with storerooms that acted as buttressing for the outer walls. Of particular interest was the north–south gallery, 4 m wide and some 40 m long. This long passageway linked corridor R1 with the antechamber of the Hypostyle Hall. All the corridors had red plaster flooring.

Guardrooms and guarded passageways

In each courtyard, 'guard posts' consisting of two rooms allowed for the discrete observation of movements: on the northern side, towards the Princely Apartments (980–981), and on the southern side, towards the 'stores' (952–953). The positions of these posts and their fields of view were such that no movement would go unobserved by the guards' vigilance.[44]

'Guard posts' and 'guarded passageways' were identified on corridor R4: one (784–783) between the King's Apartments and this corridor, the other (935–937) to the eastern extremity of the same corridor, which continues north towards the 'gallery' 865 giving access to the 'stores' and the Central Court (C2).

The apartments

Apart from that of the King, we can distinguish two types of apartment: on the one hand, apartments that could be called functional, on the other hand, vast and complex apartments reserved no doubt for members of the royal family; they often had a ceremonial room.

The functional apartments

An apartment of three or four rooms, without a specific layout, gave onto each of the four courts. We could see its occupant as exercising a specific function in relation to the activities of this particular structure. In Court C3, the apartment occupied the south-eastern corner; in Court C2 (855–859, 867–868), the central

207
The Residence
Official apartments (red),
princely (white), royal (blue)

part of the P2 building complex; in Court C1, rooms 873–874, 899–903. In the small courtyard A, the apartment only had two rooms (901–902) of building complex P1.

The 'Princely Apartments'

The apartments that we have classified as 'princely' are completely different: they were organised around courtyards in the north-western quarter of the Residence where their remains, as we have said, were almost indiscernible (D, E, F, G).[45] Group G had two large ceremonial rooms 23 m long. These apartments were accessible via corridor R4 which opened on to the north-western corner of Court C3. D and E had square courtyards (378 and 381); of these there remain only a few walls and tiles on red-coated floors. The large baked brick tiles were of unusual size (48 cm in E; 49 cm in D) in this sector, possibly in line with the system of measurement recognised by Hesse for the Artaxerxes period. Court D measured 14.1 x 13.8 m. Mecquenem saw a Hypostyle Hall in F, which the presence of a few fragments of a small column base (43 cm high) did not suffice to establish.

To the south of corridor R4, five apartments repeated the same floor plan; they each covered about 800 m² and had two courts: the first court, about 20 m², gave onto two rooms of the same size to the south; the second, about 150 m², was flanked, to the south, by two ceremonial rooms which copied the architectural layout of the Royal Apartments on a smaller scale.

The 'ceremonial rooms'

The most complex layout is that of the Royal Apartments with its three rooms which we called: 'vestibule', 'antechamber' and 'King's chamber' (753, 752 and 751). These rooms and their ancillary rooms formed an entity whose main part was made up of two, long, adjoining halls, open in the middle of their long sides, and flanked at their extremities by small transverse rooms. This design allowed a large space to be covered when the only known method of roofing was the vault. Ghirshman and Gasche observed the use of this technique at Susa from the middle of the second millennium BC. It was characterised by the presence of pilasters towards the extremities of each of the long halls, which led archaeologists to refer to them as *salles à quatre saillants*.[46]

208

**Detailed plan of the preserved area
of the women's quarters**

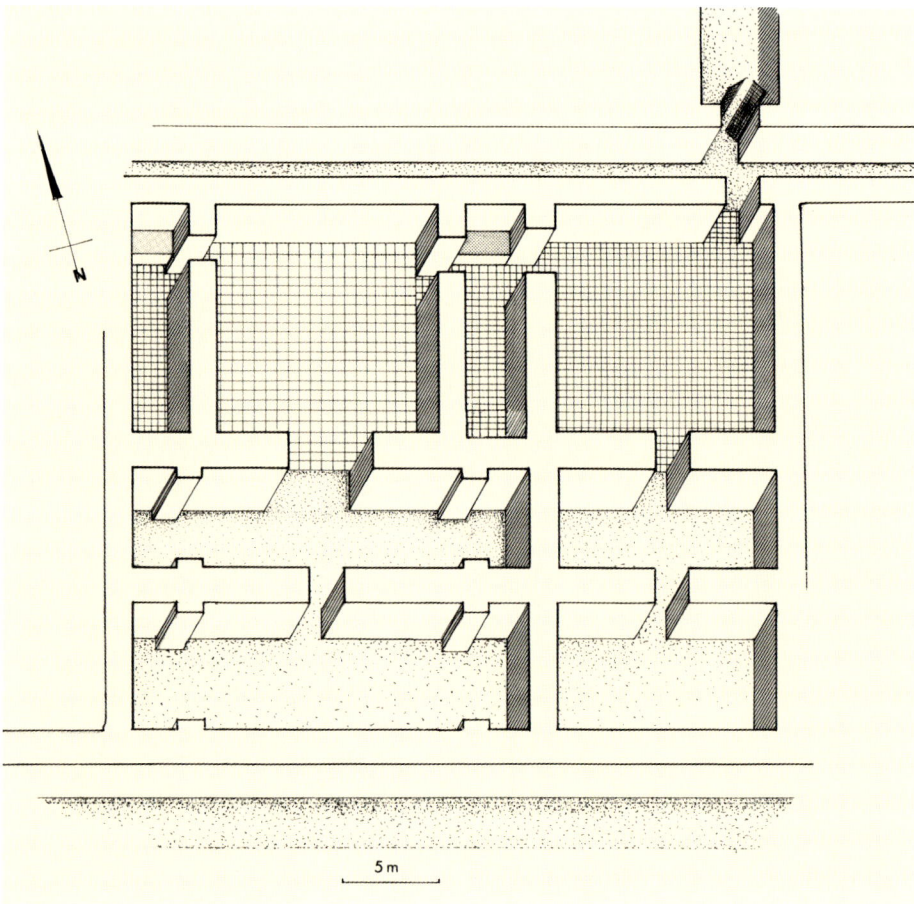

209

Axonometric view of the women's quarters

The Residence
The 'chancellery': the western block, linked to the Acropolis, could have been reserved for regional affairs

The 'stores' or premises of the 'chancellery'

To the east and west of the King's Apartments were two complexes: the surface area of the complex to the west was equal to that of the Royal Apartments (around 2,000 m²), while that to the east was larger at 2,500 m². The internal organisation of the two blocks was similar but with a few differences. Schematically, each presented a cluster of rooms around north–south and east–west axes, made up of one long room and a small court; in each block, eight units were laid out in two rows; the northern row was separated from the southern row by a transverse corridor (855, 1400). In each block, the southern units were slightly longer than those of the northern row (13 m versus 9.5 m in the eastern block; 13.5 m versus 11 m in the western block). The walls were not very thick (four bricks = 1.3 m), and the floor of these chambers and corridors was red plaster, like that in all the rooms and passageways of the private area.

These blocks could be isolated by closing their doors. Access to the eastern block was gained from the Central Court (c2), access to the western block from the 'small court' (A); in both cases via three doors, the central door being the widest (2.4 m). However, the narrow lateral doors (1.2 m) had the advantage of being in the axis of the internal north–south corridors, whilst the central doorway only led on to the (northern) transverse gallery. This gallery opened into the vestibule (753) of the King's Apartments: in the east via chamber 762, and in the west via chamber 763. As to the middle corridor, it provided communication with the antechamber (752) of the King's Apartments: to the east via room 759, to the west through room 764. We will come back to the possible function of this complex which J. Perrot interpreted as being the location of the chancellery.

1. This impression has been reinforced, for instance, in the northern part of the Hypostyle Hall, by major displacement of the foundation gravel of the corner towers due to post-Achaemenid excavation.

2. It seems that there was no attempt here to reach virgin soil. The latter is a little lower, as shown by Ghirshman's trench slightly to the east.

3. A century later, the Hypostyle Hall and related buildings of the Shaur Palace of Artaxerxes II (R. Boucharlat and A. Hesse, this volume, ch. XII), rest on a layer of gravel some 2 m thick.

4. PERROT and LADIRAY, 1972.

5. It is supposedly here that the 'lion frieze' was found, having in its fall apparently smashed through the paving. N. Chevalier, this volume, ch. XIII: 82–83.

6. This little channel ran into the main drain, thus leading to the latter's discovery; it then continued west to the river.

7. The discovery of the bottom of this channel was revealed by the 1968 collapse at 2.75 m below the surface. We had not then recognized it for what it was. It consisted of six courses of baked brick, bonded with bitumen, over a width of 2.2 m and preserved for a distance of over 10 m.

8. MECQUENEM, 1947: 30–31.

9. Mecquenem mentions that around these foundations 'below a level of gravel some 50 cm thick, we came across gravel mixed with fragments of brick; and so we recovered parts of panels depicting a winged bull. It seems, therefore, that this backfill took place after a change in the original plan; the glazed bricks had evidently suffered from long exposure to the elements'. This leads one to suggest that the masts may have been replaced or removed under Artaxerxes II, during the restoration of the Hypostyle Hall and the Residence.

10. DIEULAFOY, 1893: 238, fig. 129 below, note 40.

11. These stone door sockets were 'approximately square, measuring some 15 cm each side and 8 cm thick. In the upper surface there was a central round hollow about 6 cm in diameter and 16 mm deep; the weight is about 25 kg' (MECQUENEM , 1947: 30). A door socket from the gate in the NE corner of the East Court [c3] is in the Louvre in Paris (R4). We left another *in situ* in the doorway that leads from the King's apartments to the long corridor giving access to the apartments of the royal family. Another has been noted by Rémy Boucharlat in the Shaur Palace.

12. It is possible that there were seated lions (J. Perrot, ch. VII).

13. MECQUENEM, 1947: fig. 13, 1. For the foundation plaque, see above, ch. IV and also ch. IX.

14. J. Perrot, this volume, ch. VII: 243. These stones were photographed *in situ* by M. Pillet (p. 168) and were found displaced, as were those in the entrance to the Residence.

15. N. Daucé, this volume, ch. XI; A. Hesse, this volume, ch. V. One should allow for 100 bricks per cubic meter.

16. See 'Marks and Stamps' in this volume, ch. XII.

17. A string-line dipped in water can be used instead of a spirit-level if it is stretched taut until the water drops no longer move along it. This practice is still used nowadays in Iran.

18. MECQUENEM, 1947: 10 and Pillet, in N. Chevalier, this volume, ch. III.

19. R. Boucharlat, this volume, ch. XII.

20. See 'The wall of Artaxerxes II', 205.

21. It was noted in the Palace of Nebuchadnezzar at Babylon by R. Koldewey (KOLDEWEY, 1914).

22. MECQUENEM, 1947: 35, fig. 15.

23. Mequenem noted a small square base (0.75 m) surrounded by paving, in the south-west sector of the Residence, but in an uncertain stratigraphic context. It may be post-Achaemenid.

24. This layout is known in the East from the beginning of the first millennium BC.

25. It was not possible to draw a stratigraphic section due to lack of time. This would have provided a definite answer, but the existence of a ramp in the axis of the Gate does not support the suggestion of a ditch full of water.

26. PERROT, LADIRAY and VALLAT, 1999.

27. F. Vallat, this volume, ch. IX: xsa; and Perrot, this volume, ch. XIV.

28. STEVE, GASCHE and DE MEYER, 1990: 31–32; STEVE, VALLAT and GASCHE, 2002: col. 396 and 486.

29. PERROT and LADIRAY, 1974.

30. This chapter: 142.

31. The plan and layout of these foundations suggest the figures of winged, human-headed bulls, as in the Gate of Xerxes at Persepolis.

32. F. Vallat, this volume, ch. IX: xsd.

33. See below.

34. J. Yoyotte, this volume, ch. VIII.

35. MECQUENEM, 1947; Perrot, ch. VII, 234.

36. MECQUENEM, 1947.

37. This Hall was identified by Loftus in 1852 and has been described many times. Here it has only been subjected to checks relating to the position of the doorways and the nature of the foundations.

38. The excavation of the door-sockets has produced some bronze nails which may have been used for fixing bronze plaques to the leaves of the doors. One of these plaques was found and described by Jane Dieulafoy on the Ville Royale tell (DIEULAFOY, J. 1888: 228).

39. This feature is frequently paralleled in contemporary palatial buildings at Persepolis and Babylon.

40. See J. Perrot, this volume, ch. VII.

41. Mecquenem had already had doubts concerning his theory of a southern entrance to the Residence after the discovery of these remains and, even more so, after the exploration, in 1946, of the large baked-brick wall which supports the south-west corner of the platform. He was aware that 'the gravel platform must extend some 35 m south of passageway R4', but for all that, he did not modify his overall plan with the main entrance to the south.

42. Mecquenem's measurements are shorter. As his plan indicates, they were taken between the small walls of unbaked brick that enclosed the gravel foundations.

43. MECQUENEM, 1947: 32, 50. On this side we have had to raise a high and long wall of bricks to contain the earth.

44. In C1, in the north-east corner (871–872); in C3, in the north-east corner (1502).

45. Pillet produced different reconstructions (N. Chevalier, ch. III); Mecquenem (MECQUENEM 1947: pl. I and II) and Ghirshman (GHIRSHMAN 1968b).

46. H. Gasche, this volume, ch. XIII.

The foundation wall of Artaxerxes II

Jean Perrot

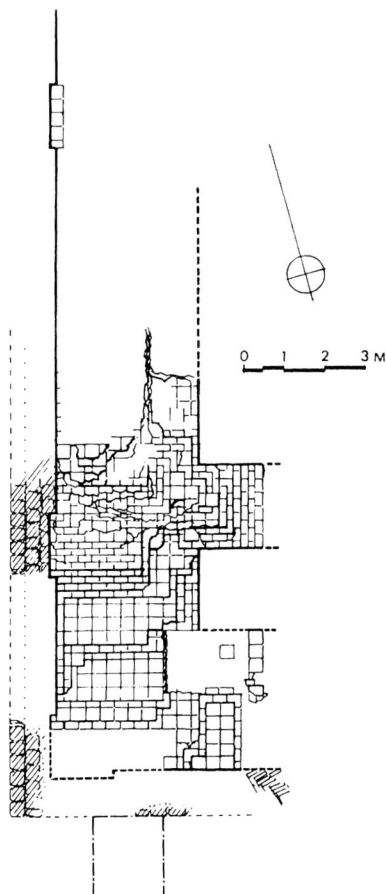

Plan of the south-western corner of the foundation wall of the Residence

On the western edge of the Apadana tell a large, baked-brick wall, bonded with bitumen, has for a long time intrigued excavators. It was recognised in 1912–1913 by Maurice Pillet who left some interesting photographs;[1] and described by Roland de Mecquenem, who in 1946 excavated towards the south.[2] The wall was the object of a detailed plan by Hermann Gasche in 1966. From the evidence, it is a re-foundation of the western wall of the Residence. The inside face is linked to the gravel by extensions at mid-height; it is also tied to the foundations of the internal walls of the Residence. On the outer face of the wall, there are twin pilasters every 9 m (3.5 m apart, these pilasters are five bricks wide and protrude by one half-brick); these projections decorated the external wall of the Residence; underground, the pilasters are masked by a mud-brick wall about 1 m thick, itself buried into the solid mass of a retaining wall of the terrace of the Apadana. At its top, the retaining wall is still 10 m wide as it had to accommodate the parapet walk. It is clear that the building of the large, baked-brick wall is part of a general rebuilding project of the western edge of the terrace. It seems that the terrace must have eroded over several metres and with it the western wall of the Residence. That event could have taken place in the second half of the fifth century BC, at the same time perhaps, as the fire that temporarily put Darius' Apadana out of action.

Under the large, baked-brick wall, Mecquenem indicated the presence of 'mud bricks with reliefs of archers' and of 'tiles stamped on their surface with the name of Darius' (Mecquenem, 1947: 17–19; these tiles are visible in the photograph by M. Pillet and indicated as such). In 1946, he discovered 'in the block of masonry' which ran along the wall towards the south, 'tiles stamped with the motif of the lion passant'. This motif is not known in Darius' building works in any other part of the Apadana tell, but Rémy Boucharlat and Albert Hesse found it frequently in the 1970s whilst excavating and studying the Shaur Palace. It is therefore

Malefaçons du mur

*Banquette en briques estampillées (ornes)
au nom de Darius 1er*

Pilastre-contrefort

(14)

Mur D'enceinte de l'Ouest Briques cuites d'un pied

reasonable to surmise that the building of the large, baked-brick wall, with its stamped tiles, was the work of Artaxerxes II; his intervention on the Apadana tell is established by the inscription carved onto the bases of the Hypostyle Hall and also by the presence of two column bases which supported the awning in the 'Small West Court' (Mecquenem's Court A); their measurements are identical to those of the bases of the columns of the Shaur Palace.

The importance of these works poses questions as to whether the residential part of the palace was habitable over several decades between the reigns of Artaxerxes I and Artaxerxes II; this situation reinforces the impression of emptiness which Achaemenid Susa gives in the last third of the fifth century BC.

212
Photograph taken by Maurice Pillet in 1913 showing the bricks stamped with the name of Darius under the baked brick wall of Artaxerxes II
former Maurice Pillet collection.
© Musée du Louvre/Christian Larrieu

213
The wall of Artaxerxes II
Preserved to a height of more than 2 m
despite a degradation of the upper courses
due to the pilfering of materials, this wall was
found nearly 3 m under the floor level of the
palace (18.25) at level 14.48; it still reaches
level XVII.34. Its width varies between 3.6 m
(10 bricks) and 2.75 m towards the middle

1. Fig. 224.
2. MECQUENEM, R. 1917: 11–12.

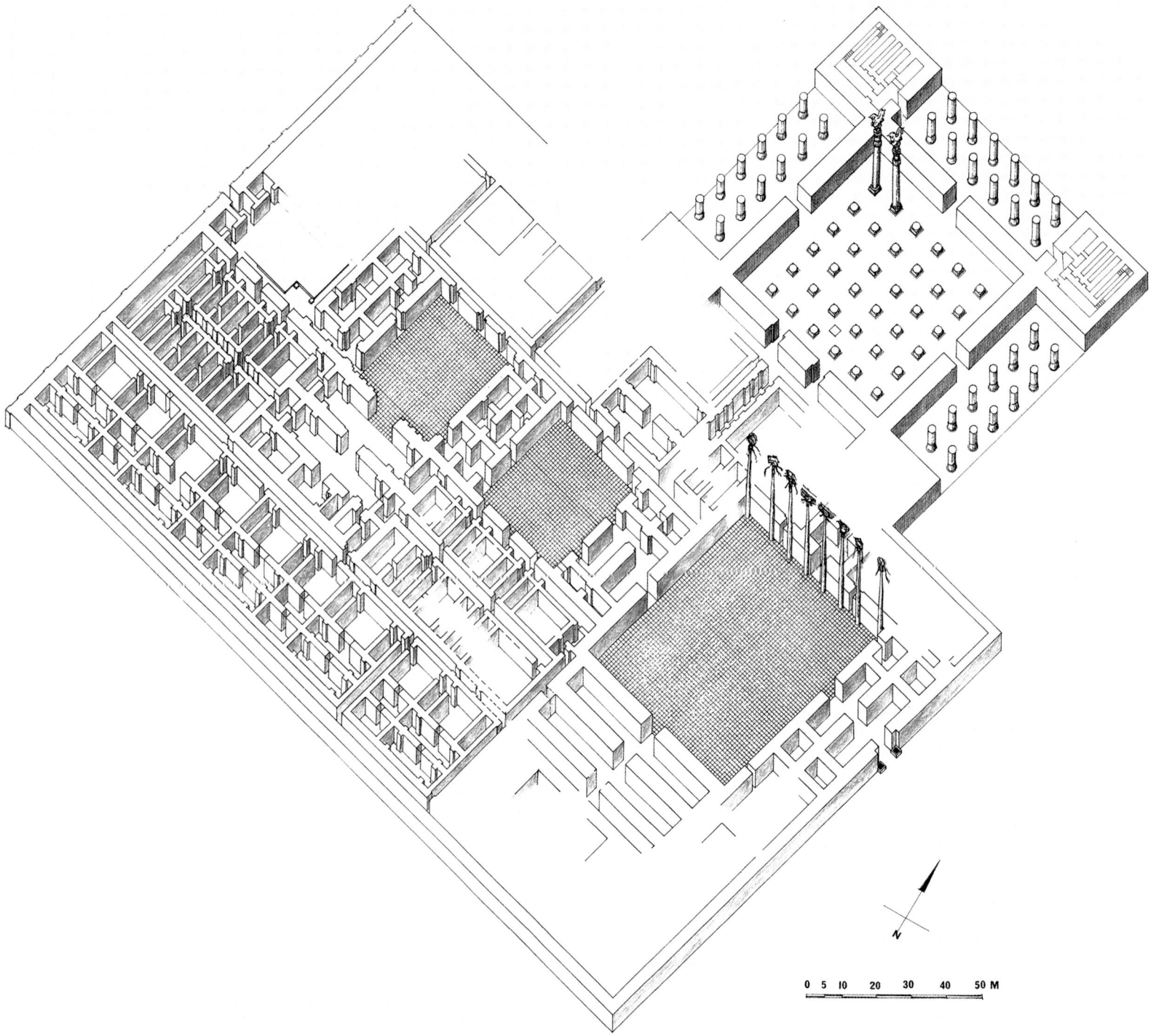

214
Susa Palace
Axonometric view of the Residence and the audience hall
drawing by Anne Ladiray

7 Restoration, Reconstruction

Jean Perrot

To excavate the remains of a monument and draw up the plans is one thing; it is another to reconstruct the elevations and the forms beyond a simple axonometric projection. There are many questions regarding dimensions, methods of roofing, the general aspect, the ornamentation. The plan can suggest ratios of proportion; other ratios can also exist between ground and facade, between built structures and decorative detail. In a more general way, all reconstruction must respect the classical rules of stability, commodity and harmony. We can also have recourse to existing buildings, whilst taking into account their surroundings and their purpose.

VAULTS OR CEILINGS?

The first issues, when looking at a plan of the Residence with a view to reconstruction, are those regarding the height of the walls and the roofing of the large halls: are they vaults or ceilings? The question does not concern the roofing over of the corridors and the smaller rooms where the vault is the simplest and the most economic solution, but the important rooms, such as the vestibule and the antechamber of the King's Apartments. The plan here can help us with some kind of answer as to the nature, the form and the spacing of the supports (walls or columns). It was noted, for example, that the beams of the Apadana (square, with sides of 75 cm) have a span of at least 8 m and perhaps 20 m. The width of the great halls of the Royal Apartments is more than 9 m; were the Babylonian masons capable of vaulting a span of almost 10 m with mud brick? According to Diodorus of Sicily and Strabo, the stone barrel vault with voussoirs was invented in around 470 BC by Democritus of Abdera; before this date, stone architecture would only have known the corbelled vault (the best example being in Egypt 2,000 years earlier, that of the pyramids). The first stone arcades in Greece go

215
The baked brick wall footings allowed for the restoration of the niches and pilasters of the wall, as here, at the entrance to the King's Apartment

back no further than the fifth century BC; the pointed barrel vault does not appear there before the third century BC. It is not the same for vaults made of mud brick. Strabo recognises that this form of roofing was invented in Mesopotamia where 'due to a lack of wood' it became the norm. The Royal Tombs of Ur in the third millennium BC were described as vaulted; but were these true vaults? From the thirteenth century BC, the ziggurat of Tchoga Zambil, in Susiana, shows keyed vaults in mud brick, although admittedly the spans were narrow.

A particular technique put into practice to roof over the funerary crypts with mud brick was present at Susa in the second millennium BC.[1] It consisted of spacing out the roof with vertical sections, the tiles of the first section resting obliquely on the end wall of the room which served as a form of centring; the weight and the forces exerted on the wall were relatively feeble. The following sections lent against the first, the barrel progressing slowly in this way from the end. In the case of a long room, one could conceive that, when built from the two extremities, the 'rollers' met towards the middle of the room where their point of contact allowed for a skylight. No example of vaulted covering of great importance before the sixth century has been observed and recorded in Mesopotamian archaeology, but according to Victor Place, the excavator of the eighth-century BC palace of Sargon at Khorsabad, halls 32 m long and 8 m wide must have been vaulted in mud brick.[2]

216
Modern construction of a vault with inclined segments
BESENVAL, 1984: fig. XXX

217
above

**Roofing over of the extremities
of an Elamite long room**
According to Hermann Gashe, site A,
Ville Royale, second millennium BC

below

**Sketch of the method followed in
the large halls of the Residence**

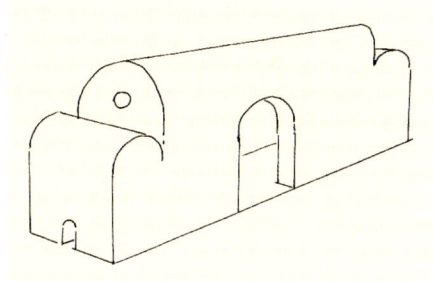

The stability of a vault depended on that of the walls that supported it and the control of the oblique forces. The lateral force could be reduced on a keyed vault by gently heightening the level of the barrel; the weight of the vault could be lightened by reducing its thickness; the use of well-tempered earth mixed with lime could give the mud brick qualities similar to those of baked brick, making it naturally waterproof. In the case of the adjoining long rooms, the lateral forces of the vaults counterbalanced each other and were cancelled out above the middle wall. The forces could be mitigated at the ends by the vaults of the small transverse rooms; as these vaults were narrower and lower than that of the long hall, the top of the end wall was unobstructed and could be opened up to provide light and ventilation.[3] Whether this method was of Mesopotamian or Susan origin, we can only say that it was the logical development of mud-brick building technology.[4] Although this arrangement of long transverse rooms does not necessarily mean that they were vaulted, in the absence of wood they represented the only way to vault a vast space. So much so, that their appearance on a plan can generally be taken as evidence for a vaulted ceiling.

At Susa, the Residence's first excavator, Mecquenem, was in favour of ceilings (it seems that the discovery of a piece of burnt beam on the ground of the antechamber of the Royal Apartments may have influenced his judgement).[5] Ghirshman and Gasche declared themselves in favour of vaults; for the reasons indicated above, this is the position we will take. We must admit that the construction of a vault with a 9.5 m span is quite an achievement, but the Babylonian masons brought to Susa by Darius were no doubt amongst the best. They operated in Susiana in a natural environment that was familiar to them, with a material which, for them, had no secrets. The instructions they may have received regarding the layout of the Residence were not beyond their skills.

EVIDENCE FOR THE RECONSTRUCTION

In the Hypostyle Hall, the columns were around 20 m high; this was therefore also the height of the walls of the Central Hall. These walls were 15 bricks thick at their bases, thus just a little more than 5 m. Based on a rule of three, it should be possible to deduce the height of the walls of the Residence from their thickness, which we know. Another indication could come from the width of the passages and doorways. In stone structures, such as at Pasargadae or Persepolis, the width-to-height ratio of the openings is 2:5 at the very least; a door 3 m wide would be 7.5 m high. We could not apply this ratio to mud-brick constructions. To judge from the preserved Mesopotamian monuments, the ratio is closer to 1:1.5 so that a passage 5 m wide would be 7.5 to 8 m in height. There may be examples of a larger ratio, but from an aesthetic point of view we could not go below 1:1.5. If one adds to this measurement the radius of the vault of the hall to which this door gives access, plus that of the thickness of the vault and the height of the parapet, one gets an average height of around a dozen metres. Let us take the King's Apartments as an example: the entrance to the vestibule measures 9.5 m wide so its height, exceptionally, could be around 15 m. The vault of the vestibule springing above the arch of the entrance, and the width of the vestibule also being 9.5 m, its vault, at its apex could be 4.75 m higher; the terrace above would therefore be around 20 m from the ground. This height, which corresponds to that of the columns of the Hypostyle Hall, is of an order that is appropriate for the king's house. Therefore, above the mass of buildings of a height of 12 to 13 m, would emerge: 1. the Hypostyle Hall, 2. the Royal Apartments and 3. the great halls to the south of the East Court (c3).

The reconstruction of the audience hall poses another problem, that of the relative height of the porticoes to the central hall. 'It is not certain', writes Mecquenem, 'that the outer order was lower than the inner one; a difference, however, would have allowed for lighting the Hypostyle Hall from the top … But neither Xerxes' hypostyle (at Persepolis), nor the columned hall depicted on the royal Achaemenid tombs showed a difference in height of the terraces.'[6] On this last point we notice that the 'palace façades' that ornament the royal tombs are simple porticoes with only one row of columns; we should not therefore rush to conclusions as regards the porticoes of the Hypostyle Hall (we must remember, however, that they depicted only the double-headed part of the Achaemenid column's capital). As far as the lighting of the Hypostyle Hall through its walls is concerned, we must remember that these walls were 5.2 m thick at the base and that even if they produced some results, openings in their upper reaches would resemble tunnels rather than windows: this would have produced some ventilation, but would not have been so good for lighting. With the doors open, the eastern light could have been sufficient to produce the chiaroscuro effect that the majesty of the place required. Openings in the ceiling are also a possibility.

Another observation can be made concerning the relative heights of the central hall and the porticoes that surrounded it. It is linked to the problem of rainwater run-off. The violent spring storms in Susiana are normally accompanied by massive rainfall. Precipitation of 10 cm is often registered. We could not imagine

218
Main door of the north wing of the East Court
reconstruction by Héritage Virtuel

219
The Hypostyle Hall
reconstruction by Héritage Virtuel

220
**Column capitals of the north portico
of the Hypostyle Hall**
sculptor Pascal Coupot;
reconstruction by Héritage Virtuel

221
**Northern façade of the Hypostyle Hall
giving onto the garden and pool**
reconstruction by Héritage Virtuel

the gutters of the central hall spitting tons of water onto the fragile terraced roofs of the porticoes. These terraces were made of a layer of clay mixed with straw (*kāguel*) which it was necessary to renew on a regular basis; this had been the manner of roofing over buildings in Susiana since the fourth millennium BC. The central hall and the porticoes must then have been covered to the same height, with the rainwater flowing towards the edges of the roof whence it was thrown as far as possible from the base of the walls by the gutters. One can imagine these waters channelled towards a pool in the middle of the gardens which occupied several acres of the northern part of the Apadana tell.[7]

As to the question of access to the Hypostyle Hall via ramps or staircases, we have no evidence of a changing level between the ground of the Hypostyle Hall and that of the area that surrounded it. The trenches perpendicular to the northern and eastern porticoes revealed no platform and no retaining wall.[8] The floor of the Hypostyle Hall was the same level as that of the Residence.

STOREYS IN THE CORNER TOWERS OF THE APADANA

These square (25 x 25 m) mud-brick towers had an internal measurement, at ground level, of around 15 x 15 m; the walls were 5 m thick (15 bricks), they were over 20 m high and carried the weight of the portico roofs. One can imagine the internal layout of the ground floor for the southern towers of the Apadana based on the observed model at Persepolis, a model derived from the fort of Nush-i Jan on the Iranian plateau in the seventh century BC.[9]

Taking the north-eastern tower of the Apadana as an example, the staircase could have been built against the southern wall, starting at the south-western corner (near the passages towards the porticoes). It was 12 to 13 m long and possibly 2 m wide (including a low parapet of 30 cm = one brick); there was a 20° slope rising to a height of around 5 m which would be that of the first floor; the landing, 2 x 2 m, encroached on the thickness of the wall which was thereby reduced from 5 to 3 m, a thickness that the wall would maintain with the staircase rising to the second floor (around 10 m) and up to the top. At the second floor a new landing of 2 x 2 m was taken, this time, from the northern wall which, in its turn, lost 2 m thickness with the flight to the third floor. Access to the terrace was from the third floor, and due to the occasional nature of its use, via a ladder, and an exit protected by a hut, most likely in the south-western corner. The thickness of the parapet of the terrace (crenellated or not) was no greater than 1 m (three bricks); the space at the top of the tower could be some 500 m² against the 200 m² for the ground floor. The latter was vaulted and the floor of the first floor was in beaten earth; the second and third floors had wooden floorboards across beams supported by posts (possibly six per floor), one directly above the other, the base resting on a beam supported by the walls which enclosed the ground floor.

On the ground floor, the walls were windowless; but from the first floor onwards, once they were only 3 m thick, one could conceive narrow openings for light and ventilation: on the first floor, in the eastern wall, in the eastern and northern walls on the second and third floors. The load-bearing southern and western walls did not have this layout.

MULTI-STOREY SUSA?

The reconstruction of the Residence brings up the age-old question of a *piano nobile* above what we have called until now the 'stores', on either side of the Royal Apartments. There, where we have identified the chancellery, Pierre Amiet put forward the idea of an additional floor whilst pointing out that 'the privileged location of the "stores" intimately associated with the ceremonial rooms, was strange, even incongruous' and that the real function of these stores could only 'logically' be to 'serve as foundations for Princely Apartments';[10] the absence of a staircase to access them was due, according to him, to 'lacunae in the plans'. There remain, it is true, some gaps in the floor plans of the 'stores', as there are in other areas of the Residence, but at no point amongst these can there be the possibility of establishing the existence of a ramp or stairwell. The building of a ramp would have required a long corridor at an 18° incline (10 m for 3 m), or a central pillar for a stairwell with steps at least 3 m wide (as is the case in the Darius Gate). There are staircases at Susa; we recognised them with no trouble at the Darius Gate. No doubt they also existed inside the corner towers of the Hypostyle Hall, as we have seen above.[11]

The walls of the 'stores' are not very thick (4 bricks = 1.35 m) but they could support a vault, even an additional floor, although not the small courtyards. Even so, a storey here would be aberrant from the point of view of access and traffic flow, as an axonometric projection makes it easy to realise: the passageways were blocked between the high walls of the Royal Apartments to the west and those of the great halls which rose to the south of the East Court (c3). In contrast, the height of the 'stores' (our chancellery), with their thin walls and narrow doorways, could not have been greater than 5 or 6 m. Taking into account the average height of the various structures other than the ceremonial halls (estimated height of around a dozen metres) we could envisage that the rooms and passageways of the chancellery were surmounted by small, intercommunicating, upper chambers, but without access to neighbouring buildings; if we are talking of the chancellery, these rooms could have been accessible from the small courts via wooden staircases or ladders. They could have served as storerooms for the archives, like the casemates at Persepolis, but one would find it hard to see them as a floor of Princely Apartments.

The idea of building additional storeys comes to mind fairly naturally in areas where wood is the main building material: for example in the mountains of the Zagros, of the Taurus, of Assyria or of Mediterranean Syria. This was not the case in lower Mesopotamia where one built with reeds and earth; the houses lie squat around courtyards. It is from this tradition of the lower lands that we have the Residence at Susa, a work of the Babylonians. The only buildings of Darius' Susa capable of carrying upper storeys were those which, like the Apadana, came from

224
The Darius Gate
watercolour sketch by Daniel Ladiray

225
The reconstructed Propylaeum (24 x 24 m)
reconstruction by Héritage Virtuel

the Iranian tradition, or those like the Propylaeum or the Gate that demonstrate this same mountain tradition in their structural form. We can picture the presence of upper rooms in these buildings but, in the case of the Residence, the proposition of living quarters at upper levels seems like an architectural misinterpretation.[12]

THE PROPYLAEUM AND THE ARTISANS' GATE

The reconstruction of the Propylaeum does not only raise the problem of its height. The meeting here of a mountain tradition, in the form of porticoes flanking a Babylonian-style vaulted structure, leaves a question hanging concerning the upper form of the entrance and exit passageways: full arch or Egyptian cornice? As for the Artisans' Gate, the only problem it poses is in relation to its particular situation, isolated at the top of the glacis. Its terraced roof could have covered the whole building or there could have been separate roofs above the small lateral halls; the first solution seems the more likely.

THE DARIUS GATE

The reconstruction of this building of 40 x 28 m poses a problem regarding its façade; this had been eroded, along with its foundations, over several metres below the level of its floor. The position of the entrance door has nonetheless been determined by the regular pattern of the walls of the central hall and even of what foundations survive,[13] which on either side of the entrance must have supported heavy sculptures. The question concerns the presence, on the façade side, of rooms or stairwells replicating those on the Esplanade side. Staircases on the façade side would require projections of at least 2 m on either side of the gateway.

Another question: did the staircase identified on the western side give access to the terrace of the building or to rooms above the lateral halls? As to the height of the structure, an indication is provided by the probable presence of columns;

226
The Residence complex
Audience hall, the Acropolis and the River Shaur in the background
watercolour sketch by Daniel Ladiray

227
The Darius Gate (40 x 28 m)
Two of the four columns of the central hall have disappeared

228
The Darius Gate during restoration

since their square sockets have sides measuring 1.52 m, the diameter of their shafts would be 1.2 m (they were 1.65 m in the audience hall) which could translate, for the Gate, as a height of 12 to 15 m. The column shafts could have been made of wood. The few fragments of fluted shafts found in the sector of the Gate during the excavation seem to have come from the Hypostyle Hall.[14] We found no capitals corresponding to columns of medium size.

THE ORNAMENTATION OF THE STRUCTURES[15]

The edifices were imposing primarily because of their mass; the floor plans show harmonious ratios which were probably reflected in their vertical proportions. The general aspect was certainly austere; the pink ochre of the Susiana soil only reacts to the soft light of sunrise and sunset. The mud brick generated soft shapes, without angles or noticeable reliefs. We should not imagine cornices or large windows in mud-brick structures. As far as it could be reconstructed from the recesses that show the baked brick courses, the architectural ornamentation was limited to simple niches on either side of the vestibule entrance of the King's Apartments and in some doorways where the jambs had moulded frames. The walls of the Darius Gate and of the Propylaeum were the only ones to have stepped recesses: the Gate, inside the central hall; inside and outside the Propylaeum. The foundations of the baked brick western wall of the Residence, restored by Artaxerxes II,[16] displayed signs of pilasters. These, no doubt, ran the length of the wall, but it is not certain whether the motif was repeated on the other external walls of the structure. In the Residence courtyards, the siliceous brick panels make up the main ornamentation against a possibly whitewashed background.[17] The question here mainly concerns the extent of the surfaces covered by the bricks.

There could have been paintings in the interiors (traces were found on the walls of the Shaur hypostyle hall),[18] and probably also tapestries and wall hangings. The floors of the private areas were red – a colour that did not appear in the range of siliceous bricks.

The ornamental brick panels

For technical and aesthetic reasons, it is unlikely that the courtyard walls were completely covered in ornamental bricks. One can consider the problem as one of energy and resources. Each brick, of each panel, required a considerable amount of work: preparation of materials, moulding, colour application, repeated firing, assembly etc.[19] These transformations took time and required a highly qualified workforce; no doubt several workshops worked simultaneously, but there were limits as to their numbers and their production capacity. From a technical point of view, we must take the weight of the baked brick panels into consideration and their bonding to the mud-brick walls. At ground level, these panels rested directly against the courses of the wall, which they protected. The situation was different for the friezes, where they had to be 'hooked' into the wall itself.[20] A good place was above the base of the vault which covered the room; an overload of the wall at this point helped compensate for the oblique pressure of the vault.

The total length of the walls of the four principal courts of the Residence was around 600 m over an average height of 10 to 12 m – thus a surface area of about 6,000 m². To cover the entire surface of the walls would have required 200,000 to 500,000 bricks (30 bricks per m²). When faced with this number, we must remember that the old excavations recovered around 12,000 ornamental bricks.[21] These bricks, of baked or sintered clay, were friable. Many, no doubt, have completely disappeared but we can estimate that one in ten still remain,[22] which leads us to the production of 100,000 bricks, a considerable number all the same. We might reach the same figure, from an aesthetic point of view, by limiting the decoration in each courtyard to a low band 2 to 3 m high and a frieze of 2 to 2.5 m, including the frame. This design would be comparable to that which has been observed in the Assyrian palaces with their wide bands of vertical stone slabs decorated with reliefs, protecting the base of the walls.

With the exception of the 'lion frieze' excavated by Dieulafoy in a sector that is considered to have been close to the north-western corner of the East Court (c3),[23] we have no certainty as to the distribution of the decoration. The bricks were heavy and it is unlikely that they were carried far from where they had fallen. Even so, concentrations of ornamental bricks have been reported here and there by excavators; hence elements of the 'archer' frieze were discovered *in a heap* in the eastern sector of the Residence, while others were used in the construction of water channels during the Islamic period (the 'aqueducts' of de Morgan).[24] They were frequently reused in the foundation walls of the Parthian period; bricks and

229
The archer frieze
reconstruction by Marcel Dieulafoy

230
The majority of the glazed bricks were found on the edges of the Residence, often in the foundation walls of the Parthian period

231
Examples of glazed bricks

fragments of bricks constituted an excellent infill material for the foundations. However, we cannot exclude the possibility that the finds of ornamental brick could have preserved a link to their initial distribution, but this should be treated with circumspection.

Stone ornamentation

With the exception of the Egyptian statue of Darius installed at the Gate by Xerxes at the beginning of his reign, and the copy that this king must have made to be placed symmetrically, Susa at the time of Darius seemed not to have known works sculpted in stone other than the capitals of the Apadana and eventually the figures at the entrance of the Gate.[25] The sculptured stones recovered by Mecquenem mainly came from the southern sector of the Ville Royale tell at the location called 'Donjon'.[26] Today, after the discovery of the Palace of Artaxerxes II on the opposite bank of the Shaur, we can believe that they were ripped from this structure, abandoned and pillaged from the Seleucid period onwards.[27] These pieces, of mediocre artistic quality, were in the iconographic tradition of Persepolis. Their number at Susa, in the fourth century BC, is a sign of both great richness and a general improvement in communications.

The statuary

Sculpture in the round was not a form of expression alien to Achaemenid art but it was faithful, certainly in its initial phase, and also at Pasargadae, to the Elamite and Assyrian traditions of high and low relief. At Susa, where the stone had to be imported, bitumen and bronze were often the sculptor's preference.

Restoration of the statue of Darius

Executed in Egypt around 490 BC, the statue could have been transferred to Susa as early as 487 BC because of the troubles along the Nile Valley at the time;[28] but it is more likely to have been in 484 BC by order of Xerxes following the revolt.

232
Pieces of carved stone slabs in low relief found by Mecquenem in the area of the Donjon where they seem to have been reused, probably coming originally from the palace of Artaxerxes II (405–369 BC) on the right bank of the Shaur

233
Fragment of a face from a royal statue (?) of uncertain date, found in 1913 (above).
Foot belonging to a person wearing laced shoes (below).
MECQUENEM, 1947

Proposals for the reconstruction of the head and shoulders were made by G. Azarpay and S. Razmjou.[29] There is a question regarding the headdress of the king as to whether it is Persian or Egyptian. The second possibility is not one to be discarded, given the 'Egyptianizing' model given to the Egyptian sculptors.[30] Even so, the Persian nature of the clothing, the weapon and the jewellery that the king wears, and also the commissioning of a 'portrait', leaves little room for what might appear, on Darius' part, as a concession, even if he did not hide his pride in being Pharaoh.

As to the ratio of the head to the body, the 'restorers' suggested conforming to a rule. The attempt by Azarpay in this direction, in seeking to define a Persepolis principle based on the works in relief, be they in stone or in brick, seems to have little foundation; the data are insufficient. The Egyptian sculptors, in this domain, followed their own standards. The reconstruction must be harmonious; it must also lean, as Ladiray proposes, against the pillar at its back.

Other statues at Susa

Pieces of statues in grey stone belonging to sculpted human figures were found 'on the Apadana tell':[31] the provenance is only indicated by a short reference in the excavation report of 1913. Mecquenem stated in this note that 'these works did not take place without bringing to light some interesting documents, amongst which were two fragments of a colossal Achaemenid statue, one showing the mouth and beard, the other a shod foot'. He wrote later:[32] 'The whole forms a royal statue which, according to the dimensions of the shoe, could be 3 m high'.[33] This is far from being correct.

The first thought to come to mind in this context is that the 'face' could come, if not from a human statue, then from an animal sculpture with a human head. The dimensions, however, of this 'face', and also those of the head (which can easily be reconstructed; being about 30 cm it does not exceed the norm), are too small to belong to one or other of the known types; and for the same reasons, to a local replica of the Egyptian statue of Darius.

234
Reconstruction of the upper part of the Darius Statue
as suggested by Daniel Ladiray

235
The form of the robe, with the folds rising in a zigzag to a peak between the legs, appeared in Iran during the first decade of the fifth century BC

This face is that of a statue, but it cannot be *royal* if, along with Mecquenem, we attribute the 'foot' to it. The dimensions of it are not an issue; reconstructed, it measures no more than 40 cm (which is close to the 50 cm of the feet of the Egyptian statue); but it wears a common shoe, with laces, whilst kings generally wore slippers.[34] Besides, how should we explain this 'flying' foot which would only get a foothold on its missing toes? Finally, only the face fragment could belong to a royal statue, but we still do not know which king it represented.

From a chronological point of view, the 'Egyptian' statue brings interesting information concerning western influence on Achaemenid sculpture. It is seen in the appearance of the 'zigzag' movement given to the bottom of the Persian robes when they were lifted above the feet by a pin fastened under the belt. This characteristic mode, or fashion, unknown at Pasargadae under Cyrus, became the norm at Persepolis at an imprecise date given what we know of the progression of the works at the time of Darius. He does not seem to have completed any of the monuments of the Persepolis Terrace; we can ask ourselves, however, at what date the sculptors (Ionian, Carian, Egyptian) began their decorative work and developed this arrangement of folds which became the classic style. The Egyptian statue of Darius, however, was executed according to the template and probably according to a model which could only have been established by the sculptors working at Persepolis; this means that at the date of execution of the statue around 490 BC certain norms of Achaemenid sculpture, reflecting western influence, had already been fixed.

In 1947 Mecquenem also published two fragments of a statue in grey limestone showing the vertical folds of a Persian robe with the traces of a cuneiform in-scription (DSn) translated as: 'Darius the King has ordered this sculpture to be made', followed by a request for protection – only the name of the king and the verb are clear – the word 'sculpture' is conjecture.[35] These fragments are of a robe, one at the height of the right knee (if it is judged from the beginning of the folds), the other at the bottom of the clothing where one finds the characteristic 'Achaemenid pleat'. Given their nature and their dimensions, these two pieces could come from the local stone replica of the Egyptian statue; we would only be able to confirm this, however, if the few words preserved had been inscribed in a passage, not by Darius, but by Xerxes, whose general meaning was: '[this is the copy of the statue which] Darius, the King, ordered to be made' in Egypt. Its position at the Gate would then not give rise to any particular question.

Did other statues exist? The possible positions are very limited; at the Gate, entrance and exit, the places are occupied, as we have seen above. At the entrance to the Residence, two large supporting stones (2.3 x 2.3 m) are in position.[36] Care-fully prepared, they both have 1.65 x 1.25 m rectangular cut-outs ready to accommodate bases with these dimensions (nearly double those of the base of the Egyptian statue). Of these statues, however, we have no trace. Given the proportions of their bases we could imagine seated animals, possibly lions.

236
Two fragments of the robe of a statue in local stone
Probably the replica which Xerxes commissioned at Susa of the statue of his father (which he brought back from Egypt) to be placed as a counterpart to the first at the Darius Gate. The trilingual inscription which these fragments carry must be attributed to Xerxes. As for the inscription on the Darius Statue, its vertical position, one side with less writing, and the content itself of paragraph 2, suggest that it may have been added at Susa itself, with the statue lying flat before its installation

237
The entrance gateway of the Residence was flanked by colossal statues of which only the bases remain; on the inside are the sockets for the gate hinges

238
Direction of movements from the outside towards the Residence complex-audience hall and, inside the Residence, towards the Royal Apartment

FUNCTION OF THE STRUCTURES

The discoveries of the Darius Gate, of the Propylaeum and the Artisans' Gate changed the overall picture one might have had of Achaemenid Susa. A new image comes into focus, the plan of each building suggesting a particular function.

The main entrance must have been to the west, on the banks of the river, between the Acropolis and the Apadana tells. Briant mentioned the existence of a quay for boats coming from Babylonia or the Persian Gulf.[37] The fort of the Acropolis, whose bastions and walls must have been more than 40 m above the plain, constituted the strong point in the defensive system of the place. This was completed by a bastion at the north-west corner of the Apadana terrace and perhaps a few structures at the extreme south of the Ville Royale tell.[38]

The Artisans' Gate pedestrian gateway, placed at the top of the glacis, accessible via a ramp, must have answered the needs of a population displaced to the north-east of the tells towards the only place free from flooding that could accommodate the camps of the foreign workers; the neighbouring areas, to the north and south, are damp; they are in an old tributary of the Shaur.

The space of some hectares between the three mounds, at the centre of the site and level with the surrounding plain (Dieulafoy's 'Parade Ground'), had the capacity to accommodate the arrival of a troop and its baggage train before it was billeted to the east on the Ville Royale tell, easily accessible from this point. At the top of the rise, on the left, the Propylaeum marked the entrance to the residential complex. This small building, whose position was dictated by the topography, stood on its own.[39] Its orientation, at right angles to the Darius Gate, and its access conformed to a contemporary norm of Achaemenid urban architecture. It was found at Persepolis with the 'Unfinished Gate'. At Susa, the Propylaeum was a place of welcome, of selection and sorting; it marked the limit of the reserved area and provided new arrivals with the benches of its porticoes.

The causeway gave way to a passage about 10 m wide and 40 m long, in the axis of the Darius Gate. This earthen embankment was, apart from being the fortification walkway, the principal entrance to the Apadana terrace (the other being the outer curtain wall).

The Darius Gate was an imposing structure of 1,200 m². Its four-columned central hall acted as a formal reception area; it was a place of greeting and information, where palace rumours were spread.[40] Here the visitor could await his introduction to the king.

The Esplanade is impressive due to its size. The view extends way beyond the austere walls of the Residence. To the left it encounters the Acropolis fortifications; to the right, it stretches all the way to the tall porticoes of the audience chamber, the gardens, the plain and the distant horizon enclosed by the snowy chain of the Zagros Mountains.

From the evidence, the Hypostyle Hall is a place of assembly, reception, an audience hall or, if one so wishes, the throne room. The probable position of the throne is marked on the ground by a large square slab which is to be found on the north–south axis of the building, between its fifth and sixth rows of columns. The central hall (nearly 3,000 m² of living space) could accommodate over 1,000 people, the main access apparently being from the northern door where the inscription of Artaxerxes II would later greet them (A2sa). Inside, we can picture the king enthroned in a ray of light, surrounded by his entourage against a sparkling backdrop of accumulated treasures. In the background, on either side, the two southern doors give onto a long corridor, 5 m wide, between the two southerly towers and on to rooms that could have served to store the royal furnishings when these were not needed for ceremonies. The hypostyle halls were very symbolic of royal establishments; they appear to have been indispensable to the exercise of power. When Artaxerxes II decided to spend more time at Susa, where Darius' Apadana was in ruins, his first concern was to build a temporary audience chamber on the other bank of the Shaur. As at Persepolis and later at the Shaur Palace, the Hypostyle Hall of Susa was completed by outbuildings; here, rooms that could have served as places of rest and relaxation between receptions.

The Residence

The Residence was made up of two parts: the first, around the 'East Court' (C3), brings together the services; the second developed around three courts: the 'Central Court' (C2) which gave access to the chancellery; the 'Honour Court' (C1), onto which opened the King's Apartments; and the small 'West Court' (A). Rooms and passageways had carefully polished red plaster floors.

The East Court

The entrance to this first courtyard (3,500 m²) was via a chambered gateway whose entrance must have been flanked by statues of which only the supporting stones remain.[41] The two rooms of this gateway were 215 and 160 m² respectively, and they were capable of accommodating more than 100 guards. The courtyard was tiled. One's gaze would have been immediately drawn to the northern side by eight large masts standing in the corners and at either side of the three doors. These masts, following the example of those found in front of Egyptian and Mesopotamian sanctuaries, may have been topped by religious or dynastic symbols. The three rooms behind them were small (70 m² for the central room). These could have been repositories for images, ensigns or banners which, according to historians, would have been carried at the head of processions during the king's journeys. The top of this wall would have carried Dieulafoy's 'lion frieze'.

239
North façade of the East Court (C3)
with eight 'masts'
reconstruction by Héritage Virtuel

240
In the East Court excavated by Mecquenem
the stone supports of the masts that flanked
the northern façade were discovered
at a depth of around 2 m

241
**On the north façade of the East Court
nearly 2 m under the floor of the courtyard,
large stones held the bases of the eight masts
which flanked the north wing**
(see page 145)

In the north-western corner of the courtyard was the chambered gateway leading to the audience chamber via the 'royal passage' (s) which was 5 m wide and some 40 m long.[42] This official passageway, with regular projections, must have allowed the king, coming from without, to reach the audience hall without having to go through the residential quarters. The same gateway also gave access to corridor R1 leading directly to what are termed the 'Princely Apartments'.

On the southern side of the 'East Court', under an awning of which we only have the foundations, there would have been two enormous rooms (360 and 390 m²)[43] with large tiled floors. They could have accommodated the king's horses, the women's carts, baggage and equipment. The court was under surveillance by an officer whose four-room apartment opened out onto the south-east corner.

The private area of the Residence was accessed towards the middle of the western side of the court via a gateway of lesser importance than the first and with the peculiarity that the passageway that opened in the middle wall was a chicane so as to block the view of one court from another. One entered here into the zone of the red floors. The double exit of this gate onto the Central Court was due perhaps to protocol.

The Central or Inner Court

The Central Court (C2) was the crossroads of internal traffic. Smaller than the first courtyard (1,120 m²), it was tiled in the same fashion. The lodgings (four rooms) of the high functionary who controlled it, ran along the western wing. In the rooms opposite, two 'guardrooms' watched over the northern doors giving onto corridor R1 and the 'Princely Apartments' and to the south onto the 'chancellery'. In the south-western corner of this internal court a third 'chambered gateway' gave access to the 'Honour Court' (C1); the rooms of this third gateway were no more than 60 m². The width of the passageway was reduced from 4 m to 3.5 m.

The 'Honour Court' or the courtyard of the king's household

The Honour Court (C1) had practically the same dimensions as the Central Court (1,000 m²), but the floor was covered in large tiles (50/51 cm). On the north side, three doors (giving onto corridor R1 and the 'Princely Apartments') were watched over from the east by a 'guard post'. In the west wing were the duty officer's quarters (four rooms). The access portal to the king's vestibule opened wide (9.5 m wide by some 15 m high) to the south. As a whole the Honour Court had more decoration, with niches on either side of the entrance to the vestibule. All the doorways that opened onto this courtyard had recessed frames; all are associated with foundation boxes. The mural decoration was undoubtedly in keeping: various motifs and representations of mythical animals – lions and winged bulls, sphinxes and griffins – according to the accounts of the first excavators.[44]

242
**South façade of the Honour Court (C1)
and entrance to the Royal Apartment**
reconstruction by Héritage Virtuel

243
The King's Apartments
The dimensions of the vestibule
and the antechamber are 36 x 9.5 m.
The location of the foundation tablets
is indicated by the arrows

The Royal Apartments

In the heart of the Residence, the Royal Apartments were centred around the 'King's chamber' (751) where one supposes he would have retired. This room, of relatively modest dimensions (70 m²), contained an alcove with a tiled floor which could have held a ceremonial bed.[45] A throne could also have been placed at its centre. The room, together with the 'antechamber' (330 m²) and two annexes strictly speaking constituted the Royal Apartments. They were separated from the vestibule by a 6 m-wide double door. When this door was open, the view extended from the King's chamber into the Honour Court.[46] The stone tablets carrying the foundation charter in Elamite and Babylonian were found under the walls of the King's chamber (their position is marked on the reconstructed walls) on either side of the entrance. The version in Old Persian was perhaps on the wall of this room, a wall which had eroded. In the King's chamber the alcove tiles were photographed *in situ* by Pillet and the court was excavated by Mecquenem.

The Chancellery

The premises of the chancellery were made up of two blocks of rooms whose red floors suggest that they were an integral and frequented part of the Residence. It is worth noting that the doors could be closed from within the chancellery. Without denying its role as an archive store, the internal layout (long rooms with associated small courtyards) was more favourable to an activity such as that of the numerous cohorts of scribes and multilingual translators in the direct and permanent service of the king and an omnipresent administration.[47] The layout of the rooms, and their relation to the Royal Apartments, answers the question about the functioning of an administration. That we did not find a mass of tablets in this area, occupied long after the time of Alexander, was not surprising.

244
**The western block of the chancellery
and the south-western corner of the
reconstructed Residence**

245
**The passageway from the western block of the chancellery
to the antechamber of the Royal Apartment**

246
Corridor R1 skirts the chancellery to the east
It is guarded at its entrance onto the Central Court (C2)

The north-western quarter of the Residence

Jean Perrot

The archaeological data for this sector are essentially those collected by Mecquenem (plan I, D.E.F) and published by him in 1947. These data do not seem to allow for the reconstruction proposed by Pillet in 1913, after only one season of excavation, in the course of which he could not give to all parts of the Residence the extreme care devoted to the small West Court (Court A). Moreover, it was not the only example of his brilliant imagination. Mecquenem would use part of Pillet's proposition in his reconstruction, but he saw in F a Hypostyle Hall rather than a court (the 'Lions Court'), D and E becoming 'halls' when their dimensions (15 x 14 m) seem to exclude the possibility of a single span roof. Ghirshman followed Mecquenem in 1968, re-establishing the courtyards. More recently, some have wanted to see 'twin pavilions' in this sector, independent of the Residence; others have talked of 'temples'.

The internal organisation of the Residence and its perfect coherence suggest more simply a row of four apartments in this sector, slightly larger than the apartments of the southern row but organised around a courtyard. Using this hypothesis, their relative independence (they are accessed directly from the East Court by corridor R1) could suggest that they were quarters reserved for men; one cannot exclude that they may have been for the use of the royal spouses who seem to have enjoyed a certain liberty.

Whatever the use of this area, the stratigraphic examination of the remains shows without a doubt that it was the object of important renovation works with plans overlaying the initial layout which permitted the identification of foundation walls and red floors. In the historical context of the area, it was obviously tempting to attribute this renovation to Artaxerxes II, to whom we no doubt also owe the reconstruction of the western wall of the Residence and the Small West Court (Court A).

247
North sector, north-west of the Residence
Plan of the remains by Mecquenem

248
North sector, north-west of the Residence
Reconstruction of the sector by Pillet (1913)

249
North sector, north-west of the Residence
Reconstruction by Mecquenem (1947)

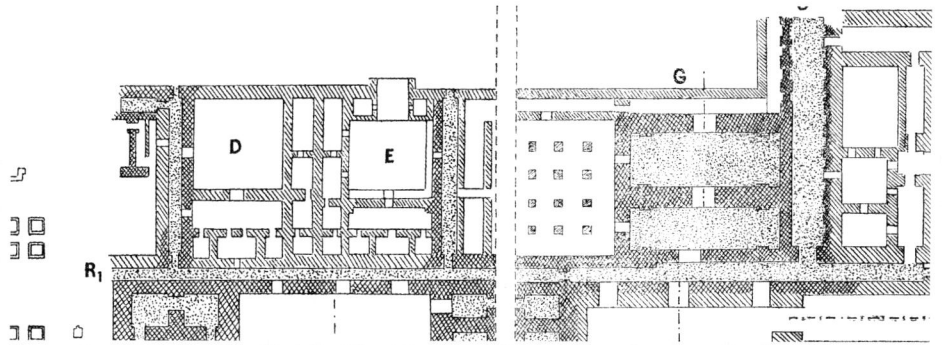

250
North sector, north-west of the Residence
Reconstruction by Ghirshman (1968)

251
North sector, north-west of the Residence
Reconstruction by Perrot-Ladiray

'Women's quarters'

In the south-eastern corner of the royal antechamber, a 'guarded passageway' gave access to the long corridor R4 which opened out onto what one might call the 'women's quarters': five identical apartments, each about 800 m², with rooms, small courts, sanitation and ceremonial rooms.[48] This same corridor, R4, went around the 'chancellery' to the east and opened out, via another 'guarded passageway', onto its northern gallery and the Central Court. This hallway allowed communication with the great halls to the south of the East Court (C3) via a small door, found walled up and already identified by Pillet. The passageway could guarantee discreet communications between the 'women's quarters' and the outside. This part of the Residence suffered from the erosion that swept away the southern edge of the Apadana terrace. What remained, however, does not show signs of renovation, unlike the apartments situated to the north of corridor R1 which were remodelled, to the west, probably by Artaxerxes II. Ploughed by the trenches of Loftus and Dieulafoy,[49] the ground here was excavated by Mecquenem and re-examined in 1913 by Pillet. Both drew plans and a fantastical reconstruction. Area H, 'Lions Court' for Pillet who placed here the frieze found by Dieulafoy (generally situated in the north-western corner of court C3), became, for Mecquenem, a Hypostyle Hall. Some saw in this area 'temples', while others (in D and E) saw 'twin pavilions' independent of the Residence; all are unacceptable propositions in view of the foundations.

The reason why we propose to see in this quarter apartments reserved for men is that they benefited from a relative independence; they could be accessed directly from the East Court via corridor R1. Even so, one could see in them an extension of the women's quarters, reserved for the royal spouses close to the gardens.

252
Floor tiles of the loggia giving onto Court A coming from the Honour Court

253
Small West Court (A)
Reconstruction of the loggia canopy by Maurice Pillet (1913)

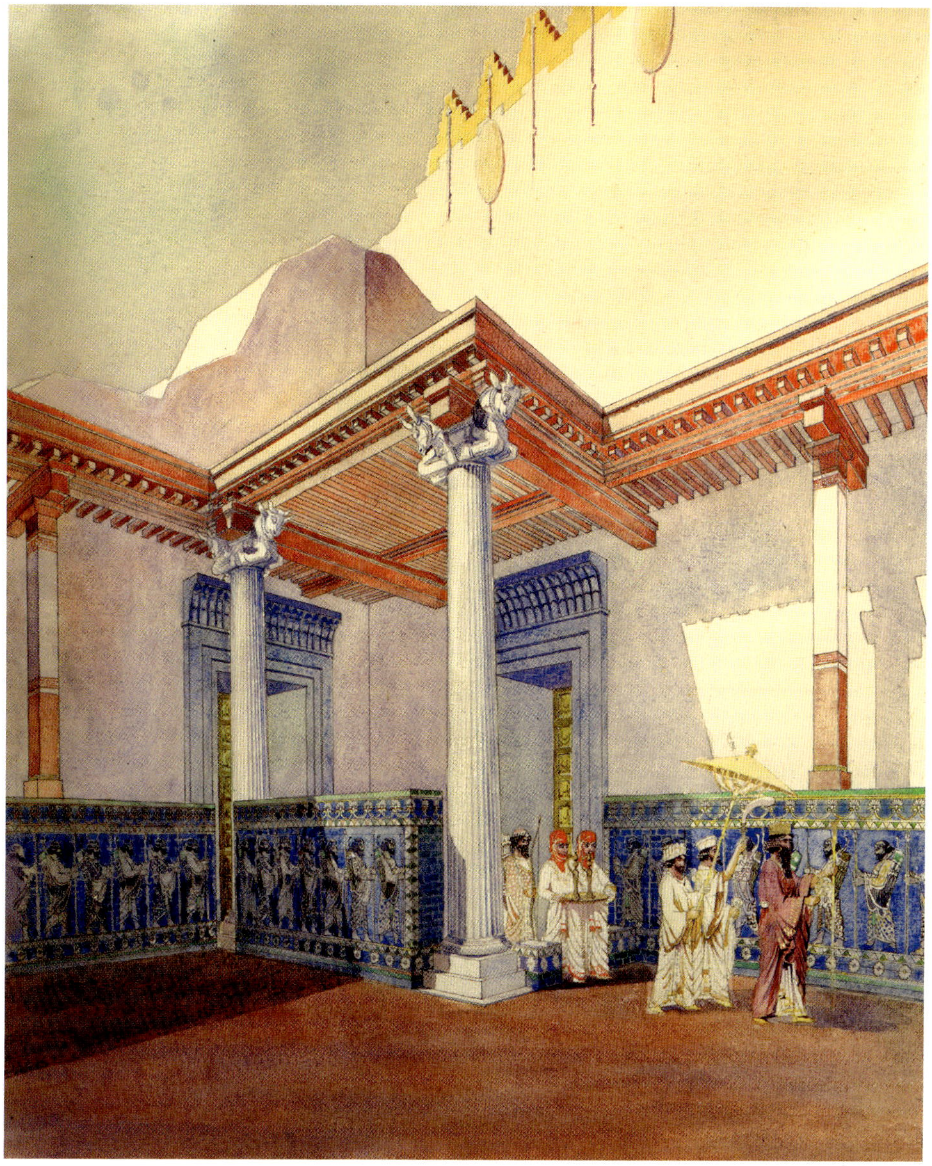

The Small West Court

Mecquenem saw this courtyard (A) as a 'very large hall' (28 x 20 m). He could have been impressed by the fact that, under the grey plaster which covered the floor, there appeared, in the south-east corner, fragments of red flooring which he normally came across in the halls and passageways: the conclusion was evident. Pillet had previously described this space, in a sector that he recorded in 1913, as a courtyard: the 'court of the columns' in consideration of the two square bases supporting, in the south-east corner, some form of canopy, which Mecquenem called a 'vestibule' or 'porch', measuring 6 x 4 m and tiled with 33 cm tiles. The tiling continued along the south and east walls of the court: 1.85 m wide to the south and 2.37 cm to the east, resting on a 'mortar covered in a light brown substance … The interior row of these tiles, fired, showing a sky blue glazed surface'. These observations, also made by Pillet, led him to propose the reconstruction pictured above.

One could indeed see this canopy over the courtyard, from which it is separated by a low glazed brick wall, as offering the king, when coming from the Honour Court, the possibility of a symbolically protected encounter with people admitted to the Residence through the small door L1 that opened on the western side onto the wall-walk connected to the Acropolis; that is to say, connected with the officers in charge of the administration, the Treasury and the garrison.

Clearing of the floor tiles
laid over the original red floor

RESTORATION

The restoration works on the Apadana tell benefited from the help and care of Jean Martin, 'Compagnon de France' (guild of master craftsmen), attached to the Office for the Protection of Architectural Heritage of Iran, and that of A.B. Tilia, in charge of the restoration works at Persepolis, called to Susa for the consolidation of the Darius statue before its transfer to the museum in Tehran. The digital images presented in this book may appear somewhat austere but we are, with the Residence at least, confronted with buildings of mud brick and this material poses special demands.[50]

255
Manufacture of mud bricks
for the reconstruction of the walls

256
Ancient restoration
Plaster flooring covering
floor tiles of the Residence

257
Moving the column drums coming
from the east portico of the Hypostyle Hall

258
**Placing a column base
in the central hall of the Darius Gate**

259
**Fragment of a capital from the central hall
of the Hypostyle Hall preserved *in situ***

260
Lifting of the statue
Work undertaken by Jean Martin, master
craftsman ('Compagnon du Tour de France'),
assigned to the Susa mission, assisted by the
foreman, Abbas Ettemadi

261
**A.B. Tilia, head of the restoration team
at Persepolis, strengthens the statue by
implanting three steel bars**

1. Regarding this matter, see the complete study by R. Besenval (BESENVAL, 1984: 123).

2. H. Gasche, this volume, ch. XIII. Iranian masons were consulted and certainly believed that a span of 10 to 12 m was feasible.

3. When making comparisons, the small rooms that close off the long rooms are to be considered as an integral part of the architectonic module 'à quatre saillants'.

4. The module comprising long rooms side by side was described at Susa by Ghirshman and Gasche in the context of the mansions ('grandes maisons') of the second-millennium BC. Gasche, this volume, ch. XIII.

5. 'The two great rooms (752 and 753) were covered by a ceiling; their width of 9.25 m is not a problem, because in the Hypostyle Hall the gap between the rows of columns is about 8 m and presupposes beams of that length […]. We believe that only the passages were vaulted.

6. MECQUENEM, 1947: 33.

7. Such an image accords with the interpretation of the word 'apadana' by P. Lecoq who prefers to translate it as 'water reserve'; the word 'apadana' would be restricted to a 'building which had such a facility', LECOQ, 1997: 115.

8. Ghirshman had already reached this conclusion, and trenches and sections to the north and east have confirmed this (ch. VI: 198–201).

9. R. Boucharlat, this volume, ch. XII.

10. AMIET, 1944.

11. Certain motifs decorating the ornamental bricks suggest their presence at Susa.

12. Not to mention the suggestions of a mezzanine in the Apadana that presupposes openings through walls 5 m thick! The idea, proposed by Mecquenem (MECQUENEM, 1947: 20–41), of placing stone columns on an upper floor, above the unbaked-brick walls of the ground floor, is incongruous.

13. It should be noted that the interplay of stepped niches together with the presence of tiles up to the base of the walls seems to exclude the presence of a bench along the sides.

14. The width of the fluting is the same.

15. We have preferred the use of the word ornamentation rather than decoration because the former still has an undeniable symbolic meaning.

16. D. Ladiray, this volume, ch. VI.

17. When Jane Dieulafoy excavated the lion frieze, she found it crowned by blue crenellations which stood out against the white wall (N. Chevalier, this volume, ch. III). Fragments of unbaked clay bearing traces of colour were reported by D. Ladiray at the Darius Gate (ch. VI), and Ghirshman mentioned others at the Apadana.

18. R. Boucharlat, this volume, ch. XII.

19. N. Daucé, this volume, ch. X.

20. J. Dieulafoy noted baked bricks at the back of the lion frieze which were intended to key the ornamental bricks into the wall (DIEULAFOY, J. 1888).

21. There are about 6,000 in the Louvre and an equal number distributed between the museums at Susa and Tehran. We ourselves only found a few dozen glazed bricks (now deposited in the Susa Museum stores).

22. Prehistorians calculate the frequency of a given type of pottery vessel on a site on the basis of the number of fragments of the type that have been collected and then work out the indices of fracture established for each type of vessel on an experimental basis (according to size, fragility, etc.). Here the problem is different, but we believe that we can suggest a ratio of 1:10.

23. This was not Pillet's view, who placed it more to the west (Pillet's plan, ch. III: 95).

24. MECQUENEM, 1947: 3.

25. The size of these foundations and their type suggest an oblong shape of considerable weight, like that of the Assyrian winged human-headed bulls. Those of the Gate at Persepolis are 6 m long and 5.50 m high; those of the entrance to the west are winged and human-headed; those of the east entrance are plain bulls.

26. MECQUENEM, 1947.

27. R. Boucharlat, this volume, ch. XIII and J. Perrot, this volume, ch. XIV.

28. See J. Yoyotte, this volume, ch. VIII.

29. AZARPAY, 1995; RAZMJOU, 1988.

30. J. Yoyotte, this volume, ch. VIII. Statuettes of pharaohs of the Nubian dynasty wear a non-Egyptian headdress.

31. We define a 'statue' as a work of sculpture in the round depicting a whole living person.

32. MECQUENEM, 1947: 47, pl. V, 2, 3.

33. PARROT, 1957: 249; ROOT, 1979: 111; LUSCHEY, 1983: 195; AZARPAY, 1987: 187, fig. 3.

34. At Bisitun, however, he wears sandals.

35. MECQUENEM, 1947: pl. V, 4–5.

36. Ch. III, photograph taken by M. Pillet.

37. The hydrographic network cannot now be identified. Dieulafoy travelled along the River Diz as far as Kaleh Bender, about 50 km south of Susa. see Briant, this volume, ch. I: 19.

38. R. Boucharlat, this volume, ch. XII: the 'Donjon'.

39. No other traces of buildings were registered at this level (which corresponds to Level VII of Ghirshman's trench nearby). The 'Ville Royale' tell and the Apadana terrace are also at the same level.

40. In the Book of Esther 2:19 and 21, 'Mordecai was sitting at the king's gate' to pick up the news and gossip (New International Version of the Bible, with Apocrypha).

41. D. Ladiray, this volume, ch. IV.

42. This sector is very poorly preserved due to the trenches of Dieulafoy ('tranchée des lions'?) and of Mecquenem. The existence of a door is, however, highly probable based on the archaeological remains, as well as the 'royal passage' and the internal layout of the Residence. M. Pillet had already indicated it on his plans.

43. To the extent that it is possible to restore this sector thanks to the electronic surveys of the foundations and small fragments of tiling.

44. J. Perrot, this volume, ch. XIV. This courtyard would be that where Esther, having 'put on her royal robes … stood in the inner court of the of the palace, in front of the king's hall. The king was sitting on his royal throne facing the entrance' (Esther 5:1); see also note 40.

45. This alcove may be the original location of the famous 'golden vine' presented by a rich Lydian to Darius in 513 BC on the occasion of the latter's journey through Asia Minor.

46. It is generally agreed that the author of the story of Esther knew Susa and the layout of the royal Residence, either because it was still inhabited in the second century BC, or because the story was based on an earlier tale. See notes 40 and 44.

47. It is in this sector, close to the Central Court, that the famous Old Persian tablet (DSf) was found. It provides the earliest 'foundation charter of the Palace'. Scheil (SCHEIL, 1929) provided too vague a description of its provenance: 'the great Persian tablet which was found in its natural place, the Apadana'. This has resulted in many scholars being misled. The tablet was found in 1912 in part of the Chancellery, near a block that supported a door socket (Mecquenem's 1912 report to the Ministère des Affaires Etrangères).

48. D. Ladiray, this volume, ch. VI.

49. MECQUENEM, 1947: fig. XX.

50. They are the work of Pierre Rupp and Loïc Thirion Lopez from the firm Héritage virtuel.

The Statue of Darius
after cleaning and restoration
National Museum of Iran, Tehran

8 The Egyptian Statue of Darius

Jean Yoyotte

'HERE is the stone statue which Darius the King ordered to be made in Egypt so that it may be seen and that whomsoever should see it in the future will know that the Persian Man holds [var. 'has taken'] Egypt.'[1] Thus is it proclaimed in the three usual languages of Achaemenid power on the right-hand side of the pleated gown worn by the sovereign.

The famous statue, which in 1973 became one of the glories of Iran and of the National Museum in Tehran, was found at the entrance of an access building to the Apadana terrace, a structure built by Darius and finished by Xerxes. It stood with its back against the right-hand door-jamb. Archaeologists agree that a statue of similar dimensions would have stood symmetrically on the opposite side of the doorway.[2]

Unfortunately, the upper part just above the elbows was missing. Complete, the monolithic statue and its base must have measured some 3 m in height, perhaps more if a crown or the *pschent* of the pharaohs topped the usual Persian hairstyle.[3]

The still imposing section which survives is in a very good state of preservation. The polish of the stone has not been altered by exposure to air, or by burial. There is only one break, at knee level, resulting no doubt from the pressure of the earth. The right-hand fist was broken and the bent elbow of the left-hand arm is chipped. These breaks cannot be explained by ground pressure and so are probably due to hammer blows wrought by humans.[4]

The Persian dress is the same, standardised, as on the reliefs of Persepolis.[5] The originality of the statue is that it provides a three-dimensional representation of 'Achaemenid drapery'. A sheathed dagger is held in the belt. The left arm is folded over the chest, the hand holding a lotus flower stalk; the right arm hangs down beside the body (it is hard to tell what the king held in his fist).[6] Nevertheless, this effigy adds precious details to the rather austere image that the reliefs of the palace portray: bracelets adorned with bovine heads, lines of winged bulls carved

263

Statue of Darius I
Grey metamorphic rock (*Greywacke*) from the quarries of Wadi Hammamat in Egypt
height preserved 2.46 m (probable height about 3.5 m) • base height 51 cm • length 104.3 m • width 64.2 cm
after STRONACH, 1974a: 61–63

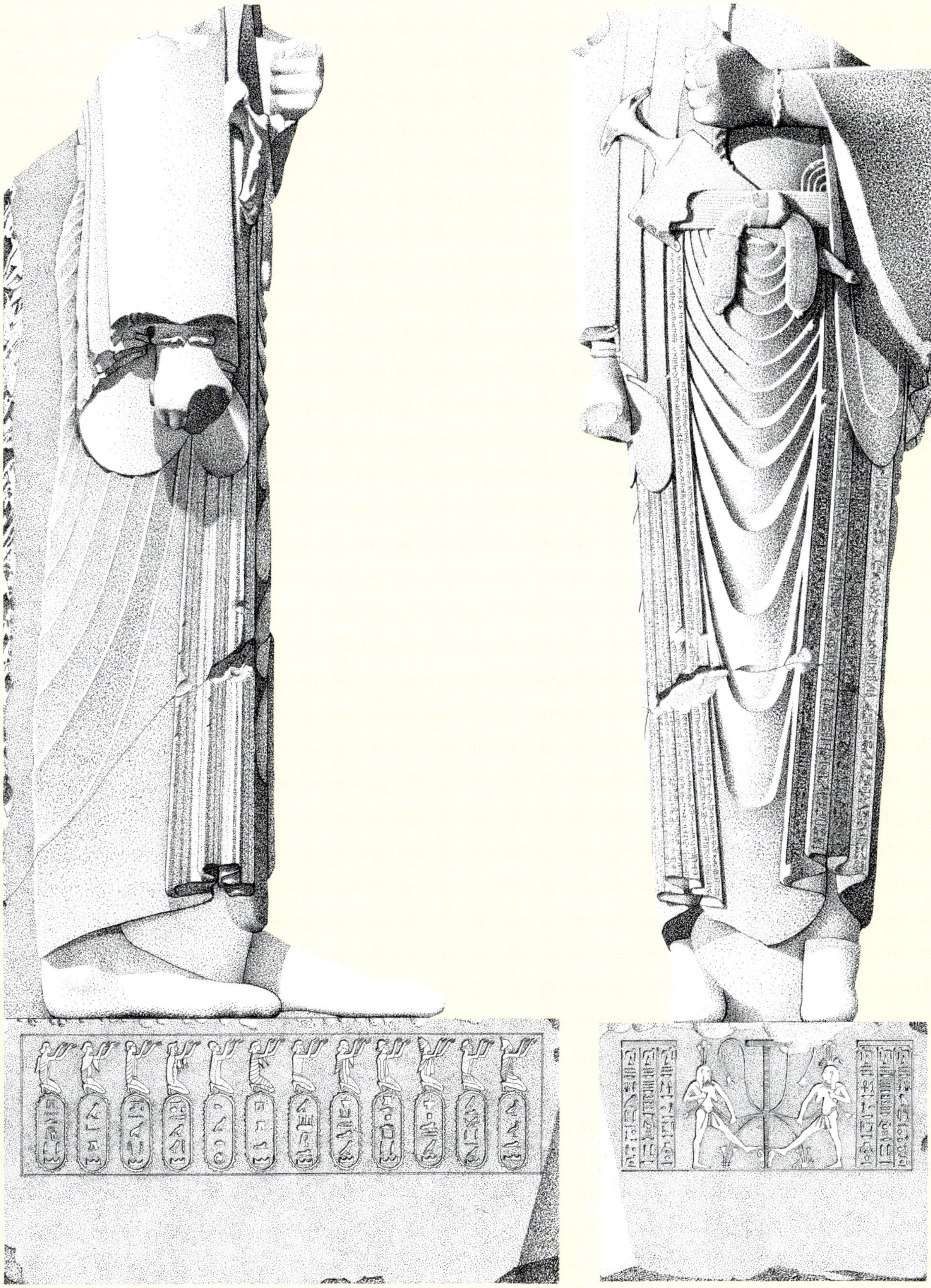

264
The torso and scabbard for the dagger

on the sheath of the dagger, beads at each end of the belt. The shoes are the same elongated type as on the reliefs at Persepolis.

The king is represented with his left leg forward, the right arm down hard against his side; the fist closed round a short 'baton'. The left arm is folded, the forearm held against his chest. The left-hand, damaged, holds a flower with a long stalk (broken) which could be a lotus flower.

The king wears the ceremonial dress of the Persians, that is to say a garment with long sleeves, gathered in at the waist with a belt; the cloth of the left-hand sleeve hangs straight down in front and forms two folds at the back; the right-hand sleeve has four folds, two in the front of the sleeve, two in the back. These sleeves were apparently cut obliquely: the longer part, inside, has two rounded ends; a wide hem is visible on the rearmost end of the left-hand sleeve.

A large belt, knotted at the front, was made of supple material. Each thickened end terminates in a small knob and carries an Egyptian inscription with the name of the king. At the back, the belt is smooth, in contrast with the front which is decorated with fine incisions; herringbone patterns alternate with rows of small ovoids. Above the belt, on the left-hand side of the figure, small, tight concentric folds seem to indicate that the fabric of the robe was pinched and lifted under the belt. Robe and sleeves were probably cut from the same piece of cloth. Underneath the belt, on the front of the garment, a series of rounded folds fall in a cascade. Tighter towards the top, they widen towards the bottom of the robe. On each side of these folds, from the belt to the level of the ankle, there are four vertical folds. They gather at the bottom and end in a zigzag.

On the sides and at the back, on either side of the dorsal pillar, the fall of the dress' folds forms a circular pattern that widens towards the bottom. The lower hem is executed in such a way that the front and back of the costume fall nearly to the same height.

As in the large reliefs of Persepolis and of Naqsh-i Rustam, the king wears fitted shoes without laces. A small arch on the outside of the foot corresponds with the inner arch, whilst a little dent behind the little toe helps to give the shoe an unusual look.

Special attention is given to the dagger, which is carried diagonally in the belt. The weapon has a large horizontal guard extending to one side. The simple hilt ends in a narrow crescent-shaped pommel. The upper and lower parts of the scabbard are decorated with incised bands of ladder-pattern framing triple files of winged bulls. The lack of finish on the incised surfaces suggests that they were to have been decorated with metal or paste. The triangular extremity of the dagger is undecorated.

Thin round bracelets ornamented the wrists; that on the left-hand wrist is damaged but, judging by the one on the right, it is clear that both ends must have been decorated with calves' heads.

The four folds on the left-hand side of the figure have the longest of the five Egyptian texts on the statue, whilst those on the right-hand side carry cuneiform texts in three languages: Old Persian, Elamite and Babylonian. The position of these cuneiform lines does not make them easy to read, as one has to tilt one's head sideways to decipher them. By contrast, an Egyptian only had to follow the correctly placed, vertical columns from top to bottom to read the text offered to him.

The base has three inscriptions in Egyptian. Text 3 (five lines) appears on the upper face of the base in front of the right foot. Text 4 is on the two short sides of the base on either side of the 'genies' personifying Upper and Lower Egypt. On the long sides, the 'Fortress cartouches' give the names of the 24 nations of the empire. The kneeling figures, who represent the nations, differ from one another

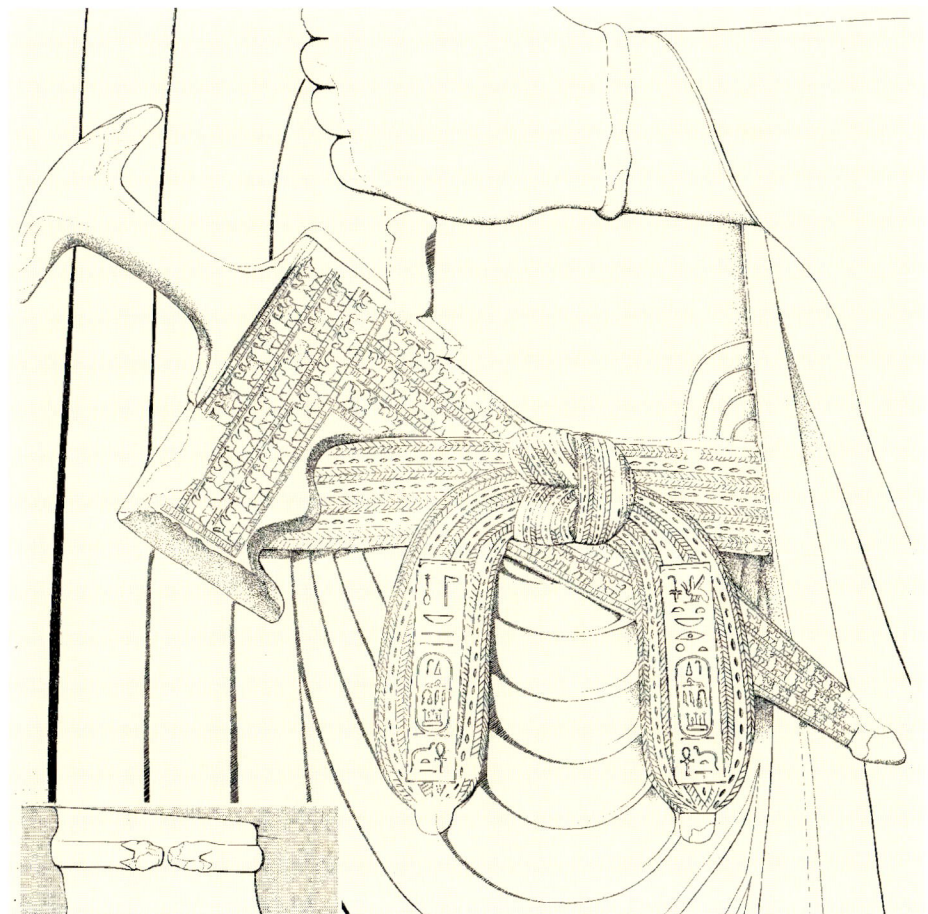

265

The scabbard for the dagger
Decorated with friezes of winged bulls.
The ends of the belt have metal plaques with
the name of the king. The ends of his bracelets
are decorated with heads of young calves

by their national costume, their headdress and their hairstyle: the people of Iran and the North on the left-hand side of the base; the people of the west and the south on the right-hand side.

The two sides of the robe hang down forming large pleats, four on each side of the body. These vertical bands serve as surfaces for the carved inscriptions which identify and describe the representation of the king, cuneiform to the right, and Egyptian hieroglyphs to the left.[7] The state of preservation of these signs is admirable: there are only five gaps due to damage in the Egyptian texts, which can be easily restored.

The Darius statue of Susa is the first known product of large-scale Achaemenid statuary, commissioned by the king in accordance with his wish to have himself portrayed projecting an image of his supreme power.[8] He ordered this statue to be made by his Egyptian subjects. Seen from a distance, this monumental effigy imposed itself, thanks to its typical costume, as 'an unambiguous representation of Persian power', in all its strength and quietly assured.[9] But from close up we can see that this Persian work, if not ambiguous, was certainly ambivalent. On the most visible part, the belt ends, the name of Darius was carved, but in Egyptian hiero-glyphs. To the left (text 1a) we read: 'the King of Upper and Lower Egypt, master of the observance of rites, Darius, may he live for ever'. To the right (text 1b), 'the perfect God, master of the Two Lands, Darius, may he live forever'. What is more, a long vertical hieroglyphic inscription runs on the left front of the robe, and the base is decorated on all its faces with images belonging to the pharaonic portfolio, or which are adapted from this repertoire: they are abundantly captioned with hieroglyphs.

The geometric way that this sculpture was carved in three dimensions is typically Egyptian, the three sides of the body being worked like three independent reliefs. In his static walk the figure leads with the left foot. At the back of the figure's body rises the usual dorsal pillar, symbol of the protective presence of the personal god of the individual portrayed. Finally, as we will see later, the stone in which this full-length portrait of the great king was carved was excavated from a quarry in the Eastern Desert between the Nile and the Red Sea.[10]

Because of its dimensions and sculptural form, this exceptional work proves to be a commemorative monument to the Great King, a manifesto first destined for the people who would see it in Egypt and, from the reign of Xerxes at least, for the Persians and subjects passing by the Elamite residence of the Great Kings.

266
Emphatic titulature of Darius 'King of Kings', Wadi Hammamat
G. GOYON, 1957: pl. 34

DARIUS I, SECOND PHARAOH OF THE TWENTY-SEVENTH DYNASTY

The Egyptian historian Manetho counted the Persians as legally forming the Twenty-seventh Egyptian dynasty. Carrying on from the Saite dynasty, the indigenous pharaohs, entrenched in Sais and the Libyan borders, managed to withstand the Persian forces several times with the help of the Libyans. Nevertheless, as far as we know, during nearly 120 years the majority of the provinces remained in submission to the Great King.

After the establishment of Cambyses at Memphis, followed by a visit to Sais, the Achaemenid, master and overseer of everything, defender of the organised world against the Barbarians, was recognised by the most eminent Egyptian thinkers as the fulfilment of the ideal pharaoh, whose functions he performed: to assure the security and prosperity of a united Upper and Lower Egypt, on the one hand by administering people and goods, and on the other by maintaining the divine cults in the temples.[11] After Cambyses, Darius assumed the financial affairs which had been those of the Saites of the Twenty-sixth Dynasty (even though the Temple revenues were given over to the royal purse).

267
The Nile Valley
with Wadi Hammamat and
the Nile Canal to the Red Sea

The priests of Memphis and Heliopolis, to signify that they recognised the global sovereignty of the dynasty from Iran, immediately wrote Cambyses' name in the cartouche, then that of Darius, the knot signifying all that the sun circumscribes in its course. Moreover, in demotic documents the Achaemenid name was preceded by the title of 'pharaoh'.

Traditionally the royal titulary was composed of five elements, each followed by a name, the last two in cartouches, the 'prenomen' adopted on his accession and proclaiming a formulaic attribute of the sun, and the name of 'son of Ra', which was none other than the name – 'nomen' – that the king had since his birth. It seems that a complete royal titulary was put together for Cambyses, but only the initial Horus name and the two cartouches are confirmed. The five names of Darius are only known thanks to a monumental double band on the Temple at Hibis (Kharga Oasis), a titulary that speaks volumes.[12] In some of the temple's panels, the Persian king was endowed with a first cartouche confirming that he was 'loved by Amun-Ra master of Hibis, master of the scimitar (*khpesh*)' eventually abridged to 'loved by Amun-Ra'.[13] Thus, even in the monument which he had founded and whose ornamental illustrations were particularly rich and learned, the distant Iranian pharaoh did not benefit from the canonical royal titulary in force under the indigenous dynasties. This belittlement may stem from the fact that the de facto accession had not been followed by the theological consultations and reflections which fixed the new monarch's programme.

268
The valley of Wadi Hammamat
J. COUYAT, P. MONTET, 1912

Both on the large and small objects made in the name of the king and in the inscriptions of individuals, the denomination of Darius was radically shortened to his only original name, an austerity echoing the omnipresent egotism in his communications. In practice the scribes engraved only the name 'Darius', surrounded by a cartouche and preceded by the titles, or sequence of titles, which introduced the prenomen in the ancient form: 'King of Upper and Lower Egypt and Lord of the Two Lands' or 'perfect God, Lord of the Two Lands' and, rarely, 'Master of the Rites'.[14] Of the traditional royal titles, only those expressing universal domination were kept, and a few lines from Year 4 also, reminding us that Darius was both 'the King of Egypt' and 'the King (*wr*) of Kings (*wrw*) of foreign countries'.[15]

It was not always necessary to translate the titulary of the Achaemenids into Egyptian; the phraseology of the earlier imperialist pharaohs had already expressed the same pretensions. According to an inscription dating from 496 BC, the Persian was designated as 'the King of Upper and Lower Egypt, the perfect God, Lord of the Two Lands, the son of Ra, Lord [of the crowns]', sovereign of sovereigns, possessor of power, 'Darius, living like Ra'.[16] This titulary inserted in sequence two qualifiers which were part of the old repertoire: the dignity of 'sovereign of sovereigns', which the major figures, Amenhotep III and Ramesses II had so formidably represented, corresponding to the Iranian 'King of Kings', and the banal 'Master of power' which was consistent with the exploits of Darius as warrior and war chief.[17]

At the end of 44 years in power, Amasis had left Egypt in excellent condition. Cambyses had massacred far fewer than Herodotus would have us believe. Darius, who would hold this country of advanced political culture for 34 years, found competent and trustworthy administrators in place and was content with subordinating them to a satrap of Achaemenid stock. This is how the *senti*, a form of prime minister responsible for the economy, 'the director of the scribes of the Council', and other scribes accounting for all manner of things, remained the cogs of the central administration, at least in what concerned temple goods and personnel.[18] In addition, Darius attached certain indigenous dignitaries to his retinue. Udjahorresnet of Sais remained amongst his physicians and was sent from Susa to Sais on a charitable mission. Ptahhotep's curriculum vitae is a magnificent illustration of the presence of an Egyptian amongst the 'king's men'.[19] It seems that this man, holder of several priestly titles at Memphis, came to administer the personal treasure of Darius in Iran, and the surviving statue presents him in Persian dress, above which he wears a pectoral displaying the adoration of the gods of Memphis, and a torque ending in rams' heads, a typical product of Achaemenid goldsmithing.

When Cambyses arrived on the scene, there already existed the seeds of what became a lasting defamatory opinion amongst the intelligentsia,[20] partly due to opportunism, an effect of their old loyalist ethic but also, for others, to intellectual conviction. The real developments brought to the economy under Darius, notably thanks to the development of *qanat*s in the Libyan oases, must have contributed to an improvement. Darius' personal contacts with the local population were certainly also influential.

The memory of Amasis had been maligned by Cambyses, his grave desecrated, his effigies mutilated, and his cartouches censored. As the epitaphs of the Apis in the Serapaeum confirm, and also a quantity of private monuments, Amasis was rehabilitated by Darius, who claimed to have inherited his work. Just as Cambyses had been, so the new Great King was instructed concerning the indigenous gods and myths. Diodorus Siculus counted Darius amongst the great Egyptian legislators, and not without reason. After eulogising his virtues and wisdom he continues: 'in Egypt he consorted with the priests and participated in their studies on the subject of theology and the events described in the sacred books'.[21] The image can seem somewhat forced, but such an approach on the part of Darius, who was in his way a thinker believing in his gods, and a moral writer, is plausible. We have seen that eminent Egyptians, supposedly expert in sacred knowledge, were amongst his closest retinue.[22]

Nothing allows us to pinpoint at which moment in his reign these consultations took place. We know from Polyaenus[23] that Darius, in order to bring the satrap Aryandes to heel, arrived following the death of an Apis – that, it must be

269
Front face of the base
The two halves of the united world (*sma-tawy*) support the Great King

270
The statue *in situ* showing the
double fracture that follows the
geological fault lines in the stone

admitted, was buried in Year 4 (518 BC).[24] But another occasion is more likely,
notably when the king came to deal with the canal between the Nile and the Red
Sea, some time between 495 BC and 491 BC.

The Egyptian scribes and their Persian contacts noted without difficulty the
analogies between their respective conceptions of what constituted royal power:
under the benediction of the supreme God who shines in the sky, to ensure the
reign of a just order amongst men. The 'profession of faith' in Ahuramazda figured,
translated into traditional Egyptian at the beginning of the Kabret Stele.[25] The
Susa statue brings together the major conclusions of the meeting between two
polytheistic cultures.[26]

THE STONE FROM WHICH THE DARIUS IS STATUE IS MADE

The stone from which the statue of Susa was carved was recognised by Jean Trichet
as *greywacke* (from the German *Grauwacke*), often called schist or also basalt in

271
Wadi Hammamat quarry showing natural fracture lines in the stone
The inscriptions are identified by the white labels
G. GOYON, 1957

Egyptological literature, and *bekhen* in Egyptian.[27] This hard and compact rock is a fairly dark grey once polished, shading to green.[28] It appears on the surface on the edges of Wadi Hammamat, the beautiful gully which, crossing the Arabian Desert at its shortest point, constituted a comfortable route between Koptos, on the Nile, and the Port of Kosseir, on the Red Sea.[29]

The patron of Koptos, called 'the Koptite', who in appearance resembled Min, the ithyphallic god of Panopolis, was considered the master of the routes which left from his town. Those who worked in the *greywacke* quarry or in the area, as well as travellers to or from the Red Sea, happily prayed to the one that the Hellenistic Greeks would call 'Pan of the good journey'. From the time of Cambyses to that of Artaxerxes I, the Persian princes (*erpa*) of Koptos, first Atiyawahi, and then Ariyawrata, his brother, would leave standardised inscriptions on the walls of the quarry, so as to be 'with Min' and the other divinities of the region. It would be wise to admit that nothing allows us be precise about the motives for the governors' visits (inspection of the gold mines nearby, police operations, journeys to the port of Kosseir?).

The *bekhen* of Hammamat had been used by the Egyptians since the earliest times. From the Sixth Dynasty, the overseers of the expeditions sent to bring back this stone recorded their passage on the walls of the quarry as a form of detailed statement or, more briefly, as dated and signed graffiti. Quarrymen and other workers left modest inscriptions.[30] The steep mass of the vein is naturally fragmented, by horizontal and diagonal cracks, into parallel epipedic blocs.[31] This material, hard to cut and heavy to move, was not practical as building stone.[32] It was used to make large public ornaments. The expeditions of varying size, organised with military precision, came from the capital by boat down to Koptos and then followed the Wadi to the quarry, a distance of some 90 km. The stones were chosen – they were detached by metal bar and no doubt carved – and they were conveyed (perhaps hauled across ground lubricated with mud or carried by beasts of burden) to the embarkation point at Koptos, whence they were shipped to their destination at the sculpture workshop. Under the Twenty-sixth Dynasty the sculptors and engravers particularly appreciated the harder and darker stones for statues of kings and private individuals, large mummy shaped sarcophagi, low walls and so forth. A significant number of monuments made from *greywacke* have reached us from this period. This taste continued amongst the great nobles under the reign of Darius as is illustrated by the traditional kneeling block statue of the *senti* Horudja,[33] and that of the treasurer Ptahhotep dressed as a Persian.[34] The quarry at Hammamat was particularly actively exploited between Years 26 (496 BC) and 30 (492 BC) under the care of the superintendent of works Khnemibre.

KHNEMIBRE, OVERSEER OF WORKS

This figure was sometimes designated by the traditional title 'Overseer of all the king's works', who could lend himself to all forms of enterprise.[35] In his inscriptions, he in fact carried two titles of state: 'Overseer of Works of Upper and Lower Egypt' and 'Director of Works in the entire land' elaborated into 'Director of the work of slicing the mountain in all the land (or in all the *Jebel*)', so quarrying contractor. The first title concerned the temples and sculpture workshops of Egypt, the second concerned royal enterprises in the empire. Khnemibre would have participated in the realisation of Darius' palaces at Susa and Persepolis. By 496 BC he had almost 30 years' experience under his belt. He could have been older than 50 and must have enjoyed a certain notoriety in the world.

A sequence of three titles make explicit the responsibilities incumbent upon him during the course of an operation: 'Leader of the great Artisans', 'Troop Leader' (that is to say of drafted labour) and 'Leader of the Archers' (no doubt a foreign military escort). Without doubt the movements and transport over ground would have benefited from the services of the royal navy, which suggests that Khnemibre, *servant of the King*, did not operate under the supervision of the satrap or take his orders from the Persian governor of Koptos.[36] An inscription retrospectively dated to the 44th and last year of Amasis mentioned the visit of the Overseer of Works Ahmes-si-Neith and his eldest son Khnemibre (the father and son having been named after the cartouched names of Amasis), but the official arrival of our entrepreneur to the site of Wadi Hammamat did not happen until 30 years later, in the Year 26 of Darius (496 BC). This same year he had no fewer than four inscriptions carved, one of which is a prestigious genealogy of Overseers of Works which, from disciple to master, created Khnemibre's professional ascendancy going back to the Third Dynasty. When returning via Koptos he dedicated an altar of *greywacke* to Orisis bearing Darius' name.

Khnemibre then made frequent visits to Wadi Hammamat during a four-year period: twice in 495 BC, once in 494 BC and once in 492 BC. In the stereotypical graffiti that he had carved, he saw no reason to specify that he had come to quarry, but he wished to 'stay for eternity' with Min, Horus, Isis and other gods of the region. One of the inscriptions of Year 26 (496 BC) and that of the altar enumerate a long series of sacerdotal titles before detailing the technical functions of the Overseer of Works. The two sequences start with 'the divine father of 'On' [=Heliopolis], 'the divine father of the White Wall' [= Memphis]. Although the rank of the divine father was quite modest, these were the two titles which figured on the impressions of the official seal of Khnemibre on unbaked clay bullae found at Memphis, along the White Wall, seat of the Persian administration.[37] Because of his experience, Khnemibre was awarded the 'the official title' of 'pure' (*uab*) which allowed him to officiate in the temples of Sais, Heracleopolis and Athribis. In contrast, of his eight honorific titles of 'prophet' (or 'servant of the god'), the

272
Offering table in the name of Darius dedicated to Osiris of Koptos by Khnemibre
Museum of Egyptian Antiquities, Cairo (JE 4839).
POSENER, PDPE, pl. XVI

first was attached to the cult of the leonine goddess Sekhmet at Heliopolis itself. The other seven put him in the service of the gods of the northern part of the Heliopolite Nome, those of the area known as *Troia* (now Tourah), on whom depended the famous fine limestone quarries that had been for ever exploited on behalf of the sanctuaries and tombs, and which were still very active under the Saites. We must add that his priestly domain of activity, from Heliopolis in the North to Tourah in the south, placed him in contact with Babylon of Egypt (in what is now Coptic Cairo), the strategic site of a Persian garrison which controlled the Memphis crossroads.

The profession of stone technician in the service of the king and the gods did not prevent but rather required the mastery of extended religious knowledge and a firm grasp of classical Egyptian lapidary writing (hieroglyphs) and cursive (hieratic). We should remember that this was a period when certain archaic forms were in fashion. Indeed, Khnemibre was one of the 'scribes of the divine book at Heliopolis'; Herodotus tells us that the greatest intellectuals of the country were to be found in this town.[38]

Darius decided to commission his monumental 'portrait' from the Egyptian artists who were to treat it according to their graphical traditions and label it in their writing according to their own theology. Strong loyalty and a fine political intelligence were expected of the eminent workshop overseer who would have to ensure his sculptors carved a uniquely Achaemenid and pharaonic image.

The choice of the luxurious *bekhen* stone used to carve Darius' image leads us to Wadi Hammamat. Wadi Hammamat, in turn, leads us to Knemibre, the very erudite superintendent of Darius' works. It is hard not to attribute to this Egyptian the concept of the statue of Persia, with its epigraphic ornament and the geopolitical iconography on the base.

THE DATE AND CIRCUMSTANCES OF THE STATUE'S CREATION

The name of Darius first noted as 'TRYWŠ', was transcribed 'ENTRYWŠ' in the hieroglyphic inscriptions from around 495 BC and until the reign of his son Xerxes.[39] It is this last written form which we find on our statue, as on the three stelae discovered in Wadi Tumilat and at Suez. Thus we can place these monuments in the last third of the reign, a period when the canal from the Nile to the Red Sea was dredged and reopened; a period when Darius seemingly came to Egypt in person.[40] We have already noted that the superintendent of works, Khnemibre, operated at Wadi Hammamat between 496 BC and 492 BC.

Rose granite stelae with hieroglyphs and trilingual Persian texts, not to mention at least one in purely Persian style, were erected along the length of the canal.[41] Important remains of three of the Pharaonic stelae have been discovered at Tell el-Maskhutah (Pithom),[42] Kabret[43] and near Suez,[44] but the accounts on them are unfortunately riddled with gaps. Upstream and downstream, from stele to stele, we can identify the stages of the enterprise. At the start Darius collected intelligence.[45] Contact was made with the prince or princes of Shaba (in which we can identify the kingdom of Saba). Then the king defined the objective of joining the two seas and this link was realised according to his wishes.

The enterprise was started by Necho II (610 BC to 595 BC) as recounted by Herodotus (II, 158–159). A wide navigable canal from the Pelusiac branch of the Nile would have allowed Egyptian boats from Memphis to look for incense amongst the inhabitants of the 'shores of Punt', that is to say the coast of Kushite Sudan, between the latitudes of the modern-day Port Sudan and the Eritrean frontier.[46] In this way the Egyptians would no longer be dependent on the Arab caravans that brought the spices of Southern Arabia up to Gaza and beyond.

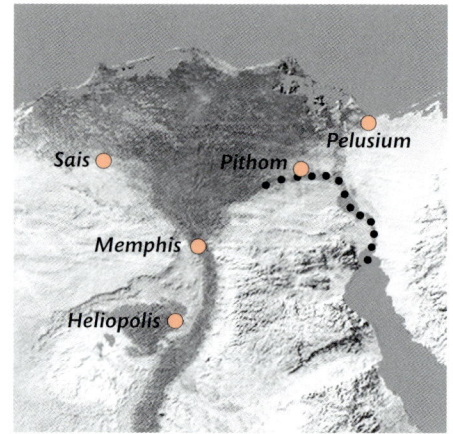

273
Route of the canal (dotted line) **linking the Pelusiac branch of the Nile to the Red Sea**
Three statues of Darius were positioned along the length of the canal

274
facing page
The stele of Tell el-Maskhuta
near Pithom
G. PSENER, 1936: pl. IV.

PIERRE & J.J.CLERE

This competition ended with the Persians who, perhaps from the reign of Cyrus and certainly under Cambyses, held Gaza and then made the Arabs, if not subjects, then at least auxiliaries.

Darius' enterprise, as written on his stelae in Persian and in Egyptian, went much further than that of the Saite ruler, 'From a river by the name of Piru [Egyptian P3 Itrw, 'the River'] which runs in Egypt towards the sea which comes from Persia, this canal was dug as I ordered and the boats sailed from Egypt, via this canal, to Persia according to my pleasure'.[47] Amongst the fragments of sentences from the stele of Kabret it can be discerned that, once this canal was finished, 24 (or 32) seafaring boats (knb.t) laden with produce (inw) sailed to Persia.[48] This flotilla would have rounded the tip of the Arabian Peninsula – a journey of more than 6,000 km between little known shores. The reality of this 'unthinkable circumnavigation' has been called into question without good reason.[49] This exceptional enterprise had the goal of taking symbolic possession of the seas which lapped at the western shores of Darius' domain. In the East, its equivalent was the circumnavigation of Scylax of Caryanda by navigating from the mouth of the Indus to the Gulf of Suez.[50]

The Pithom–Susa maritime link, a long voyage not without risks, and not very profitable in the transport of goods, cannot have been undertaken often. One can imagine that the transport of the statue took place via this route, but other itineraries are also conceivable.[51]

THE INITIAL DESTINATION

In the trilingual declaration, Darius had not stipulated in which spot he had ordered the statue to be placed so that it might be visible to all. By contrast, the Egyptian dedication (text 3) indicates that the memorial (mnv) preserved his memory 'close to his father, Atum, Heliopolitan lord of the two lands, Ra – Harakhte' – this long formula being the conventional designation of the sun, Ra, creator and supreme regulator of the organised world. How though, can we comprehend in cartographical terms this theological location which must have referred to an important temple of Atum? The principal 'house of Atum', third holy city after Thebes and before Memphis, was *On*, Heliopolis for the Greeks. The cosmological system of the City of the Sun had from the third millennium BC served as a framework for the royal religion and later for all the local theologies and rituals. Herodotus noted that the Heliopolitans were the most learned inhabitants of the country, which confirmed the place held by the sages and the magicians of the old city of Ra in the Egyptian tales. On my first reading, my reaction was to situate the original location of Darius' statue in this famous City of the Sun.[52] This hypothesis was adopted as a certainty in the magisterial *Histoire de l'Empire perse* by Pierre Briant.[53] However, we must put this theory aside and instead agree with the conclusions of Edda Bresciani.[54]

Everything leads us to think that the chosen site was the homonym of Heliopolis, which was in the Wadi Tumilat, midway between the eastern Nile and the Bitter Lakes. Its full name 'The House of Atum Lord of Tjeku' (Tjeku was the name of the region the wadi ran through) was abbreviated to 'The House of Atum' (*Pr-Itmw*) – hence the transcription *Patoumos* by Herodotus (II, 158); *Pithom* in Hebrew. According to Exodus 1:11, *Pithom* is one of the two towns that the Hebrews built with bricks.[55] This definition of 'store city' agrees with its presumed activities in the Persian period. It has been identified at Tell el-Maskhuta.[56] It was an important customs and police post on the Necho Canal which became the Darius Canal, *alias* 'The Canal of the Pharaohs'.[57] Furthermore, a cross-route cut obliquely through the north Sinai Desert to the end of the wadi.

THE KING'S EULOGY

The king's eulogy, which was carved on the folds of his clothing (text 2) was similar in all except a very few words to that which figured as a preamble at the beginning of the stele of Tell el-Maskhutah which contained a description of the preparation of the works. The left-hand side of this broken stele is lost; the version from Susa allows us to fill the gaps almost completely. The upper part of the stele of Tell el-Maskhutah, where we usually see the king in the presence of the gods, is taken up by motifs which normally are at the bottom of walls and on the plinth of royal effigies: the representation of the union of the Two Lands (text 4). Underneath, in two convergent lines, 'Fortress cartouches' showing the countries united under the Persian Empire (text 5a and 5b), symbolised here by identical figures raising their arms in adoration. The same composition appeared at the top of the stelae found at Kabret and at Suez. In other words, the decoration which normally represented the terrestrial universe on the base where Darius marched triumphantly was moved to the top of the stelae, since these easily decipherable symbolic images were visible from a distance.

Thus the Egyptian statue of Darius, made for the inauguration of the canal, was placed at the entrance to the *temenos* of Atum so as to be visible to those who journeyed via the wadi or those who came to visit the administrative or temple services.

The Egyptians prioritised south over north, and west over east. The countries of the Iranian subcontinent and their northern neighbours are depicted on the left side of the base. The western possessions and the African margins of the empire are on the right. According to this arrangement of the decoration, the figure of Darius was planned so that it would have faced north or west.

CIRCUMSTANCES AND DATE OF INSTALLATION AT SUSA

Two hypotheses can be advanced with regard to the date and the circumstances of the transfer of the monument from Pithom to Susa: either the transfer took place during the reign of Darius or that of Xerxes.

We know that in 487/486 BC, the Prince of Sais and of the Libyan borders, having become the Pharaoh Psamtek IV, managed to extend his power into Upper Egypt.[58] This conquest implied that he had taken Memphis, but there is nothing to confirm to what degree he expelled the Persian forces from the Arabian borders, thus leading the satrap to evacuate the precious effigy of the Great King.[59] Darius died in November 486 BC. Forthwith, Xerxes personally led his army to reconquer the Kingdom of Egypt (484 BC). We know of very few votive objects marked with his cartouche (the contrast with the prodigiousness of Darius in this matter is striking). He was admittedly called 'pharaoh' in the demotic records – and his successors after him[60] – but no temple would thereafter show another Achaemenid officiating in the service of the indigenous gods. At Susa, the statue therefore no longer signified that Darius had also been the predestined child of Ra. It was there to remind the world that the Persian had taken Egypt by the grace of Ahuramazda and his military might.

WHICH ROUTE FROM PITHOM TO SUSA?

Whatever the dates and circumstances of the transfer of the statue to the royal city of Susa, the question must be asked as to how and by what means this heavy stone was transported (a question which could be asked of all the exotic stone used at Susa, notably the large piece of rose granite which lies in the remains of the Apadana). The result is there. There are no doubts that the engineering

275

The Kabret stele
on the bank of the Nile–Red Sea Canal dug by Darius
G. POSENER, 1936: pl. V.

practices in the service of the Great King were highly advanced, having at their disposal the 'pharaonic' competence of the Egyptian superintendents. To attempt to reconstruct the journey precisely would just multiply in vain the many divergent hypotheses and uncertain calculations.[61]

Just as the raw block had been sent to the sculptors overland from the quarry, and then by boat to the workshop, so the monument must have been transported by amphibious means. From Pithom the statue could have easily been loaded onto a barge and floated down the canal, either to the Pelusiac branch of the Nile to reach the Mediterranean and a Phoenician or Palestinian port, or towards the Gulf of Suez and the Red Sea.

Both these alternatives are of equal validity. One hesitates to imagine that the cargo trireme or sailing ship might have ventured with its precious load into an interminable circumnavigation along the little-known shores of the Arabian Peninsula. In contrast, the journey to a port in Palestine (Akko) or Lebanon (Sidon) would have been short, safe and familiar to sailors, whether Egyptian, Phoenician or Greek. From there they would have had to cross overland to the Euphrates, as did the great Lebanese trees destined for the royal buildings in Iran.[62] They would have eventually re-embarked on the Euphrates and via Lower Mesopotamia would have reached Susa over land and water.

276
Possible routes (sea, river and road) for the transport of the Darius Statue from Pithom to Susa

277
Stone relief from the Palace of Ashurbanipal at Nineveh showing Phoenician boats transporting logs from the Lebanon

278
The name of Darius is carved on the belt ends, but in Egyptian hieroglyphs

on the left
The King of Upper and Lower Egypt, master of the accomplishment of the rights of Darayaouesh, may he live eternally (1a)

on the right:
The perfect God, master of Two Lands, Darayaouesh, may he live eternally (1b)

279
Jean Yoyotte and François Vallat
with the Darius Statue on its discovery

THE THEOLOGICAL EULOGY OF DARIUS THE GREAT

The accumulation in one person of the central omnipotence of the Persian and the no less central function of Son of Ra-Atum was explicitly affirmed in a traditional Egyptian *encomium* (text 2). Using mythological allusions to the victories of Ra over the forces of chaos during the genesis of the world, it emphatically recalls the providential predestination, the innate virtues and the triumphal vocation of the monarch representing God on earth.

In its vocabulary and poetic structure this classical composition could be glorifying any Egyptian king if the titulature, which acts as an epilogue, did not tell us that the 'King of Upper and Lower Egypt Darius' was 'the Great, the King of Kings, the Supreme Chieftain of the Earth [in its totality, the son of the] father of a God Hystaspes, Achaemenes, who rose as King of Upper and Lower Egypt on the throne of Horus of the living'. Ever since the Middle Kingdom, the title of 'father of God' was conferred on an individual whose son, an ordinary subject, had obtained supreme power. Whether he were a 'royal son' born of an established king of a line of kings, or a new man, the myth of theogony required that he had been predestined once he had been conceived, his mother having received the visit of the solar God who had taken on the appearance of the husband of the woman. Thus Theban Zeus, from Boeotia, disguised himself as Amphitryon to make love to Alcemene and to father Heracles. For the respectable theologians of Memphis and Heliopolis the same doctrine must have 'legitimised' Cambyses, son of Cyrus and of Cassandane, but also the authentic *'offspring of Ra'*, as it was written in his prenomen cartouche.[63]

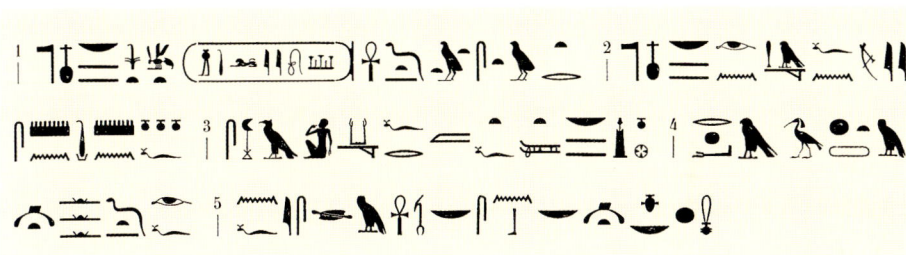

280
The Egyptian inscriptions on the statue of Darius
The theological eulogy (top)
The dedication (middle)
Sma-tawy speech (bottom)

The goddess Neith and the bow

The lead physician Udjahorresnet, the eminent courtier originally from Sais, who had welcomed Cambyses and had initiated him into the mysteries of his temple, had finally found himself in Elam, from where Darius sent him home, giving him the means to restore the House of Life and make its services available to all.[64] One may believe that just as he had addressed Cambyses, he had talked of the goddess Neith, mistress of the town, one of whose principal aspects was that of Sagittarius, riddling the adversaries of Ra and nasty demons with her arrows. The *encomium* of Pithom does not fail to mention that the Achaemenid, a skilled archer like all true Persians, has these skills and his weapon by the grace of the patron of the Twenty-sixth Dynasty. The quality of infallible archer was a fairly current theme in the royal eulogies dating from the Middle Kingdom. It was especially appropriate to grant him a cosmic range.

The theological eulogy

Text 2:

> [fold-1] *The perfect God, acting by his own hand, the sovereign, Regent of the two crowns of the North and the South, he who inspires fear in the heart of humans, possessor of prestige in the face of anyone who sees him, whose power has conquered each of the Two Lands and who acts in conformity with the orders of the God. The son of [...], The offspring of the God Atum, the living image of Ra, he who has been placed by him on his (own) throne to bring to a successful conclusion that which he had started here below.*
>
> *The perfect God who rejoices in truth [fold-2], he who Atum Lord of Heliopolis elected to be master of all that defines the solar disc, because he knows he is his son, his guardian. He ordered him to conquer each of the Two Lands and the goddess Neith gave him the bow she holds to slay all his enemies, acting as she had done for her son Ra, the first time, so that he may be vigorous in pushing back those who revolt against him, to reduce [fold-3] those who rebel against him in each of the Two Lands. The strong king, full of prestige, master of power like he who presides at Letopolis, master by (his own) hand, when he enters the fray, shooting precisely without his arrow ever missing [fold-4] the target, he whose strength is like that of the God Montu.*
>
> *The King of Upper and Lower Egypt, master of the Two Lands [Darius] – may he live forever! – the Great (King), King of Kings, the supreme Lord of Earth [in its totality, the son of) the Father of a God Hystaspes, the Achaemenid, he he who appeared as King in Upper and Lower Egypt on the throne where Horus reigns over the living, like Ra at the head of the gods, eternally*

The dedication

> [1] *The perfect God, master of the Two Lands, King of Upper and Lower Egypt Darius – may he live forever! – Image made as an exact resemblance of the* [2] *perfect God, master of the Two Lands, which his Majesty made so that a durable monument to him might be established* [3] *so that we may remember him with his father, Atum, Heliopolitan Lord of the Two Lands,* [4] *Ra Harakhte for all eternity. May he accord him in* [5] *recompense all life and all strength, all health, all joy as Ra (enjoys).*

THE UNION OF THE TWO LANDS

The Egyptian monarchy was conceived as dual.[65] The Kingdom was made up of the union of the 'Two Lands' (t3wy), the Upper being upstream of the point of the Delta, the Lower downstream from Memphis, the capital. Furthermore the king had to defeat attackers, raiders or invasions of people from strange lands by maintaining them 'under his sandals'. The unity and security of Egypt were concurrently symbolised on the base of the royal statue by traditional images.

On the front is the union of the Two Lands, the *sma-tawy*.[66] Two water genies identifiable as Hapi, the power who made the waters rise, tightly knot the stalks which rise from two symmetrical clumps around the hieroglyphic sign for the verb 'reunite' (sm3); on one side is the papyrus, emblem of Lower Egypt, on the other the lotus, emblem of Upper Egypt.[67]

On the sides are the chained lines of the enemies of Lower and Upper Egypt, often represented by their name inscribed on the inside of a 'fortress cartouche' (a crenellated oval depicting the plan of a fort) which overlies the torso of a man with ethnic characteristics.[68] The two motifs have been taken up again on the base of the Susa statue of Darius, but 'updated'.

281
Inscription no. 2 on the folds
of the left-hand side of the robe

282
Detail of inscription no. 2

283
**Dedication on the top
of the base of the statue**

284
**Detail from the Karnak relief
showing four of the Asiatic territories
conquered by Sheshonq I**
from *OIC in Tanis, l'Or des Pharaons*

The *sma-tawy*, is depicted twice, carved in *bas-relief* on the front and only incised on the back. The composition itself, as well as the lines which pronounce the 'Niles' (text 4) conform to the traditional model. The genies of prosperity give the king 'all life and prosperity, all health and all joy, Upper and Lower Egypt in adoration of his beautiful face and all the flat countries and all the mountainous countries reunited under his sandals' (text 4). The significance, however, was widened: Upper and Lower Egypt, that is to say the entire civilised world, included mountainous countries, until now home of hostile barbarians,[69] but henceforth peaceful subjects whose collaboration offered them a share of central power.

The sma-tawy

Speech:

> *I give you all life and all strength*
> *All stability, all health and all joy*
> *I give you all the countries of the plain*
> *And all the countries of the mountains reunited under*
> *Your sandals*
> *I give you Upper and Lower Egypt*
> *who offer their adoration to your beautiful face*
> *Like that of Ra, eternally.*

On the two sides of the base, 24 countries within the empire are laid out in symmetrical rows. To the left (east for the Egyptian), the countries of the Iranian subcontinent. On the right (the west), the western possessions and the southern margins of the empire. The name of each land is written in a fortress cartouche but above, its population is depicted by a figure characterised by his costume, headdress, facial hair and the profile of his face, his features. The list (texts 5a and 5b) is parallel to those which make up the cuneiform inscriptions of Darius.[70] It must be said, however, that the four last names of the right-hand list use Egyptian terms for the Arabs, Egypt itself, Libya and Nubia.

Here, the representation of the peoples *under the feet* of the king, analogous with the *union of the Two Lands*, was radically rethought to conform to Persian ideology. With the scene having been set by Darius' proclamation of universal

285
**The *sma-tawy*, symbol of the union of
the Two Lands, emblem of Upper and
Lower Egypt**

286
Front of the base of the Darius Statue
representing the union of the Two Lands
of Upper and Lower Egypt

287
**The throne bearers on the front
of Darius' tomb at Naqsh-i Rustam**
Ghirshman archives

domination,[71] a composition had been created which figured on the façade of his tomb at Naqsh-i Rustam[72] and on the door jambs of the Tripylon at Persepolis.[73] The large relief which shows above the king seated or standing under the sky has a colossal replica of the throne as a base. Between the throne-legs and spread over two or three rows, are human figures in high relief who represent the various ethnicities of the empire, and raise their arms to support the lands over which the Great King reigns. The Egyptian artists elegantly drew and captioned this 'nation-bearer' motif in their own manner, a symbol of their subjection to, and their cooperation in, the prosperity of the pacified empire.

THE WORK OF ART

After having shaped the block of *greywacke* using rock hammers, the sculptors carved the figure of the standing king, shaped the vertical folds of his clothing and carved the detailed ornamentation of his belt and his dagger. The wrought iron tools they had at the time must have been up to the task. Polishing must have been done with sand, according to a painstaking traditional method. The hieroglyphs and images destined to adorn the base, drafted on papyrus by learned men, 'scribes of form' (the illustrators), were skilfully transferred to the stone with ink. Then the 'chisel handlers' who were not necessarily literate, carved them faithfully. One must suppose that the team included a carver of Babylonian origin who was capable of accuately tracing the triple cuneiform text, using Egyptian tools. The customary in-depth aesthetic analysis is impossible due to the state of the monument whose upper section is missing. We cannot determine, for example, if the body followed the aesthetic canon of Egypt or of Persepolis.

The Persian grip over the whole country, over the fertile valley, as well as over the two deserts, had not unduly affected the production of stone ornaments, hard stone statues and sarcophagi or limestone votive stelae.[74] However, the exotic commission from Darius was without precedent for the workshops – or almost. Since the beginning of a return to the old traditions, during the course of the eighth century, royal iconography in sculpture in the round had been confined to a few types of representation: the pharaoh standing, sitting or kneeling, bare-chested and wearing only the short pleated loincloth, as in earlier times. Strict though the tradition was, foreign dress was sometimes added. Under the Twenty-fifth 'Nubian' Dynasty that ruled both Egypt and Kush, the artists of Thebes and Memphis came to endow these figures with a headpiece sporting two *uraei* and a pendant depicting the ram's head of Kushite Amon. For the rest, however, the clothing of the Nubian kings remained the short sober loincloth.

It is probable that in daily life the Saite pharaohs dressed according to the fashion of their times (under Amasis, the dress of the nobles consisted of a large kilt, wrapped around the torso and knotted level with the sternum).[75] It is evident that, for his part, Darius demanded a lifelike 'portrait' showing him clothed in Persian dress, the dagger held in a minutely decorated scabbard under his belt. From what we can see the Egyptian artists produced an authentic image of the robe. We can wonder about the model they used: a statue made of wood, clay or bronze? Why not the King himself in Persia or during his visit to Egypt? Or better still, the reconfiguration in three-dimensions of a two dimensional high relief from one of the Iranian palaces?

The issue of sources is also a problem with regard to the representation of the empire's populations. It is implausible that the Egyptian artists could have studied, one by one, live subjects of the 24 regions. Rather, one can imagine that they based them on national facial characteristics and of headdress and clothing as they saw them in high relief at Susa or at Persepolis. In the history of pharaonic

288
The dorsal pillar of the Darius Statue

art, the base of the Darius statue offers the only official representation known of far-flung foreign nations dating from the 'Saite-Persian' period. In contrast to the New Kingdom, to our knowledge the Saite period had never depicted foreigners, either on the walls of their temples erected by kings in the service of the gods or in the funerary chapels of private individuals.[76]

Because of its size, the statue of Achaemenid workmanship communicates the incommensurable power of Darius at the world's epicentre. The Egyptian drawings succeed in marrying the symbolism of the union of the Two Lands of the Nile and the coming together of all the nations and supporters of the conqueror blessed by the heavens. This was a juxtaposition of two cultures, an elegant convergence without attempt at hybridisation, due to a connivance between the conqueror and the conquered.[77]

The height of the Persian immediately drew the onlooker's gaze to the top. At head height and looking at the ground, the passerby saw the signs and images produced by the learned practitioners of the 'writing of the words of God', loyal

289

Peoples of the west and south
from right to left: Kemi (Egypt), the land of the Tjemehu (Libya), the land of the Nehesy (Nubia), Maka, Hindu (India).
right-hand image: Hakor (the Arabs of the north-west), Kemi (Egypt)

290

Peoples of the west and south
from right to left: Babylonia, Armenia, Sardis (Lydia), Cappadocia, Skudra, Ashur (the Syrians), Hakor (the Arabs from the north-west), Kemi (Egypt)

291
People's of the east and the north
right to left: Persia, Media, Elam, Aria, Parthia, Bactria, Sogdia, Arachosia, Drangiana, the Sattagydes, Chorasmia, the Saka of the marshes and of the plains

servants of the sovereign. Notwithstanding the authoritarian tone of his declaration, Darius must have been proud to hold Egypt, long admired as a land of wisdom, science, fine art and the mysteries of the divine universe.

Who is the author of this monument? The sovereign who commissioned it or the master craftsman who carved it? The theological concepts which the hieroglyphs express and the union of the Two Lands, pure products of Egyptian theology, result in a sincere recognition of the providential character of the accession. Or, viewed the other way around, the indigenous 'decor' illustrates the acceptance by the Persian of his status as pharaoh. It makes us forget that the exploitation of the peasants' work and the heavy taxes for the benefit of the gods making profit for the king's household were a continuation of the pharaonic regime.

1. F. Vallat, this volume, ch. IX.

2. The lower part of a man's face in the round, from the moustache to the jaw, had been found at Susa (GHIRSHMAN, 1963b: 140, fig, 189). After study it would appear that this fragment came from a statue carved from the local grey basalt and which must have measured some 3 m high (STRONACH, 1972: 245–246).

3. David Stronach considered this option (STRONACH, 1972: 243–244).

4. RAZMJOU, 1988. In an article written in Persian and which has been available to me only in its brief English summary, the author attributes the major damage to Alexander's troops 'who also destroyed the name of Darius in the hieroglyphic text on the statue'. This assertion cannot be sustained. Darius' cartouche appears four times on the statue. It is clearly visible in the dedication (text 3), and is ostensible twice on the belt (text 1). In text 2, line 4, only the last sign survives, but the damage is simply the result of a break in the stone which has nothing to do with vandalism.

5. Analysis of the dress by D. Stronach (STRONACH, 1972: 241–246 and 1974a: 64–67).

6. The small diameter of the cylindrical object cannot be that of a stick. I would rather suggest a papyrus scroll, perhaps enclosed in its *mekes* case, a document that was supposed to contain an inventory of the universe as transmitted to the king by the supreme god.

7. The signs written from right to left on this vertical text orientate it towards the king.

8. According to legend, Darius had wished to set up a statue of himself at the entrance to the temple of Ptah at Memphis. In view of the colossal statues that the mythical Sesostris had set up, Darius' statue would also have been huge, but he seems to have given up this project (Herodotus II, 110; this anecdote was repeated and expanded by Diodorus Siculus I, 58.3). The heads of some small statues depicting Persians have been found in Egypt, but the existence of monumental copies of Darius' Susa statue (BRIANT 1996: 989) remains purely speculative.

9. The expression '*sans ambiguité*' is Briant's (BRIANT, 1996: 499–500). Udjahorresnet and other Egyptian scholars who drew up the royal titulary of 'Pharaoh Cambyses' and 'Pharaoh Darius', affirming their divine nature and highlighting the beneficent deeds of the Achaemenids, are relatively silent about the fact that this foreign dynasty's domination was the result of military conquest. However, the ambiguity is reciprocated, with the Great King formally accepting his role as Egyptian sovereign, blessed by the gods of the Egyptian peoples. Indeed, as far as we know, Darius had taken possession of Egypt without having to fight the Egyptians.

10. See p. 247.

11. STILL and YOYOTTE, 2000: 14–22.

12. GARIS DAVIES, 1953: pl. 48–49 ; CRUZ-URIBE, 1988: 154–155. We should remember that the Hibis temple was built during the last third of Darius' reign and could well have been connected with the creation of *qanat*s in the Southern Oasis. For the Great King's dedications, see BARDINET, 2008: 282–283.

13. GARIS DAVIES, 1953: pl. 47.

14. The titles normally introducing the birth name 'Son of Ra, Lord of the Crowns' (POSENER, 1936: no. 30) are also extremely rare.

15. Serapaeum Stelae, Louvre 319 and 320

(POSENER, 1936: 39, n. *a*).

16. GOYON, 1957: pl. XXXIV, no. 109, left. Regardless of what the editor has proposed, pp. 118–120, the inscription of Governor Atiyawahi, on the right, is not contemporary with the text of Year 26.

17. See also text 2, fold 3, line 3. In Wadi Hammamat the same leonine title is given to Psamtek II in a graffiti commemorating the victory of his troops over the Ethiopians, *RdE*, 8 (1951): 238, n. 6; *BIFAO*, 50 (1952): 197, n. 5.

18. Concerning the *senti* see VITTMANN, 1998: 296–298 ; PERDU, 1998: 179.

19. POSENER, 1936: 91–96 ; JANSEN-WINCKELN, 1999: 163 ff.

20. At the time of Inaros' revolt in 464 BC, 'the Egyptians who had not taken part in the revolt' withdrew to Memphis 'with the Medes and the Persians' (THUCYDIDES, 1964: 758).

21. Diodorus Siculus I, 95. 4–6 according to the translation by Pierre Bertrac (1993), p. 175. We cannot tell what language these scholars spoke to each other (Aramean?, Babylonian?), either directly, or through specialist interpreters.

22. We regret the contempt in which Briant (BRIANT, 1996: 92–93 and 497) holds the statesman and scholar Udjahorresnet, and the contractor Khnemibre who was probably one of those responsible for the creation of the Darius Statue, and may even have conceived it. Although their lists of titles and functions may seem verbose and inflated, they provide objective information as to their responsibilities and activities.

23. *Stratagemata*, VII, 11.7.

24. Surviving epitaph (POSENER, 1936: 5 and 39 n. *a*).

25. There were major improvements to the entrances to the Serapaeum in Year 31 (491 BC). VERCOUTTER, 1962: 73, note G.

26. POSENER, 1936: 79.

27. TRICHET and POUPET, 1974 ; TRICHET and VALLAT, 1990. At a time when the Arabian Desert was inaccessible, this inscribed stone chip, Hammamat no. 99 of Necho II, removed by vandals and sent to a Parisian antiquarian by a Luxor antiquities dealer, has enabled the quarry to be identified.

28. KLEM and KLEM, 1993.

29. For general views, see André Bernand (BERNAND, 1992: 58–74 and pl. 10–13).

30. COUYAT and MONTET, 1912 ; GOYON, 1957. In 1987–1989, three IFAO expeditions, directed by Annie Gasse, undertook the archaeological exploration of the site and completed an exhaustive survey of the hieroglyphic and demotic inscriptions, with the collaboration of Didier Devauchelle: *BIFAO*, 87 (1987), p. 316–321 ; 88 (1988), p. 205–206; 89 (1989), p. 313–314, 318.

31. See *BIFAO*, 88 (1988), pl. XXIV.

32. It is naturally out of the question that Atiyawahy, the Persian governor of Koptos, could have been asked 'to supply stones for the construction sites of Kharga' (BRIANT, 1996: 497). The Hibis Temple, built in the oasis in the name of Darius, was constructed of local stone.

33. BOTHMER, 1960: no. 61, figs 143–146.

34. *Ibid.*, no. 64, figs 151–153. See also no. 65, figs 154–157, the 'Director of the King's craftsmen in silver and gold, Psamtek-sa-Neith'.

35. The inscriptions of Khnemibre were edited, with

commentary, by POSENER, 1936: 88–116, no. 11–116. GOYON, 1957: 118, no. 109, pl. XXXVI, left, with no. 108, p. 117, being the lower part of graffiti no. 20 (POSENER, 1936: 113).

36. Pierre Briant (BRIANT, 1996: 497) doubted, in 1996, that the titulature of Khnemibre could correspond to 'the powers assigned to this Egyptian' since the exploitation of the quarry was directed by Atiyawahy (see above, note 32) since, according to him, a 'position of leadership or initiative' could only have been held by a Persian (BRIANT, 1996: 92–93). The case of the 'governor' (*senti*) in *Rylands Papyrus 9*, which is no longer identified as the Persian satrap, but undeniably an Egyptian diocete, highly placed in the management of the kingdom's economy, has led the historian (BHA ch. II, p. 123, note 251) to cease minimizing to such an extent the responsibilities that important Egyptian functionaries retained during the reign of Pharaoh Darius.

37. British Museum 48927 (HALL and REGINALD, 1913: 292, no. 270; YOYOTTE, 1972b: 220, n. 7). A large number of letter and parcel sealings, including those of Persian seals, were found discarded in the Memphite fortress.

38. Herodotus II, 3. The priests of Heliopolis often figure in historical novels of the Late Period (as, for instance, Potiphar in the biblical tale of *Joseph*; Gen. 39:1).

39. POSENER, 1936: 162–163. Add the variant *Trywhš* (GOYON, 1957: 118–119, no. 109).

40. It is striking to see, judging from the script, that the greatest number of small objects dedicated to Darius, and found throughout Egypt, are dated to the period between 495 and 486 BC.

41. Summary in POSENER, 1936: 48–50. The fragments of the three stelae were at one time in the Ismaïlia Museum, but have now been transferred to the Port Said Museum.

42. POSENER, 1936: pl. IV.

43. POSENER, 1936: pl. V.

44. POSENER, 1936: pl. XIV.

45. The allusions to the 'residence' that 'Cyrus has built' (POSENER, 1936: 60–61) are enigmatic. They might refer to Darius' place of residence in Persia. Posener noted that 'the absence of any royal title before the name of Cyrus is strange' (POSENER, 1936, 60–61 n. *h*). However, F. Vallat has pointed out (see ch. II: 54–66) that the name of the said Cyrus appears in none of Darius' Cuneiform inscriptions.

46. For the location of Punt, see POSENER, 1973: 300–374; POSENER, 1977: 337–342.

47. François Vallat, this volume, ch. II: 38–39.

48. The conclusion reached by Posener on the basis of Scheil's translations (POSENER, 1936: 77 and 180–181.

49. SALLES, 1998: 96–97.

50. Herodotus IV, 44 (BRIANT, 1996: 397, 495).

51. See fig. 276.

52. YOYOTTE, 1972a: 263; STILL and YOYOTTE, 2000: 17.

53. BRIANT, 1996: 229–230, 492, 494, 973 and 989. A collection of radical criticisms which recent research has rendered obsolete. In BRIANT, 2001: 201, note 423, the Heliopolitan provenance is firmly retained.

54. Most recently in BRESCIANI, 1998: 103–111. BRIANT, 2001: 126, note 423 arbitrarily assigns to E. Bresciani '*her unstated conviction* that the statue was transported to Susa by sea directly from the Red Sea', which would have led her to choose Pithom rather than Heliopolis.

55. The other 'store city', called *Ramses*, cannot be identified with the famous residence of Ramses II, the 'House of Ramses' (situated at Qantir) which was a large open town, including a royal palace, princely villas, stables, workshops, temples, harbour facilities, etc. Ramses depot is more likely to have been located near Tjaru (*Hebwa*) in the eastern Delta.

56. The House of Atum was originally situated in the western part of the Wadi Tumilat (Tell el-Retabeh). It was moved eastwards under Psamtek I. The naos, sphinx and statues of Ramses II were then transferred to Tell el-Maskhutah (Holladay 1982).

57. The re-establishment of this means of access to the Red Sea under Ptolemy II was well known to Greek historians (Diodorus, Strabo), and was recorded on the so-called Pithom Stele found at Tell el-Maskhutah. See Christophe Thiers's reconsideration of the evidence and of the problems relating to the 'Canal of the Pharaohs' (THIERS, 2007: 107–117).

58. PESTMAN, 1984. Publication of the texts: VLEEMING, 1991.

59. This was what François Vallat had already suggested in 1974 (VALLAT, 1974a: 161–170). Halliday's admittedly very restricted stratigraphic excavation at Tell el-Maskhutah barely reached a level of burnt remains which he related to the events of 486 BC.

60. On the stone vessels found at Susa and Persepolis, the cartouche of Xerxes is followed by the title *pr ꜥȝ pȝ ꜥȝ*, translations of the Persian title 'Great King'.

61. For general information on the roads, see P. Briant (BRIANT, 1996: 395–396 and 954–955).

62. Compare the 'Foundation Charter', DSf §9.

63. POSENER, 1936: 12, n. r.

64. The Vatican Naophorous (POSENER, 1936: 21–25).

65. Pascal Vernus in VERNUS and YOYOTTE, 1996: 66–67.

66. There is a vast bibliography concerning this concept (see my remarks in *CRIPEL*, 11 (1989: 127–128). We must remember that the name of Horus, bestowed on Cambyses, had been precisely *smȝ tȝwy* (epitaph and sarcophagus of the Apis buried in 524 BC, POSENER, 1936: 30–36, no. 3-4).

67. Fragment of the seat of a statue of Psamtek II HODJASH and BERLEV, 1982: 113, 114, 115 and 116, no. 113.

68. Personifications of Palestinian towns taken from the great scene of Sheshonq I at Karnak.

69. For the equivalence of *tȝwy = oikumene* in Roman times, see QUAEGEBEUR, 1975: 112–113.

70. BRIANT, 1996: 185–186.

71. Cf. F. Vallat, ch. IX, DSe.

72. GHIRSHMAN, 1963b: 230–231, fig. M179; BRIANT, 1996: 222–225. This composition would be repeated on the tombs of his successors.

73. GHIRSHMAN, 1963b: 198–199, fig. 246; BRIANT, 1996: 231, fig. 15–16.

74. Do not trust the article by J.A. Josephson (JOSEPHSON, 1997).

75. This garment was previously and wrongly thought to be of Persian origin because it was thought to be exclusively restricted to statues of the XXVIIth Dynasty. However, it was well known under Amasis and could easily have survived under the first Persian kings (BRESCIANI, 1967: 273–280).

76. Comparative material remains to be found among representations of Carians and Syrians on the funerary stelae produced at Memphis in workshops aimed specifically at these groups of foreigners. Some sample cosmetic spoons that can be attributed to the Saite-Persian period represent authentic depictions of Syrian dress (WALLERT, 1967: pl. 37).

77. Contrary to what P. Briant would have us believe (BRIANT, 1996: 499–500) neither Egyptian texts, nor Egyptologists have maintained that Darius owed his power 'to the good favour' of Udjahorresnet and his equals'. For Egyptian thinkers of this type, the 'legitimacy' of the Twenty-seventh dynasty, supported by a military occupation, certainly did not depend on their 'good favour'. It was certainly not based on the aristocratic status of their family in Iran, but on their predestination by Ra who had engendered them.

Peoples and countries of the empire

Jean Yoyotte

A t Naqsh-i Rustam and at Persepolis, the personification of the countries which support the Great King number 28, even 30, whilst, on either side of our image of Darius, the two series of fortress cartouches only show 24 'nation-bearers'. This difference is not significant: the space being limited, the names of ethnic dependencies have been omitted: Caria, the two from Ionia, Scythia and Gandhara.[1]

In a kneeling posture, arms lifted to the heavens, each figure is elegantly carved in Egyptian fashion. The infill detail remains schematic and the depiction of clothing seems incomplete in some areas (they were perhaps originally painted). It is unlikely that the Egyptian illustrators sketched live models, typical representatives of the 24 regions. It is more plausible to suppose that they noted and, in their own manner, 'reinterpreted' the facial features, headdresses and clothes of the various nations, as they had seen them in high relief at Susa and Persepolis.

More than half these peoples are dressed in long, full hanging robes forming large pleats; some wore baggy trousers. Since these pleats are different from the tight pleats of the royal *shendjyt* and the traditional Egyptian loincloths, it is likely that the creators of the statue were inspired by Ionian sculpture, of which examples were known at Memphis.[2]

By comparing these illustrations with others depicting nations carrying Darius and with the line of tribute bearers at Persepolis, it appears that the base of the statue offered original sartorial variation, some of real ethnographic interest and some no doubt fanciful but which aesthetically create a picturesque diversity.

To the left, symbolically north and east of the epicentre where the Great King was, were named the countries occupying Iran and its Afghan borders, followed by the mention of the Scythians of the steppes bordering on the empire, from the shores of the Black Sea to Central Asia.

To the right were the possessions situated to the west of Iran, starting with

292
**Distribution of the peoples
on the base of the Darius Statue**
facing west: Persia, Media, Elam, etc.
facing east: Egypt, Arabia, Ethiopia, etc.
drawing by Daniel Ladiray

Mesopotamia, the immediate neighbour, and passing by Anatolia and the lands west of the Euphrates, to arrive in the Egyptian sphere and then complete the outline of the Persian Empire with the coasts of Oman and India.

THE LEFT-HAND SERIES: THE IRANIAN WORLD

The left-hand series started with the western edge of Iran and, progressing towards the east, listed all the territories according to designations which define both topographic realities and large ethnic groups, continuing to the Afghan mountains and between the Caspian and Aral Seas. It ended with a cursory mention of the Scythians. There were two types of dress, more or less conventional: in long robes with short wide sleeves were the Persian, the Elamite, the Arachosian; wearing the *kandys*, with the sleeves thrown back over the shoulders were the Medes, the Aryans, as well as the Cappadocians in the right-hand series. The others only seem to wear a short loincloth, pleated or not. With the singular exception of the Persians, all these Iranians had more or less full beards finishing in a point, conforming with the Egyptian-drawn model of an Asiatic (Syro-Palestinian).

The Persian, the Aryan and the Parthian turbans were all wound round the head several times. The Medes wore the round bonnet that is so characteristic of the nation in the ceremonies at Persepolis. The headdresses of several Iranians were accompanied by removable earflaps. The representative of Drangiana wore a form of balaclava.

I. *Persia*

Fars, the leading Iranian region, with Pasargadae, Persepolis and the royal necropolis at Naqsh-i Rustam, the seat of Achaemenid power. Its populace was

293
Peoples of the north and the east

represented by a man whose costume, though certainly of Persian style, was not that of Darius and his nobles, but that of ordinary subjects. Nonetheless, the relative importance of the Persian, the dominant ethnicity, was denoted by the bracelets he wears on his wrists.

II. *Media*

The Median nation is represented by a man quite understandably wearing the long costume of 'Median' type, the *kandys*, whose sleeves were thrown back over the shoulders and wearing the characteristic round bonnet with earflaps.

The lands of the Medes, an Aryan race with close links to the Persians, occupied a large band of territory running from present-day Kurdistan to the southern shores of the Caspian Sea. In the seventh century BC the Medes, led by a king, constituted a strong military power which was allied to Babylon and took part in the annihilation of Assyria. The royal capital was at Ecbatana (Hamadan).

Pierre Briant seriously doubts the existence of this empire, seeing it as an invention of Herodotus, an illusory pastiche of the empire founded by Cyrus.[3] But how else can we explain the prominent place of the Medes in Achaemenid expression, with the reliefs of Persepolis establishing a form of parity for the sake of protocol between Median and Persian nobles? According to Darius, Media provided workers and artists for the Susian building sites and gold plate for the Great King.[4] Nonetheless it would not be appropriate to speak of 'Median art'.

Numerous historians agree that this invading Median nation really made an impression on the world over a 60-year period between 615 BC and 550 BC, before Cyrus brought about the pre-eminence of the Persians on the back of their expansion. This is how the name of the Medes obscured that of the Persians in the vocabulary of neighbouring nations. From the Greek we have retained the expression to qualify the aggressive enterprises of the Persian kings: the 'Median Wars'.[5] The Egyptians spoke of the 'Medes' when referring to the Achaemenid dynasty and used this term for foreign soldiers. The genealogy of the nations in Genesis 10:2 refers only to *Madai*.

III. *Elam*

The figure representing the third 'nation' of the empire and Darius' main power base is notable for his use of Persian costume. Although the Assyrians had brutally put an end to the Neo-Elamite dynasty (around 639 BC), the ravages had not destroyed the Elamites' language or culture. The highlands of Elam and the plain

| XXIV | XXIII | XXII | XXI | XX | XIX | XVIII | XVII | XVI | XV | XIV | XIII |

294
Peoples of the south and the west

of Susiana having become domains of the Achaemenid family, Darius I set up a major power centre in the old royal city of Susa. According to the Canal Stelae, going to Susa was to go to 'Persia'.

IV. *Aria*

The figure, wearing a high turban like the Persian, is the first of a series of men wearing Median-style dress, all depicting the camel-herding nations who occupied the Iranian plateau and its oriental and northern confines. The territory of the Arians, to the north-east, corresponded more or less to Khorasan, spanning the border between Iran and Afghanistan (with its capital Herat, which would succeed Alexandria in Aria).

V. *Parthia*

The lands of the Parthian tribes extended from the southern shores of the Caspian Sea to the Arian borders. A nomadic, camel-breeding population.

295
Base of the Darius statue
Persia and Media, Elam and Aria

VI. *Bactria*

This territory, upstream of the Oxus (Amu Darya), corresponded more or less to the southern point of modern-day Uzbekistan. Bactra (today Balkh) was the eponymous capital. The country was powerful and very prosperous, even before its annexation by the Persians, and remained so afterwards, with camel-breeding, agriculture and high-quality artisanal work. Bactria delivered gold to Darius.

VII. *Sogdia*

Between the Oxus and the Jaxartes (Syr Darya), prosperous Sogdia was on the extreme north-eastern border of the empire. Its territory was in present-day Uzbekistan. The capital, Maracanda, was none other than the future Samarkand. Sogdians supplied carnelian and lapis lazuli (imported from Badakhshan).

VIII. *Arachosia*

Alexander would confront this difficult region when he transformed the satrapic capital into an Alexandria of Arachosia, located at Kandahar in Afghanistan, close to the Pakistani border. Camel-breeding and the importation of ivory from India were the major commercial activities.

IX. *Drangiana*

Situated between Aria and Arachosia, Drangiana corresponded more or less to Sistan in the south-west of Afghanistan. It was well irrigated and well cultivated under the Achaemenids.

296
VI. **Bactria**

X. *The Sattagydians*

The country called *sadagudj* in Egyptian, *Thatagus* in Persian and *Satagusu* in Babylonian in the lists of Darius was otherwise only known from Herodotus (III, 91), according to whom the Sattagydians were a group of tributaries associated with the inhabitants of Gandhara. The central mountain chains of Afghanistan along the rivers of the Helmand and the Arghandab have been suggested as the location for these peoples.

XI. *Chorasmia*

A vast frontier zone extending between the Caspian and Aral seas in what is now Uzbekistan. This ancient toponym survives today in the form *Khwarezm* (whence the ethnic name *Al-Khwarizmi* by which the great mathematician who gave his name to algorithms was known). Chorasmia delivered horses and turquoise. The figure in a short garment(?) wears a bonnet with earflaps.

XII. *The Saka*

'The Saka of the marshes (and) the Saka of the plains', otherwise known as the Scythians whose tribes occupied the northern margins of the empire, from the Black Sea to the marshes that form the deltas of the Oxus (Amu Darya) and the Jaxartes (Syr Darya). The first mention of the Saka was written phonetically, but the second, as well as the designations for the two types of Scythians on the Pithom Stele, were noted by the Egyptian word *sk*, 'destructor', apparently a pertinent etymological word game. The Scythian bonnet with earflaps, similar to that of the Chorasmian, is distinguished by a crest.

297
XII. **The Saka**

XIII. *Babylon, otherwise known as Mesopotamia*

The ancient cultural and political metropolis of the Akkadian world headed up the list. It became a hegemonic centre of Persian power under Darius, The name *Babilu*, Babylon, here probably denoted the whole of Mesopotamia, from the Persian Gulf all the way to the upper reaches of the two rivers, Herodotus' Syria (see *infra 17 Ashur*).

The Babylonian is, as usual, bearded and wears a long robe. The shape of the tiara that he wears manifestly recalls the 'white crown' which the pharaohs wore as kings of Lower Egypt.[6]

XIV. *Armenia*

Darius provided the first known confirmation of this ethnic and topographic name for the high mountain region, backing onto the Caucasus which, despite its fundamental historical unity, was dismembered by Turkey and what was previously the Soviet Union – the native Armenians having been massacred or expelled by the Turks in modern times.

The Egyptian hieroglyphs transcribe the Old Persian *armina* whilst the Babylonian retains the name of *Urartu* by which the Assyrians referred to the powerful kingdom of *Biainili* which threatened and stood up to them from 832 BC to 714 BC. Yerevan (*Erebuni* in Urartian), capital of the present-day Republic of Armenia, was founded by King Argishti I (787–766 BC).

The consonantal notation '*rrt* for the Urartu in Armenian and in Hebrew was arbitrarily vocalised into '*Ararat* in the Masoretic Bible.[7] This form remained piously inscribed in the toponymy of Christian Armenia and in international cartography. The Armenian wears a bonnet whose earflaps are folded up over his head.

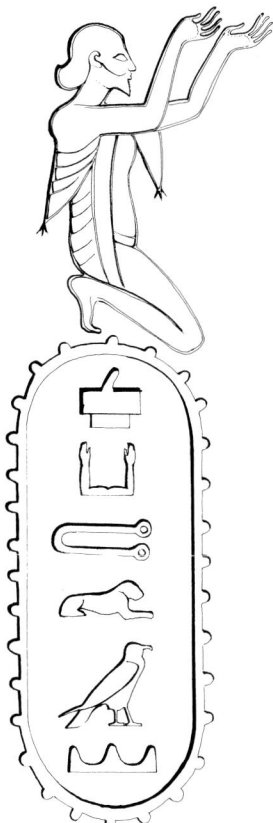

XV. *Lydia*

The name of *Saparta*, otherwise known as Sardis, the capital of the extremely wealthy kingdom of Lydia, covered the whole of the western part of Anatolia, from the Aegean to the Halys bend. This land united over 15 peoples, some of whom had formed states that preserved their respective languages and culture.

It was vocalised as *Sepharad* by the biblical prophet Obadiah (verse 20) speaking of the people of Jerusalem deported to Lydia. Later, when the name of Sardis was forgotten, it would come to designate distant Spain, and today refers to all southern and oriental Jews.

XVI. *Cappadocia*

The eastern part of Anatolia, which had escaped Lydian expansion, was called *Katpadukya*, Cappadocia in the broader sense. It is possible that Cilicia was also included. According to Herodotus (I, 72) its inhabitants were called 'Syrians' by the Greeks. The Cappadocian wears a similar headdress to the Armenian, and a *kandys* identical to that of the Medes (no. 2).

XVII. *Skudra*

No headdress, a small goatee and a shawl, all denote an undifferentiated Asian, whilst other representations of nation-bearers give them crested hats which cover the cheeks, and a cloak similar to that of the Scythians. It is generally acknowledged that they were the Thracians of Europe.[8]

XVIII. *'Ashur', the Syrians*

In Old Persian *aqura*, Babylonian *assur*, Armenian *'swr*, this western domain of Darius was called Assyria. The Assyrian state and empire had been brutally crushed by the Babylonians and Medes in 612 BC. Meanwhile, Western Syria, which had been wholly absorbed as an Assyrian province, preserved the name of *Ashur* in the imperial vocabulary as well as in the Egyptian (*'išr*).[9] Thus Armenian script was called 'the writing of the land of Ashur' in Egyptian.[10]

Excepting the Phoenicians of the Lebanon, its inhabitants, according to Herodotus (VII, 63) 'called Assyrians by the Barbarians, were called Syrians by the Greeks'. He revealed the presence of Syrians at the Cappadocian frontier (III, 91) and wrote of the abundance of 'Syrians of Palestine' whose lands extended across the northern Sinai to Lake Sirbonis (I, 105; II, 104; III, 5).[11]

When the 'Foundation Charter' mentions the cedarwood from the Lebanon which 'the Assyrians transported to Babylon' and that 'from Babylon the Ionians and Carians transported them to Susa', we should understand that it was the Syrians who carried the wood to the Euphrates.[12]

XIX. *The Arabs*

The trilingual cuneiform list of the nation-bearers places Arabia between the Syrians of Trans-Euphrates and Egypt.[13] In the Egyptian version of this list provided by the statue, a passage begins in which the neighbouring peoples of Egypt are designated by Egyptian expressions. Such was the case with the country which the Egyptians called *Hakor*, a denomination well attested by the name borne by the Pharaoh *Achoris*.[14] The horsemen and camel riders of the north-west of the Arabian Peninsula were faithful auxiliaries of the Persians in controlling the access routes to Egypt.

The ample pleated robes and the shawl of the figure, comparable to that of the Thracians, were no doubt the result of an arbitrary convention.

XX. *Egypt*

The Egyptian is, as normal, dressed in a short-sleeved robe, lightly traced. According to habit, his hair was cut short and he was clean-shaven. The country name, *kemi* (etymologically, 'the black land') was mechanically inscribed in a fortress cartouche.

XXI. *The Libyans*

In Old Persian *Putaya,* in Babylonian *Puta*, in Hebrew *Pwt*, transcriptions of the term *pyt* (vocalised *Païet) one of the first mentions of which can be found in a political passage by Pharaoh Osorkon II (around 874 BC – 850 BC), who was of Libyan origin, to designate the peoples of Marmarica and Cyrenaica.[15] The scribes who transposed the list of peoples, in accordance with the archaistic fashion of the time, wrote of 'the land of the Temehu' – a traditional expression going back to the Old Kingdom.[16]

The Libyan is bare-headed and his beard is thick and pointed. The carving of his clothing was close to reality if one compares it with the images of Libyans that the New Kingdom has left us.

XXII. *The Ethiopians*

Another archaic expression, 'the Land of Nehesy', corresponded to the cuneiform *Kuysiya*, otherwise known as the land of Kush and called the Kingdom of Ethiopia

300
XVIII. 'Ashur'

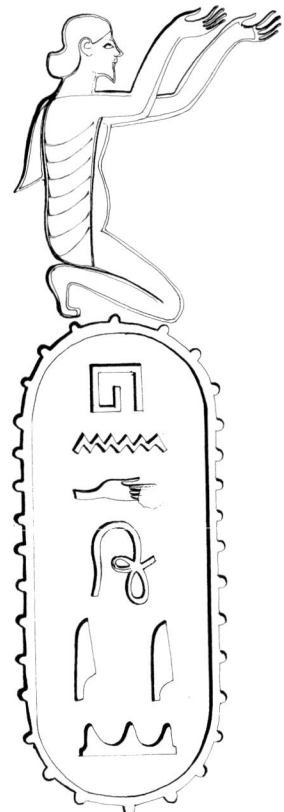

301
XXIV. India

by the Greeks. The mention of these two place names, and particularly the second, which extended Darius' domination towards the African interior, conveys an excessive pretension. At the start the archaic expression 'Lands of Nehesy' denoted Lower Nubia, but had come to be applied to the more northerly regions of the Nile Valley. As for the name *Kush*, the name originally of a kingdom based in Dongola, then of a vice royalty which extended to the fourth cataract, it was internationally famous since the eighth century BC, when the Napata monarchy, having given Egypt its Twenty-fifth Dynasty, intervened deep into Palestine before being dramatically overthrown by the Syrians and then pushed back by the Saites into its native Sudan. Separated from Egypt by the aridity of the Batn-el-Hajar, the kingdom of Kush – the one which would hold the Persian Cambyses in check – subsisted upstream of the third cataract. Without ever renouncing their status as Kings of Egypt, the Napatans ensured the south of their kingdom prospered, where a second residence at Meroë was developed.

The theoretical border between Egypt and Ethiopia was situated at the latitude of Hierakonpolis, a little downstream from the first cataract.[17] During the Saite-Persian era, the garrisons charged with controlling the passage and watching over the Nubians were installed at Elephantine and Aswan. Persian power which had extended its control up to the second cataract of the Nile (Doginarti) was able to extract tribute from the Nehesy of Lower Nubia in the form of gold, and in recruiting soldiers amongst them. However, the implicit identification of the 'Land of the Nehesy' with Kush is fallacious, Darius not having annexed any more than the Saites even the smallest part of the distant kingdom of Napata and Meroë.

The illustrator exaggerated to the point of caricature the Black African traits which he gave the Ethiopian. This anthropological type, however, was not the only one, and was probably not in the majority in the Kingdom of Kush. The long pleated clothing of the Sudanese contrasted with the supposed poverty of the Syrian.

XXIII. *Maka, Oman*

The hieroglyphic *Mag(a)* is a transcription of the Old Persian *Maka*. This toponym is generally accepted as the name for the shores of Oman and the entrance to the Persian Gulf.

The clothing of the representative of this marginal region to the south-west of Iran is similar to that of the Indian, despite the distance which separates the Gulf from India.

XXIV. *India*

In Egyptian *Hndwy*, in Old Persian *Hindu*. The lists of Darius include Gandara and, according to classical sources, the Achaemenid domination extended to the middle valley of the Indus. As Herodotus recalled, it was on the instructions of the Great King that the Carian sailor, Scylax of Caryanda reconnoitred the course of the river to the sea and then explored the coasts of Iran and Arabia, after which, Herodotus reports (IV, 44), 'Darius subdued the Indians and opened the sea to his ships'.

The Indian's costume was as conventional as that of the man from Oman.

1. This section is largely based on the work of Michael Roaf (ROAF, 1974).

2. H. Luschey has supplied interesting information (LUSCHEY, 1976: 210–212).

3. BRIANT, 1996: 36–37.

4. See F. Vallat, this volume, ch. IX, Dsf § 2.

5. This name is derived from Herodotus IX, 64.

6. As noted by John Baines (BAINES, 1974: note 153).

7. 'The mountains of Ararat' (Genesis 8:4) where the expeditions of fundamentalists continue to search for Noah's Ark. The kingdom of Ararat is among the invaders from the north (Jeremiah 51:27).

8. HENKELMAN W. and M. STOLPER: *Identity and ethnicity in the Persepolis tablets: The case of the Skudrians.* In P. BRIANT and M. CHAUVEAU (eds), 2007.

9. COLIN, 2004: 224–233.

10. Similarly, Thucydides states that messages seized from a Persian emissary were written 'in Syrian characters' (*History* IV, 50).

11. The 'Father of History' applied the name Assyria to the whole of Mesopotamia, including both Nineveh and Babylon (I, 106, 178; III, 92).

12. See F. Vallat, this volume, ch. IX, Dsf, x 9.

13. See F. Vallat, this volume, ch. IX, Dse, x 3.

14. POSENER, 1969: 148–150.

15. Statue Cairo CG 1040 (JACQUET-GORDON, 1960).

16. For Libyans in the Persian period see Frédéric Colin (COLIN, 2000: 90–94).

17. The name Kush (Greek Kusis), now Dush, would be expanded at an indeterminate date to include the southern extension of the southern oasis, which was so well treated by the Persians.

language, such as the foundation plaque DSaa (Babylonian) or had a quadrilingual inscription, such as the Darius statue, of which one side of the robe and the plinth were decorated in Egyptian hieroglyphs. That said, the Egyptian text was not a translation of the trilingual cuneiform inscription – it was totally independent.[1]

Here we should note that these different inscriptions have been translated by P. Lecoq,[2] albeit with some differences. To start with, his translations were biased towards the versions in Old Persian whilst those presented here give precedence to the Elamite. Consequently, there are some divergences in the interpretation of facts in certain passages. The summary bibliographic references refer to the *editio princeps*, generally to the epigraphists of Susa (V. Scheil, M.-J. Steve, F. Vallat) as well as the two principal corpuses, that of F.W. Weissbach (trilingual)[3] and that of R. Kent (Old Persian).[4]

Moreover, it is important to recognise that we are totally ignorant of provenances based on the records from excavations preceding those directed by Roman Ghirshman. Scheil confirms this in his introduction to *Inscriptions des Achéménides à Suse*: 'Apart from the large Persian tablet, which was found in its original location, the Apadana, the fragments of marble tablets were scattered across every corner of the ruin, Apadana, Acropolis, Ville Royale, Donjon, etc. It therefore seems futile to try to indicate a precise location for the provenance of each.'[5]

V. Scheil was right when dealing with isolated fragments, but wrong when the plinths or bases of the columns seemed to be still *in situ*. In most cases, however, even the inscriptions found in their original location do not permit us to identify the buildings, such is the confusing terminology. To take just one example, we can cite the text of Artaxerxes II who called his palace *hadiš* in Old Persian but *taçara* in Elamite and Babylonian, even though this was a term of Iranian origin.

THE INSCRIPTIONS OF DARIUS AT SUSA

DSe

A trilingual inscription known only from fragments: 12 in Old Persian, 5 in Elamite and 3 in Babylonian. The translation is from the Babylonian text which Scheil called 'Conquests and politics of Darius'.[6]

[§ 1,1–5] *The great god is Ahuramazda who created this earth here, who created the sky there, who created man, who created the happiness of man, who made Darius king, first king of many, first lord of many.*

[§ 2, 5–8] *I am Darius, the Great King, King of Kings, the king of peoples of all origins, the king of this great far-flung land, the son of Hystaspes, the Achaemenid, a Persian, son of a Persian, Aryan of Aryan descent.*

[§ 3, 8–22] *And Darius the king says:*
By the grace of Ahuramazda, here are the peoples that I have conquered outside Persia. They obey me; they bring me tribute. What I order them to do, they accomplish. They respect my law: Media, Elam, Parthia, Aria, Bactria, Sogdiana, Chorasmia, Drangiana, Arachosia, Sattagydia, the Macians, Gandhara, India, the Amyrgian Scythians, the Tigrakhauda Scythians, Babylonia, Assyria, Arabia, Egypt, Armenia, Cappadocia, Lydia, the Greeks who guard the sea, the Scythians across the sea, the Carians.

[§ 4, 22–29] *Darius the king says:*
Much of the harm that had been done, I transformed into good. The nations which fought amongst each other, whose people killed each other, these, by the grace of Ahuramazda I ensured that their people did not kill each other any more and I reinstalled each in their own country. Presented with my decisions, they respected them so that the strong neither strike nor rob the poor.

[§ 5, 30–36] *Darius the king says:*
By the grace of Ahuramazda many enterprises which beforehand had not been accomplished, I made good.
I saw that the fortifications which had once been built at Susa had gone to ruin. But I raised them up. They are in fact new works that I have built.

[§ 6, 36–38] *Darius the king says:*
May Ahuramazda protect me, with all the gods, as well as my house and this text that has been written!

These lines represent an aspect known elsewhere, in his homage to Ahuramazda (1) and in his list of countries (3) which respect the laws of the king. He is more original when he speaks of morality (4) and more especially when he speaks of the poor state of the buildings at Susa and the reconstruction of its walls (5).

DSf

Foundation charter of the palace.[7] Trilingual fragmentary inscriptions: 13 fragments in Old Persian, 12 in Elamite, 27 in Babylonian.[8]

[§ 1, 1–4] *The great God is Ahuramazda who created this earth, who created the sky, who created man, who created the happiness of man, who made Darius king, first king of many, first lord of many.*

[§ 2, 5–7] *I am Darius, the Great King, the King of Kings, the King of peoples, the King on this earth, the son of Hystaspes, the Achaemenid.*

[§ 3, 7–11] *And Darius the king says:*
Ahuramazda, who is the greatest of gods, created me himself, conferred royalty on me himself, gave me this kingdom himself, which is large, and which, due to its men and its horses, is beautiful.

305
The Elamite foundation tablet (DSz)
Lines 1–20

[§ 8, 26–32] *And the beams of cedar wood were brought from a mountain called Lebanon. The Assyrians transported them as far as Babylon, and from Babylon the Carians and the Ionians transported them to Susa. And the yaka timber was brought from Gandhara and from Kerman.*

[§ 9, 32–37] *And the gold, which was worked here, was brought from Sardis and Bactria.*
And the precious stones, such as the lapis lazuli and the carnelian, which were worked here were brought from Sogdia. And the turquoise which was worked here was brought from Chorasmia.

[§ 10, 37–42] *And the silver like the ebony were brought from Egypt.*
The decorative elements with which the terrace was painted were brought from Ionia.
And the ivory, which was worked here, was brought from Ethiopia, India and Arachosia.

[§ 11, 42–46] *And the stone columns which were carved here, were brought from a village called Hapiratush in Elam; the artisans who worked this stone were Ionians and from Sardians.*

[§ 12, 46–52] *The goldsmiths who worked the gold were Medes and Egyptians.*
And the men who carved the wood were Sardians and Egyptians.
And the men who made the bricks were Babylonians.
And the men who decorated the terrace were Medes and Egyptians.

[§ 13, 53–56] *Darius the king says: by the grace of Ahuramazda at Susa, much excellent work was ordered, much excellent work was executed. May Ahuramazada protect me as well as my people.*

306
The Elamite foundation tablet (DSz)
Lines 25–44

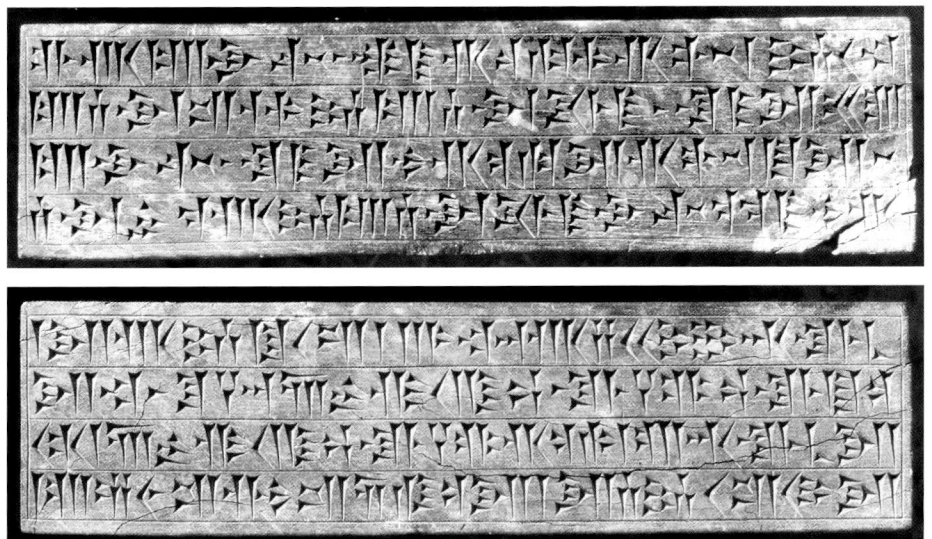

307
The Elamite foundation tablet (DSz)
Lines 45–48 and 53–56

308
The Babylonian foundation tablet (DSaa)
Lines 1–14
National Museum of Iran, Tehran

309
The Babylonian foundation tablet (DSaa)
Lines 35–37
National Museum of Iran, Tehran

There are three main differences between this and the DSF foundation plaque. The first is the absence of the name of the king's father, Hystaspes when asking for Ahuramazda's protection. Next, the depths of the foundations dug for the palace are different in DSF: on the one hand 40 cubits, on the other 20, whilst here they have been uniformly dug to 20 cubits, which implies that DSZ was produced for a different palace from that of DSF. Finally, the text is different from its Babylonian counterpart DSaa, both found *in situ*.[10]

DSaa

Foundation tablet written in Babylonian discovered at the same time as DSZ (on either side of the same passageway) but the texts are different: DSZ is more complete, DSaa is abridged.[11]

> [§ 1, 1–3] *I am Darius, the Great King, King of Kings King of nations, King on this earth, the son of Hystaspes, the Achaemenid.*
>
> [§ 2, 3–10] *And Darius the king says:*
> *By the grace of Ahuramazda, the palace which is built here, it is I who built it. Where the palace was built, its foundations were dug until I reached the bedrock and with gravel, over 20 cubits, were filled.*
> *On the rubble, the palace foundations were raised.*
>
> [§ 3, 11–17] *Here are the materials which were used for this palace: gold, silver, lapis lazuli, turquoise, carnelian, cedar wood, wood from Maka, ebony, ivory and the relief decorations. All the columns are of stone.*

310
Reverse of the Babylonian tablet (DSaa)
lines 18–31
National Museum of Iran, Tehran

[§ 4, 18–31] Here are the countries which brought the materials and decorations of this palace: Persia, Elam, Media, Babylon, Assyria, Arabia, Egypt, the Countries of the sea, Sardis, Ionia, Urartu, Cappadocia, Parthia, Drangiana, Aria, Chorasmia, Bactria, Sodgia, Gandhara, Scythia, Sattagydia, Arachosia, Quadia.

[§ 5, 32–40] Darius the king says:
By the grace of Ahuramazda, the materials and decoration of this palace were brought from afar and I designed the layout. All that I have done, all this, it is thanks to the protection of Ahuramazda that I have accomplished it. Ahuramazda will protect me until I have accomplished all.

DSab

Statue of Darius. Trilingual inscription on the folds of Darius' robe (right-hand side). An Egyptian hieroglyphic inscription on the folds of the king's robe and another adorns the statue's plinth.[12]

[§ 1, 1] The great God is Ahuramazda who has created the earth here, who has created the sky there, who has created man, who has created the happiness of man, who has made Darius king.

[§ 2, 1–2] Here is the stone statue which Darius the king commanded to be made in Egypt, so that he who should see it knows that the Persian Man holds Egypt.

[§ 3, 2–3] I am Darius, the Great King, King of Kings, King of peoples, King over this great land, the son of Hystaspes, the Achaemenid.

[§ 4, 3] Darius the king says:
May Ahuramazda protect me, also that which I have made!

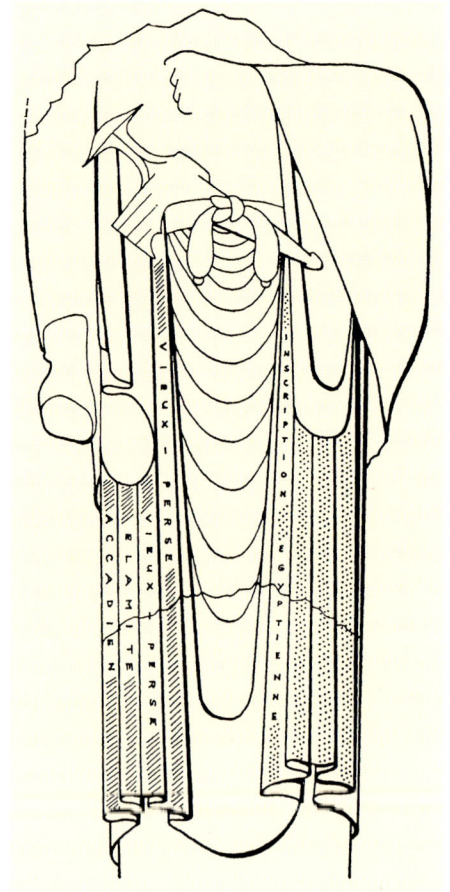

311
The statue of Darius showing the position of the cuneiform inscriptions on the folds of the robe (right-hand side of the statue)

312
The trilingual cuneiform inscription on the folds of the right-hand side of the robe
See F. Vallat, this volume, ch. 9

313

Copy of inscription DSab
on the robe of Darius
Each paragraph represents one line:
the first four for the Old Persian;
the next three for the Elamite;
the last three for the Babylonian

314
Column base of the Propylaeum portico
inscribed with the name of Xerxes (XSa)

315
Xerxes' inscription (XSa) in Old Persian on
the base of column 5059 of the Propylaeum

316
The Darius Gate: Xerxes' inscription
(XSd) on a base of the central hall

INSCRIPTIONS OF XERXES

XSa

Trilingual inscription on the bases of round columns from a palace called *hadiš* in Old Persian, *ulhi* in Elamite and *bitu* in Babylonian: four fragments of Old Persian, four in Elamite, three in Babylonian.[13]

> *Xerxes the king says:*
> *By the grace of Ahuramazda, the king Darius,*
> *my father, built this palace.*

XSb

Bilingual inscription on a column base for the palace called *hadiš* in both Old Persian and Babylonian.[14]

> [§ 1, 1–2] *I am Xerxes, the Great King, the King of Kings, King of Nations, King of the Earth, the son of King Darius, the Achaemenid.*

> [§ 2, 2–4] *Xerxes the king says:*
> *Darius the king built this palace, he who was my father.*
> *By the grace of Ahuramazda, me, I completed it.*

XSd

Trilingual inscription on the bases of the columns of the monumental gate.[15]

> *Xerxes the king says:*
> *by the grace of Ahuramazda, the King Darius,*
> *my father, built this gate.*

The word 'gate' is rendered *duvarthi* in Old Persian, *el* in Elamite and represented by the Sumerogram KÁ for *bâbu*.

XSe

Babylonian inscription on a column base.[16]

> [§ 1–2] *I am Xerxes, the Great King, King of Kings, King of Nations, King of the Earth, the son of King Darius, the Achaemenid.*

> [§ 2, 2–5] *Xerxes the king says:*
> *All that I did here, and all that I did elsewhere*
> *On Earth, all was done by my hand; all that I did,*
> *I did by the grace of Ahuramazda.*

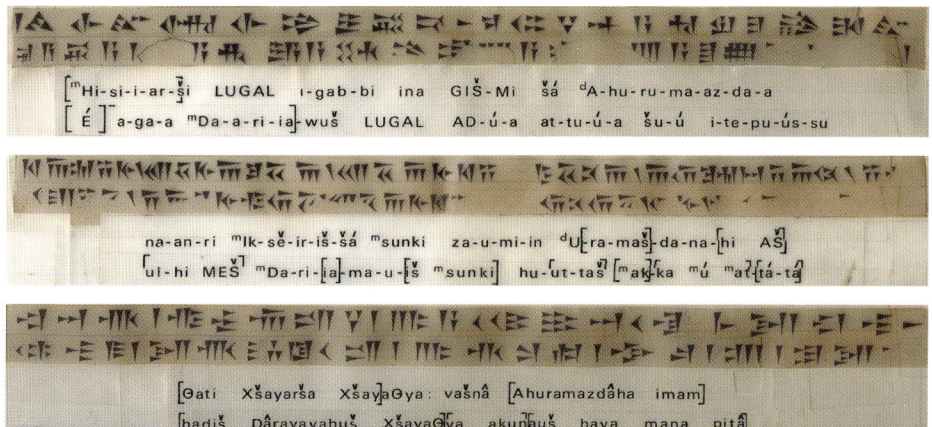

[ᵐHi-si-i-ar-ši LUGAL i-gab-bi ina GIŠ-Mi šá ᵈA-hu-ru-ma-az-da-a
[É] a-ga-a ᵐDa-a-ri-ia-wuš LUGAL AD-ú-a at-tu-ú-a šu-ú i-te-pu-ús-su

na-an-ri ᵐIk-se-ir-iš-šá ᵐsunki za-u-mi-in ᵈU-ra-maš-da-na-[hi AŠ]
[ul-hi MEŠ ᵐDa-ri-[ia]-ma-u-[iš ᵐsunki hu-[ut-taš [mak-ka mú ᵐat-[tá-ta]

[θati Xšayaršá Xšayaθya: vašnā [Ahuramazdāha imam]
[hadiš Dārayavahuš Xšayaθya akunauš haya mana pitā]

Transcription, transliteration and translation of the Xerxes inscription (XSa) on the column bases of the Propylaeum

The palace decoration of Susa in the Louvre

Béatrice André-Salvini

The Persian collections in the Louvre are unique thanks to the sumptuous polychrome decorations of the Susa palace. Marcel Dieulafoy discovered the most important fragments in 1885 and 1886. From June 1888 two panels of archers, the lion frieze, a decorative element from a ceremonial staircase and the monumental stone capital of a column from Darius' audience chamber were all exhibited in a room on the first floor of the Perrault colonnade.

In 1908, Roland de Mecquenem resumed the excavation of the palace; he brought back important collections of bricks to the Louvre, including a new series of archers. The discoveries of that season allowed the reconstruction of a bestiary both real and fantastical, composed of six decorative panels in moulded, unglazed bricks, figuring two bulls, two griffins and two lions walking both left and right (height 1.6 m; length 1.9 m–2.12 m); two panels each figuring two composite animals facing each other, forming the griffin frieze, reconstructed from polychrome bricks found reused in the first courtyard of the palace (height 1.65 m; length 4.17 m and 4.2 m); two sphinx panels: human-headed lions, seated, facing forwards, wearing the Persian crown and supporting the winged disc, emblem of the dynastic god Ahuramazda, which must originally have decorated projecting pilasters;[1] a panel with a winged bull in polychrome bricks (height 1.92 m; length 1.83 m).

In 1936, the Persian monuments were brought down to the ground floor of the north wing of the Cour Carrée, where they stand today. The 'Dieulafoy archers' and the sections of the lion frieze were displayed back-to-back according to the ornamental model established by Dieulafoy, and integrated into the architecture of their new palatial home, as they had once been in the Palace of Darius I. In 1947, after an eight-year closure due to the war, the single panels with other decorations were spread throughout the rooms according to the availability of space and, above all, based on decorative considerations.

319
The capital (AOD 1)
during restoration at the Louvre in 1887
Musée du Louvre
© RMN/Hervé Lewandowski; Franck Raux

320
**General view of the Louvre galleries
containing the decoration of the Susa palace**
Musée du Louvre/Étienne Renault

The restructuring of the Department of Oriental Antiquities, inaugurated on 9 October 1997, allowed for the use of those areas that benefited from natural light.[2] The reorganisation according to the dimensions and categories of the works of art meant a more spacious presentation of the architectural decor and, by regrouping the decorative themes, a more coherent historical layout. There was also an attempt to evoke the imposing atmosphere of the royal palace, rather than suggest an arbitrary reconstruction, since the original location of most of the decorative elements is uncertain.

The restoration methods of the end of the nineteenth century and beginning of the twentieth century, determined the layout of the new 1997 display which respected the now historical restoration work, unless it was incompatible with reality or an understanding of the work.

THE CAPITAL

When the capital was first displayed in 1888, beams (made of chipboard to make them lighter) were placed in the form of a cross on the back of the bulls, so as to represent the beams that supported the roof of the audience chamber at Susa. In 1937, the capital – cut into three pieces – was brought down to the room it is in now. The section patterned with an egg-and-dart type of motif which, until then, had decorated the base of the voluted section, forming the same separation as between the top of this section and the twin-headed bulls, was removed. A grey, uniform coating was applied to the surface. In 1996, the removal of this coating revealed the light, grey-veined limestone and the restored sections. The horns and the ears are fake. Examples of these anatomical parts belonging to much smaller bulls allowed the restorers in the Louvre, at the end of the nineteenth century, to reconstruct them on the large bull. Dieulafoy found traces of a red substance and

321
**General view of the Louvre galleries
containing the decoration of the Susa palace**
Musée du Louvre/Étienne Renault

a trace of gold in the tear duct of one eye. This piece, exhibited at the Louvre, no longer has any trace of gold, but fragments of red were discovered on the bull's cheek whilst the coating was being removed.

THE DECORATIVE RELIEF

The lion frieze is the only complete ornamental group found at Susa. The rebuilding and restoration of the three lions and two forequarters, as well as the floral surround, were executed at the Louvre (panel height 3.6 m). The methodology used by Dieulafoy to reconstruct a procession of nine archers from the bricks he had was based on that provided by the lions and shows that the desire to create a majestic effect was paramount in the reconstruction of the royal palace. The separation into two panels was due to the constraints of technical presentation.[3] The archers, dressed in rich robes with decoration representing crenellated fortresses on a white background or rosettes on a yellow background, which Dieulafoy chose to alternate, converge on a fragmentary inscription relating to the foundation of the palace. The height of the figures was determined by the logic of assembling the bricks, but Dieulafoy extended the height four bricks above the spear tips, reinforcing the monumentality of the frieze. Originally the brick faces abutted; Dieulafoy, however, assembled them in alternating courses with large alternating joins. The pieces of real brick drown in a mix of coloured plaster and mortar. The changes to the lions were highlighted by a darker outline, giving the impression of an illusionist's mosaic.

The work of reconstruction accomplished between 1913 and 1920 respected archaeological truth far more and had an ethic of simplicity. The 'Mecquenem archers' were put together as separate panels without a floral frame and with a lance height two bricks lower.[4] Only the polychrome panels with the fantastical animals, found in small numbers and which one can suppose were presented as pictures, were reconstructed with floral and geometric surrounds that formed a discreet frame. There was an attempt to make the restored sections visible, and at the same time a scientific concern emerged. On their arrival at the Louvre in

1913 the bricks were oven-dried to remove all traces of humidity and ensure that the surface would adhere. Analyses were carried out in the ceramics laboratory at Sèvres. To recreate the missing sections of the archer and animal friezes it was decided to make moulds from existing bricks. Thus the original parts and the lighter reconstructed sections are easily discernible to the detriment, on occasion, of aesthetic considerations.

For the baked-brick panels, the plaster bricks were treated to give the impression of terracotta. The restoration was done hastily. In some panels as much as half the content is modern, despite original bricks existing amongst fragments brought back to the Louvre.

The 1995 restoration consisted of consolidating the bricks and the pigments and lightening the older restorations, allowing the freshness and sparkle of the original colouring to shine through where it had been preserved.[5] The variations of tone were emphasised, highlighting the fact that the lion frieze and the sections of the monumental staircase had an overall sea-green hue, whilst the archers, the griffins and the sphinx had a turquoise-blue background.

The tone for the new decoration is set by the column capital of the Apadana as well as the file of archers and the lions brought back by Dieulafoy, whose composition has not been changed for technical reasons. Twenty 'Mecquenem archers', in separate panels, have been arranged in a procession heading towards the 'Dieulafoy archers'. Their restoration into superimposed files relates to technical issues; but the height thus reached is in harmony with the monumental pieces put together by Dieulafoy within floral and geometric surrounds, towards which they process in two long parallel friezes. This collection of 30 archers evokes the power of the Persian Empire, which was manifest in the decoration that covered the walls of the royal palace at Susa over a length of several hundred metres. This new reconstruction favours a superimposed separation of the two clothing motifs rather than an alternating one.[6]

The panels of fantastical animals have been placed on high so as to recreate an ornamental arrangement which existed in the Palace of Darius. As a focal point, the six decorative animal panels in unglazed moulded brick, representing two bulls, two griffins and two lions, have been arranged on three levels and opposite each other, according to a realistic monumentalist presentation, close to the reliefs of the Ishtar Gate built by Nebuchadnezzar II at Babylon, a source of inspiration for the Persian artists.

To complete the inventory of architectural decoration from the Persian period, the showcase contains pieces belonging to the ornamentation of the palace at Susa. Objects illustrating the arts and furniture as well as the languages and writing of the Achaemenid Empire evoke court life in this palace whose construction was recounted by Darius in his foundation charters. Stone fragments complement the decorative architectural fragments of the palace of Susa.

1. H. 0.87 m; L. 1.18 m; a third example was later reconstituted and is now in storage at the Musée Borély in Marseille.
2. The design and architectural creation of the galleries were entrusted to the Pylone architectural practice.
3. H. 4.75 m; panel H. 1.85 m; L. 0.70.
4. Archer: H. 1.66 m; L. of one panel: 3.75 m; H. of the archers: 1.90 m.
5. The restoration was the work of Michel Bourbon.
6. Various bricks show that the choice of dress was more important and included at least one further floral motif. Three other archers were deposited in foreign museums: in the Vorderasiatisches Museum in Berlin (1936); in the British Museum in London (1958); and in the museum in Tehran (1959). The bricks kept in the store and recently rearranged, have enabled the partial reconstitution of animal motifs in unglazed terracotta.

Bibliography

The Galleries
Béatrice ANDRÉ-SALVINI, 'L'empire perse-achéménide. Fin VIe–IVe siècle av. J.-C.' in *Louvre. Guide du visiteur: les antiquités orientales*, Paris, RMN, 1997, pp. 181–200.
Béatrice ANDRÉ-SALVINI, 'Les salles perses au Louvre', in L'Iran et la Perse. Les nouvelles salles du Louvre', *Le Monde de la Bible* 106, September–October 1997, pp. 58–63.
Béatrice ANDRÉ-SALVINI and Michel BOURBON, 'Le décor en briques polychrome du palais de Darius Ier à Suse dans les collections du Louvre', *Coré*, no. 9, November 2000, pp. 16–26.

Manufacturing techniques
Alexandre BIGOT, 'Les frises du palais de Darius et leur fabrication', *Comptes rendus de l'Académie des inscriptions et belles-lettres*, 1913, pp. 274–280.
H.-A. VASNIER, 'Observations sur la reconstitution des frises rapportées de la Susiane par la mission Dieulafoy', *Mémoires de la Société nationale des Antiquaires de France*, vol. LXV. 1906.

10 The Fired Arts

Annie Caubet

*The men who made
the bricks were Babylonians
the men who decorated the wall
were Medes and Egyptians*
DSf § 13

Susa is a unique case in the Persian world due to the variety and extent of its fired art techniques – meaning the industry of vitreous materials. Faience, frit, glass and glazed ceramic (see the glossary below) result from using a high percentage of silica mixed with fluxes and colours. These various techniques were used in the Susa palace with spectacular results, the largest and most famous being the glazed brick murals which were used to create the archers, the lion frieze in the East Court, mythological monsters and numerous stylised floral decorative elements. In addition, many other creations using this technique were brought to light in the excavation of the palace: tableware, statuettes, jewellery, amulets, offerings to the gods and items of worship.

It may seem paradoxical to compare the majestic wall decoration of the panels with, for example, tiny pendants in the shape of the Wedjat protective eye. They all stem, however, from the same family of technical procedures, using economical and fairly easily procured materials such as sand, lime and alkali, but requiring workers and artists with a high degree of knowledge, perfectly mastering the kiln and the inherent properties of different ingredients. But who were these technicians, these artists? Babylonians, Medes, Egyptians? The foundation texts of Darius and his successors were rather discreet on this point. A close examination of the products of this type allows us, however, to follow several leads.

AN ANCIENT TRADITION

First of all, we must remember that the old Elamite metropolis of Susa, chosen by Darius as one of his capitals, was home to a long-established industry that had wide experience in very high-quality production. From the end of the fourth millennium BC, amulets and pendants made of siliceous clay began to appear, covered in a blue-green glaze with copper. At the end of the third millennium BC, the artisans ventured to mould small shell-like dishes, or ridged goblets similar to their normal ceramic repertoire. The most significant inventions were in the second half of the second millennium. In the fourteenth century BC, in the neighbouring capital of Chogha Zanbil, Untash-Napirisha created architectural elements, tiles and circular pommels used for attaching square plaques to the walls, in baked clay covered in a copper glaze; blue- and white-coloured glass formed part of the decoration, in the form of 'eyes' inlaid in the tiles or juxtaposed tubes applied on doors as a sort of mosaic. In the twelfth century BC, the Shutrukid dynasty built several monuments to Inshushinak, patron god of Susa. In the dedicatory inscription they gloried in the fact that they built them with special bricks called *u-pa-at-ak-ti-in-ni-ma*, a term that we can translate as glazed or enamelled brick.[1]

> I, Shilhak-Inshushinak, son of Shutruk Nahhunte servant of the well-loved Inshushinak, King of Anshan and of Susa; the kings, my predecessors, had built this gate in baked bricks; I, Shilhak-Inshushinak, made it in enamelled bricks. There I inscribed my name![2]
>
> The effigies of Shutruk Nahhunte my dear father, of Kutir Nahhunte, my older brother, of myself and the Lady Nahhunte-utu, my dear wife, in glazed bricks.[3]

324
Lion from the 'processional way' at Babylon, reign of Nebuchadnezzar II (605–562 BC)
Glazed terracotta; height 1.05 m, length 2.27 m
Musée du Louvre, Department of Oriental
Antiquities AO 21118 (on loan from the
the Vorderasiatisches Museum of Berlin)
© RMN/Franck Raux

325
Lion *passant* to the left
Discovered by Marcel Dieulafoy in 1866
© Musée du Louvre/Christian Larrieu

Of these buildings, there only remain loose bricks of glazed siliceous clay bearing fragmentary inscriptions, and traces of reliefs in the shape of faces, hands or feet, but it is possible to reconstruct the design of a decorated chapel with a frieze of characters from the royal family. From the twelfth century BC, the Elamites were therefore capable of creating large mural decorations by assembling moulded bricks, each carrying part of the inscription or the relief decoration; the process meant that large surfaces could be covered using a limited number of moulds, around a dozen for each motif or figure. Susa was not the only capital of the second millennium to exploit this decorative architectural technique: the Kassite and Assyrian sovereigns used it too. It was still in fashion amongst the great empires of the first millennium, in Assyria, at Babylon; at Susa, in the eighth and seventh centuries BC the Neo-Elamite dynasty followed the traditions of their predecessors, before Darius produced an extraordinary new development.

ARCHITECTURAL ORNAMENTATION

As we will see, the palace at Susa mainly used siliceous bricks with a coloured glaze and, in lesser numbers, baked mud bricks with reliefs, which were used only for mythological animal motifs: winged bull, griffin, lion. The first were faithful to the traditional processes inherited from the great innovators of the second millennium: the famous archers and the other coloured decorations owed much to local Elamite traditional know-how. For its part, Mesopotamia used only clay bricks, both with and without a coloured glaze; at Babylon, Nebuchadnezzar undertook the first stage of construction of the Processional Way with a decoration of terracotta bricks in relief. Forced to raise the level of the works due to the rising water table, the king then decorated the Ishtar Gate, the Processional Way and the palace façade with clay bricks covered in cobalt blue, white and yellow glaze. The imagery, characterised by the absence of human figures, was entirely devoted to symbols of the Babylonian pantheon: the bull, lion, dragon and other designs.

At Susa, Darius' foundation texts proclaimed that 'the men who made the bricks were Babylonians'. The Babylonians were very probably the creators of the rare baked clay panels moulded to represent mythological monsters. This part of the decoration of the palace at Susa, which was limited to the symbolic animals, was almost certainly inspired by the monuments at Babylon, where this semi-regular layout of isolated symbolic figures already existed.

The preference for 'vignettes' adopted at Susa for all the decorative techniques was totally at odds with the narrative and continuous character of Assyrian art, the other source of inspiration for Achaemenid art. The palaces of the Assyrian capitals at Nimrud, Nineveh and Khorsabad were ornamented with stone reliefs figuring tales and historical episodes linked by the background landscape. An inscription acted as a 'subtitle' to the image and helped to clarify the propaganda message destined for the viewer. This spectacular scene-setting was adopted by Darius at Persepolis for the immense parade of people who had come to pay allegiance to the Great King. From this point of view, Persepolis is closer in spirit to the Assyrian palaces than is Susa. Between Persepolis and Susa there was not simply a difference in primary materials, stone at Persepolis, brick at Susa; the tenor of the message written on the walls of the palaces varied discreetly between the two, perhaps an indication of a subtle evolution in the concept of royalty.

Thus the architectural decoration of the Persian palace at Susa is testimony to the presence of several parallel traditions, some inherited from an Elamite past, others borrowed from Babylon. The new imagery, which barely overlaps with that of Persepolis, is enriched by updated building techniques and the revitalisation of age-old *savoir-faire*.

326
Glazed tile known as the Horned Lion
Discovered 1947
Musée du Louvre (Sb 3336)
© Musée du Louvre/Franck Raux

The ornamental bricks

Noëmi Daucé

When the enamelled pieces came out of the earth,
still damp from the freshness of the soil,
it seemed as though I were witnessing
the resurrection of sapphires and turquoises
enveloped in the golden rays of the Susa sun.
J. DIEULAFOY, 1888: 276

It was with great enthusiasm that in 1888 Jane Dieulafoy described the renaissance of the ornamental brick decoration at Susa in her journal of the excavations. William Kennett Loftus might have found the first remains a quarter of a century earlier, but it was the excavation directed by Marcel Dieulafoy that revealed how diverse they really were. Later, excavations from the end of the nineteenth century into much of the twentieth century enriched the collections (of the Louvre) and confirmed, if confirmation were needed, the originality of the architectural decoration at Susa during the Achaemenid period.[4]

Other sites, notably Persepolis and Babylon, have admittedly left evidence of brick decoration of the same period, but in much smaller quantities. At Susa, the decorative programme of Darius' Residence was almost entirely carried out in this medium. The location of the old Elamite capital, in a plain devoid of stone, was the determining factor, since it was with the help of the materials at hand – sand, clay and water – that the artisans working on the Susa site formed thousands of bricks, thereby reviving techniques inherited from the Elamite and Mesopotamian worlds.

The ancient sources did not comment on the magnitude of the decoration; only with the progressive build-up of the collections could their extent be appreciated. Despite over a century of excavations, however, and the discovery of several thousand bricks, there are only two publications dedicated to their study:

these ingredients, in principle easily available at Susa,[12] were mixed in colossal quantities. If one only considers the preserved collections, this is more than 55 tons of sand and some 2.5 tons of lime which were needed for their manufacture. The components were mixed with water so as to achieve an elastic clay, mouldable to the shape of the bricks.

None of the moulds destined for the manufacture of the bricks has been found during the various excavations. Only the study of the collections therefore allows us to retrace the different steps taken to make the bricks.

The siliceous bricks without relief (A.2) were no doubt moulded in simple wooden frames made up of four planks of the same dimensions as the brick, like a truncated pyramid. Placed on the ground or on a reed mat,[13] these moulds were filled with clay, with care taken to leave no intervening gaps. The top surface was then scraped to remove any excess clay before removing the mould from above. Thus the brick took on its final shape which, after air drying, was made durable when fired.

The manufacture of bricks with relief (A.1 and A.3) was more complex. In the first instance, the artisans had to create a prototype of each motif in relief (archers, servants, confronted sphinxes and animals *passant*) whose dimensions conformed, right from the start, to the standard measurements applied to the architectural elements. These prototypes were no doubt modelled in clay then baked in order to facilitate the moulding process. In anticipation of the alternate joint facing, they were then cut to the number of bricks required for the final panel. The result was a number of individual pieces in relief from which one could make multiple moulds. These casts, rectangular in shape and made from terracotta, were then added to the wooden, truncated-pyramid frames and made up the fifth face of the moulds destined to create bricks in relief. We do not know how these different elements fitted together; perhaps they slotted together thanks to a system of grooves. The bricks could then be released from the mould simply by removing the wooden frame.

Once the bricks were hardened in the fresh air, they were fired once to obtain a biscuit, on which the glazes were then added. Some siliceous bricks were unglazed, and their manufacture completed at this stage. The extent of the decoration implies the use of large-capacity ovens; however no trace of such has remained at Susa. Built on part of the site and probably on its periphery, they may have been destroyed at the end of the building works. The granular, sometimes friable aspect of the bricks indicates a firing temperature of between 900 and 1,000°C,[14] an estimate based on the build-up of grains of silica that never reached their fusion point. The material used in combustion to reach these temperatures could have been provided by straw or brushwood collected in the immediate vicinity.[15]

The choice of a siliceous clay, rather than terracotta, was a judicious one: it shrank at the same rate as the glaze that covered it, and it avoided the phenomenon of crackling inherent in Mesopotamian production. The glazes, fine layers of glass applied in a liquid state onto the surface of the bricks, were composed of silica to which alkaline fluxes (soda or potash) were added to lower the fusion point. The addition of metallic oxides provided colour.[16] The chromatic range of the Susa reliefs is limited to the use of blue, green, yellow, white and brown glazes obtained respectively by using copper oxide for the green and sky-blue; cobalt oxide for the deeper blue; lead-antimony for the yellow and orange; calcium-antimony for the white and manganese-antimony for the brown and the black.[17] Variations in the proportions of the metallic oxides used allowed the artisans to obtain tints of different intensity. One might be astonished by the absence of red, the colour used at Susa as much for the walls of the internal rooms of the Residence as for the mural paintings of the Shaur Palace.[18] If the bricks have often lost their brilliance, following the decomposition of the alkalis, their colours are well preserved.[19]

The layering of the glaze required two stages. The relief contours were traced using a dark glaze coloured with manganese oxide forming compartments or *cloisons*. This stage, of paramount importance, then allowed the filling in of the pre-defined *cloisons* with coloured glaze without the colours mixing. The outlines must have been applied freehand, using cones which must have been filled with a thick but runny glaze which could be piped through a small hole at their tip. The vitrification temperature of this glaze would certainly have been higher than

334
**Cloisons and glazing;
horn of griffin passant to the left**
Siliceous brick; height 8.5 cm,
width 18 cm, depth 9 cm
Susa Museum

the others so as to ensure its preservation in later firings. The coloured glazes were then applied as liquids into the pre-formed compartments using paintbrushes, and then fired again to harden them. Applying these glazes to the relief bricks meant mastering their viscosity so that the colours did not pool in the cracks. Finally, as the colour-runs on the sides of the bricks show, the bricks were placed end-on and face-up in the kilns. Some bricks with several decorated sides were submitted to repeated firings.[20] At the end of this operation the different elements of the reliefs were brought together before being integrated into the brickwork of the Susa Residence.

The baked mud bricks

The baked mud bricks with reliefs (B.1) reveal original manufacturing practices which at present have no equivalent. Due to age and modern handling, the face carrying the relief has sometimes separated from the main body of the brick, revealing the use of two distinct materials. The part in relief was moulded using a very fine clay where the aggregate is invisible to the naked eye, whilst the body of the brick was made up using a more common building earth mixed with roughly chopped straw.

These observations indicate that the moulding operations took place in two stages. Concave moulding blocks, made using similar techniques to those explained above, were first filled with fine clay. Finger marks are sometimes found on the surface of the plaques that have come unstuck.[21] They were intended to increase the bonding surface with the building earth forming the brick body. The second stage is more uncertain. Traces of rush mats are consistently present on the top surface of the bricks.[22] These mats were placed on the ground so as to prevent the building earth from sticking to it when it was being poured into the moulds. The imprints therefore indicate that the moulding of the brick body was done flat. The terracotta mould, once filled, must have been tilted vertically, thus forming the fourth side of the wooden mould into which the building earth had been poured. To make the extraction from the mould easier it is assumed that frames that could be dismantled were used. Once they had been placed in their moulds the bricks were left to dry outside before being fired at fairly low temperatures, as the straw used as a temper was often not completely burned.

Glazed baked mud bricks (B.2) are also present in the collections. Rarely mentioned in the publications, they were, however, found in fairly large numbers: in one of his reports Mecquenem mentions ten crates.[23] The stores at the Shush-i Daniel Museum contain fragments of them. These bricks, with or without reliefs, combined the two manufacturing techniques previously described: their body is

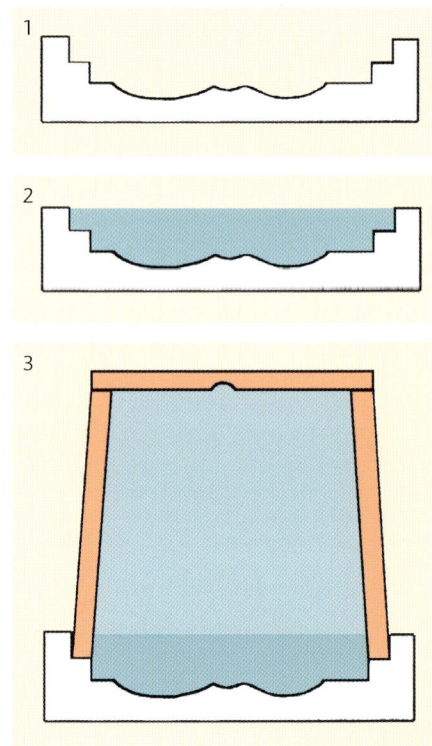

335
Manufacture of baked mud bricks with relief
1. Matrix with concave mould, obtained from a terracotta prototype.
2. Filling of the mould with a fine clay.
3. Cross-section of a composite mould combining a terracotta matrix and a wooden frame
drawings by Noëmi Daucé

336
Glazed baked mud brick
height 8.5 cm, width 17.5 cm, depth 13 cm
Shoush-i Daniel Museum, Susa

337
Artisans' marks identified by W.K. Loftus
Travels and Researches in Chaldaea and Susiana,
London, 1857, p. 398

made of the same materials as the baked mud bricks, but a glazed decoration is applied, apparently similar to that of the siliceous bricks. It has been suggested that these bricks were destined to act as substitutes for missing or damaged sections of siliceous brick panels. Seeing the permanence of the decorative techniques during the Achaemenid period,[24] why would the eventual gaps not be filled with siliceous bricks? We can therefore only observe the existence of glazed baked mud bricks with reliefs; their role remains largely undetermined.

The artisans' marks[25]

The main player in bringing to light the wealth of ornamental brick decoration at Susa, Marcel Dieulafoy, recalled the difficulties he encountered in reconstructing the panels, notably those of the archers,[26] which had been dismantled in the distant past and the bricks scattered. The complexity of the motifs and their assembly would no doubt have posed the same problems for the workers responsible for their assembly and the implementation of the decoration at the heart of the Residence, if a system of guide marks had not been put in place.

These appear on the top of the glazed siliceous bricks (A.1 and A.2). They were painted using the coloured glazes which covered the bricks, and they are placed right next to the face. On whole bricks, three of these marks can be observed: one in the centre, the two others at the ends. Of very different shape (circle, hatched lines), they vary from one brick to another following what appears to be a numerical system. Given the frequency of reuse and the almost systematic dispersal of the bricks at Susa we cannot now suggest a reconstruction. However, following similar examples observed on the Neo-Assyrian and Neo-Babylonian decorative bricks,[27] the central marks would indicate the course; the end marks indicated their position within the course. Intended for the masons working on-site, they were sketched by the artisan brick makers during the layering of the coloured glazes, before the final firing. They are testimony to the perfect production line which takes later stages into account during the manufacture of the bricks themselves.

As Loftus remarked in 1852, two other categories of mark were on the top surface of the siliceous bricks. The first, traced with a point into the soft clay, can be found anywhere on the surface of the brick and do not seem to follow any directional rules. They were applied just after the moulding and can be attributed to the brick workshops, the first stage in the production line. As such, and with a limited number of workshops, it is not surprising to find groups of similar markings. They are unfortunately too often clipped, the majority of the bricks having been sawn a third of the way along their depth so as to lighten the convoys which brought them back to the Louvre,[28] and therefore cannot be studied. in the second category, which is rarer, the bricks are marked with the glaze used for the compartments. Although they are of more modest dimensions, they are more complex in their motifs, including swastikas and radial circles, for example.[29] The marks may have been used to check the work of the artisan ceramicists after the bricks had left the kilns. As with the siliceous bricks, the baked mud bricks with reliefs (B.1) also had artisans' marks, but placed on the sides and backs. Thus, a vertical band in slight relief can be found on the backs of some bricks preserved in their entirety. Similar to the marks found on the most common baked mud bricks, they were carved into the wooden frames used as moulds. They could have one or several marks of this type, allowing the production of different brick workshops to be distinguished.[30] By contrast the absence of guide marks is surprising because the motifs on the baked mud bricks are as complex as the animal friezes on the siliceous bricks.

The production line

The fragmentary nature of most of the bricks does not allow for a systematic study of the artisans' marks. It does, however, clarify the status of the artisans responsible for the brick decoration at Susa by indirectly illustrating the different stages in the production line and highlighting the intervention of three different successive teams: brick makers, artisan ceramicists and masons. The marks of the first two groups, who do not have any involvement in the installation of the reliefs, can be understood only in relation to a meticulous control of production and output. The Achaemenid sources confirm this administrative yoke; the Persepolis tablets describe the allocation of workers into divisions of tens and hundreds, placed under the orders of an overseer who reported to a treasurer or under-treasurer, who distributed rations and salaries.[31] The identity of the artisans was often touched on in the official inscriptions from Susa. More than once (DSf and DSz) Darius attributed the manufacture of the bricks to the Babylonians and the ornamentation of the walls to the Medes and Egyptians. Attempts have therefore been made to attribute the conception of the decorations to one group or another. However, the specialisation of the tasks indicates an altogether different reality and drastically reduces their role, whatever their origin. There is no doubt that the Achaemenid rulers had recourse to experienced and qualified artisans who possibly came from regions where the decoration of bricks had a long tradition. However, they did no more than apply an artistic programme conceived in the immediate confines of the king's royal entourage.[32]

338
Engraved and painted marks with glaze on the top face of a brick
Glazed siliceous brick, geometric motif, height 8.4 cm, width 33.7 cm, depth 34.4 cm
Shoush-i Daniel Museum, Susa

339
Archers of Darius
Musée du Louvre (Sb 3317, Sb 3320)
© RMN/Hervé Lewandowski

The bricks and their decoration show the traces of outside intervention. As has already been highlighted, the contours used to separate the different coloured glazes were made freehand. In the case of the decorative friezes there is a notable lack of mistakes and a remarkable regularity in the lines. This can only be explained by the use of stencils whose dimensions adhered rigidly to the standards of measurement. For example, the chevron friezes are made up of a succession of equilateral triangles half a foot wide. G. Azarpay has highlighted the fact that standardised grids were also applied to the more complex motifs, no doubt the archers and the animals *passant*.[33] These choices were not made by the artisans, but probably by the designers of the decorative programme at Susa, who controlled the motifs and technical methods, and chose their location in the Residence.

THE ICONOGRAPHIC PROGRAMME[34]

Darius inaugurated a new form of architectural decoration at Susa, entirely derived from the expression of imperial ideology. All narrative theme is abandoned in favour of conceptual motifs which are multiplied over and over in friezes and panels, embodying the universalist and immutable ideal of the dynasty in power. With the exception of the frieze of the lions *passant*, the Susa bricks which made up this decorative scheme were found reused in later structures: Seleucid, Parthian and Sassanian. The initial position of the panels is at the very least uncertain, even if the concentration of bricks in certain sectors can be considered as an indication of their location. The study of the iconographic programme allows for a differentiation of two categories of decoration. The first, restored as friezes or panels in the modern era, were found in the heart of the Residence or in its immediate vicinity. The second, too fragmentary for any reconstruction to be contemplated, testifies to the presence of ornate stairways which were probably in the vicinity of the Hypostyle Hall.

The decoration of the Residence

The archers, who have established the reputation of the architectural decor at Susa, constitute the commonest motif within the brick collections, of which the Louvre alone has nearly 2000 pieces, whole or fragments of bricks. For the main part these are glazed siliceous bricks with reliefs (A.1). The panels are the result of modern reconstruction; Dieulafoy proposed to reconstruct them in 21 courses whilst Mecquenem, adopting a more minimalistic approach, limited them to 19.[35] The figures wearing Persian ceremonial dress file towards the right or the left, armed with long spears whose butts rest on their leading foot, a bow (and a quiver) which gives them their name.

Near the archers, Dieulafoy unearthed glazed siliceous bricks (A.2) inscribed in Old Persian, Babylonian and Elamite. He apparently identified the names, inscribed in Old Persian, of Darius and Utana (Otanes),[36] one of the seven conspirators who took part in the removal of Gaumata-Smerdis in 522 BC. Mecquenem also discovered inscribed bricks, full of gaps, which, according to him, reproduced the trilingual text called the foundation charter of the palace.[37] At least some of the archers converged towards this inscription. From the large concentration of bricks next to the eastern gate of the Residence, the reliefs could have been on the external façades or the walls of Court C3. In addition, the presence of bricks covered in glaze on two adjacent faces indicates recesses along the line of figures, probably level with the gates.

The celebrity of the panels displayed in the Louvre galleries has often eclipsed some of the discoveries illustrating other series of archers which differ

340
Head of an archer with white skin
Glazed siliceous brick, decorated in relief; height 8.5 cm, width 34.5 cm, depth 17 cm
National Museum of Iran, Tehran, no. 2548

341
A small archer
Glazed siliceous brick without relief; height 6 cm, width 16.5 cm
Musée du Louvre (Sb 3332)
© RMN/Franck Raux

iconographically and/or technically. Thus, whilst the majority of the archers have brown skin, bricks of a similar format, discovered in sectors far from the Apadana,[38] confirm the presence of white-skinned archers. These also appeared on glazed bricks without relief (A.2); they are very rare, and are distinguished by their small dimensions, and their height varies between 6 and 7 cm. As Dieulafoy remarked, these figures extended over nine courses, faithfully reproducing the archer frieze on a smaller scale (55 to 59 cm in height). Their location as well as their date remains uncertain.[39] Finally, the archers were also depicted, but more rarely, on glazed baked mud bricks (B.2). Most of these were found around Room A during the excavations directed by Mecquenem.[40] These bricks, which seemed to him ancient, could in fact belong to a stage of restoration of the architectural decor after the reign of Darius. The archer motifs, an Achaemenid innovation, appeared during the reign of Darius and, in contrast to the friezes of animals *passant*, they had no precedent in the Mesopotamian iconographic repertoire. Some of the detail was inspired by older traditions, and in this was faithful to the syncretism that characterised Persian Achaemenid art. Pierre Amiet thus identified, in the figures' attitude, a use of Elamite iconography from the first half of the second millennium BC,[41] whilst the anatomical and clothing details were inspired by Mesopotamian and Elamite influences.[42] The identification of the archers, who are found in great numbers on the reliefs of Persepolis, is always debated. When they were discovered, Dieulafoy considered them part of the king's elite troops, the Immortals, described several times in Herodotus' *Histories*. However, this attribution was not unanimous; the archers were sometimes relegated to the ranks of simple guards of the royal residence whilst Amiet detects a more conceptual representation, that of 'the Persian people at arms'.[43] For Perrot they represent the nobility of Susa whom Darius wanted to honour in this way.[44]

The sphinxes

Bricks (A.1) discovered in the north-eastern corner of Court C2, allowed Mecquenem to expand the repertoire of restorations with a new motif: two human-sphinxes, seated winged lions, confronted, with heads turned away under the winged sun disc. Four panels, the fruits of a collaboration between Mecquenem and Pézard, were put together without knowing if they reproduced the original layout. Scattered bricks preserved in the stores of Shush-i Daniel make it possible that at least another two panels originally existed.

The composition was deployed over 14 courses, three bricks wide (1.2 x 1.17 m). The winged sun disc that dominates the scene is a motif of Egyptian origin, adopted by the Hittites and the Syrians before coming back into favour during the Achaemenid period. For Pierre Briant,[45] this may symbolise the god of the royal family, Ahuramazda, whilst Pierre Amiet[46] relates it to a superior dynastic principle, the 'glory' of the king. In the lower section, the two seated sphinxes confront each other, heads turned away. Their long beards, together with the three stylised horns which are drawn on the sides of their tiaras, belong to the conventions representing deities. The interpretation of this motif, common on the bas-reliefs of Persepolis as well as on contemporary seals and coins, remains uncertain at Susa. Nor has the original location of the panels been ascertained. They must have projected slightly from the walls, as shown by bricks glazed on adjacent sides.[47]

Lions, griffins and winged bulls

In contrast to the archers, the zoomorphic motifs are distinguished by the uniformity of their dimensions. All the animals are 14 courses high and six bricks

342
Ornamental bricks from the archer frieze
Musée du Louvre (AOD 488)
© RMN/Hervé Lewandowski

343
Panel of opposed sphinxes
Apadana, Darius Residence, Court C2.
Glazed siliceous bricks, decorated in relief;
height 120 cm, width 117 cm

344
**Frieze of lions passant restored
by Marcel Dieulafoy**
Glazed siliceous bricks, decorated in relief
Musée du Louvre (AOD 489)
© RMN/rights reserved.

long (about 1.25 x 2 m), which suggests they were built at the same time.[48]

The frieze of the lions *passant*, was discovered by Dieulafoy in his excavations, sunk into the tiling of a courtyard (Pillet located it in 'H' on his plan); it would have crashed from the top of a northern wall. The lions, made of large, glazed, siliceous bricks,[49] filing to the left and to the right, are framed by decorative motifs bringing the height of the panels to nearly 3.5 m. Crenellations, drawn and painted, crowned this decoration.[50]

Griffins and winged bulls, adopting the same pose as the lions, completed the architectural decoration of the Residence. The first were found in a wall of the Parthian era built to the north-east of Court C3, whilst the second, less often attested,[51] were discovered in two sectors: to the east in the vicinity of the frieze of lions *passant* and to the west in Court A. All these motifs are also found on baked bricks with reliefs (B.1) and, more rarely, on painted baked mud bricks (B.2). Only six baked mud-brick panels with reliefs were reassembled: each one figured one of the animals *passant* to the right and another to the left. However, the remains preserved in the stores of the Louvre, as well as in those of the Shush-i Daniel Museum, indicate that some of them, most notably the lions, were reproduced several times, perhaps deployed in registers[52] or in long friezes.[53]

It is in the friezes of *passant* animals that Mesopotamian influence manifests itself most acutely: these friezes revive the memory of Babylonian works of a century earlier,[54] but now the symbolic content seems somehow to be missing.[55] The pose of the lions and of the Susa 'apocalyptic monsters' reproduces that of the Mesopotamian antecedents, although handled differently for the sake of greater stylisation. The anatomical details, muscle mass and articulation are now pretexts for decorative developments which, with the juxtaposition of enclosed coloured fields, recalls the cloisonné techniques used in contemporary jewellery. Only the baked mud-brick friezes show a greater finesse in detail, with the quality of the clay and the absence of glaze allowing the depiction of the reliefs to be refined.[56]

345
Griffin *passant*
Glazed siliceous bricks, decorated in relief

346
Winged bull
Glazed siliceous bricks, decorated in relief
Musée du Louvre (Sb 3328, 3329, Sb 3330)
© RMN/rights reserved

The zoomorphic motifs were unlikely to have been limited to the lions, griffins and winged bulls *passant*. Dieulafoy had already mentioned fragments of lounging and seated lions,[57] whilst Mecquenem referred to the fragments of a crouching griffin.[58] The bricks which would have composed this motif were published in illustrations, but have not as yet been found in the stores. By contrast, other materials have added to the Achaemenid bestiary. Essentially these are baked mud bricks with reliefs (B.1) – these are objects of recent research, whose motifs do not correspond to those which had previously been listed. Amongst these, S. Maras has identified relief fragments which possibly belonged to a standing lion, others to a beast in combative pose and to a winged animal still unidentified. Finally, J. Nguyen and myself have also identified bricks illustrating the presence of a hybrid animal, no doubt a griffin, similar to those engaged in the fight against the figure encountered on certain doorjambs at Persepolis.

OTHER DECORATIVE MOTIFS

Motifs of plant or geometric inspiration, traced onto glazed bricks without reliefs (A.2), constitute, along with the archers, the largest part of the Achaemenid brick collections. There were three different Perrot categories. The first is made up of motifs inspired by plants which were arranged in friezes of different heights: rosettes or palmettes linked by semicircular ribbons. The second category contains geometric elements: essentially chevrons and two-colour lines which separated different motifs. Lastly came a motif combining both plant and geometric elements: palmettes rising either side of a frieze of concentric circles linked by parallel bands. The lion frieze, found along a length of 4 m,[59] gives an understanding of how the decorative bricks were put together: the rows of rosettes or palmettes, set between geometric friezes, framed the figurative motifs almost overwhelming them with their abundance. It was, using this example, that Dieulafoy reconstructed the frame of the archers panel. Later, more minimalist reconstructions were suggested by Mecquenem, but they do not correspond perhaps, to the exuberance of the original architectural decor. Finally, we can also suppose that some decorative friezes were made to underline the architectural features: doors and passages at the heart of the Susa Residence.

The Servants

Some 30 siliceous bricks with or without relief (A.1 and A.2), and siliceous without glaze (A.3) revealed the presence of the servants motif at Susa. They were discovered as one-offs scattered across the Apadana and Acropolis tells as well as the Donjon. It is possible that they were originally destined to decorate staircases. Because of the low numbers and the diversity of materials used, these bricks were often studied individually. The iconographic unity, however, requires them to be read as a group. Until now no reassembly has been possible, but the more common reconstructions represent figures extending over a height of nine courses (about 72 to 76 cm in height).[60] With the help of some anatomical and clothing details, servants, successively Persians and Medes, climb a staircase, adapting their progression to the slope. Some bring tableware, others animals and some offerings. This theme, well illustrated at Persepolis and generally associated with banqueting, is also reproduced at Susa on stone reliefs, discovered at the Donjon and the Shaur Palace.

During the course of the excavations that he led from 1929 to 1933 at the Donjon, Mecquenem discovered several siliceous bricks without glaze (A.3) re-used as tiles in a floor which he attributed to the Sassanian period. These bricks,

347
Reconstruction of a frieze of decorative elements
DIEULAFOY, 1893: fig. §80 or pl. XIII

348
Fragments of glazed bricks thought to belong to figures of servants climbing a staircase
drawing by Audran Labrousse

remarkable in the fineness of the reliefs, represent servants in profile, facing left and right. The head of a servant facing left can be recognised, as can fragments of clothing, the head of a lamb and the right arm of a servant who holds a lid with care.

The Dieulafoy 'parapet'

In the spring of 1885, Dieulafoy discovered decorative bricks from an Achaemenid parapet in a trench to the south-west of the Apadana. Other bricks collected later confirmed the presence at Susa of one or several staircases with decoration similar to those at Persepolis. We do not know their original location.

From the bricks which had been discovered, Dieulafoy rebuilt the parapet of a staircase made up of bricks with several glazed faces. It is decorated on the front face with a Lotus frieze. This motif, which can be deployed over a variable number of courses, allowed difficult surfaces to be filled in, such as the acute angles of the partitions.[61] The sides are covered with brown and yellow spirals. Friezes of rosettes and chevrons were laid out obliquely, highlighting the slope. They also framed the servants frieze and the animal combat scenes. Finally, merlons, which Dieulafoy believed crowned the staircases, were made of the same siliceous clay as the bricks. They had glazed decoration of a blue or white arrow on the front face, painted in an illusionist manner on glazed bricks without reliefs (A.2) that perhaps surmounted the archer friezes.[62]

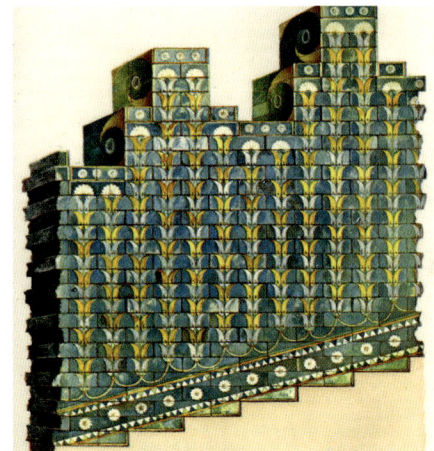

349
Projected reconstruction of a staircase banister
DIEULAFOY, 1893: pl. VIII

Small faience objects

Annie Caubet

SMALL SCULPTURE IN THE ROUND

During the Persian period, the handling of vitreous materials also enabled the development of the refined creation of small statues designed for personal devotion. A fine fragment of a statue of an Egyptian goddess in faience, found in the palace at Susa, is a testimony both to the quality of these techniques in vitreous materials and to the ascendancy of Egyptian art at Susa and in the empire.[63] The demon Bes, already a favourite subject for amulets, was also frequently represented in the form of small statuettes or vases. The flasks in the shape of Bes were probably designed to contain cosmetics or medical/magical potions, for private and individual use. Only small fragments have been found at Susa, but intact examples from the Levant and Egypt give an idea of these creations, marked, like the amulets, by the softening of the lines and the decorative arrangement of the beard and hair. As well as these images of deities and demons, images of sovereigns were also created in vitreous materials. The famous head crowned with a merlon diadem, made of 'Egyptian blue' frit and discovered at Persepolis, is the most famous vestige of what must have been small royal portraits; were they made as diplomatic gifts? Were they used in the palaces? A royal head in green faience, wearing a crenellated crown and preserved in a New York collection, had belonged to a sphinx, symbol of royal power. Was it part of a piece of furniture, or the support for a bowl or a throne?

A goddess in blue faience[64]

This attractive fragment represents the thighs of a feminine figure moulded in a tight tunic; a hand is laid flat on the left leg, slightly forwards. The statue rests against a dorsal pillar, on which there are remains of Egyptian hieroglyphs. It is possible to read 'priest', according to the museum record established by Pierre

350
Fragment of a statuette of a goddess
Discovered by Mecquenem at the Donjon.
Blue faience; preserved height 14.5 cm
MECQUENEM, 1933: 7–8. Musée du Louvre,
Department of Oriental Antiquities (Sb10214)
© Musée du Louvre/Georges Poncet

Amiet. The total height of the statue can be estimated at more than 50 cm, thus about one-third life size; this size is exceptional for a faience object, and this alone represents a tour de force.

Technologically, this piece is of an exceptional quality. The siliceous clay of the main body of the piece is of a very fine grain, and the glaze which covers it is in extremely thin layers, with the hue best preserved where the legs meet, where it is thickest. The artist has obviously taken account of the variations in thickness and colour of the glaze to accentuate the curves of the female body. The canon of beauty is slender but firm, as is the hand with the long squared fingers. According to Geneviève Pierrat-Bonnefois and Sylvie Guichard (Louvre, Département des antiquités égyptiennes) the image is very probably that of a goddess, perhaps one with a lion's head. The work is manifestly that of an Egyptian artist. There is a question mark over the date. If she had been found in Egypt, she could have just as well be dated to the Saite period (seventh and six centuries BC) as to the Persian period. Her presence at Susa suggests the second hypothesis. Was she imported from Egypt or was she made *in situ*? The masterpieces in vitreous material found at Susa show that its various techniques were perfectly mastered there; everything suggests that she was made at Susa by an Egyptian artist working for the Persian Empire. The Palace of Susa has given us many other figurines of Egyptian divinities, as well as a large number of amulets which testify to the strong presence of Egyptian belief at Susa. There were numerous Egyptians in the heart of the empire, artists and specialist workers, functionaries and envoys, interpreters and scribes. They needed to be surrounded by familiar objects. The statue of the goddess, meanwhile, assumes a special status amongst all these trinkets due to its size. It is, after the Darius statue, another Egyptian work of art made for the Great King, the largest Egyptian statue at Susa. Was she made for the devotions of the sovereign?

TABLEWARE

The Palace of Darius was looted of its movable treasures – precious metals, ivories, gems – of which only the smallest fragments remain.[65] The gold plate has disappeared. The pillage, however, did not touch the vitreous tableware. As with the architectural decor, the techniques are varied and made use of 'faience' (or siliceous clay covered in glaze), frit, clay ceramics and glass. For tableware, the production of siliceous paste faience, inherited from the Elamites, carries on, but polychrome ceramics, so characteristic of the Neo-Elamite period, disappear in favour of pale

green glazes. The repertoire of shapes is inspired by those of metalwork, with a predilection for ridged and gadrooned cups; the rhyton (or drinking horn) with an animal's head nozzle was used in ceremonial banquets. Entire services must have been offered to the guests, in gold, in ivory and in different vitreous materials.

The tableware of the Persian period saw the development of a new technique, that of clay ceramic with glaze. This was used for a clay vessel traditionally turned, to which the artisan had managed to make a glaze adhere. This technique represents a considerable advance as it made it possible to turn a larger quantity of vases. The application of siliceous glaze on clay requires a perfect understanding of the mechanical properties of the components so as to allow the body and the surface to adhere. The invention of this technique goes back to the end of the second millennium BC and occasional examples appear during the Neo-Elamite and Neo-Assyrian periods. In the Persian period, and especially in Seleucid and Parthian times, glazed ceramic vessels became the fine tableware par excellence of Mesopotamia and Iran.

Cultic pottery

Several examples of a form of 'balustered' vase have been found in the palace of Susa. They are identical in shape but of various colours and of different materials: they exist in blue faience, in green faience and in 'Egyptian blue' frit. All have traces on the neck that indicate that their mouths were made separately, either in the same material or, more probably, in precious metal. They were long interpreted as elements of architectural decor, balusters. Their small number, fewer than five, excludes this hypothesis, as do the dimensions of the aperture, which are large enough to allow liquid to be poured. In reality they are a type of libation vase well known in Egypt, with an elongated body, a short, narrow, cylindrical neck supporting a thick horizontal mouth, which is often manufactured separately. We do not know what these receptacles were used for at Susa. We simply note the presence at Susa of a traditional Egyptian vessel adapted to the needs of the Persian palace. We also find rhyta (animal-shaped drinking vessels), a type widespread throughout the empire.

354
Small cups in the shape of bivalve shells
Musée du Louvre (Sb 753, Sb 14418)
© Musée du Louvre/Christian Larrieu

TOILETRY OBJECTS AND INSTRUMENTS

Model shells in green faience were found at Susa. It is likely that they were make-up containers. The attraction for shells, real or imitations in precious materials, had been around for a long time in the Orient: thus in the third millennium BC the royal tombs of Ur had models of seashells in gold and silver used to hold cosmetics. At Susa itself, a faience pot in imitation of a bivalve, dates from the last quarter of the third millennium BC. This revival of an inspiration from nature can also be observed in the number of small bone, ivory and faience instruments of the Persian period, characterised by a handle in the shape of an animal: leonine, bovine or equine. There were only fragments at Susa, but examples of these small precious objects have been brought to light in various regions of the empire, notably in the Levant and Egypt. Stylus and quill-trimming penknife handles go back to Assyrian prototypes. On the reliefs of the palace of Sargon II at Khorsabad, for example, these small instruments are tucked into the clothing of court dignitaries.

AMULETS

Large numbers of amulets were found in the Persian levels of Susa. They are carved either with magic symbols, animals or protective demons. They are protective talismans of Egyptian origin, a category that had spread throughout Egypt and the Levant since the second millennium BC. The finds at Persepolis and Susa allow amulets of a similar type, found elsewhere, to be attributed to the Persian period as they have new characteristics compared with the works of the New Kingdom or the start of the first millennium BC. The glaze is now light green in colour, very fine and of a slightly different style. The magic eyes, the Wedjat, are two-sided plaques. The lion heads seen face on have an elongated muzzle, the mane locks are neatly arranged into a ruff. The Egyptian demon Bes appears on a number of amulets, generally in the form of a grimacing, leonine mask, tongue out, with lion's ears and a high crown of feathers. Bes is a familiar figure, well known in Egypt and the Levant since the New Kingdom. He regains popularity in the first millennium BC and large numbers of amulets styled in the same way as those from Susa have been found in the Levant, in Cyprus and in Egypt. In comparison to the older prototypes, Bes' appearance undergoes discreet stylistic changes, noted in the softening of the lines of his face; the figure loses his forceful and leonine character to become kindly; the beard and hair are dressed in a very refined way, with a large number of locks laid out symmetrically. The examples at Susa allow some works found in the Levant to be attributed to the Achaemenid period. It is reasonable to suppose that the new favour shown to this protective demon during

GLOSSARY

Archaeological faience
The term 'faience' (the name of the clay pottery covered with a lead glaze with an addition of an oxide of tin to the slip produced in Faenza in Italy) is misused by archaeologists to designate objects in glazed siliceous clay. Partially vitrified by a firing at high temperature, the clay is made up of around 95 per cent silica, in the form of quartz grains or crushed flint to which fluxes are added so as to lower the fusion temperature of the silica. These fluxes are sodium or potassium-based, either through the mineral natron (naturally occurring sodium carbonate) or plant ash.

Glazed clay ceramic
Clay pottery onto which a glaze is applied. The procedure, invented in the Levant at the end of the second millennium BC, became more wide-spread during the Iron Age and then the norm for fine tableware during the Hellenistic period.

Glaze
A vitreous layer similar in composition to glass and coloured using metal oxides. The glazes from the Ancient Near East were alkaline. The first lead glazes appeared during the third century BC in the eastern Mediterranean and spread throughout the Roman world.

Frit
In archaeological literature this term defines the results of diverse fusion operations via sintering or the aggregation of siliceous elements into a vitreous stage. If unglazed, frit is often coloured from within by metallic oxides. The best known is 'Egyptian blue'.

355
Amulets
Musée du Louvre (Sb 3571, Sb 3585)
© Musée du Louvre/Annie Caubet

the Persian period goes hand in hand with the renewal of its appearance, the result of the formal syncretism so characteristic of Achaemenid art.

The study of various products of vitreous art at Susa and in the Persian world allows us to uncover several common traits. The architectural decor at Susa was entirely original in terms of iconography and composition, even if it borrowed from local traditions at the technical level. It is also peculiar to Susa that nothing of this kind has been found elsewhere in the empire.

By contrast, the production of tableware and small objects in glass, faience and frit are of international character; objects of the same type found in Iran, Egypt and the Levant are all very similar; it is almost impossible to distinguish the origin of these works. Can this internationalism be put down to the policy of systematic transfer of artists? Born and educated in the different regions of the empire, these artists and specialists adapted their know-how and their repertoire to a new ideology.

All the categories of works born of the fired arts, architectural decor of Susa – tableware, instruments, statues – are distinguished by a high level of technical and aesthetic perfectionism which makes them immediately identifiable as belonging to the Persian period, whilst all along being inspired by the ancient Egyptian, Assyrian and Babylonian traditions. These designs were entirely assimilated, renewed and transformed to take on a distinct Persian character which influenced the works produced across the vastness of the empire.

1. AMIET, 1976; CAUBET, 2003.
2. MALBRAN-LABAT, 1995: no. 50.
3. LAMBERT, 1978.
4. N. Chevalier, ch. III.
5. LABROUSSE, 1972: 138.
6. MOOREY, 1994: 319.
7. None of these bricks it complete, so that we do not know their original length.
8. A. HESSE: 1972.
9. RAZMJOU, 2004: 385.
10. A. Caubet: this volume, ch. X: 301–304.
11. CAUBET and KACZMARCZYK, 1998: 25–26.
12. Mecquenem (MECQUENEM, 1947: 95) mentions the presence to the north of Susa of a s mall quarry of pebbles which, when burnt, might have provided the necessary lime. However, blocks of limestone brought from quarries in the Zagros, or stone debris from the Hypostyle Hall could also have been used.
13. SAUVAGE, 1998: 21.
14. CAUBET and PIERRAT-BONNEFOIS, 2005: 13.
15. SAUVAGE, 1998: 24.
16. CAUBET and PIERRAT-BONNEFOIS, 2005: 13.
17. CAUBET and KACZMARCZYK, 1998: 25–26.
18. R. Boucharlat, this volume, ch. XII. LABROUSSE and BOUCHARLAT, 1974: 83.
19. ANDRE SALVINI, 2000: 17.
20. Thus one can see the trickles of glaze crossing each other perpendicularly on the sides.
21. BOURGEOIS, 1992: 285.
22. This relates to the upper face of a brick which then became the bottom of the brick when the bricks were assembled into panels.
23. Mecquenem, 1913 Archives: AN F17/17 225.
24. See R. Boucharlat concerning the silicious bricks of the Shaur, this volume, ch. XII.
25. A. Hesse, this volume, ch. XII: 360.
26. DIEULAFOY, 1893: 280–281.
27. READE, 1965: 39.
28. MECQUENEM, 1980: 22.
29. Loftus (LOFTUS, 1857: 398) thought they were to indicate the orientation of the motifs, but one cannot see why, in that case, the signs were so complex.
30. HESSE, 1972: 223 and this volume, ch. XII.
31. BRIANT, 1996: 442–444.
32. ROOT, 1990: 115–139.
33. AZARPAY, 1994: 169–184.
34. Very early the question arose as to whether the king was represented. M. Dieulafoy was the first to suggest that he might be shown on a very large, but fragmentary brick on which the head of a figure with a long beard could be seen. Upon finding, close by, fragments of a winged disc, probably from the same composition, he was obliged to abandon his hypothesis. Thereafter, some bricks were readily attributed to the royal figure. J.V. Canby (CANBY, 1979: 315–320) believed such a fragment showed the king in a victorious posture similar to that of Darius on the Bisitun relief. However, neither the dimensions, nor the colours confirm this suggestion. It has since been accepted that the brick in question is more likely to belong to the procession of servants ascending steps. Annie Caubet has recently suggested that certain fragments might represent members of the royal entourage such as guards, bearers of a parasol or a fly-whisk, thus attesting indirectly to the presence of the king in the compositions, perhaps comparable

to some Persepolitan scenes (CAUBET, 2007: 133–134). For the time being, we must be content with underlining the absence of representations of the king within the context of Achaemenid bricks.
35. In both cases, the figures are 17 bricks high, and only the height of the spears is affected by these different proposals.
36. DIEULAFOY, 1893: 274.
37. MECQUENEM, 1947: 54.
38. In 1885, Dieulafoy excavated the first of them in the 'tumulus oriental' (= Ville Royale), where they had served as covering for a funerary urn of Parthian date, according to the excavator. Later, during his excavations at the Donjou, Mecquenem found another example.
39. However, their iconographic similarity to bricks from the Persian building in Babylon enabled them to be attributed to the reign of Artaxerxes II.
40. MECQUENEM, 1947: 54.
41. AMIET, 1988, fig. 81; J. Perrot, this volume, ch. xiv.
42. MUSCARELLA, 1992: 227.
43. AMIET, 1998: 129.
44. J. Perrot, this volume, ch. xiv.
45. BRIANT, 1996: 260.
46. AMIET, 1988: 132.
47. RAZMJOU, 2004: 386 and CAUBET, 1992: 224.
48. Only the bricks of the frieze of lions *passant* do not conform: the beasts are only seven bricks high However, to the extent that the height of those bricks is twice the height of the others, the size of the animals remains identical to that of the others.
49. The visible face is 17 bricks high. Some fragments in the stores indicate that they were also reproduced in a more traditional format (H. 8.5 cm).
50. DIEULAFOY, 1893: 276.
51. Mecquenem (MECQUENEM, 1947: 64) also recalls the difficult reconstruction of the single bull panel displayed to the public. He also mentions bricks indicating the presence at one time of a winged bull moving towards the left.
52. CAUBET, 2007: 130.
53. Recent research, led by the writer, has shown the frequent repetition of a brick with the same motif, thus indicating the presence within the French and Iranian collections of at least twelve lions moving towards the left. Nevertheless, only a single lion could be reconstructed, as the other pieces were far too small.
54. A. Caubet: in the present chapter, 301.
55. This casts a doubt on J. Perrot, ch. xiv: 460–461.
56. DIEULAFOY, 1893: 274.
57. DIEULAFOY, 1893: 37.
58. MECQUENEM, 1947: 82.
59. DIEULAFOY, 1893: 274.
60. LABROUSSE, 1972: 138.
61. They are used in the same way on the carved reliefs of Persepolis.
62. The fight of the lion and the bull, which appears several times on the stair façades at Persepolis, seems also to be related to the ceramic decoration of the Susa stairs. Dieulafoy mentions ten bricks that are 'painted without relief' (doubtless silicious glazed bricks) that reproduce this scene. However, the surviving collections do not confirm this, apart, perhaps, from a brick in the museum in Tehran (MECQUENEM 1947: fig. 52, no. 5) which he attributes to a figure of a crouching lion, but it could just as easily be part of a composition showing the fight between the lion and the bull.

This motif also appears on baked bricks with relief (B.1). Mequenem found one during the Donjon excavations in 1932.
63. See J. Yoyotte, this volume, ch. VIII: 327–329.
64. Mecquenem's 1933 report: 7–8, in the archives of the Département des antiquités orientales in the Louvre.
65. P. Amiet, this volume, ch. XI: 330.

Wedjats of the Apadana

Jean Yoyotte

A human eye and its painted eyebrow, underlined by a schematic rendering of the feathers on the cheek of a falcon; it figures the two eyes of the sky, both the eye of Horus, the moon, and the eye of Ra, the sun. This figure symbolises the perpetually renewed plenitude of the days as well as the monthly restitution of the wholeness of the night star. Regularly reproduced as an amulet, it constituted for many the best of the talismans for vigour and long-term well-being. It is called *wdȝ.t* (wedjat). Although Egyptian terms describing the eye are feminine (like the Latin *pupilla* and the Greek *korè*), French Egyptology treats the word wedjat as a masculine word.

Over the years, many wedjats were discovered in the earth cleared by the excavators of the Apadana, most of them broken and now dispersed between Tehran, Susa and the Louvre. All are identical in shape, dimension and material and very different from the small amulets recovered from the tombs and houses of individuals. They are large amulets (H. 41 x L. 65–67 mm), perforated on each side to allow them to be worn on a necklace. They are made of a fairly friable faience, and the surface is most often turquoise, sometimes lapis lazuli blue in colour. The detailed outline of the celestial eye is carved both on the front and the back (one side showing 'the right eye', that is to say the sun, the other the 'left eye', the moon).

As Mecquenem wrote in 1912, these groups of wedjats would have been part of the foundation deposits. The excavation of the palace of Darius in 1910–1911 'revealed two curious foundation deposits, one containing a large quantity of small clay bullae, all carrying the same Achaemenid seal impression; the other, a considerable number of Egyptian amulets in blue clay, "Oudjah" [*sic*] and images of the God Bes, no doubt brought back from a campaign in Egypt and buried in the foundations of the palace as charms'. The two examples published here were found in Apadana East in 1972–1973.

356
A Bes in international Persian style, from Egypt
Musée du Louvre (E10929). © RMN/Hervé Lewandowski

357
**Wedjats found on the Apadana tell
during the excavations of 1969–1979**

The small God Bes, with the feathered head, combative protector of mothers and children, is a common apotropaic agent. It is possible to imagine that these typically Egyptian amulets, talismans in current usage, were placed by the Egyptian employees of Darius, both for their own protection and for that of the royal works (they are certainly nothing like the foundation deposits of pharaonic temples).

It should be noted, however, that the foundation wedjats of Susa, which unlike the Bes and other figurines, constitute one or a series of identical models, have a cosmological symbolism, representing both the Sun and the Moon.

However, a detailed inventory of the Egyptian faience objects discovered at Susa has yet to be made, as has a compilation of archival data in relation to their location.

358
Painted terracotta vase
height 22.8 cm, length 30 cm, width 10.5 cm
Ghirshman excavations, Achaemenid village
© National Museum of Iran (8485)

11 Decorative Arts at Susa during the Persian Period

Pierre Amiet

T he recent discovery, to the north of the Ville Royale, of royal constructions isolated from all habitation – the Propylaeum and the monumental gate in front of the entrance of the palace – has revealed the unexpected extent of what appears to be a vast palatial complex of the Great Kings of Persia at Susa. It has in addition, however, indirectly raised the long unrecognised or at least implicit question of the urban character of the town in the Persian period – that is to say, the existence of a settlement for the civilian population. Previously, at the end of the Neo-Elamite period, after the intervention of Ashurbanipal in 646 BC, the town had been densely populated, both at the future location of the Palace of Darius and on the Ville Royale mound. Despite the lack of architectural remains, which were poorly identified at the beginning of the twentieth century, this occupation was well illustrated by the richness of the objects found in tombs explored by Mecquenem.[1] In addition, the archives discovered on the Acropolis and 'underneath the Apadana' confirmed an 'Iranian', or more exactly Persian, and even royal presence, on the eve of annexation by the great Cyrus, without, however, any precise evidence.[2] Nevertheless, it is clear that there was no habitation around the Propylaeum and the Darius Gate, which seem to have been isolated on the *tabula rasa* which the Ville Royale had become. P. de Miroschedji, however, noted both the Neo-Elamite occupation and the scarcity of Persian occupation.[3] This explains why the first excavators attributed the everyday objects they found, essentially the Neo-Elamite pottery, to this latter period. The terracotta figurines also testify to this scarcity: there are fewer than ten examples for the Persian period against hundreds for the Neo-Elamite period.[4] Persian weapons, known from the representations on the Persepolis reliefs, are represented by only modest pieces of harness at Susa: bridle attachments in the shape of small horns, made of limestone or gypsum alabaster, reproducing the original models carved from wild boar's teeth.[5] And what can be said about the rich Achaemenid metal

359
**Architectural ornament
in the shape of a bull protome**
Terracotta; height 22 cm, width 17 cm
Musée du Louvre (Sb 3080)
© RMN/Franck Raux

360
Bronze cauldron
height 26.3 cm, diameter 41.4 cm
(Morgan excavations)
Musée du Louvre (Sb 13757)
© RMN/Franck Raux

tableware, abundantly represented on the Persepolis reliefs, or the fine examples in museums, generally without provenance? At Susa only one deep bronze bowl, without decoration, survived the pillage.[6] The decorative arts of the Persian period, notably the ceramics, were practically all found by R. Ghirshman outside the Ville Royale,[7] and only around the edges of the artisans' settlement; this seems to indicate a surprising demographic deficiency and therefore raises questions about the fate of the Elamite population. Were they forced to flee? If so, where to? Were they reduced to forced labour for the massive royal construction programme? This is an unverifiable hypothesis, but the questions need to be asked.

Ghirshman was lucky to find two rare tablets in his 'Persian village'; these are private records of the period,[8] which we now know must be linked to a tablet imported from Persepolis, inopportunely published with the Neo-Elamite archive of the Acropolis.[9] We still do not know whether it was originally found with the other tablets. The signet rings, used exclusively in the 'village', confirm by their use on bullae the spread of Aramaic (usually on desiccated papyrus), of which a few graffiti have survived at the Donjon, transferred onto a masonry coating.[10] The poor quality of carving on cylinder seals, with a few rare exceptions, never ceases to amaze because it is evident among discoveries made since the beginning of the archaeological excavations at Susa in official as well as private sectors.[11] This suggests, along with the absence of cuneiform archives, a surprising lack of administrative activity, unlike the traditional or non-Susian sources. Coins are extremely rare, both at Susa and Persepolis. In addition to two silver shekels deposited in the princely tomb, which were minted in the Phoenician town of Arwad at the end of the fifth century BC,[12] some other silver coins were found in the early excavations, the majority from Phoenician towns, in a small hoard found at the Donjon.[13] This scarcity is probably due to the looting of the palaces, but also to the lack of coinage in circulation in Persia and Mesopotamia, though very evident in the Levant and Asia Minor.

Cheap Egyptian imports and Egyptian-influenced glazed pottery in the 'village' as elsewhere,[14] reflect a form of Egyptomania at the court, which imported a huge quantity of luxurious and predominantly Egyptian tableware. Meanwhile, a wider eclecticism was manifest in the ivories thrown into the well of the Donjon,[15]

not far from where the small hoard was found and from the wall with Aramaic graffiti, suggesting an official presence in this area during the Persian period.[16] From the same well came a fine fragment of Greek black figure ware, to which must be added a series of painted potsherds found on the Acropolis at the beginning of the excavations,[17] modestly testifying to imports from the Greek world.

OBJECTS IN STONE

That the palaces of Susa were abandoned is enough to explain why virtually none of their decorative objects has been found in the ruins, and that their fragments should be scattered across the site.[18] That said, in 1850, William K. Loftus found a 'collection of broken alabaster vases' on the Acropolis, some with Xerxes' inscriptions,[19] and whose stacking could not have been accidental. Later, Marcel Dieulafoy and then above all Jacques de Morgan discovered other similar vases on the same site;[20] these were undoubtedly of Egyptian origin and (when complete) bore a quadrilingual inscription, some by Darius, many by Xerxes and one by Artaxerxes.[21] Some of the vases, however, were inscribed with the name of Nebuchadnezzar II and his successors,[22] which for a while seemed to confirm the impression of a Neo-Babylonian domination of Susa.[23] On the other hand, the presence of inscribed fragments in archaic Hebrew suggested another interpretation.[24] The Babylonians must have brought home such vases as loot, all the while importing others from Egypt for their use,[25] after which the victorious Persians took these prized objects and deposited them in their treasuries at Susa, Persepolis and probably elsewhere.[26] They added other objects, such as the giant bronze knucklebone brought back from Ionia. It is therefore clear that there was a store of royal objects on the Acropolis that also housed hardstone cups, unknown in Iranian petrography and, no doubt, also imported from Egypt.[27] To these uninscribed fragments must be added other scattered finds, some carrying the remains of a probable quadrilingual inscription of the Persian kings.[28] These cups were not as fragile as the alabaster vases and they seem to have been broken intentionally, like similar ones in the treasury at Persepolis whose fragments remained grouped together. All this tableware is surely of Egyptian origin.

Neo-Babylonian urns and alabaster vessels[29]

Six alabaster vases, all in pieces, are identifiable thanks to their Babylonian inscriptions which at least mentioned their capacity and, more often, the royal palace from which they came. They are distinguished by a higher collar than those of the Persian period; the larger ones can be defined as urns, in contrast to the alabastra that are, strictly speaking, made to be held in one hand. The kings mentioned are Nebuchadnezzar II, Amel-Marduk and Neriglissar.

Urns and alabastra of the Persian period

Although all the royal vases were broken, others, uninscribed, survived intact or complete. Three shapes can therefore be identified:

A. A large urn with a wide, low and straight neck; only one example exists,[30] one of the few vases inscribed with the name of Darius, and only in Egyptian.
B. Ovoid urn with a flared, straight neck; only one example in this shape has been found, with a quadrilingual inscription by Xerxes (Year 11).[31]
C. Urns and alabastra with a wide, flared neck; they are widely distributed, with variations. The largest vase to have survived has an almost flat base; it is

364
Upper part of an alabastron with two handles
Inscribed with the name of Nebuchadnezzar II (605–562 BC). Alabaster; height 15.4 cm, diameter 9 cm
Musée du Louvre (Sb 608)
© RMN/Christian Larrieu

365

Fragment of red figure vase showing an Amazon with an inscription, 'Lylamis' (?), painter of Sotades. Athens, circa 460–450 BC

height 5.2cm, length 11.4 cm (Morgan excavations, 1898)

366

Fragmentary veined alabaster vase with Persian, Babylonian, Elamite and Egyptian inscriptions of Xerxes (485–465 BC)

preserved height 19.3 cm, diameter 16 cm

367

Uninscribed vase with two handles

Alabaster; height 31 cm, diameter 26 cm

probable that the large inscribed vases, mostly with the name of Xerxes, were squat with sloping sides. However, more pronounced ovoid shapes are also attested,[32] as well as the elongated form characteristic of classic alabastra. A small fragment of marbled black and green serpentine revealed a unique variation on alabaster.[33] Other fragments, in pure white gypsum alabaster, belonged to more unusual vases, with handles in the shape of ducks' heads, also attested at Persepolis.[34]

Hardstone cups

Only a few fragments of this royal tableware survive (they are fully described in our contribution to a volume published in honour of Jean Perrot).[35] Only three fragments bear the remains of seemingly quadrilingual inscriptions by Xerxes. They are made of different stone, hard, green or, more rarely, black: feldspathic sandstone, serpentinite or dolerite composed of feldspar and brownish-black pyroxene. The largest vessel must have had a diameter of around 28 cm; the rim is flat with a thin band in relief below it; the base was in the shape of a flat disc. Other, uninscribed fragments, found by Jacques de Morgan, are in red marble or red and yellow breccia. Some had a simpler shape, without a flat rim, with or without a band in relief below. They can be paralleled by fragments of very large, white marble cups found by Marcel Dieulafoy, as well as square basins.

Decorated cups

The most elaborate series was carved either in grey or black schist or in an artificial material obtained by hardening bitumen with ground calcite powder. This kind of mastic was used at Susa from the start, but mainly during the Early Dynastic Period (first half of the 3rd millennium BC) and the dynasty of the Simashki (late 3rd to early 2nd millennium BC). It is therefore possible that the fragments of the Persian period were of local manufacture. Other than a fairly simple schist cup with a ringbase, it has not been possible to restore more than one other hemispherical cup, which must have had three bovine legs decorated on their upper parts with a row of loops. Six scattered legs of felines and bovines belonged to similar cups of small dimensions, very finely crafted and comparable to the vases of Persepolis.[36]

Objects in blue composition, called 'Egyptian blue'

An artificial material imitating lapis lazuli appears in Susiana during the Untash-Napirisha period (second half of the 2nd millennium BC);[37] we do not know if there is evidence of its use at Haft Tepe. It is attested by several cylinder seals and scattered fragments that cannot be dated precisely but which are probably of similar date.[38] Two small discoid fragments, on one of which a few Old Persian signs survive, can be linked to an object discovered at Persepolis where it was identified with a mural 'nail' with the trilingual inscription: 'Pommel in lapis lazuli made in the house of Darius, the King'.[39] It was probably only the base of the pommel, crowned by the pommel proper, to which some baluster-shaped objects could have corresponded, made in a similar but harder material.[40]

The same material was used for the carving of several scattered objects: a baluster-shaped vase and two small, fragmentary cups and some smooth plaques for revetment,[41] apparently destined to decorate small items of furniture. Two square plaques bear floral decoration carved with hollows, possibly for inlay. A blue glass fragment in the shape of a flat fan with elaborate floral decoration is probably of later date.

368
Egyptian blue vase
Musée du Louvre (Sb 2792)
© Musée du Louvre/Annie Caubet

369
**Fragment of a bowl of Xerxes I with the
royal titulature in Old Persian and in Elamite**
Dark green feldspar; reconstructed diameter 13.1 cm, height 2.5 cm
Musée du Louvre (Sb 548), © RMN/Franck Raux
drawing by Pierre Amiet

370
**Vase with Egyptian inscription
in the name of Darius I, year 34 (488 BC)**
preserved height 21.1 cm, diameter 32.4 cm
Musée du Louvre (Sb 515)
© Musée du Louvre/Maurice and Pierre Chuzeville

Various sculptures

A series of thin plaques, all broken, sculpted in low relief, is carved in a soft, light-green or sometimes darker stone, which Gustave Jéquier called 'stéatoschiste'.[42] They were found over a wide area, despite their stylistic similarity. These plaques are quadrangular or circular; the first are sometimes perforated, possibly allowing them to be fixed to small items of furniture such as chests; the others, by contrast, do not seem to have been perforated and are not moulded on the sides, which distinguishes them from a very similar object found at Pasargadae which strongly resembles a lid.[43] The four known fragments of discs have a rosette in the centre, some surrounded with a series of petals, which are also found in the decoration of a quadrangular plaque.[44] These last, also evident at Pasargadae,[45] associate the central rosette with a floral decorative band, sometimes with birds; as at Pasargadae, a purely animalistic decoration can also be found; the hindquarters of a lion, with the muscles defined in the Achaemenid tradition, can be identified. A disc was decorated with a band of gazelles more softly executed. In addition, a series of much cruder plaques in grey schist illustrates a popular variant of decorative art. Animals and figures were represented with an infantile clumsiness. Irregularly shaped fragments reveal that there were also openwork versions.

Very different is a small relief in grey-green limestone found at the Donjon and representing a gazelle in the best Neo-Elamite tradition.[46] Finally the gazelle-shaped handles or hilts of two objects (a weapon and a thick pin), with long grooved horns, conform to the tradition illustrated on the Neo-Assyrian reliefs.[47]

THE ACHAEMENID IVORIES

Amongst the precious materials assembled for the construction and decoration of his palace at Susa, Darius did not fail to mention ivory, brought from Ethiopia, India and Arachosia,[48] even though at Persepolis only the Ethiopians are represented bringing elephant tusks.[49] No tribute bearer, however, brings worked or decorated ivory objects comparable to the items of goldwork so obligingly illustrated. Only a few pieces of such objects were found at Persepolis.[50] In contrast, in 1935, whilst

373
Limestone relief of a gazelle
Height 13.5 cm, width 15 cm, depth 2.1 cm
(Mecquenem excavations, Donjon, 1932)
Musée du Louvre (Sb 3782)
© Musée du Louvre/Christina Larrieu

374
Fragments of round plaques in schist
Musée du Louvre
(Sb 3776, Sb 3770, Sb 3771, Sb 3777)
© RMN/Franck Raux

emptying a well dug under the palace attributed to Artaxerxes I and to Darius II at the Donjon, Mecquenem brought to light an important collection of scattered fragments, mainly of ivory, schist and faience, which seem to have been torn from the objects to which they had been attached before being discarded, already very incomplete.[51] The stylistic diversity of these ivories corresponds to the different provenances of the raw ivory. Four different series can be distinguished: Syro-Phoenician, Persian, Egyptian and Greek, nicely illustrating the eclectic taste of the Persian court.

Syro-Phoenician series

Some fragments reveal that the long-established tradition in the countries of the Levant from the ninth to the seventh centuries BC had not been lost with the fall of the Assyrian Empire, which had assembled the largest number of examples in its palaces.[52] This tradition, a little weakened it seems, survived in the theme of the 'Lady at the window',[53] which is identifiable in the baluster capitals framed by the remains of uprights. In the same way, the stylised trees with openwork volutes which framed decorated panels of animated figures, or stood in rows between mythical beings,[54] were reproduced with variations that confirmed the weakening of the creative tradition. The same probably applies to fragments of very finely carved wings, originally possibly framing the solar disc.[55] A small, almost complete plaque, decorated with simply carved rosettes, is very similar to that which was found in the sarcophagus of Eshmunazar at Sidon, but owes nothing to that tradition; it nevertheless confirms continuing Levantine influence with regard to the use of ivory to decorate furniture and precious caskets.

375
Ivory plaque decorated with volutes
height 5.5 cm, width 2.3 cm
Musée du Louvre (Sb 9174)
© RMN/Franck Raux

Persian series

Other than a few fragments of small plaques, used in the same way as those from the Levant, Persian ivory art in the true sense is distinctive in that it is represented essentially by grooming products: mainly combs and feminine statuettes used as handles or containers. It has been possible to link four fragments of the same type of composite object with the separate parts fixed by peg and mortise and glue, the adjacent surfaces being cross-hatched to facilitate the bonding. These include the body of a woman clothed in a pleated robe bordered with small roses and leaving the chest apparently bare. The breasts were applied, as were the (missing) arms. The heels of the pointed shoes were hidden by the robe that fell to the ground at the back, corresponding to a small square base. It can be linked with a very fragmentary head, a little out of proportion, which harks back to the Syro-Phoenician tradition.[56] The figure wore large pendant earrings in the form of crescents, and generally a sort of cylindrical *polos* similar to those worn by naked women on ivories found at Nimrud.[57]

The statuettes that one can thus reconstruct are very close to those in bone and especially in bronze of Levantine provenance during the Persian period.[58] A minuscule statuette, 2.7 cm high, represents a woman dressed in a pleated robe with two large front panels replacing the sleeves. We do not know if she is a one-off or was integrated into the decoration of another object. The combs are usually double, in the shape of a rectangular central plate, bordered on both sides by two tooled uprights, decorated with a row of tongue motifs ending in elongated animal heads. These uprights could have been gold-plated. The central plate could have been composite, made of pieces fixed with the help of small tenons, like those of the statuettes. This plate was decorated in low relief with a simple frame or a double frame with the tongue motif or with rosettes alternating with

376
Minuscule statuette of a woman enveloped in a large cloak
Ivory; height 2.7 cm, width 1 cm
(Mecquenem excavations, Donjon, 1935)
National Museum of Iran, Tehran (no. 11808)

377

**Fragmentary composite statue
of a woman in a pleated dress**
Ivory; body with a Persian pleated robe;
height 10.7 cm, width 1.4 cm, depth 2 cm
(Mecquenem excavations, Donjon, 1935)
Musée du Louvre (Sb 3728)
© Musée du Louvre/Maurice Chuzeville
drawing by Pierre Amiet

378

**Window balustrade of Syro-Phoenician
type known as 'Woman at the Window'**
height 2.1 cm, width 4.9 cm, depth 0.35 mm
Musée du Louvre (Sb 9212)
© RMN/Franck Raux
drawing by C. Florimont

379

**Ivory comb fragment decorated
with an animal in front of a palm tree**
height 4.4 cm, width 3.3 cm

380
Parts of a comb decorated with Persian heroes fighting and overcoming monsters
Ivory; height 6.5 cm, width 3.3 cm
(Donjon, 1935)
Musée du Louvre (Sb 3729)
© RMN/Franck Raux

381
Fragments of a comb decorated with a monster attacking a winged bull, and a monster attacking a human-headed, winged bull
Ivory; height 6.3 cm, width 4.4 cm
(Mecquenem excavations, Donjon, 1935)
National Museum of Iran, Tehran (no. 42811)
drawing by Pierre Amiet

382
Ivory and gold comb with a representation of the king as a hero, subduing a standing lion
height 14.4 cm, width 10.5 cm
(Morgan excavations, bronze sarcophagus from the Acropolis, 1905–1906)
Musée du Louvre (Sb 9095)
© RMN/Franck Raux
illustration, Pierre Amiet

double palmettes, resembling simplified fleurs-de-lys. The decorative theme was borrowed from the traditional Mesopotamian repertoire, as interpreted by the Persians: winged bulls and human-headed, winged lions attacked by a monster with the head of a bird of prey, and the 'Master of the Animals' transformed into a personification of the Persian and Median peoples. It should be noted that the palm tree has been rendered naturally, as on the Darius cylinder seal and not like the old 'Sacred Tree'. The quality of the carving of these combs is of unequal quality in summarily carved very low relief, implying a certain diversity of artist or workshop.

Egyptian ivories

The Egyptian ivories are clearly of a superior quality, even if they too are sometimes of uneven quality. For the main part they must have been used as decorative plaques applied to furniture and chests, like the Syro-Phoenician ivories. Other than a lion goddess, they largely represent gift bearers, in conformity with the traditional repertoire of tomb artwork. They include the head of an Egyptian carrying an animal on his shoulders, in low relief, and a smaller one of a Nubian calf-bearer in a sharper relief of equal delicacy. These themes were used in Egypt before the Persian period.[59] This manifestly Egyptian work is, however, associated with rosette borders characteristic of Persian art, which suggests the existence of a mixed workshop of Egyptian artists working for the Persians.

383
Fragments of Egyptian-style plaques

right
A calf carrier
Ivory; height 4.1 cm, width 3.4 cm (Donjon, 1935)
© Musée du Louvre/T. Olliver

far right
A Nubian kid carrier (far right)
Ivory, height 3.4 cm, width 4 cm (Donjon, 1935)
Musée du Louvre (Sb 3723)
© Musée du Louvre/T. Olliver

1. MECQUENEM, 1922: 124 ff. and 1943: 35 ff.

2. SCHEIL, 1911: 1–298 and 1929: 301–309.

3. MIROSCHEDJI, 1987: 32 ff.

4. MARTINEZ-SÈVE, 2002a: 74–79.

5. AMIET, 1998.

6. CURTIS and TALLIS, 2005: no. 110.

7. GHIRSHMAN, 1954; STRONACH, 1974b: 243 ff.

8. GHIRSHMAN, 1954: 19 and 79-82. Others include: JOHANNÈS, 1990: 173–180 and AMIET, 1973: pl. XVI–XVII, no. 72–76.

9. MUSCARELLA, 1992: no. 191.

10. AMIET, 2001: 244.

11. AMIET, 1972: 284 ff.

12. G. ELAYI and J. ELAYI, 1992.

13. ALLOTTE DE LA FUYE, 1928: 65–74; ALLOTTE DE LA FUYE, 1934: 21 and 78–82. For the entire treasure, see MECQUENEM, 1934: 77.

14. PÉZARD and POTTIER, 1926: 141, no. 347; MECQUENEM, 1947: fig. 24; GHIRSHMAN, 1954: pl. XVII.

15. AMIET, 1973.

16. MECQUENEM, 1934: 77.

17. JÉQUIER, 1900c: pl. V, and R. Boucharlat, ch. XIII, p. 373.

18. BOUCHARLAT, 1990a: 225–233.

19. LOFTUS, 1857: 409–413 and CURTIS, 1993: 26–27, pl. 11b and 19a.

20. DIEULAFOY, 1893: 435–436; MORGAN, 1900: 93, fig. 137; JÉQUIER, 1900c: 129–130, fig. 314–317; *id.* 1905b: 171.

21. G. Posener catalogued all the fragments bearing Egyptian inscriptions (POSENER, 1936: 137–151).

22. PÉZARD and POTTIER, 1926: 80, no. 132–134.

23. DHORME, 1933: col. 959.

24. CLERMOMNT-GANNEAU, 1906; AMIET, 1990: 213, 217, no. 1.

25. VON BISSING, 1941.

26. SCHMIDT, 1957: 81 ff.; STRONACH, 1978: 228.

27. JÉQUIER, 1900c: 135, fig. 344–347.

28. AMIET, 1990: no. 3–4, 7.

29. Louvre sb 608: SCHEIL, 1905: 56 and SCHEIL, 1905: 96 and 96; sb 4114 (with missing indication of the capacity); sb 525 (capacity: 4 qa 4sa).

30. JÉQUIER, 1905b: 171, fig. 47; PÉZARD and POTTIER, 1926: 81, no. 142 (Louvre sb 515); POSENER, 1936: 139, no. 38.

31. PÉZARD and POTTIER, 1926: 80, no. 136; POSENER, 1936: 141, no. 43 = Louvre Sb 561.

32. Louvre Sb 648 (H. 0.283 m; diam. 0.0163 m). PÉZARD and POTTIER, 1926: 80, no. 139.

33. AMIET, 1990: no. 2.

34. SCHMIDT, 1957: pl. 48, no. 8b and 8c.

35. AMIET, 1990: 213–224.

36. SCHMIDT, 1957: pl. 5 (3) and 56 (1; 3; 4).

37. MOOREY, 1985: 188 ff.

38. PORADA, 1970: no. 113, 121; AMIET, 1972: no. 2043, 2044, 2051. Plus a small fragment of an applied plaque(?) decorated with volutes.

39. SCHMIDT, 1957: pl. 42: 27.

40. MECQUENEM, 1943: 40, fig. 34–3 = Louvre sb 2792 (H. 0.203 m; max. diam. 0.059 m); sb 2793 (H. 0.203 m); base diam. 0.059 m; max diam.: 0.062 m).

41. Louvre sb 18423: diameter of largest fragment (0.12 x 0.083 m).

42. JÉQUIER, 1900c: 136, fig. 354. MECQUENEM 1943: 76, fig. 63 (1–9).

43. STRONACH, 1978: pl. 116 and 227.

44. For the 'tongues' see AMANDRY, 1966: 69, n. 85.

45. STRONACH, 1978: 230, fig. 100 (7–8) and pl. 167 b and c.

46. MECQUENEM, 1947: 89, fig. 57: 1932 excavations.

47. HROUDA, 1965: pl. 22 (21, 22, 26).

48. VALLAT, 1971: 58 and F. Vallat, this volume, ch. IX: xsf.

49. SCHMIDT, 1953: 90.

50. SCHMIDT, 1957: pl. 40 (1–2).

51. MECQUENEM, 1943: 76; MECQUENEM, 1947: 88–89; AMIET, 1972: 167–191 and 319–337.

52. BARNETT, 1982: 43–55.

53. WINTER, 1981: 111, 116, pl. XIII d and c; BARNETT, 1982: 48, pl. 50b.

54. BARNETT, 1982: pl. 47b, 55.

55. MALLOWAN and HERRMANN, 1974: pl. C–CIII.

56. Plus a beardless face: AMIET, 1972: pl. IV (1).

57. For example: BARNETT, 1982: pl. 43d, 44c.

58. See the incense-burner stand: ZAYADINE, 1986: 156, fig. 11.

59. For example: DUNHAM, 1950, pl. XXXIV.

60. PÉZARD and POTTIER, 1926: 234–235.

61. REINACH, 1892: 124–125 and PFUHL, 1923: no. 626–627, p. 786 ff.

62. BECATTI, 1947.

63. BARNETT, 1982: pl. 67, p. 66. MASSON and PUGAČENKOVA 1956–1959.

The Acropolis tomb

Constance Frank

I n February 1901, Jacques de Morgan discovered on the Acropolis a bronze coffin in the shape of a bathtub. 'Hard up against the ruins of an Elamite wall' and 6 m below present ground level,[1] it was orientated north–south. Nearby another bronze vat of the same type was empty apart from an ivory comb.[2] In the first burial, the presence of two silver shekels from Arad in Phoenicia, a satrapy of the empire, allow the burial to be dated to the end of the fifth century BC.[3]

These are the only Achaemenid funerary remains discovered at Susa. The two sarcophagi were found 4 m south of a square-plan building, with tiled floors built with glazed bricks. The foundation charters which were found there showed that it was a Neo-Elamite temple built by King Shutruk-Nahhunte II (716–699 BC).[4] The only building attributable to the Achaemenid period in the neighbourhood was a large mud-brick wall on the edge of the tell, running north–south over the Neo-Elamite remains.[5]

THE TOMB AND THE DECEASED[6]

There are very few documents giving details of the funerary architecture and its immediate surroundings other than Morgan's descriptive remarks, which leave little room for interpretation. We learn, therefore, that the neighbouring substrata were composed of ceramic potsherds, ashes, burnt bone and brick fragments. These bricks, of the same type as those of the Achaemenid rampart discovered nearby, had fallen inside the tub. Morgan therefore hypothesised that the coffin must have been inside a collapsed vaulted hypogeum.[7] This observation led him to suppose also that the tub had not been covered.[8]

The only graphic document we possess relating to the tomb is a watercolour painted by Morgan. It is not known if it was done *in situ*, and its reliability might therefore be questioned. Nevertheless, certain remarks relating to the disposition

387
Plan of the remains discovered on the Acropolis tell
MORGAN, 1905: fig. 66

388
Jacques de Morgan, *The Acropolis Tomb*
Watercolour
MORGAN, 1905

389
Bronze sarcophagus
height 56 cm, length 1.65 m, length at the bottom 1.29 m
MORGAN, 1905: fig. 67

of the bones give us some idea of the body's position. The body was placed on its back, lower limbs extending straight down; the bent arms had been brought up to the chest.[9] The sex of the deceased is not known, but due to the slenderness of the skeleton and especially the nature of the material deposited, Morgan presumed that the body was that of a woman.

The question of the social identity of the deceased also remains a mystery. The literary evidence from texts postdating the Achaemenid period tells of the richness of the tombs of the Achaemenid kings and the sumptuousness of the clothing, textiles and jewellery which accompanied them into the afterlife.[10] The remarkable furnishings of the tomb at Susa, made more exceptional thanks to the unique character of the discovery, led naturally to its discoverer hypothesising about its occupant. The quantity and the splendour of the jewellery encouraged Morgan in his idea that the deceased could only be a woman.

However, it must be admitted that in antiquity men and women both used make-up and perfume and could wear identical jewellery;[11] but, despite the number of textual attestations, archaeological discoveries are rare. As to the iconographic records, they are rich but partial; more often than not they represent men who are part of, or linked to, royal circles. It is probable that one of the main pieces of jewellery from the tomb, the torque, would have been worn only by men (at least, this is the case in the illustrations we have). It may be the same for the lion-head bracelets.[12] The necklaces made of simple rows of beads of semi-precious stones are not represented on relief sculpture.[13] Other ornaments present in the tomb at Susa are depicted in the monumental decorations; these are gold granulated beads, generally pierced.[14] They can be seen at the end of locks of hair on the tribute bearers sculpted on the reliefs at Persepolis.[15] These elements would suggest that the occupant of this tomb, despite the absence of weapons, was a man. However, the round earrings were equally worn by women, as the ivory statuette discovered at Susa can attest.[16]

THE OBJECTS

Thanks to the watercolour and the descriptions of the excavators, the layout of the objects inside the coffin (no objects were noted near the tub) is known. The material is divided into two groups – the objects worn, such as jewels and items of adornment; and the objects placed next to the body, such as stone and metal tableware. Regarding the ornaments, we know that two gold buttons were worn on the left-hand side of the chest.[17] The earrings were discovered on either side of the jaw. Amulets were scattered with other beads and must have belonged to a necklace. The tableware was made up of two alabaster vases with the large horizontal lips of Egyptian type and a flared silver bowl, of a shape wide-spread in the Achaemenid period.[18]

Bead necklaces and pendants

The necklaces were mainly made up of beads and amulets of precious stone. A petrographic study was made by Françoise Tallon, who noted the use of some 15 materials in their manufacture: rock crystal, amethysts and smoky quartz as well as agate and jasper; banded stones such as onyx and sardonyx, flint, haematite, marble and breccia. Frit, an artificial material, was also used, as were fine pearls.[19] For each necklace, the artisan seems to have played with the colour, opacity and texture of the stones by alternating them, sometimes by adding gold beads, pendants or gold-mounted beads.

The epigraphic records tell us from which regions of the empire these materials were imported.[20] Thanks to the foundation charter of Darius I found at Susa, we learn that the gold came from Bactria, the lapis lazuli and the carnelian from Sogdiana (Afghanistan),[21] and turquoise from Chorasmia (Turkmenistan).[22] As for the pearls, they were certainly imported from the Persian Gulf. In this same inscription it is said that the goldsmiths were Medes or Egyptians.[23]

Inlays

This technique, also called cloisonné, was used for the decoration of several gold objects, including the extremities of the torque and the bracelets, the two buttons and the earrings. Many inlays fell out during the excavation because of the decomposition of the adhesive holding them in position.[24] The inlays were made of carnelian, lapis lazuli, turquoise and also, but exclusively for the lions' head decorating the torque and specifically for the eyes, mother-of-pearl. The appearance of the stones sometimes varies in the intensity of their colour and their texture. It has not been determined if this variation was due to their different origins, and therefore quality, or to a chemical change in the stones resulting from the length of time they have been underground.[25]

Cloisonné was also used for the decoration of the pendants in the shape of boots, made up of two assembled leaves of gold, and for the discs used as spacers between the beads of the pearl necklace.

The metalwork

Another technique used was granulation. Just as decorative as cloisonné this technique was used particularly on the beads and the buttons. The beads are made up of a cylinder onto which are soldered two to four rows of gold grains. This technique is also used for the 'head-dress beads' and was also applied to the upper part of the pendants decorated with cloisonné.[26] Granulation had been known since the first half of the third millennium BC in Mesopotamia, as testified by the jewels from the tombs of the royal cemetery of Ur. Nearly 2000 years later its usage could be found again in the neighbouring region of Assyria, at Nimrud, in tombs dating to the start of the eighth century BC. It is not possible, however, to attribute a Mesopotamian origin to this technique, as the same goldsmithing motifs and the same manufacturing techniques were known and widespread. Not only were Medes and Egyptians well known for their ability to work the precious

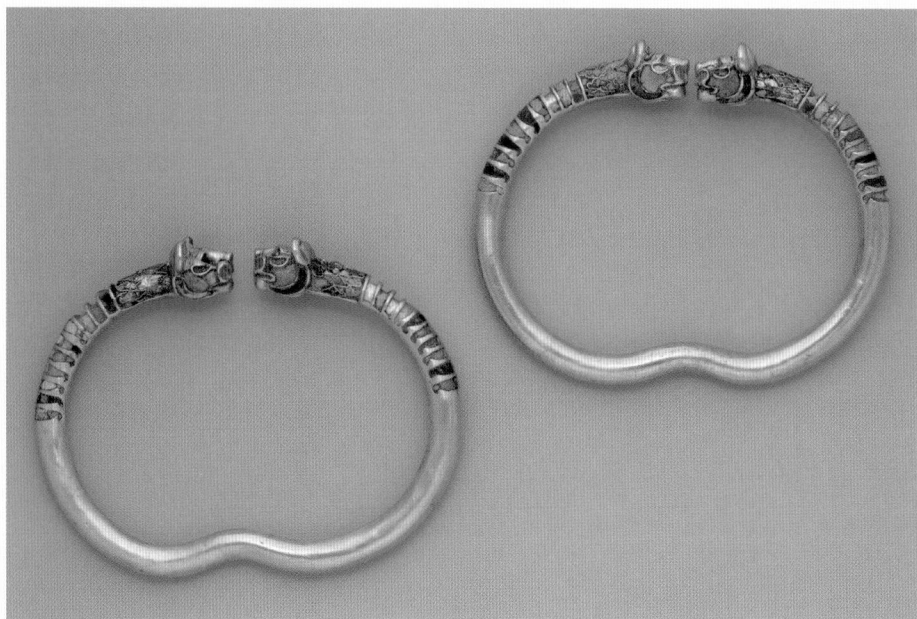

390
Two bracelets
Gold, lapis lazuli, turquoise and mother-of-pearl
6.4 x 7.9 cm

391
Jewellery discovered in the Acropolis Tomb

1 Gold beads with granulation (hair ornaments); outer diameter 5.5 mm
Musée du Louvre (Sb 19364)
2 Necklaces of semi-precious stones (agate, turquoise, lapis lazuli, carnelian) and gold beads with granulation
One of the necklaces has two small pendants
Musée du Louvre (Sb 2768 and Sb 19355)
3 Torque: gold, lapis lazuli, turquoise, mother-of-pearl; internal diameter 20.2 cm
Musée du Louvre (Sb 2760)
4 Necklace with inlaid pendants: gold, lapis lazuli, turquoise and carnelian; length 70 cm
Musée du Louvre (Sb 2763).
5 Amulets
Musée du Louvre (Sb 19358, Sb 19359, Sb 19360, Sb 19361)

© RMN/Christian Jean

392
Silver bowl
diameter 18.4 cm
Musée du Louvre (Sb 2756)
© Musée du Louvre/Oi Cheong Lee

393
Bead necklace
Musée du Louvre (Sb 2767)
© RMN/Christian Jean

394
Earrings
Gold, lapis lazuli, turquoise and mother-of-pearl;
height 4.1 cm, width 4.4 cm
Musée du Louvre (Sb 2764, Sb 2765)
© RMN/rights reserved

395
Buttons
Gold, lapis lazuli, turquoise and carnelian;
diameter 2.1 cm
Musée du Louvre (Sb 2766)
© Musée du Louvre/Oi Cheong Lee

396
Alabastron
height 21 cm, diameter 9.1 cm
Musée du Louvre (Sb 524)
© RMN/Frank Raux

397
Silver amulet in the shape of a falcon
Musée du Louvre (Sb 4201)
© Musée du Louvre/Chuzeville

metal, so were the Scythians, the Lydians, the Carians and the Armenians. The gold torque (of more than 20 cm in diameter) and the bracelets,[27] whose ends are in the shape of lions' heads, were realised thanks to the lost-wax process. The body of the torque was therefore formed of two tubes 1.27 cm in diameter. Cavities had been cut into the heads of the lions so as to apply the fragments of stone creating the beast's coat. The cylindrical part behind the head was also made in cloisonné, forming a sort of lapis lazuli net depicting a mane; the next part (from the collar of which the inlays have disappeared) must have suggested the animal's breast.[28] The same technique was used for the bracelets, although the decoration of the head was slightly simplified. The hoop of the bracelets was made from one single piece, onto which the heads of the lions were then fixed.[29] Other smithing techniques can be identified in the tableware. The silver bowl rested against the side of the coffin. This form of drinking cup, shallow but sharply flared, was widely used during the Achaemenid period. It can also be found in gold. The tableware is, generally, formed by beating. However, the weight of the piece discovered in the tomb (562 g) tended to prove that it was cast.[30] Indeed, the outside decoration is not found on the inside, as would have been the case with tableware decorated using repoussé. The decoration of this type of piece is fairly stereotyped, and is more often than not floral decoration (here a rosette on the outside and a lotus at the bottom of the inside) from which radiate, on the outside, 40 leaf motifs. The details are incised.[31] On this piece a raised narrow band is placed between the body and the rim. The metalwork, as well as the ornamental themes (notably the rosette and the leaves), directly recall the works of the Neo-Assyrian goldsmiths.

The bronzes of the Acropolis

Jean Perrot

Bronze knucklebone[1]

Discovered in 1901 on the Acropolis of Susa by Jacques de Morgan, this bronze knucklebone, made by the lost wax process, was probably brought back to Susa at the beginning of the fifth century BC by the soldiers of Darius who had pillaged and destroyed the great sanctuary of Apollo at Didyma. The inhabitants of Miletus were deported to Susa (Herodotus, VI, 19–20) before being sent to the Persian Gulf. The knucklebone has a Greek inscription, crudely chiselled, recording its dedication to Apollo by Aristolochos and Thrason as produce of the harvest tithe for the sanctuary of the god. It carries the name of the man who cast it, Pasikles, son of Kydimeneus. The object was probably a weight, and has two handles, one on the top and the other on the side. The use of knucklebones was widespread in the Greek world; they were used as gaming pieces, or as a means of consulting the oracles or even as offerings to the deities.

Bronze weight in the shape of a lion[2]

Discovered near the knucklebone weight on the Acropolis of Susa in 1901 by Jacques de Morgan. This weight has a loop handle in the tradition of the Assyrian weights of the eighth century BC. These weights would have been used to weigh the tributes to be given to the satraps. They have been found in different areas: Pasargadae, Kerman and as far as Afghanistan. They often have a trilingual inscription where the royal titulature is accompanied by an indication of the weight. Darius would have created a scale of pyramidal weights in diorite or basalt. The basic measure was the *Karša* or talent (a little over 40 g); there are weights of 2 *Karša*, of 60 *Karša* and 120 *Karša*.

1. HAUSSOULIER, 1905. ANDRÉ-SALVINI and DESCAMPS-LEQUIME, 2005.
2. MORGAN, 1905: 171–177. ANDRÉ-SALVINI and DESCAMPS-LEQUIME, 2005.

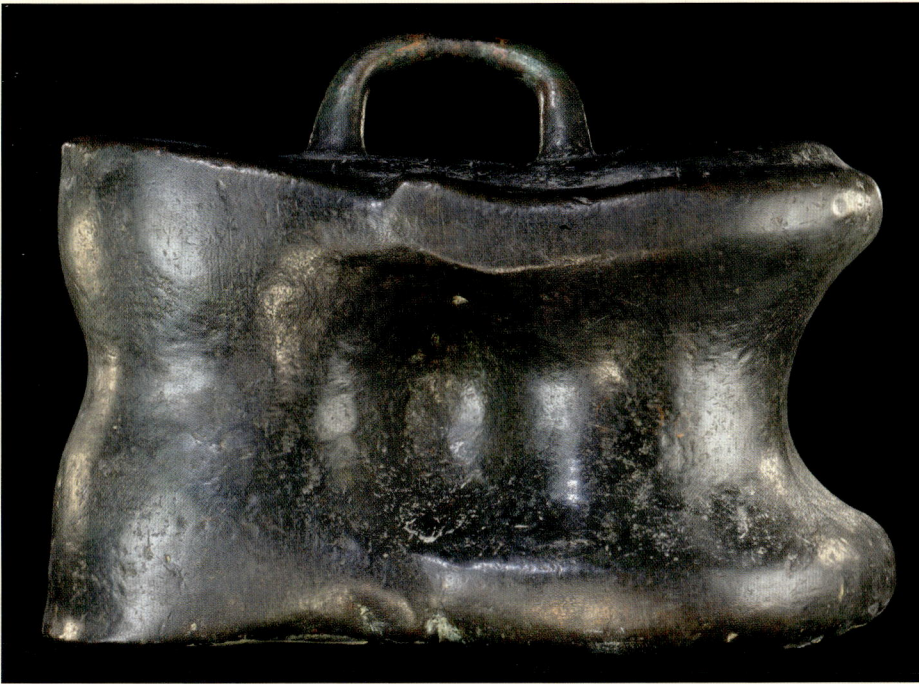

398
Large bronze knucklebone
height 27.5 cm, length 39 cm, depth 24.5 cm; weight 93.7 kg
Louvre (Sb 2719)

399
Bronze weight in the shape of a lion
height 30 cm, length 53 cm; weight 121 kg
Louvre (Sb 2718)

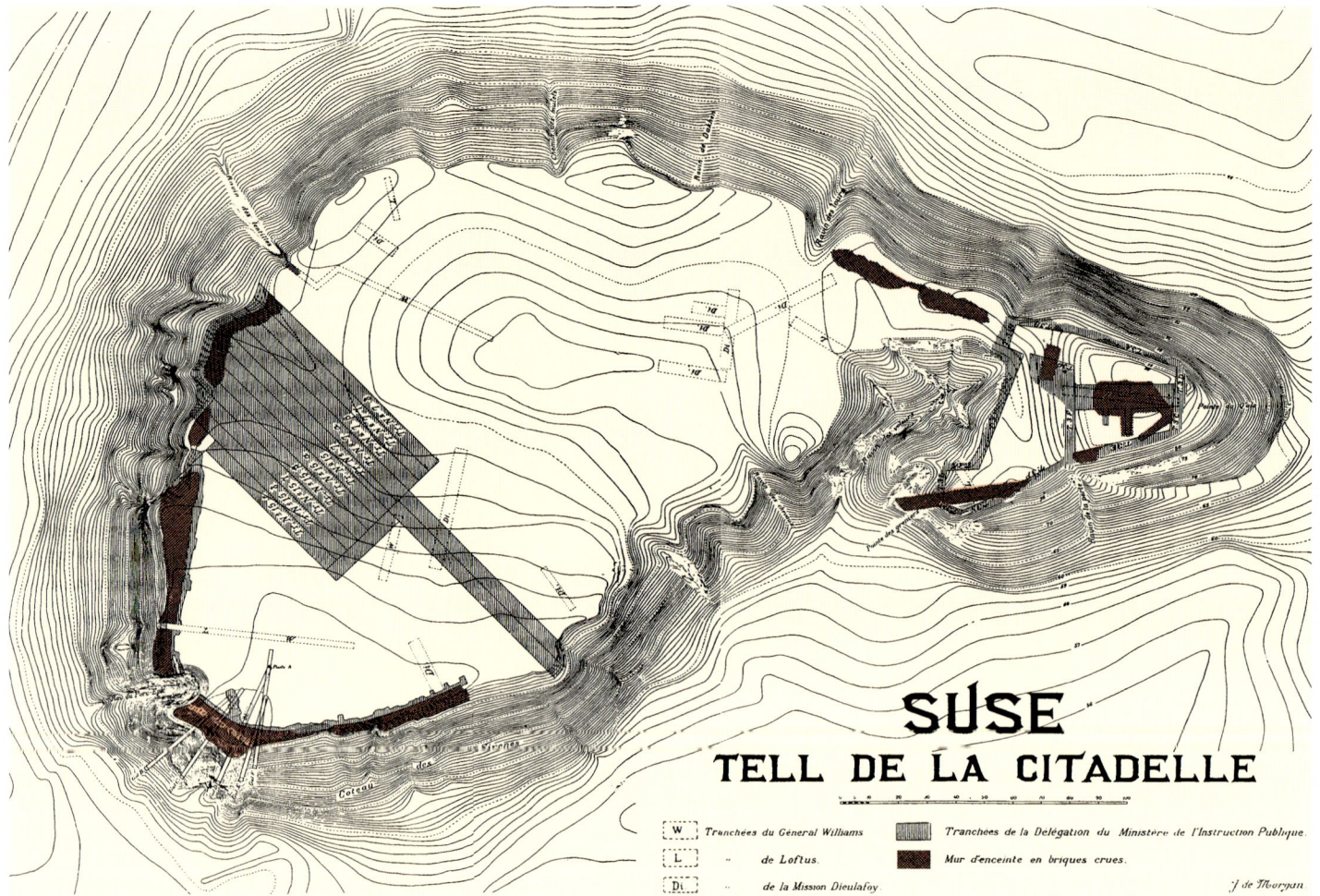

SUSE
TELL DE LA CITADELLE

W	Tranchées du Général Williams		Tranchées de la Délégation du Ministère de l'Instruction Publique.
L	" de Loftus.		Mur d'enceinte en briques crues.
Di.	" de la Mission Dieulafoy.		J. de Morgan

400

**Plan of the Acropolis showing the trenches dug
by Morgan during the two first seasons of excavation**

The remains of the Achaemenid mud-brick walls are shown in red.
The external face was never determined

MORGAN, 1900: plan II

12

Other Works of Darius and His Successors

Rémy Boucharlat

The discovery of the Palace of Darius during the first excavations of the nineteenth century and the unearthing of the Achaemenid walls enclosing the three highest tells of Susa have long satisfied the reader of classical sources and the Bible in search of the capital of the Persian kings.

'Three enormous piles of earth, well separated and quite distinct one from the other, rise before us; the most imposing, that whose summit appeared to dominate the whole tell, the *Kalé Chous*, rises 36 m above the level of the Shaur', wrote Jane Dieulafoy.[1] Even before the construction of the Château by Jacques de Morgan, one of the tells had been nicknamed château or fort because it dominated the two others by more than 15 m and had steep slopes. It reaches a height of 19 m above the level of the Hypostyle Hall at the northern and south-eastern points of the Acropolis. Marcel Dieulafoy saw it as the site of an acropolis with rather fantastic defences, but he took into consideration the height and the shape of the tell, while also giving the name *acropole* to the group of three tells, the subject of his book *L'Acropole de Suse*. He also calls the Acropolis tell *Kaleh-è Chous*.[2]

THE SUSA ACROPOLIS AND THE ROYAL TREASURES

It would be good to have a description, even a short one, of the remains of the wall of the Acropolis, but the excavation led to only a few observations which Jacques De Morgan summarised in several, often rather inaccessible, publications.

Before the excavations, the summit of the Acropolis tell was not flat. The general shape of the tell is a crude triangle with a promontory in the north-east and, in addition, in the central part, a depression open to the East. The edges were turned up to the south and the west.[3] The dimensions of the summit are estimated to be 300 x 180 m (not including the promontory where the château was to be built).[4]

401
The Acropolis tell (Qaleh Chous)
photographed by Marcel Dieulafoy in 1886

The construction

Jacques de Morgan, who undertook the extensive excavation of the Acropolis in search of the oldest levels, quickly found the Achaemenid wall under the surface and on nearly the entire perimeter of the tell; he identified it only thanks to its very broad outline: 'the edge of the tell was in this area [east south-east], like everywhere else, crowned by a large mud-brick wall slavishly following the uneven terrain, and I think I can attribute it to the Achaemenid period. The wall, unique and very irregular in its direction, as in its thickness, formed the only defence of the citadel.'[5] Nothing, not even traces of towers, would justify the extremely complex reconstruction which Marcel Dieulafoy had suggested several years before.

In the sector where the Achaemenid tomb was found, the wall has shallow foundations. On other parts of the tell, by contrast, the wall cuts through the 'Anzanite' (Elamite) levels.[6] The level of the base of this wall is indicated at different points, therefore it is at datum point 28 m, more often at 30 m altitude, or even at 31 m above the level of the plain (so +2 m above the water table).[7] However, the only published stratigraphic section that shows the wall is not located on the plan,[8] and it appears 2 m under the surface, at datum point +28 m and with a height of 5 m, thus with its base at 23 m. This only erroneous point could be due to the substrata being lower locally, or possibly to an error in Morgan's trench which was not carefully planned, but represented by a schematic sketch. As all the other information is fairly consistent, we will take datum level to be +30 m above the water table for the base of the wall. It is a fairly meagre foundation, only 2 to 3 m below the floor level. These were 12 to 15 m above the floors of the Palace of Darius. Consequently, if the wall was 10 m high, its summit was at least as high as the roof of the Hypostyle Hall of Darius.

The thickness of the wall was very variable. It was around 4 m in the trench mentioned above but, according to Jacques de Morgan, in other places it was 6 to 8 m, even though the exterior face was never preserved. The maximum thickness was 12.5 m near the southern tip,[9] to the extent that we can wonder if there did not exist one or more reinforced parts at the extremities, perhaps towers. The line of the wall is not known precisely, despite a trench dug by Morgan along the inside face over more than 220 m to the south and the east, and the unearthing of the wall in the northern trenches. The wall is known over only a quarter of the perimeter.[10]

The date of the wall and its abandonment

The building technique was not documented; a report by Morgan mentions that on the tell's edges there were 'sections of the curtain wall built of mud bricks 0.2 x 0.32 x 0.46 m'.[11] These brick dimensions are fairly improbable at Susa for the Achaemenid and later periods. A final observation is made by Morgan: the wall was cut into, at least in the west, by constructions dated to the Greco-Persian period, easily identifiable by associated Hellenising objects, of the sort that would have been abandoned soon after the time of Alexander.

This information is one of the most certain chronological clues which we have for dating this wall to the Achaemenid period. It is the only important, post-Elamite construction on the Acropolis tell, situated stratigraphically above the monuments of the eighth to seventh centuries BC. As to the *terminus ante quem* it is level with, or covered by 'poor constructions' in which the material appears, from the evidence, to be of the Seleucid and Parthian eras. It is thanks to this chronological bracket that the wall can be dated, in all likelihood, to the Achaemenid period.

402

This cross-section by Morgan shows that the Achaemenid curtain wall was founded very high up on top of 15 m of archaeological levels on the Acropolis tell, over 10 m above the floors of Darius' Palace on the Apadana tell
MORGAN, 1907: fig. p.9

The observations of Morgan as to the abandonment of the wall are important for the history of Susa; indeed, the citadel of Susa was mentioned several times, not only by Alexander's historians, but later still at the end of the third century BC, during the revolt of Molon. In this last case, there is no confusion between the town (Greek *polis*) which Molon conquered and the Citadel (Greek *akra*) which the governor Diogenes had laid siege to before him (Polybius, v.48.14).

Was the Citadel the location of the store of royal treasures?

According to a long-standing tradition amongst the classical authors, the Achaemenids accumulated rather than invested. Quintus Curtius (v.2.11) wrote: 'as soon as he had entered the town (*urbs*) of Susa, Alexander extracted from the treasures an incredible amount of currency: 50,000 silver talents, not coined, but in crude ingots. Numerous kings, over the ages, had amassed immense fortunes which they assigned to their children and their descendants; in the space of one hour they passed to the hands of a foreign king'. The author, who repeated his predecessors, did not indicate the particular place where this treasure was stored, but equally does not mention the 'several palaces and treasuries' of the Persian kings at Susa that Strabo had referred to. Diodorus (xvii.56.1) was hardly more precise: 'Alexander took possession of the town (*polis*) and the treasures stored in the royal palace (*basileia*)'. No writer spoke of the treasures being guarded in a fortified place.

The material brought to light during the excavations of the Acropolis, from the trenches of W. K. Loftus and Marcel Dieulafoy, but mainly during the period of complete clearance by Jacques de Morgan, evidently did not show traces of treasures which would have been preserved but it did include remarkable records.

403
Horns and ears of bulls from the capitals of the Hypostyle Hall, found scattered in a baked brick cistern on the Acropolis tell
Pillet archives
© Musée du Louvre/Christian Larrieu

Amongst the architectural elements belonging to the Achaemenid period, a bell-shaped column base inscribed with the name of Xerxes was found at the beginning of the excavations.[12] Of course, other fragments of stone architecture have been mentioned in individual reports but not enough to let one believe in the existence of a columned building. The other sectors excavated at Susa delivered much the same. A curious phenomenon, however, is the abundance of fragments of horns and ears of stone bulls, remains of Achaemenid capitals, particularly numerous and concentrated in what was, it seems, a mud-brick cistern, perhaps a well, built during the Elamite period, but used and transformed much later.

Stone vases, hardstone cups and alabaster bottles were relatively numerous on the Acropolis in comparison with the other sectors at Susa.[13] Other luxury tableware, sherds of Greek red-figure ware, were found in one location, it would seem, during the first excavation.[14] Finally, two very remarkable objects were found on the southern flank of the Acropolis: the bronze lion weight and the bronze knucklebone weight, inscribed in Greek.[15] These luxury items would indicate that the area of the Acropolis, the most protected area at Susa, was not only a refuge or seat of the garrison, but also a place where objects of value were secured.

THE 'PALACE' DONJON

Since the excavations of Roland de Mecquenem between 1928 and 1933, the remains of the southern point of the Ville Royale, architecture, architectural elements and objects have been the subjects of discussions which, unfortunately, were not based on solid fact. The very badly preserved remains represent several periods of occupation. Also, the excavations were undertaken and published in a very summary way. The poor data available were often used to back up contradictory hypotheses; they have been re-examined in detail by L. Martinez-Sève who was able to demonstrate that this sector was still occupied at the beginning of the sixth century AD, basing his dating on a Roman bust.[16]

The excavations

At the origin of all speculation was the presence in this area of numerous and obvious Achaemenid architectural elements and inscriptions which led to the hypothesis of a royal Achaemenid building in this privileged spot. As early as 1852 Loftus, the discoverer of the Apadana, had found at the Donjon, 'another columnar edifice'.

Marks and stamps on fired clay products

Albert Hesse

BRICK MARKS

While meticulously measuring the terracotta architectural elements, bricks as well as tiles, we had an opportunity to observe certain details of their manufacture and installation, especially a particularly discreet marking system.

On the Apadana tell we find terracotta bricks (1 foot square) marked on four sides *in situ* in certain well-preserved parts of the walls. The marks are original, and consist of one to three bars across in relief which were produced by a corresponding notch in the construction mould. By looking at their position on the side and in distinguishing between the lower and upper faces, one can tell that they form a repertoire of five different motifs. The marked bricks represent at most a quarter of the total production of bricks. Yet by considering only the production without markings, we can confirm the presence of a minimum of six workshops (in the restricted sense of one mould per workshop and not taking into account that one mould can give two different marks according to the direction in which it is used). The measurement of all identified marked bricks allows a very precise distinction to be made between three of the workshops, with a very small dispersion for each, but shows that the hypothesis of one workshop for all the bricks without marks, with a much wider dispersion, is certainly underestimated. The presence of these marks across all the points of the Apadana terrace where the brick appears is a new clue to the remarkable homogeneity of the construction, because the mark with centred bar not only appears in the construction of the Hypostyle Hall but also in the Residence.[1]

This homogeneity is also confirmed if the identical marks observed by Noëmi Daucé on the unglazed ornamental relief bricks are taken into account.[2] The existence of one large workshop producing the different but related construction materials must therefore be entertained.

404
above left
Bricks with vertical ribs in relief
Darius constructions on the Apadana
photograph by Albert Hesse

405
above right
Stamped motif of lion *passant*
Susa collections, unknown provenance,
probably foundation of the west wall
of the Residence
photograph by Albert Hesse

THE STAMPS

Throughout the excavations at Susa, a relatively large number of terracotta material was found carrying a mark which can be described in general terms as an 'animal *passant*' and which can sometimes be identified as a lion, or at least feline. There are some three sources of records which can be examined: the ancient finds of the Apadana tell,[3] the group of stamps housed in the stores at Susa,[4] and, most importantly, the tiles discovered at the Shaur Palace.[5]

On the Apadana tell, the excavations of the 1970s did not allow for any study of such stamps, neither on-site (floors of Court C1 to the west of the Residence in tiles of one cubit or of Courts C2 and C3 to the east, in 1-foot bricks), nor even scattered. There were some found earlier, however. As Mecquenem noted: 'amongst the brick tiles we found five pieces of the lion passant to the right'. We cannot add to this because one or other of these lions, which he already seemed to know about, can probably be found, but without the possibility of identification. In the stores at Susa, 20 stamps with a great variety of animals *passant* were found: only three types have a duplicate from the same stamp. These stamped bricks have an inventory number but no indication of provenance. Four of them were produced from the same mould in a setting at the end of a stalk; they were no doubt from another period. Some animals are very clearly lions, others may be badly drawn lions or dogs or even goats, mostly *passant* to the right. They appear in relief on the base of a stamp which was more often than not rectangular, sometimes oval. The stamp was often badly impressed and identification is not always certain due to the softness of the terracotta onto which it was applied and from which it could have been badly removed. In these conditions, the dimensions of the stamp outline, clearer than the relief, can be an excellent complementary criterion in distinguishing or linking certain impressions.[6] It is important to note that the supports, often broken, on which these stamps were applied are exclusively bricks.

The Shaur Palace is a major source of information as it is the only place where the impressions could be observed *in situ* on the tiled floors. A well-made lion *passant* to the right was usually found when the stamp (rectangular 7.2 x 8.4 cm) was well applied, on tiles of one cubit (average sides of 46.6 cm) which belonged to the Hypostyle Hall: 268 examples are certain; 86 others, hard to read, probably belong to this type.

406
above left
**Floor tiles in the Shaur Palace
stamped with the lion** *passant*
photograph by Albert Hesse

407
above right
**Squares marked in the middle
of a small circle, Shaur Palace**
photograph by Albert Hesse

There is little doubt that these marks are Achaemenid; that they were therefore exclusively from the period of Artaxerxes II is not so certain inasmuch as the tiles of this palace pose multiple and complex homogeneity problems which are difficult to relate here in detail.[7] Indeed, the Hypostyle Hall of the Shaur Palace has tiles without marks from two different provenances according to their dimensions, stamped tiles 'lion *passant*' in a rectangular stamp, and finally tiles marked strangely in the centre by a simple small circle seemingly obtained by applying the end of a tube. In other areas (Building III, court 639) this circular mark, applied on bricks of one foot this time, is mixed with a small number of bricks without marks,[8] some with animal stamps (lion or barking dog *passant* to the left) in a large oval. It is interesting to note that this oval stamp on bricks of one foot, like some others found *in situ* or scattered across the palace, is represented in the corpus of the stores described above.[9]

If one adds to this that several tiles of this palace are also made in terracotta of one foot, it is clear that the supply of materials is extremely disparate and was not made especially for the building. This mix of production looks like an indication of recycling in several areas, more for the construction than for the restoration of the floors.[10]

This disparity in appearance must have obstructed the builders right from the start, and this may explain why it is possible to see a coating in several areas, used to harmonise the floor over the tiles. The stamps, which we do not know for certain whether they were decorative, symbolic or simply workshop marks, were then lost from sight. Their frequent imperfection, as well as their feeble contribution to decoration in the case of the small circles and finally their coating, would point towards this last hypothesis.

1. HESSE, 1971.
2. N. Daucé, this volume, ch. X.
3. MECQUENEM, 1947: 18.
4. HESSE, 1973.
5. R. Boucharlat, this volume, ch. XII.
BOUCHARLAT and LABROUSSE, 1979.
6. HESSE 1972; BOUCHARLAT and
LABROUSSE. 1979.
7. HESSE 1972; BOUCHARLAT and
LABROUSSE, 1979.
8. BOUCHARLAT and LABROUSSE,
1979, fig. 24.
9. HESSE, 1973: pl. IX, no. 7.
10. From the places where pieces for reuse
could have been obtained, we should absolutely
exclude the buildings of Darius on the Apadana
mound, as attested by the absence of stamps
and the dimensions.

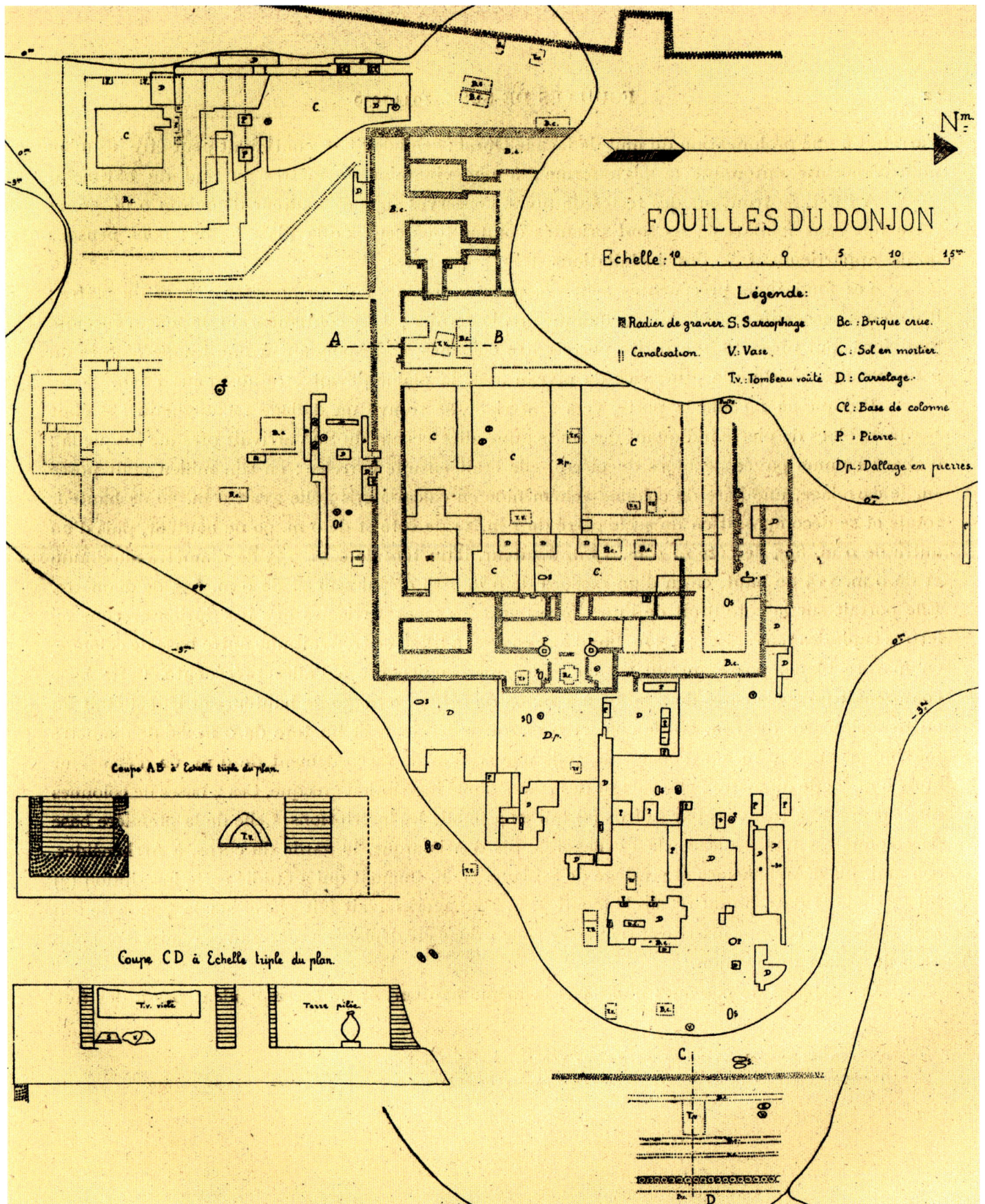

FOUILLES DU DONJON

Echelle: 10 . . . . 0 . . . . 5 . . . 10 . . . 15

Légende:

Radier de gravier   S: Sarcophage   Bc: Brique crue.

Canalisation.   V: Vase   C: Sol en mortier.

T.v: Tombeau voûté   D: Carrelage.

Cl: Base de colonne

P: Pierre

Dp: Dallage en pierres.

Coupe AB à Echelle triple du plan.

Coupe CD à Echelle triple du plan.

408

The only plan of the excavations of the upper layers of the Donjon

It brings together diverse architectural elements, most of which are modest structures that reuse existing materials such as column bases and pieces of stone plinth, glazed bricks of the Achaemenid period or Greek inscriptions. From this complex plan there emerges a rectangular structure of which the mud-brick foundation survives between two gravel sleeves. Surrounded by Achaemenid architectural debris, this construction, whose foundation techniques vaguely recall those of the palace of Darius, suggested that there had been a palace in this spot.

MECQUENEM, 1934: 60

None of the stone elements, however, was *in situ*. Some had been reused in more recent buildings, others had been dispersed: fragments of fluted shafts, small column bases, plaques and 'cornices' (actually wall plinths). Better still, Loftus brought to light bell-shaped bases one of which had a trilingual inscription of Artaxerxes II (A2sb), a base which Dieulafoy rediscovered and brought to the Louvre as well as two square bases, one with 1.14 m sides, (like those of the Shaur,[17] and also the small Court A of the Residence of Darius),[18] the other with sides of 1.05 m; both had an inscription in Greek. These bases were rediscovered by Mecquenem during his excavation which brought to light at least two other square bases with sides of 95 cm; one has a trilingual inscription by Artaxerxes II (A2sb), the same as that which the inscribed fragments from the Shaur Palace carry.[19] In addition, other evidence of Achaemenid architecture appeared: two orthostats of half-height figures climbing a staircase, like those of the Shaur Palace; other *bas relief* fragments and the decorated limestone plaques; no less than 50 pieces of plinth, reused as floor tiles, the decorated pieces face down;[20] not counting the large numbers of glazed bricks, whole or broken.

Traces of the Seleucid and Parthian periods were equally very numerous, also reused as building materials: a dozen pieces of sculpture, some from the Hellenistic period, but all the others, with the exception of a Roman bust, Parthian in date.[21]

The Achaemenid fragments reused during the Parthian era could have been found *in situ* or, it was thought, taken from the ruins of Darius' Palace. An apparently convincing argument appeared to support the thesis of an Achaemenid

409

Fragment of a stone plinth intended to decorate the base of the mud-brick walls
height 43 cm, length varying between 28 to more than 40 cm

About 50 pieces were found at the Donjon, reused as floor tiles, front face down. They were probably taken from the Shaur Palace, where several pieces were found although none was *in situ*

410
**Fragment of an orthostat in grey limestone
found at the Donjon, representing at half
life-size the bottoms of the robes of two
figures, one carrying an unidentified object,
the other a spear**
MECQUENEM, 1947, pl. VI, 2

building in this location – the identification at certain places of foundations in gravel pits. This technique at Susa is an innovation of the Achaemenid period, largely put into practice, as we have seen, in the buildings of Darius and Xerxes and, using a different technique, in that of Artaxerxes II at the Shaur Palace. At the Donjon, the excavator could observe that the foundations of the walls were dug 2.55 m deep, then a layer of gravel 75 cm deep was poured into the trench. Above this, a course of baked bricks (sides of 31 cm) was laid, then courses of mud bricks with sides of 32 cm, forming a foundation 1.75 m deep which reached ground level. In plan, the space between these foundation walls and the sides of the wider trench was filled with gravel. This foundation technique was different from that which was used for the Palace of Darius, but the objection is that the implementation was not uniform at the Residence, at the Darius Gate and the Propylaeum.[22] The implementation was less elaborate at the Donjon, but there again, the Shaur Palace, with its continuous layer of gravel foundations for each building, indicates the use of a simpler technique.

Meagre results

In the meandering, unedited excavation reports and the publications by Mecquenem, we note that there are several buildings, but discovered less than 3 m under the surface, of which we do not know their stratigraphic relationship. In the south-west was a small, almost square, construction of 9 x 10 m, in mud brick, where the fragments of the upper level were in terracotta bricks and tiles, and the lower level was a 'lime and gravel floor which once had been painted red', according to the excavation report, a technique well identified for the floors of the Residence of Darius, but these floors are described later, not as 'concrete', but as plaster painted red.[23] Some 'fine Achaemenid mud bricks' were identified near them. Further to the east, mud-brick foundations 2.2 m wide resting on a layer of shingle, like those mentioned above, were found. Without going into detail, this area was abundant with pieces of column shafts and capitals; fragments of copies of Darius' foundation charter (DSf); a trilingual inscription by Xerxes; a round base with a trilingual inscription by Artaxerxes II (A2sb); a Darius (I or II) tablet inscribed in Elamite; staircase orthostats; fragments of plinths; stamped bricks with lion and horse motifs; a sandstone stele with hieroglyphs; and numerous glazed bricks.[24] To the north of this building, the two Achaemenid-type bases with a Greek inscription, already seen by Loftus, rested on the tiled floor.

A more important building stands out from the descriptions and the rare finds of the excavators. It was a rectangular construction, 54 x 36 m,[25] floored with terracotta tiles covered in plaster. The main door was to the north. There would have been another opening to the south. A large central space could be observed, a courtyard, 40 x 29 m,[26] where the floor was partly made of stone tiles, amongst which were reused fragments inscribed in Greek. The west wing, 16.6 m wide, was more important than the east wing (8.6 m wide). Only the main walls had foundations, using a mass of mud bricks resting on a layer of gravel; the other walls had no foundations or only had mud bricks as foundations.

In the other buildings, outside and to the east, which were labelled as 'common', some walls were founded on rows of large stones, of which some were parts of Achaemenid stones.

Such is the available data: unedited reports, a published general plan and two summary stratigraphic sections. Despite the complete excavation of the area there is no coherent overall plan available. The outline of the foundations and the walls describe several distinct buildings probably belonging to different periods up to the Sassanian era, as Mecquenem thought, and as was confirmed by Martinez-Sève. The excavator identified, amongst the recycling, some 'marble tiles' in a paved alley, 'often debris of ancient Parthian steles', of which one was inscribed.[27] It was a Greek inscription dating from the beginning of the Christian era, on a plaque obtained by sawing a floor tile.[28] It is clear that part or all of the buildings and repairs were largely post-Achaemenid.[29]

Lack of space and no traces of a palace

The available data apparently led to the consideration of the existence of an Achaemenid building, such as some people wished to find there. It is what a lot of excavators thought when searching for the building which would have replaced Darius' Apadana, damaged under Artaxerxes I. Other than the occasional remains of some large walls, the Donjon revealed Achaemenid type, round and square column bases, the inscriptions of several sovereigns and other architectural elements, such as stone plinths and glazed bricks. In addition, potsherds were found in this area, characteristic of the fifth and fourth centuries BC, as well as Aramaic graffiti of the same period. Finally, a nearby well delivered a collection of ivories, generally broken, produced in various parts of the Achaemenid Empire and probably deposited there towards the end of the fourth century BC.

411
Greek inscription carved on a square column base of Achaemenid type, reused upside down
Found at the Donjon where the majority of the Greek documents of Susa were found. It is datable to the end of the third or the first half of the second century BC. It is in honour of a certain Arrheneides 'Strategist of Susiana', Governor of Susa and of the region for the Seleucid kings
Susa Museum

These remains are undeniably Achaemenid, in particular the architectural fragments. Amongst these, can be noticed not only the column bases but fragments of shafts. However, other than Darius' Hypostyle Hall no other Achaemenid building with stone shafts is known. The fragments from the Donjon were therefore brought from the Apadana. On this basis it can be doubted whether the other architectural elements were in their original location at the Donjon.

Other arguments can be advanced against the hypothesis of a royal palace: the lack of space offered by this southern point of the Ville Royale (110 x 60 m), which could not even have contained the Hypostyle Hall of Darius, and more obviously, the absence of any important building. The only building known, in the centre, covered barely 1800 m². It was organised into several rooms of modest proportions, around a space in the centre, with no indication that it was covered; it was probably a courtyard. The hypothesis of a temporary royal palace is weak, more so because there was no important room which could have played the part of an audience chamber.

Nonetheless, the Donjon area could have been occupied during the Achaemenid period, perhaps by the elite, as the ivories thrown in the well and other rare Greek and Egyptian objects testify. As to the other objects, also Achaemenid in origin, they were probably taken from the Palace of Darius and perhaps from that of the Shaur after the collapse of the empire. From the Seleucid period and over several centuries, the area of the Donjon was an important location, and it may even have been the location of public and religious buildings, as several Greek inscriptions testify.

Discoveries post-1968

New data surfaced in an unexpected manner in 1968 when the plain to the west of the tells, on the other side of the river Shaur, was cultivated. The bulldozer used to level the area hit several round column bases, much smaller than those of Darius' Hypostyle Hall. Excavation was agreed upon jointly by the Susa mission and the centre for Iranian archaeological research. Six excavation campaigns and three seasons of electronic prospecting produced the general plan of a new complex of around 4 hectares, facing Darius' Palace.

There were many new elements: the first evidence of a true palace outside the walls of Susa; a work of the fourth century BC, much later than Darius, because inscriptions allowed most of the construction to be attributed to Artaxerxes II; a plan showing solutions until then unseen in Achaemenid architecture; fragments of stone architecture, rare on the tells of Susa; characteristic new techniques; and lastly, the first examples of Achaemenid figurative painting. In addition, it was clear that this palace of the last century of the Achaemenid era had been built in several stages.

Several years later, in 1977, a stone staircase of Achaemenid manufacture was found not far from there, in the basement of a house in the modern town of Shush. This assembly of recycled Achaemenid blocks, which could have come from the Shaur Palace, was the first evidence of a stone staircase at Susa.

These architectural remains, along with the Palace of Darius, make up the totality of the evidence for the activity of the builders of the Achaemenid sovereigns at Susa. The column bases found in isolation here and there in a radius of several kilometres around the tells of Susa are far from certain clues. That they were moved to be reused after the Achaemenid period is the most likley hypothesis, but their original emplacement was not necessarily in one of the known palaces. If there had been Achaemenid buildings other than the palaces of Darius and Artaxerxes II, the image that we have of Achaemenid Susa would be different.

412

The Shaur Palace in 1971
The Hypostyle Hall on the right with the round column bases, on the left the northern portico with the square column bases. In the background, on the right, the Acropolis tell on which stands the Château

THE SHAUR PALACE

The palace outside the walls gets its name, given to it by archaeologists, from the river which runs alongside it today – the same river which once ran further to the east, at the foot of Darius' Palace. Whatever the case, a bridge must have been necessary to reach it from Darius' Palace but no trace of one has been found. The entire area is flat and it is only the ruins themselves which, until the excavations, created a small projection 2 m high which Marcel Dieulafoy had already identified.[30] The location of this complex, unlike that of Darius' Palace situated 18 m above the river, was very favourable to its integration in an easily irrigable, to the point of floodable, area.

The flat topography of the plain did not limit the builders and allowed them to conceive a complex at least 220 x 150 m, with open-air spaces inside and perhaps others, greater still, outside. The most important, in the middle (70 x 60 m maximum), could have been a large courtyard, or more probably a garden. The reconstruction of the whole in elevation is made difficult by the poor preservation of the remains; indeed, only three buildings retained elements of their elevation, whilst the evidence for three or four others is only their foundations. The built

413
The Shaur Palace in 1971
Seen from the Susa tells after two seasons of excavation. The remains of the Hypostyle Hall and of the northern portico are already unearthed. Beyond it extends the flood plane of the Karkheh river which flows 2 km further on

sections, on foundations of shingle and stones, contrast with the outside or open-air spaces, without foundations, as the geophysical surveys conducted in 1971, 1974 and 1977 under the direction of Albert Hesse were able to show. These surveys, using the electrical resistivity method on the 2 m deep shingle foundations, provided a textbook case: they were undertaken whilst a constant dialogue was maintained between surveyors and archaeologists, and the results were often very clear. Some of the boundaries of the foundations were interpreted with as much clarity by the prospectors as the archaeological soundings provided by outlining the foundation plan of most of the buildings. It was these surveys which allowed the reconstruction of the whole, whilst the excavations alone would have missed the whole western section of the plan and definitely made it impossible to understand the whole. To be convinced, it is enough to compare the plan of the excavated sections with that of the parts reconstructed using the plan made from surveys conducted by Hesse.

The excavation

As revealed by the surveys and excavations, the Shaur Palace, viewed from the river, consisted of a hypostyle hall in front of a complex which was oriented similarly to the Palace of Darius (16° east), but with a principal axis perpendicular to it; this hall was surrounded by porticoes on all four sides. Behind and on either side of this hall, the building complex must not have been as tall as the hypostyle hall. The southern building has disappeared, the northern structure is partially preserved, organised around a tiled courtyard. Behind the hypostyle hall, to the west, a portico gave access to a central, un-roofed area, enclosed to the south and the west by buildings which no longer exist; and to the north originally by a long building. This building was completely rebuilt during a second phase, according to a very different plan, constructed on a 2 m-high terrace: a central columned hall with two porticoed, perpendicular façades, one opening onto the garden and the other on to a courtyard. Of the other buildings, further to the west we only have a general outline of the foundations; equally, it is from the shingle foundations that the curtain wall, which protected the hypostyle hall to the east, can be reconstructed.

Electrical resistivity survey of the Shaur Palace

Albert Hesse

From 1970, the Shaur Palace was the object of the first geophysical investigations, with a fruitless attempt at magnetic measurements. Most of the electrical resistivity survey took place the following year, between 2 and 18 March 1971. It was completed in February 1974. Then, in February 1977, there were several extensive exploratory profiles when it turned out that, at the limits of the archaeological soundings for the recognised building, there were adjoining structures also built on foundations. The totality of the work having been published in an article dedicated to this survey,[1] it is sufficient here to recall its main results.

As has already been mentioned in Chapter 5, the first issue which must be tackled when engaging in an electrical survey is that of the distance between the

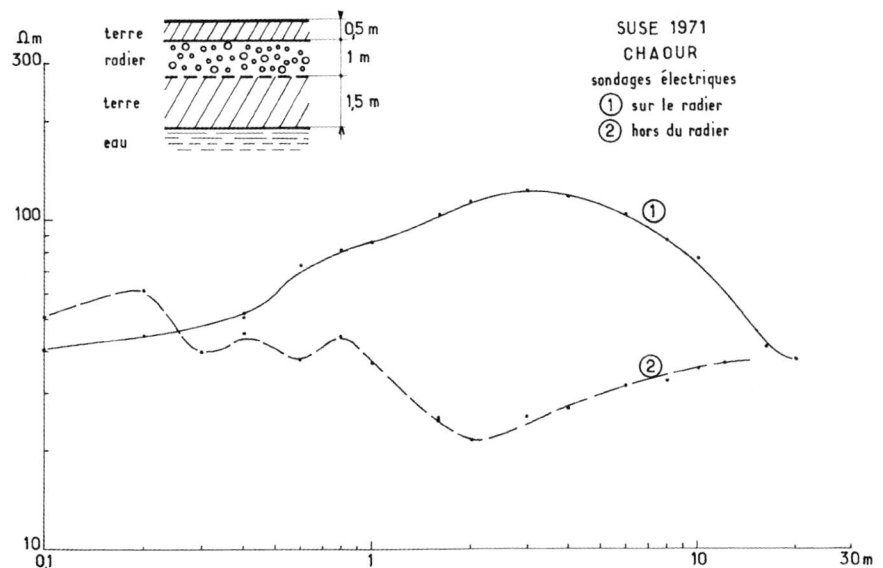

SUSE 1971
CHAOUR
sondages électriques
① sur le radier
② hors du radier

Two preliminary geophysical surveys of the Shaur Palace
1. conducted on the foundations
2. conducted outside the foundations
drawing by Albert Hesse

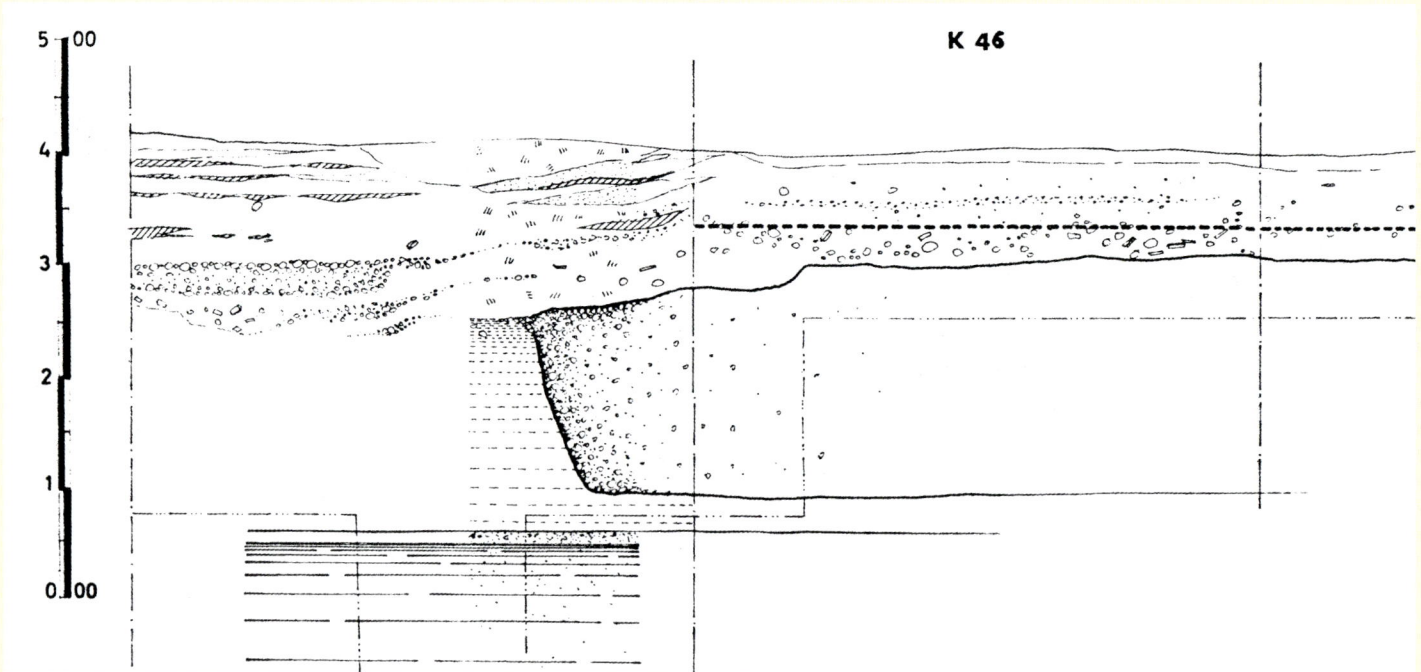

415
Cross-section of the *galette* foundations of the Shaur Palace
At the time of the observations the foundations reached down
almost to the level of the water table
drawing by Albert Hesse

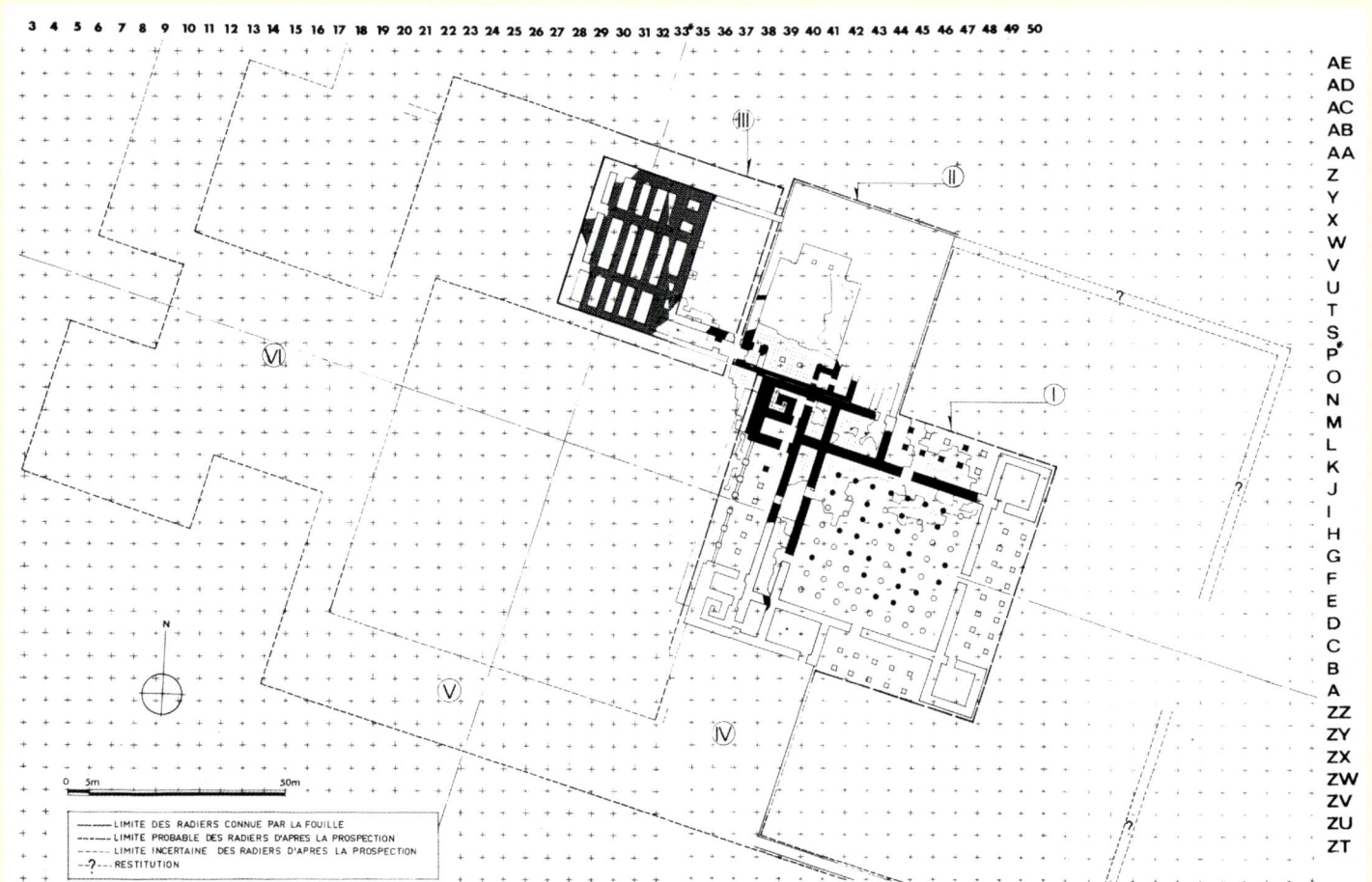

416a
The Shaur Palace
Each of the three buildings was built on a foundation layer of gravel (see resistivity levels, facing page).
The Hypostyle Hall, probably surrounded by porticoes on all four sides,
projected forward from the complex towards the Darius Palace 300 m to the east

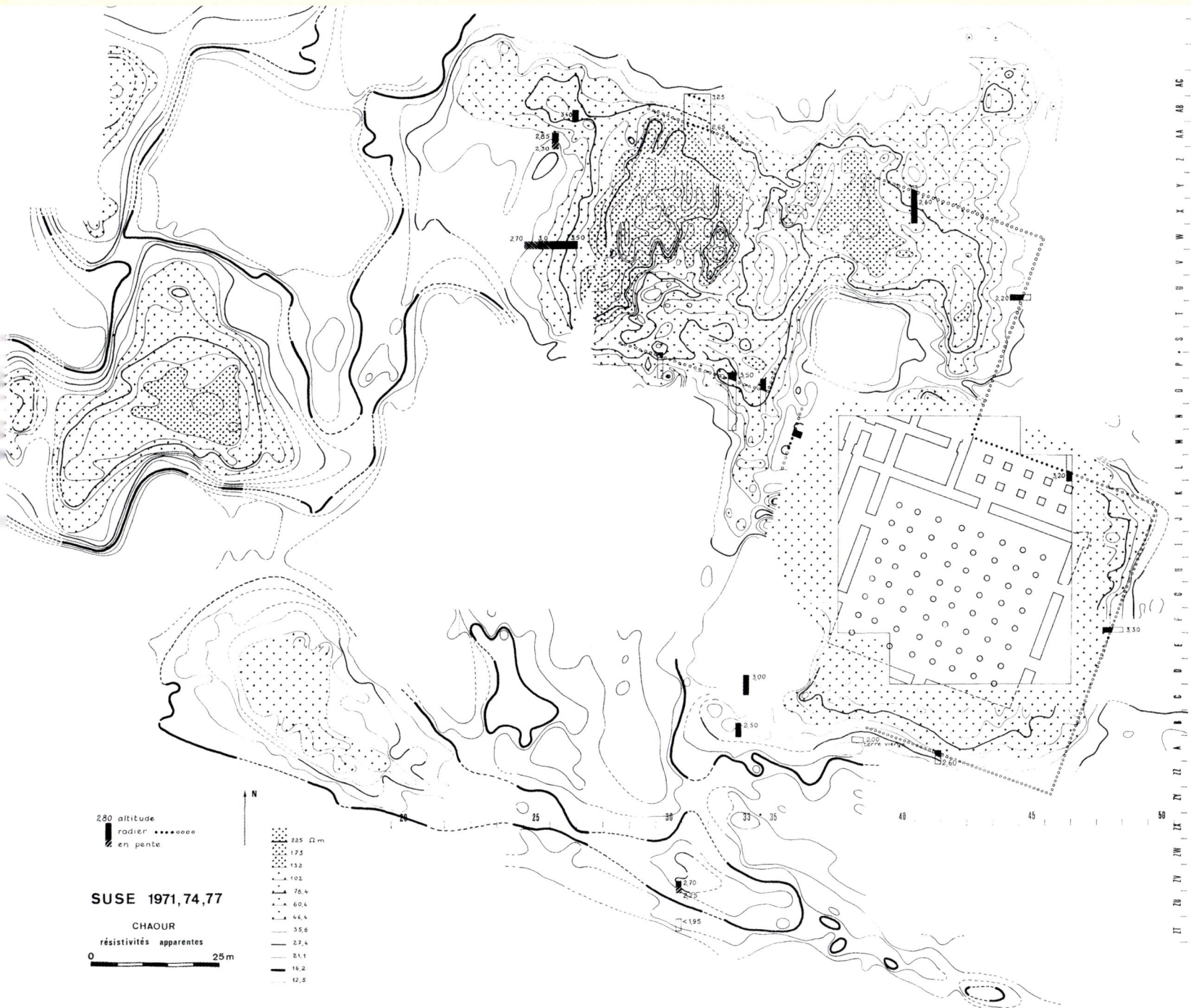

416b
Resistivity levels of the Shaur Palace

electrodes, because the depth of the investigation is directly dependent on this factor. The technique of electrical sounding easily allows adjustment to be made by running two tests, one on the structure to be explored, the other outside it.

The results here were more reliable due to a regular horizontal stratification. By luck, the first excavations had just revealed how ideal the site was for resistivity surveying – with a near continuous high resistivity layer of foundation gravel sandwiched between two conductive layers: the relatively consistent silt of the archaeological layers above, the water table below.

Two soundings were therefore made in this area. It is clear that these diverge at the depths where structures were encountered, but come together again at the extremities when the terrains at upper and lower depths were little different. One can then choose between two extreme values (minimum and maximum), the compromise of an 'optimum' allowing the drawing up, without too many measurements, of a sufficiently detailed image of the buried structure. The distance between the electrodes was therefore chosen at 2.5 m. This application of the method in almost ideal terrain conditions, called 'tabular', as required by the theory, showed that the procedure was highly appropriate.[2]

The plan obtained not only contributed to the direction of further stages of excavation, but also gave an overall image of one of the major aspects of the construction: the foundations which, without the survey, would only have appeared in occasional verification soundings. The resistivity zones, whether they were indicated with a thick line or, for the stronger ones by a series of dots, clearly show the right angled nature of Building I and Building II. The courtyard which separates them did not need foundations and is clearly identified by a zone of low values.

The biggest contribution which this survey has brought to archaeological knowledge mainly concerns the picture which it gave us of the overall plan of the Shaur Palace. If it had been solely down to the excavation, the appearance of the palace would have been very different. It would have represented only a small part of what the resistivity plan indicates. On the western edge of the cleared building, two well localised anomalies, symmetrical to the axis of the Hypostyle Hall, revealed the magnitude of this concept. Maybe it opened onto gardens or individual pavilions which were suggested towards the west by some other anomalies of high resistivity rather badly described by a few isolated profiles hastily created. To the south and in relation with one of these structures, a large linear anomaly stretches towards the east: it was not fully surveyed because of its length, but it might possibly be a curtain wall enclosing the palace on a vast plan of several hectares. Very eroded, perhaps less sturdily built than elsewhere, all these structures were only checked by excavating at certain points. Several amongst them, unfortunately, remain hypothetical because of the interruption of the excavations in 1978.

1. Hesse, 1979b.
2. The project has, indeed, been a good teaching example in a manual we prepared at the time: HESSE, 1978.

418

**Schematic plan of the shingle foundations
of the three excavated buildings**
The oldest are those of Building III, very
elongated; they must have supported a
structure of which only traces survive

Building techniques and materials

Like the Palace of Darius, mud bricks, terracotta bricks and tiles for the floors and grey limestone for the column bases were the basic materials for the buildings of the Shaur Palace. Gravel and shingle were used in the foundations. The plaster, which left few traces in Darius' Palace, is present on the walls and the floors of the Shaur; on the other hand, the red plaster floors, as found in the Residence, are completely absent. Elements of painted plaster have been found at different points, but if the location of some decorations is certain, the same cannot be said for the glazed bricks and the grey limestone orthostats. There were so few remains that the elements originally planned for this palace cannot be confirmed. There must have been wood, for the column shafts in particular, but none remains.

The foundations and the drainage

The foundation techniques used were not as elaborate as those of Darius' Palace. Here the footprint of each building was dug into the compact clay soil of the plain to a depth of 2.3 m for Building I, more than 2.5 m for Building III, but only 1.5 m for Building II. Each trench was then uniformly filled with shingle. When seen in section, the exterior boundaries of these shingle layers form a very neat bevelled edge. The sides were wider than the outside walls of the buildings by 1 to 2 m. The foundations did not reflect the elevation, unlike those at the Palace of Darius. In one building (Building II), the foundations do give an indication of the floor plan: the shingle layer is reduced to a depth of 30 cm under the building's courtyard and is even nonexistent in the centre. This was no doubt intentional, as the absence of foundations caused the tiles to subside from the outset, so as to allow rain water drainage. The presence of drains near the exterior to the east and the west confirms this building technique.[31]

At the same time as the foundations were being completed, drains were being fitted out, as in Building II; more often outside the foundations, as in Building I, alongside the central garden; or between the foundations of Buildings II and III. A more complex system was identified to the north of Building III: it was made up of two drains, belonging to two different phases, the most recent corresponding to the restoration of the terraced building. They are constructions over 1 m deep with an internal conduit 30 cm wide and 40 cm high. A layer of earth was spread over the shingle to seat the walls and the floors, except for the column bases where coarse-grained sand was used to allow the levels to be adjusted.

The walls

The walls were made of mud brick, without baked-brick foundations as was the case in Darius' Palace. Their thickness varied according to the importance of the building: from four and a half bricks (1.5 m) to six and a half bricks, the bricks measuring 32–33 cm per side and 10 cm thick. The wall faces then had three coatings of mud plaster, successively finer – the last 4 mm thick and recognisable by its greenish hue.

A layer of plaster was applied over these coatings to the base of the walls. It was found in the Hypostyle Hall; to the west of it in the long hall and the portico; also on the end wall of the portico of the courtyard of Building II; finally, outside, on the eastern face of the terrace of Building III. Above this smooth and bare plinth, the painted decoration started in some areas.

None of the preserved passageways had doors. Only one example of a hinge, with its bronze socket sealed with lead, was found, but completely out of context, in a trench of Building III.

419
General plan of the remains of the Shaur Palace
Representing around a third of the surface constructions

420

The northern portico of the Shaur Palace with columns on square bases and the central hall with round bases
This layout is the opposite of that of Darius' Apadana

421

The bottom section of the walls of the main hall was covered by an 80 cm high layer of plaster, forming a plinth
It was in front of this north wall of the hall that were found, face down, the fragments of paintings which must have decorated the walls above the plinth.

The column bases

It must be noted straightaway that only the column bases were made of stone. The shafts and the capitals, if these last existed, must have been made of wood; but nothing has been found. The material used was a grey Zagros limestone, of the same mediocre quality as that used for the columns of the Apadana of Darius. It is possible to see the sense of economy which led certain round bases to be constructed using not one monolithic block, but two drums, with either horizontal or diagonal joins. In the first case, the two drums were held together in the centre by a steel tenon set in lead; in the second case, they were held together using three tenons set around the periphery. Some bases showed traces of old repairs, some possibly as far back as the construction phase. The cracks are held together using steel staples buried into rectangular cavities or gently dovetailed. Similarly, the breaks were carefully re-carved into regular shapes which were then filled by skilfully shaped pieces. The mends could be masked with grey cement, which has sometimes survived in the cracks.[32] This colour clue, added to the polish, shows that the bases were not painted. It is true that splashes of blue paint were found at the bases of several column bases but the paint covered, not the carefully polished stone base, but most likely the wooden shafts.[33]

Round, bell-shaped bases, as well as square bases had several different templates. In Building I, the round bases of the Hypostyle Hall and the square bases of the northern portico, all follow the same pattern: 1.14 m in diameter or side; the diameter of the shafts were therefore the same (92 cm), as well as the total height of the base (70 cm); indeed 1.14 m is almost half the size of the bases of the Hypostyle Hall of Darius.[34] On the other hand, the square bases of the western portico of the Shaur Palace were smaller (92 cm); none of the other bases, round or square, generally broken, was found *in situ*, so that their original location is unknown. It is possible, however, to conjecture that the two bases of the southern portico of Building II were square and also measured 92 cm per side; indeed, by chance, amongst the fragments found there, four were of this type and were inscribed, each in one of the three cuneiform languages referring to Artaxerxes II inscription (A2sd). Elsewhere, for example in the area of Building III, two incomplete bases and some fragments, all found out of context, came from three round templates and three square templates. Thus not only did they use different modules or decorations according to the buildings, but also in one building, such as Building I, round and square bases could be found, the latter having at least two different templates. This diversity also occurred in the Apadana at Susa and in that of Persepolis, where the bases of each of the three porticoes have different decorations.[35] Palaces P and S at Pasargadae already had very different dimensions for the square bases of the Central Hall, that were much larger than those of the porticoes.[36]

The floors: bricks and tiles

All the preserved floors were tiled, both in the halls and the courtyards; they do not show any traces of red painted plaster, well known in Darius' Residence and in some buildings at Persepolis, such as the restored Harem building where some of the fragments of the original flooring was preserved, as well as in the Achaemenid palace of Babylon.[37] The terracotta floor bricks were then covered in a layer of plaster, possibly painted, of which there remains no trace.

Two forms of floor covering are attested, one using tiles with sides of 46 to 47.5 cm and around 8 cm thick; the others, smaller baked bricks 32 x 32 x 8 cm — the same size as the mud bricks. The reason for choosing one or the other of these shapes is not clear; indeed, tiles are most in evidence in the hypostyle hall and in the northern passageway, but also in different areas of the western parts of the

TYPE B

422
Drain cover and column base from the Shaur Palace

423

The best-preserved round column bases were in the north-west part of the Hypostyle Hall

Although complete, they show evidence of cracks present at the time of their installation. These faults were hidden by a layer of plaster. Other bases were made up of two drums tied with an iron crampon in the centre. Others still had been carefully repaired by the insertion of extra pieces

424

The traces of blue paint found at the foot of certain bases come probably from the wooden shafts which were plastered before being painted

In comparison with the staircases at Persepolis the one of the Shaur had the peculiarity of being covered, as indicated by the rooms forming a vestibule at the foot of the staircase and especially the thickness of the walls around it (1.4 and 1.9 m), too thick to be just parapets. In this case, the tiled courtyard to the north of the staircase was carefully isolated from the rest of the complex.

Building III would have consisted of a square central hall, with a portico to the front and a room to the back; the central hall would have been flanked by long rooms and, to the east, a row of small rooms and a portico was added. Thus reconstructed, the plan is not incongruous with Achaemenid architecture, although precise parallels are too few to amount to much. There are two examples at Persepolis that can be cited: the plan of the building known as the Harem, today transformed into a museum, or that of the small building between the Treasury and the rampart.[44] In the proposed reconstruction, the presence of the eastern portico and the positioning of the staircase, here at right angles to the terrace wall, as well as its roof, would be more original.

This building on a terrace is much more than an architectural tweak, it represents an important re-engineering which intervenes at the moment of the conception of the other buildings, at least those which were preserved (Buildings I and II) or even after their construction. The clues are in the rubbish thrown into the ditches dug in the foundations or in the filling up of the caissons with fragments of column bases, glazed bricks and an intact door socket, rejects from the building phase of the other structures, unless all this debris came, more simply, from the first Building III.

A stone staircase discovered to the north of the palace

The answer to the staircase giving access to the terrace, admittedly hypothetical, came several years after the excavation in 1977, with the fortuitous discovery of a new testimonial to Achaemenid architecture found 800 m north on the left bank of the Shaur. Six grey-limestone steps, similar to those of Achaemenid build, were found at a shallow depth. The stonework: pick carving, anathyrosis, worked with tooth-edged chisels, the polishing of visible parts, all indicated the characteristic techniques of the Achaemenid period.

No wall and no architectural element were found around the staircase. It was about 1.4 m wide and 90 cm high. Each step was made up of one, two or three blocks. All the pieces had moved, but they were manifestly arranged to make up a staircase. Some of the blocks originally had another function than that of a step: one was re-cut from a fragment of fluted column shaft; another was a large floor tile with a projecting border on four sides, a border which two other blocks have; another has preserved half of the seating for a dovetailed staple; finally the steps are not all the same length and some blocks were re-carved for their new usage.

There are two clues as to the date: firstly, the piece which would have belonged to a drum of a column shaft can have had no other possible provenance than Darius' Hypostyle Hall, the only structure with column shafts that we know at Susa, unless it was a discarded block; secondly the ceramic material identifiable belonged partly to the Achaemenid tradition, but mainly to the third century BC. That the staircase itself should have been put together and in place in the post-Achaemenid period does not exclude the possibility of an Achaemenid structure in this place, modified or transformed afterwards, but it is more likely that the elements had been taken from the Shaur Palace. If we accept this hypothesis, one question remains: in this last case, was the staircase made up by recycling older pieces or had these elements of column shaft or bordered tablet been added to the staircase blocks?

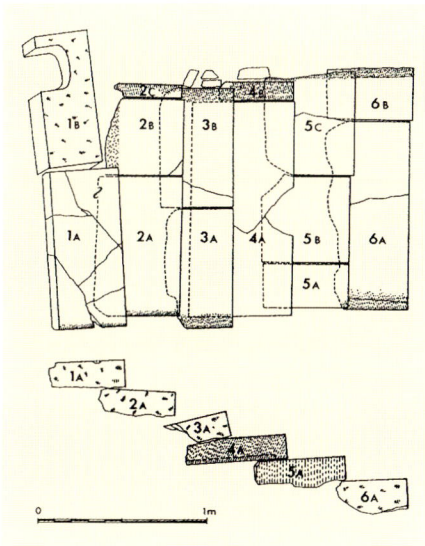

429
Axonometric view of the preserved part of the Shaur Palace
The central part, with no foundations, must have been a garden.
On the other two sides, the structures are barely suggested,
as their existence is based only on the traces of the pebble
foundations determined by geophysical surveys.
drawing by Daniel Ladiray

430
**Reconstructed in the garden of the Susa Museum, this small staircase of six steps,
1.4 m wide, was fortuitously found in a well to the north of the Shaur Palace**
The various elements are heterogeneous and certain blocks have been reused.
The whole was poorly laid on earth without foundations. It could represent the
remains of the staircase of Building III of the Palace, more than 3 m wide and
which must have had more than 15 steps.

431
Orthostat with a half life-size figure
climbing a staircase, wearing a long
pleated tunic, carrying a form of tray
with a duck's head terminal
52 x 25 cm, thickness 14 cm
Susa Museum

432
Hand holding a spear or bow

433
Fragments of bas-reliefs

above left
An archer in a short tunic climbing a staircase
Found on the surface in the area of the
Shaur Palace; preserved height 25 cm

above right
Representing an archer

WALL DECORATION

With the very remarkable exception of the paintings, the other elements of wall decoration were never found *in situ*; in addition there are so few of them, whether they be large stone blocks or parts of plinths or glazed bricks, as to make their use as decoration in the Shaur Palace very hypothetical.

Low relief sculpture

Low relief sculpture is represented above all by a complete orthostat 56 cm high with a figure climbing a staircase to the left; he wears a long pleated robe in the Persian fashion and carries some sort of tray with a duck-head end. This type of tribute carrier is well attested at Persepolis, at Darius' Palace and at that of Xerxes, seemingly sculpted to the same scale,[45] but the tray that the Shaur figure carries is very like an isolated case found at the Susa Donjon. Other testimonials to sculpture are small fragments belonging to a short skirted archer climbing a staircase to the right, the other a fragment of pleated robe at half scale,[46] a scale similar to that of the glazed brick figure representations 72 to 76 cm tall.[47]

The upper part of a block showing the head of a figure wearing rounded headwear but with pleats on the sides, perhaps a Mede, does not belong to an orthostat but to a parapet as the upper face of the block shows: partially visible, worked and very thick. This fragment may have been a parapet piece bordering, for example, the small eastern portico of Building III; it could not have decorated the staircase giving access to the terrace because this has been reconstructed as roofed. By contrast the staircase may have been decorated by large half-scale orthostats, such as the tribute bearer climbing a staircase and discussed above. Is it truly possible, however, to propose such a reconstruction with so few preserved elements?

The three plinth fragments pose the same problem of provenance. These wall pieces with vertical channels have a projecting cornice decorated with rosettes. The area of the Donjon provided several dozen pieces, with the decorated part face down, as they had been reused as floor tiles after the Achaemenid period. The row of rosettes was at the top: the upper border was narrowed to receive a course of bricks or other blocks, and only one border was worked and polished. The channels were not polished right to the extremity as the last centimetres were hidden by the ground.

The paintings

The fragments were found fallen on the ground of the north-western part of the Hypostyle Hall, and the best preserved reveal Achaemenid mural painting for the first time. There is no doubt that for a long time traces of colour on low relief sculpture at Persepolis had been known, but until then no fresco or painting on dry surfaces, and only a few non-figurative elements at Pasargadae. At Persepolis, stone sculpture in low relief showed the polychromy of the figures, the winged discs and the decorative borders; the surfaces of plaster column shafts confirmed geometric decorations. The colours were varied: black, white, blue, red, green and yellow. At Pasargadae, the little-known discoveries of E. Herzfeld had already shown colours on clay with some blue, some green, some yellow and two reds.[48] At Susa, at the Darius Gate, traces of blue and red paint were found on fragments of mud plaster. Elsewhere, at Persepolis as at Susa, the excavators sometimes brought to light potsherds used as pallets, indicated by the deposits of pigment preserved on the inside, two different reds and one blue.[49]

In the Hypostyle Hall of the Shaur, three painted representations are sufficiently well preserved that we may recognise the heads of figures almost life size, shown in profile as on the low relief sculpture at Persepolis. One is the head of a Mede; the other is that of an Arachosian, the third, of which only the face is visible, is not identifiable.

The analysis of certain pigments has shown that the blue had a base of copper oxide, one of the reds was ferrous oxide, but the vermillion red had been obtained from cinnabar (mercury ore). This use of the ore was unknown until then in Iran.

The glazed bricks

The 300-odd fragments of glazed brick dug up in the excavations were never found *in situ* but dispersed amongst different buildings. For the most part, they belonged to bricks similar to those of the compositions in the Residence, based on their dimensions, scale and style, and the same holds true elsewhere at Susa, at the Donjon and in practically every other area which was excavated. No report from older excavations omits to mention in passing the discovery of 'enamelled bricks', sometimes in great numbers. It is, however, unlikely that this decorative technique was used throughout Susa; it is because glazed bricks were found in great numbers in two sectors where Achaemenid architecture (Shaur) or supposedly Achaemenid (Donjon) survived, that it is sometimes proposed that there was ornamentation in that location, in addition to that of the Residence of Darius, but nothing proves this. At the Shaur, however, some fragments differ from all the panels and fragments confirmed in the Residence – they differ in scale and representation and in some rare cases, in the motifs represented. On the other hand, certain fragments can be linked to bricks found at the Donjon.[50] It should probably be concluded that there existed a workshop at the time of Artaxerxes II.

To conclude, as far as wall decoration is concerned the only paintings that are without doubt in their original location are the figure representations in the Hypostyle Hall of the Shaur, and in certain passages from it, and in Building II surfaces which were possibly uniformly blue, because it was the only colour found, without traces of any motif.

Inscribed fragments

Amongst the 14 fragments of inscribed base recovered on the Shaur tell, several lay on the surface; the others were found during the excavation of the palace destruction layer – but never *in situ* – or in the post-Achaemenid level and even in ditches of the Islamic period. The concentration of four of these fragments in the

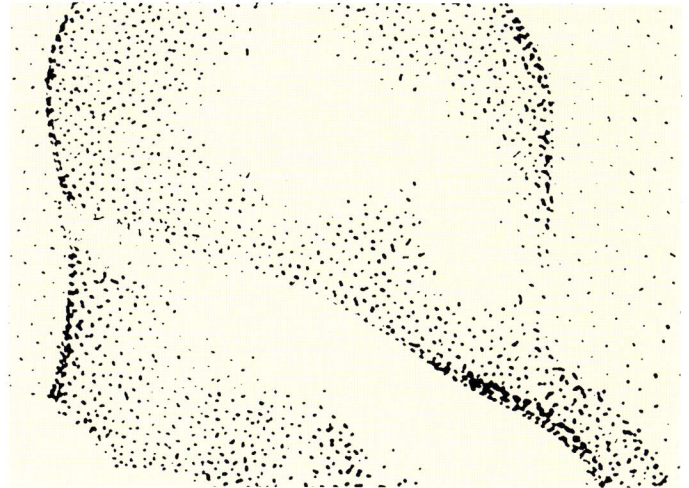

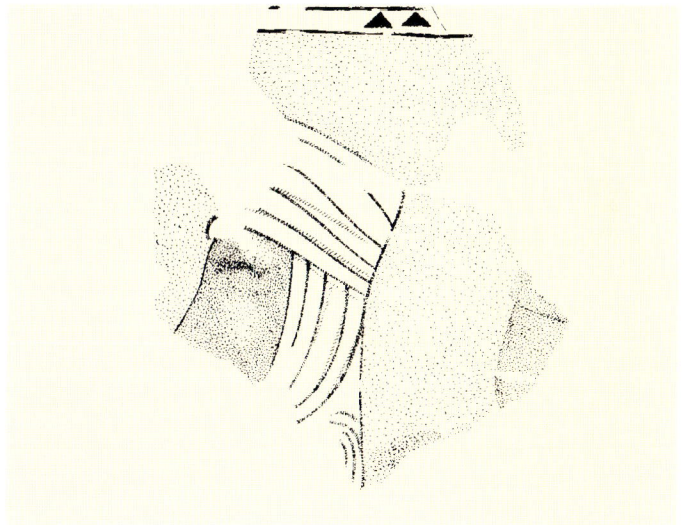

434
Fragments of restored mural paintings
Size of fragments 50 cm. Both were on a blue background,
the predominant decorative colour, also used on the columns

top left and right
Detail of a head wearing a rounded bonnet of the Median type

above left and right
A head covered with a *bashlyk*, the headdress of the Arachosians

435
Fragments before restoration

above left
Head of an Arachosian

above right
A bare head, barely distinct, above which the border of the panel is made
up of a series of red and white alternating triangles. In front of the figure,
an indistinct object

Fragment of a square column base whose precise location in the Shaur Palace is unknown
It has an Old Persian (below) and Babylonian (left) version of the Artaxerxes II inscription (A2Sd). This inscription is attested elsewhere in the palace through several different versions. The structure mentioned is not specified in the Babylonian and Elamite versions while the interpretation of the Old Persian version is still controversial: palace or 'paradise'

southern portico of Building II led to the reconstruction of two inscribed bases of medium size (92 cm sides). The Shaur Palace was subject to at least two phases of construction, followed by repair works of greater or lesser importance. As to the inscription fragments, they all belong to one trilingual inscription, that of Artaxerxes II (A2Sd). In these conditions, one must attribute the majority, if not the entirety, of the construction and repair of the palace to him; a predecessor or successor would not have failed to advertise his own works.[51]

All other fragments of this inscription – be they those found at the Shaur, or those from a base preserved in the stores of the Susa Museum – were studied by François Vallat who concluded that the A2Sd inscription was repeated on at least eight square bases, probably all trilingual. However, nearly all the inscribed bases found at the Shaur whose dimensions can be determined were of the medium template (92 cm); one other was of a smaller size (80 cm).[52] This leads one to conclude that neither the large square bases of the northern portico nor, probably, those of the symmetrical southern portico were inscribed. Where were these inscriptions carved? The two bases from the small southern portico in Building II were very probably inscribed, as several fragments were found in the area. In addition, we can also suppose that the bases of the western portico of Building I, which are of medium-size, or even those of the eastern portico, that have completely disappeared, were inscribed, but we have no indication of this. As for Building III, nothing is known of the initial building, neither the shape, nor the dimensions of the bases of the two reconstructed porticoes which leaves the way open to all hypotheses.

The other buildings and unbuilt spaces

The meagre details that we have about the other buildings of the Shaur Palace are thanks to the electronic survey results and a few control soundings. These surveys provided the outlines of several constructions and conversely indicated in the middle of the complex a large area without any foundations which was interpreted as a garden due to its dimensions. Structures which enclosed the garden to the west and to the south can only be said to be less important than Buildings I and III (initial build). Also, the existence of the wall which would have enclosed the Hypostyle Hall to the east is only suggested by a long and thin electrical anomaly following the orientation of the structures; it was only found to the south-east of the Hypostyle Hall, but was not looked for on the other two sides.[53]

THE FUNCTION OF THE SHAUR PALACE

The discovery of the Shaur Palace, a century after the first excavations of Darius' Palace in the middle of the nineteenth century, revealed the existence of at least one other royal complex at Susa, this time outside the perimeter defined by Darius. That this palace was private in character is very probable from its floor plan and its location in the plain outside the walls – but what was its function?

The possible answers depend on three different pieces of data: the certain dating to Artaxerxes II from the A2sd inscription; the repair work to Darius' Hypostyle Hall which, according to the inscription of Artaxerxes II A2sa, was damaged during the reign of his grandfather Artaxerxes I; and finally the occurrence of the Old Persian term, thought to read *paridaida* in the A2sd inscription.

At Persepolis, nearly all the Achaemenid sovereigns added a structure to those of their predecessors or completed a building started before them. There is nothing like this at Susa, despite what Strabo reports regarding the palace and the treasury which each monarch would have built. The Shaur Palace is a unique royal construction, undertaken after Darius, despite the problematic 'Donjon Palace'.

The Shaur Palace – a replacement for the damaged Hypostyle Hall?

The explanation often given for the building of the Shaur Palace is that of a columned hall, erected by Artaxerxes II whilst he repaired or rebuilt the hypostyle hall of his ancestor Darius. The project would have then been far more modest, as this new Hall was only roughly a third of the size of that of Darius and half its height. One can object that if the latter had only been damaged, the Residence itself had not been touched.[54] Why also build a 4-hectare complex so far from the Residence if the audience chamber alone with its annexes was to be replaced? In addition, it is known that the Persian kings had other, very standard, solutions for receptions and banquets, such as the royal tents which often served, not only whilst the king was not in one of his residences, but very probably also when he stayed in one, installing himself outside the prestigious buildings when large numbers of people were to be received.[55]

Stranger still, in the replacement palace hypothesis, how should we explain the time lapse between the hypostyle hall being out of service from an undetermined date during the reign of Artaxerxes I (465–425 BC) until the building of the Shaur Palace by Artaxerxes II after 404 BC, the year of his succession, or after 401 BC, the date of his victory over his brother Cyrus the Younger which allowed him to confirm his position? Let us not forget the history of the construction of the Shaur Palace. It probably started with the initial phase of Building III, which consisted only of the foundation of the rectangular floor plan, 55 m or even 70 x 44 m, with the short eastern side facing Darius' Palace. It was only after a second phase, perhaps soon after the first project, but not immediately,[56] that the Hypostyle Hall and perhaps the other buildings were conceived.

The impression is given of a project limited to one residence or pavilion far from the official palace, very probably in a lush environment which allowed its situation almost level with the river, and not that of a palatial complex with multiple, indispensable functions: reception, residence and administration. In conclusion, there can be no reason to link the fire at Darius' hypostyle hall and the building of the Shaur Palace.[57]

A pavilion and a palace outside the walls in a park

If the construction of this new palace did not respond to an imperial necessity, the hypothesis remains of that of a royal whim. To escape from the enclosed world of Darius' Residence, and at the same time profit from a pleasant environment, one needed to descend from the tells of Susa and step outside Darius' walls. The plain fitted these criteria: unlimited space and easy access to water. It is here that we must bring up the question of a term which is only used in the Old Persian version of the A2sd inscription of the Shaur; for a long time it was read as *paradayadam* (*paridaida*), which corresponded to the famous Persian 'paradise'. This interpretation was not a new one; it had been known at Susa for a long time from trilingual inscribed fragments of this same A2sd inscription, discovered on the tells of Susa and published in 1929 by Vincent Scheil. The term 'paradise' has most often been understood as an enclosed area, and from there, as an orchard, but also deer park, hunting grounds etc. The fortune of the word paradise is well known: it passed into Greek under the form *paradeisos*, came back to the Orient as *farâdis/firdaus* in Arabic, taken up as *ferdôws* in Persian and *pardis* in modern Persian or indeed as *pardês* in Hebrew. The Persian parks and gardens gained the admiration of the classical writers after Xenophon for Sardis and elsewhere; they are often called 'paradises'. Later, but harking back to an older event, Diodorus Siculus (2, 13, 1–2) eulogises the paradise designed by the Babylonian Queen Semiranis near Bagistana Mountain (Bisitun) which had a circumference of 12 stadia. It remains to be said that a precise definition of the word 'paradise' cannot be given. Indeed, it seems to cover several realities, from garden to hunting park. It was a source of pleasure and an area which produced fruit, vegetables, and meat from domestic and wild animals.

The Old Persian word in the Artaxerxes II inscription is reconstructed from **pari-daida *p-r-i-d-i-d-a*,[58] but in reality there is no proof of it in this form in the A2sd. Written *p-r-d-y-d-a-m*, it was read as *paradayadam* and translated as 'paradise'. Formerly translated by François Vallat as 'pleasant retreat', basing himself on R.G. Kent's edition of the Old Persian inscriptions, the term was later interpreted as 'outside the walls' by M.-J. Steve.[59] These two interpretations were rejected by P. Lecoq who translated the word as 'I have consecrated';[60] for him, indeed, it was not conceivable that the king had transformed a palace into a hunting park, but this function was not the only one, as we have seen. Lecoq had another objection, it was the script which was faulty. Today, the translation 'paradise' has been rehabilitated thanks to new solid explanations, but this is not unanimous.[61] The rest of the inscription in the three languages is not of any great use in defining the construction because one finds *hadiš* in Old Persian, *taçara* in Elamite and in Babylonian, terms which, according to the inscriptions at Persepolis, seem to have been interchangeable and imprecise.[62] They were translated by the general term 'palace' or simply 'building'.

Whatever the translation or the interpretation proposed for the Old Persian term being discussed, we can see that all three can be adapted to the possible function of the Shaur Palace. Indeed, we do not know if the inscription deals with all or one part of the Shaur complex, if it concerns the built areas or the complex in its entirety, including the gardens, which seems more probable according to two of the three interpretations proposed. Also, did what was thus defined have a precise function – official and administrative; residential and leisure or several of these functions?

As we lack an explanation based on the problematic inscription, we can, instead, see what can be learnt about the Shaur Palace through its plan and the history of its construction. It was originally a fairly modest building, a small palace or pavilion, which would have been the Building III in its original form;[63] based on its location, this structure may or may not have been in an enclosed compound, but it was probably in the middle of a garden or a park. The project then increased in scale when the original building was reconstructed according to a new plan, smaller but elevated on a terrace, and especially by the addition of other distinct buildings, of which one was the Hypostyle Hall. The whole was spread over a site of more than 3 hectares, always in the middle of vegetation. This creation did not have the luxury and the quality of that of Darius, but it was not the result of a hasty decision: materials were especially commissioned for this palace, column bases, floor tiles and perhaps orthostats – unknown in Darius' Palace – and some of the glazed bricks; furthermore some pieces could have been imported. The knowledge and the techniques of Darius' century were still alive, despite the changes in the templates for the column bases, the bricks and the floor tiles.

According to the only inscription known on the site, Artaxerxes II was the palace's creator, very probably as we know it today, but was he the king who chose the location? If, as we suppose, a pavilion or small palace (Building III in its initial form) preceded the whole, it is not impossible to think that one of his predecessors had the idea of landscaping the area as somewhere pleasant, far from the Palace of Darius, amongst the vegetation and close to the water. In this case, no king from Darius I to Darius II can be excluded. It remains the case that Artaxerxes II is, after Darius and Xerxes, the Achaemenid sovereign who was the most interested in Susa, based on the testimony of the surviving inscriptions: he restored Darius' Hypostyle Hall, that had deteriorated between 25 and 50 years earlier, and built the Shaur Palace, and why not other structures of which we have no evidence? The Shaur Palace complex would therefore be a remarkable illustration of the interest that this sovereign had for Susa; his long reign (404–359 BC) left him an ample amount of time to build this palace which he wanted to be a verdant space easily developed in a park or a garden set in the middle of the fertile plain.

The Ayadana and the question of fire temples

Marcel Dieulafoy excavated this now completely vanished monument in 1886, 4 km north-east of Susa, which he interpreted as an Achaemenid, Zoroastrian fire temple of the fourth century BC. *Ayadana* harked back to the term translated as 'house of the gods' used by Darius in the Old Persian and Babylonian versions only of the inscription of Bisitun. The king boasted of having rebuilt the temples destroyed by Gaumata. Happy to have an archaeological testimony which corresponded to the sacred texts, the historians and theological historians adopted Dieulafoy's interpretation until the 1970s. Thus, during nearly a century, the Ayadana of Susa was unanimously recognised as the most complete example of a 'fire temple' of the Persian era, the prototype for Zoroastrian temples from the Achaemenid period and several centuries later.

437
The site of the Ayadana in 1971

appropriated to qualify the building he excavated. Indeed, he used it unduly as no records indicate that this word defines a specific place of fire or idol worship. The representations of worship on the scenes at Persepolis, on rock reliefs and seals, do not tell us about the locations concerned. The famous low relief sculptures above the royal tombs show a scene without context at whose centre is the king, standing on some form of enormous throne carried by the nations of the empire, lifting his arm in front of an altar placed on a stepped pedestal on top of which a fire burns. Between the king and the altar there floats a crowned bust coming out from a winged disc, who is not necessarily Ahuramazda.[82] A religious scene, without doubt, where the king is the only figure in front of the fire, but was it a real religious rite or just a dynastic one?

This representation can be found in other places on numerous seals impressed on tablets at Persepolis, mainly from Darius' reign. It is not always, however, the king who is represented, often it is a figure or even two men, no doubt priests who then face each other on either side of the altar on which burns the fire. The altar which carries the fire is the only component which relates to a rite, but the scene is an abstract one with no landscape or architecture.[83]

The temples of Achaemenid Persia remain to be discovered

The unique archaeological record which would testify to worship in the open air, as spoken of by Herodotus, has been known for a long time at Pasargadae. Set away from the palaces, there are two cubic stone pedestals, 8 m apart. One is placed on a stepped dais and has sides of 2.8 m and a height of 2.1 m; its top forms a slight depression. The other is slightly smaller and the same height, but more importantly it has steps to the top. Were they two altars to two gods, in which case, which ones? Today, the scene represented by the low relief sculptures of the royal tombs is the one preferred: a pedestal for the fire, the other a dais for the king which he reaches via the stairs.[84] If the interpretation of the scene is seductive, the shape of the altars, very different from those represented in the carvings, is less so, and has never been found elsewhere in Persia.[85]

Amongst the other Achaemenid monuments, very few are interpreted as temples, even fewer as fire temples. At Persepolis, a small installation in the open air which adjoins the Palace of Darius is sometimes considered as a place for libations because of a gutter and a few channels carved into the rock.[86] Equally, the lines of figures carrying objects on the stairs of this palace, similar to those which the adorn the stairs of the Apadana are interpreted as carriers of offerings for worship. One hypothesis, which is a long way from being unanimous, considers the whole of Darius' *Taçara* as a religious monument.[87] Another building situated at the foot of the Persepolis Terrace has sometimes been called an Achaemenid temple. This 'temple of the Frataraka' consists of a square hall with four columns in which a pedestal decorated with mouldings is set in the centre near the back. The hall is surrounded by long, very narrow rooms on four sides; behind one of these a very off-centre portico with four columns constitutes the entrance to the main hall. There are not many similarities with the *Ayadana* of Susa. If the hypothesis of a temple with images is probable, with the pedestal seemingly destined to carry a statue, the hypothesis of a fire temple is based on nothing. Furthermore, for this discussion the Achaemenid era must be excluded: the pedestal with mouldings has its origins in Hellenistic art; furthermore, the shape of the column bases was unknown to the Achaemenids; finally the shape of the mud bricks of the walls is characteristic of the post-Achaemenid period.[88]

Another building has often been suggested as a temple, or Persian fire temple: the tower at Naqsh-i Rustam, opposite the rock tombs, as well as its almost complete replica at Pasargadae which is in fact the older of the two. At Naqsh-i

442

At a short distance from the Pasargadae site are two monolithic blocks more than 2 m in height; a staircase adjoins one
They are often compared to the bas-relief representations on the royal tombs at Persepolis and Naqsh-i Rustam (see fig. 443 below), showing the king on a stage facing a fire-carrying altar
photograph by Rémy Boucharlat

443

Bas-relief above the royal tomb north of Persepolis (Artaxerxes III ?)
This is identical to all the tombs of his predecessors. It represents the king on a platform carried by the peoples of the empire. Mediator between man and the gods he faces an altar on which burns a fire. The scene is surmounted by a winged bust probably representing the royal 'glory' rather than the god Ahuramazda

Rustam it is easy to note that the small high chamber, accessible by a staircase of 30 steps, had neither vent-hole in the roof nor windows, which makes the hypothesis of a permanent fire inside very improbable, even if we know that, as in the Zoroastrianism temples of today, it consisted of a pile of embers. The hypothesis of a temple is not convincing, nor is that of a tomb. On the other hand, using an extract from Plutarch (*Artaxerxes*, 1, 3) who wrote that each king had to go to Pasargadae for his coronation to be 'elevated' to kinghood, the tower has been proposed as the location for this ceremony. At Pasargadae, the dynastic cradle, as it was the residence of the founder of the dynasty, the tower would then have been both a royal and a religious monument insofar as royalty was linked to Ahuramazda. If the hypothesis is seductive for the tower at Pasargadae, what did the Darius era, identical tower at Naqsh-i Rustam represent? The repetition of the same rite near the new royal residence, or a strongroom where dynastic objects were stored?[89] Whatever they were, these two towers were neither fire temples nor temples for images.

The problem of Persian temples therefore still remains. We do know, however, that less than two centuries before Cyrus, an Iranian population from the central Zagros, called Medes, had temples. One of these was excavated between 1969 and 1978 at Nush-i Jan, situated a few dozen kilometres from the modern town of Hamadan; it was dated to the end of the eighth century BC and was in use until the end of the seventh century BC.[90] It is a sort of mud-brick tower, shaped like a lozenge with stepped walls. The interior space, which was cruciform, had an antechamber and an access stairway to the floor above it, then a principal, triangular room decorated with blind windows, very sheltered from prying eyes in the light of day. In the corner of this room there was a stepped altar made of mud brick, whose top formed a shallow bowl which was full of ash. This layout led this building at Nush-i Jan to be seen as a Median fire temple, supposing that the altar had a fire burning at all times.[91]

Was fire the object of worship?

The question as to the function of the monument at Nush-i Jan is still unanswered, as it could have been a *fire temple* just as much as a place of worship in the presence of fire, an *instrument* of worship. It was certainly a place of worship, because the archaeological data indicates that the building was not abandoned but deconsecrated by careful infilling. This event took place before 600 BC, so well before the Achaemenids.[92] Since the discovery of Nush-i Jan, other contemporary buildings in the same province of Hamadan and in a region further to the east on the Iranian plateau, have been identified and partially excavated. The plan is rarely attested, the internal layout even less so, but it was observed that these constructions were all intentionally back-filled with care, possibly at the same time as the Temple at Nush-i Jan. The pre-Achaemenid period, though in fact very poorly understood, is actually better recorded archaeologically in terms of religious monuments than the Achaemenid period itself. It would be an error, however, to conclude that these did not exist during the reign of the Great Kings; one must only admit to an almost complete ignorance of Persian religious practices.

Other than the Palace of Darius and that of the Shaur, the totality of architectural and epigraphic data at Susa is meagre and mostly very uncertain.[93] Is this a consequence of the limits of archaeology and epigraphy, or a reality? Royal Achaemenid Susa seems fairly void of buildings; in that respect it is very different from the Royal Court at Persepolis, with its terrace covered in a dozen buildings erected over nearly two centuries, not counting the visible buildings and some still buried at the foot of the terrace to the south.[94] As at Persepolis, where Achaemenid buildings are discovered bit by bit or identified in the plain in a radius of 4 to 5 km

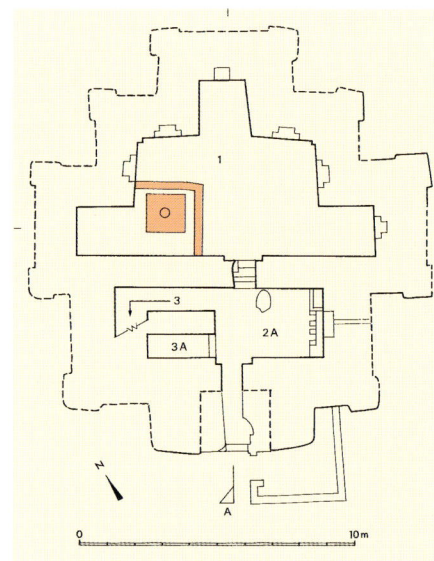

444
Temple of Nush-i Jan in the region of Hamadan, Median period (end eighth to seventh century BC)
The top of the modest mud-brick altar had a central depression in which ashes were found. The altar was placed in the main room, not in the centre but to the left of the entrance
STRONACH, ROAF, 2007: fig. 2.2 and pl. 18c

445

Square tower in dressed stone, known as Kabah-i Zardusht since the Middle Ages, opposite the royal rock tombs of Naqsh-i Rustam

It has sometimes been interpreted as a Persian temple. Built in plain masonry, with only a very small room on the top floor, without ventilation or openings (the windows are blind) it would have been difficult to perform religious rites and certainly to maintain a permanent fire.

photograph by Rémy Boucharlat

around the terrace,[95] perhaps one must suppose that some isolated column bases found at Susa and around the tells mark the location of royal or princely edifices that no longer exist. The diversity of the dimensions and of the bases would point in this direction. Could one also evoke the diversity of techniques for the mural bricks, with or without glaze, with or without reliefs; as well as the scale used to represent figures: life-size or half scale? It is also possible to imagine that this heterogeneity can be attributed to re-use.

Considered as a whole, the remains of the Persepolis plain offer a much broader picture of ancient Parsa than that offered by the Terrace. They stretch over an area of 6 km, from the Terrace to the necropolis at Naqsh-i Rustam.[96] Can it be supposed that Achaemenid Susa also had such a large extent? The hypothesis, currently unconvincing due to a lack of evidence, cannot be definitively discarded.

Mercury in the walls of the Shaur Palace

Rémy Boucharlat

It was a real surprise to the excavators of the Shaur Palace when, in 1971, they discovered drops of mercury in a liquid state and small air pockets with iridescent walls, traces of oxidised mercury inside some of the mud bricks of the western wall of the hypostyle hall.

The hypothesis that a modern object containing mercury (such as a thermometer) had been dropped was quickly abandoned when the wall was taken to pieces. The mercury was present not only on the surface but well into the depths of the bricks over a height of eight courses, spread over three or four bricks in each course down to the foundations of shingle, which also bore traces. The deposit was intentional, as was shown by an experiment using part of the kilogram of liquid mercury that had been recovered. Some 200 g were deposited into a hole made in a brick during the manufacturing stage; 200 g were mixed with the mud of another brick. After drying the bricks for three days, it was observed that, in the first test, the mercury had moved through the brick through the cracks that had been formed during the drying, whilst, with the second test, the mercury had spread throughout the whole brick in the form of small drops and small inclusions, as in the old bricks.

The mercury was obtained by roasting its ore, cinnabar (mercury sulphide) used elsewhere to produce red vermilion pigment, used in the mural paintings of this same palace. Cinnabar mines were exploited before the Hellenistic period in Cappadocia (Strabo XII, 2, 10) and near Laodicea on the Lycus. One of the uses of cinnabar was in the composition of a binding cement. Elsewhere, the gilding of metallic vases with mercury by amalgam was a technique known in the Orient alongside hammering. The kilogram of mercury found on the ground of a house at Al Mina in Syria was destined for this use; this discovery was dated either to the turn of the fifth to sixth centuries BC or to the Hellenistic period.

446
Mercury droplets in the brick core

The discovery of mercury in the Shaur Palace shows that already under the Achaemenids cinnabar mines were being exploited; the closest to Susa, according to twentieth-century geographical data, were those situated near Hamadan and in Azerbaijan near Takht-i Suleiman.

The intentional presence of mercury in the Shaur Palace cannot be explained other than as a foundation rite. This rite generally took place towards the beginning of the construction; the deposit was placed either in the foundations themselves or in the corner of the structure, or again in the doorways, but the rules were not very precise. At the Shaur Palace, the deposit was placed in the wall elevation, from the base up; furthermore, it is neither in the axis of the hypostyle hall, nor in the corner, nor in a doorway.

As to the material used in the foundation deposits, there was a large diversity including liquids, ordinary but symbolic foodstuffs (bread, beer) or odd shapeless objects. The mercury was certainly a rare and surprising material, which can explain its unique ritual use.

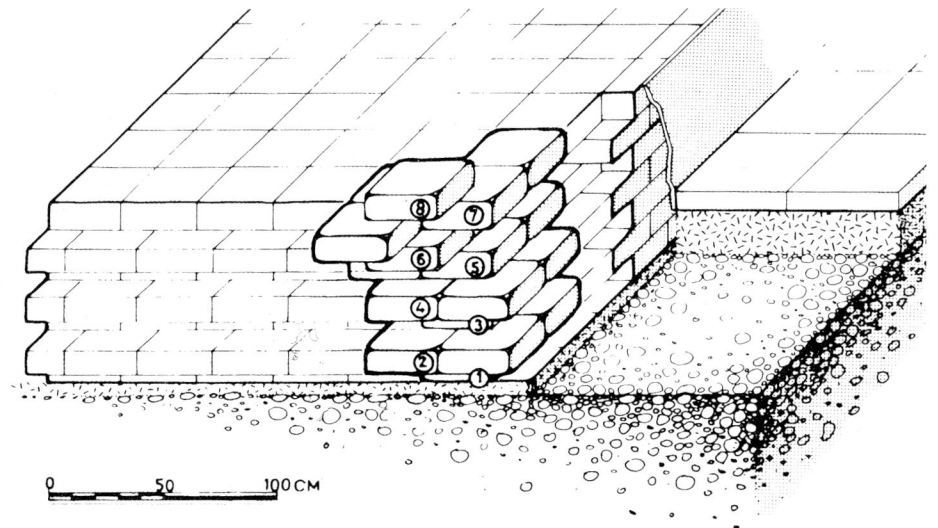

447
Diagram showing the position of the bricks with mercury droplets

448

Persepolis: south-west corner of the Terrace
The retaining wall, more than 14 m high, was built with large
blocks but sometimes used the recut natural rock. It was crowned
by alternating, large and small merlons decorated with an arrow
in the centre and capped with a row of indents and tall spikes,
an Elamite inheritance
photograph by B.-N. Chagny

13 Susa in Iranian and Oriental Architecture

Rémy Boucharlat

The art and architecture of the Achaemenids, the last manifestation of the arts of the ancient Orient before the time of Alexander the Great, are surprisingly innovative, especially in Iran. One of the most striking traits was the extensive use of stone columns, which allowed vast surfaces to be covered. Achaemenid art was also astonishing in the way it borrowed from different cultures of the empire: Greek (Lydian-Ionian), Syrian, Egyptian and Mesopotamian styles could be found in Persian palaces. These styles were so clearly borrowed that some concluded in the past that Persian art lacked inventiveness, manifested a culpable heterogeneity and marked the decline of Oriental art.[1]

Such borrowings from other cultures are certainly numerous and they are as perceptible in architecture and sculpture as in the applied arts such as glyptic and goldsmithing. Even so, if one is prepared to move beyond first impressions and, further, to question the *raison d'être* of this borrowing – rather than the influences – a sense of the procedure can be discovered, which has been defined as a 'positive eclecticism'.[2] From his initial distant conquests onwards, Cyrus, the first master of the Achaemenid Empire, was able to appreciate the architectural and artistic creations of the conquered countries, whether they were older or contemporary with his passage. Cyrus and his successors appropriated figures and symbols, often transforming them in vocabulary and techniques. The Great King's objective was to translate a message, largely innovative and ideological compared with his Mesopotamian predecessors, into architecture, representation and ornamentation.

From Pasargadae onwards, through architecture and sculpture, Cyrus created a form of narrative. Numerous features at Pasargadae, more numerous and more important than one may think, heralded Susa and Persepolis. After Cyrus, and beyond the enigmatic Cambyses – who, however, may have left some traces[3] – the Palace of Darius at Susa is one of the important monuments of Persian architecture.

449
**Pasargadae was the site chosen by Cyrus as a residence
at 1800 m altitude in the heart of his country of birth**
It is at first sight a vast park whose centre was occupied
by a formal garden as indicated by the stone channels
photograph by B.-N. Chagny

450
**The Persepolis Terrace, laid out on the flanks
of the mountain, occupied about a dozen hectares.
Today, it appears covered in buildings.**
This density which contrasts with the layout of
Pasargadae is the result of building enterprises by
Darius and his successors during more than 150 years
photograph by B.-N. Chagny

In all its aspects, location, distribution and type of buildings – Propylaeum, Gate, Hypostyle Hall, Residence – internal and external architecture, ornamentation, the palace as a whole is an example of the king's visual programme. The original project of the royal quarter on the Terrace at Persepolis, the work of the same king, was no doubt conceived at the same time as the one at Susa. Persepolis, on the other hand, seems to have had different objectives and the result was certainly different.

The history of Achaemenid architecture, of which the palace at Susa is part, was not therefore a simple evolution of one site into another and cannot be reduced to the three complexes of Pasargadae, Susa and Persepolis. Not only did the Persian kings build elsewhere in Persia in modern-day Fars – and not only 'pavilions' – but they also created works outside their region of origin. We know this from Ecbatana, in Media, where up to the present day almost nothing has been found. At Babylon, the work of Achaemenid kings was not limited to the small 'Persian Palace' of Artaxerxes II, a hypostyle hall with a portico. As Hermann Gasche suggests here, in a new study, Achaemenid Babylon from Darius, if not earlier, was marked by the profound transformation of some of the enormous buildings constructed by their Neo-Babylonian predecessors such as Nebuchadnezzar. This last case perfectly illustrates the complexity of the process which transformed Persian architecture from Cyrus down to Alexander the Great; Achaemenid kings certainly borrowed from Babylon, but they also introduced the Iranian hypostyle hall, modest at Babylon and, if we are to believe Gasche, they re-adapted an architectural solution known in the Neo-Assyrian and Elamite palaces. In the area of decoration also, new techniques for making glazed bricks, different from the Neo-Babylonian method, were introduced to Babylon from Susa.[4]

SUSA IN ACHAEMENID ARCHITECTURE

The governing of the Achaemenid Empire from several places of residence has often intrigued historians, and it has been accepted that the kings did not have one or several capitals, but several residences, and that the mode of government was that of a 'itinerant state', as Pierre Briant has demonstrated.[5] The kings elected several locations to establish a residence in which they invested heavily. The case of Pasargadae, the oldest, built from the 540s BC onwards, has not prompted any questions as it was presumed to be the unique residence, being older than the other locations, namely Susa and Persepolis. Actually, it is likely that Cyrus had already officially lived in other political centres such as Babylon and possibly Ecbatana, but he does not seem to have built there. Darius' strategy is less easy to understand today, because he chose as his residences Susa – re-founding a town many thousands of years old – and Persepolis, a new creation; the works were planned seemingly at the same time. The other royal residences at Babylon and Ecbatana were undertaken at an unknown date, but, from the reign of Darius on, can be seen as a desire to perpetuate the continuity of predecessors, whilst being a manifestation of power in non-Persian countries.

THE SIMULTANEOUS CHOICE OF SUSA AND PERSEPOLIS

Specialists generally consider Susa to pre-date Persepolis.[6] However, as the possible gap between the beginning of the two residences is a matter of a few years, neither the archaeological facts nor the epigraphic evidence allows for such a clear-cut decision. Records used by Briant provide indications, but they remain imprecise;[7] Darius is at Susa around 519 BC, but does he live there? Also, according to a tablet from Persepolis, the royal residence of Susa, whether or not complete, is clearly mentioned in 500/499 BC. This gap of some 20 years could correspond in the first case to the initial development works on the Terrace and, in the second case, to the completion of what we call the Residence.

For Persepolis, a chronological piece of evidence for the beginning of the construction is given by two foundation deposits of the Apadana: next to the inscribed gold and silver plaques were found Croesus standard coins, gold Lydian coins and Greek coins, the most recent being dated to around 500 BC. These coins give the *terminus post quem* for the start of the building of the Apadana walls, but not the date of the first works on the Terrace. It is obvious that the layout over 12 hectares followed by the building of the platform for the Apadana preceded the construction of the Hypostyle Hall by several years. We can be certain that the start of the works was before 509 BC, the date of the oldest of the thousands of tablets inscribed in Elamite found in the Fortification Archive.[8] According to B. Jacobs, the very first works on the Terrace at Persepolis could be dated to very soon after Darius' seizure of power, that is to say soon after 519/518 BC, which would make them more or less contemporaneous with the re-foundation of Susa.[9] The progress of the two sites in parallel cannot be dated more precisely, but in both cases, the building of the Hypostyle Hall only started several years after the beginning of the terracing works. In any case, it must be remembered that in the years which followed the consolidation of his power, Darius launched two almost simultaneous programmes, which presumes considerable human and material means.[10]

The climate argument, different for the plain of Susa and for the high valley of Persepolis at 1600 m altitude, was drawn upon many a time by ancient writers to explain the king's mobility. It was certainly not the most important factor in Darius' choice,[11] all the more so since this choice had to be revised in accordance with Darius' geopolitical schemes relating to the royal residences. If Persepolis, and Pasargadae before it, had been at the heart of the Persian nation, Susa was without doubt in largely familiar territory, but also the major town in the ancient, powerful kingdom of Elam on the plain. In an effort to impose himself and to show himself in conquered countries, the palace of Babylon was installed in the ancient Neo-Babylonian palace of powerful Nebuchadnezzar who reigned over the Near East several decades before Cyrus. Achaemenid Ecbatana, which has yet to be discovered, was the Median capital until the reign of Cyrus. On one of the hills of the modern town of Hamadan, the 11 seasons of excavations by M.R. Sarraf between 1983 and 1999 brought to light an urbanism that was grandiose in its size and regularity, but we know today that it did not belong to the Achaemenid period. The excavator was not able to be sure of the foundation date – he suggested the early Median period – nor the duration of the complex's use – until the Sassanian period, he thought. M. Azarnoush and R. Biscione, who reopened a detailed excavation in 2004–2006, were able to definitively show that this urbanism was from the Parthian period and certainly no earlier.[12] It is true that fragments of Achaemenid column bases were found at Hamadan, some here and there in the excavation, and even from the brief French excavations of 1913,[13] but always recycled; others, more or less complete, sometimes inscribed, in the town and round about; today they are preserved in the local museum.[14] The existence of royal Achaemenid buildings on one or other of the hills of Ecbatana is indisputable; but it remains for them to be discovered.

The almost simultaneous beginnings of Susa and Persepolis must be taken into account in all attempts to compare the architecture of the two residences and their history, without preventing comparisons with the remains of other royal residences. This palatial architecture was very new at Susa, on the Iranian plateau and partly at Babylon, and it is therefore interesting to understand from what traditions it benefited and from where were borrowed the very varied concepts which Persian sovereigns saw in the territories of their immense empire.

451

Persepolis: stone chest containing the foundation inscriptions of the Apadana, on gold and silver sheets
SCHMIDT, 1953: fig. 43b

452

Grey limestone column bases from Ecbatana (now Hamadan), Achaemenid in shape and technique.
The royal palace has as yet not been found
photograph by Rémy Boucharlat

453

Pasargadae: Palace P, often called the 'residential palace'; a hypostyle hall bordered by two long porticoes.
In the background between the columns, the stone tower, a 'twin' to that at Naqsh-i Rustam. In the distance, the hill extended by a stone platform built under Cyrus.
photograph by Mission archéologique franco-iraniennede Pasargades et Persépolis

THE ARCHITECTURAL INNOVATIONS OF PASARGADAE

At the Pasargadae site, the royal constructions known today are grouped in two or three complexes disseminated over dozens of hectares. This is an immediate contrast with the compact aspect of Persepolis and Susa, which has long been recognised, to the point where people have wanted to see Pasargadae as a form of encampment scattered with a few prestigious, palatial, religious and defensive buildings, a recollection of the nomadic life of the Persians to which Cyrus would have been attached.[15] This romantic vision is without foundation. Furthermore, a very different image of Pasargadae comes from the most recent research; other buildings, still buried, have been identified, whilst the whole central part of the site must have been developed, transformed into a park split by an artificial river or a large basin. The housing, or a part of it, was also identified behind the citadel. It comprised large architectural units with sides of more than 30 m.[16] These developments and stone constructions were due to Cyrus, between around 550 BC and his death in 530 BC. Darius finished some buildings and built on the platform, so we are unaware of what Cyrus had planned to build there – most probably his residence.

The platform dominates the site from some 30 m and is made up of a natural hillside called Tall-i Takht and a considerable extension obtained by building walls with large dressed stone blocks, the whole covering an area of 2 hectares. This platform is located on the top of the hillside and held by a retaining wall, with foundations halfway down the slope, which rises to a maximum height of 14.5 m; the same dimensions are found in the walls of the Terrace of Persepolis and are close to the height of that at Susa.[17]

The official part was located 800 m away on the plain; it comprised several ceremonial buildings, without terracing to elevate them, but each building rested on imposing foundations made from enormous limestone slabs. These halls (a total of around 6,000 m² of covered spaces) were therefore distinctly separated from the residential area on the platform that was envisaged by Cyrus; a series of constructions comprising an isolated tower and a large stone building close the gap somewhat. The function of this complex may have been dynastic or religious.[18] The complex was planned and commissioned by a single person – Cyrus.

One of the possible reasons for this loose layout was the development of a vast park, of which only a small section is known with any precision, a rectangular garden defined by a double line of stone channels. The interior is subdivided into

454

Pasargadae: north-west corner of the retaining wall of Cyrus' platform
The technique of large embossed blocks was already in evidence in Assyria, but their assembly with joints held together with clamps set in lead illustrates the intervention of artisans and masons from Ionia and Lydia called to Pasargadae around 540 BC. Furthermore, numerous masons' marks are comparable with those on the monuments of Miletus in Asia Minor
photograph by Rémy Boucharlat

two parts by a channel. Around this regular garden, the recently recognized layout was arranged either side of an artificial river, channelled between two stone banks, or at least a large basin.

It can be seen that the general organisation of the site at Pasargadae has nothing in common with a plain covered in tents. This latter form of habitation is not excluded for certain categories of the population, such as the army or groups of artisans, but Pasargadae was above all a royal residence, divided into distinct sectors, the principal one being a vast space developed as parkland in which stone buildings were placed.[19] In this respect, Cyrus' residence is a complete break with the arrangement of Mesopotamian palaces.

The appearance of the porticoed hypostyle hall and the monumental gate

The column, sometimes in stone and resting on a stone base, is one of the great innovations of Pasargadae. The technique of using rows of intermediate supports between two walls of a room – wooden posts had long been used – was a feature of pre-Achaemenid Iranian architecture but was unknown in Mesopotamia for covering vast surfaces. The post was used in the Orient well before the Achaemenid period, although it was limited to façades and porticoes, but the discoveries of the second half of the twentieth century in western Iran showed the important evolution of this type of support. It had already been developed at Hasanlu in Iranian Azerbaijan from the ninth century BC. Meanwhile, in parallel, the neighbouring kingdom of Urartu had a preference for large stone pillars. The post was taken up in the central Zagros, around Hamadan in the eighth and seventh centuries BC, where the multiplication of rows – six rows of five posts – allowed a span of 25 m for the largest hall at Godin Tepe, thus 600 m².

In the last years of the twentieth century, archaeologists were obliged to note that the hall with several rows of posts was not exclusive to the Zagros. In eastern Arabia, in the present-day United Arab Emirates, several buildings were discovered

455

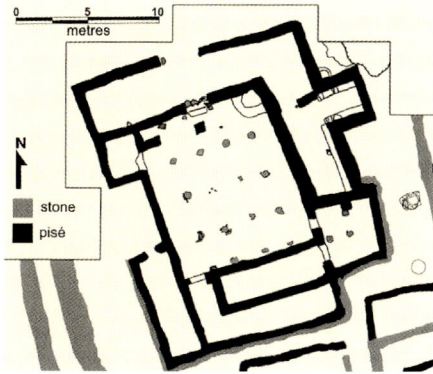

Constructions recently discovered in the United Arab Emirates (Muweilah, Sharjah, eighth century BC)
Room with wooden columns resting on flagstones. Area C
MAGEE, 2001: fig. 2

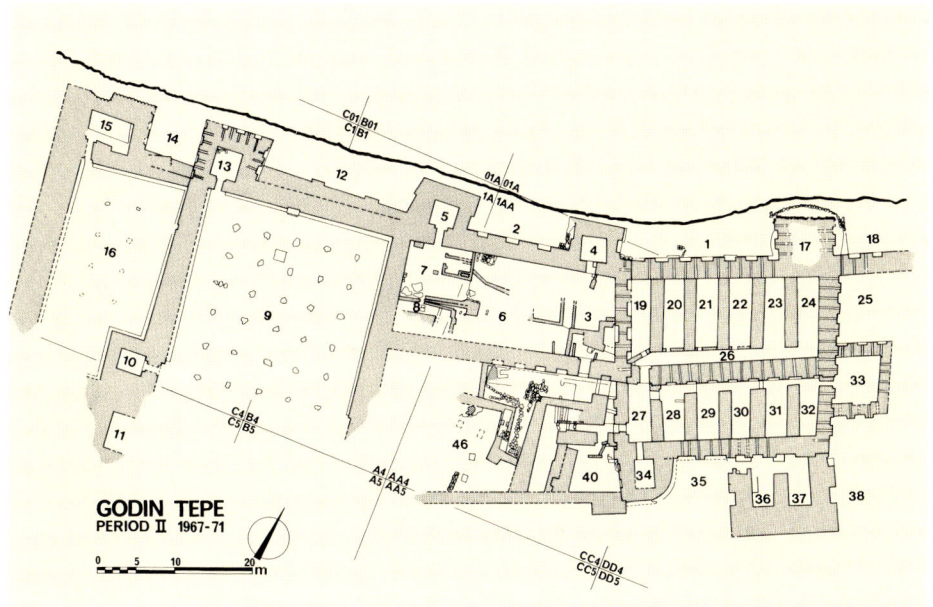

456

Godin Tepe: before the appearance at Pasargdae of the true stone column the support had been a simple wooden pole standing on a flat stone as at Godin Tepe in the seventh to sixth centuries BC
YOUNG LEVINE, 1974: fig. 87

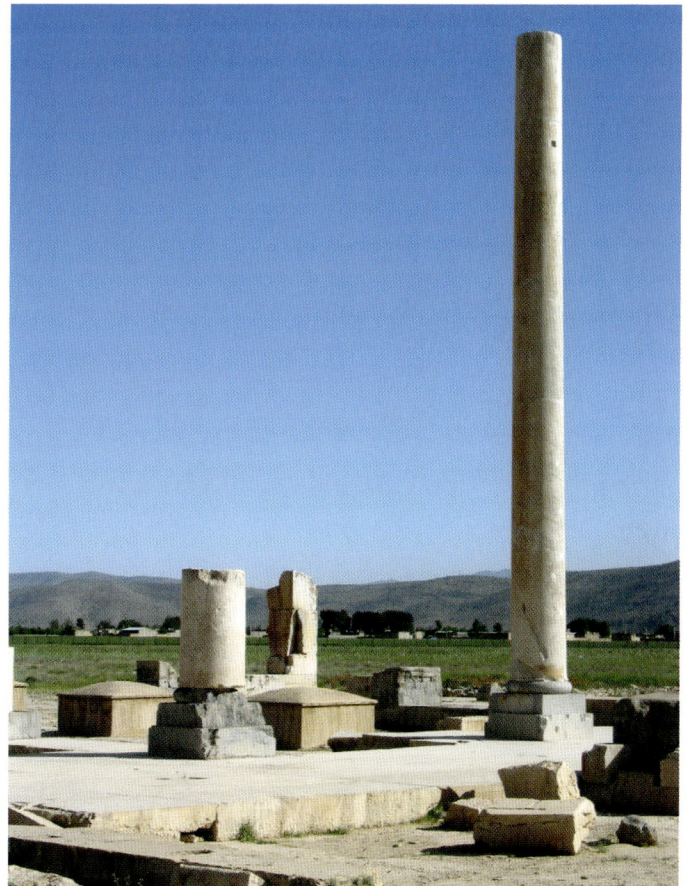

457

The columns of Pasargadae are made up of smooth shafts whose drums measure several metres in length on a two-stepped base playing on the contrast between black and white limestone
Mission archéologique franco-iranienne de Pasargades et Persépolis

458
Palace P at Pasargadae
photograph by B.-N. Chagny

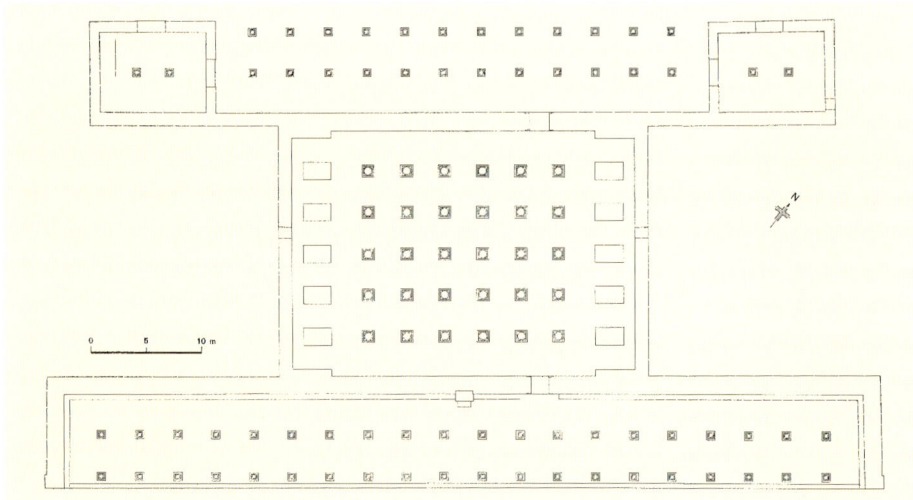

459
Plan of Palace P
STRONACH, 1978: fig. 41

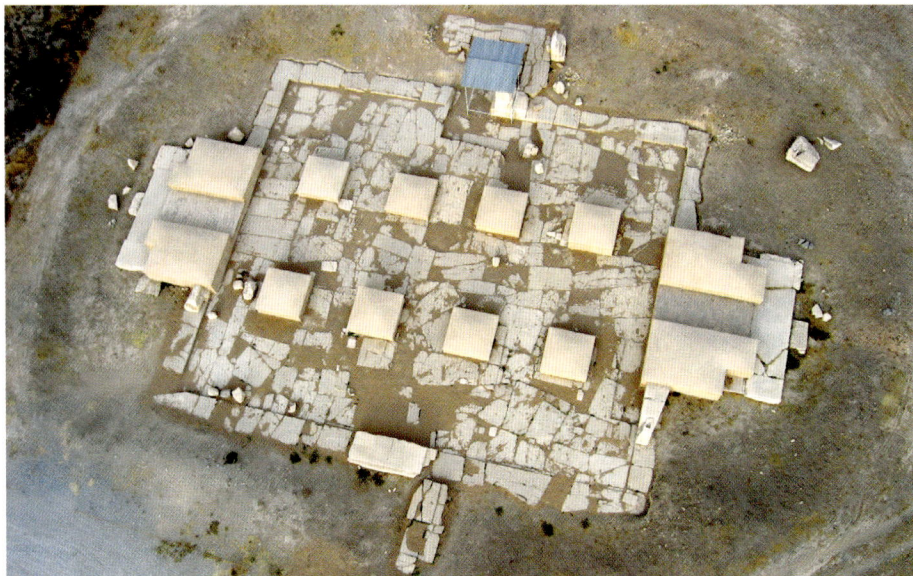

460
Gate R at Pasagadae
With two rows of four columns,
protected here against the frost
photograph by B.-N. Chagny

composed of a hall with three rows of four or five posts, although it must be said that the halls were more modest, no greater than 12 m at their widest.[20]

The pre-Achaemenid halls with posts were rectangular, except at Godin Tepe; they remained so at Pasargadae, around 32 x 22 m for palaces P and S, thus 700 m² each, as well as in the hall of the first palace of Borazjan attributed to the reign of Cyrus. The column proper, made of stone and set on a stone base, appeared at Pasargadae in the middle of the sixth century BC. For historical reasons, it is more likely that it derived from the posts of the Zagros than from those of Arabia. It assumed a functional and decorative role previously unknown elsewhere in the Orient. In the Greek world – continental Greece and Ionia – the decorative column was used for colonnades and temple porticoes; in Achaemenid architecture it was used to cover large halls, as in the three principal hypostyle spaces at Pasargadae, Gate R and Palaces P and S. The whole system was in place: base and capital, already decorated, shaft of several drums. The Ionian influence is indisputable for the bases, of which some in Palace P adopt a template recently created at Miletus. On the other hand, the capital with animal protomes was the Persian adaptation of the Assyrian protome, which normally formed the door jambs of monumental doorways. These Pasargadae capitals are not well known, since only small fragments survived and remained unpublished for a long time.[21] They belonged to bulls, as at Susa and Persepolis, and to horses, an animal which would no longer be represented after Pasargadae.

The portico, used in the façades of several buildings at Hasanlu but without lasting influence in the Zagros, appeared in its simple form at Pasargadae, this time under Ionian influence. Four porticoes surround the central hall of Palace S, but only two over-extended porticoes line the long sides of Palace P. The absence of hinge sockets at Pasargadae indicates that the openings were only passageways, which nonetheless could be closed with canvas.

Gate R at Pasargadae visually marked the entrance into the royal space, as did the Darius Gate at Susa and the Xerxes Gate at Persepolis. Yet at Pasargadae it was far more than a gate: it was a complete building with a rectangular external plan whilst the internal room with two rows of four columns was almost square, measuring 26.4 x 22.2 m. The innovation lies not only in its size and shape, but also in the lack of defensive structures. Not only were entrance and exit made by simple passages but there was no aperture in the walls and the absence of ramparts was remarkable.[22] The gate thus represented the journey from the external world towards an internal, royal space, with a sharp contrast between the arid vegetation and disorder of the exterior and the orderly layout of the park or garden which started as one passed through the gate.

The continuity of Pasargadae at Dasht-i Gohar, near Persepolis

The creations of Cambyses (530–522 BC), between Cyrus and Darius, remain an unresolved question. It is most likely, however, that it was Cambyses, before Darius, who chose the region of Persepolis to establish a new residence. He was the creator of several monuments situated 3 km north of the Persepolis Terrace, a stepped platform very similar to that of the foundations of Cyrus' tomb, and near it, a 700 m² rectangular hypostyle hall, surrounded by porticoes, like those of Pasargadae and perhaps other, little-known buildings, discovered at the beginning of the 1970s.[23] The hypothesis of a date shortly after Cyrus comes from the shape of the stepped platform, of the rectangular shape of the hypostyle hall and the simplicity of the column bases. David Stronach suggested that Cambyses had envisaged this new, undefended and carefully planned residence as a 'garden capital' following the model of Pasargadae.[24]

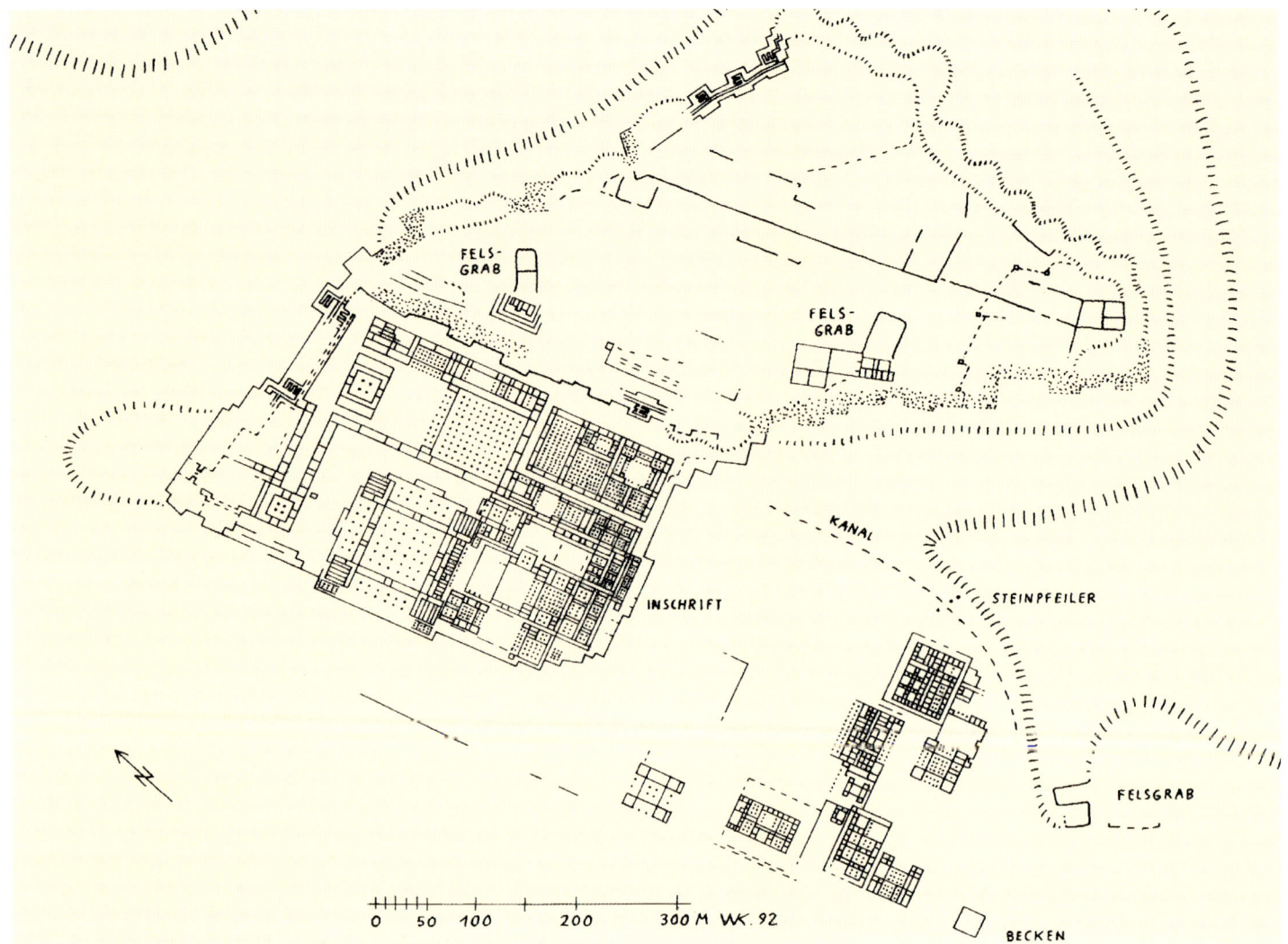

461

Overall plan of the known constructions at Persepolis
The 12-hectare terrace constitutes only a part of it, at the foot of the mountain. The mountain is defended along its crest by a fortification. The Royal Quarter extends to the south of the terrace with partially excavated stone structures
KLEISS, 1992, Abb. 1

PERSEPOLIS

The extent of the buildings on the Terrace at Persepolis, almost entirely excavated, should not make us forget those which rose immediately at the foot of the Terrace and which have only been partially uncovered; this almost doubles the built area, without counting the development which took place on the slope of the mountain. At Susa the terrace had to be built on top of an earth mound. At Persepolis, Darius' choice was different. He backed the Terrace against the mountain, which must have been heavily cut into. This operation simultaneously furnished building materials. As at Susa, the terrace was not the highest point in the area because the mud-brick fortifications, which ran along the ridge of the mountain, dominated the palaces and the hypostyle hall by several dozen metres,[25] more so than the battlements of the Susa Citadel.[26]

Coincidence or not, the Persepolis Terrace was built to the same height as those of Pasargadae and Susa – 14.5 m.[27] It also covered the same surface area as that at Susa. The Terrace dominated another part of the royal quarter, partially identified to the south. Persepolis perfectly illustrates the desire for ostentation, as the maximum height of the supporting wall corresponded to the floor level of the Apadana, the Hypostyle Hall, itself elevated 2.5 m on a platform – a feature which does not exist at Susa.[28] Likewise, the palaces of Darius and Xerxes at Persepolis were built on a specific platform. On the other hand, the ground level was much lower in other official buildings: 11.7 m only at the Gate of All Nations, that of Xerxes and in the Hall of a Hundred Columns; lower still at less than 10 m in the Treasury to the south.

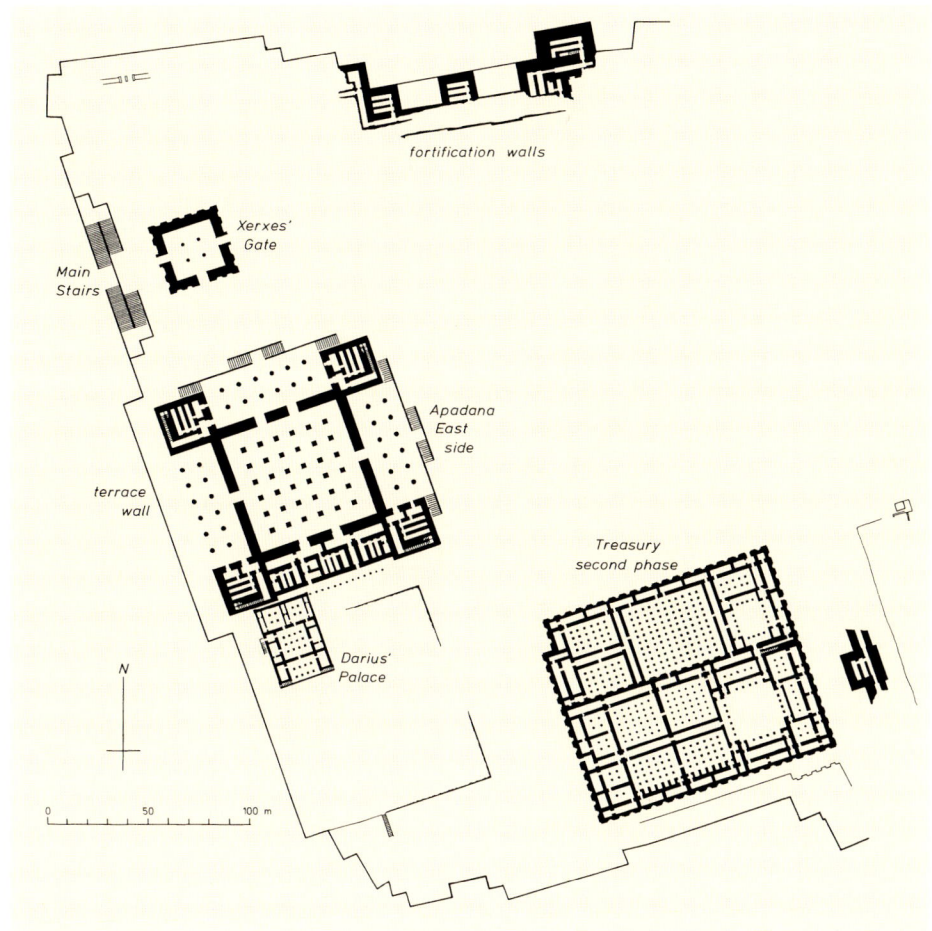

462
Persepolis: state of buildings on the terrace at the start of Xerxes' reign
Darius built the Treasury, his small palace and a section of the fortifications. He started the construction of the Apadana and perhaps that of the monumental gate, works finished by his son Xerxes
ROAF, 1983: fig. 152

The Persepolis built by Darius, from what we know, is reduced to four buildings representing less than 3 hectares spread across the Terrace: the Apadana, to which the building called the Palace of Darius practically adjoined and which, from the modesty of its size and its floor plan, could not have been his residence; the Treasury which occupied about a hectare to the south-east, and perhaps the beginning of the monumental gate to the north, which replaced an initial project in which the access was situated opposite, to the south. Fortifications would be added to the north, of which the towers offered numerous, narrow, usable rooms. If Darius had foreseen other buildings, we would have only traces as part of the realisations of his son Xerxes: both together cover barely half the Terrace. It is probable that open spaces were planned, developed as gardens or large courtyards. It was their successors who would finish the project by filling the larger part of the Terrace as we know it today. The open areas remained an important but scattered element, unlike at Susa where the Hypostyle Hall was open on three sides, as was the eastern side of the Residence.

The foundations and the drainage: a gigantic effort
Amongst the developments prior to the building works, the care taken with the foundations and the drainage at Persepolis was as remarkable as at Susa. The techniques put into practice were different, because they were largely dictated by the substratum and the materials available. The layout of the foundations of Persepolis used the natural bedrock or the accumulated debris taken from the mountain. The importance given to the drainage network was remarkable for its 1.5 m deep drains at the foot of the mountain, some carved into the rock, others built into the foundations. The secondary channels were smaller, around 40 cm wide and 30 to 80 cm deep, but always carefully carved or built in stone.[29]

When looking at the foundations, Persepolis, like Susa, is distinct from Pasargadae, due to the importance given to the doorways of which the massive door sockets survive. At Persepolis, however, some entryways are simple passageways, the gates being reserved for access from outside or towards important spaces. It was only the openings of the Gate of Xerxes, those giving access to the Hypostyle Hall, or those to the central halls of the Palace of Darius and of Xerxes which had actual gates. At the Treasury also, some of the doorways had gates. Elsewhere on the Terrace, the openings are only passageways, which, curiously, is the case with the Hall of One Hundred Columns, even if the only direct access to this hall was from the north through the only portico. As we have seen at Susa,[30] the door sockets were crudely worked, buried blocks, whilst at Persepolis, the socket blocks at the Apadana were probably visible, decorated with an enormous rosette around the cylindrical cavity in which the socket rested.

At the same time as the substructures were being finished at Persepolis and Susa, before or during the building of the walls, or even after this operation, foundation deposits were laid, but in different places at each location: the inscribed tablets which were found at Persepolis were in coffers placed underneath the walls in two corners of the Apadana, or audience hall; at Susa, those that were found *in situ* were in the passageway heading towards the King's Apartments. The example of the Shaur Palace suggests prudence with the value and siting of possible deposits: the mercury deposit,[31] if it really was a ritual gesture, was made in mud bricks, in the elevation of a wall but not in its middle, and was not accompanied by an inscription. Based on this example, the place chosen would not always be obvious to us and the materials deposited were not always limited to gold or inscribed stone; it is also what a number of Mesopotamian examples, older than the Achaemenids, showed. The disappearance of virtually the entire elevation of the walls at Susa and, by contrast, the better state of preservation of those at Persepolis, which because of this have not been excavated, suggest that there may have been deposits (as yet undiscovered) that marked the construction or repair of each building or part of a building.

With the distribution of the buildings, the royal quarter of Persepolis is distinctly different from that at Susa, but one must remember that the first is the result of several different building phases, stretching over more than a century for the most important, whilst the second is the work of Darius, finished by Xerxes.

The monumental gate

We pass from rectangular to square in the plans of the hypostyle halls, but also in the plans of monumental gateways. The Gate of Xerxes at Persepolis was a construction measuring 36 x 36 m, comprising a single hall, 25 m square with four columns; the smooth walls had an inset bench. The room had two doors in its axis and another towards the Apadana. At Susa, the path taken was slightly different; the Darius Gate was a rectangular construction of 40 x 30 m, but the tetrastyle central hall was a 21.2 m²; the walls were decorated with recesses. The whole was flanked by two long rooms with staircases at the corners. On this basis it did not have side entrances but only two passages in the principal axis. This would have been the plan of the unfinished gate at Persepolis. Yet another solution was adopted for the Propylaeum at Susa: 24 m² of which the central part was made up of two long adjoining rooms (12.8 x 4.7 m) without columns. The walls were decorated with stepped recesses, like those of the hall in the Darius Gate. There were two entrances preceded by porticoes and it was flanked by small side rooms.[32]

The floor plan of Building 'E' at Persepolis, at the foot of the south end of the Terrace, attributed to Xerxes, differed slightly from that of the gateways: in

463
Persepolis: the door sockets in metal in which the posts of the heavy gates of the Apadana turned were held in enormous stone blocks
The floral decoration around the socket here indicated that the block was visible, whilst at Susa it was hidden
SCHMIDT, 1953: fig. 47B

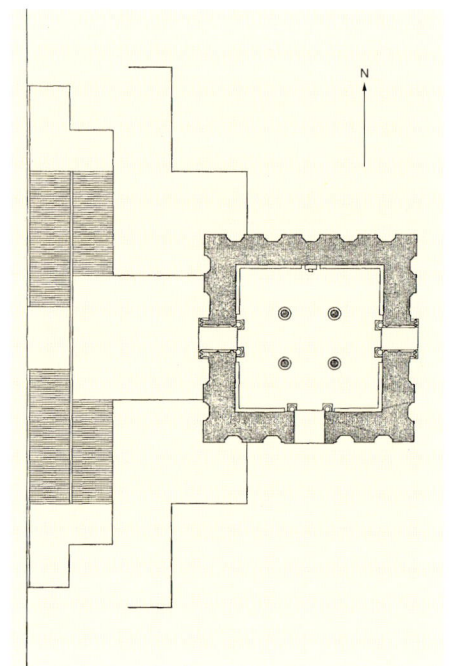

464
Plan of the Gate of All Nations at Persepolis
SCHMIDT, 1953 : fig. 26.

465

The Gate of All Nations at Persepolis, also known as the Gate of Xerxes – a trilingual inscription indicates that it was Xerxes who had the gate built
The central hall has four 20 m columns. Its east and west doors (see fig. 464) were flanked by composite animals with human heads in the Mesopotamian manner. As at Pasargadae, the gates had no defensive function, but marked the entrance onto the Terrace, into the Royal Quarter.
photograph by B.-N. Chagny

a building 40 m square, the tetrastyle Central Hall was also square with sides of around 20 m; on three sides it opened onto small, two-columned porticoes, the fourth gave access to small rooms. No monumental gateway was identified at the Shaur Palace, but, as previously mentioned, the possibility cannot be excluded.

In other Achaemenid palaces, still being excavated, such as those of Borazjan, near Bushire, 300 km to the south of Persepolis, and Nurabad, in western Fars, it would be interesting to see if a structure corresponding to an isolated gateway were present.[33]

Ever since Pasargadae the monumental gateway was a characteristic feature of Achaemenid architecture; it was an edifice completely isolated from all other buildings, set well to the fore of the residence or the hypostyle hall. At Susa it was open on two sides, three at Persepolis and even four at Pasargadae. It was no longer an opening in the ramparts or in the massive façade which delimited the royal perimeter. It marked a clear break with past traditions; abandoning the gate as a compulsory and protected passageway, it became a symbolic entrance, while still preserving Neo-Assyrian-style representations of winged monsters.[34] The gates of Assyrian palaces such as Nineveh or Khorsabad, or those of Babylon – the Ishtar Gate for example – formed part of the town or palace walls; they were the only passageway that allowed access inside a defined perimeter. The Achaemenid gateway created a new symbolism indicating free and peaceful access into the royal enclosure, but through an impressive monument.

466
Persepolis: the unfinished gate
The second passageway after the Gate of All Nations, was reserved for those who were going to the Hall of One Hundred Columns. Its layout is incomplete; the hall of four columns, flanked by two long halls, recalls the plan of the Darius Gate at Susa
photograph by B.-N. Chagny

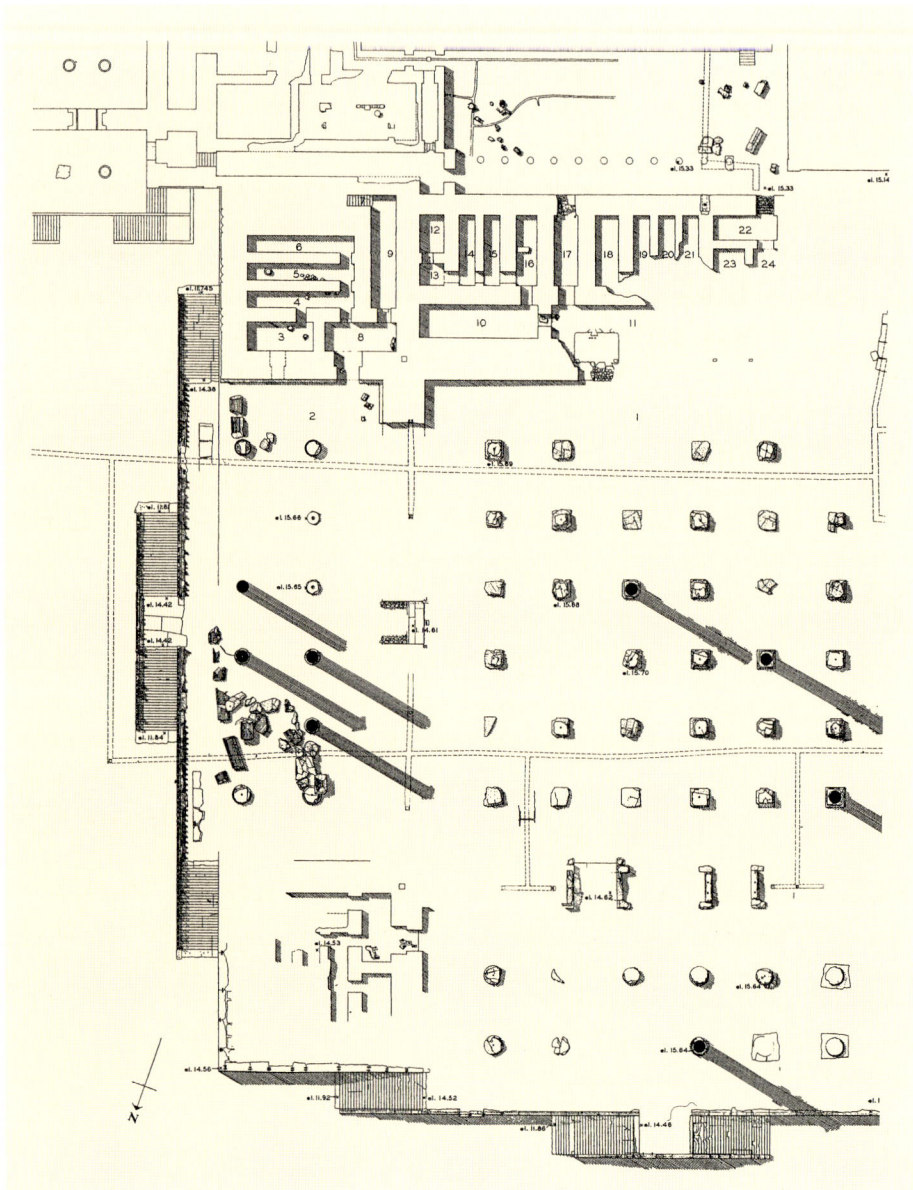

467
Persepolis: view of the southern sector of the Apadana showing several groups of narrow parallel rooms traversed by two long passageways
SCHMIDT, 1953: fig. 29

The hypostyle hall

The hypostyle halls of Susa and Persepolis are very similar in plan, dimensions and order of the column bases: square in the main hall, round and bell-shaped in the porticoes which flanked them on three sides. Unlike those at Pasargadae and Dasht-i Gohar the hypostyle halls were now perfectly square, with sides of 60.5 m on the inside at Persepolis, thus 3,660 m²; the whole of the building with its porticoes formed a 112 m square. The distance between columns, which at Palace P was no more than 3.5 m and slightly more than 6 m in Palace s at Pasargadae, was extended to over 8.5 m in the hall and porticoes at Susa and Persepolis; the columns, including capitals, reached a height of 21 m.

The fourth side, without portico, gave access to a less official area. At Persepolis this sector consisted of three groups of four narrow, parallel rooms, like those that occupied the corner towers.[35] These groups of rooms were accessed via a long hallway divided into two sections, parallel to the sides of the hypostyle hall. From the material found at Persepolis, these served as storerooms. Two of these narrow spaces were corridors which crossed from the hypostyle hall towards the back into a porticoed courtyard flanking the Palace of Darius. This layout was different from that of the Hypostyle Hall of Darius at Susa where, on the very badly preserved fourth side, the passageway leading to the Residence was at right angles to the hall, through unknown structures. In its access to an interior courtyard, the Apadana at Persepolis resembles more closely Building I at the Shaur Palace, a century later. Indeed, in this hypostyle hall, a large open air space was accessible through a long room.

It is not possible to reconstruct the fourth side at Susa, virtually all traces having disappeared. Conjecture is only possible through extrapolating the evidence at Persepolis. A hypothesis formed by Pierre Amiet, and recently taken up by D. Huff, postulates that the fourth side could have been the substructure of an upper storey. Both suggest that the stairs, present in all the corners, were too important to provide access to the Terrace alone; furthermore, it is hard to imagine narrow halls more than 15 m in height in the towers; if the staircases gave access to an upper floor, this may not have been limited to the towers, but could have spread over the whole southern end. What type of rooms might be reconstructed on this floor? Storerooms or administrative quarters mirroring the floor plan below, as Jean Perrot believes? Or apartments?[36] In this last case, the spaces must have been larger than the narrow rooms at floor level. In favour of this hypothesis, D. Huff noted that small column bases were found in the excavations of this sector. They cannot have come from the Hypostyle Hall, nor from the narrow rooms in which they would have been useless. They could have fallen from the upper storey, which would have been made up of large rooms with rows of posts on these small bases, resting on the walls of the narrow rooms which were 1.2 to 2 m thick. Pursuing his hypothesis, D. Huff saw this as the real royal residence of Persepolis which, together with the hypostyle hall, comprised the true palace. It should be noted that the residence would then constitute an interior space of nearly 100 x 20 m. Neither the highly hypothetical reconstructions nor the interpretations of function are valid at Susa, where this whole area has disappeared, because the Residence is a distinct complex, though linked to the Hypostyle Hall. But why not imagine an upper storey at Susa as at Persepolis, quarters where the family and retinue could be close to the Hypostyle Hall?

THE OTHER BUILDINGS OF PERSEPOLIS AND THE RESIDENCE AT SUSA

If the Achaemenid architecture of the columned halls seems homogeneous, despite much inventiveness and development over time, this is not the case for the rest of

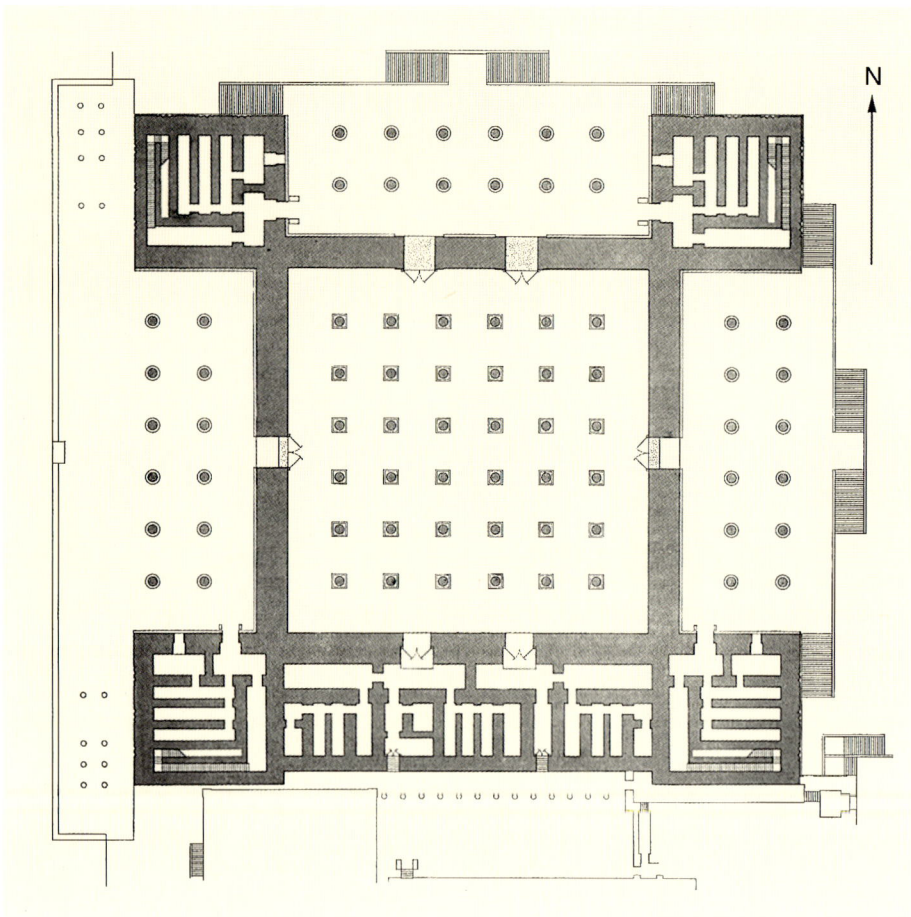

468
Persepolis: plan of the large Hypostyle Hall (Apadana)
SCHMIDT, 1953: fig. 30

the palace. Leaving aside Pasargadae, where the plan of the Residence is unknown – if one was planned by Cyrus on the Tall-i Takht – it can be seen that Darius' choices were fundamentally different at Susa and Persepolis. At Susa the Residence forms a block 220 by 150 m, with a complex but well-organised internal floor plan, as highlighted by Jean Perrot.[37] Arranged around several courtyards disposed along the same access, the King's Apartments were isolated from the other sections of the complex, which adjoined one another but were distinct. At Persepolis, if one admits that the Palace of Darius and the Treasury are part of the residence, in the sense of a ceremonial palace (the other buildings are later than Darius), the founder's programme was both more limited and less compact, even if a rapid decision was taken to change the plan of the Treasury and especially to considerably extend its area.

The fact remains that at Persepolis the buildings were individual and relatively accessible from the exterior whilst at Susa the Residence formed a compact block well protected from the outside. This difference and the layout of each unit suggests that Persepolis was not a residence similar to that at Susa: none of the 'palaces' was habitable, each was just designed to host a reception or banquet for a few dozen people, corresponding to the desire of each king to leave his mark. The complex made up by the individual 'palaces' and the Treasury of Persepolis, which was the administrative part of the palace, would have been the much larger counterpart to the eastern section of the Residence at Susa. These apartments are lacking at Persepolis, particularly the king's apartments, unless we follow D. Huff.

It must be asked whether the sovereign and the court lived on the Terrace during their stay at Persepolis. If this was not the case where did they then reside? And where did the permanent administrators of the Fars satrapy live? The southern section could be a suggestion, at the foot of the Terrace, but amongst the half dozen buildings excavated, isolated one from the other, as the 'palaces'

469
Persepolis: the large Hypostyle Hall
photograph by B.-N. Chagny

470
Persepolis: The 'Darius Palace'
photograph by B.-N. Chagny

projections – an ancient Elamite trait – but one known also from first millennium Mesopotamia. As for the disposition of the groups of rooms that flanked the Royal Apartments, the question of their origin is linked to that of their function: offices of the chancellery according to Jean Perrot, storerooms according to Pierre Amiet, for whom these were the supports of an upper storey. Amiet showed that the formula of storerooms juxtaposing ceremonial rooms had been well attested from the second millennium BC onwards – at Mari for instance, where such rooms are able to support a floor above, a hypothesis which J. Margueron also supports vigorously.[41] But what was this floor, a question already asked in the context of the organisation of the south side of the Hypostyle Hall? Storerooms at the most, thinks Jean Perrot, who points out that this hypothetical storey was cut off by the Royal Apartment which rose to roof level. For Pierre Amiet, the hypothesis of a 'noble floor' is plausible, a theory based on the plan of the long parallel rooms of large edifices in Urartu and of the pre-Achaemenid buildings of the Zagros, also on the Neo-Assyrian examples studied again by J. Margueron, who makes this hypothesis his own. The question of an upper floor can be postulated, as can its layout, for the enigmatic Building G at Persepolis, situated level with the Treasury, but lower than the 'palaces', where long narrow rooms, 2.4 m wide and walls 1.4 m thick, are preserved.[42] Why should we have such a plan if it were not for an upper floor, because everywhere else in this area of stores and chancellery offices there was a bias towards rooms with columns? The excavator E.F. Schmidt reconstructed a floor here, followed by his architect F. Krefter, and many more after them.[43]

The Persepolis Treasury may provide an answer to the argument put forward by Jean Perrot over the impossibility, very real at Susa, of movement on the upper storey, either side of the Royal Apartments. Indeed, the southern part of the Terrace at Persepolis, dedicated to warehousing and administration, was divided into non-communicating sections, and what is called the Treasury proper was itself organised into several sections without communication between them. This division of spaces, confirmed for warehouses, could also have been desired at Susa for apartments assigned to different categories. Here we enter into the domain of speculation.

Perrot advanced an argument further restricting the hypothesis of an upper floor on either side of the Royal Apartments at Susa: the absence of traces of stair-cases and the impossibility of finding locations for them in one or other of the narrow rooms, because all had traces of red plaster floors. If it had been proved that not one of these narrow spaces could have contained a staircase and that there were no other means in the interior or around this complex of reaching an upper storey, the hypothesis would have had to be abandoned. For the rooms located to the north-west, based on the data collected by Pillet in 1913, Mecquenem had indicated on his overall plan two pavilions comparable to twin apartments of the South Palace at Babylon, as Pierre Amiet has pointed out to me. But this section seems to have been a reconstruction because Mecquenem himself did not always show it on his plans. Having not found any traces of it, Perrot preferred not to indicate it on his plans.[44]

THE DECORATION

Another difference which people are happy to highlight between the royal residences, relates to the wall decorations, stone bas-reliefs at Persepolis and Pasargadae, and glazed brick panels at Susa. The differences were certainly im-portant but, on each of the two sites chosen by Darius, if one of the techniques was dominant, it did not exclude the other. Panels of glazed brick have been

GREEN   YELLOW   BLUE

474
Persepolis: reconstructed glazed brick panel with various decorative motifs

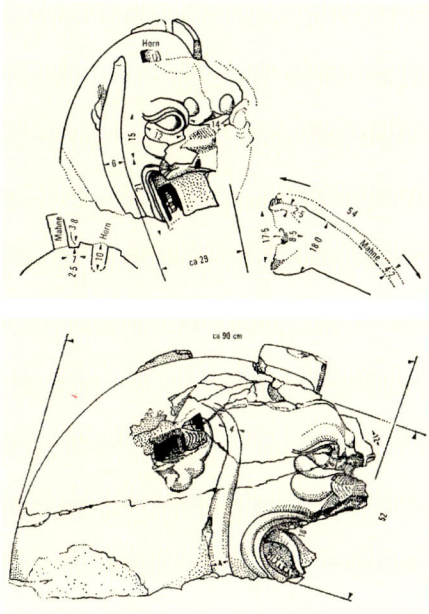

Pasargadae: pieces of stone column capital
Herzfeld excavations
STRONACH, 1978: fig. 29 a–b

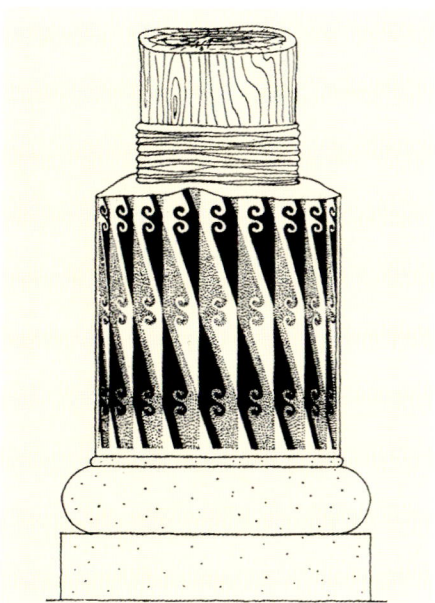

**Persepolis: wooden post covered in blue
and red painted plaster**
SCHMIDT, 1953: fig. 20

confirmed at Persepolis itself, as well as other monuments in the plain, a large number on a tell going by the evocative name of Tall-i Ajjori (baked bricks).[45] By contrast, the art of bas-relief is represented at Susa, modestly it is true and, furthermore, after Darius – a few orthostats were found in the Shaur Palace and there are others at the Donjon, perhaps taken from the Shaur. All have been dated to the reign of Artaxerxes II.

Another characteristic must be mentioned: unless we are mistaken, the glazed brick panels only decorated the Residence at Susa,[46] whilst at Persepolis the stone bas-reliefs are present in both the official buildings and in the so-called residential structures. On the other hand, at Persepolis glazed brick decoration does not appear in the palaces, but only in the Apadana, on the outside on the south-east and to the north, as decorative friezes interspersed with inscribed panels.[47]

Materials necessary for the making of glazed bricks needed to be available at Persepolis as at Susa, as well as the colours which, all things considered, must have been easy to transport.[48] The works we know of at Persepolis were modest and non-figurative, but there was also an inscription by Xerxes (XPg) in both Old Persian and Babylonian, found near the Apadana.[49] The decoration of glazed bricks, as evidenced at Persepolis and a few other sites such as Ecbatana, was completely new on the Iranian plateau, whilst the technique had long been used at Susa and is also confirmed in Neo-Babylonian Babylon. The panels at Susa, however, illustrate new techniques: siliceous bricks not only in terracotta, and the true use of cloisonné to create a finer drawing; this technique can be found at Persepolis and Achaemenid Babylon. Yet again at Babylon, but not Persepolis, human figures appear during the Achaemenid period, both full scale and half scale, most likely representing spearmen like the 'archers' at Susa. In this case, it was Susa which influenced the palace at the beginning of the fourth century BC at Babylon.[50]

If the components of glazed bricks are not so dependent on the local environment, the same cannot be said for stone, usage of which at Susa under Darius was limited to the component elements of the columns, whilst at Persepolis the use was extended to the door, window and recess frames. The distance from the quarries was probably one of the reasons for a restricted use of stone at Susa, but it was not a total constraint, because the bas-reliefs at Persepolis, which demanded a high quality limestone, required the working of quarries 30 km away from the Terrace.[51]

It was in architectural stone decoration that Greek (Ionian) influence was the most marked. As demonstrated by C. Nylander, in a book tellingly entitled *Ionians in Pasargadae*, this influence was very perceptible at Pasargadae, but it continued through to Persepolis and Susa in a manner that is less immediately visible, in the form of influences, mainly shapes, from the Levant and Egypt. In the use of techniques, a Lydio-Ionian influence is present from Pasargadae to Persepolis and at Susa. As an example we can cite the stone markings, although we do not know whether they were made in the quarries or by the masons. The repertoire of markings identified on the large carved blocks for the platform at Pasargadae was partly comparable with that on the Ionian monuments, seals, coins and painted vases.[52] The column bases at Persepolis and Susa each carried one or more markings, quite different from those at Pasargadae, but comparable with each other.

Stone wall decoration

Of the stone wall decoration at Susa, there exists a small number of staircase steps and parapet fragments, plaques and parts of plinths. These pieces did not exist in the Residence and the Hypostyle Hall, which highlights an important difference with Persepolis and Pasargadae. Indeed, as Pasargadae shows, bas-reliefs appeared at the start of the Achaemenid period; the sculpted fragments are more numerous than is often thought: besides the guardian monsters at Gate P and the capitals of the Gate and in Palace s, bas-reliefs decorated the door jambs in the three structures. The most famous is the 'winged genie' of the eastern passageway of the Gate, but the representations of figures, royal or often mythical, are numerous in other buildings.[53] After Cyrus, Persepolis saw an extensive use of the bas-relief with other depictions, whilst Darius' Susa has no examples, unless we can surmise that this absence is due to the ravages of humans and time.

Finally, painting is another decorative technique which, this time, unites Pasargadae, Susa and Persepolis, and does not allow for differences between plain and mountain. At Persepolis, traces of polychrome were detected on the stone and on the plaster coating of the wooden columns,[54] whilst the evidence for painting is very limited at Pasargadae and at Susa where it is only in evidence on mud brick. The use of polychrome, which was a very ancient tradition in the Orient, marked all the important Achaemenid constructions. Paintings may have covered a less extensive surface area than was claimed by nineteenth-century writers, particularly in the upper parts of the building exteriors at Persepolis,[55] but the most recent research has found considerable evidence: besides the visible remains on the columns, numerous and varied traces were identified on the bas-reliefs whether figurative or geometric.

The fragments of figural wall paintings found at the Shaur Palace remain unique, even though clues to painted decoration are confirmed in the structures of Darius at Susa, in the form of pigments on mud brick and potsherds which were used as pallets. The paintings of the Shaur, depicting figures in profile, sometimes in front of a cypress tree, could have played the same role as did the bas-reliefs at Persepolis, but without totally replacing them because their usage was less extensive and there were also stone orthostats. Finally, and no doubt from necessity, paintings depicting a row of figures were placed inside the Shaur hypostyle hall, which confirms its official nature, whilst the bas-relief friezes at Persepolis were always on building exteriors.

STRUCTURAL SIMILARITIES AND DIFFERENCES

The three palace complexes show strong similarities which are, for the most part, innovations in oriental architecture: monumental gateways with columns, isolated from other structures; large reception buildings with columns; these halls appeared to be very open, surrounded by several porticoes, isolated and without links to other buildings. The hypostyle halls of Persepolis and Susa, very similar to each other, marked a change of scale compared with Pasargadae and Dasht-i Gohar as well as a move from rectangular to square. At that time and later, at the foot of the Persepolis Terrace, the square plan still dominated in the most important structures.[56] The plan of the hypostyle hall of the Shaur Palace was also square, despite a slight difference of 3 m in the lengths of the sides.

The differences of concept and layout of the three residences are evident. At Pasargadae, the residence, planned by Cyrus on the platform, was distinctly separate from the reception rooms.[57] The Residence at Susa adjoins the Hypostyle Hall; it was compact and organised around several courtyards. Persepolis contained several structures very distinct from each other, even when they were nearby, and these had a central columned hall and at least one portico. The wall decorations, especially their relative importance, can vary partly according to the local natural resources; on the other hand, the techniques were not very different from one site to another. More significant were the location of the decorations and the depictions, which differed even at the two contemporaneous sites of Susa and Persepolis.

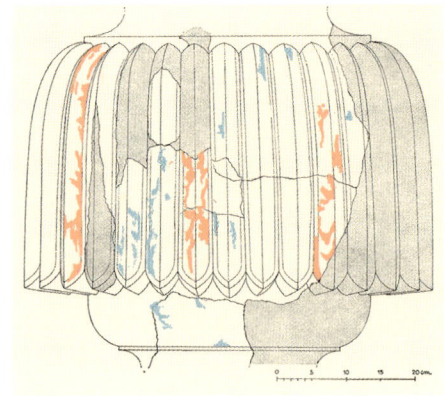

477
Capital with traces of paint
TILLA, 1978: fig. XX

The differences, and conversely, the similarities between the residences, amongst which that of Babylon must be included, can be attributed to several factors, including chronology and the contemporary local environment and traditions; these are not as open to discussion as that of the function, or the functions of each of these.

If the relative chronology of Pasargadae compared with Susa and Persepolis is clear, with a 30-year head start for the first, the respective dates for Susa and Persepolis lead to the conclusion that they were largely contemporaneous, at least at the start of the enterprise and its unfolding under Darius and Xerxes. The formative period of Achaemenid architecture, which Jean Perrot would like to identify at Susa, seems to me more marked at Pasargadae, where determinative elements appeared, such as the independence of each royal structure – even a dispersal at Pasargadae – the stone columned hypostyle hall, the animal-protome capitals, the multiple porticoes, the monumental gate without ramparts, the figural sculpture on the door jambs. These are innovations from the reign of Cyrus, some of which take up Lydian-Ionian and Mesopotamian themes, all completely new in the regions of Persepolis and Susa. One must stress the absence of stone-working traditions in these regions before Cyrus. In previous periods, including during the great Middle Elamite period, buildings were made of mud brick or baked brick, with stone only used as natural blocks or rubble. It was therefore a complete importation of forms and techniques that Cyrus decided upon, many of which came from distant western Asia Minor. One must not, however, forget the probable role played by traditional architecture from Urartu, a powerful kingdom at the juncture of the Zagros and the Elburz ranges, between the ninth and the beginning of the six century BC, whose buildings in large stone blocks were often faced with beautifully dressed stone. As regards the figural and decorative motifs from Mesopotamia, it is probable that the Persians knew some of the elements, as shown by discoveries from the pre-Achaemenid period (around 600 BC) such as the Arjan tomb in ancient Elam, in eastern Khuzestan, on the border with Fars. These elements, of which several appeared at Pasargadae, would be equally important at Susa and Persepolis, probably also at Babylon, but of the latter we have no trace.

LOCAL ENVIRONMENT AND TRADITIONS

The local environment and the traditions which are partially linked to it create differences between the architecture of Achaemenid sites but are less of a constraint than might appear. Stone was abundant in the Pasargadae region and at Persepolis, as well as in Borazjan, where quarries were identified, but the quality of the stone varied, which sometimes meant long journeys of up to 30 km at Persepolis for the bas-reliefs. At Susa, the use of stone was more limited, not so much because of the distance of resources as by the absence of a tradition; it remains that there, too, royal prerogative allowed for the execution of stone column bases and capitals of the same quality as at Persepolis. Similarly, the stone necessary for the column bases found in the small Persian palace at Babylon, and in other areas where there must have been structures of this period, had to be transported a long way.

Clay, a basic material, was also commonly used on all the sites, in the form of mud and baked bricks. The relatively simple techniques of building walls and, above all, the construction of vaults were known in Fars, Khuzestan and Mesopotamia. On the other hand, the glazed brick panels which the Elamites and Mesopotamians knew were a novelty at Persepolis. The use of wood in the form of long beams to cover the hypostyle halls, an innovation in all the regions of Persian residences, was only possible, from Pasargadae onwards, due to the power and extent of the empire which allowed imports from regions best provided with large trees. All things considered, the different materials and techniques used in Achaemenid architecture appeared across nearly all the sites. Chronology, local environment and traditions were not constraining factors from the moment the Great King willed these developments. The differences in the different areas must therefore be attributed to choice, that is to say the function the sovereign wanted to give each of his structures.

Compared with the organisation of the Mesopotamian, the Syrian or Babylonian and most probably the Elamite palace, Cyrus broke completely with the past at Pasargadae, which owed nothing to the Fars traditions (about which we admittedly know very little). He separated his residence and his ceremonial buildings and did not adopt an urban enclosure or a closed palace, such as characterised the Mesopotamian towns and palaces which he certainly would have seen. Further, he created the isolated monumental gate. Of course, he could show his power through a theme cultivated by his predecessors, but which was not dominant: the mastery of nature. To develop the landscape over dozens of hectares, transform a wasteland of rough terrain and scrub into green spaces, flat and partly organised along straight lines, was a major innovation. The Assyrian gardens, which we know mostly through representations, as well as the famous Hanging Gardens of Babylon, which remain to be identified with any certainty, were not on this scale. They were contained in the palace, whilst at Pasargadae, it was the ceremonial structures that were integrated into the park or garden.

Darius maintained all these elements, both in architecture and in the development of open-air spaces. These are not as visible today at Susa and Persepolis as they are at Pasargadae, but there is no reason to doubt them, such is the extent of the open spaces inside the site of Susa and around it, as with the 6 km that separate the Terrace of Persepolis and the royal necropolis at Naqsh-i Rustam. The Terrace at Persepolis itself, which appears today almost completely covered by built structures, must have had many open spaces in Darius' initial conception.

The differences seem to establish two types of structure: on the one hand, Pasargadae, Borazjan and Persepolis, on the other, Susa and Babylon.[58] This is much more than a difference between mountain and plain – Borazjan was at a low altitude, in the Persian Gulf region – and only minimally is it a difference between Persian lands and the lands of ancient empires. It is tempting to see a difference between the ceremonial spaces that are preserved only at Pasargadae, Persepolis and no doubt Borazjan, and the places where the residential and administrative areas are still visible, as at Susa and Babylon. There is no doubt that residential quarters existed in the first three sites, whatever their shape and decoration, but they are little known, or unknown; on the other hand, ceremonial spaces were built at Susa: the Hypostyle Hall and a part of the Residence, the Gate, and at Babylon, where only the 'Persian Palace' survives. Differences there certainly are, and also evolution during the first century of the Achaemenid Empire, especially a real homogeneity of conception, always grandiose, as the Persians wished it to be, whatever the price in men, rare materials from distant lands, and in quality of execution. No one doubts that, other than some differences in the structures found, this homogeneity of royal projects would be more obvious if we knew each 'residence' in its whole context of built and developed spaces.

If we consider the Terrace at Persepolis as a ceremonial architectural ensemble, and not as a dwelling, the royal residence itself remains to be discovered, as well as the quarters of the satrapy chancellery staff and the workmen attached to the permanent building site which was Persepolis. At Susa, the royal residence is now better understood, but the urban surroundings of Achaemenid Susa, if they ever existed, cannot be guessed at.

1. Happily, our western way of looking at things has changed since J. de Morgan wrote 'Achaemenid art, if we can qualify as art the incoherent mixture favoured at the court of the successors of Cyrus, which was merely a composite of Assyrian, Egyptian, Phoenician, Greek, Lycian, Cappadocian, Phrygian [...]. These diverse elements were, most often, brought together in the worst possible taste; they are rarely grouped in an agreeable fashion' (MORGAN, 1905b: 46).

2. NYLANDER, 1979: 355.

3. See above, pp. 419–420.

4. See below, H. Gasche.

5. Briant, ch. I, this volume, p. 11.

6. Briant, ch. I, this volume, p. 10.

7. Briant, ch. I, this volume, p. 11.

8. STRONACH, 1989: 442 ff.; STRONACH, 2001: 103: N. 40.

9. JACOBS, 1997a. M. Roaf (M. ROAF, 1983: 150–152, 157) leans towards a date at the beginning of the fifth century BC for the earliest work on the Terrace. D. Stronach (STRONACH, 2001: 103), on the contrary, favours a date well before 500, because many years would have been required for the construction of the Terrace. The almost simultaneous beginning of the two enterprises, which is suggested here, is also favoured by Briant (BRIANT, 1996: 180–181).

10. J. Perrot, this volume, ch. XIV, p. 454.

11. P. Briant, this volume, ch. I, pp. 5–7.

12. In all his reports, M.R. Sarraf maintains this indecisive position (most recently SARRAF, 2003: 273–274). For the new excavations, see the first clues provided in a note by R. Biscione (BISCIONE, 2005). Since then, a detailed report in Persian has been published by M. Azarnoush (AZARNOUSH, 2007).

13. CHEVALIER, 1989. The excavators have also noted fragments of column shafts and glazed brick.

14. KNAPTON, SARRAF, CURTIS, 2001. The inscriptions belong to the reign of Artaxerxes II, without forgetting those that are not on column bases, but on gold and silver plaques bearing the names of Ariaramnes and Arsames, ancestors of Cyrus, at the beginning of the sixth century BC, and a further one in the name of Darius. Some consider these as authentic, belonging to the period of these kings, whereas others believe them to be 'forgeries' made during the reign of Artaxerxes II (LECOQ, 1997: 124–126).

15. HERZFELD, 1935: 28; HANSMAN, 1972: 110.

16. This recent evidence derives mostly from the geophysical surveys carried out between 1999 and 2008 (BOUCHARLAT and BENECH, 2002).

17. STRONACH, 1978: 15 and fig. 5.

18. BOUCHARLAT, 2003.

19. We should also consider later Iranian palaces, of which that of Safavid Isfahan is the best known.

20. BOUCHARLAT and LOMBARD, 2001; MAGEE, 2001.

21. The fragments were found by E. Herzfeld in 1928; they were examined much later on the basis of his notes (STRONACH, 1978: 61–62, fig. 29 and pl. 55; CALMEYER, 1981).

22. The most one might suggest is an enclosure behind the Gate, as mentioned by D. Stronach (STRONACH, 2002: 96), following E. Herzfeld's observations. Recent geophysical prospection would tend to confirm the absence of a rampart there, where the garden may well have begun (BOUCHARLAT

and BENECH, 2002: fig. 2).

23. KLEISS, 1971b; TILIA, 1978: 73–80; STRONACH, 1978: 100–101.

24. STRONACH, 2001: 100–101.

25. Overall plan (KLEISS, 1992: Abb. 1) and reconstructions (KREFTER, 1971: Taf. 1–3 and Beilage 34).

26. R. Boucharlat, this volume, ch. XII, p. 378.

27. The floor of the palace is 18 m above water-level; the level of the plain in Achaemenid times must have been some meters above water level.

28. J. Perrot, this volume, ch. VII, pp. 182–185.

29. The overall plan of Persepolis (SCHMIDT, 1953: fig. 21) gives a clear idea of the drainage network of the terrace. For details, see *ibid.*, fig. 32 to the south of the Apadana, figs 66 and 69 in the Treasury, figs 75–77, 88.

30. D. Ladiray, this volume, ch. VI, pp. 146–148.

31. R. Boucharlat, this volume, ch. XII, pp. 395–396.

32. The city gate, or Porte des Artisans, does not belong to the same category. Its plan is clearly defensive, and its location on the glacis marks the limit of royal Susa.

33. On this last, see the first observations of the archaeologists who have reopened the excavation of this building (POTTS *et al.*, 2007).

34. HERZFELD, 1929: 5; STRONACH, 1978: 44–47, 51.

35. SCHMIDT, 1953: 72–78.

36. AMIET, 1994: 3. D. Huff (HUFF, 2005: 375–377) sees in this arrangement, which he restores in the Persepolis Apadana, a link between the pre-Achaemenid and Islamic periods. Indeed, Huff interprets the narrow, parallel spaces of pre-Achaemenid fortresses at Tepe Nush-i Jan and Godin Tepe, which might also be storerooms, as substructures for official or residential rooms which could have been huge and required beams that rested on the parallel walls. This hypothesis, among others, was examined by the excavators of Nush-i Jan (STRONACH and ROAF, 2007: 127–128). D. Huff further considers the Sassanian Palace of Ardashir at Firuzabad as an example within the same context of Iranian continuity. In that palace, the high, domed halls on the ground floor are surrounded by apartments that are half the height and he even cites, for the Safavid period, the halls and galleries that surround the central hall of buildings in Isfahan.

37. J. Perrot, this volume, ch. xiv, pp. 458–459.

38. STRONACH, 2001: 103. J. Perrot, however, believes that the plan had been well considered. The height of the walls depended on the total completion of the system of foundations and drainage, and this would have taken several years to accomplish.

39. H. Gasche in this chapter, p. 438.

40. This was recognized in Palace D, to the west of the present Museum (SCHMIDT, 1953: fig. 114), and has also been proposed for southern part of the Apadana. Whether or not these rooms supported a superstructure, it remains the case that their layout ties in well with the system of narrow storerooms.

41. AMIET, 1974: 71. J. Margueron has long argued in favour of the reconstruction of upper storeys in some parts of many Mesopotamian palaces, and has recently demonstrated this in the context of the 'Throne-Room Suite' of Neo-Assyrian palaces (MARGUERON, 2005). He believes that only the Throne-Room itself occupied the whole height of the building, whereas adjacent rooms of different sizes had upper floors with rooms that could have

had several rows of wooden beams resting on the walls of narrow storerooms on the ground floor.

42. SCHMIDT, 1953: fig. 113–114.

43. SCHMIDT, 1953: 269; KREFTER, 1971: 78–80, Beilage XXXVI.

44. Compare, on the one hand, the plan of Susa (MECQUENEM, 1947: Plan I or TALLON, 1997b: 109) and the plan of Babylon (KOLDEWEY 1990, Abb. 70a), and on the other hand the earlier plans of Susa and that shown here (Perrot, this volume, ch. VII).

45. TILIA, 1978: 84–85, pl. LII–LIII, with white, yellow, blue and green colours – some in slight relief.

46. One could have suggested stair panels; these would have enabled the possible extra height of the Hypostyle Hall to be crossed. However, a study of the foundations show that this reconstruction would be impossible (J. Perrot, this volume, ch. VI, pp. 200–201).

47. SCHMIDT, 1953: 70–71. It has been possible to reconstruct the inscription to the north, which belongs to Xerxes who declares having completed what his father had begun.

48. N. Daucé, this volume, ch. X: p. 305.

49. LECOQ, 1997: 100 and 256. The Susa glazed bricks are rarely inscribed; the exception is the Darius trilingual (DSM), found already by Dieulafoy, which gives a list of nations (DIEULAFOY, 1893: 284, fig. 192, pl. XII; LECOQ, 1997: 239).

50. For Persepolis, see SCHMIDT, 1953: 71; for Babylon, see HAERINCK, 1973: 118–122 who provides a good summary of the results of R. Koldewey's excavations; INVERNIZZI, 2008: 242–245.

51. Certain quarries at Persepolis are close to the terrace, and some are even on the terrace. However, the quarries of Majdabad, that provided the stone for the sculptors, is barely closer than the quarries used by the craftsmen of Susa (CALMEYER, 1990).

52. BOARDMAN, 1970 and 1998.

53. As noted above. HERZFELD, 1929; STRONACH, 1978; CALMEYER, 1981.

54. SCHMIDT, 1953: fig. 72J; TILIA, 1978: 31–39.

55. PERROT and CHIPIEZ, 1890: 712, 713 and 730.

56. TAJVIDI, 1976: fig. 22.

57. The Achaemenid ruins of Borazjan, to the north of Bushire, are attributed to Cyrus. New, still unpublished excavations, show that the complex is not restricted to the building previously excavated, but that its layout is probably similar to that of Pasargadae, with several buildings separated by several hundreds of metres in a space now occupied by a palm-grove, thus hampering excavations.

58. In this last case, the Neo-Babylonian buildings that survived in the time of Cyrus were probably vital in maintaining local architecture, but not to the extent of preventing one of the kings from profoundly modifying certain parts, as demonstrated by H. Gasche.

The small column bases

Rémy Boucharlat

Small stone column bases, partial or complete, were found individually on the tells of Susa and around the site, testimony no doubt to palaces or small structures now vanished. The majority of them date from the Achaemenid period. Some were inscribed, and more often than not had square rather than round bases. The bell-shaped bases (also referred to as campaniform) were the easiest to differentiate thanks to their decoration; the square bases were distinguished mainly by their size.

The diversity of their provenance is astonishing; easy to transport because of their relatively light weight, they were probably reused where they had been found, at a time that it is sometimes possible to determine. Their concentration in a specific location, however, does not allow us to favour one or other sector of the site or its surrounding area. In three cases, several bases were found in the same area. These findings by Ghirshman at the Ville Royale (site A) were Achaemenid; they were disparate, some square and others round. Amongst the four, ribbed, bell-shaped bases, at least two are decorated with ovoids on the top. Their diameter is around 50 cm. The building which reused these bases, of which there must have been around 14, would have dated from the end of the Parthian era.[1]

At the southern end of the Ville Royale, at the Donjon, the square bases found by Loftus and by Mecquenem are different one from the other. They were reused in a Seleuco-Parthian structure, as indicated by the Greek inscriptions which two of them have: one is in grey and the other in white limestone. Could the latter have been a post-Achaemenid imitation? Two other square bases were smaller (95 cm). We must remember that two different templates (114 cm and 95 cm) were evident in the Shaur Palace. Round bases also came from the Donjon; one was inscribed with the name of Artaxerxes II (A2sb). The other bases brought to light were isolated, difficult to locate and rarely described. The very rapid urbanisation

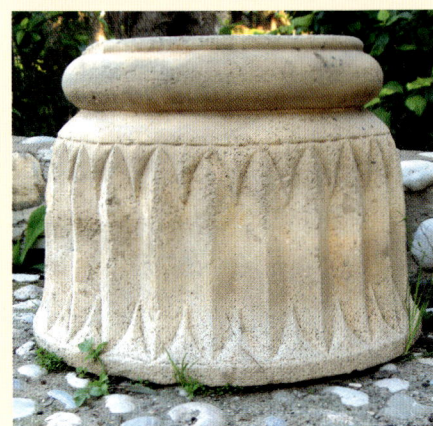

478
Reused column bases from the Ayadana
Haft Tepe Museum.

479
Transporting a small column base
J. DIEULAFOY, 1888

of the town of Shush since the 1960s has been the occasion of new discoveries, but it is probable that not all were reported. Finally, next to these partial or whole bases, the older excavations regularly brought to light scattered limestone base fragments.

The inscriptions

The inscriptions suggest the existence of structures built during the entire Achaemenid period, but their known sponsors were Darius and a few successors: Xerxes, Darius II and Artaxerxes II. Their inscriptions incorporate the terms *taçara* or *hadish* which cannot be translated only by the words 'house' or 'building'. Hence we have the *taçara* built by Darius (DSd) and the 'columned building' another inscription by the same king (DSg). Xerxes also mentions a structure which remains unlocated (XSb). An inscription of Darius II (perhaps D2Sa) and those of Artaxerxes II (A2Sb and A2Sd) are mentioned to support the hypothesis of an Achaemenid palace at the Donjon. Artaxerxes II also mentioned a building (A2Sc) with a staircase which has not been identified.

TABLE 4
Classes of small column bases

	Height	Diameter	Round bases with/without egg-shaped decoration	Places of discovery (bases not in situ)	Inscription Author
Square bases					
1.14 and 1.03	0.70	0.92	—	Donjon	—
0.91–0.925–0.96	0.47	0.70	—	Shaur, building II	A2Sd
	0.42	0.67	—	Shaur surf	A2Sd
	0.48	0.45	—	Donjon	A2Sd
Round bases					
0.80–0.82	0.60	0.69	with	Shaur, building II	A2Sd
			with	Donjon	A2Sd
			without	Donjon	A2Sd
0.63–0.68–0.71	0.43	0.50–54	?	Residence, salle F	—
			without	Ayadana	—
			with	Ayadana	—
0.51–0.54	0.42	0.46	with	Acropolis	XSa
		?	with	Ville de Shoush	—
			with	Ville royale A	—
		0.43	? incomplete	Shaur	—

1. GHIRSHMAN, 1976: pl. XLI, GASCHE, 2002; STEVE, VALLAT and GASCHE, 2002: 510 and fig. 8

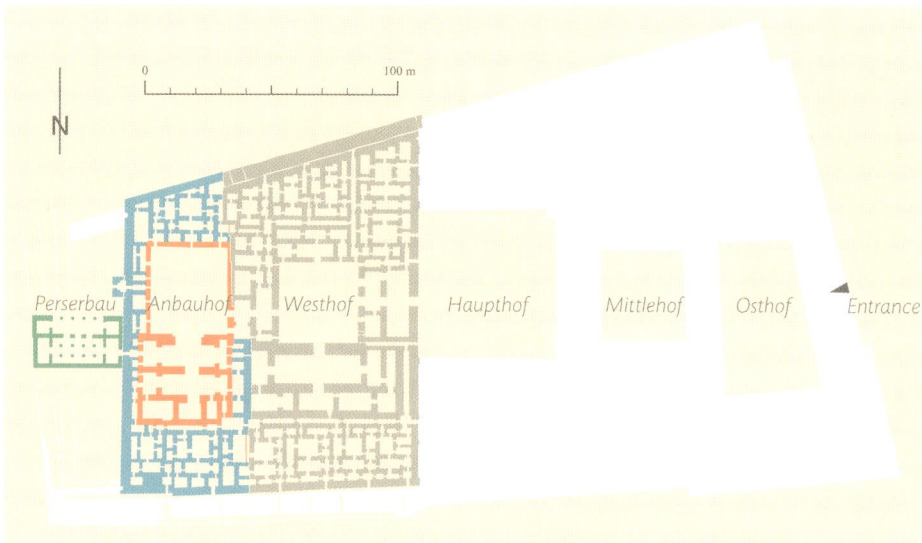

480
**Babylon: plan of the Südburg
with detail of the apartments around
the Westhof and the Anbauhof**
The red walls indicate the section which
is the object of the present enquiry
after KOLDEWEY, 1931:
pls 2, 20, 22, 23, 25 and 28

Building work of Artaxerxès II

Achaenimid constructions (probably Darius I)

Older Achaemenid constructions
(probably of Cyrus)

Walls of the 'Achaemenid Palace'
of Susa superimposed onto the
plan of the *Südburg* of Babylon

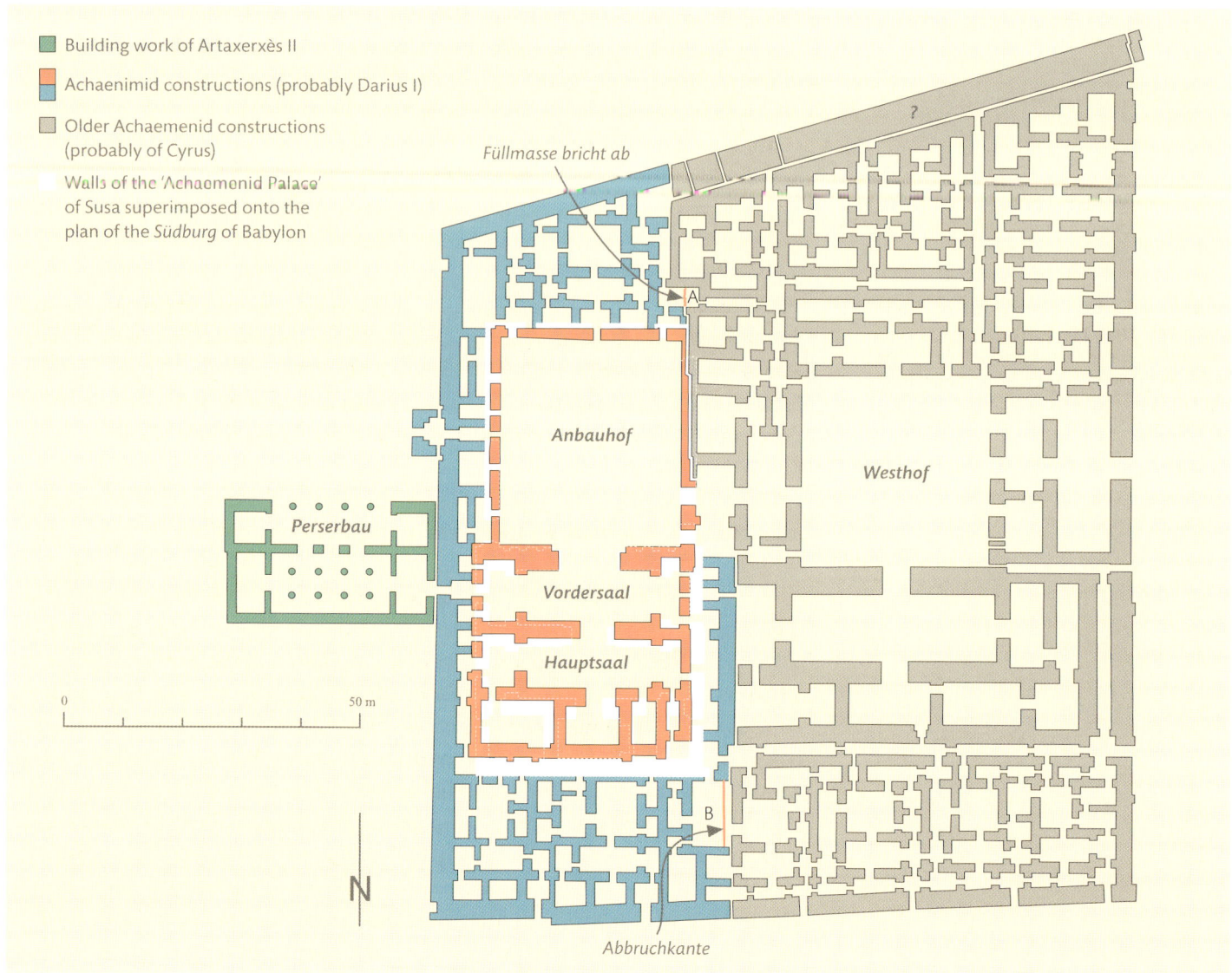

481
**Babylon: the Westhof, Anbauhof
and the Perserbau in the Südburg**
Note the breaks between the red walls
and the grey walls as well as the long break
in the eastern wall of the Anbauhof
after KOLDEWEY, 1931:
pls 2, 20, 22, 23, 25 and 28

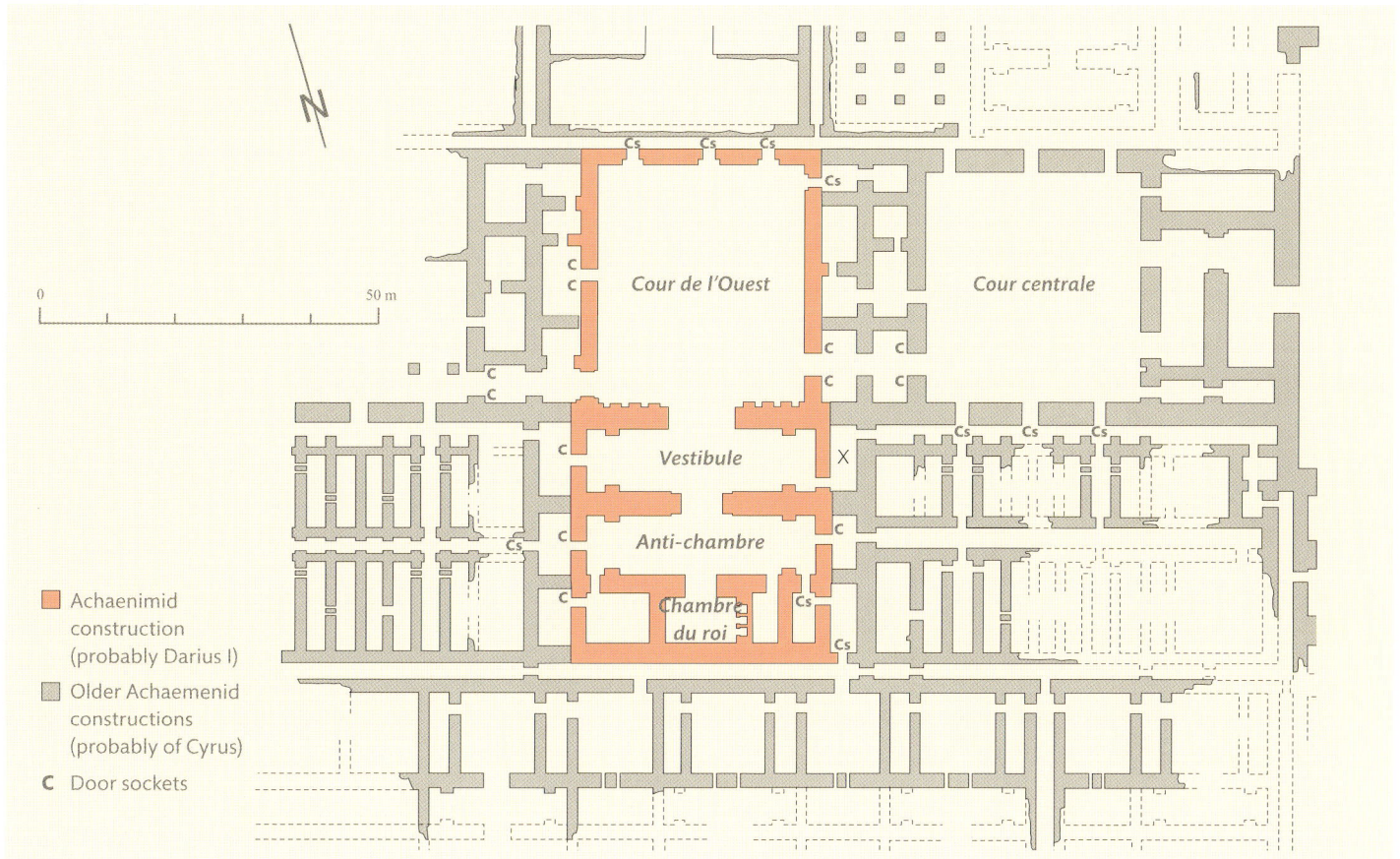

482

Susa: the Central Court and the West Court of the Achaemenid palace
The door sockets identified in the 'West Court' show that access to the spaces outlined by the red walls was protected, with the exception of that marked 'X'.
after KOLDEWEY, 1931: pls 2, 20, 22, 23, 25 and 28

As for the slightly earlier Neo-Assyrian halls, they did not respect – as we have already said – the two co-existing features of the Chaldeo-Persian hall. This does not prevent us from seeing there a local version, but without roots in Assyria; it is then delicate to propose – as did Roaf[16] – a sort of stage between the halls of Babylon and a Susian version originating nearly a millennium before.

The halls of Susa built between 1600 and 1400 BC

It is at Susa that one finds the oldest evidence of the four-pilastered hall. In an article dedicated to Susian architecture, Roman Ghirshman pointed out their appearance in level XIV of his site A, situated less than 150 m to the east of the complex built 1,100 years later by Darius the Great.[17] It was still in use in levels XIII and XII and in early level XI, about 1400 BC, but in a residence of which only the foundations have survived.[18] Later, in levels X and IX, we do not find them amongst the very meagre structures of the end of the second millennium BC.

All the examples of site A respect the special features defined at the beginning of this investigation: four pilasters disposed symmetrically towards the extremities of the long sides and an opening onto the courtyard significantly larger than for a normal door. Except for the more modest house C, the opening in question never had door sockets; it was therefore unlikely that there was a door between the courtyard and the four-pilastered hall dating from the second millennium BC. On the other hand, we do not encounter a second hall behind the first, but we are dealing here with domestic architecture, not that of a palace, even though five of the seven residences excavated each covered an area of more than 1500 m² and though the area of one of them could have been greater than 2200 m². Other than at Susa, the hall with four pilasters has been identified at only one second millennium BC site: Qatna, in western Syria.

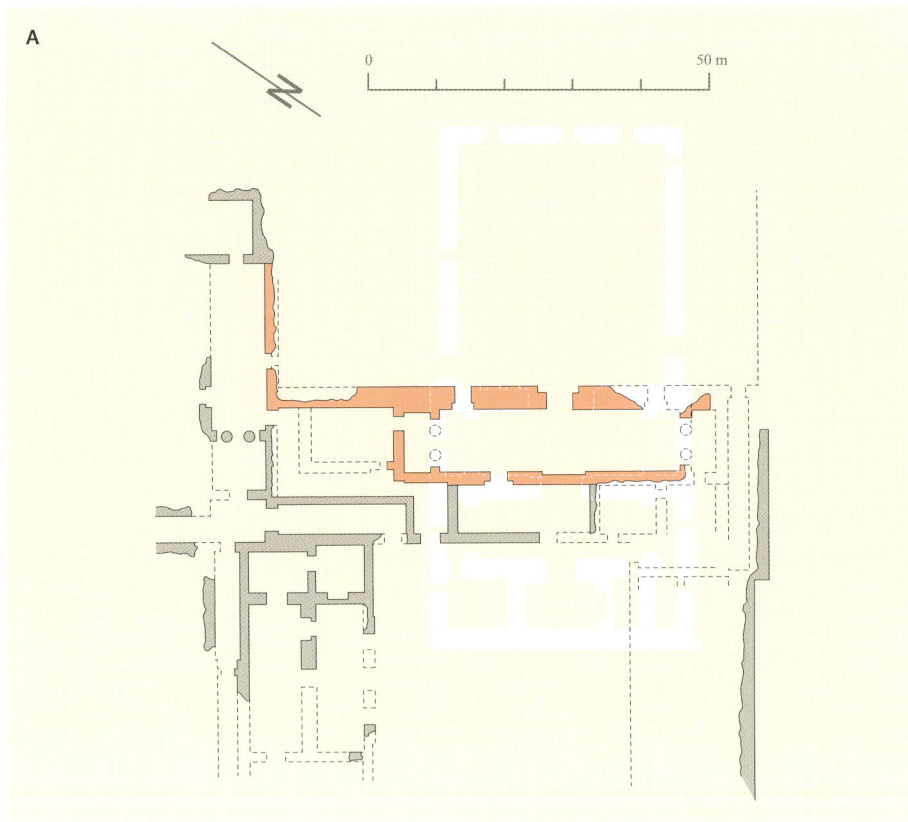

A

0   50 m

B

0   50 m

Neo-Assyrian structures

Walls of the 'Achaemenid palace' of Susa superimposed on the plan of Nineveh

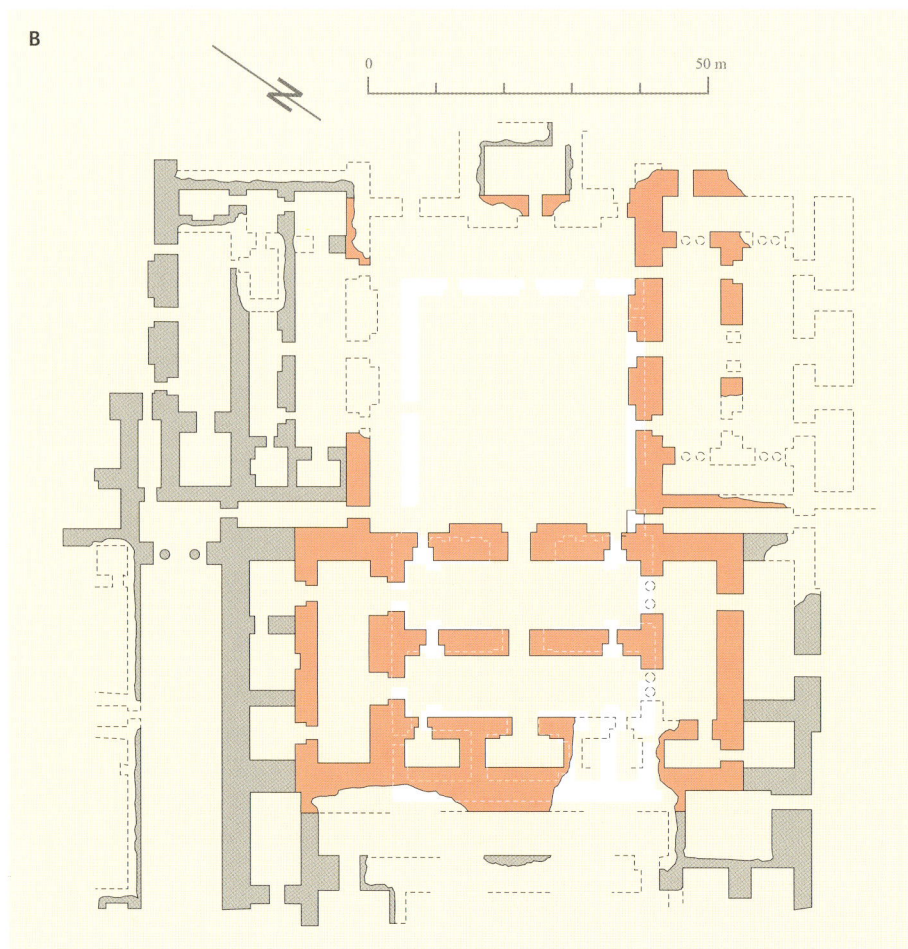

483
Nineveh

above left
A: section of the North Palace of Ashurbanipal (668–627 BC).

left
B: section of the South West Palace of Sennacherib (704–681 BC)

The restored columns between the pilasters of Hall M (Ashurbanipal) and in the body of the building in red of Sennacherib's palace were probably inspired by those which are in evidence between spaces P and B of Ashurbanipal's palace and 48 and 49 of that of Sennacherib

READE, 1998–2001: figs 11 & 12

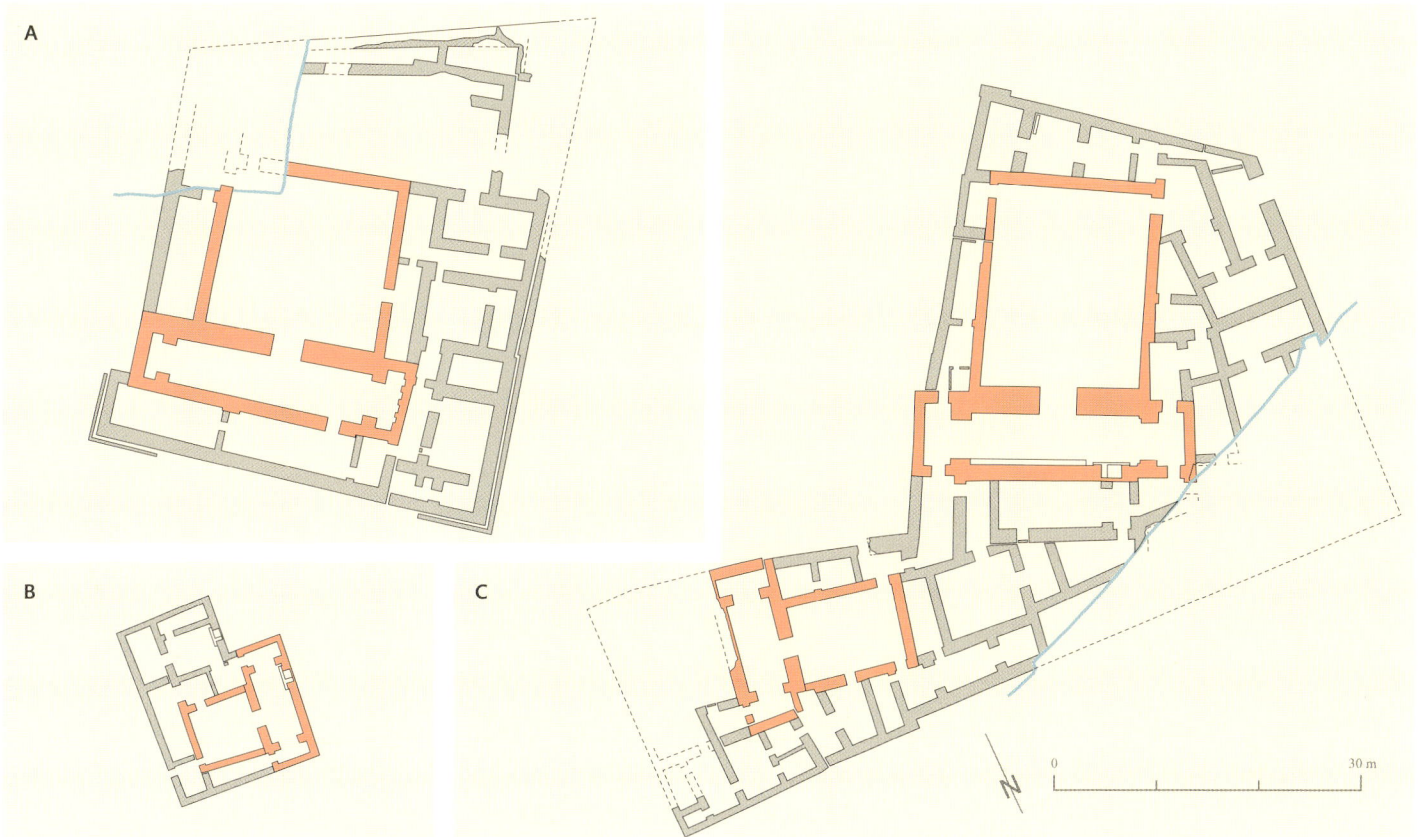

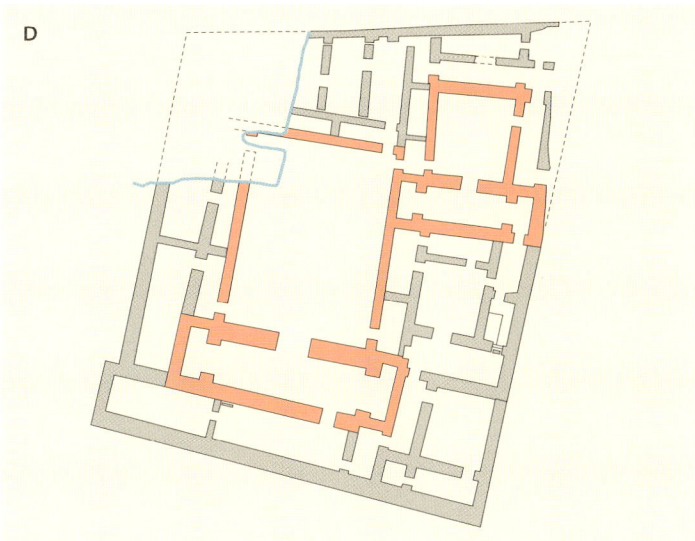

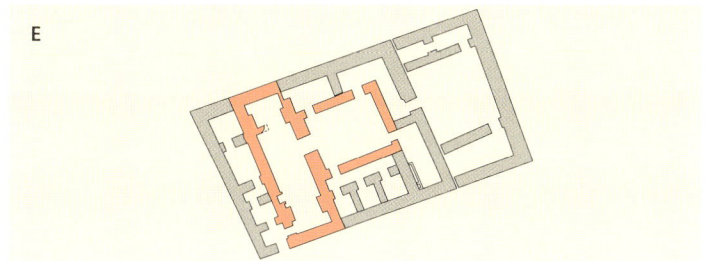

484 **Susa: Ville Royale, Ghirshman's site A**

A, B Reconstruction two large residences of level XIV (*c.*1640–1570 BC)
C Reconstruction of a house of level XIV (*c.*1640–1570 BC)
D Reconstruction of the large residence of level XIII (*c.*1570–1500 BC)
E Reconstructed plan of the residence of late level XII (*c.*1500–1440 BC)
F1, F2 Reconstructed plan of the two successive buildings of the large residence of early level XII

The dates refer to the new chronology base (fall of Babylon in 1499 BC)

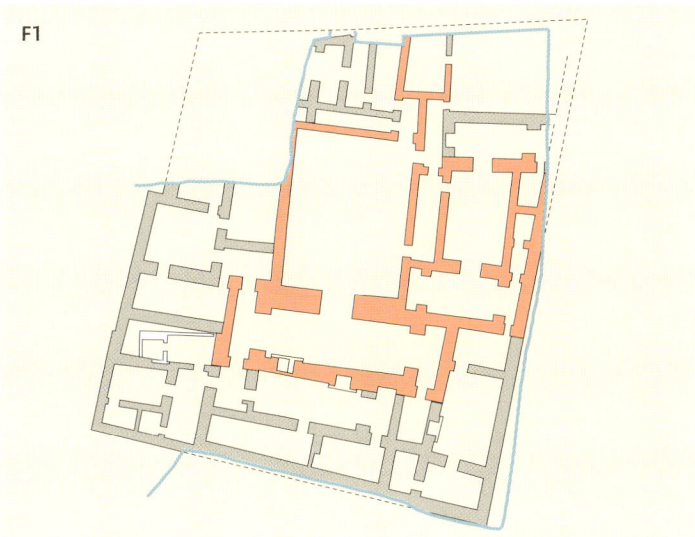

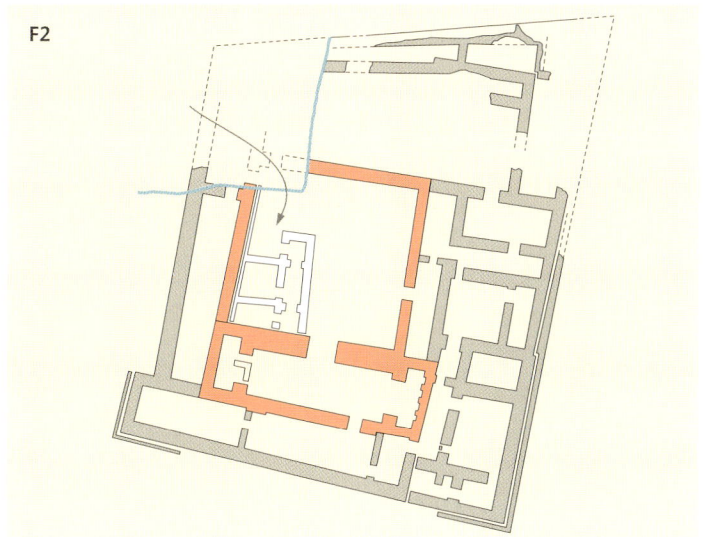

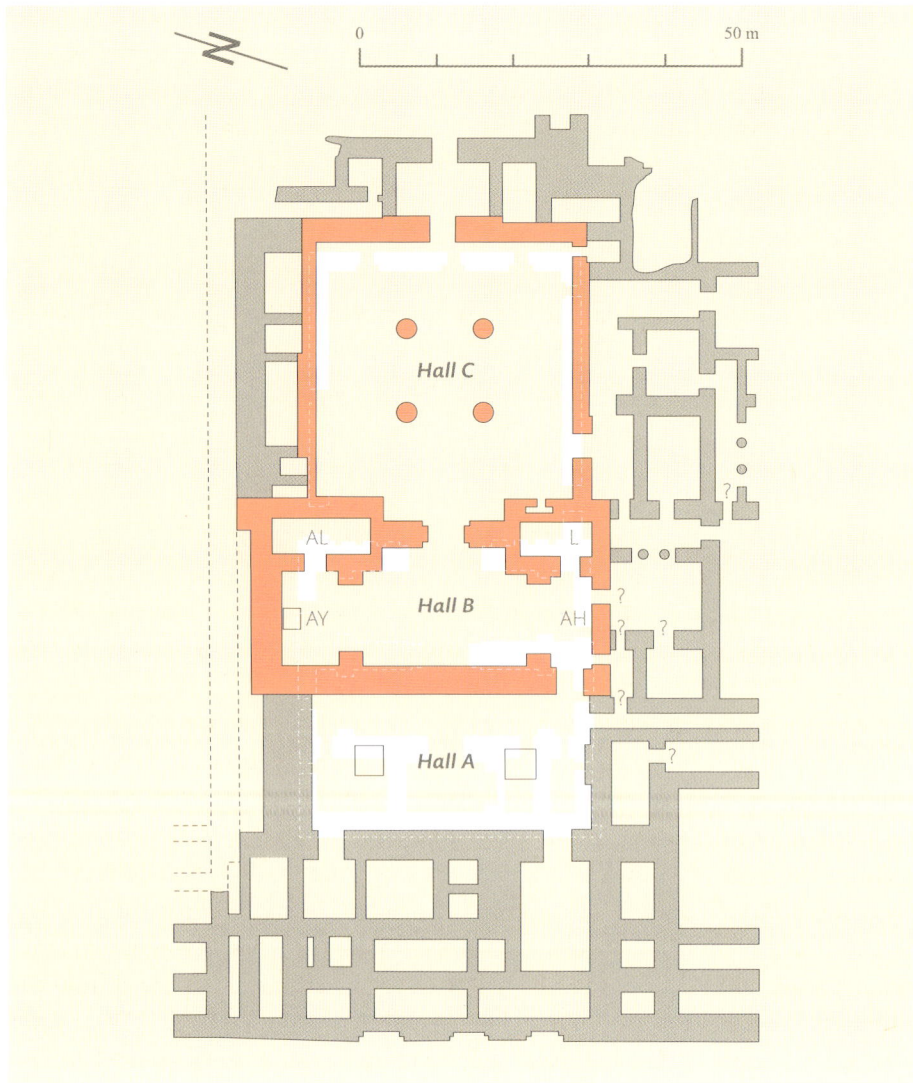

☐ Walls of the 'Achaemenid palace' of Susa superimposed on the plan of Qatna

? Reconstructed door

485
Partial schematic plan of the royal palace at Qatna, middle of the second millennium BC
Syria: excavations of 1924–29 and 1999–2005. The covered Hall C here replaces the Assyro-Suso-Babylonian courtyard; elsewhere, two rooms (AL and L) were inserted between Halls B and C. An archive was found in a niche in the wall at P
after MORANDI BONACOSSI and EIDEM, 2006: fig. 2

The hall of the Royal Palace of Qatna ('Hall B')

This hall from the middle of the second millennium BC was interpreted by the excavators as the throne room of the palace, built more than 1,100 km to the north-west of Susa.[19] Its width, that is to say its span, was never equalled in this type of structure, which bears witness to an excellent mastery of the technical constraints.

Despite its geographical distance, the design of 'Hall B' at Qatna was very close to those of the Susian halls whose origins were a little older: two pairs of pilasters divided the space into three unequal surface areas and one opening – around 5 m wide without door sockets – gave onto a vast covered space, 'Hall C', which here occupied the place of the courtyard in the more easterly palaces. The only difference was the presence, at Qatna, of two rooms, 'L' and 'AL', squeezed between Halls 'B' and 'C' on either side of the central opening; this layout resembled slightly that of a pylon, but does not affect the two co-existing features of the four-pilastered hall.

The similarities between the halls of Susa and Qatna are so surprising that they bring about the theory of exchanges between these two regions, however distant one from the other. With the exception of architecture, however, no elements of material culture support this conjecture. François Vallat, meanwhile, suggested a rethinking of several records found in the old excavations and published in 1949 and 1950 by Jean Bottéro. Certain words and personal names mentioned in these records could have been of Elamite origin, such as *Naplimma, Urpazana, puhu*;

indeed *Lullu* and *Idadu* could equally be Elamite names. Furthermore, the goddess NIN.É.GAL appeared as the principal divinity of Qatna in one of these records, which Thomas Richter dated to the end of the fifteenth century or beginning of the fourteenth century BC.[20] Coincidence or not, it was also the period of the four-pilastered hall in the palace, approximately when NIN.É.GAL was worshipped independently at Chogha Zanbil in Susiana, confirming the importance of this site as a royal stopover;[21] but, without simplifying unduly, it is important to recall that the hall with four pilasters was not known in the architecture of this new town.

The clues brought together here do not prove an alliance between Susa and Qatna, but they do not negate possible contacts between the two towns in the middle of the second millennium BC when troubles and dynastic changes brought ruin to the great empires of the centre and the east of the Near East.

The period between 1400 and the end of the sixth century BC

We have just seen that the hall with four pilasters was not attested at Chogha Zambil, in its palaces of the fourteenth century BC, or in the more recent and rudimentary structures published by J. Michalon;[22] but the architecture of this site distances itself from the traditions of the previous period and perhaps deserves a new, more subtle, approach than that which has been accorded it until now. These halls do not appear either in the constructions of the neighbouring site of Haft Tepe, contemporaneous with early level XI at Susa, but the Iranian excavations reached neither the palace nor the residential quarters.

Apart from a few incomplete religious buildings found on the Acropolis at Susa, no edifice built between around 1400 and the end of the sixth century BC survived the murderous picks of the ancient excavators. For all that, this lack of information does not allow us to deduce that the hall with four pilasters disappeared from the Susian architectural repertoire in which it had been well established. We cannot conclude, therefore, as Michael Roaf did,[23] that the 2,000-year-old model at Susa was reintroduced by the Neo-Assyrian architects into their palaces, and that from these it was copied at Babylon, Lachish, Persepolis and even Susa, where it originated. This strange journey has no merit other than to stimulate a different approach.

To summarise, one would have to admit that the available data only confirms the origins of the hall with four pilasters: Susa, with several examples built around 1600 BC and one, slightly more recent hall at Qatna in western Syria. The subsequent path, passing by the Neo-Assyrian variations through to the Chaldeo-Achaemenid period is not documented. We would not be much mistaken if we saw, at the outset, a fairly popular architectural layout at Susa. The unique example found in Syria does not negate this hypothesis.

THE SÜDBURG: A NEW EXAMINATION OF THE RUINS

When Robert Koldewey began work in 1899, he lavished considerable resources on this site whose *intra muros* area covered 975 hectares. The excavations were to surpass ordinary expectations, but the techniques used often hindered detailed stratigraphical analysis of the remains. On the other hand, the minutiae of the architectural data and the attention accorded to certain anomalies are precious tools in our investigation.

Nebuchadnezzar II (604–562 BC) realised a building programme at Babylon which most certainly transformed the urban landscape left by his father Nabopolassar (625–605 BC). We owe to him the building or the rebuilding of three large palaces known as the Sommerpalast, Hauptburg and Südburg, the last having more than 600 rooms.[24] In the Südburg, better documented than the others, the activities of the successors of Nebuchadnezzar were relatively modest, but their reigns were shorter; the remains brought to light, and also the inscriptions, concur in revealing that they did not undertake works as prestigious as those of their predecessors. From the reign of his son, Amel-Marduk (561–560 BC), only two inscribed brick fragments came from Koldewey's excavations.[25] Neriglissar (559–556 BC) had, according to the Cambridge Cylinder,[26] rebuilt the palace.[27] However, as five of the six duplicates of certain passages from this inscription and this king's stamped bricks come from areas situated around the Westhof and the Anbauhof,[28] Neriglissar's reconstruction work could easily have been limited to the western sector of the Südburg. Later, the enigmatic Nabonidus (555–539 BC), though very active in the country, would build relatively little in the capital.[29] In the Südburg, according to Koldewey he repaved the Mittelhof and all the large courtyards of this complex,[30] according to a text re-edited by the same author.[31]

Surviving records suggest that when Cyrus the Great (549–530 BC) entered Babylon in 539 BC, the town did not put up any resistance, but we know of no work of his in the palaces there.[32] The same observation goes for the successive sovereigns between Cambyses (530–523 BC) and Darius II (423–405 BC).[33] On the other hand, François Vallat[34] convincingly attributes the Perserbau to Artaxerxes II (404–359 BC),[35] the only Achaemenid to whom the sources ascribed any architectural activity in the palace at Babylon. Later, Alexander the Great would make the ancient capital the centre of his empire for some months; he would live and die in its royal residences.[36]

The data above provides the following information:

- The oldest palace, that of Nabopolassar (625–605 BC), is not useful for our investigation; Koldewey attributed a certain number of walls to this building which is mainly known from an inscription by his son and successor.[37]
- Nebuchadnezzar II (604–562 BC) built and restored the palaces at Babylon.
- Neriglissar (559–556 BC) rebuilt the Südburg, or more likely its west wing.
- Nabonidus (555–539 BC) seems to have only undertaken minor works.
- Artaxerxes II (404–359 BCC) built a 700 m² *hadiš or taçara*[38] on a clay and sand embankment[39] next to the Südburg; it is an insignificant area compared with the 4.56 hectares of the Südburg.
- On returning from his expedition to India (324 BC), Alexander the Great lived in the palaces of Babylon; if he was able to do so, they cannot have been in ruins.

Thus we learn that the works of the last three Chaldeans on our list extended over 60 years. After the exile imposed on Nabonidus, there would have been a gap of at least 135 years before Artaxerxes II added a small edifice to the Südburg. For the palace itself, the known records do not show any architectural intervention by the Achaemenid sovereigns. Nevertheless, Koldewey attributes several sections of missing wall in the Haupthof to a more recent period.[40] He is notably followed by Haerinck,[41] who, because of a certain analogy with an Iranian model, sees in it 'a building probably dating from the Achaemenid period'; we could also mention the two modest columns of the small Court 36, to the south of the Hauptburg,[42] but it is hard to give a precise date for these two structures due to the lack of more pertinent chronological evidence.

Finally, on his return from India, thus 215 years after the negligible work by Nabonidus, Alexander, according to this hypothesis, occupied the brick palaces constructed by Neriglissar and Nebuchadnezzar. This is not very likely; even a strong stone fortress such as the 'tower of David' at Jerusalem, was rebuilt or modified at much shorter intervals!

486
Susa: the two halls with four pilasters ('salle à quatre saillants') and the King's Chamber seen from the West Court of the Achaemenid Palace
In the foreground is the 9.5 m wide passage which links the court to the vestibule; in the centre the two figures are looking at one of the two enormous hinge sockets between the vestibule and the antechamber

487
Susa: to the south of the West Court (excavated by Mecquenem), the vestibule, the antechamber and the King's Chamber restored in 1970

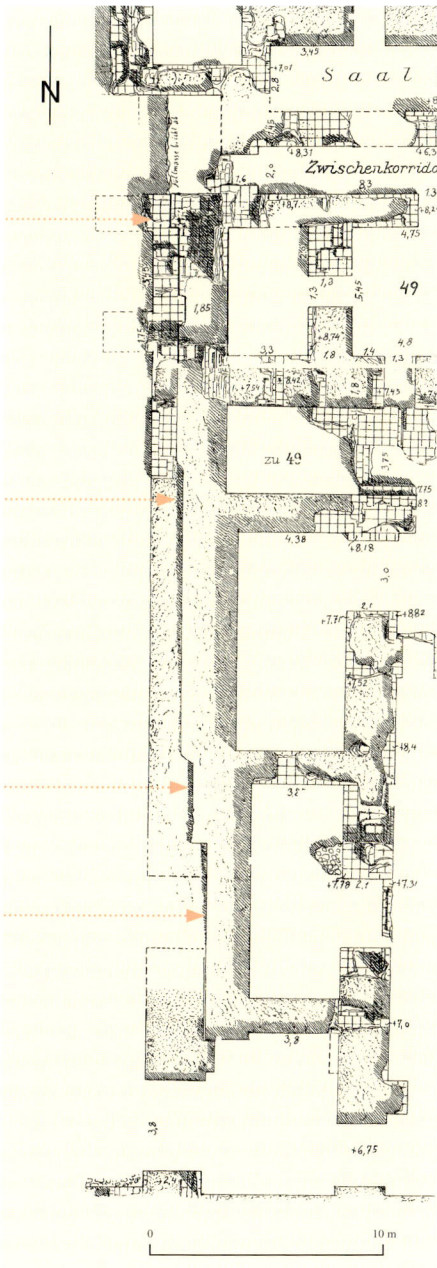

488

Babylon: Südburg: amalgamation of parts of two original plans of the Anbauhof
The red arrows indicate the fracture line identified by the excavator in the eastern wall of the Anbauhof.
KOLDEWEY, 1931: pl. 20 and 25

We cannot therefore accept that a complex as prestigious as this was not re-modelled during the two centuries of Persian occupation when it was, several times, between Nebuchadnezzar and Nabonidus – a period three times shorter. It is even less credible that the Persian court would have sojourned regularly in the ancient capital, in its existing condition, particularly when it was in the heart of a region of remarkable economic growth.

Unfortunately, bricks were subsequently pillaged at the site and therefore reliable stratigraphic information was destroyed. Koldewey partially circumnavigated this issue by producing data in extraordinary detail; his plans, however, did not illustrate the palace from the time of Nebuchadnezzar, but a more complex state with numerous anomalies which must be attributed to the reconstructions or remodelling following this king. But these works are often difficult to date.

The Südburg thus reveals several irregularities. Amongst the most visible, we must identify the northern and southern segments of the surrounding wall whose methods of building changed three times;[43] Towards the centre of the complex, the monumental gateway linking the Mittelhof and the Haupthof was built in such a way that it cut the access to an alleyway which led to a whole complex of living quarters. Finally, the Westhof and the Anbauhof, and their outbuildings, also presented singularities which will now be examined.

A separate quarter in the palace

The wedge-shaped wing around the Westhof and the Anbauhof has a different plan to that of the more eastern sectors of the palace. One does not find there, or does so much less, the long corridors which lead to the complexes to the north of the three eastern courts.[44] Elsewhere, the plan is more homogenous, even if there are irregularities which we will examine later, the walls are more robust and the whole is enclosed by a wall which, despite numerous doors, gives the impression of being an interior enclosure. But the most useful clues for our investigation, the most interesting also, can be found towards the middle of this wing (see fig. 481, p. 438).

Indeed, the east wall of the Anbauhof, illustrated in detail there, presents a clear fracture line along two-thirds of its length. To the north and the south of it, all the way to the enclosure wall, the black walls never connect with the grey walls;[45] furthermore, Koldewey identifies 'limits of intrusion' in the loci (named 'A' and 'B' on the plan), their infill being on the Anbauhof side. These observations are important, because they teach us, without possible doubt, that the Anbauhof sector – that is to say the black and red walls – was built after those of the Westhof. The question is therefore the following: who built these two distinct units of the west wing of the Südburg reproduced on Koldewey's plan?

More recent installations are often concealed under older remains

According to Koldewey,[46] Nabopolassar's Old Palace was under the Westhof, but its plan is not known; in reality, its existence is hypothesised from the passage of an inscription of Nebuchadnezzar which mentions both the reasons for the restoration of his father's work and the manner in which it was done. Despite the fragility of his hypothesis, Koldewey in the end reconstructed five phases of building work in the western sector of the Südburg;[47] all are the work of three Chaldean kings: Nabopolassar, Nebuchadnezzar (three phases) and Neriglissar; if we add the work of Nabonidus indicated above, the new scheme still does not contain any architectural activity after the Neo-Babylonian period.

In another passage, Koldewey wrote that the bricks found around the Anbauhof carried Neriglissar's stamp;[48] one of them was even *in situ* in a section of wall which probably fell after materials were pillaged. Nevertheless, according to the excavator, this block must have belonged to the upper part of a wall because the bottom and the foundations had bricks stamped by Nebuchadnezzar. He deduced that the fallen block came from the palace built by Neriglissar mentioned in the Cambridge Cylinder and of which the Germans found six duplicates of certain passages: two in embankments to the south of the Anbauhof and three in embankments to the south and north of the Westhof; the sixth fragment came from Homera mound.[49] The five examples found in the Südburg lead us to digress a moment.

We know the altimetrical levels of the pavements that are apparently the most recent of Nebuchadnezzar; from the east to the west of the Südburg, the levels are the following (in metres above the water table):

- Around 13 m in the Osthof.[50]
- 12.3 and 12.8 m in the Mittlehof.[51]
- 12.52 m towards the eastern limit of the Haupthof.[52]

When one passes into the Westhof, the bricks of the most recent pavement preserved are not inscribed and they are at around the 8 m level, thus 4.5 m lower than those of the neighbouring Haupthof;[53] and this pavement is therefore not contemporary with the others, but it could belong to an older structure than that of Nebuchadnezzar or his father. Finally, in the Anbauhof, no floor level has been preserved, but the walls here were particularly roughly treated by the looters; they rarely rise above the 6 m level.[54]

If one admits that the floors of the Südburg must have been on a more or less horizontal plane towards the end of the reign of Nebuchadnezzar, it must have been between 12, even 11, and 13 m. Up till there, there is no reason not to find bricks of Neriglassar in walls situated below this level, as his reconstruction could have been made from the foundations, as mentioned in the Cambridge Cylinder. There is no reason not to find a collapsed section of wall with a Neriglissar brick in these deep levels, the section having collapsed for a number of reasons. It is more curious to find only one inscribed brick, the proportion being higher in walls *in situ*. Should we envisage a reuse for this brick in a build after Neriglissar? The question is not without interest, because the five duplicates of Neriglissar's cylinder all come from the embankment situated under the level of Nebuchadnezzar's floor level. We must also look at three hypotheses:

1. The duplicates were intentionally deposited during the construction works of Neriglissar. This is unlikely as these fragmentary objects are scattered in the embankments of two different residential units, the Westhof and the Anbauhof, built one after the other according to the data gathered above. Otherwise, we do not know of any particular layout relating to these objects. We should also note that the Neriglissar stamped bricks come from the Anbauhof sector.
2. They fell haphazardly when the bricks were being looted. This is also improbable because the looters generally emptied the walls and foundations of their substance without touching the rubble and embankments which could be found on either side of the structures. This looting technique was clearly recognised in the excavations of the defensive works built by Nebuchadnezzar II to the north of Sippar.[55]
3. The documents came from embankments used for the infill between the foundations of a new structure. In this case the duplicates of the Neriglissar cylinder could only have come from the debris recovered during the demolition

KINGS OF BABYLON	
BABYLONIANS	ACHAEMENIDS
Nabopolassar 539–529 BC	
Nebuchednezzar II 604–562 BC	
Amel-Marduk 561–560 BC	
Neriglissar 569–556 BC	
Labasi-Marduk 556 BC	
Nabonidus 555–539 BC	**Cyrus II** 539–529 BC
	Cambyses II 528–522 BC
	Bardiya 522 BC
Nebuchednezzar III 522 BC	
Nebuchednezzar IV 521 BC	**Darius I** 522–486 BC
	Xerxes I 486–465 BC
	Artaxerxes I 465–425 BC
	Xerxes II 425–424 BC
	Darius II 424–405 BC
	Artaxerxes II 405–359 BC
	Artaxerxes III 359–338 BC
	Arses 338–336 BC
	Darius III 336–331 BC
MACEDONIANS	
Alexander the Great 330–323 BC	

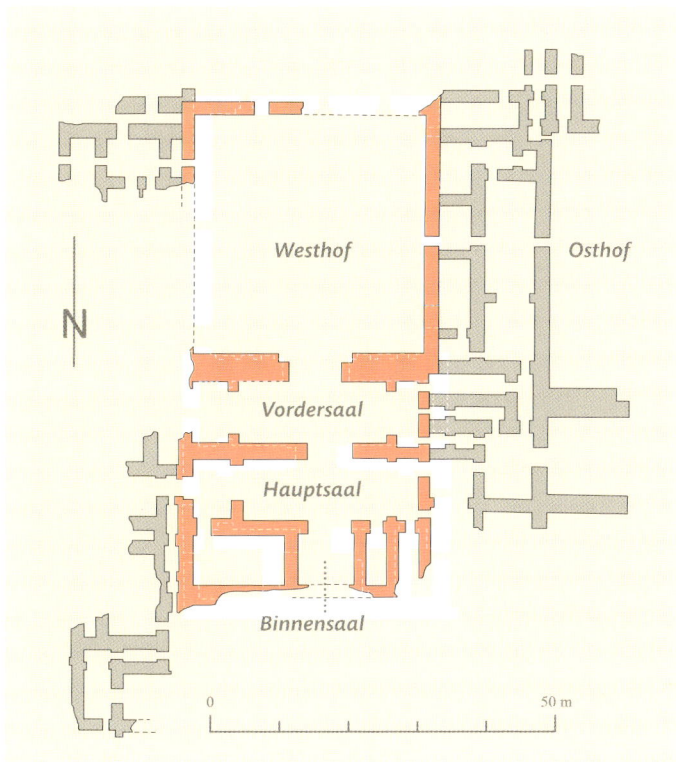

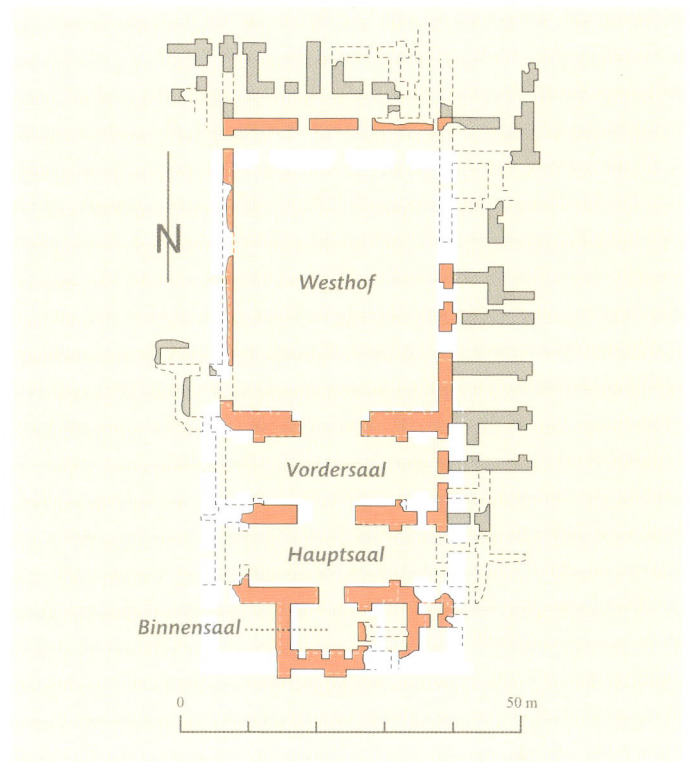

489
above left
Babylon: the West Court of the Hauptburg
above right
Babylon: the West Court of the Sommerpalast
KOLDEWEY, 1932: pls 8 and 32

▢ Achaemenid construction/reconstruction

▢ Walls of the 'Achaemenid palace' of Susa
superimposed on the plans of the
Haupburg (left) and the Sommerpalast (right)

of one of his buildings, in this case his 'palace' localised in the western sector of the Südburg, by Koldewey.

Only the last of these three scenarios can be upheld. It confirms, if needed, a reconstruction already revealed by other observations which we have described above. On the other hand, it does not provide us with the name or names of the new builders, but it guarantees that this reconstruction is later than those which the sources attribute to Neriglissar. Since his successors Labashi-Marduk and Nabonidus left no traces in this sector of the palace, there is only one conclusion: it was the Persians who remodelled the western wing of the Südburg.

CONCLUSIONS AND CONSEQUENCES

After the Chaldean building works of sometimes overweening ambition, the sources only mention a discreet pavilion of the Achaemenid period (Perserbau). However, a new study of the evidence has brought to light that the two residential units of the west wing of the Südburg, the Westhof and the Anbauhof, were successively built or rebuilt after the Neo-Babylonian period; we only lack the names of the patrons.

In this new scenario, Artaxerxes' pavilion (Perserbau) proves to be a useful reference; the organisation of the floor plan, the precise parallelism of its walls with the complex around the Anbauhof, but also the fact that it adjoined it, all these observations indicate that the pavilion was the last to be built. A second reference point is no less important: we have already seen that the complex around the Westhof was earlier than that which would be centred around the Anbauhof. We therefore obtain the following chronological order for the different sites:

1. After the fall of the Chaldean Empire (539 BC), building of the residential unit around the Westhof; to the west, this complex encroached on the space which the future complex around the Anbauhof would occupy (black and red walls on the plan above).

2. Building of the complex around the Anbauhof. The eastern wall of its great courtyard was partially boxed in by those of the older complex around the Westhof; the other walls are never connected to those of the previous complex.
3. The building of the Perserbau by Artaxerxes II (404–359 BC).

This outline informs us that the Westhof and the Anbauhof were built between 538 BC at the earliest and 405 BC at the latest; in other words, these works took place between the Babylonian reign of Cyrus the Great (539–530 BC) and that of Darius II (423–405 BC) but the sources do not mention any architectural activity in the palaces during this period. However, Darius I (522–486) and his son Xerxes (485–465) were great builders, the first at Susa and Persepolis, the second above all at Persepolis; unfortunately, this fact still does not unmask the identity of the king or kings who built at the Südburg. We must therefore go back to the beginning of our investigation where we find a useful point of reference for our enigma: the hall with four pilasters.

First we must recall that at Susa the architecture of this hall stretches its roots back beyond the middle of the second millennium BC, but we know of no works between this ancient date and the end of the sixth century BC. On the other hand, the similarity between the original model and the halls constructed by Darius I in his complex at Susa – begun at the beginning of his reign[56] – is so remarkable that it is hard to imagine such a long absence of this theme in the architectural repertoire of Susa, especially as we are sadly lacking in archaeological observations for the whole of this period. Thus we are not stretching the truth too much in attributing to the Great King, more so probably than to his son Xerxes, the realisation of the residential complex around the Anbauhof. By deduction it is to Cambyses or more likely to his father Cyrus – who anyway restored the huge wall of Babylon[57] – to whom we must attribute the older complex around the Westhof.[58]

But the Persian sovereigns would not rest there: the other two palaces of Babylon, the Hauptburg and the Sommerpalast also have large halls with four pilasters behind their western courts; because they are incomplete, these complexes are evidently less documented by the excavations.

For the Hauptburg, Koldewey indicates, however, that the base of the four pilasters was not at the same level as the significantly deeper base of the walls.[59] Is this evidence of a restoration? Considering the state of the records, it is difficult to pronounce definitively, but the similarity of these halls, always situated to the south of the most westerly courtyard of the palaces of Babylon and Susa, does not allow us to view other creators than those who were in the service of the Achaemenid sovereigns. Furthermore, the Sommerpalast – also attributed to Nebuchadnezzar II by the excavator – reveals at the same time as the halls with four pilasters, another indicator of a late date which is not uninteresting. George Stoops, father and son,[60] carried out petrographic analyses of several fragments of these 'red floors' found in the palaces at Babylon and Susa. The study notably shows that the sample from Susa is very close to a fragment from the Perserbau of Babylon, built by Artaxerxes II; knowing that this same King rebuilt all or part of the Palace of Darius at Susa, we cannot but congratulate ourselves on this pertinent crosscheck. As for the fragment taken from the Sommerpalast, it is, along with two other samples from Babylon of unknown provenance, of a higher quality;[61] could this 'Summer Palace' be the work of one of the forebears of Artaxerxes II?

In any case, those responsible for the ambitious modern reconstruction of the Südburg at Babylon have paid homage to their powerful and henceforth worrisome neighbour in the East.

490

The Südburg at Babylon: reconstructed state of the Vordersaal behind the Anbauhof
Since the area suffered heavily from the looting of foundation bricks, the Iraqi restorers have kept a difference of level which never existed. It should be noted that the staircase is built of breeze blocks, thus introducing another anomaly to the visitor. The modern walls are also distinguished from the ancient walls as the first are interspersed with bricks carrying a grandiose dedication in Arabic based on a Babylonian model: 'on the occasion of the festival of the victorious Saddam Hussein the President of the Republic – may Allah protect him! The servant of glorious Iraq, the restorer of its renaissance.'
Translation by C. Janssen

1. The Sommerpalast owes its name to the wind channels (*bad-gir* in Persian) that the excavator thought he had identified in the thickness of some of the walls (KOLDEWEY, 1932: 51 and 54), channels which, in Iran, Iraq and the Gulf, were or still are used for cooling – including some residential rooms.

2. This area and the following one, rounded to the nearest square metre, are established on the basis of the plan by Koldewey (KOLDEWEY, 1931: pl. 24) and are only used here for comparison. The Hauptburg halls are slightly larger (approx. 190/290 m²) as are those of the Sommerpalast (approx. 195/310 and 175/280 square meters, according to KOLDEWEY, 1932: pl. 5 and 32).

3. We shall not discuss here the roofing of these spaces, but refer to Gasche and Birchmeier (GASCHE and BIRCHMEIER, 1981) for the technical aspect of this question deduced from the earliest examples excavated at Susa. Koldewey favoured vaults for these rooms, but Heinrich (HEINRICH, 1968 and 1971) vigorously rejected this solution for reasons which are not always linked to technical constraints.

4. KOLDEWEY, 1931: 116. In the Hauptburg, the same opening measures only 7.55 m, but this dimension is still too wide for a door (KOLDEWEY, 1932: 11); in the Sommerpalast it measures 9 m (KOLDEWEY, 1932: 54).

5. In the Palace of Darius I at Susa, for example, the doorway between the vestibule and the antechamber was 6 m wide and was equipped with two heavy door-sockets that testify to the existence of double doors.

6. Houses and large residences excavated in the Merkes quarter of Babylon are particularly good examples of private architecture; see Reuther (REUTHER, 1926: pl. 17) for an overall view.

7. Attributed to the King's apartments by Koldewey (KOLDEWEY, 1931: 109) as empirically as he had assigned the halls behind the Anbauhof to those of the queen.

8. MALLOWAN, 1962.

9. KOLDEWEY, 1911: pl. 3.

10. See recently MARGUERON, 2004, fig. 177 (phase P–2) and fig. 189 (phase P–1); during the most recent phase, P–0 (fig. 194), the two pilasters are clearly longer, but they continue to separate the 'Most Holy Place' from the 'Sacred Enclosure'.

11. GASCHE *et al.*, 1998; all the dates of the second millennium BC used in this section refer to the new Low Chronology, with the date of the Fall of Babylon in 1499 BC.

12. BATTINI and CALVET, 2003.

13. Level xv of Ghirshman's Chantier A (GHIRSHMAN, 1967: fig. 2).

14. For a more complete discussion of the Assyrian palaces, see TURNER, 1970.

15. See more particularly AMIET, 1973: 71; AMIET, 1997: 80; BOUCHARLAT, 1997b: 65; and also CALMEYER, 1994b: 143 who unconditionally advocates the Babylonian character of the western part of the Palace of Darius at Susa. Sarre (SARRE, 1923 16–18), while admitting Babylonian influence, also emphasises Susian characteristics.

16. ROAF, 1983.

17. GHIRSHMAN, 1965b.

18. For the plan of these foundations, see STÈVE *et al.* 1980: fig. 8.

19. I should like to thank Michel el-Maqdisi, director of the excavations in the area where 'Hall B' was found, for the information he gave me during an informal conversation in Paris. He dates the occupation levels

of this area to the Late Bronze Age, 'towards the middle of the second millennium BC.' The dating of the palace varies to some extent depending on the opinions of one or other team associated with this project. For an update on the matter, see PFÄLZNER, 2006: 164.

20. RICHTER, 2006, 161; and p. 160 for a more precise chronological framework, 'towards the end of the fifteenth century BC'

21. STÈVE, 1967: no. 47. At Susa, NIN.É.GAL already appears in the texts of Ebarat II (SCHEIL, 1908: no. 5, 7, 8 [seal], 45–46 and 59, and SCHEIL, 1939: no. 5), but these earlier attestations are not as relevant to the present discussion. Surprisingly, the attestations of NIN.É.GAL in Susiana do not appear in the article by BEHRENS and KLEIN, 1998–2001.

22. For the plan of the palace, see GHIRSHMAN, 1968a: pl. 11, 13 and 14.

23. ROAF, 1973.

24. KOLDEWEY, 1931: 28.

25. KOLDEWEY, 1990: 89.

26. BEZOLD and SCHRADER, 1892: 70.

27. See Carl Bezold in SCHRADER, 1890: I R67.

28. KOLDEWEY, 1931: 32.

29. For further information see BEAULIEU 1989: 38–41 and 113–114. See also a reference to a 'house of the Crown Prince' in a contract dated to Year 7 of Nabonidus (STRASSMAIER, 1889: no. 265).

30. KOLDEWEY, 1931: 32.

31. KOLDEWEY, 1990: 80. As we shall see, this cannot even so refer to anything other than the three great courts of the Südburg, as no pavement with Nabonidus bricks was found in the Westhof, and no pavement at all was found in the Anbauhof.

32. He did, however, restore the great wall of Babylon, the Imgur-Enlil; see BEAULIEU, 1989: 38–39, and LECOQ, 1997: 185.

33. As regards the problems relating to the construction of a house of the the Crown Prince, referred to in a contract of Year 24 of Darius I (UNGNAD, 1907: no. 135), see now Vallat (VALLAT, 1989: 5 and n. 24): 'it is in CAD that the correct translation is to be found: "to the workshop of the house of the son of the king"'. Nothing, therefore, suggests that Darius built this 'house', especially as it might refer to the *house of the Crown Prince* already referred to in a document of Year 7 of Nabonidus (STRASSMAIER, 1889: no. 265) and which might still have been standing in the time of Darius, as only 50 years separate the two texts. It is, however, the first of these texts which was used, without citation, by Edwin M. Yamauchi (YAMAUCHI, 1990: 193) in order to affirm that 'as early as 498 BC [= Year 24 of Darius I] we have a reference to the building of a Palace [by Darius I] at Babylon for the king's son'. Pierre Briant (BRIANT, 1996: 182) also informs us that Darius I 'had built a new palace at Babylon', but he too fails to give a reference because there are none; the existence of this mysterious 'house of the Crown-Prince' may have inspired Briant's formula. On p. 694 of the same work, the author mentions, still without a reference, the construction of a palace by Artaxerxes II, but in this case it can only refer to the pavilion known as the Perserbau. As we have seen, the documentation at our disposal does not allow us to deduce architectural activity by Darius I in Babylon, but we must recall the presence of fragments of a stone relief – with inscriptions and various depictions – found in the Hauptburg area and brought together by Ursula Seidel (SEIDL, 1976,

1999a and b). These fragments show undoubted affinities with the relief that the Great King had carved on the cliffs at Bisitun at the beginning of his reign.

34. Vallat's approach (VALLAT, 1989) rests on a comparison of the texts from Babylon with those, more complete, from Susa. Thus he was able to establish (p. 5) that at least three of the 14 fragments found at Babylon can certainly be assigned to Artaxerxes II, whereas none can be ascribed to Darius I, to whom several scholars have sought to attribute the *Perserbau* (for references see p. 3, notes 2–4).

35. For a detailed analysis of the *Perserbau* see Haerinck (HAERINCK, 1973) and his note 2 for a list of earlier publications; in note 4, replace 'la longueur du palais' by 'la largeur du palais' [i.e. replace 'length' by 'width'].

36. Plutarch, *Alexander* 76, and Arrian VII, 25.

37. See the translation by Claus Wilcke in KOLDEWEY, 1990: 120.

38. A comparison between one of the inscribed fragments from Babylon and Inscription A2sd from Susa has enabled Vallat (VALLAT, 1989: 4, n. 20) to state that the Perserbau is a '*hadiš*' or '*taçara*', as the two words are synonymous, and not an Apadana, as has often been stated.

39. KOLDEWEY, 1931: 120.

40. KOLDEWEY, 1931: 77, pl. 2.

41. HAERINCK, 1987: 141.

42. KOLDEWEY, 1931: 95, pl. 15.

43. KOLDEWEY, 1931: pl. 2.

44. KOLDEWEY, 1931: pl. 2.

45. On Koldewey's general plan (KOLDEWEY, 1931: pl. 2) the walls are bonded at the south-east corner of locus 50, but this is not the case on more detailed plans.

46. KOLDEWEY, 1931: 94.

47. KOLDEWEY, 1931: 95.

48. KOLDEWEY, 1931: 32.

49. KOLDEWEY, 1931: 35–36.

50. KOLDEWEY, 1931: 68.

51. KOLDEWEY, 1931: 76.

52. Koldewey (KOLDEWEY, 1990: 79–80) summarises the situation regarding this difference in level, but it is of no interest in connection with our enquiry.

53. We know that there were important improvements to buildings in several parts of Babylon. See especially Bergamini (BERGAMINI, 1977); however, these building works distract us from the focus of our enquiry.

54. See KOLDEWEY, 1931: pl. 20 and 23–25. We should note in passing that the floor of the *Perserbau* – built more than 150 years after Nebuchadnezzar – was at level 13.41 m, but the Esplanade to the north of it was 2 m lower (11.42 m); KOLDEWEY, 1931: 120–121.

55. See GASCHE, 1989, especially figs 3.1 and 3.2 which explicitly show the trenches created by the looters.

56. The exact date of this complex is not known; we therefore follow the reasoning adopted by STÈVE *et al.*, (2002–2003: col. 487–488) because at present there is no convincing argument for situating the beginning of this construction later than the reign of Darius.

57. See BEAULIEU, 1989: 38–39 and LECOQ, 1997: 185.

58. This proposal contradicts the date suggested by

Koldewey for a large tomb containing a sarcophagus, found in the exterior wall of the *Westhof* unit, near the northeast corner of house 47 (KOLDEWEY, 1931: 105, pl. 2, 25 and 30). Indeed, the excavator attributes this pillaged burial to an important dignitary from the beginning of the reign of Nebuchadnezzar II or that of Nabopolassar, or even of Nabopolassar himself. More recently, Ursula Moortgat-Correns (MOORTGAT-CORRENS, 1996) has suggested that this could be the tomb of Nabonidus, if one accepts the version of Berossus, according to which the last king of Babylon would have been sent to live in one of the eastern provinces of the future Persian Empire, and would have outlived, in exile, both Cyrus and Cambyses. Moortgat-Correns' hypothesis would fit in with the chronological framework proposed here. However, it is unlikely that the successor of Cambyses, Darius the Great, would have accepted the human remains of Nabonidus in his palace, in a wing built by Cyrus or Cambyses, and buried according to funerary rites that were alien to the Persians. Whatever the situation may have been, the shape of the sarcophagus is attested in Achaemenid times, and even later (HAERINCK, 1980: 55 and 60, and pl. 5 and 7). Furthermore, one could suggest that the tomb was that of a Babylonian dignitary who was buried in the palace after it had been vacated by the Persians.

59. KOLDEWEY, 1932: 11.

60. STOOPS, 1994.

61. STOOPS, 1994: 484.

Darius at Persepolis

Jean Perrot

Carved into the mountain which dominates the Marvdasht plain in the heart of Persia, the Terrace of Persepolis has no residential palace; when the king was in Fars his tent was pitched in the plain or in a palace which remains to be discovered. The Persepolis Terrace was a political centre; the Persian tribes assembled there around the personage of the king; communing in a sentiment of vainglorious pride, they could be conscious of their national identity and military superiority. 'This nation, [wrote Darius on the south wall of the Terrace] this Persian nation: that Ahuramazda granted me […] Thanks to me, Darius the King, it fears no other' (DPd).

Persepolis: the Terrace in 1971
in the foreground, the
Hall of One Hundred Columns

The feeling of domination by the Persian tribes seems to be marked, however, by an evident tendency to associate, at least in images, and not without arrogance, their Median and Susian or Elamite cousins in their glory.

Essentially created by Xerxes, the iconographic repertoire of Persepolis, drafted under Darius, casts the mythical monsters aside to make room for man. The lion-bull coupling owes its life only to the triangular composition of the motif, adapted to the bottom corner of staircases. In the doorjambs, the rampant griffins are stabbed by the daggers of a Persian man. Henceforth, royal law coexists with traditional religious law.

Long files of tributaries, bearers of products from their countries, lined the walls of edifices, but in picture only. Some 1,000 km from Babylon, Persepolis was only accessible to Persians and their kin. The historians of this age do not seem to have known about it; their writings only mentioned it after its destruction by Alexander the Great – a destruction which, as some have thought, signified to the recalcitrant Persians the end of imperial grandeur or, more probably – as Diodorus and others after him explained – that Alexander wanted to 'avenge the Hellenes, appease the spirits of the ancestors and make the Persians pay for the invasion of Greece, the destruction of Athens and that of its temples'.

492

Persepolis: door jamb in the Hall of One Hundred Columns

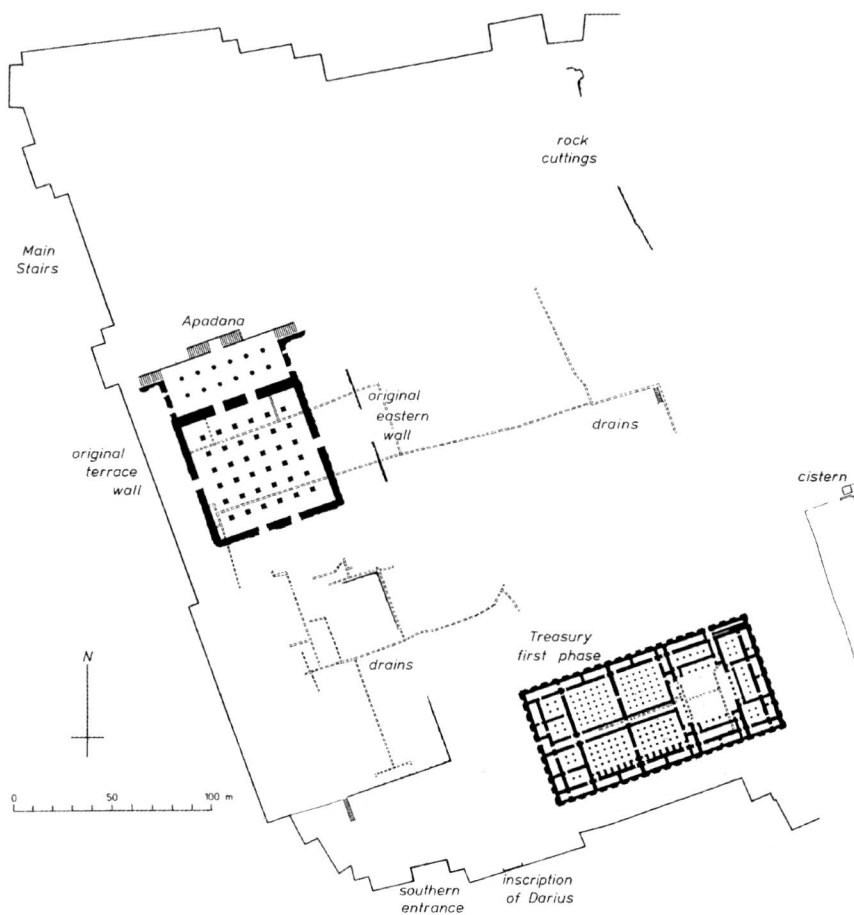

493

Plan of Persepolis Terrace
This plan published by Michael Roaf (1983) shows how the work on the Persepolis Terrace had progressed by the end of the reign of Darius. It shows the large Hypostyle Hall (Apadana) which was started around 515/510 and whose porticoes, the staircases and the ornamentation had not yet been completed; and a first phase of the Treasury. The small palace of Darius (taçara) on the southern side of the Apadana was no doubt being built; it was finished by Xerxes (XPe) who seems to have been interested in Persepolis even before his investiture in 486 BC. The great decorative themes of Persepolis were already set (servants or tributaries), and the Ionian and other sculptors were hard at work

Bibliography:
SCHMIDT, 1953; POPE, 1957; GHIRSHMAN, 1957; SHAHBAZI, 1976; KLEISS, 1981; ROAF, 1983; MOUSAVI, 1992.

14

Darius in his Time

Jean Perrot

In the conclusion to *Contribution à l'étude du palais achéménide de Suse,* published in 1947, Roland de Mecquenem wrote: 'The current work had the aim of making the present state of our knowledge on the subject known without claiming to have exhausted it; it even shows some gaps; we hope that one day they will at least be reduced.' My colleagues and I make this conclusion our own after ten seasons of excavation (from 1969 to 1979) followed by research, international conventions and exchanges. We do not bring definitive answers to all the questions; however, the new archaeological data clarify a number of points concerning a palace often mentioned but never seen or understood.

These data show the rapprochement of two architectural traditions – that of the Mesopotamian plain and that of the Iranian plateau; of two building methods whose juxtaposition converges, like that of the visual arts, towards elegant solutions. The palatial complex at Susa appears today as an exceptional witness to a key phase in architectural development from the sixth to the fifth centuries BC. Whether public or private – because architecture is linked to the events of human life – architectural remains at Susa can contribute to a better understanding of this period; in the same way, the inscriptions and decoration of the palace shed light on the ideology of Darius I, a personality who is sometimes confused with that of his successors.

In the first chapter of this book, Pierre Briant brought to our attention the limited nature of ancient records and the weakness of contemporary literary testimony. Herodotus was not the contemporary of Darius but that of Artaxerxes I, who reigned from 465 BC to 424 BC, after the long reign of Xerxes. Herodotus was no doubt the first of the historiographers, but he was not a historian; he lived a long way from Susa, a victim of the phenomenon of polarisation of which we are guilty when we say 'Moscow' meaning Russia, or 'New York' or 'Washington' meaning the United States. We cannot reject Classical sources wholesale; their interpretation, as Briant highlights, leads to reflection and discussion; but we cannot give them preference over archaeological realities, even if these have their limits. The deciphering of Elamite tablets from Persepolis is a precious source of information concerning daily life at the time of Darius; but their contribution is not so great as to present Susa as 'the' capital of the Persian Empire. The royal inscriptions show quite clearly that, other than during the reigns of Darius and Artaxerxes II, Susa played only a secondary role in the empire – that for which the city had been created, at the crossroads of the network of major roads of economic and military interest, as part of a complex strategy of imperial organisation.

In the following pages we will come back to the reasons for the choice of Susa and to the technical and architectural constraints imposed by this choice; to the timescale of the works and their relation with the royal inscriptions; to the decoration of the Residence and the ideology to which it attests; to the economy and life of the palace. Iranian architecture's place in Middle Eastern architecture has been discussed above by Rémy Boucharlat and Hermann Gasche.[1] The Darius inscriptions were reviewed in their Elamite versions by François Vallat, with the implications of his new readings.[2] Whilst reporting on the building activities of the king, the inscriptions also allow a glimpse of other aspects of his personality.

THE PROJECTS OF DARIUS

Darius as a young prince no doubt campaigned in Egypt at the side of his royal cousin, Cambyses, who then became the first pharaoh of the Twenty-seventh Dynasty. He could have discovered the temples of the Valley of the Nile with their colossal statues, and more certainly the pyramids, already 20 centuries old; these images nourished his imagination; when the moment came, they would dictate his actions. Did he already dream of supreme power and the means of seizing it, alone or with others? Could he already foresee a universal empire? In the circumstances it is unlikely that his first concern was to hurry to Susa to install the capital of this empire.

His seizure of power in 522 BC unleashed revolts that shook Persia and Media whilst reviving tribal and clan conflicts. The rebellion extended to Elam and Babylonia, leading to military engagements that required his personal intervention; from Babylon, he recaptured Ecbatana and Media, where a hard struggle took place; several months of tough fighting were necessary to eliminate the Median pretender. It was only then that Darius, gathering his forces, began the reconquest of his own country. The first two years of his reign were thus marked by much turmoil. In Elam, after two initiatives led by Persians, a third revolt, in 519 BC, was led this time by Elam. It is hard to imagine that, in these circumstances, large-scale enterprises could have been undertaken at Susa or Persepolis before this date.

When Darius came to power it was very probably in his own country that he envisaged the building of a capital, in the mountains of Fars, where as a child he had been moved by the tales of Cyrus' victories, the fall of Lydia, the capture of Babylon. Fars is the heart of Persia. Darius knew Pasargadae, which was still under construction; it was a place that Cambyses himself had already decided to abandon in favour of Dasht-i Gohar near Persepolis.[3] Returning to Pasargadae, Darius may well have been underwhelmed by the edifices that his memory had earlier magnified and which he found no longer measured up to his new ambition.

It was not sufficient to seize power; it was necessary to hold on to it. On a military level, Darius understood the importance of swift communications. The unity of the Empire and his control depended on information and the quality of his road network. Between Fars and Babylonia there are nearly 1000 km! – 45 days' march for troops with weapons and baggage; possibly even more for all the royal cortège. Susa was halfway. Darius knew Susiana; he had had many occasions to cross it. He knew the advantages of Susa, its tells, its history, linked to its geographic position at a crossroads of routes to Babylonia and the Persian Gulf, the Sea of Oman and the Indian Ocean, that is, towards India, Egypt and Ethiopia. Susa was the gateway to Persia. But the old Elamite capital was only a shadow of its former self. Unlike most of the towns of the Empire, Babylon, Ecbatana and others, Susa no longer had a suitable royal residence; it was important to remedy the situation quickly.[4]

The building of Susa was part of a programme of great works on an imperial scale, all with different objectives. The creation of Persepolis had a political motive; the digging of the canal from the Nile to the Red Sea was an economic decision. The palatial complex at Susa satisfied three different needs: that of a stopping-place, a protected way-station, on the long route between Fars and Babylonia; that of an administrative centre for the Susiana satrapy; and finally that of a place where power could be properly exercised when the King, with his court, would choose to stay there, if only to take advantage of the natural resources of the region and the mildness of its winter climate.

The beginning of the works

Taking into account the political and security situation, the works could scarcely have started at Susa (and at the same time Persepolis) before the second or third year of Darius' reign, that is to say around 520/519 BC. It was only then that, as regards Susa, the order could have been given to fell the cedars in the Lebanon and the *yaka* wood in the Kerman Mountains, as well as that to extract the stone from the Abiradu quarries in the Zagros Mountains, some 50 km from Susa, on the edge of the Mesopotamian plain. What must have struck the builders arriving at Susa was 'neither the beauty of the town nor its prestige', but the imposing mass of its hills, of its three tells, formed by the accumulation of ruins of an occupation over three millennia old. No doubt there existed, further to the east, at the foot of the Zagros range, positions that were 'naturally stronger',[5] but the Susa which would be developed would still be capable of resisting the attacks which she would have to suffer after the disappearance of the empire.

The first care of the builders would no doubt have been to fortify the Acropolis tell, which offered a good command post, and install a garrison charged with guarding the stores of precious materials, the movement of people and the camps of foreign workers. The edges of the Ville Royale tell were then also carved into an embankment; the glacis of the tell was raised and the strong retaining walls of the terrace were built, which would support the Residence and the audience hall. The manufacture of mud bricks destined for the infrastructure, the glacis and the boxing-in of the foundations began. It is difficult to determine the number of men used in these works. We cannot imagine this without calculating at the same time the rations required and the scope of the project. The banked curtain wall and the mud-brick walls linking the tells must have represented the movement of half to one million cubic metres of earth, which would have required the labour of several thousand men, displaced or recruited locally, during a period of two to three years.[6] At the same time, enormous stone cylinders,[7] ready to be used, were rolled over a distance of 50 km; 4,000 tons of stone would be necessary for the columns of the Hypostyle Hall and for the stone supports of the door sockets. Elsewhere, hundreds of tons of gravel had to be raised from the neighbouring riverbeds. After felling the trees in the Lebanon (around 800 trunks at least 20 m long for the main beams of the Hypostyle Hall), it must have taken many months to transport and float them over more than 1,500 km; the same must be true for the transport of the wood from Kerman destined for the door frames and furniture. We must also take into account the climatic conditions in Susiana. In the summer, the daily temperatures could reach 50°C.[8]

Once the infrastructure works had been completed, work on the different buildings began: the monumental gateway, Residence, audience hall and so on. The first two courses of the walls were in baked brick; the walls then rose using mud brick; their widths varied from 4 to 15 bricks (that is to say 1.4 m to 5.2 m); their height would be on average 12 m but they reached 20 m and more in the Hypostyle Hall. Some 200,000 baked bricks were necessary for the wall courses and 100,000 tiles for the paving of the courts and the Esplanade. The private area of the Residence, that with red floors, must have required nearly two years of work alone. As to the construction of the Hypostyle Hall, it could have stretched over a decade and no doubt more, after the erection of its 72 columns, 20 metres high and weighing some 50 tons.[9]

The construction phases at Susa and the royal inscriptions

It is not unrealistic to try to relate the royal inscriptions to the construction phases.[10] Before Darius, there were no traces of Achaemenid settlement. Cyrus II, on his way to Babylon in 539 BC, would have passed by without stopping. The town was not mentioned in the great Bisitun inscription; if Darius had intended to make Susa the seat of imperial power, the town and region would have figured more prominently in his thoughts. François Vallat thinks that paragraph 58 of the Bisitun inscription implies that the works were already under way at Susa; the king would not have mentioned it for fear that one might think that he was 'exaggerating' or 'lying'.[11] But it is difficult to imagine that in the socio-political conditions of the first years of his reign, as he raced from battlefield to battlefield, from one extremity of the empire to the other, that the King would have been concerned with gathering valuable resources in a hostile environment. The fortification of the Acropolis, the embankments of the Ville Royale tell, the building of the Apadana terrace and the great mud-brick walls linking the tells must have taken at least two years. Around 517–516 BC, the building works might have reached a stage where they could have been in accord with the following inscription of Darius (DSe, 33–36): 'I saw the fortifications (which at Susa) had once been built go to ruin; me, I raised them again. It is in fact completely new fortifications that I have built.'[12]

Two more years at least would go by before the great work of the Residence would be finished, at least its private quarters. The inscription known as the 'foundation charter of the palace' (DSf)[13] could have corresponded to this new phase. It would have coincided with a visit or brief stay by the King at Susa. After a long preamble, DSf has a detailed description of the foundation works of the walls as well as a list of materials brought by the nations who worked them; the King expresses his satisfaction with the work accomplished: 'at Susa, much excellent work was ordered, much excellent work was done' (DSf, 14); finally, the King asked Ahuramazda's protection for him and his father, Hystaspes; from which we can conclude that his father was still alive.

DSf is generally considered as an act of political propaganda; this inscription was destined to be seen, as demonstrated by the numerous copies found at various points of the site in different forms: for example, stone tablets, clay tablets, cylinders, and notably on a stone tablet preserved at the Louvre 'whose inscribed sides, are perforated through the middle to secure an axle which, resting on some feet, must have allowed the stone to pivot so as to facilitate its reading; the stone is hard to handle due to its weight'.[14] This tablet must have been found in the confines of the palace. It was most probably written before 515 BC.

In 1970, we found two versions of this text, one in Elamite (DSz), the other in Babylonian (DSaa). These two stone tablets were laid 'in the wall foundations' of the king's chamber, on either side of the entrance; *above* the rubble and *below* the baked brick courses in the wall. They describe, however, the palace as complete, whereas, according to their location, it was just beginning to be built. The Elamite text (DSz) is similar to DSf but without the cosmogenic first verse. The Babylonian text (DSaa), after a short titulature, presents a shortened version of the building works and a dry enumeration of materials and nations. The two texts end in an invocation to Ahuramazda but do not mention the king's father, Hystaspes. As regards the foundations, they mention trenches 20 cubits deep and not '20 and 40 cubits' as in DSf. In their essentials, however, they take up the themes of DSf. Both, like DSf, refer to a finished palace: 'the palace which is at Susa, I built it' (DSaa § 2–6) and DSz adds 'Me, I made this offering to Ahuramazda' (DSz § 5).[15] The reference to foundation trenches of 20 cubits can be explained in the present case because, in the sector of the royal apartment where these tablets were found, the 'bedrock' was reached within a few metres depth whilst in other places of the terrace the foundations sometimes stretched to nearly 10 m. According to François Vallat, the absence of the name Hystaspes can be explained by the death of Darius' father around this date; a date which, in view of other considerations, M.-J. Steve had already proposed placing around 515–514 BC.[16] From an epigraphic point of view, the time difference between DSz and DSf is not very great, the same as the difference between DSaa and the great inscription at Bisitun.[17] It remains to explain the surprising stratigraphic position of these two tablets.

For François Vallat,[18] DSz and DSaa can be placed in the corpus of 'unreadable' documents; that is to say, documents destined not to be read, be they buried in the wall or far from view like, for example, the inscriptions of Bisitun on the flank of a cliff at a height of over 60 m, or even those of Xerxes above the 'Gate of All Nations' at Persepolis; these inscriptions were destined exclusively for the deity. That the palace was complete or not would be of secondary importance – only the intention needed to be taken into account. It is difficult, however, to imagine the Great King, enemy of 'the Lie', deceiving Ahuramazda by writing, even as the palace had yet to reach ground level, 'me, I made this offering to Ahuramazda'; and also omitting the cosmogenic introduction.

The following explanation could be proposed: around 515–514 BC, Darius was at Susa; he proclaimed his satisfaction with the work accomplished (DSf). His attention was then drawn to the fact that, at the beginning of the works no one had sacrificed in a good and proper fashion, by the local custom of a foundation deposit.[19] The text of the inscription DSf, still being written, would have been copied and adapted; DSz and DSaa would have been laid out by the scribes and carved on stone tablets, on all six sides. Cuts in the long introductory text were inevitable, despite the skill of the carvers. These cuts have to be interpreted, whilst always bearing in mind that these records were destined neither to be seen nor read. New circumstances are then brought into account, like the death of Hystaspes which would have occurred around that time; and also the fact that the deposit was destined for a sector where the foundations were shallower. The insertion of tablets under the walls would have been a minor operation in itself; to dig a recess, move several baked bricks from the courses, insert the tablets and then proceed with a quick replastering would only have been a matter of a few hours. It is indeed this operation which is suggested by the data and photographs of the discovery; the baked brick courses are replaced in this sector by an alignment of broken bricks.[20]

THE PRINCIPLES OF SUSIAN ARCHITECTURE

The palatial complex at Susa can be considered as being part of the formative phase of the development of Achaemenid architecture, if one understands by that qualification the elegant convergence and juxtaposition of elements borrowed from architectural traditions differentiated by their natural environment or that which created them. Essentially, it means two ways of building; one in the Mesopotamian plain having only clay as a material; the other, mountain-based, Iranian, accustomed to working with both stone and wood; both subject to standards of stability, practicality and eventually beauty; both are open to outside influences. It is thus, that after the conquest of Western Asia by Cyrus II, the technical and cultural contribution of the Ionian stonemasons was strongly felt at Pasargadae.[21]

At Susa, Darius' vision and circumstances would provoke the meeting of both traditions; the Iranian was found transplanted into an environment to which it did not belong; Susa became a form of testing ground where new architectural forms were elaborated. The operation became complex: on the one hand there was the royal demand for grandeur, which led to the buildings being expanded in size and in position; on the other, there was the nature of the ground and the necessity of raising heavy structures on the soft earth of the tells, in a region beset by earthquakes. The morphology of the site made things even harder: it proved necessary to flatten one of the three tells to obtain the requisite surface on which to establish the Residence. The complex at Susa therefore takes on a particular character which must be taken into account in all attempts at comparison. On this basis, Susa still belongs to the formative phase of Achaemenid architecture, in the same way as Pasargadae.

Stability

The Babylonians elevated monuments and houses on low terraces to ensure they were out of reach of flooding. Their experience inspired the development of a system of foundations at Susa which was inspirational to the point that the inscriptions of Darius would describe them in detail. Each wall was founded on a strong caisson made of gravel taken from the neighbouring rivers, a process which ensured both the watertightness of the ground and the stability of the walls destined to carry fragile mud-brick vaults. Flexible according to the weight of the buildings and the nature of the terrain, this system, Susian rather than Achaemenid, and resource-hungry, would remain tied to Susa itself, to the strength of the edifices and to that of the builders. Its use at the Apadana by the Iranian architects was a sign of their adaption and close cooperation with local tradition; their efforts also extended to the organisation of the space and the planning of the edifices. The move of the Hypostyle Hall to a square plan corresponded to anxieties over stability which led to a narrowing of the porticoes. Conversely, stone and wood would become part of the construction of the Gate and the Propylaeum, the plans of which originally belonged to the Mesopotamian tradition. The Residence was not affected, as it had no columns. Built by masons called to Susa by Darius in the urgency of the first few years of his reign, it was typical of Babylonian architecture of the time, with its long vaulted halls, supported by small transverse rooms at the extremities, in a manner already attested at Susa and more generally in the plain from the second millennium on.[22]

Practical arrangements

Whilst deciphering the floor plans of the large Assyrian and Babylonian palaces can sometimes leave one perplexed in the face of an ensemble of modules of ceremonial courtyard, rooms and halls without any apparent specific function, the palatial complex at Susa stands out for its readability. First is its organisation of space. Its design resembled that of Assyrian and Babylonian palaces but with the slight difference that it carried the mark of a new logic, as though, with the extension of the empire at the turn of the sixth and fifth centuries BC, rationality was affirming itself.

Susa was the administrative centre of a satrapy; the province had a governor who probably resided with the garrison and its commander on the Acropolis where the royal 'treasury' was likely located.[23] In the absence of the King, the Residence was guarded and maintained. Four officers each occupied a billet in each of the courtyards. When the King and his retinue sojourned at Susa the region sprang into life as is shown by the Persepolis tablets for the years 500/499 BC. In the first years of his reign, Darius' suite was no doubt nothing in comparison to the long trains which the chroniclers of the Great King's successors would take pleasure in describing. It numbered several thousand people with the family entourage, servants, councillors, scribes and bodyguards. Whilst the soldiers were billeted on the 'Ville Royale' tell, the King and his cortège journeyed along the causeway, through the Gate and onto the Esplanade. The king's horses and the women's chariots entered into the first court of the Residence.[24] Flags and banners or standards were deposited in the 'chapels' or 'altars of rest' on the northern side of the court. Horses and chariots were housed in the stables and sheds in the outbuildings and large halls to the south of the courtyard; from these halls the women could gain their apartments by a discreet door and via the long corridor R4. The king could directly access the audience hall by the gate in the north-western corner of Court C3 and by the 'royal passage' (s); the princes could reach their apartments by the same gate and passageway R1. Alternatively, the king crossed the Central Court, where the chancellery staff would stay, to reach the Honour Court and his apartments. By then he would have gone through seven gateways from his entrance into the place – seven large, but well-guarded gates.[25] On its own, the entrance to the Residence with its two large halls could accommodate more than 100 men. The 'King's room', by contrast, was modest (70 m²): it comprised a bed in an alcove and, most likely, opposite the entrance, a seat for receptions and small ceremonies. On either side of this room there may have been conveniences. From the door separating the antechamber from the enclosed vestibule, the total area of the royal apartment, with antechamber and dependencies, did not exceed 500 m². This apartment was linked, to the south, via an unguarded passageway to corridor R4 which led to the 'women's apartments'. To the east and the west, the antechamber communicated with the chancellery.[26] In addition, from the loggia of Court A, the king had the possibility of discreetly, and without direct contact, meeting the Acropolis personnel: governor, treasurer, officers and so on could access this court via the battlements and gate L1. When the king stayed at Susa, the population of the Residence can be estimated at 1,000 people, servants and guards included. The need for water could be easily satisfied by wells, reaching the water table.[27] Provisions could be stored in the villages of the region and delivered according to need, as indicated in the Persepolis tablets.[28]

Beauty

We do not know what the exterior of the structure looked like but we should remember that mud-brick walls do not lend themselves to the tricks of light and shade that can be created by the recesses and projections of baked-brick architecture. The whole must have been one of great austerity. We have taken into account this observation in our reconstructions, which are deliberately minimalist.

As to the height of the buildings, the columns of the Apadana, whose heights are known, can serve as a benchmark, along with the technical indications provided by the thickness of the walls and the width of the doorways. There must have existed a harmonious relationship between the various elements of the plan.

We have no idea how the rooms of the Residence were appointed other than the fact that, in the private area of the Residence, the floors were plastered with a highly polished wine-red coating. The walls may have been whitewashed, enlivened by tapestries (a few glazed tiles decorated with fine geometric motifs suggest this). The stone furniture comprised seats, benches and canopies; we have some fragments of this, but it is not possible to attribute them to one period or another. In the courtyards, the glazed brick panels enlivened the austerity of the mud-brick walls.

The purpose of this decoration was naturally to embellish, to make pleasant; but it aimed at more than mere ornamentation – it also added character to the whole. We are in the habit of talking about the animal representations at Susa as though they had lost all symbolic value, which is probably not correct. This impression could have come about because the images of lions, griffins and winged bulls appear today as somewhat incongruous in an environment of which we have a preconceived idea based on views of Persepolis; these animalistic representations must be put back into their context which is that of the Babylonian palace. The Babylonian masons decorated the Residence, the private area at least (the part with red floors), according to their practices and beliefs; they could not shock in Susiana, whose culture was traditionally linked to that of Babylonia. This repertoire would be reconsidered by Darius on the completion and decoration of the exterior Court (c3).

A NEW IDEOLOGY

Towards 515 BC, when the private part of the Residence was completed, Darius visited the site – a visit which could correspond to the carving of DSf. According to this text, Darius was satisfied with what he saw. He found there an artistic form of expression and a symbolism to which his eye and his mind had become accustomed during his childhood. This art is that of the times of Cyrus; it reflects the dominant religious thought of the Babylonian world in the second half of the sixth century BC. At Susa, land of the glazed brick, it found a new vitality. The drawing of the animal figures is livelier, more naturalistic, more convincing than at Babylon but the symbolism remains the same. In fact, a change was made at Susa itself by Darius, perhaps, during this visit to the site and around this date. What the king sees no longer corresponds to his thoughts and even less to his ideology.

At least, it is a suggestion which one could make. What would the reaction of the Great King have been before the works already completed at the Residence? For François Vallat, who supports the Elamite version, the King said: 'at Susa much excellent work was ordered, much excellent work was done [DSf, 14].

For P. Lecoq, referring to the Old Persian: 'much beauty was ordered, much beauty was made'. The translations differ on the word 'fraša', an Old Persian word which the Elamite version is content to transcribe. Etymologically speaking, wrote P. Lecoq, 'fraša' is 'what is presented, what has developed, then figuratively 'eminent, excellent'. The word is generally translated as 'beautiful' to designate the eminent quality of what was created by Ahuramazda. P. Lecoq also uses it for what is built by Darius; whilst noting that 'beautiful' is the opposite of ugly, another word (atara) is preferred. Playing with the words:

the distinction between 'excellent' and beautiful' is not an indifferent one. 'Excellent' carries a judgement of value; 'beautiful' signals an aesthetic emotion. One could say, if one wanted to reconstruct the scene, that if Darius had aesthetic emotions in front of what he had before his eyes, this signifies that he rediscovered with pleasure what he had been taught as being beautiful; this would also mean that Assyrian and Babylonian art had not evolved over the course of the previous decades.

It is then that he would have decided on a new programme to be applied immediately to the decoration of the exterior Court (c3), still a building site, a programme that would project on the walls a magnified image of Susian nobles, carriers of the symbols of power, the bow and the lance. The time was one for rapprochement with an Elamite nation which in fact had never been an enemy. The decision was political but it also revolutionised artistic expression. In the following period, on the walls of Persepolis, the mythological monsters practically disappeared; they only fill in the bottom angles of staircase ramps and some door embrasures. Henceforth, the image of man imposed itself: dignitaries, carriers of offerings, servants – we are witnessing a profound change of theme; henceforth, the repertoire is in better accord with royal ideology.

OTHER BUILDINGS OF DARIUS AT SUSA

It has often been written that Darius' palatial complex at Susa was completed by Xerxes, which now seems unlikely. Xerxes' interest in Susa seems to have diminished rapidly, his attention moving to Persepolis. The inscriptions he left at Susa are simple signatures (xsb, xse) other than those concerning the Gate and the Propylaeum (xsa and xsd) which, moreover, recall that these buildings were the work of his father. When Xerxes participates in a building, he make certain to record it: 'what I have done and what my father has done' (xsa, xsb, xsc and xsf); or 'what I have done, I have done it' (xsa). Unlike his father, he had a strong propensity to write his name (up to 14 times on a small building at Persepolis), whilst Darius does not sign the bases of the Apadana columns.

We can ask what led Xerxes to inscribe the bases of the columns at the Propylaeum Gate. One explanation could be that once he had become king he installed the statue of his father at the Gate and the replica which he had commissioned at Susa, and the works took on a certain importance; he might have worried then that in the minds of visitors or his contemporaries he, Xerxes, was the creator of the monument or that he wanted to pass as such. The Gate inscriptions would then have had the aim of clarifying the situation. In the same flash of probity and filial piety, he would have done the same at the Propylaeum. One should readily admit that the Propylaeum does not date from the first decades of the fifth century BC, but this is not the case with the (Darius) Gate which, because of its position, must have been the first structure completed on the terrace of the Apadana, to which it was the principal access. Darius' name has been found on the bricks and on several small column bases (DSc, DSd, DSf, DSz).[29] DSd lays claim to the construction of a *taçara* and DS mentions a 'building with columns'. These bases are small in size and could not have belonged to anything other than secondary buildings which have disappeared. The remains of structures were found on the Acropolis but it is not possible to attribute them to one king or another.[30] It is possible to claim that, from the time of Darius, at the southern point of the Ville Royale tell, at the point called Donjon, there existed an installation, possibly for military purposes, as well as several pavilions at the Shaur site. We should be careful, however, not to see 'residences' behind each column base; there are no 'miniature Royal Achaemenid residences'. The buildings which accompany the large hypostyle halls are outbuildings, areas of rest, and not strictly speaking, residences. An Achaemenid residential complex cannot be conceived other than spread over several hectares. On the tells at Susa there is no place for a residence other than that which we know of. The surveys undertaken on the Ville Royale tell did not reveal anything which could be interpreted in this way. When he felt the need to replace Darius' Apadana temporarily, during the period of its restoration, Artaxerxes II built the interim hall outside the walls on the western bank of the Shaur.[31]

THE TIME OF DARIUS (522–486 BC)

Darius' architectural and artistic creations at Susa obviously do not allow, in themselves, the definition of an ideology. Susa is not the fulcrum of his thoughts. Contrary to Herodotus' writings, Susa was not the place where power was seized; Susiana was not the realm in which his mind and character were formed. For this young and charismatic warlord, an eminent member of the Persian nobility and of the royal family, one can imagine a general culture on the scale of the vast territories which he had already travelled; for him, as for all Persians, Greece was at the ends of the world. The universe was determined by the networks of exchange which extended from the Nile to the Indus and from the Caspian to the Sea of Oman; a world which was seeing the last gasps of the great Sumero-Akkadian and Egyptian civilisations and where the intellectual centres of Ionia and Western Asia shone. The cradle of philosophy, of arithmetic and of sciences was not Athens but more so Miletus, where Thales brought back from Egypt and from Babylonia the foundations of geometry; or Samos which saw the birth of Pythagoras. The logic of the times was not yet that of Aristotle; the epic had not yet made way for history as Thucydides would understand it, nor had myth been replaced by clear and theoretical concepts. Darius' contemporary was Hecataeus, the author of the *Genealogies* and *Travels around the Earth.*

At Babylon, which opened up to Cyrus in 539 BC, amongst the exiled Jews, the author of the exalted verses of the Book of Isaiah had sprung to the fore. To the east of the Caspian Sea, where the message of Zarathustra had perhaps already become blurred,[32] China with Confucius and Nepal with Buddha produced, in different regional environments, ideas similar to those of the westerners and which, like them, would influence humanity through the ages. The second half of the sixth century BC appears to have been dominated by the religious thoughts of the Orient, through new currents and a new approach to the principle of sovereignty.

Beliefs and practices

We know very little about the beliefs, practices and rites of the peoples of the Persian Empire at this time. Everything suggests, however, that in Iran, under Darius, the old religions clung on. Susa and Elam retained traces of the old Elamite pantheon with the names of Humban, Napirisha, Simut and Napazaba.[33] Humban is often mentioned in the Persepolis tablets, which also mention Iranian, Elamite and Babylonian deities. The royal administration paid for their priests; it even distributes what they were to offer as sacrifices (wheat, flour, wine). The powers-that-be seem to have regulated religious practice, if not the beliefs, in a spirit which was that of the politics initiated by Cyrus. On the Persepolis tablets relating to cultural activity, the name of Ahuramazda only appears rarely, which leads to questions about the place, let alone the existence of an official cult surrounding Ahuramazda. Susa has revealed no trace of such a cult; the situation seems to have been the same on the Persepolis Terrace. The only cultural scene involving Darius is that on the front of his rock tomb at Naqsh-i Rustam where he is in the presence of what is generally interpreted as a fire altar.[34]

Ahuramazda

The name Ahuramazda is not an invention of Darius, or even the Iranians. The name was known by Indo-Iranian groups (Aryans) coming down from Central Asia towards the south, to the west and to the east of the Caspian Sea, in the direction of India and the Iranian plateau, from the end of the second millennium BC. For P. Lecoq, linguistic data shows 'irrefutably' that these groups formed one and the same nation. We do not know, however, what their concept of the divine could be and what Ahuramazda or other deities could represent for them. The name Ahuramazda appears in eastern Iran in the *Gathas* of the *Avesta* and in western Iran with the inscriptions of the first Achaemenid kings.[35] Mazda corresponds to the Sanskrit *Mehda* which is translated as 'wisdom', whilst the word *ahura* has its equivalent (*asura*) in Indian records where it qualifies a category of sovereign deity. Ahuramazda is generally translated as 'Wise Lord'; one can, however, ask if there is not some prejudice here in personifying an entity which, for Zarathustra, was essentially of the spiritual and philosophical character. 'Great wisdom' or 'supreme wisdom' would perhaps be a better answer. We should be less indifferent to this translation, the more so as already the Old Elamite iconography, as can be seen notably at Jiroft in the third millennium BC,[36] seemed to hesitate in personifying the concept of the divine, in great contrast to what can be observed in Mesopotamia and Egypt at the same time. The iconography of Jiroft seems to convey the search for an equilibrium, an inner peace, a finality which one finds in this formula of 'the happiness of man' in the inscriptions of Darius' Palace. One might see a trace of the process of acculturation by the Persian tribes mixing with the natives on the Iranian plateau in the first half of the first millennium BC.

Ahuramazda and Zarathustra

Without entering into the controversy that divides religious historians on the historicity of Zarathustra, we must recall briefly that the prophet is reputed to have rejected the practices and rites of the traditional Aryan religion, as well as the deities of its pantheon, with the exception of Ahuramazda who incarnated his concept of the divine. Ahuramazda created the world through thought and it is through thought that humans can approach him. He is surrounded by seven divine entities, the Amesha Spenta, through which he intervenes in the world; they are qualified 'good thought, justice, immortality, devotion'. Ahuramazda is also the father of two twin spirits, one kindly, the other destructive; these spirits do not oppose each other; they offer choice to man. The writings attributed to Zarathustra, the *Gathas*, form the oldest part of the *Avesta*; they are 'chants' or 'poems' whose comprehension is not always guaranteed; their ideas would take on, through Mazdaism, and also through Judaism, a more elaborate and systematic form. It would, however, be imprudent to go back through time and attribute to Zarathustra what the more recent *Avesta* would bring.

Darius and Ahuramazda

For Darius, Ahuramazda was the 'God of the Aryans'; he was 'the greatest of the gods'. His name reappeared in the inscriptions as a leitmotif, a recurring point. Ahuramazda appeared to Darius like a protective and creative force. Like the Near Eastern deities, he created the sky, the earth and man; he is 'a god of the sky'; he grants sovereignty, as Ashur and Marduk did for the Assyrian and Babylonian kings. In the first years of his reign, Darius seems to have endorsed without problem the symbolic Assyrian and Babylonian astral symbol (Sun, Moon, Star). At Susa, he accepted, in the decoration of the first part of the Residence, an iconographic repertoire which was still that of Nebuchadnezzar and his successors. We have seen that nearly a decade would go by before he affirmed his own ideology. Ahuramazda also made 'beautiful things' whose enumeration brings us closer to Iranian reality. He created a nation and a country 'of good men, of good horses and of good chariots' (DSs); enough to ensure 'the prosperity of man' and of the warrior.

The relationship of Darius with Ahuramazda was specific in that it did not tolerate any social intermediary. Like the pharaohs, Darius is the only intercessor between Ahuramazda and the people. The elimination of Gaumata, and with him of the Magi and their class, was not accidental; the obvious tension, on a religious level, would manifest itself again under Xerxes, after the death of Darius, and the Magi would finally return in strength under Artaxerxes II, together with Mithra and Anahita.[37] Between Darius and Ahuramazda, there was total connivance. Darius' devotion is incontestable; his respect of transcendental forces was profound, mixed with love and fear; his constant worry of being reassured over the legitimacy of his power leads one to ask if he did not entertain doubts on the subject himself.

A short inscription on a baked brick from Susa, of imprecise provenance (DSk), is currently translated as 'I (am) Ahuramazda's, Ahuramazda (is) mine'. The dative is unarguable, but the interpretation must not be prejudged. J.-M. Steve saw in these words, which do not repeat the customary phraseology of the royal ideology of the great inscriptions, the most convincing affirmation of Achaemenid Zoro-astrianism.[38] He wrote: 'In the Susian context, it is difficult not to see there, in the face of a population which remained faithful to other religious traditions, a pro-clamation in which Darius affirms his intimate conviction: a non-aggressive mono-theism which opens the door to a certain tolerance'. To qualify Darius' religious thought as Zoroastrian or Mazdaean makes no great sense due to the difficulty in defining Mazdaism in its earliest phase. We note that elsewhere, in the centuries that followed, Mazdaism would have little success in south-western Iran.

As for monotheism, at the turn of the sixth and fifth centuries BC we are still a long way from a clear concept. Darius allowed himself to be presented in Egypt as 'perfect God' in his pharaonic titulature; but in his inscriptions he referred to 'other gods'. We cannot help but see a certain semantic or political finesse; we must not confuse monolatrism and monotheism; true monotheism does not appear until the fourth century BC in the very particular conditions in which the Jews, exiled from Babylon to the limits of the Persian Empire, found themselves; and this monotheism, as is highlighted below by Jean Soler, was ethnocentric.

SUSA AFTER DARIUS

After the death of Darius I, his son, Xerxes, seems to have lost interest in Susa, as its construction was complete, and turned his attention to Persepolis where works had been delayed by the building of the Terrace. Susa continued to play its role as a way-station and regional administrative centre for the satrapy. The Palace of Darius I was maintained. It would not have survived an abandonment, however brief, as the terraces had to be remade every year.[39] After Xerxes (486–465 BC), Artaxerxes I (465–425 BC) only leaves indirect traces at Susa, and there is a brief inscription of Darius II (425–405 BC). Throughout the period from 480 to 400 BC,

Susa gives the impression of being an 'empty shell'; the second half of the century would see the accidental destruction of the Apadana; and also, no doubt, the crumbling of the western edge of the Apadana terrace, carried away by bad weather.

According to Babylonian sources, the Susian agglomeration consisted of an active market, but its territorial extension was limited; it barely extended beyond the three large tells, and only towards the north where the 'Artisans' tell' was beginning to take shape. We are a long way here from the thousand hectares of Babylon or even the large spaces of Pasargadae, Ecbatana or Persepolis. Susian archaeology reveals nothing about an urban organisation under the Achaemenids; it is strange not to find more traces of daily life, when we can follow the development of the city, generation after generation, over the millennia which precede and follow.

On an artistic level, the fourth century BC saw signs of decline, particularly in sculpture.[40] The orthostats found in the 'Donjon' by Mecquenem,[41] stones which, in all probability, were taken from the Shaur Palace of Artaxerxes II,[42] follow the Persepolis repertoire (notably the motif of the servant climbing the stairs) in a careless and feeble style. Stone seems to have been more current at Susa,[43] a sign, no doubt, of greater wealth; it remained, however, a rare material; the columns of the audience hall of the Shaur Palace were wood covered in painted plaster, and makeshift repairs to their bases were badly concealed under yellow paint.[44] Building works remain vigorous – the baked brick foundation wall which Artaxerxes ordered to be erected to support the western edge of the Apadana terrace is impressive – but on the whole, the builders appear to have been more conscious of efficiency than grandeur.[45] The production of ornamental bricks was always to the fore,[46] but they were of smaller dimensions and inferior quality. They were found in greatest numbers in the western sector of the Apadana Terrace, restored by Artaxerxes II. In a neighbouring area, the paintings which decorated the walls of the hypostyle hall of the Shaur Palace get our attention more due to their rarity than their quality.[47]

We can seek the reasons why Artaxerxes II was interested in Susa. The first, no doubt, was the necessity to preserve its evident use as a relay station. The central geographic position of Susa in the Empire must also have been of strategic interest, well before Strabo mentioned it five centuries later. Specific political conditions, possibly personal reasons, must have intervened in the choice of Artaxerxes II, a choice which contributed significantly to placing Susa on the horizon of the chroniclers.

The 'winged disc' and Ahuramazda

Jean Perrot

A t the top of the scenes sculpted into the rock at Bisitun, a bearded figure, dressed as a Persian, rises halfway out of a ring, flanked by the large wings and fan-tail of a bird of prey; with his raised right hand he exchanges a greeting with King Darius.

This construct, a derivative of the old Egyptian solar symbol, was introduced in the first millennium into the Assyrian and Babylonian world by the Phoenicians. The flying figure was Ashur, the great Assyrian god, or Marduk, great god of the Babylonians; we cannot dismiss outright the idea that this is Ahuramazda, great god of the Aryans, especially as in the first years of his reign, Darius did not reject Mesopotamian symbols – as proved by the mythological monsters of the Susa Residence.

494
The figure in the winged disc at Persepolis

An image has its own life and, especially when the theme travels, its significance can change; here we do not lack reasons to discard the idea of a figure with divine properties. For one, the figure's headdress does not have horns; also, when Iranian tradition escapes from Mesopotamian influence, it does not have a reputation of personifying or representing the divine concept in animal form. Darius venerated Ahuramazda who, for him, represented forces greater than his own power, but his concept of divinity seems pure and theoretical, much like that of Zarathustra and that of the great Oriental religions to come. The figure with whom the king seems to be exchanging a sign of intimacy was therefore more likely an entity of propitiatory, familial or clannish character.

This figure was copied, executed in the same fashion, on the front of Darius' rock-cut tomb at Naqsh-i Rustam; the identical symbol was found on those of his successors. The motif is heavy, with thick rectangular wings; an appearance which cannot be attributed to the quality of the rock which, elsewhere, is carved with fine cuneiform inscriptions.

The motif appears again with a bird-like lightness on the stone walls at Persepolis next to the primitive winged disc which probably does not have the same significance. In this initial shape it is present at Susa on several glazed-brick panels of uncertain date, linked with sphinxes who wear the horned tiara.

495
The figure in the winged disc at Bisitun

496
The figure in the winged disc at Naqsh-i Rustam

Bibliography:
SHAHBAZI, 1974; GNOLI, 1974;
ROOT, 1979; LECOQ, 1984.

Persians and monotheism

Jean Soler

Two verses of the Book of Isaiah mention Cyrus, the Persian god who liberated the Jews from their captivity in Babylon (44:28 and 45:1). In the same passage, expressed more clearly than anywhere else in the Bible, is the belief in a single God. What link is there between these two pieces of data?

A direct causality must be excluded: the Persians of the Achaemenid period were not monotheist; nor were the Jews. No more were they during the time of the exile – between the years 597 and 539 BC, after the destruction of Jerusalem and its temple by the Babylonians – than during the life of Isaiah, two centuries earlier – which evidently makes it scarcely credible that he was the author of the text where the name Cyrus appears. This does not mean that the Persians did not play a role, indirect but decisive, in the adoption of monotheism by the Jews.

> *1. Now in the first year of Cyrus King of Persia, the Lord stirred up the spirit of Cyrus King of Persia, that he made a proclamation throughout all his kingdom, and put it also in writing, saying,*
> *2. Thus saith Cyrus King of Persia, The Lord God of heaven hath given me all the kingdoms of the earth; and he hath charged me to build him an house at Jerusalem, which is in Judah.*
> EZRA I:I–2

NATIONAL GODS

We know today that monotheism does not go back as far as Moses – not to mention his ancestor Abraham – as the three religions of the only God maintain. It is under the domination of the Persians that the Jewish people conceived of monotheism and made it the central dogma of their religion. Until then it had taken on a form which was the rule in the region, 'monolatrism': a specific cult dedicated to one of the gods with which the people had concluded an alliance and who, by this fact, became a national god; this is without denying the existence of other gods, who were for this nation secondary gods, whilst they might be national gods for other people. In conflicts between nations, the god of the victor was presented as stronger than the god of the vanquished – and, therefore as the greatest of the gods, and why not as the creator of the sky and the earth? From this point of view there was no difference between the religion of the Jews and the religion of the Persians. When the Hebrews led by Moses managed to escape pharaoh's army by crossing the Red Sea, they intoned a praise of thanksgiving to Yahweh, the god who revealed himself to Moses as the one who had made a pact with Abraham, Isaac and Jacob, and had just shown himself to be greater than the gods of the Egyptians: 'Who is like You, O Lord, among the gods?' (Exodus 15:11).

On their side, when the Achaemenids want to thank their national god for having beaten numerous gods to become 'King of Kings', they carve inscriptions such as 'Ahuramazda is the great God, who created this earth here, who created the sky there, who created man, who created the joy of man, who made Darius King, unique King of many…'[48] or 'Ahuramazda the great, who is greater than all the gods, Who conferred royalty upon the King Darius on this great earth where there are numerous nations…'[49] The national god is the greatest of the gods, but he is not the only one. Elsewhere, Darius does not fail to also thank 'the other gods who exist'.[50]

A Messiah called Cyrus

The propensity of the peoples of the region to attribute their victories or their health to their national god – which is also the case with the Assyrians and Assur or the Babylonians and Marduk – led the deported Jews to think that they owed their liberation to their own God, Yahweh. The exodus from Babylon took place alongside that from Egypt in biblical legend. For this to be credible, Cyrus had to have acted under the orders of Yahweh. This is what the anonymous author affirmed, when, at an unknown date, he inserted pages into the collection of sayings attributed to Isaiah (he himself wrote nothing) which tell both of Cyrus and the belief in one God: 'It is I, Yahweh, that saith of Cyrus, He is my shepherd, and shall perform all my pleasure: even saying to Jerusalem, Thou shalt be built; and to the temple, Thy foundation shall be laid.' Thus spoke Yahweh to his anointed (literally, his 'Messiah'), 'to Cyrus, whose right hand I have holden, to subdue nations before him; and disarm kings, that thou mayest know that I, Yahweh, which call thee by thy name, am the God of Israel. For Jacob my servant's sake, and Israel mine elect, I have even called thee by thy name: I have surnamed thee, though thou hast not known me. I am Yahweh, and there is none else, there is no God beside me' (Isaiah 44:28; 45:1–5). Despite this last verse, definitely monotheistic, the perspective was still ethnocentric. It was the god of the Jews who expressed himself, and his only interest was the good of the Jews, not that of humanity. When other peoples were mentioned, it was to say that Israel would have its revenge on them after centuries of humiliation, under the hegemony of the Assyrians and the Babylonians after them. All the peoples will rally to the God of Jerusalem: 'even to him shall men come; and all that are incensed against him shall be ashamed. In the Lord shall all the seed of Israel be justified, and shall glory' (Isaiah 45:24–25).

This is what the author makes the national god say, in the exaltation brought about by the long awaited, but miraculous fall of Babylon, and with the hope, maintained during the exile by the prophets Jeremiah and Ezekiel that the return to Jerusalem by the Jews deported by the Assyrians and the Babylonians to various countries would be the prelude to the reconstruction of a great and powerful kingdom, as had been the case with David and his son Solomon.

> *I saith of Cyrus, He is my shepherd, and shall perform all my pleasure: even saying to Jerusalem, Thou shalt be built; and to the temple, Thy foundation shall be laid.*
>
> *Thus saith the Lord to his anointed, to Cyrus, whose right hand I have holden, to subdue nations before him; and I will loose the loins of kings, …*
> *I am the Lord, and there is none else, there is no God beside me*
>
> ISAIAH 44:28; 45:1–5

THE RELIGIOUS POLITICS OF THE PERSIANS

This hope was perhaps provoked or heightened by the politics of the Persians, who after they had conquered the Babylonians, allowed exiles of all nationalities to regain their countries and worship freely. No particular treatment was reserved for the Jews. Furthermore, in each of the countries brought into the empire, the Persians put themselves under the protection of the national god, whilst always only attributing their victories to Ahuramazda alone. The Darius statue discovered at Susa in 1972 had hieropglyphs where the king presented himself as a pharaoh, son of Ra-Atum 'perfect God'. But the other inscriptions, in the three official Achaemenid languages, give thanks to Ahuramazda for the fact that 'the Persian man holds Egypt'. On a clay cylinder brought to light in the ruins of Babylon in 1879, the Babylonians explain the fall of the town through the infidelity of their king to the national god Marduk, who had called on a foreign king, Cyrus, whose 'hand he had seized', whose 'name he pronounced', to give him 'kingship over the whole world'. Cyrus then speaks to affirm that he 'venerated Marduk' and prided himself on having liberated all the deported populations and re-establishing their religions.[51]

To speak of the duplicity of the Persians would be an error. In a polytheistic world it was normal to be wary of angering any god and to be reconciled with the deities who could help you. If, as a bonus, one obtained the thanks and submission of their faithful, then all was fair in love and war!

Cyrus' edict taken up by Darius

Cyrus' edict cited in two books of the Bible has therefore every chance of being authentic, even if the spin given it is fallacious. The second Book of Chronicles finishes and the Book of Ezra starts with the same lines: 'Now in the first year of Cyrus king of Persia, that the word of Yahweh by the mouth of Jeremiah might be fulfilled, Yahweh stirred up the spirit of Cyrus king of Persia, that he made a proclamation throughout all his kingdom, and put it also in writing, saying, "Thus saith Cyrus king of Persia, The Lord God of heaven hath given me all the kingdoms of the earth; and he hath charged me to build him an house at Jerusalem, which is in Judah. Who is there among you of all his people? His God be with him, and let him go up to Jerusalem, which is in Judah, and build the house of Yahweh, God of Israel, he is the God, which is in Jerusalem" ' (Ezra 1:1–3 and Chronicles II 36:22–23). For the Persians, it was obvious: Yahweh was only one god amongst others, designated either by his religious characteristic – a 'god of the sky' like Ahuramazda himself – Herodotus had remarked on it – or by his ethnic and geographic characteristics – the 'God of Israel', the 'God of Jerusalem'. What was more remarkable was that it was the same for the Jews. The books of Ezra and Nehemiah, virtually the only documents we have on the history of the Jews after their return to Jerusalem, always presented Yahweh as a God of their people, never as the only god who existed.

But Zerubbabel, and Jeshua, and the rest of the chief of the fathers of Israel, said unto them, Ye have nothing to do with us to build an house unto our God; but we ourselves together will build unto the Lord God of Israel, as king Cyrus the King of Persia hath commanded us. Then the people of the land weakened the hands of the people of Judah, and troubled them in building, And hired counsellors against them, to frustrate their purpose, all the days of Cyrus king of Persia, even until the reign of Darius King of Persia.

EZRA 4:3–6

Very soon after the time of great hope began the time of disillusionment. Despite Cyrus' edict, the Temple was not able to be built during his reign by the returning community due to internal dissent. The 'people of the country', an expression designating the non-Jews and the Jews who remained in Palestine who had intermingled, as opposed to the 'children of Israel' or the 'people of Judah', or the repatriated – wanted to participate in the reconstruction of the Temple, but they were excluded with the following argument: 'Ye have nothing to do with us to build an house unto our God; but we ourselves together will build unto the Lord God of Israel, as king Cyrus the king of Persia hath commanded us' (Ezra 4:3). From this came the resentment and manoeuvring that prevented the project from being realised. Under the reign of Cyrus' successor, Cambyses (530–522 BC), the Persian king who conquered Egypt, no progress was made. It had to wait until the accession of the next king, Darius (522–486 BC), for the building works to really start. The governor of the satrapy asked the king for confirmation of Cyrus' edict quoted by the Jews. Darius ordered a search of the royal archives. At Ecbatana, the ancient Median capital, which became one of the Achaemenid capitals along with Susa and Babylon, a 'cylinder' was found on which Cyrus gave his instructions that the Temple of Jerusalem should be rebuilt at the king's expense, that is to say, through raising taxes in the region (Ezra 6:1–8). And Darius ordered that it be done as Cyrus had commanded. Thanks to which the Temple, of modest proportions and free of the artistic decorations which had adorned the Temple of Solomon, was inaugurated in 515, a quarter of a century after the capture of Babylon by Cyrus and the liberation of the Jews who had been deported.

The misery of the Jews

The prophet Haggai is a good witness to the situation of the Jews returned from Babylon: 'You expected abundance and there was little' (Haggai 1:9). In addressing the people in the name of Yahweh, he says, 'If it is so, in King Darius' second year' (Haggai 1:1), thus in 520 BC, it was because the temple had not yet been built. When it was, the rain and the harvests would return. And the Jews would usher in a new era: 'I will shake up all the nations, then the treasures will flow from all the nations and I will pile glory upon this temple, said Yahweh of the armies. To me the silver! To me the gold! Oracle of Yahweh of the armies' (Haggai 2:7–9). Not only would the Jews have a new king, but he would be the most powerful of the kings: 'I will overthrow the thrones of kingdoms and destroy the power of national kingdoms' to grant power to Zerubbabel, a descendant of David named by the Persians as governor of Judaea, 'for it is you that I have chosen, Oracle of Yahweh of the armies' (Haggai 2:22–23). For this Jewish prophet, it was no longer the Persian king who was 'the anointed' (the Messiah) of Yahweh, but a Jew called to supplant him. Alas! Nothing of the kind happened. The situation of the Jews was no better once the temple had been built and Zerubbabel disappeared from history. The Persians refrained from re-establishing the king. Why would they have done so – Judaea was nothing but a group of villages in a 30 km radius around a town in ruins.

For Jerusalem at this time was indeed still in ruins and underpopulated, much as Nebuchadnezzar had left it in 586 BC. The Jews of the Return must have settled in villages.

The cupbearer of Artaxerxes

The town was not rebuilt until the reign of Artaxerxes I (465–424 BC), thanks to Nehemiah, a Jew who was the cupbearer to the king. We must note in passing the confidence manifested by a Persian king towards a non-Persian. Of all the people who approached a king, the cupbearer was the one who could most easily poison him. Nehemiah, solicited by the Jews of Judaea who had sent a delegation to Susa, asked if the king could grant him a temporary mission such that he might go and rebuild Jerusalem, starting with its ramparts and repopulating it progressively. This mission, towards the middle of the fifth century BC, was followed by another, several years later, to sort out social problems. It was completed by a different mission, granted no doubt under Artaxerxes II (404–359 BC) to another Jew, Ezra, a scribe-priest, whose family, like that of Nehemiah, had preferred to stay in exile (only a minority of the deportees had taken advantage of Cyrus' authorisation).

The role of the Bible

Ezra took the road to Jerusalem with a caravan – more than a century after the first of Jews desirous of returning to the country of their ancestors. On his arrival, he promulgated 'the book of the Law of Moses which Yahweh had commanded to Israel' (Nehemiah 8:1). By means of an authoritative 'writ', the intention was to give a religious and legal framework to the community of Judaea, as well as to the Jews dispersed throughout the empire. This document, the core of the actual Bible, served the understandable interests of the Persians as well as that of the Jews. The importance for the Persians was that each ethnicity should be well organised and not tempted to revolt. To this end, the traditional laws which governed them were tempered by royal power. The Books of Ezra and Nehemiah – they are by the same hand and form a whole whose chronology has been mixed up – insist on the first measure imposed by Ezra: the outlawing of mixed marriages. Indeed, since the return of the first repatriates 'the holy race mingled with the peoples of the land', which explains the 'wrath of the god of Israel', of 'Yahweh, our God', who made 'slaves' of us even though he had gained 'the favour of the kings of Persia'. To obtain his pardon it was necessary to no longer pollute themselves through contact with non-Jews: 'give not your daughters unto their sons, neither take their daughters unto your sons, nor seek their peace or their wealth for ever: that ye may be strong, and eat the good of the land, and leave it for an inheritance to your children for ever' (Ezra 9, 2:12).

There is no trace of monotheism in these texts but always the hope that the national god, if one were to scrupulously observe his laws, would re-establish Israel to the greatness which had been hers at the time – largely mythical, as proven by archaeology – of David and Solomon.

If the Jews were still not monotheists at the beginning of the fourth century BC, when did they become so and why?

THE INVENTION OF MONOTHEISM

The hypothesis to which I have come is that monotheism arose through the misfortune of the Jews. The renouncing of mixed marriages and the expulsion of foreign spouses and their children, the respect of the innumerable commandments of Moses, the first of which requires no other god than Yahweh, did not improve the fate of the Jews any more than had the reconstruction of the Temple. During the two centuries of the Persian Empire, Judaea was only a minuscule district in a satrapy that extended from the Euphrates to the Nile, without a king, without independence, without an army, without prosperity. The Persian inscriptions that mention the twenty or so nations making up the empire, such as the Assyrians, the Babylonians, the Egyptians and the Arabs, never mention the Jews. None of the prophecies which had fed their expectations materialised. Doubts over the real power of the national god were inevitable, particularly because the Jews must have learnt, starting with those who were close to power, such as the cupbearer Nehemiah or Ezra, that the Persians attributed their success to their own god, Ahuramazda, and in no way to Yahweh.

Add to this that there was no way to curse the Persians, as they had done with the Assyrians and the Babylonians who had served as instruments of Yahweh to punish his unfaithful people – this is what the prophets explained – and who had been chastised in their turn for having made Jewish blood run. There was nothing for which the Persians could be reproached. They had been caring towards the Jews. For what reason would Yahweh want their loss? Their domination had perhaps been determined to last forever. Should it be concluded that the greatest of the gods was not Yahweh but Ahuramazda? During the course of the fourth century BC, about which we know nothing precise concerning Judaea – whilst in Greece it is the century of Plato and Aristotle – the Jews no doubt faced a deep crisis. Either Israel had to abandon its god and adopt the god of the victor, as many peoples have done in history, and thereby renounce its identity, so much had religion and ethnicity become intertwined, or it had to find a completely new explanation, capable of saving both its god and its identity. This revolutionary idea was monotheism.

If there existed only one god, there was no need to pit the gods against each other, wondering which was the greatest. Specifically, there was no longer a need to distinguish between the god of the Persians and the god of the Jews. He was the same, unique God. Now he favoured the Persians, one day he would favour the Jews.

The bringing together of the two deities was facilitated by their points in common. Ahuramazda and Yahweh were gods of the sky, creator-gods of the earth, and gods which were not represented in human form.

This change of religion in the Jewish people came about slowly, progressively, without being attributable to any one prophet in particular. The writer, whose monotheistic verses were inserted into a passage of Isaiah which mentions Cyrus, was certainly not a prophet, the 'second Isaiah', as has been claimed since the eighteenth century AD. A prophet of whom we know nothing, even the name, would be an anomaly in the Bible. Furthermore, it is unlikely that this scribe lived at the time of Cyrus. The Jew who would have had the original idea of a monotheistic doctrine was not listened to, because the following generations forgot even his name. The moment had not come for this radically new idea to find fertile ground and to surmount hardships. In a similar way, certain Greeks of antiquity claimed that the earth rotated around the sun, as well as on itself, or even that matter had an atomic composition, but they were not followed by their people, because these ideas did not respond to a need and did not help solve any problem.

The birth of monotheism towards the end of the fourth century BC was limited to the Jewish people. The Persians had no reason for changing their religion. One does not change a winning religion. But could the monotheist mutation have taken place elsewhere, other than with the Jews and at another time, in other circumstances than under the domination of the Persian Empire? I think not.

1. R. Boucharlat, this volume, ch. 12 and 13.

2. F. Vallat, this volume, ch. 9 and Appendix.

3. R. Boucharlat, this volume, ch. 13: 417–418. The Marv Dasht Plain, where Persepolis is located, had, together with Anshan (Tall-i Malyan), always been at the very heart of Elamite civilisation.

4. Even before Cyrus II had passed through Susa in 539 BC, during the period known to archaeologists as Neo-Elamite IIIB (605–539 BC), Elam was no more than a collection of small cities that were completely independent of any central authority. A few hundred economic tablets written in Elamite and dated to the seventh–sixth centuries BC were found on the Acropolis. Some bear Iranian names from which it can be deduced that some Persians were already settled at Susa and in its surroundings. Other tablets refer to the making of weapons and spears, the working of wool and the presence of weaving and dyeing workshops (STEVE, VALLAT and GASCHE, 2002–03: 554). When Darius arrived, Susa was politically at its lowest ebb, and its diminished population only inhabited parts of the tells. One might even suppose that the simple announcement of a royal project to establish a fortress at Susa may have led to the third Elamite uprising, headed this time, not by a Persian, but by the Elamite Aoamaita.

5. Strabo, XV 3

6. Based on an average daily production per man of 3 cubic metres.

7. From 2 to 3 m in diameter and 3 to 5 m long.

8. Abadan, on the north coast of the Persian Gulf, is known to climatologists as the 'hot pole', just as Murmansk in Siberia is the 'cold pole'. The region's climate has barely changed since the fourth millennium BC; however, the population may have fluctuated according to vegetation and farming. Today, with the development of huge fields of well-irrigated sugar cane, life has become easier during the summer season. A century ago, there were only a few tribes of nomads in Susiana.

9. The Persepolis archives note the departure from Susa of 416 stonemasons on the eve of the king's arrival in the 22nd year of his reign (P. Briant, this volume, ch. 1: 15–16).

10. Although F. Vallat (VALLAT, 2002: col. 488) notes the difficulty in relating inscriptions to buildings because of destruction wrought by succeeding generations of occupants; few inscriptions have been found in situ and the terminology used by the scribes to identify different buildings is confusing.

11. § 58 'There are many other things that I have done which are not written in this inscription … for fear that what I have done might seem too much to the one who may read this later and he might think it was untrue', Appendix: 483, § 58.

12. There is one reservation, however, concerning the mention of 'at Susa'; it corresponds to a break in the tablet. The restoration is plausible as regards the spacing and the fact that the tablet was found at Susa. It has to be noted, however, that the reference to Susa breaks the unity of a text of which the general theme is the pacification of the empire.

13. F. Vallat, this volume, ch. 9. It is within the confines of the Residence, and not of the Hypostyle Hall, that in 1912 was found the famous Persian tablet with the text of the 'Foundation Charter of the Palace'. (Report on the excavations sent by Mecquenem to the Foreign Ministry). V. Scheil confused the 'Apadana tell' with the Hypostyle Hall (Apadana).

14. VALLAT, 1972b, St Ir 1, 5.

15. F. Vallat, this volume, ch. 9.

16. STEVE, 1974. W. Hinz proposes a date around 510 BC (HINZ, 1976).

17. F. Vallat, this volume, Appendix.

18. F. Vallat in litteris.

19. Other than tiny objects placed in the foundation deposits near doors of the Honour Court C1 of the Residence.

20. See J. Perrot, this volume, ch. 4: 104, fig. 87.

21. Egyptian influence is particularly clear if we take into account the headdress of the winged figure at the gates of the palace. F. Vallat, this volume, ch. 2; fig. 20.

22. H. Gasche, this volume, ch. 13.

23. In comparison with Pasargadae, where the different parts of the complex are dispersed, the compact block of the Residence-Apadana calls to mind that of Neo-Assyrian palaces. It may be due to technical constraints imposed by the nature of the largely artificial platform on which rise heavy buildings; the stability of these buildings diminishes in relation to the distance from the central core, made up of the ancient levels of the tell.

24. The wheels of the carts have marked the paving of the monumental Gate on the way out to the Esplanade, see ch. 6, this volume, fig. 177.

25. No particular significance should be attached to this number, particularly to number 7, even though its importance in Iranian cosmology is well known.

26. The west bloc was accessible from the Acropolis by means of the battlements and postern L1 which may have been reserved for the local administration.

27. Mecquenem draws attention to a stone-built well in the Central Court but without indicating its exact position. It is a detail worth recording, that until 1963 water was brought to the Château by a donkey making constant return trips between the house and the river.

28. P. Briant, this volume, ch. 1.

29. See P. Lecoq (LECOQ, 1997: 110). These bases measure from 0.75 to 0.91 m in diameter, as against almost 2 m for those of the Apadana. See also pp. 434–435.

30. R. Boucharlat, this volume, ch. 12: 359–360.

31. Concerning this building and its place in Susa's history, we should note that it was built rather curiously in the floodplain of the Kherka, between the Shaur and that river that flows at some distance to the west of the tells (see the satellite view of the area: 18–19). The engineers of Artaxerxes II were not ignorant of the risks from flooding when building in this area (as we experienced in 1969), or even of the permanent risk from the high water-table affecting floors and walls. They ensured the waterproofing of the building by raising it on a layer of gravel some 2 m thick. Such foundations were not necessary for a building which was relatively light. The choice of the site does, however, need some explanation. It consists of an assembly hall with the usual dependencies (rooms for resting, and probably green surroundings) of the Apadana type that seems to have been essential for the exercise of a particular type of power under the rule of the Great Kings. However, at Susa, when Artaxerxes II decided to stay there, at least during the appropriate season, the Apadana of Darius required repairs which could be foreseen as lasting many years, hence the need for a temporary replacement building. As the tells of Susa could not provide sufficient space for a second hall and its annexes (the 'Ville royale'

tell was probably occupied by the troops which accompanied the king), it was therefore necessary to build extra muros, but as close as possible to the old Residence occupied by the king and his court. This necessary proximity must have dictated the final choice on the west bank of the Shaur, but in the floodplain of the Kherka; this was temporarily acceptable despite the calculated risk of flooding at approximately ten-year intervals. Such a situation would explain the somewhat relaxed construction of the Shaur Palace and its relatively scant decoration.

32. Considering the linguistic state of the texts attributed to him (the Gathas of the Avesta) Zarathustra would have lived at the beginning of the first millennium BC. However, according to one tradition, he died aged 77 some 258 years before the death of Alexander the Great.

33. STEVE, VALLAT and GASCHE, 2002–03.

34. Mecquenem drew attention to an architectural piece from the 'Donjon' (MECQUENEM, 1947) that he thought might have belonged to a fire altar, which is likely; however, this piece is probably no earlier than Artaxerxes II. R. Boucharlat, this volume, ch. 13: fig. 440.

35. LECOQ 1997, p. 155, n. 2. This word also occurs in the Avesta as a noun used for designating gods and names.

36. PERROT and MADJIDZADEH, 2003.

37. The religious crisis was not instigated by Darius; it is interesting to go back to the reign of Nabonidus and his troubled relationship with the Babylonian priests.

38. STEVE, 2003: 556–557. 'Lines 3–5 of DSk have a syllogistic brevity: "man: AM/AM ha: adam / AM m: ayadaiy", which can be translated literally: "mine is Ahuramazda / I shall sacrifice to Ahuramazda".' F. Vallat, this volume, ch. 2 and 10.

39. The Residence was doubtless occupied from time to time by his successors, and more regularly by Artaxerxes II while the Apadana was being restored, and was temporarily replaced by the Shaur hypostyle hall. Nearly a century later, the palace welcomed the family of Darius III; Alexander the Great is also supposed to have been married there!

40. All the carved paving stones found at Susa can be attributed to the time of Artaxerxes II. The use of the stone became popular, notably for plinths and for some stair-treads imitating what was being done at Persepolis.

41. MECQUENEM, 1947.

42. R. Boucharlat, this volume, ch. 12: 371.

43. The stone stair treads found in the village of Shush-i Daniel a few hundred metres from the Shaur Palace, probably came from there (R. Boucharlat, this volume, ch. 12: 378).

44. R. Boucharlat, ch. 12: 381.

45. J. Perrot, this volume, ch. 6: 205–207.

46. N. Daucé, ch. 10: fig. 322.

47. R. Boucharlat, ch. 12: 390–391.

48. LECOQ, 1997: 217.

49. LECOQ, 1997: 229.

50. LECOQ, 1997: 210.

51. I commented on the inscriptions of the cylinder and the statue in SOLER, 2002: 69–71.

Susa and the Bible

Jean Perrot

THE BOOK OF ESTHER

> *Now it came to pass on the third day, that Esther put on her royal apparel, and stood in the inner court of the king's house, over against the king's house: and the king sat upon his royal throne in the royal house, over against the gate of the house.*
>
> *And it was so, when the king saw Esther the queen standing in the court, that she obtained favour in his sight: and the king held out to Esther the golden sceptre that was in his hand. So Esther drew near, and touched the top of the sceptre.*
>
> ESTHER 5:1–2 KJV

There is a real possibility of a link between the lines from the 'scroll of Esther' and Susian archaeological reality as it appears today, with the location described and the internal layout of the royal apartments at the heart of the Residence; the discovery of the monumental Gate allows us to answer several questions relative to the comings and goings of Mordechai and his contacts with Esther, his pupil. This picture is certainly not enough to establish the historicity of the Book of Esther and Esther's relationship with the Palace of Darius–Xerxes (Ahasuerus), but it explains some difficulties of which the least would be the reconstruction of the journey which the queen would have taken between the 'women's quarters' behind the King's apartments and the inner court (C1). (One could admit, it is true, that the 'Princely apartments', to the north of the court, were also allocated to the women, notably to the royal spouses). No one can doubt the sources of the Book of Esther, a knowledge of the arrangement of the royal palaces of the period and the customs of the Achaemenid court; the memory was still vibrant during the Parthian period.

497
Claude Vignon, *Esther before Ahasuerus*
oil on canvas
Musée du Louvre, paintings department
© RMN/Franck Raux

Originally, the Book of Esther was a form of profane novel preserving an oral tradition and writings in Hebrew, Greek and Aramaic (several snippets of the last have been found amongst the Dead Sea Scrolls) reviving the memory of an oriental diaspora, and proving the presence at Susa of a Jewish community. It was later, at the end of the second century BC, following the catastrophe of the first Jewish war, that these stories were compiled and re-oriented by the keepers of the collective memory of the Jewish people,[1] conscious of constructing a positive view of the past by bonding the figures of Esther and Mordechai more closely to the prestigious history of Achaemenid Persia. From this point of view, it is not without interest to note that, through all the levels of interpretation, 'Susa the citadel' remains at the heart of the places of memory of the Jewish diaspora of the Near East.

Greek text

It was in the days of Ahasuerus, the Ahasuerus who reigned from India to Ethiopia over 127 provinces. In these days, as the King Ahasuerus sat on his royal throne at Susa the citadel, the third year of his reign, he made a feast for all his ministers and servants. The generals of the Army of the Persians and the Medes, the nobles and the provincial governors were in his presence, when he exhibited to them the richness of his royal splendour and the magnificent brightness of his grandeur, during a great number of days: 180 days!

And when these days were accomplished, the king made for the whole population who were at Susa the citadel, from the greatest to the smallest, a seven day feast. In the courtyard of the garden of the Royal Palace. These were white and purple violet linen drapes held fast with sea silk and purple crimson to silver rings and to alabaster columns, gold and silver divans placed on tiles of porphyry, marble, mother of pearl and black marble.

498
**Mosque of the 'Prophet Daniel'
at Shush-i Daniel**

Drink was offered in gold cups of different shapes and the wine was poured with a royal liberality. But according to the instructions, no one was forced to drink because the king had prescribed to all the stewards of the house to act according to everyone's pleasure'. For her part, the Queen Vashti made a feast for the women in the royal house of King Ahasuerus.
ESTHER 1:1

THE BOOK OF DANIEL

The tomb sheltered by the small mosque of Shush-i Daniel is reputed by local tradition to be that of the biblical prophet; this tradition probably rests on the verses of the Book of Daniel (8:1–2). 'I looked into the vision; so, whilst I was looking, I was at Susa the citadel, which is in the province of Elam. I was looking into the vision, and I was near the river Ulaï' (The Ulaï of Babylonian and Elamite records, the Eulaios of the Macedonians, yet we still do not know whether it is a reference here to the Shaur or the neighbouring Kerkha.)

If the geographic framework is relatively precise, the events to which it alludes are less so. They are disparate tales belonging to theology as much as a history that one can place in the middle of the first half of the sixth century BC (Daniel, a young Jew exiled to Babylon interprets a dream of Nebuchadnezzar). The story was written down during the Seleucid period, as the presence of Persian and Greek terms attests; it no doubt precedes the death in 164 BC of Antiochus IV, persecutor of the Judaeans.

The book of Daniel is no less a testimony to the mentality and the ideas of an Oriental diaspora mixing the religious traditions of Babylonia, Persia and Hellenistic Greece. Its author appears to know all of the great themes of Mazdaism (the 'Almighty' appears as a dispenser of wisdom). Several centuries after Isaiah, he proclaims an absolute monotheism with force.

Bibliography:
SMITH, 1963. ELLERS, 1974. KUHRT, 1983–1990.

1. There is a detailed Exposé of the question in STEVE, 2003: col. 590–595 citing J.-C. Picard

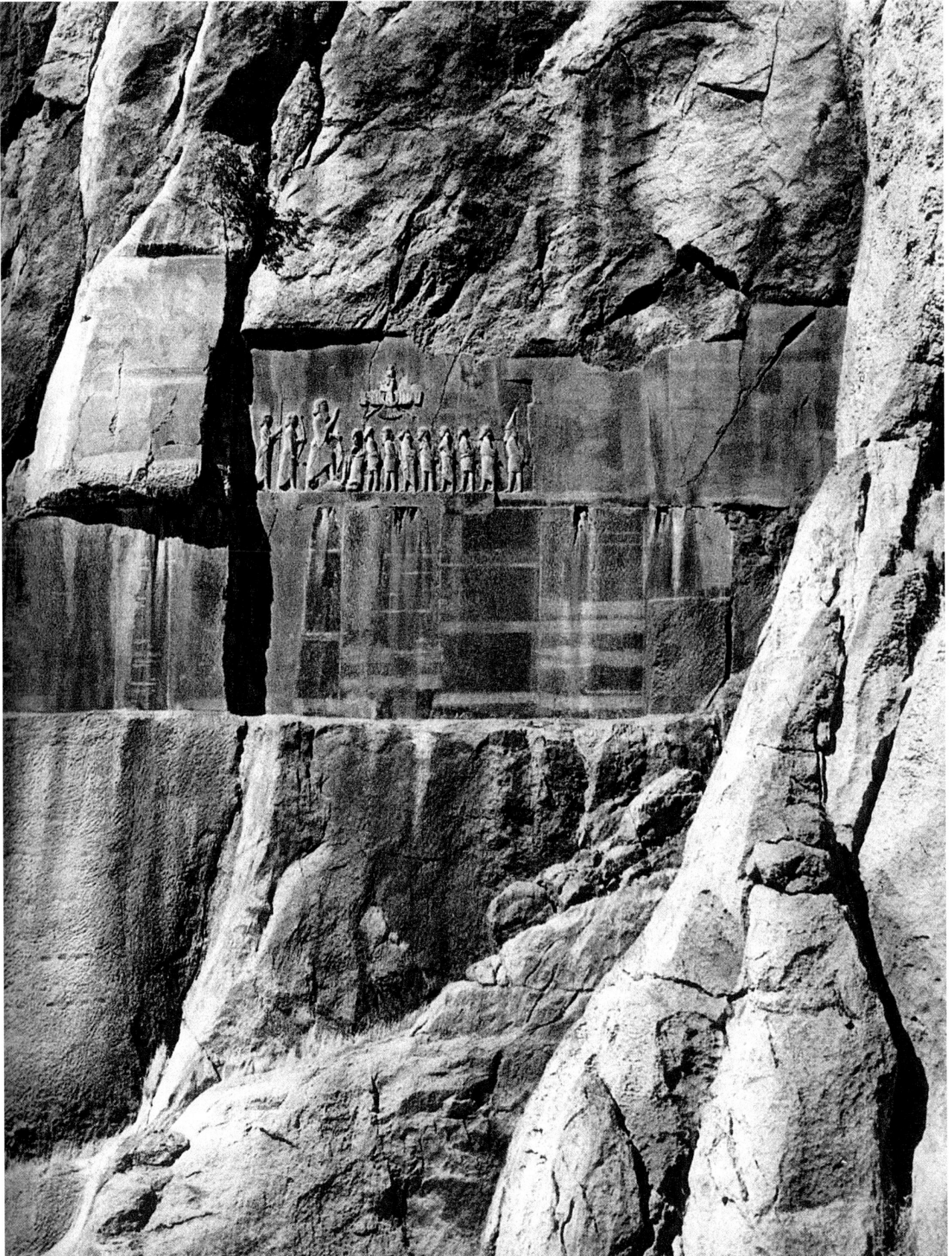

499
The Bisitun rock with the relief and inscriptions of Darius I

Appendix
The inscriptions of Darius at Bisitun (DB)

François Vallat

Translation of the Elamite version

Darius' inscription carved onto the cliff face at Bisitun was inscribed like most of the royal Achaemenid inscriptions in three languages: Old Persian, Elamite and Babylonian. The translation proposed below favours the Elamite version except of course for paragraphs 71 to 76 which only exist in Old Persian. For the translation of the Old Persian version I have referred to P. Lecoq[1] and for the Babylonian version to Fl. Malbran-Labat.[2]

The present translation is as close as possible to the Elamite version. It follows the classical numbering, that of F.H. Weissbach.[3] The omission of the formula 'And Darius the King says:' noted at the beginning of several paragraphs of the Elamite version has been added between square brackets as it figures on the Old Persian version.

However, we have decided against labelling the protagonists with the Greek names given to us by the Classical writers. Thus, for the Smerdis of Herodotus (III, 61–62, 67, 68 etc.) we have kept with the reading Bardiya of the Old Persian because this name is written Bar-ti-ia in Elamite and Bar-zi-ià in Babylonian.

So as not to overburden the text, we have decided not to indicate the eroded passages or to note the variants which, generally, add nothing to the general content of the translation.

This inscription recounts the facts and actions of Darius during the year which followed his accession to power (§ 1–69). The Old Persian version narrates the details of certain campaigns which happened during the second and third years. The essentials, however, are made up by the eight first paragraphs in which Darius produces proof of his legitimacy. The more enigmatic passages of this inscription have been explained, specifically, in chapters 2 and 9.

§ 1
And Darius the King says:
I am Darius the Great King, King of Kings, King in Persia, King of the peoples, the son of Hystaspes, grandson of Arsames, the Achaemenid.

§ 2
And Darius the King says: My father was Hystaspes; Hystaspes' father was Arsames; Arsames' father was Ariaramnes; Ariaramnes' father was Teispes; Teispes' father was Achaemenes.

§ 3
And Darius the King says:
For this reason we are called Achaemenids.
(So) from long ago we have been noble.
From long ago our family has been royal.

§ 4
And Darius the King says:
There were eight of our family who were kings before me;
I am the ninth; nine in two lines have we been kings.

§ 5
And Darius the King says:
By the grace of Ahuramazda, I am King.
Ahuramazda bestowed the kingdom upon me.

1. LECOQ, 1997.
2. MALBRAN-LABAT, 1994.
3. WEISSBACH, 1911.

§ 6

And Darius the king said:
Here are the peoples who claim to be mine.
By the grace of a Ahuramazda, I am king over them:
The Persians, the Elamites, the Babylonians,
the Assyrians, the Arabs, the Egyptians,
the Sea People, the Sardisians,
the Ionians, the Medes, the Armenians,
the Cappadocians, the Parthians, the Drangians,
the Aryans, the Chorasmians, the Bactrians,
the Sogdians, Gandara,
the Scythians, the Sattagydes, Arachosia, Maka.
In all 23 peoples.

§ 7

And Darius the King says:
these peoples claim to be mine,
by the grace of Ahuramazda, they do my bidding,
they bring me tribute.
What I order them to do, be it night or day,
they execute.

§ 8

And Darius the King says:
Within these countries, the man who is loyal,
   him I reward well;
He who is hostile, I punish him greatly.
By the grace of Ahuramazda within these countries
   my law is respected.
What is told to them by me, they execute.

§ 9

And Darius the King says:
Ahuramazda conferred this kingdom upon me
and Ahuramazda aided me until
I had secured this kingship.
By the grace of Ahuramazda, I hold this kingdom.

§ 10

And Darius the King says:
This is what, by the grace of Ahuramazda, I did
after I received the kingdom.
One named Cambyses, son of Cyrus, of our family
he held the kingdom.
This Cambyses had a brother called Bardiya,
of the same mother and the same father as he.
And this Cambyses killed Bardiya.
Once he had killed Bardiya, the people did not know
that Bardiya had been killed.
Then Cambyses went to Egypt.
The people then became hostile because the lie
was propagated in that country and also in Persia,
and also in Media and also in the other countries.

§ 11

[And Darius the King says:]
And then, a man, a Magus called Gaumata,
this man, in the region of Naširna,
on a mountain called Harrakatarriš, revolted.
It was the 14th day of the month of Mikannaš
   when he rose up.
This man lied to the people saying:
'I am Bardiya, the son of Cyrus, the brother of
   Cambyses.'
Then all the people revolted against Cambyses and

went over to him (Gaumata),
the Persians and the Medes as well as the other
   countries.
It was the ninth day of the month of Karmapattaš.
It was thus that he revolted against Cambyses.
It was then that Cambyses died his own death.

§ 12

And Darius the King says:
This kingdom that Gaumata the Magus had taken
   from Cambyses,
this kingdom had belonged to our family from
   long ago.
Thus Gaumata the Magus took it from Cambyses.
Also from the Persians and the Medes and the other
   peoples,
he took from them and made them his possession.
He took the kingdom.

§ 13

And Darius the king says:
There was no one, neither Persian nor Mede,
nor person from our family who could have taken
the kingdom from Gaumata the Magus (for)
the people feared him greatly.
He killed many people who, before,
had known Bardiya. It is for the following reason,
   that he killed many people: 'so that they cannot
   divulge that I am not Bardiya, the son of Cyrus.'
And no one dared do anything against Gaumata
   the Magus
until I came. Then I prayed to Ahuramazda.
Ahuramazda aided me. By the grace of Ahuramazda,
   the 10th day of the month of Bagiyatiš, then,
   with few men, I killed Gaumata the Magus as
   well as the men who were his principal followers.
   It was in a town by the name of Sikayahuvati, in
   the region of Nisāya in the country of the Medes,
   it is there that I killed him and robbed him of
   the kingdom. By the grace of Ahuramazda,
   I am King because Ahuramazda gave me the
   kingdom.

§ 14

And Darius the King says:
The kingdom which was torn from our family,
I brought it back and put it back in its place, as it
   had been before. And I rebuilt the sanctuary of
   the god which Gaumata the Magus had destroyed.
   And I returned to the people the fields and the
   flocks and the servants – thanks to the courtiers –
   which Gaumata the Magus had taken from them.
   And I reinstalled the people to their positions, be
   it Persians, Medes or the other peoples, as they
   had been before. What had been taken away,
   I returned.
By the Grace of Ahuramazda, this is what I did.
And I accomplished tasks until I had put our palace
   back as it had been. And I accomplished so many
   tasks, by the grace of Ahuramazda, it was as though
   Gaumata the Magus had not moved anything in
   our palace.

§ 15

And Darius the King says:
This is what I did after I took the Kingdom.

§ 16

And Darius the King says:
Once I had killed Gaumata the Magus,
then, an Elamite called Haššina, the son of
   Ukpatarranma,
revolted in Elam saying: 'I am King over the
   Elamites.'
So the Elamites revolted against me.
They went over to this Haššina.
So he he became King over the Elamites.
And a man called Nuditbel, a Babylonian,
the son of Hanara, rose up in Babylon.
He lied to the people saying:
'I am Nebuchadnezzar, the son of Nabonidus.'
So all the people of Babylon went over to Nubitbel.
Then the Babylonians revolted. This man became
   King of the Babylonians.

§ 17

And Darius the King says:
Then I sent a message to Elam.
This Haššina was taken and sent to me.
Then I killed him.

§ 18

And Darius the King says:
Then I went to Babylon against this Nuditbel
who said: 'I am Nebuchadnezzar'.
The troops of this Nuditbel, on a river called
   the Tigris,
There were deployed and held the banks of
   the Tigris.
So the troops were placed by me on wineskins.
I placed some on camels.
Others were placed on horses.
Ahuramazda brought me aid. By the grace of
   Ahuramazda
we crossed the Tigris. In this place I crushed
   the Army of this Nuditbel.
It was the 26th day of the month of Hašiyatiš
   on which we thus joined battle.
I killed many soldiers there.

§ 19

And Darius the King says:
Then I went to Babylon
but before I had reached Babylon,
in a town called Zazan, situated on the Euphrates,
   there,
this Nuditbel who said: 'I am Nebuchadnezzar'
came against me with his troops. He had decided
   to offer battle. So we gave battle. Ahuramazda
   brought me aid. By the grace of Ahuramazda
   there I crushed the army of this Nuditbel. It
   was the second day of the month of Hanamakaš
   on which we thus joined battle. I killed a large
   number of Nuditbel's soldiers and those that
   fled into the river were taken by the waters.

§ 20

And Darius the King says:
Then, this Nuditbel, with a few riders left by fleeing.
He went to Babylon. So I went to Babylon.
By the grace of Ahuramazda, I took Babylon
   and seized Nuditbel.
Then I killed this Nuditbel at Babylon.

§ 21

And Darius the king said:

Whilst I was at Babylon,

these people revolted against me:

the Persians, the Elamites, the Medes, the Assyrians,
    the Egyptians, the Parthians,
    the Margians, Sattagydia and the Scythians.

§ 22

And Darius the king says:

A man called Martiya, the son of Zinzakriš,

in a town by the name of Kuganakā, located there in
    Persia,

revolted amongst the Elamites. He addressed the
    people saying:

'I am Ummannuš, the king of the Elamites'.

§ 23

And Darius the King says:

And then I, I approached Elam. The Elamites
    feared me.

This Martiya who called himself their chief,
    they seized him and killed him.

§ 24

And Darius the King says:

A man called Pirrumatiš, a Mede, revolted amongst
    the Medes.

He addressed the people saying: 'I am Sattarita of
    the family of Cyaxares'.

So the Median troops of the palace revolted against me.

They went over to him. He became king amongst
    the Medes.

§ 25

And Darius the King says:

The Persian and Median troops that I had amongst
    me were few. Nonetheless I advanced against the
    Army of the Medes.

A Persian called Midarna, my servant, I made their
    chief and I told them thus: 'Go! The soldiers who
    do not wish to be called mine, kill them!'

So Midarna, with the army, went to Media.

When he arrived amongst the Medes in a town
    called Maruš,

there in Media, he gave battle.

The one who was the chief of the Medes was not
    there. Ahuramazda aided me. By the grace of
    Ahuramazda, my troops killed a large number of
    enemy soldiers. It was the 27th day of the month
    of Hanamakas on which they thus joined battle.
    Then my army did nothing else. In a country
    called Kampanda, there in Media, they waited
    until I arrived amongst the Medes.

§ 26

And Darius the King says:

One named Daduršiš, my servant, an Armenian,
    I installed in Media. I told him thus: 'Go! Kill
    those soldiers who do not wish to be called mine!'
    So Daduršiš went. When he arrived in Armenia,
    the enemy had assembled. They advanced against
    Daduršiš. Battle was inevitable. So Daduršiš
    gave them battle in a town called Zūza, there
    in Armenia. Ahuramazda aided me. By the grace

of Ahuramazda my army killed a large number
of enemy soldiers. It was the eighth day of the
month of Turmar on which they joined battle.

§ 27

And Darius the King says:

A second time the enemies assembled. They advanced
    against Daduršiš. Battle was inevitable. So near a
    fortress called Tigra, there in Armenia, they gave
    battle. Ahuramazda aided me. By the grace of
    Ahuramazda my troops killed a large number of
    enemy soldiers. It was the 18th day of the month
    of Turmar on which they joined battle.

§ 28

And Darius the king says:

For the third time, the enemies assembled. They
    advanced against Daduršiš. Battle was inevitable.
    Near a fortress called Uyama, there in Armenia,
    they gave battle. Ahuramazda aided me. By the
    grace of Ahuramazda, my troops killed a large
    number of enemy soldiers. It was the ninth day
    of the month of Sakurriziš on which they joined
    battle. Then Daduršiš did nothing else. He waited
    for me until I arrived in Media.

§ 29

And Darius the King says:

Then a Persian by the name of Maumišša, my
    servant, I sent to Armenia. I said to him thus:
    'Go! Kill the enemy soldiers who do not wish to be
    called mine!'

So Maumišša went. Once he arrived amongst the
    Armenians, the enemies had assembled. They
    advanced against Maumišša. Battle was inevitable.
    So near a place called Izzila, there in Assyria, they
    gave battle. Ahuramazda aided me. By the grace
    of Ahuramazda, my army killed a large number
    of enemy soldiers. It was the fifteenth day of the
    month of Hanakemaš that they joined battle.

§ 30

[And Darius the king says:]

For a second time the enemies assembled.

Against Maumišša they advanced. Battle was
    inevitable.

Then, in a region called Hautiyaruš, there,

they gave battle. Ahuramazda helped me.

By the grace of Ahuramazda my army killed a great
    number of enemy soldiers. It was at the end of
    the month of Turmar that they gave battle. Then
    Maumišša waited in Armenia until I arrived
    amongst the Medes.

§ 31

And Darius the King says:

So I went to Babylon and I went to Media.

Once I had arrived amongst the Medes, near a
    town called Kuntarruš, there in Media, this
    Pirrumatiš came, he said: 'I am king over the
    Medes'. He decided to give battle. So we joined
    battle. Ahuramazda aided me. By the grace of
    Ahuramazda I killed a large number of Pirrumatiš'
    soldiers. It was the 25th day of the month of
    Hadukannaš on which we thus joined battle.

§ 32

[And Darius the King says:]

Then this Pirrumatiš fled with a few riders.

He went to Rakka. So I sent my army.

From there, where he was captured, he was
    brought to me.

I cut off his nose and ears and tongue, and tore out
    one eye.

He was kept bound to my door, Everyone saw him.

Then, at Ecbatana, he was impaled.

The men who were his principal followers, at
    Ecbatana,

in the fortress, I cut off their heads and I exposed
    them together.

§ 33

And Darius the King says:

A man called Ziššantakma, a Sagartian,

revolted against me. He spoke to the soldiers thus,
    saying:

'I am King. I am of the family of Cyaxares'.

So I sent the Persian and Median troops.

A man called Takmašpada, a Mede, my servant,

I made their chief. I spoke to him thus:

    'Go! Kill the enemy soldiers

who do not want to be called mine!'

So Takmašpada went with an army. He joined
    battle

with this Ziššantakma. Ahuramazda aided me.

By the grace of Ahuramazda my troops killed

a large number of enemy soldiers and they
    captured

Ziššantakma and brought him to me.

I cut off his nose and ears and tongue, and tore
    out one eye.

He was kept bound to my door, Everyone saw him.

Then, in the region of Arbela, there, I impaled him.

§ 34

And Darius the King says:

This is what I did in Media.

§ 35

And Darius the King says:

The Parthians and the Hyrcanians revolted
    against me.

They said they were followers of this Pirrumatiš.

My father Hystaspes was amongst the Parthians.

The army abandoned him and revolted. So
    Hystaspes,

left with the troops who had remained faithful.

Near a town called Mišpauzatiš, there, in Parthia,

he joined battle with the rebels. Ahuramazda
    aided me.

By the grace of Ahuramazda Hystaspes killed
    many rebel soldiers.

It was the 22nd day of the month of Myakannaš
    when he thus joined battle.

§ 36

And Darius the King says:

Then I sent Hystaspes Persian troops from Rakka.

When these troops joined Hystaspes,

Hystaspes went on campaign. Near a town called
    Pattrigabbana,

there in Parthia, he gave battle. Ahuramazda

aided me.

By the grace of Ahuramazda Hystaspes killed a large number of enemy soldiers.

It was the first day of the month of Garmapadaš on which they thus joined battle.

§ 37

And Darius the King says:

So this country belonged to me once again.

This is what I did in Parthia.

§ 38

And Darius the King says:

A country called Margiana revolted against me.

A man called Pirrada, a Margian, they chose to be their king.

Then to one called Daturšiš, a Persian, my servant who was

the satrap in Bactria, I sent a message in which I said:

'Go! And kill the soldiers who do not wish to be called mine!'

So Daturšiš went with an army. He gave battle to the Margians.

Ahuramazda aided me. By the grace of Ahuramazda, my troops killed a large number of enemy soldiers.

It was the 23rd day of Hašiyatiš on which they thus joined battle.

§ 39

And Darius the King says:

So this country belonged to me once again.

This is what I did in Bactria.

§ 40

And Darius the King says:

A man called Mišdatta was established in a town called Turrama, in a region called Yautiya, there, in Persia. This man, the second, rose up amongst the Persians.

To the troops he spoke, saying:

'I am Bardiya the son of Cyrus'.

So the Persian troops of the palace, previously from Anshan,

all together, revolted against me. They went over to him.

In Persia, he became king.

§ 41

And Darius the King says:

So I sent the few Persian troops of the palace who had not revolted against me as well as the troops who were with me. Of one called Irdumartiya, a Persian, my servant,

I made their chief. And other troops followed me into Media. And Irdumartiya,

with the army, went to Persia. When he arrived amongst the Persians,

in a town called Rakka, there, in Persia, this Mišdatta who said: 'I am Bardiya', marched with an army against Irdumartiya.

So they joined battle. Ahuramazda aided me.

By the grace of Ahuramazda, my army killed a large number of

Mišdatta's soldiers. It was the 12th day of the month

of Turmar

on which they thus joined battle.

§ 42

[And Darius the king says:]

And then this Mišdatta fled with a few riders.

He went to Naširma. From there, once again, his army marched

against Irdumartiya. He decided to give battle.

On a mountain called Pararrakka, there, they joined battle.

Ahuramazda aided me. By the grace of Ahuramazda, my army

killed a large number of Mišdatta's soldiers.

It was the fifth day of the month of Garmapadaš when they

thus joined battle. Then they seized Mišdatta and they also seized his men

who were his principal followers.

§ 43

And Darius the king says:

So, this Mišdatta, along with his men who were his principal followers, I impaled them at Matezziš.

§ 44

And Darius the King says:

This is what I did in Persia.

§ 45

And Darius the King says:

This Mišdatta who said: 'I am Bardiya'

had sent an army into Arachosia

and had given it a chief.

One called Mimana, a Persian, my servant,

was then Satrap of Arachosia. He spoke to him thus:

'Go! Kill this Mimana and the soldiers

who say they are of King Darius'!'

So these soldiers went into Arachosia against Mimana,

those whom Mišdatta had sent. Near a fortress called Kappiššakanuš, there in Arachosia,

they gave battle. Ahuramazda aided me.

By the grace of Ahuramazda my army killed a large number

of enemy soldiers. It was the third day of the month of Hanamakaš

on which they thus joined battle.

§ 46

[And Darius the king says:]

And a second time, the enemies assembled

and gave a battle against Mimana in a region called Irtumaka, in Arachosia. Ahuramazda aided me.

By the grace of a Ahuramazda, my army killed a large number

of enemy soldiers. It was the seventh day of the month of Miyakannaš

on which they thus joined battle.

§ 47

[And Darius the King says:]

And so the man whom Mišdatta had made their chief,

he fled with a few riders. He went to a fortress called Iršada in Arachosia, the fiefdom of Mimana.

There he went. So Mimana followed him with the Army.

And he captured this man who called himself their chief,

as well as those who were his principal followers and he killed them.

§ 48

And Darius the King says:

So this country belonged to me again.

This is what I did in Arachosia.

§ 49

And Darius the King says:

Whilst I was in Persia and in Media

for the second time the Babylonians revolted.

A man called Harakka, an Armenian, the son of Haltita,

rose up in a region called Dubala,

there in Babylonia. He lied to the soldiers saying:

'I am Nebuchadnezzar, the son of Nabonidus'.

And then the Babylonian army revolted against me and went over to this Harakka. He took Babylon.

He became king over the Babylonians.

§ 50

[And Darius the King says:]

And then I sent an army to Babylon.

One called Mindaparna, a Persian, my servant,

I made their chief. I spoke to them saying:

'Go! Kill the Babylonian soldiers

who do not wish to be called mine!'

And so Mindaparna went to Babylon with an army.

Ahuramazda aided me. By the grace of Ahuramazda,

Mindaparna killed the Babylonians and took numerous prisoners

amongst them. It was the 22nd day of the month of Markašanaš

when this Harakka who said: 'I am Nebuchadnezzar' was taken.

The men who were his principal followers were taken and bound.

Then, as I had ordered, this Harakka, and the men who were his principal followers were impaled.

§ 51

And Darius the King says:

This is what I did at Babylon.

§ 52

And Darius the King says:

This is what I did, by the grace of Ahuramazda, in one single year, after becoming King.

I fought 19 battles. By the grace of Ahuramazda, I beat them. Here are the nine kings that I captured:

the first, one called Gaumata, the Magus, lied saying:

'I am Bardiya, the son of Cyrus'. This one raised up the Persians.

Then, one called Hašina, an Elamite, raised up

the Elamites, saying:
'I am king of the Elamites'.
Then one called Nuditbel, a Babylonian, lied saying:
'I am Nebuchadnezzar, the son of Nabonidus'.
This one raised up the Babylonians.
Then, one called Martiya, a Persian, lied, saying:
'I am Ummanniš, the king of the Elamites'.
    He raised up the Elamites.
Then one called Pirrumatiš, a Mede, lied, saying:
'I am Fiattarrida of the family of Cyaxares'.
    He raised up the Medes.
Then one called Ziššantakma, a Sagartian, lied,
    saying:
'I am King, I am of the family of Cyaxares'.
He raised up the Sagartians.
Then, one named Pirrada, a Margian, lied, saying:
'I am Bardiya, the son of Cyrus'. He raised up the
    Persians.
Then one called Harakka, an Armenian, lied, saying:
'I am Nebuchadnezzar, the son of Nabonidus'.
He raised up the Babylonians.

§53
And Darius the King says:
These are the nine kings that I captured in these
    battles.

§54
And Darius the King says:
These countries that revolted – those that the lie
had raised up because they (the Kings) had lied
    to the people –
and then, Ahuramazda put them back into my hands.
As I wished, I disposed of them.

§55
And Darius the King says:
You who will later become King,
protect yourself vehemently against the lie!
The man who will lie, punish him harshly,
if you think thus: 'My country must be secure'.

§56
And Darius the King says:
And what I have done, by the grace of Ahuramazda,
I did it in a single year.
    And you who later will read this inscription,
    believe what I have done,
    What is written in this inscription!
    Do not think it is a lie!

§57
And Darius the King says:
I swear by Ahuramazda that it is the truth and no lie
    that I have accomplished all this in a single year.

§58
And Darius the King says:
By the grace of Ahuramazda, there are many
other things that I have accomplished
and which are not written in this inscription,
The reason is: he who later will read this inscription
Might think that it is too much,
that which has been accomplished by me.

He would not believe it and would think it was a lie.

§59
And Darius the king says:
The ancient kings, during their reigns, did not
accomplish as many things as I have accomplished,
by the grace of Ahuramazda, in a single year.

§60
And Darius the king says:
Now believe what I have done! Tell it to the people!
Do not hide it! And if you do not hide this tale
from the people but if you tell it to them, may
    Ahuramazda
favour you as well as your family and may you
    live long!

§61
And Darius the King says:
And if, on the contrary, you hide this proclamation
and you do not tell it to the people, may Ahuramazda
kill you, and may you not preserve your family!

§62
And Darius the king says:
This is what I did in one single year:
by the grace of Ahuramazda, in one single year
    I did it.
Ahuramazda, the God of the Aryans, aided me,
as well as the gods of whom each name can be
    found here.

§63
And Darius the King says:
The reason for which Ahuramazda, the God of the
    Aryans,
aided me along with the other gods, is that I am
    not hostile,
that I am not a liar and that I'm not criminal,
nor I, nor anyone in my family.
I have followed the law and I have done no wrong,
neither to the strong, nor to the weak.
The man who installed himself in my palace,
I protected him ardently, but the one who harmed,
I punished violently. I have never harmed anyone.

§64
and Darius the King says:
You who will later become King, do not favour
    the liar,
nor the one who harms!

§65
And Darius the king says:
You who will later see this inscription that I have
    written
and these sculpted reliefs, do not destroy them but
    protect them
as long as you will have enough strength!

§66
[And Darius the King says:]

And if you see this inscription and these reliefs
and you do not destroy them
but protect them as long as you will have enough
    strength,
May Ahuramazda favour you as well as your
    family.
May you live long and
May Ahuramazda favour your enterprises!

§67
[And Darius the King says:]
But if you destroy this inscription and these reliefs,
and if you do not protect them, may Ahuramazda
    kill you!
May you not preserve your family!
And may Ahuramazda destroy all that you have
    made!

§68
And Darius the King says:
The one called Mindaparna, son of Mišparra,
    a Persian,
and the one called Huttana, son of Dakkurra,
    a Persian,
and the one called Kambarna, son of Mardunuia,
    a Persian,
and the one called Mitarna, son of Bagabigna,
    a Persian,
and the one called Hardumannuš, son of Maukka,
    a Persian.
These are the men who helped me until I had
killed Gaumata the Magus who said:
'I am Bardiya, the son of Cyrus'.
So these men aided me.

§69
[And Darius the King says:]
You, who later will become King,
Protect the families of these men.

§70
And Darius the King says:
By the grace of Ahuramazda,
I translated this inscription differently in Aryan.
It did not previously exist here.
Thus, on tablets as well as on parchment,
the people learnt that
I re-established a name and its lineage,
thanks to this very inscription which I
sent to all the lands after it was written and read
    before me.

§71
And Darius the King says:
This is what I did the second and third years
after becoming King.
A people called Elamite revolted.
A man, an Elamite called Athamaita,
they made their chief.
Next, I sent an army.
A man, a Persian called Gaubaruva,
my servant, I made their chief.
So Gaubaruva, with the army, went to Elam.
He gave battle to the Elamites.
Then Gaubaruva beat and crushed the Elamites

and he captured their chief, sent him to me.
Then I killed him. Afterwards the people were mine.

§72
And Darius the King says:
These Elamites were perfidious
And they did not venerate Ahuramazda.
I venerated Ahuramazda.
By the grace of Ahuramazda, I treated them
    according to my pleasure.

§73
And Darius the King says:
He who would venerate Ahuramazda, favour be
    upon him,
both in life as in death.

§74
And Darius the King says:
Then, with the army, I went to Scythia.
Next the Tigraxauda Scythians marched against me.
When I reached the […] Sea
I crossed it with all my army.
Next I beat the Scythians. I captured a part.
Another part, chained, was brought before me and
    I killed them.
Their chief, called Skunxa, they captured him
and they brought him to me. There I nominated
    another chief
according to my pleasure. Afterwards the people
    were mine.

§75
And Darius the King says:
These Scythians
were perfidious
and they did not venerate Ahuramazda.
I venerated Ahuramazda.
By the grace of Ahuramazda, I treated them
    according to my pleasure.

§76
And Darius the King says:
He who would venerate Ahuramazda, favour be
    upon him,
both in life as in death.

Abbreviations

AA • *Archäologischer Anzeiger*

AchHist • *Achaemenid History, Leiden*

ActIr • *Acta Iranica*

AfO • *Archiv für Orientforschung*

AION • *Annali dell'Istituto Orientale di Napoli*

AJA • *American Journal of Archaeology*

AMI(T) • *Archäologische Mitteilungen aus Iran (und Turan)*

AntK • *Antike Kunst*

AOAT • *Alter Orient und Altes Testament*

ARTA • *Achaemenid Research on Texts and Archaeology*

BAR, Int. Ser. • *British Archaeological Reports International Series*

BIFAO • *Bulletin de l'Institut français d'archéologie orientale*

CRAIBL • *Comptes rendus de l'académie des inscriptions et belles lettres*

DA • *Dossiers d'archéologie*

DB • *Dictionnaire de la Bible*

DAFI • *Cahiers de la délégation archéologique française en Iran*

DATA • *Data: Achaemenid History Newsletter*

Eos • *Eos. Commentarii Societatis philologae polonorum*

IrAnt • *Iranica Antiqua*

JA • *Journal Asiatique*

JAOS • *Journal of the American Oriental Society*

JARCE • *Journal of the American Research Center in Egypt*

JEA • *Journal of Egyptian Archaeology*

JCS • *Journal of Cuneiform Studies*

JESHO • *Journal of the Economic and Social History of the Orient*

JHS • *Journal of Hellenic Studies*

JNES • *Journal of Near Eastern Studies*

JRGS • *Journal of the Royal Geographic Society*

JSOT • *Journal for the Study of the Old Testament*

MDAI • *Mitteilungen des Deutschen Archäologischen Instituts*

MDOG • *Mitteilungen der Deutschen OrientGesellschaft*

MDP • *Mémoires de la Délégation Française en Perse*

MIFAO • *Mémoires publiés par les membres de l'Institut français d'archéologie orientale*

MMAI • *Mémoires de la Mission Archéologique en Iran*

NABU • *Nouvelles assyriologiques breves et utilitaires*

NAPR • *Northern Akkad Project Reports*

OIP • *Oriental Institute Publications*

OIS • *Oriental Institute Seminars*

RA • *Revue d'Assyriologie et d'Archéologie Orientale*

RAAsiat • *Revue des arts asiatiques*

RdE • *Revue d'Égyptologie*

RevArch • *Revue archéologique*

RlA • *Reallexikon der Assyriologie und Voderasiatischen Archäologie*

SDB • *Supplément au dictionnaire de la Bible*

SMEA • *Studi Micenei ed Egeo-Anatolici*

StIr • *Studia Iranica*

TCS • *Texts from Cuneiform Sources*

TMO • *Travaux de la Maison de l'Orient*

WO • *Die Welt des Orients*

WVDOG • *Wissenschaftliche Veröffentlichungen der deutschen Orient-Gesellschaft*

ZA • *Zeitschrift für Assyriologie*

Bibliography

ABRAHAM, K.
1997 • 'Šušan in the Egibi Texts from the Time of Marduk-nāsir-apli', *Orientalia Lovaniensia Periodica*, 28: 55–85.
2004 • *Business and Politics under the Persian Empire: The Financial Dealings of Marduk-nāsir-apli of the House of Egibi (521–487 B.C.E.)*. Bethesda: CDL Press.

ALIZADEH, A.
1985 • 'A Tomb of the Neo-Elamite Period at Arjān, near Behbahan', *AMI*, 18: 49–73.

ALLOTTE de la FUŸE
1928 • 'Numismatique', *MDP*, 20: 3–76. Paris: Ernest Leroux.
1934 • 'Inventaire des monnaies trouvées à Suse. Première partie', *MDP*, 25: 1–60. Paris: Ernest Leroux.

ALVAREZ-MON, J. and GARRISON, M.B. (eds.)
2011 • *Elam and Persia*, Winona Lake: Eisenbrauns.

AMANDRY, P.
1958 • 'Orfèvrerie achéménide', *AntK*, 1: 9–23.
1966 • 'À propos du trésor de Ziwiye', *IrAnt*, 6: 109–129.

AMIET, P.
1971 • 'La glyptique de l'Acropole (1969–1971). Les tablettes lenticulaires de Suse', *DAFI*, 1: 217–233. Paris: Association Paléorient.
1972 • 'Les ivoires achéménides de Suse', *Syria*, 49: 167–191 and 319–337.
1973 • 'Quelques observations sur le palais de Darius à Suse', *Syria*, 51: 65–73.
1976 • 'Disjecta Membra Aelamica: Le décor architectural de briques émaillées à Suse', *RAAsiat*, 32: 13–28.
1988 • *Suse, 6000 ans d'histoire*. Paris: RMN.
1990 • 'Quelques épaves de la vaisselle royale perse de Suse', in Vallat, F. (ed.), *Contributions à l'histoire de l'Iran. Mélanges offerts à Jean Perrot*. Paris: ERC, 213–224.
1994 • 'Un étage au palais de Darius à Suse ?', in Dietrich, M. and Loretz, O. (eds.), *Beschreiben und Deuten in der Archäologie des Alten Orients, Festschrift für Ruth Mayer-Opificius*. Münster: Ugarit-Verlag, *Altertumskunde des Vorderen Orients*, 4: 1–5.
1997 • 'Le décor architectural des palais achéménides', *DA*, 227: 78–83.
1998 • 'Passants et brides achéménides de Suse', *IrAnt*, 33: 143–153.
2001 • 'La sculpture susienne à l'époque de l'empire parthe', *IrAnt*, 36: 239–291.

AMIGUES, S.
2003 • 'Pour la table du Grand roi', in *Journal des Savants*: 3–59.

ANDRÉ-SALVINI, B.
1995 • 'Babylone', *DA*, 202: 28–35.
2000 • 'Le décor en briques polychromes du palais de Darius Ier à Suse dans les collections du Louvre', *Coré*, 9: 16–26.
2001 • *Babylone*. Paris: PUF, 292.

ANDRÉ-SALVINI, B. and DESCAMPS-LEQUIME, S.
2005 • 'Remarques sur l'astragale en bronze de Suse', *SMEA*, 47: 15–25.

ARUZ, J., HARPER, P.O. and TALLON, F.
1994 • *La Cité royale de Suse*. Paris: RMN.

ATAI, M.T. and BOUCHARLAT, R.
2009 • *An Achaemenid pavilion and other remains in Tang-i Bulaghi*, www.achemenet.com/ressources/enligne/arta/pdf/2009.005-loc.pdf.

AZARNOUSH, M.

2007 • 'Gozāresh kāvosh-haye lāyehshenokhtī Tappeh Hegmatāneh Hamedān' [Rapport de fouilles stratigraphiques à Tepe Hegmataneh, Hamadan], in Fazeli, H. (ed.), *Archaeological Reports (7)*
On the Occasion of the 9th Annual Symposium on Iranian Archaeology II. Tehran: Iranian Center for Archaeological Research, 19–41.

AZARPAY, G.

1987 • 'Proportional Guidelines in Ancient Near Eastern Art', *JNES*, 46: 183–203.
1994 • 'Designing the Body: Human Proportions in Achaemenid Art', *IrAnt*, 29: 169–184.
1995 • 'Proportions in Ancient Near Eastern Art', in SASSON, J.M. (ed.) *Civilizations of the Ancient Near East*. New York: Scribner's.

BAINES, J.

1974 • 'The Inundation Stela of Sebekhotpe VIII', *Acta Orientalia*, 36: 39–54.

BARDINET, T.

2008 • *Relations économiques et pressions militaires en Méditerranée orientale et en Libye au temps des pharaons. Histoire des importations égyptiennes des résines et des conifères du Liban et de la Libye depuis la période archaïque jusqu'à l'époque ptolémaïque*. Paris: Cybèle, Études et mémoires d'égyptologie, 7.

BARNETT, R.D.

1982 • *Ancient Ivories in the Middle East and Adjacent Countries*. Jerusalem: The Institute of Archaeology of the Hebrew University, *Qedem*, 14.

BATTINI, L. and CALVET, Y.

2003 • 'Construction royale, construction privée: la maison B 59 de Larsa', *Iraq*, 65: 131–141.

BEAULIEU, P.-A.

1989 • *The Reign of Nabonidus King of Babylon 556–539 B.C.* Yale Near Eastern Researches, 10. New Haven: Yale University Press.

BECATTI, G.

1947 • *Meidias, un manierista antico*. Florence: Sansoni.

BEHRENS, H. and KLEIN, J.

1998–2001 • 'Ninegalla', *RlA*, 9: 342–347.

BERGAMINI, G.

1977 • 'Levels of Babylon Reconsidered', *Mesopotamia*, 12: 111–156.

BERNAND, A.

1972 • *De Koptos à Kosseir*. Leiden: E. J. Brill.
1992 • *La Prose sur pierre dans l'Egypte hellénistique et romaine*. Paris.

BESENVAL, R.

1984 • *Technologie de la voûte dans l'Orient ancien*. Paris: ERC.

BEVAN, B.W.

2000 • 'An Early Geophysical Survey at Williamsburg', *Archaeological Prospection*, 7/1: 51–58.

BEZOLD, C. and SCHRADER, E.

1892 • *Keilinschriftliche Bibliothek, Sammlung von assyrischen und babylonischen Texten im Umschrift und Übersetzung. Vol. III, Historische Texte altbabylonischer Herrscher*. Berlin.

BISCIONE, R.

2005 • 'Hamadan-Ecbatana. Campagna 2005', *SMEA*, 47: 345–351.

BOARDMAN, J.

1970 • 'Pyramidal Stamp Seals in the Persian Empire', *Iran*, 8: 19–45.
1998 • 'Anatolian Stamp Seals of the Persian Period Revisited', *Iran*, 36: 1–13.
2000 • *Persia and the West: an Archaeological Investigation of the Genesis of Achaemenid Art*. New York: Thames and Hudson.

BODE BARON, C.A. de,

1845 • *Travels in Luristan and Arabistan*. London: J. Madden and Co.

BONGENAAR, A.C.V.M.

1997 • *The Neo-Babylonian Ebabbar Temple at Sippar: Its Administration and its Prosopography*. Leiden: Netherlands Institute for the Near East, Publications de l'Institut historique-archéologique néerlandais de Stamboul, p. 80.

BORÉ, E.

1842 • 'Lettre sur quelques antiquités de la Perse', *JA*, 13: 334–335.

BORGER, R.

1982 • *Die Chronologie des Darius-Denkmals am Behistun Felsen, Nachrichten der Akademie der Wissenschaften in Göttingen. I. Philologisch-historische Klasse*. Göttingen: Vandenhoeck & Ruprecht.

BOTHMER, B.V.

1960 • *Egyptian Sculpture of the Late Period, 700 B.C. to A.D. 100*. New York: Arno Press.
1962 • 'Corpus of the Late Egyptian Sculpture', in *Membra Dispersa*, 25th International Congress of Orientalists, Moscow, 9–16 August 1960, *Trudy*, 1: 70–74.

BOTTÉRO, J.

1949 • 'Les inventaires de Qatna', *RA*, 43: 1–40.
1950. 'Autres textes de Qatna', *RA*, 44: 105–118.

BOUCHARLAT, R.

1984 • 'Monuments religieux de la Perse achéménide: état des questions', in Roux, G. (ed.), *Temples et sanctuaires. Séminaire de recherche 1981–1983. TMO*, 7: 119–135. Lyon.
1985 • 'Suse, marché agricole ou relais du grand commerce. Suse et la Susiane à l'époque des grands empires', *Paléorient*, 11/2: 71–81.
1990a • 'La fin des palais achéménides de Suse: une mort naturelle', in Vallat, F. (ed.), *Contributions à l'histoire de l'Iran. Mélanges offerts à Jean Perrot*. Paris: ERC: 225–233.
1990b • 'Suse et la Susiane à l'époque achéménide. Données archéologiques', in Sancisi-Weerdenburg, H. and Kuhrt, A., *Achaemenid history*, IV, *Centre and Periphery*, Leiden, Nederlands Instituut voor het Naije Oosten, 149–174.
1997a • 'Susa under Achaemenid Rule', in Curtis, J. (ed.), *Mesopotamia and Iran in the Persian Period*. London: The British Museum Press, 54–67.
1997b • 'L'architecture achéménide et ses origines', *DA*, 227: 58–71.
2000 • 'Les autres palais achéménides de Suse', in Dittmann, R. *et al.* (eds.), *Variatio Delectat. Iran und der Western. Gedenkschrift für Peter Calmeyer. AOAT*, 272: 141–154. Münster: Ugarit.
2001 • 'The Palace and the Royal Achaemenid City: Two Case Studies – Pasargadae and Susa', in Nielsen, I. (ed.), *The Royal Palace Institution in the First Millennium B.C.* Athens: The Danish Institute, 113–123.
2003a • 'The Persepolis Area in the Achaemenid Period. Some Reconsiderations', in Miller, N.F. and Abdi, K. (eds.), *Yeki bud yeki nabud. Essays on the Archaeology of Iran in Honor of William M. Sumner. Monograph*, 28, 261–265 Los Angeles: Cotsen Institute of Archaeology at UCLA.
2003b • 'Le Zendan de Pasargades: de la tour 'solitaire' à un ensemble architectural. Données archéologiques récentes', in Henkelman, W. and Kuhrt, A. (eds.), *A Persian Perspective. Essays in Memory of H. Sancici-Weerdenburg. AchHist*, 13: 79–99. Leiden: E. J. Brill.
2004 • 'Pasagardai', *RlA*, 10: 351–363
2005a • 'Ernst Herzfeld and French Approaches to Iranian Archaeology', in Gunter, A. and Hauser, S. (eds.), *Ernst Herzfeld and the Development of Near Eastern Studies, 1900–1950*, Symposium at the Freer Gallery of Art and Arthur M. Sackler Gallery, Washington, May 3–5 2001. Leiden and Boston: E. J. Brill, 427–444.
2005b • 'Iran', in Briant, P. and Boucharlat, R. (eds.), *Archéologie de l'empire achéménide. Persika*, 6: 221–292. Paris: De Boccard.
2006 • 'Le destin des résidences et sites perses d'Iran dans la seconde moitié du ive siècle av. J.-C.', in Briant, P. and Joannès, F. (eds.), *La Transition entre l'empire achéménide et les royaumes hellénistiques. Persika*, 9: 443–470. Paris: De Boccard.
2007 • 'Achaemenid Residences and Elusive Imperial Cities', in Rollinger, R., Luther, A. and Wieselhöfer, J. (eds.), *Getrennte Wege? Kommunikation, Raum und Wahrnehmung in der alten Welt. Oikumene. Studien zur antike Weltgeschichte*, 2, 454–471. Frankfurt am Main: Verlag Antike.

BOUCHARLAT, R. and BENECH, C.

2002 • 'Organisation et aménagement de l'espace à Pasargades. Reconnaissance archéologique de surface, 1999-2001', *ARTA* 2002.001. www.achemenet.com/ressources/enligne/arta/pdf/2002.001-loc.pdf.

BOUCHARLAT, R. and LABROUSSE, A.

1979 • 'Le palais d'Artaxerxès II sur la rive droite du Chaour à Suse', *DAFI*, 10: 21–136. Paris: Association Paléorient.

BOUCHARLAT, R., LABROUSSE, A. and KERVRAN, M.

1979 • 'Une sucrerie d'époque islamique sur la rive droite du Chaour à Suse', *DAFI*, 10: 155–237. Paris: Association Paléorient.

BOUCHARLAT, R. and LOMBARD, P.

2001 • 'Le bâtiment G de Rumeilah (oasis d'Al Ain). Remarques sur les salles à poteaux de l'âge du Fer en Péninsule d'Oman', *IrAnt*, 36: 213–238.

BOUCHARLAT, R., PERROT, J. and LADIRAY, D.

1987 • 'Les niveaux post-achéménides à Suse, secteur nord. Fouilles de l'Apadana-Est et de la Ville royale Ouest (1973-1978)', *DAFI*, 15: 145–311. Paris: Association Paléorient.

BOUCHARLAT, R. and SHAHIDI, H.

1987 • 'Fragments architecturaux de type achéménide: découvertes fortuites dans la ville de Shoush 1976-1979', *DAFI*, 15: 313–327. Paris: Association Paléorient.

BOUQUILLON, A., CAUBET, A., KACZMARCZYK, A. and MATOÏAN, V.

2007 • *Les Objets en matières vitreuses du département des Antiquités Orientales. Catalogue et analyses physico-chimiques*. Paris: Musée du

Louvre Éditions.

BOURGEOIS, B.

1992 • 'Conservation Report', in Harper, P.O.,
Aruz, J. and Tallon, F. (eds.), *The Royal City of
Susa*. New York: Metropolitan Museum of Art,
281–286.

1994 • 'Rapport de restauration', in Harper, P.O.,
Aruz, J. and Tallon, F. (eds.), *La Cité royale de
Suse*. Paris: RMN, 281–286.

BOYCE, M.

1975a • *A History of Zoroastrianism I, The
Early Period*. Leiden: E.J. Brill. *Handbuch der
Orientalistik*, vol. 8, part 1.

1975b • 'On the Zoroastrian Temple Cult of
Fire', *JAOS*, 95: 454–465.

1982 • *A History of Zoroastrianism II, The
Achaemenid Period*. Leiden: E.J. Brill *Handbuch
der Orientalistik*, vol. 8, part 1.

BOYCE, M. and **GRENET**, F.

1991 • *A History of Zoroastrianism III,
Zoroastrianism under Macedonian & Roman Rule*.
Leiden: E.J. Brill, *Handbuch des Orientalistik*,
vol. 8, part 1.

BRESCIANI, E.

1967 • 'Una statua della XXVI dinastia con
il cosidetto 'abito persiamo', *Studi Classici e
Orientali*, 16: 273–280.

1998 • 'L'Egitto achemenide, Dario e il canale del
mar Rosso', *Transeuphratène*, 14: 103–111.

BRIANT, P.

1979 • 'L'élevage ovin dans l'empire achéménide',
JESHO, 22: 136–161.

1982 • *Rois, tributs et paysans*. Paris: Les Belles
Lettres.

1984a • *L'Asie centrale et les royaumes proche-
orientaux du premier millénaire*. Paris: ERC.

1984b • 'La Perse avant l'Empire (un état de la
question)', *IrAnt*, 19: 71–118.

1988 • 'Le nomadisme du Grand Roi', *IrAnt*, 23:
253–273.

1991 • 'De Sardes à Suse', *AchHist*, 6: 67–82.

1992a • 'Les tablettes de bois du Grand Roi et les
lettres d'Atossa', *DATA*: note 1.

1992b • *Darius, les Perses et l'Empire*. Paris:
Gallimard.

1993 • 'Hérodote, Udjahorresnet et les palais de
Darius à Suse', *DATA*: note 7.

1994 • 'L'eau du Grand Roi', in Milano, L. (ed.),
*Drinking in Ancient Societies. History and Culture
of Drinks in the Ancient Near East*. Padua: Lucio
Milano, 45–65.

1996 • *Histoire de l'empire perse. De Cyrus à
Alexandre*. Paris: Fayard.

2001 • *Bulletin d'histoire achéménide II*. Paris:
THOTM Editions.

2003 • *Darius dans l'ombre d'Alexandre*. Paris:
Fayard.

2006a • 'Retour sur Alexandre et les *kataraktes*
du Tigre. L'histoire d'un dossier (I)', *Studi
Ellenistici*, 19: 9–75.

2006b • 'Retour sur Alexandre et les *kataraktes*
du Tigre. L'histoire d'un dossier (II)', *Studi
Ellenistici*, 20: 155–218.

BRIANT, P. and **BOUCHARLAT**, R. **(eds.)**

2005 • *Archéologie de l'empire achéménide*. Paris:
De Boccard, *Persika*, 6.

BRIANT, P. and **CHAUVEAU**, M. **(eds.)**

2009 • *Organisation des pouvoirs et contacts
culturels dans les pays de l'Empire achéménide*.
(Colloquium, Collège de France – CNRS), Paris,

De Boccard, *Persika*, 14.

BRIANT, P., **HENKELMAN**, W. and
STOLPER, M. **(eds.)**

2008 • *L'Archive des fortifications de Persépolis.
État des questions et perspectives de recherches*.
Paris: De Boccard, *Persika*, 12.

CAGNAT, R.

1921 • *Notice sur la vie et les travaux de Marcel
Dieulafoy, lue le 18 novembre 1921*. Publication
de l'Institut de France, n. 2.

CALLIERI, P.

2007 • *L'Archéologie du Fârs à l'époque hellénistique.
Quatre leçons au Collège de France, 8, 15, 22 et 29
mars 2007*. Paris: De Boccard, *Persika*, 11.

CALMEYER, P.

1980 • 'Textual sources for the interpretation of
Achaemenian palace decorations', *Iran*, 18: 55–63.

1981 • 'Figürliche Fragmente aus Pasargadae nach
Zeichnungen E. Herzfelds', *AMI*, 14: 27–44.

1990 • 'Madjabad. Zur Datierung von Steinbruch-
Arbeiten um Persepolis', *AMI*, 23: 185–190.

1994 • 'Babylonische und Assyrische Elemente
in der Achaimenidischen Kunst', in Sancisi-
Weerdenburg, H., Kuhrt, A. and Root, M.C. (eds.),
*Continuity and Change: Proceedings of the Last
Achaemenid History Workshop*. April 6–8, 1990,
Ann Arbor, MI. Leiden: Nederlands Instituut
voor het Nabije Oosten, *AchHist*: 131–147.

CAMERON, G.G.

1948 • *Persepolis Treasury Tablets*. Chicago:
The University of Chicago Press, *OIP*, 65.

1959 • 'The "Daiva" inscription of Xerxes:
in Elamite', *WO*, 2: 470–476.

1960 • 'The Elamite version of the Behistun
Inscriptions', *JCS*, 14: 59–69.

1973 • 'The Persian Satrapies and Related
Matters', *JCS*, 32: 47–56.

CANAL, D.

1976 • 'Note sur un fragment de carreau décoré'.
Paris: Association Paléorient, *DAFI*, 6: 83–91.

1978 • 'La terrasse haute de l'Acropole de Suse.
Première partie: historique, stratigraphie et
structures'. Paris: Association Paléorient, *DAFI*,
9: 11–55.

CANBY, J.V.

1979 • 'A Note on Some Susa Bricks', *AMI*, 12:
315–320.

CARDASCIA, G

1951 • *Les archives des Murasu, une famille
d'hommes d'affaires babyloniens à l'époque perse
(455–403 av. J.-C.)*. Paris.

CASANOVA, M.

1993 • 'Lapis Lazuli Beads in Susa and Central
Asia: a Preliminary Study', *South Asian
Archaeology*: 137–145.

1999. 'Le lapis-lazuli dans l'Orient ancien', in
Caubet, A. (ed.): *Cornaline et pierres précieuses.
La Méditerranée, de l'Antiquité à l'Islam. Actes
du Colloque organisé au musée du Louvre par
le Service culturel les 24 et 25 nov. 1995*. Paris:
La Documentation française, 185–210.

CAUBET, A.

1992 • 'Le décor de briques achéménides',
in Aruz, J., Harper, P.O. and Tallon, F. (eds.),
La Cité royale de Suse. Paris: RMN, 223–225.

2003 • 'Le temple d'Inshushinak de Suse et
l'architecture monumentale en "faïence"', in
Potts, T., Roaf, M. and Stein, D. (eds.), *Culture

through Objects: Ancient Near Eastern Studies
in Honour of P.R.S. Moorey*, Oxford: Griffith
Institute, 325–332.

2007 • *Faïences et matières vitreuses de l'Orient
ancien: étude physico-chimique et catalogue des
œuvres du département des Antiquités orientales*.
Paris: Musée du Louvre.

CAUBET, A. and **KACZMARCZYK**, A.

1998 • 'Les briques glaçurées du palais de
Darius', *Techné*, 7: 23–26.

CAUBET, A. and **PIERRAT-BONNEFOIS**, G.

2005 • *Faïences de l'Antiquité. De l'Égypte à
l'Iran*. Paris: Musée du Louvre Éditions-Cinq
Continents.

CHEVALIER, N.

1989 • 'Hamadan 1913: une mission oubliée',
IrAnt, 24: 245–251.

1997 • *Une mission en Perse, 1897–1912*. Paris:
RMN.

2002 • *La Recherche archéologique française
au Moyen-Orient, 1842–1947*. Paris: ERC.

2009 • *Chronique des premières missions
archéologiques françaises à Suse d'après les
photographies et mémoires de l'architecte Maurice
Pillet (1912–1913)*. Tehran, co-edition Musée du
Louvre / Institut français de recherche en Iran.

CHOISY, A.

1887 • 'Les fouilles de Suse et l'Art antique de
la Perse', *Gazette archéologique*: 8–18.

CLERMONT-GANNEAU, C.

1906 • 'Deux alabastres israélites', *Recueil
d'Archéologie orientale*, 7: 294–304.

COLIN, F.

2000 • *Les Peuples libyens de la Cyrénaïque à
l'Égypte d'après les sources de l'Antiquité classique*.
Brussels: Académie royale de Belgique.

2004 • 'Transcriptions égyptiennes de termes
sémitiques: Assyriens, Israéliens et aqueducs',
in Schneider, T. (ed.), *Das Ägyptische und die
Sprachen Vorderasiens, Nordafrikas und der Ägäis.
Akten der Basler Kolloquiums: 9–11 Juli 2003*.
Münster: Ugarit-Verlag, *AOAT*, 40:
219–255.

COOK, J.M.

1983 • *The Persian Empire*. London: Schocken.

COUYAT, J. and **MONTET**, P.

1912 • *Les Inscriptions hiéroglyphiques et
hiératiques du Ouâdi Hammâmât*. Cairo:
Imprimerie de l'IFAO, *MIFAO*, 34.

CRUZ-URIBE, E.

1988 • *Hibis Temple Project I, Translations,
Commentary, Discussions*. San Antonio, CA:
Van Siclen Books.

CURTIS, J.

1985 • *Ancient Persia*. London: The British
Museum Press.

1993 • 'William Kennett Loftus and his
Excavations at Susa', *IrAnt*, 28: 1–55.

1997a • *Mesopotamia and Iran in the Persian
Period: Conquest and Imperialism 539–331 B.C.*
London: British Museum Publications.

1997b • 'Les fouilles de W.K. Loftus à Suse',
in Chevalier, N. (ed.), *Une Mission en Perse,
1897–1912*. Paris: RMN, 36–45.

2004 • 'The Oxus Treasure in the British
Museum', *Ancient Civilizations from Scythia
to Siberia*, vol. 10 (2004): 293–388.

CURTIS, J. and **TALLIS**, N. **(eds.)**

2005 • *Forgotten Empire: The World of Ancient
Persia*. London: The British Museum Press.

DALTON, O.M.

1964 • *The Treasure of the Oxus*. London: The Trustees of the British Museum (1st edn, 1926).

DAMERJI, M.S.B.

1999 • *Gräber assyrischer Königinnen aus Nimrud*. Mainz: Verlag des Romisch-Germanischen Zentralmuseums.

DANDAMAYEV, M.A.

1972 • 'Connections between Elam and Babylonia in the Achaemenid Period', in The Memorial Volume of the 5th International Congress of Iranian Art and Archaeology' (1968), Tehran: Special publication of the Ministry of Culture and Arts: 258–264.

1985 • 'Herodotus' Information on Persian and Latest Discoveries of Cuneiform Texts', *Histoire de l'historiographie*, 7: 92–100.

DE MEYER, L., GASCHE, H. and VALLAT, F. (eds.)

1986 • *Fragmenta Historiae Elamicae. Mélanges offerts à M.-J. Steve*. Paris: ERC.

DHORME, E.

1912 • 'Cyrus le Grand', *RB*, 9: 22–49.

1913 • 'La religion des Achéménides', *RB*, 10: 15–35.

1933 • *Élam, élamites. Supplément au Dictionnaire de la Bible 10: col. 960–962*. Paris: Letouzey and Ane.

DIEULAFOY, J.

1887 • *La Perse, la Chaldée, la Susiane*. Paris: Hachette.

1888 • *À Suse. Journal de fouilles, 1884–1886*. Paris: Hachette.

DIEULAFOY, M.

1884–[89] • *L'Art antique de la Perse*. Paris.

1885a • 'Fouilles de Suse. Campagne de 1884–1885', *RevArch*, 5: 48–69.

1885b • 'Expédition de Susiane', *CRAIBL*: 369–374.

1886a • 'Fouilles de Suse. Campagne de 1885–1886', *RevArch*, 8: 1-9 and 265–276.

1886b • 'Expédition en Susiane', *CRAIBL*: 369–374.

1887 • 'Fouilles de Suse. Campagne de 1885–1886', *RevArch*, 9/1: 1–9.

1893 • *L'Acropole de Suse (fouilles 1884, 1885)*. Paris: Hachette.

1913 • *Les Antiquités de Suse, découvertes et rapportées par la mission Dieulafoy (1884–1886)*. Paris: Ernest Leroux.

DOLLFUS, G. and HESSE, A.

1977 • 'Les structures de combustion du Tépé Djaffarabad, Périodes I à III', Paris: Association Paléorient, *DAFI*, 7: 12–46.

DUCHESNE-GUILLEMIN, J.

1953 • *Ormazd et Ahriman*. Paris: PUF.

1962 • *La Religion de l'Iran ancien*. Paris: PUF.

1972 • 'La religion des Achéménides', in Walser, G. (ed.), *Beiträge zur Achämenidengeschichte, Wiesbaden, Historia, Heft*, 18: 53–82.

1974 • 'Le dieu de Cyrus', *ActIr*, 3: 11–21.

1975 • *Zoroastre*. Paris: Robert Laffont (1st ed. 1948).

DUNHAM, D.

1950 • *The Royal Cemeteries of Kush*. Cambridge, Mass.: Harvard University Press.

DUSSAUD, R.

1914 • *La Nouvelle Académie des inscriptions et belles-lettres (1795–1914)*. Paris: P. Geuthner.

DYSON, R.H. Jr.

1968 • 'Early Work on the Acropolis at Susa: The Beginning of Prehistory in Iraq and Iran', *Expedition*, 10/4: 25–26

EILERS, W.

1974 • 'Le texte cunéiforme du cylindre de Cyrus', *ActIr*, 2: 25–31.

ELAYI, J. and A.G.

1992 • 'Nouvelle datation d'une tombe achéménide de Suse', *StIr*, 21/2: 265–269.

FARKAS, A.

1974 • *Achaemenid Sculpture*. Leiden: Nederlands Instituut voor het Nabije Oosten.

FONTOUR, E. and LE MEAUX, H.

2005 • 'De l'Égypte à la Perse: Figurines et amulettes', in Caubet, A. and Pierrat-Bonnefois, G., *Faïences de l'Antiquité. De l'Égypte à l'Iran*. Paris: Musée du Louvre Éditions-Cinq Continents. 153–156.

FRANCFORT, H.-P.

1977 • 'Le plan des maisons gréco-bactriennes et les structures de type " megaron" en Asie Centrale et en Iran', in Deshayes, J. (ed.), *Le Plateau Iranien et l'Asie centrale des origines à la conquête islamique*. Paris: CNRS Éditions, 267–295.

GARIS DAVIES, N. de

1953 • *The Temple of Hibis in El Khârgeh Oasis III, The Decoration*. New York: Ludlow Bull and Lindsley F. Hall, *Publications of the Metropolitan of Art, Egyptian Expedition*, 17.

GARRISON, M. B.

1991 • 'Seals and the Elite at Persepolis: Some Observations on Early Achaemenid Persian Art', *Ars Orientalis*, 21: 1–29.

1996 • 'A Persepolis Fortification Seal on the Tablet MDP 11 308 (Louvre Sb 13978)', *JNES*, 55/1: 15–35.

2002 • 'The 'Late neo-elamite 'Glyptic Style: a Perspective from Fars', *Bulletin of the Asia Institute*, 16: 65–102.

2011 • 'The Seal of 'Kuraš the Anzanite, Son of Šešpeš, PFS 93*': Susa-Anšan-Persepolis', in Alvarez-Mon, J. and Garrison, M. B. (eds.), *Elam and Persia*, Winona Lake: Eisenbrauns.

GASCHE, H.

1986 • 'Architecture d'intérieur susienne: les cheminées', in De Meyer, L., Gasche, H. and Vallat, F. (eds.), *Fragmenta Historiae Elamicae. Mélanges offerts à M.-J. Steve*. Paris: ERC, 83–109.

1989 • 'Habl as-Sahr 1986. Nouvelles fouilles. L'ouvrage défensif de Nabuchodonosor II au nord de Sippar', Ghent, University of Ghent, *NAPR*, 2: 23–70.

1997 • 'La période R. Ghirshman (1946-1967),' in CHEVALIER, N. (ed.), *Une mission en Perse*. Paris: 168-179.

2002 • 'Une résidence parthe dans le Quartier Nord de la Ville royale de Suse', *Akkadica*, 123/2: 183–189.

GASCHE, H., ARMSTRONG, J.A., COLE, S.W. and GURZADYAN, V.G.

1998 • *Dating the Fall of Babylon. A Reappraisal of Second-Millennium Chronology*. Ghent: University of Ghent and Chicago: Oriental Institute of the University of Chicago, *Mesopotamian History and Environment Memoirs*, 4.

GASCHE, H. AND BIRCHMEIER, W.

1981 • 'Contribution à l'étude de la voûte en briques crues', *Akkadica*, 24: 1–16.

GASSE, A.

1988 • 'Mission épigraphique au Wadi Hammamat', in Posener-Krieger, P., *Travaux de l'Institut français d'archéologie orientale en 1987–1988, BIFAO*, 88: 205–206.

GHIRSHMAN, R.

1947 • 'Une saison de fouilles à Suse', *CRAIBL*: 444–449.

1948 • 'Campagne de fouilles à Suse en 1947–1948', *CRAIBL*: 328–336.

1949 • 'Campagne de fouilles à Suse en 1948–1949', *CRAIBL*: 196–199.

1952 • *Cinq campagnes de fouilles à Suse (1946–1951)*. Paris: PUF, *MMAI*, 20.

1954 • *Village perse-achéménide, MMAI*, 36. Paris.

1957 • 'Notes iraniennes III. À propos de Persépolis', *Artibus Asiae*, 20: 265–278.

1963a • 'L'Apadana de Suse', *IrAnt*, 3/2: 148–154.

1963b • *Perse, Proto-iraniens, Mèdes, Achéménides*. Paris: Gallimard, *L'univers des formes*.

1965a • 'Suse du temps des *sukkalmah*. Campagnes de fouilles 1963–1964. Rapport préliminaire', *RAAsiat*, 11: 3–21.

1965b • 'L'architecture élamite et ses traditions', *IrAnt*, 5/2: 93–102.

1967 • 'Suse. Campagne de l'hiver 1965-1966. Rapport préliminaire', *RAAsiat*, 15: 3–27.

1968a • *Tchoga Zanbil (Dur-Untash) 2. Temenos, temples, palais, tombes*. Paris: P. Geuthner, *MDAI*, 40.

1968b • 'Suse au tournant du IIIe au IIe millénaire avant notre ère. Travaux de la Délégation archéologique en Iran – hiver 1966–1967. Rapport préliminaire', *RAAsiat*, 17: 1–44.

1976 • *Terrasses sacrées de Bard-è Nechandeh et Masjid-i Soleiman*. Paris: P. Geuthner, *MDAI*, 45.

GHIRSHMAN, T.

1970 • *Archéologue malgré moi: vie quotidienne d'une mission archéologique en Iran*. Neuchâtel: A la Baconnière.

GIOVINAZZO, G.

1994a • 'Les documents de voyage dans les textes de Persépolis', *AION*, 54/1: 18–31.

1994b. 'Les voyages de Darius dans les régions orientales de l'empire', *AION*, 54/1: 44.

2000–2001 • 'Les Indiens à Suse', *AION*, 60–61: 59–76.

GLASSNER, J.J.

1993 • *Chroniques Mésopotamiennes*. Paris: Les Belles Lettres.

GNOLI, G.

1974 • 'Politique religieuse et conception de la royauté chez les Achéménides', *ActIr*, 1/2: 117–191.

1980 • *Zoroaster's Time and Homeland*. Napoli: Istituto Universitario Orientale.

2000 • *Zoroaster in History*. Winona Lake: Eisenbrauns, *Biennial Yarshater Lecture Series*, 2.

GODARD, A.

1950 • *Le Trésor de Ziwiye (Kurdistan)*. Haarlem: J. Enschedé en Zonen.

GOYON, G.

1957 • *Nouvelles inscriptions rupestres du Wadi*

Hammamat. Paris: Imprimerie nationale et Adrien Maisonneuve.

GRAYSON, A.K.

1975 • *Assyrian and Babylonian Chronicles.* Locust Valley (NY), Glückstadt, *TCS,* 5.

GREENFIELD, J.C. and PORTEN, B.

1982 • 'The Bisitun Inscription of Darius the Great. Aramaic Version' in *Corpus Inscriptionum Iranicarum,* part 1, vol. 5. London: Lund Humphries.

GRIMAL, N.

1986 • *Les Termes de la propagande royale égyptienne de la xixe dynastie à la conquête d'Alexandre.* Paris: Mémoires de l'Académie des inscriptions et belles-lettres, 6.

HAERINCK, E.

1973 • 'Le palais achéménide de Babylone', *IrAnt,* 10: 108–132.

1980 • 'Les tombes et les objets du sondage sur l'enceinte de Abū Habbah', in De Meyer L. (ed.), *Tell ed-Dēr 3. Soundings at Abū Habbah (Sippar),* Leuven: Peeters: 53–79.

1987 • 'La neuvième satrapie: archéologie confronte histoire', in Sancisi-Weerdenburg, H. (ed.), *Sources, Structures and Synthesis. Proceedings of the Groningen 1983 Achaemenid History Workshop.* Leiden: Nederlands Instituut voor het Nabije Oosten, *AchHist,* 1, 139–145.

HALL, H.R.

1913 • *Catalogue of Egyptian Scarabs, etc. in the British Museum.* London: Trustees of the British Museum.

HALLOCK, R.T.

1969 • *Persepolis Fortification Tablets.* Chicago: University of Chicago Press, *OIP,* 42.

HANSMAN, J.

1972 • 'Elamites, Achaemenians and Anshan', *Iran,* 10: 101–125.

HARPER, P.O., ARUZ, J. and TALLON, F. (eds.)

1992 • *The Royal City of Susa: Ancient Near Eastern Treasures in the Louvre,* New York.

HARRAK, A.

1990 • 'The Royal Tombs of Nimrud and Their Jewellery', *Bulletin of the Canadian Society for Mesopotamian Studies,* 29: 5–13.

HAUSSOULLIER, B.

1905 • 'Offrande à Apollon Didyméen', *MDP,* 7: 155–176. Paris: Ernest Leroux.

HEINRICH, E.

1968 • 'Maß und Übermaß in der Dimensionierung von Bauwerken im alten Zweistromland', *MDOG,* 99: 5–54.

1971. 'Gewölbe', *RlA,* 3: 323–340.

HENKELMAN, W.

2008 • 'The Other Gods Who Are: Studies in Elamite-Iranian Acculturation Based on the Persepolis Fortification Texts', *AchHist,* 14.

2010 • '"Consumed before the King". Requisitions for the King and the Court in the Persepolis Fortification Archive', in JACOBS, B. and ROLLINGER, R. (eds.) *Der Achämenidenhof / The Achaemenid Court.* Wiesbaden, 777–813.

2011 • 'Parnaka's Feast', in Alvarez-Mon, J. and Garrison, M. (eds.), *Elam and Persia,* Winona Lake: Eisenbrauns.

HENKELMAN, W.F.M. and KLEBER, K.

2007 • 'Babylonian Workers in the Persian Heartland: Palace Building at Matannan during

the Reign of Cambyses', in Tuplin, C. ed., *Persian Responses Political and Cultural – Interaction within the Achaemenid Empire,* Swansea, 163–176.

HERZFELD, E.E.

1929 • 'Bericht über die Ausgrabungen von Pasargadae 1928,' *AMI,* 1: 4–16.

1935 • *Archaeological History of Iran.* London: Oxford University Press.

HESSE, A.

1970 • 'Introduction géophysique et notes techniques. N.T.2: Essai techno-chronologique sur la dimension des briques de construction', in Vercoutter, J. (ed.), *Mirgissa I.* Paris: Librairie orientaliste P. Geuthner, 1. 102–114.

1972 • 'Métrologie statistique d'éléments architecturaux des palais achéménides de Suse (briques et bases carrées)', Paris: Association Paléorient, *DAFI,* 2: 219–241.

1973 • 'Cachets à figuration animale des briques de Suse', Paris: Association Paléorient, *DAFI,* 3: 81–92.

1975a • 'Méthodes de prospection applicables aux sites archéologiques du Soudan', in Vallogia, M. (ed.) *Communications du xxixe Congrès international des orientalistes, 1973* Paris: L'asiathèque, 45–48.

1975b • 'Prospection géophysique des sites archéologiques iraniens: le cas des palais achéménides de Suse', in Vallogia, M. (ed.), *Communications du xxixe Congrès international des orientalistes, 1973.* Paris: L'asiathèque, 24–26.

1975c • 'Contribution de la géophysique (prospection et archéomagnétisme) à la connaissance de l'archéologie iranienne', in Bagherzadeh, F. (ed.), *Proceedings of the 3rd Symposium on Archaeological Research in Iran 1974,* Tehran: Iranian Centre for Archaeological Research: 301–310.

1978 • *Manuel de prospection géophysique appliquée à la reconnaissance archéologique,* Dijon: Université de Dijon, Centre de recherches sur les techniques gréco-romaines, 8.

1979a • (with D. Lemercier, R. Scheib and J.-P. Thalman), 'Des contrastes physiques à la détection dans le sol', *DA,* 39: 26–41.

1979b • (with S. Renimel and R. Boucharlat), 'Reconnaissance d'ensemble du palais du Chaour par la méthode des résistivités électriques'. Paris: Association Paléorient, *DAFI,* 10: 137–144.

1980 • 'La prospection des vestiges préhistoriques en milieu proche-oriental: une douzaine d'années d'expériences géophysiques', *Paléorient,* 6: 45–64.

1987 • *Archéomagnétisme et chronologie absolue au Proche Orient,* CNRS International Symposium, Lyon 24–28 nov. 1986, Oxford, s.n., *BAR, Int. Ser.* 379 II: 549–558.

1989 • 'Prospections et mesures géophysiques. Suse, dernières découvertes', *DA,* 38: 24–27.

1990 • 'Call it Archaeometry', in Vallat, F. (ed.), *Contribution à l'histoire de l'Iran. Mélanges offerts à Jean Perrot.* Paris: ERC, 317–319.

2000 • 'Count Robert du Mesnil du Buisson (1895–1986), a French Precursor in Geophysical Survey for Archaeology', *Archaeological Prospection,* 7/1: 43–49.

HESSE, A. and LECAILLE, A.

1974 • 'Un programme de recherches archéomagnétiques pour la période pré et proto-historique au Proche-Orient', *Paléorient,* 2/2: 502.

HINZ, W.

1968 • 'Die Entstehung der altpersischen

Keilschrift', *AMI,* 1: 95–98.

1969 • *Altiranische Funde und Forschungen.* Berlin: de Gruyter.

1976 • *Darius und die Perser: eine Kulturgeschichte der Achämeniden.* Baden-Baden: Holle.

HINZ, W. and KOCH, H.

1987 • 'Elamisches Wörterbuch in 2 Teilen', *AMI,* 17.

HODJASH, S. and BERLEV, O.

1982 • *The Egyptian Reliefs and Stelae in the Pushkin Museum of Fine Arts.* Moscow, Leningrad: Aurora Art.

HÖGEMAN, P.

1991 • *Der Ausbau von Elam zur Seeprovinz unter Darius I. (522/21–486 v. Chr.) und ihr Zustand zur Zeit Alexanders des Grossen in den Jahren 325 und 324 v. Chr. Stuttgarter Colloquium zur historischen Geographie des Altertums (2, 1984; 3, 1987).* Bonn: R. Habelt, 133–147.

HOLLADAY, Jr. J.S.

1982 • *Tell el Maskhuta. Preliminary Report on the Wadi Tumilat Project 1978–1979. Cities of the Delta III.* Malibu: Undena Publications, American Research Center in Egypt Reports, 6.

HOUTKAMP, J.

1991 • 'Some Remarks on Fire Altars of the Achaemenid Period', in Kellens, J. (ed.), 'La Religion iranienne à l'époque achéménide'. Actes du colloque de Liège, 11 décembre 1987, *IrAnt,* suppl. 5: 23–48.

HROUDA, B.

1965 • *Die Kulturgeschichte des assyrischen Flachbildes.* Bonn: R. Habelt.

HUFF, D.

2005 • 'From Median to Achaemenian Palace Architecture', *IrAnt,* 40: 371–395.

HUYSE, P.

2005 • *La Perse Antique.* Paris: Les Belles Lettres (*Guide les Belles Lettres des civilisations*).

INVERNIZZI, A.

2008 • 'Babylone sous la domination perse', in André-Salvini, B. (ed.), *Babylone. Catalogue de l'exposition 'Babylone'. Paris, musée du Louvre 14 mars–2 juin 2008.* Paris: Hazan – Musée du Louvre Éditions, 239–250.

JACOBS, B.

1997a • 'Eine Planänderung an den Apadâna-Treppen und ihre Konsequenzen für die Datierung der Planung – und Bebauungsphasen von Persepolis', *AMIT,* 29: 281–302.

1997b. 'Eine weitere Kopie des Bisutun-Relief? Zu einem Reliefziegel aus Susa', *AMIT,* 29: 303–308.

JACQUET-GORDON, H.-K.

1960 • 'The Inscription on the Philadelphia-Cairo Statue of Osorkon II', *JEA,* 46: 12–23.

JANSEN-WINCKELN, K.

1999 • 'Drei Denkmäler mit archaisierender Orthographie', *Orientalia,* 67/2: 155–172.

JÉQUIER, G.

1900a • 'Travaux de l'hiver 1898–1899', in Morgan, J. de (ed.), *Recherches archéologiques,* Paris: Ernest Leroux, *MDP* 1: 23–48.

1900b • 'Travaux de l'Apadana', in Morgan, J. de (ed.), *Recherches archéologiques,* Paris:

Ernest Leroux, *MDP* 1: 69–81.
1900c • 'Travaux de l'hiver 1898–1899',
Paris: Ernest Leroux, *MDP* 1: 111–138.
1905a • 'Fouilles de Suse de 1899 à 1902', in
Morgan, J. de (ed.), *Recherches archéologiques*,
Paris: Ernest Leroux, *MDP* 7: 9–49.
1905b • 'La représentation du lion à Suse', in
Morgan, J. de (ed.), *Recherches archéologiques*,
Paris: Ernest Leroux, *MDP* 7: 159–176.

JOANNÈS, F.
1988 • '*ig-gurki = Suse', *NABU*, 1988/1.
1989 • *Archives de Borsippa. La famille Ea-ilûta-
Bâni*. Geneva: Droz.
1990 • 'Textes babyloniens de Suse d'époque
achéménide', in Vallat, F. (ed.), *Contributions à
l'histoire de l'Iran. Mélanges offerts à Jean Perrot*,
Paris: ERC, 173–180.
2000 • *Rendre la justice en Mésopotamie: archives
judiciaires du Proche-Orient ancien (IIIe-Ier
millénaires avant J.-C.)*. Saint-Denis, Presses
universitaires de Vincennes
2005 • 'Les relations entre Babylonie et Iran
au début de la période achéménide: quelques
remarques', in Baker, H.-M., Jursa, M. (eds.),
Approaching the Babylonian Economy, Münster:
Ugarit Verlag, *AOAT*, 330: 183–196.
2006 • *Les premières civilisations du Proche-Orient*.
Paris: Belin.

JOSEPHSON, J.A.
1997 • 'Egyptian Sculpture of the Late Period
Revisited', *JARCE*, 34: 1–20.

JURSA, M.
2005 • *Neo-Babylonian Legal and Administrative
Documents – Typology, Contents and Archives*
(Guides to the Mesopotamian Textual Record 1).
Münster: Ugarit Verlag.

KABOLI, M.
2000 • *Archaeological survey at Qomrud*.
Tehran: Archaeological Research Centre.

KANTOR, H.
1957 • 'Achaemenid Jewelry in the Oriental
Institute', *JNES*, 26/1: 1–23.

KELLENS, J.
1997 • 'Les Achéménides dans le contexte
indo-iranien', *Topoi*, suppl. 1: 287–297.
2001 • 'Zoroastre dans l'histoire ou dans le
mythe? À propos du dernier livre de Gherardo
Gnoli', *JA*, 289/2: 171–184.

KENT, R.G.
1953 • *Old Persian. Grammar, Texts, Lexicon*.
New Haven: American Oriental Society, *American
Oriental Series*, 33; 1st edn, 1950.

KER PORTER, R.
1821–1822 • *Travels in Georgia, Persia, Armenia,
Ancient Babylonia…, during the Years 1817, 1818,
1819, and 1820*. London: Longman, Rees, Orme,
and Brown, 2 vols.

KERVRAN, M.
1972 • 'Une statue de Darius découverte à Suse',
JA, 260: 235–266.
1974 • 'Les niveaux islamiques du secteur
oriental du tépé de l'Apadana', Paris: Association
Paléorient, *DAFI*, 4: 21–41.
1977 • 'Les niveaux islamiques du secteur
Est de l'Apadana (2e partie). Le matériel
céramique', Paris: Association Paléorient,
DAFI, 7: 75–161.

KESSLER, K.

2002 • 'Sittake, Sittakene, Sattag', *Klio*, 29/2:
238–248.

KLEISS, W.
1971a • 'Bemerkungen zu achaemenidischen
Feueraltären', *AMI*, 6: 7–80.
1971b • 'Der Takht-i Rustam, bei Persepolis
und das Kyrosgrab in Pasargadae', *Archäologischer
Anzeiger*: 157–162.
1975 • 'Fundnotizen zu einigen Säulenbasen
aus West Iran', *AMI*, 8: 75–79.
1980 • 'Zur Entwicklung der achämenidischen
Palastarchitektur', *IrAnt*, 15: 199–211.
1981 • 'Ein Abschnitt der achämenidischer
Königstrasse von Pasargadae und Persepolis,
nach Susa, bei Naqsh-e Rostam', *AMI*, 14: 45–57.
1986 • 'Die Achämenidische Poststrasse von
Persepolis nach Susa', *AMI*: 133–147.
1992 • 'Beobachtungen auf dem Burgberg von
Persepolis', *AMI*, 25: 155–167.

KLEMM, R. and KLEMM, D.
1993 • *Steine und Steinbrüche im Alten Ägypten*.
Berlin: Springer.

KNAPTON, P. SARRAF, M.R. and CURTIS, J.
2001 • 'Inscribed Column Bases from Hamadan',
IrAnt, 39: 99–117.

KOCH, H.
1993 • *Achämeniden Studien*. Wiesbaden:
Harrassowitz.

KOLDEWEY, R.
1911 • *Die Tempel von Babylon und Borsippa
nach den Ausgrabungen durch die Deutsche
Orient-Gesellschaft*. Leipzig: J. C. Hinrichs,
Ausgrabungen der Deutschen Orient-Gesellschaft
in Babylon, 1, *WVDOG*, 15.
1914 • *The Excavations at Babylon*, London:
Macmillan.
1931 • *Königsburgen von Babylon. Erster Teil. Die
Südburg*. Leipzig: J.C. Hinrichs, *WVDOG*, 54.
1932 • *Die Königsburgen von Babylon. Zweiter
Teil. Die Hauptburg und der Sommerpalast
Nebukadnezars im Hügel Babil*, Leipzig: J. C.
Hinrichs, *WVDOG*, 55.
1990 • *Das wieder erstehende Babylon*. München:
C.H. Beck (Fünfte, überarbeitete und erweiterte
Auflage. Herausgegeben von B. Hrouda. Mit Beitr.
von W. *Andrae †, S. Fitz, A.R. George, E. Haerinck,
H. Schmid, L. Trümpelmann*, und C. *Wilcke*).

KÖNIG, F.W.
1965 • 'Die elamischen Königsinschriften', *AfO*
suppl. 16. Graz: E. Weidner.

KREFTER, F.
1971 • *Persepolis. Rekonstruktionen. Der
Wiederaufbau des Frauenpalastes. Rekonstruktionen
des Päläste. Modell von Persepolis*, 'Teheraner
Forschungen', 3. Berlin: Mann.

KUHRT, A.
1983 • 'The Cyrus Cylinder and Achaemenid
Imperial Policy', *JSOT*, 25: 83–97.

KULESZA, R.
1994 • 'Persian Deportations – Greeks in Persia',
Eos, 82/2: 221–250.

LABROUSSE, A.
1972 • 'La Charte de fondation du palais de Darius
Ier'. Paris: université de Paris III: thèse de 3e cycle.

LABROUSSE, A. and BOUCHARLAT, R.
1974 • 'La fouille du palais du Chaour à Suse
en 1970 et 1971', Paris: Association Paléorient,
DAFI, 2: 61–167.

LAMBERT, M.
1978 • 'Disjecta Membra Aelamica (II):
Inscriptions du décor architectural construit
par Shilhak-Inshushinak', *AA*, 34: 3–27.

LAMING-EMPERAIRE, A.
1952 • *La Découverte du passé*. Paris: Picard.

LAMPRE, G.
1900 • 'Travaux de l'hiver 1897-1898.
Tranchées 7 et 7a', in Morgan, J. de (ed.),
Recherches archéologiques. MDP, 1: 100–110.
Paris: Ernest Leroux.

LE BRUN, A.
1971 • 'Recherches stratigraphiques à
l'Acropole de Suse (1969-1971)', Paris:
Association Paléorient, *DAFI*, 1: 163–216.

LECOQ, P.
1974 • 'Le problème de l'écriture cunéiforme
vieux perse', *ActIr*, 3: 25–107.
1984 • 'Un problème de religion achéménide:
Ahuramazda ou xvarnah ?', in *Orientalia
J. Duchesne-Guillemin Emerito Oblata*. Leiden:
E.J. Brill, *ActIr*, 25, 2e série, Hommages et
Opera Minora, 9: 301–326.
1990 • 'Paradis en vieux perse', in Vallat, F.
(ed.), *Contributions à l'histoire de l'Iran. Mélanges
offerts à Jean Perrot*, Paris: ERC, 209–211.
1997 • *Les Inscriptions de la Perse achéménide.
Traduit du vieux perse, de l'élamite, du
babylonien et de l'araméen*. Paris: Gallimard.

LECUYOT, G.
1993 • 'Résidences hellénistiques en Bactriane,
résidences parthes en Iran et en Mésopotamie.
Diffusion ou communauté d'origine ?'
University of Ghent, *NAPR*, 8: 31–47.

LEMAIRE, A. and LOZACHMEUR, H.
1987 • 'Birāh/Birtha en araméen', *Syria*,
64/3–4: 261–266.

LE RIDER, G.
1965 • *Suse sous les Séleucides et les Parthes*.
Paris: P. Geuthner, *MDAI*, 38.

LEWIS, D.
1980 • 'Datis the Mede', *JHS*, 100: 194–195.

LINCOLN, B.
2008 • 'The Role of Religion in the
Achaemenian Empire', in Brisch, N., *Religion
and Power. Divine Kinship in the Ancient
World and Beyond*, Chicago: The University
of Chicago Press, *OIS*, 4: 221–242.

LOFTUS, W.K.
1857 • *Travels and Researches in Chaldea
and Susiana with an Account of Excavations
at Warka, the 'Erech' of Nimrod and Shush
'Shushan the Palace of Esther' in 1851–1852*.
London: Nisbet and Co.
1859 • *Lithographic Facsimiles of Inscriptions
in the Cuneiform Character from the Ruins
of Susa*. London.

LUSCHEY, H.
1976 • 'Archäologische Bemerkungen zu der
Darius-Statue von Susa', in *Akten des VII.
Internationalen Kongresses für Iranische Kunst
und Archäologie, München, 7–10 sept. 1976, AMI*,
suppl. 6: 207–216.
1983 • 'Die Darius-Statuen aus Susa und ihre
Rekonstruktion', *AMI*, 10: 191–206.

MAC GINNIS, J.
2002 • 'Working in Elam', in Wunsch, C. (ed.),
Mining the Archives. Festschrift for Ch. Walker

on the Occasion of his 60th Birthday, Dresden: ISLET, 177–181.

MAGEE, P.
2001 • 'Excavations at Muweilah 1997-2000', *Proceedings of the Seminar for Arabian Studies*, 31: 115–130.

MALBRAN-LABAT, F.
1994 • *La version accadienne de l'inscription trilingue de Darius à Behistun.* Rome, Pisa: Gruppo editoriale internazionale, *Documenta Asiana*, 1.
1995 • *Les inscriptions royales de Suse: briques de l'époque paléo-élamite à l'empire néo-élamite.* Paris: Réunion des musées nationaux.

MALLOWAN, M.E.L.
1962 • 'The Palace of Bel-shalti-Nannar', in Woolley, C.L., *The Neo-Babylonian and Persian Periods*, London: British Museum, *Ur Excavations*, 9: 41–43.

MALLOWAN, M.E.L. AND HERRMANN, G.
1974 • *Ivories from Nimrud (1949–1963) fasc. III. Furniture from SW.7. Fort Shalmaneser.* London: British School of Archaeology in Iraq.

MARGUERON, J.C.
2004 • *Mari. Métropole de l'Euphrate au IIIe et au début du IIe millénaire av. J.-C..* Paris: Picard.
2005 • 'Notes d'archéologie et d'architecture orientales 12 – Du *bitannu*, de l'étage et des salles hypostyles dans les palais néo-assyriens', *Syria*, 82: 93–138.

MARTINEZ-SÈVE, L.
1996 • 'Une statuette romaine trouvée à Suse et la chronologie du Donjon', in Gasche, H. and Hrouda, B. (eds.), *Collectanea Orientalia. Histoire, Arts de l'espace et industrie de la terre. Études offertes en hommage à Agnès Spycket.* Paris: Neuchâtel. L'Asiathèque, *Civilisations du Proche-Orient, série I, Archéologie et environnement*, 3: 171–180.
1997 • 'Les Figurines hellénisantes de Suse, contribution à l'histoire culturelle de Suse aux époques hellénistique et parthe'. Paris: thèse université de Paris I, UFR d'Histoire de l'art et d'archéologie.
2002a • *Les Figurines de Suse. De l'époque néo-élamite à l'époque sassanide.* Paris: Musée du Louvre Éditions, Département des antiquités orientales, RMN.
2002b • 'La ville de Suse à l'époque hellénistique', *RevArch*: 31–54.

MASSON, M.E. and PUGAČENKOVA, G.A.
1956–1959 • *The Parthian Rhytons of Nisa (trad. du russe Parfianskie Ritoni' Nisii, Moscou – Ashkhabad)*, Monografie di Mesopotamia, 1. Florence: Le Lettere Licosa.

MECQUENEM, R. de
Archives: Rapports de campagne. Centre de recherche historique des archives nationales, fonds du ministère de l'Instruction publique: F17 17246 (1912); F17 17247 (1913); F17 17255 (1914, 1921, 1922); F17 17257 (1934–1935); F17 17258 (1936).
1910 • 'Compte-rendu sommaire des fouilles de Suse de l'hiver 1909-1910', *Bulletin de la délégation en Perse*, 1, 1910: 44–47.
1914 • 'Communication par V. Scheil, séance du 24 avril 1914', *CRAIBL*: 219–223.
1922 • 'Fouilles de Suse, campagnes des années 1914–1921-1922', *RA*, 19: 109–140
1924 • 'Fouilles de Suse (Campagnes 1923-1924)', *RA*, 21: 105–118.
1930 • 'Les derniers résultats des fouilles de

Suse', *RAAsiat*, 6: 73–88.
1934 • 'Fouilles de Suse, 1929-1933', Paris: P. Geuthner, *MDP*, 25: 177–237.
1938 • 'The Achaemenid and Later Remains at Susa', in Pope, A.U. (ed.), *A Survey of Persian Art I*, New York, London: Oxford University Press: 321–329.
1943 • 'Fouilles de Suse', Paris: PUF, *MMAI*, 29.
1947 • 'Contribution à l'étude du palais achéménide de Suse', in MECQUENEM, R. de, LE BRETON, L. and RUTTEN, M. (eds.) *Archéologie susienne*, Paris: PUF, *MMAI*, 30, *Mission de Susiane*: 1–119.
1980 • 'Les fouilleurs de Suse', *IrAnt*, 15: 1–48.

MECQUENEM, R. de and PÉZARD, M.
1911 • 'Compte-rendu sommaire des fouilles de Suse de l'hiver 1910-1911', *Bulletin de la délégation en Perse*, 2: 51–58.

MENANT, J.
1874 • *Annales des rois d'Assyrie.* Paris: Maisonneuve.

MICHALON, J.
1953 • 'Restes de constructions à Tchogha Zembil', in Mecquenem, R. de and Michalon, J. (eds.), *Recherches à Tchoga Zembil*, Paris: PUF, *MMAI*, 33: 14–40.

MILIK, J.T.
1992 • 'Les modèles araméens du Livre d'Esther dans la grotte 4 de Qumran', *Revue de Qumran*, 15: 321–406.

MIROSCHEDJI, P. de
1976 • 'Un four de potier du IVe millénaire sur le tell de l'Apadana à Suse', Paris: Association Paléorient, *DAFI*, 6: 13–45.
1985 • 'La fin du royaume d'Anshan et de Suse et la naissance de l'Empire perse', *ZA*, 75: 265–306.
1987 • 'Fouilles du chantier Ville royale II à Suse (1975–1977). Les niveaux d'époque achéménide, parthe et islamique', Paris: Association Paléorient, *DAFI*, 15: 11–143.
1997 • 'D'où venaient les Perses? L'Iran et la Perse', *Le Monde de la Bible*, 106: 17–21 (numéro spécial).

MOOREY, P.R.S.
1985 • 'The Iranian Contribution to Achaemenid Material Culture', *Iran*, 23: 21–37.
1994 • *Ancient Mesopotamian Materials and Industries.* Oxford: Clarendon Press.
1998 • 'Material Aspects of Achaemenid Polychrome Decoration and Jewellery', *IrAnt*, 33: 155–171.

MOORTGAT-CORRENS, U.
1996 • 'Das Grab des Nabonid', *SMEA*, 38: 153–177.

MORANDI BONACOSSI, D. and EIDEM, J.
2006 • 'A Royal Seal of Ishhi-Addu, King of Qatna', *Akkadica*, 127: 41–57.

MORGAN, J. de
1900 • *Recherches archéologiques, fouilles à Suse en 1897–1898 et 1898–1899.* Paris: Ernest Leroux, *MDP*, 1.
1902 • *La Délégation en Perse du ministère de l'instruction publique 1897 à 1902.* Paris: Ernest Leroux.
1905a • *États des travaux à Suse en 1904.* Paris: Ernest Leroux, *MDP*, 8.
1905b • *Découverte d'une sépulture achéménide à Suse.* Paris: Ernest Leroux, *MDP*, 8: 29–58.
1905c • *Histoire et travaux de la Délégation en Perse du Ministère de l'Instruction publique 1897–1905.* Paris: Ernest Leroux.

1909a • *De Suse au Louvre, aventures d'un convoi d'antiquités entre Suse et la mer.* Paris: Ernest Leroux.
1909b • 'Les anciens vestiges de la civilisation susienne', *RA*, 7: 1–10.

MOUSAVI, A.
1992 • 'Pārsa, a Stronghold for Darius: a Preliminary Study of the Defense System of Persepolis', *East and West*, 42/2–4: 203–226.

MULLER, A.
1997 • *Le Moulage en terre cuite dans l'Antiquité, actes du XXIIIe colloque du Centre de Recherches archéologiques.* Villeneuve d'Ascq: Presses universitaires du Septentrion.

MUNIER, P.
1949 • 'Les faïences siliceuses et la classification générale des faïences', *Silicates industriels*, 14/8: 1–8.

MUSCARELLA, O.W.
1992 • 'The Neo-Elamite Period', in Harper, P.O., Aruz, J. and Tallon, F. (eds.), *The Royal City of Susa.* New York: Metropolitan Museum of Art: 197–214.
1994 • 'L'art et l'architecture achéménides à Suse', in Harper, P.O., Aruz, J. and Tallon, F. (eds.), *La Cité royale de Suse*, Paris: RMN: 216–219.

NUNN, A.
1988 • *Die Wandmalerei und der glasierte Wandschmuck im alten Orient.* Leiden: E.J. Brill.

NYLANDER, C.
1965 • 'Old Persian and Greek Stonecutting and the Chronology of Achaemenid Monuments (Achaemenid Problems I)', *AJA*, 694: 49–55.
1966 • 'Clamps and Chronology (Achaemenid Problems II)', *IrAnt*, 6: 130–146.
1970 • *Ionians in Pasargadae: Studies in Old Persian Architecture.* Uppsala: Almqvist & Wiksell.
1975 • 'Anatolians in Susa and Persepolis? *Monumentum H.S. Nyberg*', *ActIr*, 2e scr., 4: 317–323.
1979 • 'Achaemenid Imperial Art,' in LARSEN, M.T. (ed.) *Power and Propaganda: A Symposium on Ancient Empires.* Copenhagen: 345–359.
1991 • 'The Toothed Chisel', *Archeologia Classica*, 43: 1037–1052.

OATES, J. and D.
2001 • *Nimrud: An Assyrian Imperial City Revealed.* London: British School of Archaeology in Iraq.

PARROT, A.
1957 • *Le Musée du Louvre et la Bible.* Neuchâtel and Paris.

PERDU, O.
1998 • 'Le directeur des scribes du conseil', *RdE*, 49: 175–194.

PERROT, G. and CHIPIEZ, C.
1890 • *Histoire de l'Art dans l'Antiquité*, vol. V, *Perse, Phrygie, Lydie et Carie, Lycie.* Paris: Hachette.

PERROT, J.
1969 • 'Les fouilles de Suse et de Susiane (1968–1969)', *CRAIBL*: 551–564.

1970a • 'Recherches archéologiques à Suse et en Susiane au cours de l'hiver 1969–1970', *CRAIBL*: 352–378.
1970b • 'Suse et la Susiane. Survey of Excavations, *Iran*, 8: 190–192.
1971 • *Travaux de la Mission de Suse depuis 1969.* Tehran: Iranian Center for Archaeological Research, *Proceedings of the first Annual Symposium of Archaeological Research in Iran*: 1–3.
1972 • 'Suse, palais du Chaour, l'Apadana. Surveys of Excavations', *Iran*, 10: 181–183.
1974 • 'Historique des recherches dans le secteur Est du tépé de l'Apadana'. Paris: Association Paléorient, *DAFI*, 4: 15–20.
1975 • *Le 'palais de Suse'. Proceedings of the IVth Annual Symposium of Archaeological Research in Iran (3–8 nov 1975).* Tehran: Iranian Center for Archaeological Research, 230–231.
1977 • 'Suse, le palais du roi des rois', *Bible et Terre sainte*, 193.
1981 • 'L'architecture militaire et palatiale des achéménides à Suse', in *150 Jahre Deutsches Archäologisches Institut 1829–1979. Festveranstalt-ungen und Internationales Kolloquium, 17–22 April 1979 in Berlin.* Mainz: P. von Zabern, 74–94.
1985 • 'Suse à la période achéménide. *Actes du séminaire CNRS/NSF de Bellevaux (24–29 June 1985)', Paléorient*, 11/2: 67–69.
1987 • 'Historique des travaux à l'Apadana et à la Ville royale (Suse)', Paris: Association Paléorient, *DAFI*, 15: 1–10.
1989a • 'Suse, dernières découvertes. Un siècle de fouille à Suse', *DA*, 138: 12–14
1989b • 'Shushan habira', *Yigael Yadin Memorial Volume, Eretz Israël*, 20: 155–160.
1995 • 'Le palais de Darius à Suse', *DA*, 210: 84–96.
1998a • 'Images de l'Iran', in *Catalogue de l'exposition 'Regards sur la Perse antique'*, Le Blanc, Saint-Marcel: Amis de la bibliothèque municipale du Blanc et du musée d'Argentomagus, 13–15.
1998b • 'Birth of a City: Susa', in Goodnick Westenholz, J. (ed.) *Capital Cities: Vision Planning and Spiritual Dimensions, Proceedings of the Symposium hold in May 27–29 1996, Jerusalem, Israel.* Jerusalem: Bible Lands Museum, 83–98.
2002 • 'La fondation de Suse au IVe millénaire BC', in *Actes du séminaire 'Recherches archéologiques en Iran' (oct. 2001)*, Tehran.
PERROT, **J. and LADIRAY**, **D.**
1972 • 'Travaux à l'Apadana (1969–1971)', Paris: Association Paléorient, *DAFI*, 2: 13–60.
1974 • 'La Porte de Darius à Suse', Paris: Association Paléorient, *DAFI*, 4: 43–56.
1996 • 'The Palace of Susa', in Goodnick Westenholz, J. (ed.) *Royal Cities of the Biblical World.* Jerusalem: Bible Lands Museum, 236–254.
1997 • 'La Porte du palais de Darius à Suse', *DA*, 227: 72–77.
PERROT, **J.**, **LADIRAY**, **D. and VALLAT**, **F.**
1999 • 'The Propylaeum of the Palace of Darius at Susa', in *The Iranian World: Essays on Iranian Art and Archaeology Presented to Ezat. O. Negahban.* Tehran: Iran University Press, 158–178.
PERROT, **J. and MADJIDZADEH**, **Y. (eds.)**
2003 • 'Découvertes récentes á Jiroft (sud du plateau Iranien)', *CRAIBL*: 1087–1102.
PESTMAN, **P.W.**
1984 • 'The Diospolis Parva Documents. Chronological Problems concerning Psammetichus

III and IV', in Thissen, H. J. and Zauzich, K. Th. (eds.), *Grammata Demotica: Festschrift für Erich Lüddeckens zum 15 Juni 1983.* Würzburg: Gisela Zauzich Verlag, 145–155.
PÉZARD, **M. and POTTIER**, **E.**
1926 • *Catalogue des antiquités de Susiane (Mission J. de Morgan).* Paris: Musées nationaux, 2nd edn.
PFÄLZNER, **P.**
2006 • 'Qatna. B. Archäologisch', *RlA*, 11: 161–170.
PFUHL, **E.**
1923 • *Mahlerei und Zeichnung der Griechen.* Munich: F. Bruckman.
PILLET, **M.**
1913 • 'Le palais de Darius Ier à Suse (ve av. J.-C.)', *CRAIBL*: 641–653.
1914 • *Le Palais de Darius Ier à Suse.* Paris: P. Geuthner.
PIRART, **E.**
1996 • 'Le sacrifice humain dans l'*Avesta*', *JA*, 284: 1–36.
POPE, **A.V.**
1957 • 'Persepolis as a Ritual City', *Archaeology*, 10: 123–130.
PORADA, **E.**
1970 • *Mission de Susiane: Tchoga Zanbil (Dur-Untash).* Paris: P. Geuthner, *MDAI*, 42.
POSENER, **G.**
1936 • *La Première domination perse en Égypte: recueil d'inscriptions hiéroglyphiques.* Le Caire: Institut français d'archéologie orientale, *Bibliothèque d'étude*, 11.
1969 • *Littérature et politique dans l'Égypte de la XIIe dynastie.* Paris: H. Champion.
1973 • 'Philologie et archéologie égyptiennes', *Annuaire du Collège de France*, 73: 369–374.
1977 • 'L'or de Pount', in Endesfelder, E., Priese, K.H., Reineke, W.F. and Weig, S. (eds.), *Ägypten und Kusch (Festschrift F. Hintze zum 60. Geburstag gewidmet).* Berlin: Akademie-Verlag, 337–342.
1986 • 'Du nouveau sur Kombabos', *RdE*, 37: 91–96.
POSENER and KRIEGER, **P.**
1987 • 'Travaux de l'IFAO au cours de l'année 1986–1987', *BIFAO*, 87: 316–321.
1988 • 'Travaux de l'IFAO au cours de l'année 1987–1988', *BIFAO*, 88: 205–206.
1989 • 'Travaux de l'IFAO au cours de l'année 1988-1989', *BIFAO*, 89: 313–314.
POTTS, **D.T.**
1999a • *The Archaeology of Elam: Formation and Transformation of an Ancient Iranian State.* Cambridge: Cambridge University Press.
1999b • 'Elamite Ulā, Akkadian Ulaya, and Greek Choaspes', *Bulletin of the Asia Institute*, 13: 27–44.
2005. 'Cyrus the Great and the Kingdom of Anshan', in Curtis, V.S. and Stewart, S. (eds.), *Birth of the Persian Empire*, I. London and New York: I.B.Tauris, 7–28.
POTTS, **D.T.**, **ASGARI CHAVERDI**, **A.**, **PETRIE**, **C.A.**, **DUSTING**, **A.**, **FARHADI**, **F.**, **McRAE**, **I.**, **SHIKHI**, **S.**, **WONG**, **E.H.**, **LASHKARI**, **A. and JAVANMARD ZADEH**, **A.**
2007 • 'The Mamasani Archaeological Project, Stage Two: Excavations at Qaleh Kali (Tappeh Servan/Jinjun [MS 46])', *Iran*, 45: 287–300.

QUAEGEBEUR, **J.**
1975 • *Le Dieu égyptien Shaï dans la religion et l'onomastique.* Leuven: Leuven University Press,

Orientalia Lovaniensia Analecta, 2.

RAWLINSON, **H.C.**
1839 • 'Notes on a March from Zohab, at the Foot of Zagros, along the Mountains to Khûzistán (Susiana), and from thence through the Province of Luristan to Kirmānshāh, in the year 1836', *JRGS*, 9: 26–116.
RAZMJOU, **S.**
2001a • 'Hacking the Statue: An Analytical Study of the Damages on the Egyptian Statue of Darius I from Susa', *Iranian Journal of Archaeology and History*, 14/ 2: 3–10.
2001b • 'Des traces de la déesse Spenta Ārmaiti à Persépolis. Et proposition pour une nouvelle lecture d'un logogramme élamite', *StIr*, 30: 7–15.
2002a • 'Assessing the Damage: Notes on the Life and Demise of the Statue of Darius from Susa', *Ars Orientalis* 32: 81–104.
2002b • 'Traces of Paint on the Statue of Darius', *ARTA*, 2002/3: 1–2.
2004 • 'Glasierte Ziegel der achämenidischen Periode', in Stöllner, T., Slotta, R. and Vatandoust, A. (eds.), *Persiens Antike Pracht.* Bochum: Deutsches Bergbau-Museum, 382–393.
2005 • 'Religion and Burial Customs', in Curtis, J. and Tallis, N (eds.), *Forgotten Empire, The World of Ancient Persia.* London: The British Museum Press, 150–156.
READE, **J.**
1965 • 'A Glazed-Brick Panel from Nimrud', *Iraq*, 25: 38–47.
1979 • 'Assyrian Architectural Decoration: Techniques and Subject Matters', *Baghdader Mitteilungen*, 10: 17–49.
1998–2001 • 'Ninive (Nineveh)', *RlA*, 9: 388–433.
REINACH, **S.**
1892 • *Antiquités du Bosphore cimmérien. Bibliothèque des monuments figurés grecs et romains.* Paris: Firmin Didot.
REUTHER, **O.**
1926 • *Die Innenstadt von Babylon (Merkes).* Leipzig: J. C. Hinrichs, *WVDOG*, 47.
RICHTER, **T.**
2006 • 'Qatna. A. Nach schriftlichen Quellen', *RlA*, 11: 159–161.
ROAF, **M.**
1973 • 'The Diffusion of the "Salles à quatre saillants"', *Iraq*, 35: 83–91.
1974 • 'The Subject Peoples on the Base of the Statue of Darius'. Paris: Association Paléorient, 4: 73–160.
1978 • 'Persepolitan Metrology', *Iran*, 16: 67–78.
1983 • 'Sculptures and Sculptors at Persepolis', *Iran*, 21: 1–164.
1990 • 'Sculptors and Designers at Persepolis', in Gunter, A.C. (ed.), *Investigating Artistic Environment in the Ancient Near East.* Washington: Smithsonian Institute, 105–114.
1994 • 'Persepolis', *RlA*, 10: 393–412.
ROOT, **M.C.**
1979 • 'The King and Kingship in Achaemenid Art: Essays on the Creation of an Iconography of Empire', *ActIr*, 19.
1990 • 'Circles of Artistic Programming: Strategies for Studying Creative Process at Persepolis', in Gunter, A.C. (ed.), *Investigating

Artistic Environment in the Ancient Near East.
Washington: Smithsonian Institute, 115–139.
1994 • 'Lifting the Veil: Artistic Transmissions
beyond the Boundaries of Historical
Periodisation', *AchHist*, 8: 9–37.
2003 • 'The Lioness of Elam: Politics and
Dynastic Fecundity at Persepolis', in Henkelman,
W. and Kuhrt, A. (eds.), *A Persian Perspective:
Essays in Memory of Heleen Sancisi-Weerdenburg.*
Leiden: E.J. Brill, *AchHist*, 13: 9–32.
2011 • 'Elam in the imperial imagination: from
Niniveh to Persepolis', in Alvarez-Mon, J. and
Garrison, M. B. (ed.), *Elam and Persia.* Winona
Lake: Eisenbrauns.

ROUGEMONT, G.
2012 • *Inscriptions grecques d'Iran et d'Asie centrale.*
London: Corpus Inscriptionum Iranicarum.

SACK, R.M.
1983 • 'The Nabonidus legend', *RA*, 77: 59–67.
SALLES, J.-F.
1998. 'La mer Rouge, du vie siècle avant J.-C. au
milieu du premier siècle de notre ère', in Valbelle,
D. and Bonnet, C. (eds.), *Le Sinaï durant
l'Antiquité et le Moyen Âge: 4000 ans d'histoire pour
un désert, actes du colloque* 'Sinaï *qui s'est tenu
à l'UNESCO du 19 au 21 septembre 1997.* Paris:
Errance. 93–101.
SARRAF, M. R.
2003 • 'Archaeological Excavations in Tepe
Ekbatana (Hamadan) by the Iranian Archaeological
Mission between 1983 and 1999', in Lanfranchi,
G.B., Roaf, M. and Rollinger, R. (eds.), *Continuity
of Empire (?): Assyria, Media, Persia*, History of
the Ancient Near East – Monographs, V. Padua:
S.a.r.g.o.n Editrice e Libreria, 263–279.
SARRE, F.
1923 • *Die Kunst des alten Persien.* Berlin: B.
Cassirer, *Die Kunst des Ostens*, 5.
SAUNERON, S. and YOYOTTE, J.
1950 • 'La campagne nubienne de Psammetique II
et sa signification historique', *BIFAO*, 50: 157–207.
SAUVAGE, M.
1998 • *La Brique et sa mise en œuvre en Mésopotamie
des origines à l'époque achéménide.* Paris: ERC.
SCHEIL, V.
1905 • *Textes élamites-sémitiques, troisième série.*
Paris: Ernest Leroux, *MDP*, 6.
1908 • *Textes élamites-sémitiques, quatrième série.*
Paris: Ernest Leroux, *MDP*, 10.
1911 • *Textes élamites-anzanites, quatrième série.*
Paris: Ernest Leroux, *MDP*, 11.
1929 • *Inscriptions achéménides à Suse.* Paris:
Ernest Leroux, *MDP*, 21.
1932 • *Actes juridiques susiens (Suite: no. 166 à 327).*
Paris: Ernest Leroux, *MDP*, 23
1933a • *II - Inscriptions des Achéménides
(Supplément et suite).* Paris: Ernest Leroux, *MDP*,
24: 103–129.
1933b • *Actes juridiques susiens (Suite: no. 328 à 395).
Inscriptions des Achéménides (Supplément et suite).*
Paris: Ernest Leroux, *MDP*, 24.
1939 • *Mélanges épigraphiques.* Paris: Ernest
Leroux, *MDP*, 28.
SCHMIDT, E.F.
1953 • *Persepolis, I. Structures, Reliefs, Inscriptions.*
Chicago: The University of Chicago Press, *OIP*, 68.
1957 • *Persepolis, II. Contents of the Treasury and
Other Discoveries.* Chicago: University of Chicago

Press, *OIP*, 69.
1970 • *Persepolis, III. The Royal Tombs and Other
Monuments.* Chicago: University of Chicago Press,
OIP, 70.
SCHMITT, R.
1991 • *The Bisitun Inscription of Darius the Great,
Old Persian Text.* London: Published on Behalf of
Corpus Inscriptionum Iranicarum by School of
Oriental and African Studies.
1999 • *Beiträge zu altpersischen Inschriften.*
Wiesbaden: Ludwig Reichert Verlag.

SCHRADER, E. (ed.)
1890 • *Historische Texte des neubabylonischen
Reiches.* Berlin: H. Reuther's Verlagsbuchhandlung,
Keilinschriftliche Bibliothek, 3/2.
**SCOLLAR, I., TABBAGH, A., HESSE, A. and
HERZOG, I.**
1990 • *Archeological Prospecting and Remote
Sensing: Topics in Remote Sensing.* Cambridge:
Cambridge University Press.
SEIDL, U.
1976 • 'Ein Relief Dareios' I in Babylon', *AMI*, 9:
125–130.
1999a • 'Eine Triumphstele Darius' I aus Babylon',
in Renger, J. (ed.), *Babylon: Focus mesopotamischer
Geschichte, Wiege früher Gelehrsamkeit, Mythos
in der Moderne, 2, Internationales Colloquium der
Deutschen Orient-Gesellschaft. 24–26 März 1998
in Berlin*, Saarbrücken: Saarbrücken Drucherei
und Verlag, 297–306.
1999b • 'Ein Monument Darius' I. aus Babylon',
ZA, 89: 101–114.
SHAHBAZI, A.S.
1974 • 'An Achaemenid Symbol I: A Farewell to
"Fravahr" and "Ahuramazda"', *AMI*, 7: 125–141.
1976 • *Persépolis illustrée.* Tehran: Institute of
Achaemenid Research Publications.
SMITH, M.
1963 • 'Isaiah and the Persians', *JAOS*, 23:
415–421.
SOLER, J.
2002 • *L'Invention du monothéisme.* Paris: Éditions
de Fallois.
SPELEERS, L.
1927 • *Introduction au Catalogue des intailles et
empreintes.* Wetteren: Jules de Meester et Fils.
SOUDAVAR, A.
2003 • *The Aura of Kings: Legitimacy and Divine
Sanction in Iranian Kingship.* Costa Mesa, Mass.:
Mazda Publications.
2006a • *The Formation of Achaemenid Imperial
Ideology and its Impact on the Avesta*: 1–28. www.
soudavar.com/achaemenidimperialideology-5.pdf.
2006b • 'The Significance of Av. cithra, OPers.
ciça, MPers. cihr, and NPers. cehr, for the Iranian
Cosmogony of Light', *IrAnt*, 41: 151–185.
SPYCKET, A.
1980. 'Women in Persian Art', in Schmandt-
Besserat, D. (ed.) *Ancient Persia: the Art of an
Empire.* Malibu: Undena Publications, 43–45.
STEVE, M.-J.
1967 • *Tchoga Zanbil (Dur-Untash) 3. Textes
élamites et accadiens de Tchoga-Zanbil.* Paris:
P. Geuthner, *MDAI, Mission de Susiane*, 41.
1974 • 'Inscriptions des Achéménides à Suse', *StIr*,
3: 6–28 et 4: 135–169.
1987 • *Nouveaux mélanges épigraphiques. Inscriptions
royales de Suse et de Susiane.* Nice: Serre, *MDAI*, 53.
1992 • *Syllabaire élamite: Histoire et paléographie.*

Neuchâtel: Recherches et Publications,
Civilisations du Proche-Orient, série 2,
Philologie, 1.
2003 • *L' Ile de Khārg: une page de l'histoire
du Golfe persique et du monachisme oriental.*
Neuchâtel: Recherches et Publications.
STEVE, M.-J. and GASCHE, H.
1990 • 'Le tell de l'Apadana avant les
Achéménides. Contribution à la topographie de
Suse', in Vallat, F. (ed.), *Contribution à l'histoire
de l'Iran, Mélanges offerts à Jean Perrot.* Paris:
ERC, 15–60.
**STEVE M.-J., GASCHE, H. and
DE MEYER, L.**
1980 • 'La Susiane au deuxième millénaire: à
propos d'une interprétation des fouilles de Suse',
IrAnt, 15: 49–154.
STEVE M.-J., VALLAT, F. and GASCHE, H.
2002–3 • 'Suse' in *SDB*, 73–74: 359–652, Paris:
Letouzey et Ané.
STILL, M. AND YOYOTTE, J.
2000 • 'Une intuition de l'Universel dans les
représentations de l'Égypte pharaonique', in
*Rencontres philosophiques. Journées académiques.
Année 2000.* Paris: Éditions SCEREN: 14–22.
STOLPER, M.
1977 • 'Three Iranian Loan-words in Late
Babylonian Texts', in Levine, L. (ed.),
Mountains and Lowlands, Malibu: Undena
Publications, *Bibliotheca Mesopotamica*, 7:
251–266.
1985 • *Entrepreneurs and empire: the Murasu
Archive, the Murasu Firm, and Persian rule in
Babylonia.* Istanbul, Nederlands Historisch-
Archaeologisch Instituut te Istanbul.
1990 • 'Tobits in Reverse: More Babylonians
in Ecbatana', *AMI*, 23: 161–176.
1992 • 'The Murašu Texts from Susa', *RA*,
86: 69–77.
1994 • 'Tablette administrative élamite portant
l'empreinte d'un sceau au nom du Roi', in
Harper, P.O., Aruz, J. and Tallon, F. (ed.),
La Cité royale de Suse, Paris: RMN: 273.
STOLPER, M. and TAVERNIER, J.
2007 • 'From the Persepolis Fortification
Archive Project, 1: An Old Persian
Administrative Tablet', *ARTA*, 2007/1.
www.achemenet. com/ressources/enligne/arta/
pdf/2007.001-Stolper-Tavernier.pdf.
STOOPS, G. Sr. and STOOPS, G. Jr.
1994 • 'Petrographic Study of Red Floor
Fragments from the Palaces at Babylon and
Susa', in Gasche, H., Tanret, M., Janssen,
C. and Degraeve, A. (eds.), *Cinquante-deux
réflexions sur le Proche-Orient ancien offertes
en hommage à Léon De Meyer*, Mesopotamian
History and Environment: Occasional
Publication, 2. Leuven: Peeters,: 477–486.
STRASSMAIER, J.N.
1889 • *Inschriften von Nabonidus, König von
Babylon.* Leipzig: Pfeiffer, *Babylonische Texte*,
1–4.
STROMMENGER, E.
1957 • 'Grab', *RlA*, 3: 581–593.
STRONACH, D.
1964 • 'Excavations at Pasargadæ: Second
Preliminary Report', *Iran*, 2: 21–39.
1971 • 'A Circular Symbol on the Tomb
of Cyrus', *IrAnt*, 9: 155–158.
1972 • 'La statue de Darius découverte à Suse.

Description and Comment', *JA*, 270: 241–246.
1974a • 'Une statue de Darius découverte à Suse', Paris: Association Paléorient, *DAFI*, 4: 61–72.
1974b • 'Achaemenid Village I at Susa and the Persian Migration to Fars', *Iraq*, 36: 239–248.
1978 • *Pasargadae*. Oxford: Oxford University Press.
1985a • 'On the Evolution of the Early Iranian Fire Temple', in Duchesne-Guillemin, J. and Lecoq, P. (eds.), *Papers in Honour of Professor Mary Boyce*, Leiden: E.J. Brill, *ActIr*, 25, vol. II, 605–627.
1985b • 'The Apadana: A Signature of the Line of Darius I', in Huot, J.-L., Yon, M. and Calvet, Y. (eds.), *De l'Indus aux Balkans. Recueil à la mémoire de Jean Deshayes*. Paris: ERC: 433–445.
1989 • 'Early Achaemenid Coinage: Perspectives from the Homeland', *IrAnt*, 24: 255–283.
2001 • 'From Cyrus to Darius: Notes on Art and Architecture in Early Achaemenid Palaces', in Nielsen, I. (ed.), *The Royal Institution in the First Millennium BC. Regional Development and Cultural Interchange between East and West*. Aarhus: Aarhus University Press, *Monographs of the Danish Institute at Athens*, 4: 95–111.

STRONACH, D. and ROAF, M.
2007 • *Nush-i Jan I. The Major Buildings of the Median Settlement*. London: The British Institute of Persian Studies and Leuven- Paris-Dudley: Peeters.

TAJVIDI, A.
1976 • *Dāneštanihāy-e novin darbārey-e honar va bāstānšenāsiy-e asr-e hakhāmaneši bar bonyād-e kāvošhāy-e panjsāleh-e Takht-e Jamšīd* [*Nouvelles connaissances sur l'art et l'archéologie de l'époque achéménide d'après cinq années de fouilles à Persépolis*]. Tehran: Ministère de la culture et des arts.
TALLON, F.
1992 • 'The Achaemenid Tomb on the Acropole', in Harper, P.O., Aruz, J. and Tallon, F. (eds.), *The Royal City of Susa: Ancient Near Eastern Treasures in the Louvre*, New York: The Metropolitan Museum of Art: 242–252.
1994 • 'La tombe achéménide de Suse: Les pierres précieuses de l'Orient ancien des Sumériens aux Sassanides', in Tallon, F. (ed.), *Les Dossiers du musée du Louvre*, Paris: RMN: 113–120.
1995 • *Les pierres précieuses de l'Orient ancien: des Sumériens aux Sassanides*. Paris: Réunion des musées nationaux.
1997a • 'Les fouilles de Marcel Dieulafoy à Suse. La résurrection du palais de Darius', in Chevalier, N. (ed.), *Une mission en Perse, 1897–1912*, Paris: RMN: 46–55.
1997b • 'Le palais de Darius. La reconstitution de Maurice Pillet', in Chevalier, N. (ed.), *Une mission en Perse, 1897–1912*. Paris: RMN, 132–139.
TAVERNIER, J.
2004 • 'Some Thoughts on Neo-Elamite Chronology', *ARTA*, 2004/3. www.achemenet.com/ ressources/enligne/arta/pdf/2004.003-Tavernier.pdf.
THELLIER, E.
1966 • 'Le champ magnétique terrestre fossile', *Nucléus*, 7 1/3: 1–35.
THIERS, C.
2007 • 'Ptolémée Philadelphe et les prêtres d'Atoum de Tjékou', *Orientalia Monspeliensia*, 17: 107–117.

THUCYDIDES
Guerre du Péloponnèse, I. Paris: Gallimard (trans. Denis Roussel, 1964).
TILIA, A.B.
1968 • 'A Study on the Methods of Working and Restoring Stone and on the Parts Left Unfinished in Achaemenian Architecture and Sculpture', *East and West*, 18: 67–95.
1972 • *Studies and Restorations at Persepolis and other Sites of Fars, I*, Rome: IsMeo, *Reports and Memoirs*, 16.
1978 • *Studies and Restorations at Persepolis and other Sites of Fars, II*, Rome: IsMeo, *Reports and Memoirs*, 18.
TOLINI, G.
2008 • 'Les travailleurs babyloniens et le palais de Taoké', *ARTA*, 2008/2. www.achemenet.com/ ressources/enligne/arta/pdf/2008.002-loc.pdf.
TRICHET, J. and POUPET, P.
1974 • 'Étude pétrographique de la roche constituant la statue de Darius découverte à Suse en décembre 1972'. Paris: Association Paléorient, *DAFI*, 4: 57–59.
TRICHET, J. and VALLAT, F.
1990 • 'L'origine égyptienne de la statue de Darius', in Vallat, F. (ed.), *Contributions à l'histoire de l'Iran. Mélanges offerts à Jean Perrot*. Paris: ERC: 205–208.
TUPLIN, C.
1998 • 'The Seasonal Migration of Achaemenid Kings: A Report on Old and New Evidence', in Brosius, M. and Kuhrt, A. (eds.), *Studies in Persian History: Essays in Memory of David Lewis*. Leiden: E.J. Brill, *AchHist*, 11: 63–114.
TUPLIN, C. (ed.)
2008 • *Persian Responses Political and Cultural Interaction within the Achaemenid Empire*, Swansea.
TURNER, G.
1970 • 'The State Apartments of Late Assyrian Palaces' *Iraq*, 32: 177–213.

UNGNAD, A.
1907 • *Vorderasiatische Schriftdenkmäler der Königlichen Museen zu Berlin*, vol. 3. Leipzig: J.C. Hinrichs.
UNVALA, J.M.
1934 • *Inventaire des monnaies trouvées à Suse*. Paris: Ernest Leroux and Allotte de la Fuye, *MDP*, 25: 61–133.

VALLAT, F.
1970 • 'Table élamite de Darius Ier', *RA*, 64: 149–160.
1971 • 'Deux nouvelles Chartes de Fondation d'un palais de Darius Ier à Suse', *Syria*, 48: 53–59.
1972a • 'Une statue de Darius découverte à Suse. L'inscription cunéiforme trilingue (DSab)', *JA*, 270: 247–251.
1972b • 'Deux inscriptions élamites de Darius Ier (DSf et DSz)', *StIr*, 1: 3–13.
1972c • 'Épigraphie achéménide', Paris: Association Paléorient, *DAFI*, 2: 203–217.
1974a • 'Les textes cunéiformes de la statue de Darius', Paris: Association Paléorient, *DAFI*, 4: 161–170.
1974b • 'L'inscription trilingue de Xerxès à la Porte de Darius'. Paris: Association Paléorient,

DAFI, 4: 171–180.
1974c • 'La triple inscription cunéiforme de la statue de Darius Ier, DSab', *RA*, 68: 157–166.
1979 • 'Les inscriptions du palais d'Artaxerxès II sur la rive droite du Chaour'. Paris: Association Paléorient, *DAFI*, 10: 145–154.
1983 • 'Un fragment de tablette achéménide et la turquoise', *Akkadica*, 33: 63–68.
1986 • 'Table accadienne de Darius Ier (Dsaa)', in De Meyer, L., Gasche, H. and Vallat, F. (eds.), *Fragmenta Historiae Elamicae. Mélanges offerts à M.-J. Steve*, Paris: ERC: 277–283.
1987a • 'L'expression da-ma da-ak en élamite achéménide', *NABU*, 6.
1987b • 'Perse, Persépolis dans les textes achéménides rédigés en élamite', *NABU*, 113.
1987c • 'Le pseudo-pronom personnel *kaš en élamite achéménide', *NABU*, 114.
1989 • 'Le palais d'Artaxerxès II à Babylone', Ghent, University of Ghent, *NAPR*, 2: 3–6.
1989b • 'Les compléments phonétiques ou graphiques en élamite achéménide', *AION*, 49/3: 219–222.
1989c • 'Les inscriptions de Darius et de Xerxès', *DA*, 138: 66–67.
1990 • *Contribution à l'histoire de l'Iran, Mélanges offerts à Jean Perrot*. Paris: ERC.
1994 • 'Deux tablettes élamites de l'Université de Fribourg', *JNES*, 53: 263–274.
1997a • 'L'utilisation des sceaux-cylindres dans l'archivage des lettres de Persépolis', in Gyselen, R. (ed.), *Sceaux d'Orient et leur emploi*, Bures-sur-Yvette: Groupe pour l'étude de la civilisation du Moyen-Orient, *Res Orientales*, 10: 171–174.
1997b • 'Les inscriptions achéménides d'Iran', *DA*, 227: 48–55.
1997c • 'Cyrus l'usurpateur', *Topoi*, suppl. 1: 423–434.
1999 • 'Le palais élamite de Suse', *Akkadica*, 112: 34–43
1999a • 'Exit Préxaspès des textes de Persépolis', *NABU*, 28.
2002 • 'Suse', *DB*, 73–74: 361–651
2003a • *Les Religions à Suse. Supplément au dictionnaire de la Bible*. Fascicule 74, Paris: Letouzey et Ané: 529–620.
2003b • 'La civilisation proto-élamite, 3100–2600', *DA*, 287: 88–91.
2005 • 'L'inscription néo-élamite de Manaka […]-untaš et l'emploi des déterminatifs à basse époque', in Bernardini, M. and Tornesello, N.L., *Scritti in onore di Giovanni M. D'Erme. Saggi di colleghi e amici in occasione del suo compleanno, a c.: 1237–1242*, Napoli: Università degli Studi di Napoli 'L'Orientale', *Series Minor*, 67.
2006 • 'Atta-hamiti-Inshushinak, Shutur-Nahhunte et la chronologie néo-élamite', *Akkadika*, 127: 59–61.
2011 • 'Darius, l'héritier légitime, et les premiers Achéménides', in Alvare-Mon, A. and Garrison, M. (eds.), *Elam and Persia*, Winona Lake: Eisenbrauns.
VAN DER SPEK, R. J.
1982 • 'Did Cyrus the Great introduce a New Policy towards Subdued Nations', *Persika*, 10: 278–283.
VERCOUTTER, J.
1962 • *Textes biographiques du Sérapeum de Memphis*. Paris: Librairie ancienne Honoré

Champion, coll. 'Bibliothèque de l'École pratique des hautes études, IVe section', 316.

VERNUS, P. and YOYOTTE, J.

1996 • *Dictionnaire des Pharaons*. Paris: Noêsis.

VITTMANN, G.

1998 • *Der demotische Papyrus Rylands 9. Teil II, Kommentare und Indizes*, Ägypten und Altes Testament, 38. Wiesbaden: Harrassowitz.

VLEEMING, S.P.

1991 • *The Gooseherds of Hou (Pap. Hou). A Dossier Relating to Various Agricultural Affairs from Provincial Egypt of the Early Fifth Century B.C. Studia Demotica*, III. Leuven: Peeters.

VON BISSING, F.W.

1941 • *Zeit und Herkunft der in Cerveteri gefundenen Gefässe aus ägyptischer Fayence und glasiertem Ton*. Munich.

WAERZEGGERS, C.

2006 • 'The Carians of Borsippa', *Iraq*, 68: 1–22.
2010a • 'Babylonians in Susa. The travels of Babylonian businessmen to Susa reconsidered', in JACOBS, B. and ROLLINGER, R. (eds.) *Der Achämenidenhof / The Achaemenid Court*, Wiesbaden: Harrassowitz: 777-813.
2010b • *The Ezida Temple of Borsippa: Priesthood, Cult, Archive*, Achaemenid History XV. Leiden: E.J. Brill.

WALLERT, I.

1967 • *Der verzierte Löffel, seine Formgeschichte und Verwendung im alten Ägypten*. Wiesbaden: Harrasowitz.

WATERS, M.V.

1996 • 'Darius and the Achaemenid Line', *Ancient History. Bulletin of the Asia Institute*, 10: 11–18.
2000 • *A Survey of Neo-Elamite History*. Helsinki: Neo-Assyrian Text Corpus Project, coll. 'SAAS', 12.
2004 • 'Cyrus and the Achaemenids', *Iran*, 42: 91–102.

WEIDNER, E.F.

1931–1932 • 'Die älteste Nachricht über das persisches Reich', *AfO*, 7: 1–7.

WEISSBACH, F.W.

1911 • *Die Keilinschriften der Achämeniden*. Leipzig: J.C. Hinrichs, *Vorderasiatische Bibliothek*.

WESTENHOLZ, J.G. and STOLPER, M.W.

2002 • 'A Stone Jar with Inscriptions of Darius I in Four Languages', *ARTA*, 2002/5: 1–13. www.achemenet.com/ressources/enligne/arta/pdf/2002.005-loc.pdf.

WINTER, I.

1981 • 'Is there a South Syrian Style of Ivory Carving in the Early First Millennium B.C.?', *Iraq*, 43: 101–130.

WOOLLEY, L.

1962 • *Ur Excavations: the Neo-Babylonian and Persian Periods, Ur Excavations*, 9. London: British Museum.

YAMAUCHI, E.M.

1990 • *Persia and the Bible*. Grand Rapids: Baker Book House.

YOYOTTE, J.

1951 • 'Le martelage des noms royaux éthiopiens par Psammétique II', *RdE*, 8: 215–239.
1972a • 'Une statue de Darius découverte à Suse. Les inscriptions hiéroglyphiques. Darius et l'Égypte', *JA*, 270: 253–266.
1972b • 'Pétoubastis III', *RdE*, 24: 216–223.
1974 • 'Les inscriptions hiéroglyphiques de la statue de Darius à Suse'. Paris: Association Paléorient, *DAFI*, 4: 181–183.

YOUNG, T.C. and LEVINE, L.D.

1974 • *Excavations of the Godin Project: Second Progress Report*. Toronto: The Royal Ontario Museum, Occasional Papers 26.

ZAYADINE, F.

1986 • 'Cariatide brûle-parfum', in Amiet, P., André-Leickman, B. and Augé, C. (eds.), *La Voie royale. 9000 ans d'art au Royaume de Jordanie. Catalogue de l'exposition du musée du Luxembourg. Paris, 26 novembre 1986–25 janvier 1987*. Paris: Association française d'action artistique.

Index